Volume 2

Handbook of Work and Organizational Psychology

Volume 2

Handbook of Work and Organizational Psychology

Edited by

P. J. D. Drenth
Free University, Amsterdam

H. Thierry
Amsterdam University

P. J. Willems
Tilburg University

C. J. de Wolff
Catholic University, Nijmegen

JOHN WILEY & SONS

Chichester · New York · Brisbane · Toronto · Singapore

Library of Congress Cataloging in Publication Data:
Main entry under title:

Handbook of work and organizational psychology.

   Includes indexes.
   1. Psychology, Industrial.   I. Drenth, Pieter, J. D.
(Pieter Johan Diederik).
HF5548.8.H2655   1984   158.7   83–23316
ISBN 0 471 90344 2 (U.S. : set)
ISBN 0 471 90400 7 (U.S. : v. 1)
ISBN 0 471 90401 5 (U.S. : v. 2)

British Library Cataloguing in Publication Data:

Handbook of work and organizational psychology.
   1. Psychology, Industrial
   I. Drenth, P. J. D.
   158   HF5548.8

   ISBN 0 471 90344 2
   ISBN 0 471 90400 7   v. 1
   ISBN 0 471 90401 5   v. 2

Typeset by Thomson Press (India) Ltd., New Delhi
Printed by Page Brothers (Norwich) Ltd.

List of Contributors

Prof. Dr. Wil Albeda
Dr. Jen A. Algera
Prof. Dr. Jacques T. Allegro
Dr. Erik J. H. T. H. Andriessen
Dr. Albert van Assen
Prof. Dr. Paul M. Bagchus
Prof. Dr. J. Gerrit Boerlijst
Drs. Giel v. d. Bosch
Drs. Jan Willem Broekhuysen
Drs. George R. P. Bruining
Dr. Marc Buelens
Prof. Dr. Pol L. Coetsier
Prof. Dr. Jules J. J. van Dijck
Prof. Dr. Frans J. P. van Dooren
Prof. dr. Pieter J. D. Drenth
Prof. Dr. Maarten R. van Gils
Drs. B. Groenendijk
Prof. Dr. Aart Hazewinkel
Dr. Friso J. den Hertog
Drs. Herbert van Hoogdalem
Drs. Jaap H. Huijgen
Dr. Ir. John R. de Jong
Drs. Ben Jansen
Dr. Paul L. Koopman
Dr. Agnes M. Koopman-Iwema

Drs. Theo J. Meijman
Drs. Oscar M. Meijn
Prof. Dr. John A. Michon
Prof. dr. James F. O'Hanlon
Drs. E. Mazlies Ott
Prof. Dr. John B. Rijsman
Prof. dr. Robert A. Roe
Drs. Ph. Hans M. Sopar
Prof. dr. Henk Thierry
Prof. dr. Peter Veen
Dr. Eveat v. d. Vliert
Prof. Dr. Jos J. A. Vollebergh
Dr. Arie Vrolijk
Prof. Dr. Peter B. Warr
Drs. André F. M. Wierdsma
Prof. dr. Paul J. Willems
Prof. dr. A. Roper T. Williams
Dr. Jagnes A. M. Winnubst
Prof. dr. Charles. J. de Wolff
Dr. Harry L. G. Zanders

On January 15, 1984 our friend and colleague Paul Willems died. One of his last activities before he became ill was checking proofs for this handbook, which he did as always with utmost care and attention. We have worked together for a very long time, and we have admired and enjoyed his scholarship, his sound judgment, his helpfulness and his friendship. It is therefore that we dedicate this handbook to his memory.

PIETER J. D. DRENTH
HENK THIERRY
CHARLES J. DE WOLFF

Contents

Preface

Customarily, books begin with a preface, although in most cases it would be more appropriate to call it a postscript, a review of what happened between the original plans of the authors or editors and the actual result of their endeavor. This preface being no exception to the rule, it is written at a time when the editors are winding up their work. However that may be, it does give us the opportunity to thank all persons involved in the production of this Handbook.

The idea to produce a handbook does not usually arise overnight. When we first discussed the project—some 15 years ago—we soon came up with a number of reasons for abandoning it. The major one was, why should we even try to compete with a number of excellent textbooks produced in the United States? It seemed like we would be carrying coal to Newcastle. So, instead, three of the present editors decided to lower their sights and to aim for a more modest goal. They invited a number of colleagues to write a chapter for a volume on Work Psychology (*Bedrijfspsychologie*, 1970) and, a few years later, for one on Work- and Organizational Psychology (*Arbeids- en organisatiepsychologie*, 1973), both published in The Netherlands by Kluwer/ Van Loghum Slaterus. Although these volumes covered a reasonably large number of topics in the field, they did not claim to present a systematic coverage of the whole field of work- and organizational psychology.

The positive response to these books and the experience gained by the editors in producing them led to renewed discussions about the original plan of editing a handbook. But .more important than these positive experiences was our growing conviction that the European developments in our discipline in the preceding decades warranted an attempt at consolidating the results in a systematic survey of the domain.

Starting in 1976, various proposals on matters of content and structure were discussed and rejected until, in 1978, a proposal, reflected in the structure of the present Handbook, was agreed upon. The domain of work- and organizational psychology was divided into five sections, each containing a number of chapters of a rather general nature and a number of chapters discussing applications. Then we began inviting colleagues, most of them working in The Netherlands, with a sprinkling of experts from other countries, to write one, or more, chapter(s).

The task assigned to the authors was primarily to review the research and developments in the area of their expertise, and, secondly, to pay some attention to possible future developments in that area. If possible or necessary, they should also mention differences in views between Anglo-Saxon and European scientists. This recommendation was not intended to dissociate ourselves from differing views, but to contribute to a more complete picture of the problems at hand. To the present editors it would be gratifying if at least some of the ideas and views 'from the other side of the Atlantic' would indeed serve this purpose and help to clarify the problems we are all faced with.

Now that our work is (almost) done, the editors wish to express their sincere gratitude to all the women and men who contributed to the realization of this Handbook. First of all, we should thank the authors for their patience. Although they communicated with only one of the editors, they had, in fact, to deal with a quartet of commenting and criticizing reviewers. Each editor reviewed each text; these reviews were then discussed by all editors, which resulted in a combined evaluation of the proposed chapter. This procedure inevitably, and repeatedly, led to requests for revision. Although we have been demanding taskmasters, we do hope that we did not lose too many friends in the process and that the authors will share our conviction that the results are worth the toil.

With only a few exceptions, the editors and authors did not excel in writing in English. Anna de Haas and her colleagues did their best to save the reader the trouble of having to decipher the double Dutch some of us wrote down. We are very grateful for the good-humoured way in which she kept decoding our awkward sentences.

Finally, we wish to express our deep appreciation of all that the translators, typists, printers and publishers have contributed to the production and publication of this Handbook.

May 1983

P. J. D. DRENTH
Hk. THIERRY
P. J. WILLEMS
CH. J. DE WOLFF

Part 4

The interaction between person/group and organization

Handbook of Work and Organizational Psychology
Edited by P. J. D. Drenth, Hk. Thierry, P. J. Willems and C. J. de Wolff
© 1984, John Wiley & Sons, Ltd.

Introduction

Henk Thierry

The domain covered in this part of the Handbook concerns the meaning of organizational determinants of the work behaviour of groups and individuals and, conversely, the potential influence of that behaviour on the characteristics of and processes in organizations. As such, this domain is a good illustration of the remarkable developments that have been taking in W/O psychology during the past 10–15 years. Thus it may be noted that each subject as covered by the separate chapters has perceptibly expanded, while at the same time various themes relating to these subjects have noticeably gained in depth. These two developments cannot be dissociated from the fact that the domain of the interaction between person, group, and organization is partly or completely connected with the domains of other sciences (such as sociology, economics, political science, engineering, and business administration). This means that psychologists venturing on such domains, either in research or professionally, must acquaint themselves thoroughly with the main themes current in these other sciences.

Yet, the domain of the interaction between person, group, and organization, viewed here from the history and taxonomy of W/O psychology, cannot be considered a truly independent area. In nearly every chapter, problems are discussed that have much in common with those treated in parts 2 and 3—on the interaction between person and work, and between person and group, respectively. The insights and experiences gained from these domains are here often put to fruitful use or are being built on, but such influence also works in the reverse direction. Also the concept of 'organization environment'—the main theme of part 5—plays a major role in many chapters of this fourth part. On the one hand, this should illustrate the fact that W/O psychology has been and is confronted with a large number of new issues, not least—as we mentioned above—because of the contributions from other sciences to the study of organizations. This branch of W/O psychology is often designated 'organizational psychology'. On the other hand, we wish to emphasize that 'work psychology' and 'organizational psychology' have many things in common, both in their premises, theorizing, research methods and in (the problems of) the application of scientific knowledge. In this part, a specific field, a sub-domain of W/O psychology rather than an independent domain is at issue. Thus, we do not consider it warranted to talk about organizational psychology 'per se'.

The above might create the impression that, at least among W/O psychologists, there exists a high degree of consensus on how one should study the relationships between organization characteristics and processes on the one hand and the work behaviour of groups and individuals on the other. However, this is by no means the case. Perhaps the various authors agree most on the view that an integrated theory is at best a beckoning perspective, that the development of 'middle range' and part theories constitutes the line of march for the coming years, that longitudinal research is badly needed, and that there often is a considerable gap between research results and the concrete needs in practice.

These differences in approach become apparent immediately as one puts the question of what an organization theory is or should be. Firstly, the concept of 'organization' may be defined in many different ways. Another issue concerns the orientation of a theory of organizations: does it concern the behaviour 'of' an organization or the behaviour of (groups of) people 'in' an organization? A related issue is the kind of problems into which such a theory could or should provide better insight: is it the tuning in of the dissimilar interests of the groups involved in the organization? Is it the significance of the objectives set for the behaviour? Is it the adaptation of the organization's structure to the variability of the environment? And so on.

Probably there is just one very general problem underlying all organization theories: in what way can we, in the short or in the long run, control the environment's variability, the uncertainty and the dependence—both at the level of the organization as a whole and at that of various components? The way in which this problem is elaborated and marked is, however, extremely pluriform. The following examples are based on some typical problems: can person, organization, and environment be integrated? Do organizations have objectives that influence the behaviour of the organization's members in advance? What does 'rational behaviour' mean? Which interest groups influence the making of strategic choices? Does a decision always follow on the definition of the problem or may it also precede it? Can social and technological conditions be attuned in an equal manner?

Such examples, and others as well, not only indicate the pluriformity found in organization theories but also present a picture of the various schools that have come into existence in this domain. The latter were the main guideline in structuring part A: elements and process variables. Its five chapters present a survey of the dominant organization theories and of how criticism of earlier approaches inspired more comprehensive or, rather, more modest designs.

The areas of application—part B—have a multiple meaning in this context. Firstly, the eight chapters concerned each present a representative picture of the developments in a relevant part of W/O psychology. Thus, the core themes handled in each chapter may be viewed as independent subjects. Secondly, in various chapters the reader will come across accentuations of problems that were at issue in a more general sense in part A. In a few cases, the chapters refer straight to each other, as is the case with chapters 4.4 and 4.9 and with 4.5 and 4.8. Finally, a number of chapters (e.g. 4.11 and 4.13) include illustrations of the fact that the problems that may be encountered in designing particular aspects of the work situation—such as a remuneration system or an automated system—are (or should be) reflected in the theory formation and research on organizational structures and processes.

Handbook of Work and Organizational Psychology
Edited by P. J. D. Drenth, H. Thierry, P. J. Willems and C. J. de Wolff
© 1984, John Wiley & Sons, Ltd.

4.1. Characteristics of organizations

Peter Veen

1. CHARACTERISTICS OF ORGANIZATIONS

1.1. Introduction

In approaching the organization as an object of scientific study, the investigator must first specify what meaning is attached to the concept 'organization'. Once the characteristics of organizations have been clearly identified, the question arises as to whether these characteristics are conceptually pure, and whether or not they can be operationalized in a way that makes it possible for them to be measured. It must also be determined what their relationships are to one another.

In this chapter, the emphasis will be on the conceptual and operational problems connected with the various organizational characteristics, and on the relationships which these characteristics have with one another. It is first necessary, however, to describe the concept of organization in such a way that is clear exactly which characteristics are at issue. When we use the concept organization, we are usually thinking of an organization in which work is done (company X, hospital Y), or of interest groups (union, medical associations), or of associations formed for the coordination of certain activities (World Wildlife Fund, sports club, Red Cross).

In everyday speech we talk about the organization as a thing: something with a recognizable shape, its own identity, and a certain durability. We do not consider a group of friends who build a boat together to be an organization, even though the work they do must be organized. Their activities must be planned, and must take place in a certain sequence. Consumers do not constitute an organization

Proof. dr. Peter Veen, Oosterweg 60, 9751 PJ HAREN.

until they organize themselves in a consumers' union. When confronted with this kind of example we intuitively feel that we understand what an organization is. Yet it appears to be virtually impossible to produce an exhaustive definition for the concept of organization. Various different authors have provided descriptions—which have not, however, been either logically consistent, or exhaustive. There are a number of elements which keep reappearing in these descriptions and which can be considered as characteristics of an organization:

a. The organization is *goal-oriented*. '..., the study of organizations is regarded as possessing an essential unity; as having been dominated since its inception by the conceptualization of organizations as goal attainment devices' (Georgiou, 1973, p. 291). The official goals of an organization are formally recorded in the articles of association, statutes, and so forth.

b. The organization is composed of an association of *individuals*, who perform *tasks*, whose performance is aimed at the achievement of the goals. The organization needs specialized knowledge and/or tools, and must possess the skills needed to use it/them (*technology*) in order to carry out these tasks.

c. An organization has a certain scope/size.

d. An organization is complex. The tasks to be carried out must be distributed (differentiation), and then coordinated (integration). This differentiation and integration are made possible by the *structure* of the organization, which regulates the relationships among the various divisions and activities. The structure is *formalized*: that is, explicitly stated in written form.

e. The organization has a certain *permanence* in time.

f. How the organization functions is measured both within and from without, according to criteria of *effectiveness* (have the desired goals been achieved?) and efficiency (have the costs been kept to a minimum?) (For a discussion of these concepts see: in 't Veld, 1975, p. 232ff.)

Some of the characteristics presented here are of little use in differentiating organizations from other social groups. Virtually every social group, for example, has a goal. A distinguishing characteristic of an organization is that the goal is explicitly and formally stipulated. Almost all social groups are also structured to some extent. If we define structure as the relationships among the elements of a system (individuals, tasks, positions, and so forth), then every group with a reasonable amount of cohesion must by definition possess a structure. If no relationships exist among the elements of a group, then it makes no sense to consider that group as a cohesive whole. The effectiveness and efficiency criteria also apply to almost every form of human contact. After all, it will always be necessary to deliberate on whether or not a contact is useful or pleasurable, and whether or not the parties involved in the contact are willing to invest the time and effort required to maintain it. A real difference can be seen, however, between the serious demands which the environment makes upon an organization, and the more superficial demands resulting from informal contacts between people and groups. The organization must meet these stringent requirements in order to have sufficient resources at its disposal. As a result, the environment is an important determinant of the structure and functioning of the organization, and the environmental characteristics are often regarded as being secondary characteristics of the organization.

Size and permanence could be characteristics which distinguish organizations from other groups, if it were possible to indicate exactly how large and how permanent a social association has to be for it to be called an organization. This is not possible, however. It is primarily the technological and formalistic aspects which are the distinguishing characteristics of organizations. For example, one of the reasons why a family cannot be viewed as an organization is the fact that the organizational structure of a family is not formalized. Nor is the family characterized by the presence of specialized knowledge or tools—not, at least, in the sense that this knowledge or these tools are used for the functioning of the family as such.

The preceding reasoning must not be taken to mean that technology and formalization alone can be considered as *the* characteristics of an organization. The other characteristics also contribute to make the organization what it is. It is above all the combination of all the characteristics which determines the degree to which a social group assumes the character of an organization. The more characteristics a group possesses, and the more highly developed these characteristics are, the more it begins to assume the nature of an organization. That is: the more explicit a group is about its goals, the more it employs a highly specialized technology, the more it has a formalized structure, the longer it has existed, and the more it has explicit criteria for effectiveness and efficiency, the more it begins to assume the character of an organization.

In sections 1.2 to 1.6 we will select the following characteristics for further treatment from the list above: goals and effectiveness, technology, structure and size. In addition, the concept of environment will be given considerable attention. Permanence and efficiency are not dealt with separately. The omission of these two characteristics and the addition of the characteristic 'environment' have a primarily historic background. Permanence and efficiency as concepts have in the past been accorded little attention in the studies of organizations carried out in the social sciences. The concept of environment, on the other hand, has been a frequent object of study in the last ten years, especially with respect to its role as a determinant of the structure of an organization. This relationship between environmental characteristics and structural characteristics will be dealt with in section 2, along with the connection between the structural characteristics and size and technology.

1.2. Goals and effectiveness

1.2.1. GOALS

Georgiou (1973), in his critical discussion of the goal paradigm, observes that organizations virtually always are conceptualized as 'goal attainment devices'

(p. 291). He continues with the observation that 'Yet almost invariably, studies demonstrate the fruitlessness of understanding organizations as goal attaining devices' (p. 292). The reason for this fruitlessness is that it is not as easy as it first seems to indicate exactly what the goals of an organization are. In production organizations, for example, a multitude of goals can be distinguished, such as: the production of certain goods, making a profit, the provision of employment opportunities, offering individuals a chance to develop their full potential, growth and expansion, and long-term survival. This enumeration, which is far from exhaustive, makes it abundantly clear that an organization can have multiple goals which can conflict in part with one another (short-term profits versus development of human potential), and which can in part constitute necessary conditions for one another (profits as a necessary condition for survival). Some of the goals are laid down in articles of association and policy plans; they are embodied in part in the statements and behavior of members of the organization at various levels.

Perrow (1961) suggested as a means of addressing this problem of identifying goals that the visible actions (operative goals) of the organization be considered to be its goals: 'Operative goals designate the goals through the actual operating policies of the organization: they tell us what the organization actually is trying to do ...' (p. 856). The job of determining exactly what these 'operating policies' are, however, is not an easy one. After all, the actual functioning of the organization is determined by the interplay of the various desires and interests present inside and outside that organization. Different actors attempt to transform their interests into *the* goals of the organization. And the organization must, to a certain degree, take all these interests into account, so that the 'operative goals' can display a wide diversity. One method for determining what these interests are is to ask what the desires are of the different actors involved. In 't Veld (1975, p. 146 ff.) classified these desires in the categories 'preliminary conditions–goals–policy' (ways and means of accomplishing the goal). The category 'goals' was further divided into internal and external goals. For the Technical University at Delft, for example, he obtained with this method 22 external goals (for example, shaping the education of an engineer to meet the needs of society), and nine internal goals (for example, the promotion of a type of organization in which participants can contribute to the best of their ability at acceptable costs). Such a method makes possible a rough classification of a number of different goals, but is incapable of indicating to what degree the different goals can be harmonized with one another, or which goals are the most essential, if priorities must be assigned.

A solution for this problem is to approach the organization as an '... arbitrarily defined focus of interest' (Georgiou, 1973, p. 302), or in the words of Cummings (1977, pp. 59–60), as '... an arena within which participants can engage in behavior they perceive as instrumental to their goals.' The organization is thus transformed into a market in which valuable goods and services are exchanged for some form of payment (Georgiou, 1973, p. 306). Those who possess the skills, means and so forth which are the most essential to the survival of the organization will acquire the most power (see Hinings *et al.*, 1974). Those with the most power will see to it that their goals are afforded the highest priority in the organization. In this way the goals of the dominant coalition in the organization become *the* goals of the organization (Pennings and Goodman, 1977). Thus the analysis of the goals of the organization becomes the analysis of the power relationships within the organization, and of the power relationships between the organization and its environment.

1.2.2. EFFECTIVENESS

The consequence for the concept of goal of the approach sketched above is that the organization is the most effective for those with the most power. It should be recalled that effectiveness has been defined as the degree to which set goals have been achieved (in 't Veld, 1975, pp. 167, 232 ff.; Price, 1968, p. 3). The more successful an actor is in making the goals of the organization coincide with his own goals, the more likely it becomes that these personal goals will be realized. Yet the concept of effectiveness will remain just as multiform as the concept of goals, as long as all the actors involved are essential in some degree—however disparate—to the functioning of the organization. This means that the organization must take all these subsidiary interests into account, and that those involved will continually judge its performance in this area.

Because effectiveness is used in many studies of organizations as a criterion variable, more attempts have been made to make this concept measurable than for the concept of goals. However, few investigations have made the measurement of effectiveness itself an object of study. Seashore and Yuchtman (1967), in a study using factor analysis, and based upon existing administrative data (sales figures, personnel data, and so forth), isolated ten dimensions of effectiveness having to do with topics related to more or less traditional business economics: for example, volume of turnover, production costs and market penetration. Mahoney and Weitzel (1969), using a questionnaire, classified almost three hundred departments of different organizations according to their efficiency. Proceeding from more than one hundred variables they isolated twenty efficiency factors. In addition to the usual indices covering productivity and efficiency, they found a number of factors which emphasized aspects related to personnel policies and the functioning of the organization, such as the degree of democratic leadership, possibilities for development of personal potential, the presence of planning procedures, and so forth.

The multidimensional character of the concept of effectiveness manifested in the studies cited above is affirmed when the empirical studies which use effectiveness as a criterion variable are compared with one another. Using an analysis of 17 empirical studies as a basis, Steers (1975) identified 14 indices of effectiveness which were used in two or more of the studies. The indices which appeared most often were: capacity to adapt/flexibility (ten times), productivity (six times) and job satisfaction (five times). Campbell (1976) derived 30 indices of effectiveness from the literature, including uncommon ones such as motivation and the degree to which management controls the organizational apparatus.

This brief survey has hopefully demonstrated that the concept of effectiveness is indeed measured as multiformly as might be expected following our discussion of the related concept of goals.

The great variety in the operationalizations of the concept of effectiveness is not the only problem we have to solve when an attempt is made to compare the results of studies in this area. There are a number of other problems connected with this concept (for a review see Steers, 1975):

—A large number of measurements of effectiveness are only weakly correlated with one another, which engenders some skepticism about the construct validity of the concept.

—It is unclear what time span can best be chosen in describing the effectiveness of an organization. It is, for example, very well possible that a radical cut in costs will make short-term effectiveness seem very high. If, on the other hand, the cut in spending means that the maintenance of machines is neglected, or that necessary investments are not made, then the long-term effectiveness will be less favorable.

—Because different criteria of effectiveness can be incongruent with one another and because it is in addition unclear what importance should be afforded to each of them, it is far from clear how a general judgement of effectiveness is to be obtained. How can the effectiveness be described of a business firm where a 'slave-driving' management succeeds in achieving high productivity, but where employees are highly dissatisfied, which results in a high turnover of labor?

—A similar problem lies in the fact that effectiveness can be observed at different levels in the organization (individual, group, organization as a whole). It is not clear how the effectiveness at one level is related to the effectiveness at another level.

All these points highlight the fact that the concept 'effectiveness' is insufficiently anchored in theory.

A number of different suggestions have been made to increase the utilizability of the concept. Campbell (1977) suggests that more intensive case studies should be done of the process of formulating criteria of effectiveness within the organization, so that a better understanding can be obtained of how the organization itself deals with these contradictions. At the same time, he propagates simulation studies, aimed at a more effective examination of the interrelationships between the different components of the concept.

Evan (1976) proposed using a systems theoretical approach to obtain a systematic classification of the different effectiveness criteria. He uses three groups of indicators as a base: one group connected with the input (material, information, and so forth; I); one group connected with transformation processes within the organization, which transform the input into output (products) of the organization (T); and finally, a group connected with the output (O). A measurement within these groups can be cross-sectional (situation at one moment in time) or can measure the change that has taken place between two points in time (Δ). In each case, the index of effectiveness consists of the ratio of measurements at the same point in time from two of these groups (O/I; T/I; T/O), or of the ratio between a measurement of change and a cross-sectional measurement (for example, Δ I/I; Δ T/I, and so forth), from the same or different groups. Some examples are: profits/investments (O/I); raw materials/wastage of materials (I/O); working conditions/absenteeism (T/O). In this way it becomes possible to classify the various indicators of effectiveness, allowing for better comparisons among them.

Dubin (1976) has formulated a fundamental dilema with respect to the concept of effectiveness: the effectiveness of the organization, when viewed from within, consists of the effective use of means obtained in the environment for achieving organizational goals. When seen from a perspective outside the organization, it may be asked how functional these goals still are for the environment. For example, to what extent do these goals continue to have a socially relevant function? Making use of Dubin's example of the English producer of chastity belts which went bankrupt, this distinction means that it is possible to produce chastity belts extremely efficiently, while society has no need for them whatsoever; from this broader perspective the effectiveness has been reduced to zero, due to a total lack of demand for the product.

The production of atomic energy can serve as a more modern example. It is possible to put together an organization which, when evaluated from a perspective inside the organization, can produce atomic energy efficiently and effectively, even though the discussion about the social costs and benefits of atomic energy is still in full swing. The social effectiveness is determined on the basis of an evaluation of these costs and benefits, following which a decision is made as to whether or not additional resources will be made available to the organization.

Conclusion: It is impossible to make satisfactory use of a simple goal and effectiveness concept—on conceptual, theoretical, and empirical grounds. None has succeeded until now in formulating a rigorous approach for constructing a sophisticated goal and effectiveness concept which can be used in research.

1.3. Technology

The concept of technology is linked to the way in which an organization produces goods or services. Technology is here defined as the totality of operations which the organization uses to transform input (materials, clients problems) into output (products, services, solutions). We call this the production or transformation process.

In the words of Perrow (1967, p. 195): '... the actions that an individual

Input	Troughput	Output
material	processing/operations	products
problems	transformations making use of knowledge and other aids	solutions
questions		answers
clients/patients		ex–clients ex–patients
information	TECHNOLOGY	services

Figure 1. The concept of technology.

performs on an object, with or without the aid of tools or mechanical devices, in order to make some change in that object.' Figure 1 gives a schematic representation of this process.

The term 'technology' is not only used for production organizations, where, for example, a fabric is woven by transforming raw materials by a number of different processes (rinsing, washing, dying, weaving), but also when, for example, an advisory agency, making use of specific knowledge and procedures, contributes to the formation of a new organizational structure. This is also the case when a university library, using a system of data files, registered by a computer or otherwise, can provide an answer to the question of what information is available concerning the relationship between frustration and aggression. The term 'technology' is also applied when a psychotherapist, using a certain therapy, succeeds in transforming his depressive patient into a cheerful individual. Technological knowledge is also required for the transforming of information on developments in the market into a market strategy for the firm. It will have become clear that this conception of technology endows it with a much broader meaning than is the case in everyday speech, where the concept is primarily associated with the presence and operation of machines and installations (Perrow, 1970, p. 75 ff.; Porter et al., 1975, p. 232; van der Zwaan, 1972). In the literature, the use of the term technology in this broad sense has led to a great deal of confusion and lack of clarity. This is primarily due to the fact that different authors make use of different dimensions and categories to characterize the differences among technologies.

Perrow (1970, p. 78 ff.) constructs a classification on the basis of properties of the material (input). He makes a distinction between two dimensions:

a. The variability of the material to be processed. This dimension can be illustrated with the example of schools which cater to 'normal' children, compared to schools which are specially focused upon children with emotional and/or learning disabilities. The variability of the material (the children) which the school processes is much greater in the latter case than in the former. As a result the diversity of teaching methods will also be much greater in the latter case.

b. The degree to which the properties of the material are or are not thoroughly understood. If it is so that the behavior of a 'normal' child can be better understood than the behavior of a 'problem' child, then this would mean that in the latter case considerably more certainties and reserves would have to be incorporated into the choice of methods, and that more stringent evaluation procedures would need to be applied.

In addition to these two dimensions on the input side, Perrow distinguishes two other aspects in the production process itself:

c. The degree to which there are few or many exceptions to the normal production process. When there are few exceptions one speaks of routine technology (assembly line, confection). If goods are made to order, a more 'manual' technology will develop, which means that the production process is broken down into fewer segments.

d. The degree to which problems in the production process can be analyzed (the degree of uncertainty). It is poorly understood for some processes how they unfold, and which factors contribute to the completion of a good product. This is, for example, clearly the case for the transformation processes taking place in advisory organizations and many psychotherapies. The problems occurring in production processes, on the other hand, can often be analyzed very effectively, and can, for example, be solved with the aid of a computer (operations research, for example).

Like Perrow, the Aston group (Hickson *et al.*, 1969, 1970; Pugh *et al.*' 1969) distinguishes different aspects of the concept of technology which are linked either to the input side or to the transformation process. They make an additional distinction within the transformation process to the knowledge and variability distinction employed by Perrow: the aspect 'operations technology' by which they mean the sequence of activities and the apparatus used to carry them out ('equipping and sequencing of activities in the work flow'). With this definition they approach very closely the concept of technology used in ordinary speech. The Aston group has tried more than other authors to operationalize its technology concept. Using check lists, where the respondent must indicate whether or not certain elements are present, they measure the following aspects of technology: the level of automation of the equipment; the degree of inflexibility in the sequence and nature of the operations (work flow rigidity); the degree of specificity in the evaluation of the quality of operations and/or output; interdependence of work flow segments.

This same group of investigators (Pugh *et al.*, 1969) distinguishes two other concepts obtained from a factor analysis which at first create the impression of being technology measurements at an operational level: 'operating variability' and 'operating diversity'. A closer examination reveals, however, that these factors are primarily related to characteristics of the output and the market. The first factor indicates to what degree standards are or are not met. The second factor has to do with the degree of diversity of products and clients.

Joan Woodward, one of the first to do research in this area, appears at first to characterize the production process with reference to the output. She (Woodward, 1965, p. 39 ff.) distinguishes three types of production processes (with a number of sub-categories):

I. Unit and small batch production: low volume production and production of prototypes on the basis of the customer's specifications.

II. Large batch and mass production: with or without the use of an assembly line.

III. Process production: production of very large quantities of primarily chemical products using sophisticated equipment.

The description of the categories includes, in addition to characteristics of the customer and of the scope of the production, characteristics of the production apparatus. Woodward's classification is thus—not surprisingly—interpreted in the literature as 'technological complexity': that is, the complexity increases from type I to III. Hickson *et al.* (1970) interpret the classification in terms of production continuity (re-setting, re-tooling, re-designing), which they measure as a separate category. This interpretation points in the direction of still another emphasis that is encountered in the literature: the interdependence of the different phases in the production process. Thompson (1967), for example, characterizes different technologies more or less on the basis of the different types of dependence which exist between the production processes and/or branches of the organization. He distinguishes (p. 54 ff.):

a. *Pooled interdependence*: each part makes a separate contribution to the whole, and the whole lends support to each part. Each part must be attuned in its functioning to the other parts, and that functioning must not lead to activities which interfere with or contradict the functioning of the other parts. The completion of each of these processes is not, however, dependent upon the completion of one or all of the other processes: for example, one process does not have to wait to begin until the other has been completed. An example of this type of organization is a bank, which provides various services for its customers (checking account, stocks, mortgages). It is in the service industries in particular that this type of 'mediation technology' will be encountered (Thompson, 1967, p. 16).

b. *Sequential interdependence*: the different processes and subdivisions of the organization are dependent for their progress upon the contributions of other subdivisions. They cannot operate further if the other subdivisions do not deliver their contributions on time. The assembly line is the classic example of such a 'long-linked' technology which has developed according to this pattern (Thompson, 1967, p. 15). And the operations which are required for a customer

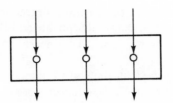

Figure 2. Pooled interdependence. (figures 2–4 based on: Van de Ven, 1977, p. 252)

to draw money from his checking account must also take place in a certain given sequence (no money if the account is found to be 'too' overdrawn).

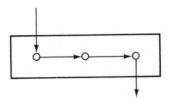

Figure 3. Sequential interdependence.

c. *Reciprocal interdependence*: with sequential interdependence, processes are only dependent upon the processes preceding them. The door of a car cannot be mounted until there is a car body, but the mounting of the body to the chassis is not dependent upon the attachment of the door. The distinguishing characteristic of reciprocal interdependence is that the contributions of the different parts are essential to one another. The programmer of analytical programs cannot do without the researcher, and the researcher cannot do without the support of the programmer. The intensive technologies (Thompson, 1967, p. 17), such as those found in a hospital, for example, are often characterized by this kind of dependence.

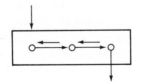

Figure 4. Reciprocal interdependence.

Considering the discussion above, it will not be surprising to the reader when we conclude that there can be observed a large diversity in the operationalizations and measurements of the concept of technology. The following dimensions can be differentiated in this area:

—*Technological complexity*: measured as degree of automation and mechanization (estimate of machinery present) and degree to which use is made of the computer (Blau *et al.*, 1976; Blau and Schoenherr, 1971; Hickson *et al.*, 1969; Khandwalla, 1974; Woodward, 1965). The measurement is usually made at organization level.

—*Task complexity*: measured at the individual level using interviews and questionnaires (Billings *et al.*, 1977), or at the level of the working group using an aggregation of individual data (Comstock and Scott, 1977; Nemiroff and Lord, 1977), or by making use of evaluations of experts working within or outside the organization (Comstock and Scott, 1977; Hrebeniak, 1974). The concept is related primarily to the complexity of the task and how well it can be overseen.

—*Variability, predictability, repetitiveness*: the meanings of these concepts are often closely related; all are connected in some way to the degree to which the transformation process can be controlled. They are measured using objective evaluation procedures, or by means of individual interviews and questionnaires. These concepts are used at an individual level (Billings *et al.*, 1977; Hrebeniak, 1974; Lynch, 1974; Mohr, 1971; Nemiroff and Lord, 1977; van de Ven, 1977), at the department level (Mohr, 1971; Overton *et al.*, 1977; Van de Ven, 1977) and at the organization level (Hage and Aiken, 1969).

Although at first glance the concepts seem to be closely related, the perceptions (subjective observations) of the factors often correlate only very slightly with one another (Hrebeniak, 1974; Mohr, 1971); in a number of cases, a factor analysis results in the orthogonal factors uncertainty and variability/repetitiveness (Lynch, 1974; Overton *et al.*, 1977).

—*Interdependence*: The concept of interdependence is used primarily to indicate the interdependence of individual tasks. The concept is measured at the individual level using questionnaires (Billings *et al.*, 1977; Lynch, 1974; Mohr, 1971), or by means of evaluations based on checklists or interviews with management (Hickson *et al.*, 1969; Van de Ven, 1977).

This survey demonstrates that technology can be characterized using a wide diversity of indices. Which characteristic is used seems primarily to be determined by which aspect of the input or of the transformation process occasions uncertainty for the organization. An important source of uncertainty for different kinds of nursing units, for example, is the type of patient that is treated. This results in the fact that the characteristics of the different types of patients are used to characterize the technology (Comstock and Scott, 1977; Overton *et al.*, 1977). In a typical production company, on the other hand, uncertainty is usually engendered primarily by the manufacturing processes themselves, and by their relationships to one another (Blau *et al.*, 1976; Hickson *et al.*, 1969; Khandwalla, 1974).

Another complicating factor is that technology is measured at the individual, task, and organization levels. The measurements are as a result often more or less specific to a particular level. The 'Requisite Task Attributes' index developed by

Turner and Lawrence (1965), for example, measures the aspects variation, autonomy, required interaction, optional interaction, required knowledge and skill, and responsibility—all at the task level. It is far from clear whether such an index can be generalized to the organization level, and how such a generalization can be made.

In addition to the wide diversity in indicators and their application at different levels, there are a number of other problems which make the technology concept more difficult to use.

—A large number of instruments have a low reliability (see, for example, Blau et al., 1976; Mohr, 1971).

—The convergent (Hrebeníak, 1974; Mohr, 1971) and discriminant (Hage and Aiken, 1969; Lynch, 1974) validity is low.

Recent research, however, has devoted more attention to the problems of reliability and validity (see, for example, Comstock and Scott, 1977; Lynch, 1974; Overton et al., 1977; van de Ven, 1977).

1.4. Structure

The concept of structure is one of the most essential concepts in the organization literature. If we look upon the organization as a system composed of a number of elements (people, machines, buildings, tasks, and so forth), which are related to one another to a certain degree, then the structure of the organization consists of all the relationships which exist among these elements (in 't Veld, 1975, p. 16). As we saw previously with the technology concept, activities take place within the organization which are directed at manipulating the input in such a way that the organization can make a product (in the broadest sense of the term) available to the environment. We call these linked activities 'processes'. Transformations are not the only processes which unfold within the organization. A variety of other processes take place in support of these production processes: communication and decision-making processes, and control (management) processes. Whenever the processes begin to exhibit a certain regularity we use the term structure, which means nothing more than that clearly distinguishable relationships can be observed among activities, and therefore among elements. Thus we speak of a communication and decision-making structure parallel to the communication and decision-making processes. In this sense, when in the course of time a structure has assumed a certain form, it is always the result of processes which have assumed a more or less settled pattern. This way of looking at the concept of structure approaches closely Allport's (1954) conception of structure as cycles of events which keep each other in existence (event-structure). This emphasizes the fact that, especially in the case of social structures, structures owe their existence to well-established patterns of behavior. The observer cannot fall back on physical structures (such as a skeleton, for example) for the recognition of such social structures, but must always depend upon the observation of behavior. This type of observation, however, very rarely takes place. The investigator usually relies upon reproduction by those involved of the various structural arrangements which are present in the organization. This is, for example, the case in the method for measuring organization structures developed by researchers of the Aston-group.

Based on a conceptual analysis (Pugh *et al.*, 1963), 64 scales were constructed, of which 32 determine the nature and scope of the specialization alone (see Pugh *et al.*, 1968, p. 71). Data were then collected by interviewing a limited number of key figures from the organization, asking them to indicate official structures and rules. The emphasis was placed in these interviews on what 'is supposed to happen', and not what 'really happens'. Data were gathered in more than fifty organizations. Wherever possible, the data were supplemented by official organization documents.

A factor analysis was then carried out on the sixteen scales '. . . that most fully represent the variables and that were most distinctive '(Pugh *et al.*, 1968, p. 82; no other explanation is given for their selection); four orthogonal factors were obtained as a result.

Factor I: Structuring of activities: standardization, role and functional specialization, and formalization.

Factor II: Concentration of authority: centralization, autonomy of the organization, percentage directly involved in production.

Factor III: Direct control of the work process (line control of work flow); ratio of subordinates/supervisors.

Factor IV: Relative size of the supportive component (percentage of administrative personnel).

These factors or very similar ones reappear in a number of replication studies, so that this classification can be used with some confidence (Child, 1972a; Inkson *et al.*, 1970a, 1970b). The only exception found by Child to a series of corroborative data was that the factors 'structuring of activities' and 'concentration of authority' were not independent from one another, but were negatively correlated.

Many conceptual classifications have been proposed in addition to this empirically-derived classification of structural characteristics (see, e.g. Indik, 1968; Sells, 1968). James and Jones (1976) derived the following representative dimensions of the concept of structure, based on a review of the existing conceptual and empirical classifications:

a. *Centralization*: The degree to which decision-making and authority are centralized or delegated.

b. *Configuration*: Indices such as number of hierarchical levels, number of subordinates per supervisor (span-of-control), number of specialists, and so forth.

c. *Formalization*: The degree to which behavioral directives, competencies, and procedures are laid down in writing (for example, function profiles).

d. *Standardization*: The degree to which activities and procedures are standardized.

e. *Specialization*: The degree of differentiation in functions, tasks and so forth (line—staff, for example).

f. *Dependence*: The degree to which divisions of the organization are dependent upon one another for the accomplishment of tasks.

They also add size as a structural characteristic to this list of dimensions. However, if structure is defined as the systematic pattern of relationships among elements, then size cannot be considered a structural characteristic.

A large number of variables are contained in the different structural dimensions; these variables overlap one another to a certain extent, and some are correlated with one another. This is one of the reasons for the criticism directed at the concept of structure. A number of these points of criticism are (see James and Jones, 1976; McKelvey, 1975; Mansfield, 1973):

a. the conceptual definitions of the various sub-concepts are ambiguous;

b. the concepts are lacking in theoretical anchorage;

c. there is insufficient exact specification of which relationships are or are not a part of the organizational structure (are friendships also considered part of the organization structure?);

d. it is unclear whether all the structural characteristics are supposed to be present in all organizations.

In addition to these theoretical-conceptual reservations with respect to the concept of organizational structure, some doubts arise with respect to the empirical studies due to the ambiguous use of multivariate techniques and the insufficiently independent measurement of the various structural characteristics.

The essence of this criticism is directed toward the ambiguous demarcation of the structural dimensions. An improvement could be achieved by combining a tightly-fitting conceptual specification of the elements and the different aspects to which they are related, as well as a systematic framework for describing the relationships. Oeser and Harary (1962) have advanced a proposal for such a system of classification. They differentiate humans (H), tasks (T), and positions (P) as elements in the organization. In their scheme they indicate what the relationship is between tasks and positions, humans and positions, among the tasks themselves, and among the positions themselves. Yet this scheme likewise fails to specify exactly what type of relationships are involved.

1.5. Size

The concept of size seems at first to be deceptively simple. The annual business supplement of an important Dutch newspaper (*NRC/Handelsblad*), in which Dutch business firms are classified according to size, demonstrates that this is not the case. It soon becomes apparent that different dimensions must be included in the analysis, such as the number of employees, the turnover, and the capital assets. There is a high degree of agreement among the different rankings. This agreement, however, is far from perfect. The index used most often in organization studies is number of employees (Kimberley, 1976). Even such a relatively simple index as this one, however, proves on further consideration to have a number of problematic aspects. It is, for example, unclear whether only paid employees are counted in determining the size of the organization, or whether volunteers are also included. What, for example, is the size of an organization where extra employees are regularly brought in at peak production periods (for a discussion see Hall, 1972, p. 110 ff.). These ambiguities have resulted in a large number of indices for measuring size. Kimberley (1976) has proposed that they be classified in four groups:

a. The physical capacity of an organization, as operationalized, for example, in the number of beds in a hospital, the productive capacity of machines, the number of square meters in a distribution center.

b. The number of employees in an organization. A number of dimensions can be introduced into this classification: volunteers—employees; full time—part time workers, permanently employed by the organization—temporarily employed. When comparing organizations, a decision must be made in advance which categories are to be included, and how they will be measured.

c. Data related to the input and output of an organization. Examples are production and turnover on the output side, and the raw materials handled (such as the number of pigs to be butchered) on the input side.

d. Resources which are completely at the disposal of the organization, such as funds for investment; ownership of property, such as land or buildings which are not being used.

Such a classification calls attention to the fact that a reason must exist for choosing a certain index. One of the most significant problems in making use of the concept of size, however, is that it is exactly a theoretical rationale for its use which is lacking in organization studies. In so far as theoretical reasons are given for the inclusion of size, they tend to support the proposition that increasing size in an organization creates problems with the communication between divisions and with their coordination (Blau, 1970). Size thus becomes one of the sources of uncertainty for the organization, which attempts to control this uncertainty as it does all other uncertainties (see section 2). A further elaboration and specification of these insights should make it possible to choose the most suitable index for size tailored to the problem which is to be investigated.

1.6. Environment

1.6.1. THEORETICAL APPROACHES

Organizations do not operate in a vacuum, but in an environment in which they fulfill certain functions. The environment will provide the resources which the organization needs to fulfill these functions just as long as these functions are of value for that environment. The organization and its environment are interdependent and therefore try to influence one another. In order to influence each other, they need to possess information about one another. For these reasons the organization has roles extending beyond its own boundaries (Aldrich, 1979, p. 243). These roles can be divided into two types:

a. External representative roles, aimed primarily at ensuring the supply of resources and at actively influencing the environment. An example would be the trustees and directors of a university hospital, who try to obtain funds for expansion or renewal from the Ministry of Education. The sales department of a goods-producing organization also falls under this category.

b. Information processing roles, which make it possible for an organization to anticipate changes in the environment. Marketing departments are a well-known example of this category. A set of directors who try to lay out a line of policy for the years ahead are also fulfilling this function.

This dichotomy is closely related to two generally accepted approaches toward analyzing the relationship between the organization and its environment. The first approach sees the environment primarily as the source of scarce resources required by the organization; the organization therefore attempts to gain as complete a control as possible over it (see Yuchtman and Seashore, 1967). The second approach sees the environment as a source of (uncertain) information which the organization needs to make adequate adjustments in its behavior.

The approach which sees the environment as a source of scarce resources implies a natural selection model, in which the organization fulfills a more or less passive role. Working within this model, it is enough to know the characteristics of the environment and to know which type of organization is suited to it to be able to explain why some organizations manage to survive. The environment allows those organizations to exist (that is, continues to make resources available) which have the 'form' (goals, structure, processes) which conforms most closely to these environmental characteristics (Hannan and Freeman, 1977). A certain combination of characteristics of the environment constitutes a kind of ecological niche, within which an organization with a certain combination of characteristics fits best. When the environmental characteristics change, new niches come into being. The familiar 'hole in the market' is an example of this phenomenon (see Aldrich, 1979, p. 112). In this approach, the accent in the description of the environment is placed on objective characteristics such as (see, among others, Aldrich, 1979, p. 63 ff.):

—Capacity (lean-rich): relative level of resources which are at the disposal of an organization (energy).

—Diversity (homogeneity–heterogeneity): the degree to which elements in the environment are or are not similar to one another (types of competitors; different types of energy).

—Stability–unstability: the degree to which the environment undergoes changes (price fluctuations, fluctuations in the harvest).

—Dispersion–concentration: the degree to which resources are uniformly dispersed in the environment (customers in the same area or not).

—Turbulence (connected–unconnected): the degree to which the environment is characterized by an increasing rate of interconnection (for example, banks with one another, or banks with the government).

—Domain–dissension: the degree to which it is recognized that an organization is entitled to a specific contribution from the environment (support from the government; legality of services rendered, and so forth).

The information-processing view regards organizations in a less passive light; it assumes that an organization will do its best to discover how it can remain in existence. Three strategies for accomplishing this end are available to organizations: 1. searching out circumstances favorable to itself, which make it possible for it to survive (searching out a niche; getting rid of old products in a new location); 2. adapting to the environment (introducing a new product on the market); 3. influencing the environment (trying to obtain protective measures for one's own product). Information is needed for action to be taken. The role played by the characteristics of the environment is primarily determined by the way in which they are perceived by an organization. In the course of this process of dealing with the environment it is faced with the following uncertainties:

a. The uncertainty inherent to the characteristics of the environment. The organization is confronted with a higher degree of uncertainty; the poorer, the more heterogeneous, and the more unstable the environment, the greater the dispersion of the elements and the more highly correlated they are with one another, and the less agreement there is about the position of the organization. This uncertainty is connected primarily to the recognizability of patterns, the predictability of changes, and the possibility of finding a place for itself.

b. In addition to this more or less objective uncertainty, localized in the environment, an organization also has to deal with uncertainty about the perception of the environment. There may be a hiatus in the information; it may be unreliable, contradictory, and unclear. Even if this is not the case and the information flow is perfect, it is still possible that no coherent patterns or predictable trends can be identified. This may be due to the fact that no such patterns are present in the environment. However, it may also be due to the fact that there are certain factors present in the organization itself which prevent trends from being recognized—for example, because an interest group in the organization refuses to see something.

c. The organization is confronted with still another kind of uncertainty when it seeks to base its action on an interpretation of characteristics of the environment. That is, uncertainly will often exist concerning the causal relations in the environment, which means that it will often be unclear what the effect of a certain line of behavior of the organization will be. If a certain action is chosen, in spite of this lack of clarity, then it will often take a long time before the effects of that action can be observed. The fact that so much time elapses before the organization obtains any feedback concerning the effect of its action is in itself responsible for an increase in uncertainty. It will, in addition, often be unclear whether or not the effects can be ascribed to the actions of the organization (see March and Olsen, 1976, p. 56 ff.).

1.6.2. MEASUREMENTS OF UNCERTAINTY IN THE ENVIRONMENT

In empirical studies in which an attempt has been made to measure the concept of environment, the emphasis has usually been placed upon the informative approach, and therefore upon the perceptions of the various characteristics of the environment. Lawrence and Lorsch (1967, p. 248), for example, making use of questionnaires, asked managers of three types of departments (production, marketing, research) in three different types of industries (plastics, food, containers) about their perception of a) the clarity of the task requirements within the various departments; b) the degree of difficulty of the tasks in the departments; c) the time which elapses before the department obtains feedback concerning the success of their functioning. They assume that the less clear and more difficult the task and the greater the time lapse before feedback is obtained, the more the uncertainty increases. This approach is clearly aimed more at measuring environmental uncertainty as experienced by departments of an organization rather than the environmental uncertainty experienced in an organization as a whole.

Duncan (1972) investigated the uncertainty associated with making decisions. He distinguishes between objective uncertainty, caused by characteristics of the departmental environment, and subjective uncertainty, caused by a lack of information. Complexity and instability were used as indices of the more or less objective environmental characteristics. A decision was considered to be more complex when more factors had to be taken into account and when more segments of the environment (for example, a greater number of other departments) were involved. The situation was called more unstable when the factors playing a role in a certain type of decision changed more often, and when new factors often played a role in a decision. Information on these points was gathered using questionnaires and interviews, so that some doubts must be entertained as to the 'real' objectivity of the indices used.

The perceived uncertainty comprised three components: a) lack of information about the environment; b) lack of familiarity with what the effects of a decision will be; c) lack of familiarity with the repercussions of the outcome of a decision for the success of the department.

The results of this investigation of a number of departments in production organizations and in research and development organizations showed that the more complex and unstable decision-making was considered to be, the greater was the increase in the perceived lack of information and lack of clarity concerning the effects of a decision, and the repercussions of these effects. This effect was related primarily to the stability factor. As expected, the research and development units perceived more uncertainties than the production units. Duncan worked within a departmental perspective, so that the enviornment of the organization as a whole plays only an indirect role.

Neither Lawrence and Lorsch nor Duncan reported reliability data for the measurement instruments they used. There are two studies in which attempts are made to obtain this type of data and at the same time to construct objective indices for the environment. Tosi *et al.* (1973) did a study involving one hundred managers of 60 business firms using Lawrence and Lorsch's questions. Parallel to this measurement of perceived uncertainty they also constructed a more objective uncertainty measurement based on fluctuations in sales figures, expenditures for research and development, and profit figures after taxes for the last ten years for the business firms in question. The correlations between the perceptual indices and the objective indices were low (.0 to .3) and inconsistent. The internal consistency of the Lawrence and Lorsch scales was also extremely low (from .1 to .5) The reliability for the entire scale is .51, which, even for research purposes, can only be regarded as marginally satisfactory.

Downey *et al.* (1975) did a study in which they used both the Lawrence and Lorsch and the Duncan measurements. In addition, they made the same measurement of fluctuations in prices and turnover figures as Tosi *et al.*; Downey *et al.*, however, did not record these figures objectively, but questioned the respondents about their perceptions of these dimensions. They also asked about perceptions of their competitors. They used the variations in the yearly predictions of the U.S. Department of Commerce concerning production figures of an industrial group for a period of ten years as a more or less objective standard of measurement. The reliability of the Lawrence and Lorsch measurements was even lower (.39) than those in the study of Tosi *et al.* The Duncan measurements of the perception of the lack of information and the lack of familiarity with the effects of the outcomes of a decision, on the other hand, exhibited a reasonable reliability for research purposes, as did the scale in its entirety (.67). The correlations between the perceptions of uncertainty according to the Lawrence and Lorsch scales, the Duncan scales, and the perceptions of fluctuations in prices and turnover, were extremely low.

In reviewing the data from these studies, we must conclude that the reliability of the scales is far from satisfactory, and that the convergent validity (correlation between related scales) is insufficient. The lack of correlations between the subjective uncertainty and the fluctuations in objective data such as turnover figures in particular leads us to question the significance of the different approaches. A problem is formed in this connection by the fact that in both the more objective and the more subjective indices the uncertainty is not directly measured, nor are direct questions asked about it; the researchers rather presume that it is correlated with changes, complexity, insufficient information, and so forth. Considering the research outcomes, it must be concluded either that our assumptions concerning these correlations are false, or that the concepts have not been measured properly, or that the wrong elements have been combined in constructing the uncertainty indices.

This brings us to another problem. In the previous discussion the tacit assumption was made repeatedly that the environment is a single coherent unit. The environment, however, is divisible into a large number of segments, each having a different relevance for different parts of the organization and each having its own dynamics of uncertainty. Friedlander and Pickle (1968), for example, distinguish the following segments: the government (local and national), the customers (market), suppliers, creditors (especially banks, and so forth), stockholders, and the employees themselves. This list can easily be expanded with other categories, such as competitors, unions, employers' associations, professional and technological developments, the labour market, and so forth (see also Duncan, 1972).

The relevance at a given moment of each of the segments for a division of the organization is determined by the nature of the problem facing the organization, and the role which the division plays in that problem. In constructing an index for uncertainty in the environment, therefore, the investigator should specify both whether measurements are objective or perceptual and the division of the organization and the segments of the environment to which the measurement is applicable. Such an approach assumes concurrently that a clear distinction can be made between the organization and the environment. This is often extremely difficult. It is, for example, difficult to determine whether stockholders are a part of the organization or of the enviroment. If the decision is made to consider them as part of the organization, the question immediately arises as to whether other suppliers of capital such as banks must also be counted as part of the organization. It is possible, as long as the stockholders do not actively work in the organization, to make an arbitrary decision to include them in the organization or not. This becomes considerably more difficult when they do work in the organization. The same is the case for numerous other intertwined aspects, which have come into being as a result of members of the organization simultaneously being members of different groups which have an interest in the organization in one way or another: the municipality, their professional association, their union, to name a few. The organization itself is also a member of groups which, again, are a part of its environment, such as associations of businesses in the same branch of trade, employers' associations, and so forth. Depending upon the interests and problems involved or upon the role played by the organization or its members at a given moment, a segment is assigned either to the organization or to its environment. Thus Starbuck (1976, p. 1071) concludes with respect to making a clear distinction between organization and environment: '... a boundary between them is partially an arbitrary invention of the perceiver ...'. He suggests that apparently the only fruitful approach to the problem will be a conceptualization in the form of a continuous series of transitions. Summarizing, we can conclude for the concept of environment as well as for the other organizational characteristics, that there exists a large number of theoretical, conceptual, and measurement problems which require the further development of theory and empirical investigation.

1.7. Conclusions

The characteristics of the organization and the environment prove to be fraught with a great number of problems:

a. *The* structure, *the* technology, *the* goals, *the* effectiveness, *the* size and *the* environment of the organization do not exist. Each of these concepts can be divided into a large number of aspects.

b. The conceptual definitions are not sharply deliniated, which often means that it is possible to divide and group these aspects unequivocally. The connection between these aspects is also unclear.

c. The aspects can be measured at different levels and can be differentiated according to the different segments inside and outside the organization. The measurements can be based upon objective data (countable or observable), but usually have their foundation in the perceptions of those involved. This has resulted in a very large number of diverse operationalizations of the concepts.

d. The convergent validity of the measurements is low: that is, measurements which are supposed to be measuring the same thing, fail almost completely to correlate with one another.

e. The reliability (especially the internal consistency) of most of the measurement instruments is also far from satisfactory.

f. It was established that virtually all the characteristics were almost completely lacking in theoretical underpinnings.

This sombre—though in the social sciences not unusual—picture raises the question of whether or not it is possible to find significant correlations among organizational characteristics. We will go into this question in section 2.

2. DETERMINANTS OF THE STRUCTURE OF ORGANIZATIONS

2.1. Introduction

By tracing whether or not a certain correlation is present between the various organizational characteristics, we can gain additional insights into the nature and significance of the characteristics. We will concentrate upon the relationship between technology, size, and environment on the one hand, and the structure of the organization on the other. The reason for this choice is that the study of organizations is in large part focused upon discovering the determinants of the effectiveness of the organization and of the behavior of individuals in the organization; the structure is presumed to be one of these determinants. And in its turn, the structure is also influenced by the factors technology, size, and environment (see figure 5).

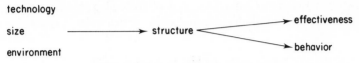

Figure 5. Determinants of structure.

Two comments should be made before the relationships among the various characteristics are discussed:

a. Taking into consideration the problems connected with each of the concepts discussed in section 1, we may expect, for this reason alone, to encounter difficulties in finding clear relations among the various characteristics.

b. Each characteristic can be divided into a large number of subordinate aspects, which, in addition, are all measured in a different way, as we saw in section 1. It is not feasible to treat all the relationships among the subordinate aspects as well as all their related problems. We have therefore opted for a method in which we examine examples of how the study of relationships among subordinate aspects has been approached. We use these examples as illustrations of the problems encountered when an attempt is made to categorize and understand these relationships.

2.2. Technology — structure

2.2.1. INTRODUCTION

The concepts of technology and structure are both extremely complex and surrounded by a full complement of problems (see section 1.3 and 1.4). There is, moreover, an additional problem: various technologies can exist side by side within a single organization. The older literature about the relationship between structure and technology usually implicitly assumed that an organization could be categorized according to one type of technology. Various authors (Comstock and Scott, 1977; Khandwalla, 1974; van de Ven and Delbecq, 1974) have pointed out, however, that a number of different technologies are present simultaneously in most organizations (for example, a computer for the administration and a conveyor belt for the production). At the task and department levels, the technology can be expected to be related to the structural characteristics at that same level (for example decision-making, number of rules). Questions arise, however, as to whether a dominant technology may be ascribed to the organization as a whole, and as to what effect the presence of a large diversity of technologies within a single organization has upon the structural characteristics. Thus, Dewar and Hage (1978) called attention to the influence which a number of different tasks and their linked technologies have upon structural factors such as specialization (differentiation) and formalization and decision-making (integration). For this reason, we will discuss the relationship between the characteristics of technology and structure at two levels: organization level and task and working group level.

2.2.2. THE RELATIONSHIP BETWEEN TECHNOLOGIES AND STRUCTURE AT THE ORGANIZATION LEVEL

At this level the relationship between technology and structure is far from clearly defined. We will illustrate this with the example of the correlation between the degree of continuity and integration (interdependence) in the primary production process on the one hand (see section 1.3) and the centralization of decision-making on the other. Hickson *et al.* (1969) and Child and Mansfield (1972) found a positive correlation between the degree of integration in the production process and the degree of centralization in decision-making. This correlation only applied for the smallest organizations (up to about 200 employees) in their sample, however. Blau *et al.* (1976) found that, proceeding from single unit production via mass production to process production (that is, increasing integration and continuity), the marketing and production decisions are more centralized, which means that the decisions are increasingly made outside the scope of the production unit. For decisions concerning employee-related affairs, however, the mass production units proved to be the most centralized.

These data demonstrate that researchers must specify the type of decisions and the size of the organization before making any statements concerning the relationship between technology and (de)centralization. It should be remembered in this respect that these are only examples, and that the number of conditional variables determining the relationship between technology and (de)centralization is presumably much more extensive. The findings reported above with respect to the connection between the integration of the production process and the centralization of the decision-making however, are, indicative for nearly all the findings concerning the relationship between technological and structural characteristics. To the extent that correlations are found, they are usually weak and contradict one another; numerous exceptions and specifications must be taken into account. Thus it is urgently necessary to develop better theoretical insights into the 'why' of these relationships. Take the study of Khandwalla (1974) as an example. He found that a greater complexity (continuity) of technology was correlated with a greater degree of vertical integration (an example of vertical integration is the buying or acquiring of a partial interest in an organization which supplies raw materials). The greater the firms' degree of vertical integration, the more decentralized they were. This correlation was stronger for firms with good results than for those with bad results. Such a finding points toward the possibility that structure makes a contribution in dealing with coordination problems, and that one solution for these problems is better than another. A theoretical idea of this type can help to point out the direction which further investigations can take. If we know which coordination problems are caused by the various characteristics of technology, and which contribution different structures can make to finding a solution for them, then better predictions can be made of what the connections between these variables will be.

2.2.3. THE RELATIONSHIP BETWEEN TECHNOLOGY AND STRUCTURE AT THE TASK AND WORKING GROUP LEVELS

The relationship between technology characteristics and the decision-making structure is a central topic at the task and work group levels as well. The technological characteristics used most often in this connection are: task complexity, task predictability, and the interdependence among tasks. The accompanying decision-making characteristics are decentralization, autonomy, and participation.

In his study of branches of local health departments Mohr (1971) found that a lower task predictability and a greater task interdependence were correlated with a greater degree of participation. Hrebeniak (1974), in a study of a number of work units in hospitals, also found that autonomy in tasks and participation in decision-making increased along with task complexity and task interdependence. In a longitudinal study of branches of employment agencies, Van de Ven (1977) observed that the greater task uncertainty and task interdependence, the more decentralization of the decision-making increased. These three studies display a gratifying consistency in their conclusion that uncertainty is correlated with decentralization and participation. Detailed analysis of these studies, however, results in a serious diminution of this gratification. The various variables prove to have been operationalized in quite divergent manners, which means that, although the studies sometimes use the same terms to indicate certain concepts, they do not always attach the same meanings to these concepts. Confusing and contradictory insights are not lacking in this area either. Van de Ven (1977), for example, demonstrates that group decisions lead to greater mutual task dependence (that is, new uncertainty), which then leads to more individual decision-making at task level, leaving the management increasingly out of the picture. This finding is in itself in agreement with the conclusion that greater uncertainty (task dependence) leads to greater decentralization. At the same time, however, it shows that decentralization can contribute to the creation of uncertainty. In their study of nursing units Comstock and Scott (1977) show that decentralization of routine decisions develops with increasing predictability of the work within a task, which contradicts the previous findings. They do find, in accord with the previous studies, that greater predictability between tasks is correlated with centralization of decision-making, at both routine and policy level.

We see at this level also that structural and technological variables must be specified further if we are to gain better insight into the relationship between the two concepts. The concept of uncertainty appears to be a central factor.

2.3. Size—structure

Child (1973b), following an analysis of data of the Aston group (Pugh *et al.*, 1969), of the data from his own study (Child, 1972a) and, when comparable, those of Blau and Schoenherr (1971), arrives at the following conclusion concerning the effect of size (number of employees): '... it is possible, from a knowledge of how many people are employed to predict with a high degree of confidence the broad outlines of formal organization structure' (p. 176). Child ascertains that as the organization becomes larger, the number of hierarchical levels increases, the number of specialistic functions increases, the standardization of procedures increases, and the centralization of decision-making decreases. The structural characteristics change parallel to changes in size, primarily as long as the organization has not exceeded certain dimensions. Once the organization has reached a certain size, the structural characteristics cease to change significantly. This is presumably due to the fact that the organization then breaks down into relatively independent divisions.

Child's conclusions are in sharp contrast to the conclusion drawn by Hall *et al.* (1967) on the basis of a study of 75 organizations: '... size may be rather irrelevant as a factor in determining organizational structure' (p. 912). In his attempt to reconcile this conclusion with the conclusions of the Aston group (Pugh *et al.*, 1968), Hall (1972, p. 119 ff.) assumes that a correlation between size and structure applies primarily within groups of organization having the same technology. This leads to the question why this is so and how size and structure are related.

Kimberley (1976) states that no answer can be given to this question without further specifying which aspect of size is correlated with which structural characteristic. He states that different aspects of size have a different relevance for different problems of the organization, with concomitant different implications for different structural characteristics. He assumes, for example, that the aspect of size 'number of employees' is primarily relevant for the problem of the social control of individuals by the organization. The implication for the structure then, is for example, that strong emphasis comes to be placed on formalization. The physical capacity of an organization, on the other hand, is primarily relevant for the problem of internal efficiency and quality, with resulting implications for differentiation and specialization in the production process. It should be clear that such an approach must be supported by a considerable degree of theory development. As indicated in section 1.5, however, such theory is only sparsely available. Implicit in many lines of argument is that size leads to problems of control. Seen from this perspective, organizational structure, when regarded as the precipitate of attempts to control this uncertainty (see section 2.5), should be correlated with aspects of size. For a fruitful investigation of this relationship, however, it is necessary to make specific predictions derived from the theoretical framework about the correlations between aspects of size and aspects of structure. Research into these relationships must be longitudinal in character in order to determine that size is a determinant of structure. It is, after all, conceivable that a well-chosen structure creates certain options for the organization, thus promoting its growth. The usual studies in this area, which correlate certain characteristics—measured at one point in time—with one another, can give no decisive answer with respect to the direction of the causality.

2.4. Environment—structure

Lawrence and Lorsch (1967) established, in their influential study *Organization and environment*, that the higher the perceived stability of the environment, the more formally structured were the sub-units of the organization. This finding is in accordance with Thompson's proposition (1967, p. 71) that 'the organization component facing a stable task environment will rely on rules to achieve its adaptation to that environment.' Lawrence and Lorsch (p. 42 ff.) also established that the sub-units in the organization had different types of structure which made it possible for them to respond with appropriate measures to the differences in uncertainty with which they were confronted. Based on this and other findings, the proposition can be put forward that the differences in uncertainty in the environment lead to two indirect effects upon the structure of the organization:

a. A division into sub-units corresponding to the differences in uncertainty in the environment.

b. A structuring of these sub-units according to the degree of uncertainty with which they have to deal.

For example, a sales division will split itself up if the big customers begin making new demands which lead to a greater uncertainty than do the demands of the small customers. This so-called 'contingency approach' (the organization's structure is dependent upon or contingent to the uncertainty in the environment) does not assume that each organization will structure itself in the same way, given a certain degree and form of uncertainty. The organization may structure itself in a number of different ways when responding to uncertainty. Some reactions, however, are considered to be better than others. Burns and Stalker (1961, p. 119 ff.), for example, assume that when there is a pronounced degree of uncertainty, decentralized decision-making and a low degree of formalization (organic organization form) will make the organization more effective. Most of the studies taking place within the framework of the contingency idea are directed towards testing this type of assumption (see also Hazewinkel, this Handbook, ch. 4.3). This means that they usually can provide no definitive answer to the question of to what degree there is a correlation between uncertainty and the structure. On the basis of the limited material available, we will attempt to delineate this relationship.

Negandhi and Reimann (1973) and Reimann (1974) investigated in two studies the correlation between the degree to which management paid attention to the environment (as an indication of uncertainty of the enviornment) and the degree of decentralization. Greater involvement with environmental segments, such as consumers, stockholders, creditors, and the surrounding community, was correlated with a greater perceived decentralization. When the involvement was extremely strong, however, a greater degree of centralization occurred once more.

In his investigation of 40 branch offices of a real estate agent Pennings (1975) found that there were virtually no correlations between subjective and objective indicators of environmental uncertainty on the one hand, and structural factors on the other. The strongest correlation existed between objective indicators of environmental uncertainty and perceived participation in and total influence on the organization (more participation and total influence are correlated with an environment in which a higher median income is earned, and in which a greater diversity of products can be distributed by the organization).

Sullivan (1977), using questionnaires presented to a sample of marketing and production managers, found no correlation between perceived uncertainty and complexity of the environment as a whole on the one hand, and perceived decentralization at division and department level on the other hand. A correlation was found for the marketing managers between the perceived *uncertainty* of the market environment and the perceived degree of decentralization. For the production managers, however, greater decentralization was correlated with a greater degree of perceived *complexity* of the task environment.

Leifer and Huber (1977), finally, ascertained that a high degree of perceived environmental uncertainty is correlated with a more organic structure (more participation, less formalization), provided that a larger number of activities take place which exceed the boundaries of the organization. This points in the direction of the proposition that the information which an organization possesses only leads to consequences for its structure when that information has been validated. Based on the findings above, the following tentative conclusions

can be drawn: a relationship appears to exist between the perceived uncertainty and complexity on the one hand, and the perceived structural characteristics (de)centralization and distribution of influence on the other (Negandhi and Reimann, Pennings). This relationship, however, is not always found to be present. Possible explanations for this are:
—The relationship is curvilinear (Reimann).
—The relationship is only found be present when the structure of the sub-unit is related to the environmental segments which are relevant to that sub-unit (Sullivan).
—The relationship is only observed when validated information has been obtained by means of boundary-exceeding activities (Leifer and Huber).

Considering the limited number of studies upon which these conclusions are based, they should be regarded as hypotheses which have as yet barely been tested. We see here once more that to the extent that there is a relationship between environmental uncertainty and centralization of decision-making, this relationship is found only under certain conditions. Theoretical insights must specify what these conditions are, and why this is so.

2.5. Conclusions

We ended our discussion of the conclusions in section 1.7 by voicing our doubts about the possibility of finding a definitive connection between the various organization characteristics, considering the myriad problems connected with these characteristics. This apprehension is amply validated by the preceding discussion. Dealing with a number of relationships by means of examples has shown that insofar as relationships can be demonstrated, they exist between component aspects of the various characteristics, under certain specified conditions. In case after case the need was felt for a theoretical rationale which would explain why a relationship exists between certain component aspects under certain conditions. Within such an approach, the concept of uncertainty will be an important explanatory concept. This concept repeatedly appears in analyses of the relationships among characteristics in an organization, and is usually linked to the problems of control confronting that organization. The basic idea behind the approach based on these concepts is that organizations attempt to survive within their environment, and that in order to do this successfully they must be able to make the uncertainty caused by size, technology, and environment more manipulable and controllable. Figure 6 presents the schema shown in fingure 5 (in section 2.1) with the addition of the concept of uncertainty.

A structure can therefore be considered in part as the result of the attempts made by an organization to control the uncertainty caused by its environment, technology, and size. Yet, the structure cannot be completely explained by the uncertainty, just as the degree of the organization's control of the uncertainty can

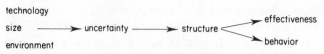

Figure 6. Uncertainty as a determinant of structure.

only be partially explained by looking at the structure (Ouchi, 1977). This is explained in part by the fact that an organizational structure is designed to control the uncertainties with which it has been familiar in the past. However, organizations are continually confronted with new uncertainties for which new answers must be found. They cannot anticipate all of these new uncertainties. Even if this were possible to a great extent, it would not be recommendable for an organization to realize in advance all the possible structural adaptations for dealing with these uncertainties. A structural elaboration of this dimension would be not only extremely expensive, but would also endanger its capacity to adapt to the unexpected events which continually take place. For this reason, an organization does not put its faith exclusively in detailed organizational arrangements, but also relies on the ad hoc actions of those in leadership positions for absorbing fluctuations and uncertainties.

The line of thought sketched above has the consequence that the association between the uncertainty caused by technology, size, and environment, on the one hand, and the characteristics of the structure on the other hand, will not be all that strong. The linkage becomes even weaker due to the fact that different structural solutions exist for the problems associated with, or resulting from, uncertainty (Galbraith, 1977, ch. 3; see also below). Each solution must, in addition, succeed in achieving a balance between different, often contradictory, demands. It is inherent in the nature of organizations that the solution of one problem often leads to the creation of a new problem (see Veen, 1980). If, for example, an attempt is made to respond flexibly to market demands, therefore eschewing rigid production schedules, the production process can be seriously disrupted. The solution chosen for dealing with uncertainty caused by a fluctuation demand in the environment creates new uncertainties in the production area. This means that ideas must be developed concerning coherent strategies for controlling uncertainties. Child (1972b, 1973a) has sketched two such strategies for the organization:

a. control via the decision-making structure;

b. control via a system of formalized and standardized rules and procedures.

The choice of strategy is determined in the first instance by knowledge of the transformation processes (technology). If there is considerable insight into how the different operations (machines) and actions (people) lead to the desired results, the choice will generally be made for control by means of formalization and standardization. If such knowledge is lacking, then a system of result control will be chosen, in which strategic and tactical decisions are centralized and output decisions are decentralized (Ouchi and Maguire, 1975). If an organization becomes too large, more and more decison making will have to be decentralized, while it attempts to ensure its level of achievement by a system of sharply defined task requirements and budgets for the organization's sub-units (Hall, 1972, p. 159 ff.).

Because the sub-units of an organization are confronted with different types of uncertainty in the environment, they will, if they are not interfered with, choose different structural solutions for dealing with these uncertainties. As a result, the problem may develop that these solutions are not coordinated with one another, thus endangering the integration of the organization. This is the familiar problem that partial solutions, which may be optimal from the perspective of the sub-unit, are no guarantee that the solution will be optimal from the perspective of the organization as a whole. A solution must be found within the organizational structure for the problem of how sub-units can be differentiated, without endangering their integration, and with it the overall effectiveness. If the sub-units of an organization can operate relatively independently of one another (compare the concept 'pooled interdependence' in section 1.3), they require only a loose form of coordination with one another. In such a 'loosely coupled' (Weick, 1976) organization it is possible to choose primarily local solutions for problems within the given task requirements, without impairing the effectiveness of the whole organization. The division structure is a well-known example of such an organization form. If, however, strong dependence exists among the sub-units of the organization, then the organization must find a balance between local adaptation and internal cohesion (Child, 1977, p. 165 ff.; Khandwalla, 1974). A well-integrated structure, which enables an organization to operate as a single coherent unit and which keeps internal uncertainty to a minimum, may considerably increase short-term efficiency. As a result, reserves are built up which are often an important prerequisite for realizing adaptations in the long run. The price paid for this is most probably loss of adaptability in the short run. Another possible strategy for the organization would be to react as quickly as possible to 'local' changes. The price paid for this strategy probably would be loss of efficiency in the short run.

It is clear from this highly condensed presentation (for an extensive discussion see Veen, this Handbook, ch. 4.2; Veen and van Haren, 1980) of a number of the theoretical ideas that try to explain the correlation between structural characteristics and other characteristics of the organization and its environment, that the problems do not become any simpler when approached in this way. Although it is suggested that certain strategies are preferable under certain conditions, it is becoming increasingly clear from the theoretical literature that in this area all roads lead to Rome, and that it largely depends upon barely specifiable interactions among variables which road will be the most promising at any given moment. Better understanding of these interactions must be obtained primarily through research which is more directly concerned with:
a. the degree to which and the way in which certain characteristics of technology,

size, and environment lead to vital uncertainties for an organization;
b. the way in which certain structural arrangements reduce, or make it easier to deal with, the uncertainty and what kind of new uncertainty is created in the process.

If these kinds of studies would have a more longitudinal character than is usually the case at present, we could determine with greater certainty the causal direction of the correlation between the structural characteristics and the other characteristics of organizations.

REFERENCES

Aldrich, H. E. (1979), *Organizations and environments*. Englewood Cliffs: Prentice-Hall.

Allport, F. H. (1954), The structuring of events: Outline of a general theory with applications to psychology. *Psychological Review*, **61**, 281–303.

Billings, R. S., Klimoski, R. J., Breaugh, Breaugh, J. A. (1977), The impact of a change in technology on job characteristics: A quasi-experiment. *Administrative Science Quarterly*, **22**, 318–339.

Blau, P. M. (1970), A formal theory of differentiation in organizations. *American Sociological Review*, **35**, 201–219.

Blau, P. M., Schoenherr, R. A. (1971), *The structure of organizations*. New York: Basic Books.

Blau, P. M., McHugh Falbe, C., McKinley, W., Tracey, P. K. (1976), Technology and organization in manufacturing. *Administrative Science Quarterly*, **21**, 20–40.

Burns, T., Stalker, G. M. (1961), *The management of innovation*. London: Tavistock.

Campbell, J. P. (1976), Contributions research can make in understanding organizational effectiveness. *Organization and Administrative Sciences*, **7**, 29–45.

Campbell, J. P. (1977), On the nature of organizational effectiveness. In: Goodman, P. S., Pennings, J. M., and associates, *New perspectives on organizational effectiveness*. San Francisco: Jossey-Bass, 13–55.

Child, J. (1972a), Organizational structure, environment and performance: The role of strategic choice. *Sociology*, **6**, 1–22.

Child, J. (1972b), Organization structure and strategies of control. *Administrative Science Quarterly*, **17**, 163–177.

Child, J. (1973a), Strategies of control and organizational behavior. *Administrative Science Quarterly*, **18**, 1–17.

Child, J. (1973b), Predicting and understanding organization structure. *Administrative Science Quarterly*, **18**, 168–185.

Child, J. (1977), Organizational design and performance: Contingency theory and beyond. *Organization and Administrative Sciences*, **8**, nrs. 1–3, 169–183.

Child, J., Mansfield, R. (1972), Technology, size and organization structure. *Sociology*, **6**, 369–393.

Comstock, D. E., Scott, W. R. (1977), Technology and the structure of subunits. Distinguishing individual and work group effects. *Administrative Science Quarterly*, **22**, 177–202.

Cummings, L. L. (1977), Emergence of the instrumental organization. In: Goodman, P. S., Pennings, J. M., and associates, *New perspectives on organizational effectiveness*. San Franciso: Jossey-Bass, 56–62.

Dewar, R., Hage, J. (1978), Size, technology, complexity and structural differentiation: Toward theoretical synthesis. *Administrative Science Quarterly*, **23**, 111–136.

Downey, H. K., Hellriegel, D. H., Slocum, Jr., J. W. (1975), Environmental uncertainty:

The construct and its application. *Administrative Science Quarterly*, **20**, 613–629.

Dubin, R. (1976), Organizational effectiveness: Some dilemmas of perspective. *Organization and Administrative Sciences*, **7**, 7–13.

Duncan, R. B. (1972), Characteristics of organizational environments and perceived environmental uncertainty. *Administrative Science Quarterly*, **17**, 313–327.

Evan, W. E. (1976), Organization theory and organizational effectiveness: An exploratory analysis. *Organization and Administrative Sciences*, **7**, 15–28.

Friedlander, F., Pickle, H. (1968), Components of effectiveness in small organizations. *Administrative Science Quarterly*, **13**, 289–304.

Fullan, M. (1970), Industrial technology and worker integration in the organization. *American Sociological Review*, **35**, 1028–1039.

Galbraith, J. R. (1977), *Organization design*. Reading (Mass.): Addison-Wesley.

Georgiou, P. (1973), The goal paradigm and notes towards a counter paradigm. *Administrative Science Quarterly*, **18**, 291–310.

Hage, J., Aiken, M. (1969), Routine technology, social structure and organizational goals. *Administrative Science Quarterly*, **14**, 366–377.

Hall, R. H. (1972), *Organizations: Structure and process*. Englewood Cliffs (N.J.): Prentice-Hall.

Hall, R. H., Hass, E., Johnson, N. J. (1967), Organizational size, complexity and formalization. *American Sociological Review*, **32**, 903–912.

Hannan, M. T., Freeman, J. (1977), The population ecology of organizations. *American Journal of Sociology*, **82**, 929–964.

Hickson, D. J., Pugh, D. S., Pheysey, D. C. (1969), Operations technology and organization structure: An empirical reappraisal. *Administrative Science Quarterly*, **14**, 378–397.

Hickson, D., Pugh, D., Pheysey, D. (1970), Organization: Is technology the key? *Personnel Management*, February, 20–26.

Hinings, C. R., Hickson, D. J., Pennings, J. M., Schneck, R. E. (1974), Structural conditions of intraorganizational power. *Administrative Science Quarterly*, **19**, 22–44.

Hrebeniak, L. G. (1974), Job technology, supervision and workgroup structure. *Administrative Science Quarterly*, **19**, 395–410.

Indik, B. P. (1968), The scope of the problem and some suggestions toward a solution. In: Indik, B. P., Berrien, F. K. (Eds.), *People, groups and organizations*. New York: Teachers College Press, 3–26.

Inkson, H. J. K., Pugh, D. S., Hickson, D. J. (1970a), Organization context and structure: An abbreviated replication. *Administrative Science Quarterly*, **15**, 318–329.

Inkson, H. J. K., Schwitter, J. P., Pheysey, D. C., Hickson, D. J. (1970b), A comparison of organization structure and managerial roles: Ohio, USA and The Midlands, England. *The Journal of Management Studies*, **7**, 347–363.

James, L. R., Jones, A. P. (1976), Organizational structure: A review of structural dimensions and their conceptual relationship with individual attitudes and behavior. *Organizational Behavior and Human Performance*, **16**, 74–113.

Khandwalla, P. N. (1974), Mass output orientation of operations technology and organizational structure. *Administrative Science Quarterly*, **19**, 74–97.

Kimberley, J. R. (1976), Organizational size and the structuralist perspective: A review, critique and proposal. *Administrative Science Quarterly*, **21**, 571–597.

Lawrence, P. R., Lorsch, J. W. (1967), *Organization and environment: Managing differentiation and integration*. Boston: Division of Research, Graduate School of Business Administration Harvard University.

Leifer, R., Huber, G. P. (1977), Relations among perceived environmental uncertainty, organization structure and boundary spanning behavior. *Administrative Science Quarterly*, **22**, 235–247.

Lynch, B. P. (1974), An empirical assessment of Perrow's technical construction. *Administrative Science Quarterly*, **19**, 338–356.

McKelvey, B. (1975), Guidelines for the empirical classification of organizations. *Administrative Science Quarterly*, **19**, 338–356.

Mahoney, T. A., Weitzel, W. (1969), Managerial models of organizational effectiveness. *Administrative Science Quarterly*, **14**, 357–365.

Mansfield, R. (1973), Bureaucracy and centralization: An examination of organizational structure. *Administrative Science Quarterly*, **18**, 477–488.

March, J. G., Olsen, J. P. (1976), *Ambiguity and choice in organizations*. Bergen: Universitetsforlaget.

Mohr, L. B. (1971), Organizational technology and organizational structure. *Administrative Science Quarterly*, **16**, 444–459.

Negandhi, A. R., Reimann, B. C. (1973), Task environment, decentralization and organizational effectiveness. *Human Relations*, **26**, 203–214.

Nemiroff, P. M., Lord, D. L. Jr. (1977), The 'FIT' between work group structure and tasks: Its influence on task effectiveness and human fulfillment. *Organization and Administrative Sciences*, **8**, nr. 4, 15–34.

Oeser, O. A., Harary, F. (1962), A mathematical model for structural role theory, I. *Human Relations*, **15**, 89–109.

Ouchi, W. G. (1977), The relationship between organizational structure and organizational control. *Administrative Science Quarterly*, **22**, 95–113.

Ouchi, W. G., Maguire, M. A. (1975), Organizational control: Two functions. *Administrative Science Quarterly*, **20**, 599–569.

Overton, P., Schneck, R., Hazlett, C. B. (1977), An empirical study of the technology of nursing subunits. *Administrative Science Quarterly*, **22**, 203–234.

Pennings, J. M. (1975), The relevance of the structural-contingency model for organizational effectiveness. *Administrative Science Quarterly*, **20**, 393–410.

Pennings, J. M., Goodman, P. S. (1977), Toward a workable framework. In: Goodman, P. S., Pennings, J. M., and associates, *New perspectives on organizational effectiveness*. San Franciso: Jossey-Bass, 146–184.

Perrow, C. (1961), The analysis of goals in complex organizations. *American Sociological Review*, **26**, 854–865.

Perrow, C. (1967), A framework for the comparative analyses of organizations. *American Sociological Review*, **32**, 194–208.

Perrow, C. (1970), *Organizational analysis: A sociological view*. Belmont (Cal.): Brooks-Cole.

Porter, L. W., Lawler III, E. E., Hackman, J. R. (1975), *Behavior in organizations*. New York: McGraw-Hill.

Price, J. L. (1968), *Organizational effectiveness: An inventory of propositions*. Homewood (Ill.): Irwin-Dorsey.

Pugh, D. S., Hickson, D. J., Hinings, C. R., Macdonald, K. M., Turner, C., Lupton, T. (1963), A conceptual scheme for organizational analysis. *Administrative Science Quarterly*, **8**, 289–315.

Pugh, D. S., Hickson, D. J., Hinings, C. R., Turner, C. (1968), Dimensions of organization structure. *Administrative Science Quarterly*, **13**, 65–105.

Pugh, D. S., Hickson, D. J., Hinings, C. R., Turner, C. (1969), The context of organization structures. *Administrative Science Quarterly*, **14**, 91–115.

Reimann, B. C. (1974), Task environment and decentralization: A cross-national replication. *Human Relations*, **27**, 677–695.

Seashore, S. E., Yuchtman, E. (1967), Factorial analysis of organizational performance. *Administrative Science Quarterly*, **12**, 377–395.

Sells, S. B. (1968), General theoretical problems related to organizational taxonomy:

A model solution. In: Indik, B. P., Berrien, F. K. (Eds.), *People, groups and organizations*. New York: Teachers College, 27–41.

Starbuck, H. (1976), Organizations and their environments. In: Dunnette, M. D. (Ed.), *Handbook of industrial and organizational psychology*. Chicago: Rand McNally, 1069–1123.

Steers, R. M. (1975), Problems in the measurement of organizational effectiveness. *Administrative Science Quarterly*, **20**, 546–558.

Sullivan, D. B. (1977), Task environments and organization structure. *Organization and Administrative Science*, **8**, nrs. 1–3, 185–202.

Thompson, J. D. (1967), *Organizations in action*. New York: McGraw-Hill.

Tosi, H., Aldag, R., Storey, R. (1973), On the measurement of the environment: An assessment of the Lawrence and Lorsch environmental uncertainty subscale. *Administrative Science Quarterly*, **18**, 27–36.

Turner, A. N. Lawrence, P. R. (1965), *Industrial jobs and the worker*. Cambridge (Mass.): Harvard University, Graduate School of Business Administration.

Ven, A. H. Van de (1977), A panel study on the effects of task uncertainty, interdependence and size on unit decision-making. *Organization and Administrative Sciences*, **8**, no. 2, 237–254.

Ven, A. H. Van de, Delbecq, A. L. (1974), A task-contingent model of workunit structure. *Administrative Science Quarterly*, **19**, 183–197.

Veen, P., Haren, Th. van (1980), Gedrag in organisaties [Behaviour in organizations]. In: Jaspars, J., Vlist, R. van de (Eds.), *Sociale psychologie in Nederland* [Social psychology in The Netherlands], *III*. Deventer: Van Loghum Slaterus.

Veld, J. in 't (1975), Analyse van organisatieproblemen [An analysis of organizational problems]. Amsterdam: Agon/Elsevier.

Weick, K. E. (1976), Educational organizations as loosely coupled systems. *Administrative Science Quarterly*, **21**, 1–19.

Woodward, J. (1965), *Industrial organization: theory and practice*. London: Oxford University Press.

Yuchtman, E., Seashore, S. (1967), A system resource approach to organizational effectiveness. *American Sociological Review*, **32**, 891–903.

Zwaan, A. H. van der (1972), Technologie binnen de organisatiesociologie: Een literatuurstudie [Technology in organizational sociology: A study of the literature]. *Mens en Maatschappij* [Man and Society], **47**, 35–53.

Handbook of Work and Organizational Psychology
Edited by P. J. D. Drenth, H. Thierry, P. J. Willems and C. J. de Wolff
© 1984, John Wiley & Sons, Ltd.

4.2. Organization theories

Peter Veen

1. INTRODUCTION

The phenomenon 'organization' is a complex and multi-faceted one. It is therefore virtually impossible to give an exhaustive definition of it. Listing its characteristics is usually felt to be sufficient. In such definitions an organization is usually described as:

—an association of individuals, whose aim is to achieve *goals*,
—in which the work is split up into different tasks (specialization and *differentiation*),
—in which the *integration* of activities takes place by means of formalized rules and a hierarchical structure (management structure);
—with a certain *permanance* in time.

(For comparable descriptions see Hall, 1972, p. 9; Katz and Kahn, 1978, ch. 3; Porter *et al.*, 1975, p. 69 ff.).

The problems of definition already indicate that it is unclear exactly what organization theories are seeking to explain: how goals are formulated, how differentiation and integration develop, how permanance is achieved? In dealing with organization theories it is necessary to continually ask what an organization actually is and what the theories are trying to explain in consequence. Consideration of the different approaches to organizations is therefore concurrently a consideration of the question as to what are the most important problems for organizations. To illuminate this phenomenon, the theories will be dealt with in order of their historical occurrence. The emphasis in this analysis will be placed on the behavior *of* organizations rather than on behavior

Prof. dr. Peter Veen, Oosterweg 60, 9751 PJ HAREN.

713

in organizations, although in the course of the analysis it will become clear that these two approaches are difficult to separate from one another. This means, for example, that theories of motivation, satisfaction, roles, conflicts, communication and such will not be taken into consideration.

2. FOUR TRADITIONAL APPROACHES

2.1. Introduction

In this section is presented a survey of the four traditional approaches to the phenomenon 'organization'. Using this survey, an attempt will be made to gain an initial insight into the set of problems which organization theories are trying to deal with, and the difficulties encountered in this process.

Attention is paid to: scientific management, the bureaucratic tradition, the human relations school, and scientific administration, in this order.

2.2. Scientific management

The 'scientific management' school (Taylor, 1911) is primarily known for its time-motion studies. The theory proceeds from a conception of organization in which goals are known, sales of goods or services no problem, and the means of production available with no problems attached (Sofer, 1972, p. 38). The approach is characterized by a concentration on repetitive tasks. Using methods of rational analysis, these tasks are dissected and measured as accurately as possible. Based upon this analysis, the task is broken down into its component parts, and then re-grouped in such a way that the highest degree of productivity (ratio: benefits/costs) possible is achieved. In this way the task-related behavior of individuals is directed toward very specific and specialized goals (March and Simon, 1958, p. 13). An important aspect of this approach is that it links remuneration to performance. Taylor proceeded from the assumption that the interests of employer and employee ran parallel. His method enabled managers ' . . . to give the workman what he most wants—high wages—and the employer what he wants—a low labor cost—for his manufactures'(Taylor, 1911, p. 10).

The techniques developed by Taylor have had a longer life than his point of departure. He himself gives four principles by which 'scientific management' distinguishes itself from regular management practice:

1. The manager systematically gathers knowledge (science) about each aspect of the employees' work. This knowledge replaces the guess work used until then in structuring the work.

2. The manager 'heartily' works together with his subordinates to make sure that the work is done in accordance with the acquired knowledge and insights.

3. The work and the responsibility are almost equally divided between manage-

ment and workers. The manager takes over all the work which he is most qualified to carry out. Previously, almost all the work and the largest share of the responsibility were allotted to the workers.

4. In this approach, the emphasis is on an intensive and harmonious relationship between the boss and his subordinates; the objective techniques which have been developed are an aid in achieving this relationship, primarily because they offer protection from arbitrary measures taken by management.

Taylor's view of work organizations is, of course, in some aspects rather dated. For example, his explanation for what according to him is the biggest problem of organizations—that is, that a worker does not work to his full capacity—is partly that the worker fears a spiral of increasing demands, and partly that management lacks the necessary knowledge. Supported by his conviction that knowing is the same as doing and his belief in unlimited growth, Taylor has developed a view which in his day was a very modern one, and whose basic assumptions still deserve our attention. Because his followers have simplified these basic assumptions, and because there has come to be a one-sided emphasis on techniques, much of his original thought is no longer found in the later versions of scientific management theory. Taylor's original version, however, very early called attention to the *problem of integrating the interests of employer and employee*. The scientific management tradition had virtually no concern for the structural and administrative aspects of organizations and has paid very little attention to the way in which subordinate tasks must be combined and arranged. In this sense, some basic organizational aspects fall outside the scope of this approach.

2.3. The bureaucratic tradition

The structural aspect of organizations is one of the points which is emphasized in the bureaucratic tradition. Max Weber is the originator of this approach toward organizations (1946, 1947). According to Weber (in the summary of Blau, 1956, p. 28 ff.), the bureaucratic organization exhibits the following characteristics:

a. The activities which take place in the organization are grouped in tasks. These tasks are grouped in positions (office). The tasks grouped together in a certain position constitute the required activities for the individual who holds that position. Everyone does a share of the work.

b. The positions are organized hierarchically. Each position falls under the supervision of a higher position. The head of a department is responsible to his boss both for his own behavior and for the behavior of his subordinates. To back this responsibility he possesses legitimate power (authority) over his subordinates. His authority is narrowly circumscribed.

c. The activities are guided by a cohesive system of rules (standardization and formalization). The system of standards must guarantee uniformity in the performance of the task, and it has a coordinating function in the sense that it regulates the harmonization of activities with one another.

d. The behavior of individuals is formal and impersonal '*sine ira et studio*', without hatred or passion, and hence without affection or enthusiasm' (Weber, 1947, p. 340). This ensures that individuals are treated justly and reasonably.

e. Work in a bureaucracy is based on technical and *professional* qualifications. There are rules for hiring and firing. Organizational loyalty is encouraged by the chance of promotion.

The bureaucratic form of organization is 'from a purely technical point of view, capable of attaining the highest degree of efficiency and is in this sense formally the most rational known means of carrying out imperative control over human beings' (Weber, 1947, p. 337). Bureaucracy is described elsewhere by Weber (1946, p. 214) as 'The fully developed bureaucratic mechanism compares with other organizations exactly as does the machine with non-mechanical modes of production.' The bureaucratic organization owes its superiority to the fact that the organization is screened, thanks to the above principles, against disruptive influences; as a result, internal processes are stabilized and routinized, and efficiency increased (Perrow, 1970, p. 59).

Merton (1957, p. 197 ff.) has pointed out that carrying bureaucratic principles to extremes can lead to disfunctional results. Because rules come to be their own justification, rigidity is promoted. Organizational behavior is directed toward the maintenance of the status quo, even when this is not the best line of behavior for the organization. What was a good rule under circumstance A, does not have to be a good one under circumstance B (Perrow, 1972, p. 31 ff.).

Selznick (1943) has stated that an informal structure exists in the organization parallel to the formal one; this informal structure contributes to the realization of a gradual change in goals. This change in goals is based on the different interests of the various divisions. It is especially when the organizational goals are not very operational that a diffuse struggle for control of the organization takes place. This will lead to the further crystallization of divisional interests, thus forming a threat to organizational efficiency.

Gouldner (1954) demonstrates that bureaucratic rules make clear to the members of an organization what the minimal acceptable contribution is. This has the disfunctional result that less is achieved than is possible, which in turn leads to closer supervision. Power, which becomes less visible through the use of rules, now becomes again more visible; tensions within the organization increase as a result. This analysis of disfunctional results shows that there are two implications contained in the bureaucratic model:

a. The assumption that the individuals in an organization identify themselves with the organization, and that their interests are identical to those of the organization.

b. The assumption that the conditions under which the organization functions remain reasonably stable.

As soon as these assumptions no longer hold, the traditional stereotype of the bureaucracy, in which the rigidity of the organization and the lack of room for maneuvering predominate, comes to the fore.

Perrow (1972, p. 7) states, however '... bureaucracy is a form of organization superior to all others we know or can hope to afford in the near and middle future.' This conclusion is justified primarily for the organization of routine tasks. Perrow counters the allegation of a lack of freedom for individuals in an organization by pointing out that the rules also provide protection from arbitrariness (compare the function of objective techniques in Taylor; see 2.2).

We see one of the essential problems of organizations loom up in the course of the analysis of disfunctional outcomes: *how uncertainty can be reduced without sacrificing flexibility*, or how efficiency now can be combined with effectiveness in the long run. The bureaucratic theory explains the efficiency, but not the flexibility.

2.4. The human relations approach

The bureaucratic approach to organizations presents a picture of how an organization seeks to protect itself from the needs and motives brought along by the individuals who comprise it. It can be seen in the disfunctional outcomes that this will never be one-hundred percent successful. In addition, individuals in organizations must cooperate with one another, which entails additional problems. 'For the larger and more complex the institution is the more dependent it is upon the whole-hearted co-operation of every member of the group' (Mayo, 1975, p. 62).

The series of investigations carried out in the Hawthorne factory of the Western Electric Company, Chicago, in the twenties and thirties directed attention to this factor, and to the human factor in general (Homans, 1951, ch. III–IV; Roethlisberger and Dickson, 1939; Mayo, 1975).

Commencing with the typical scientific management question concerning the relationship between physical working conditions and performance, the investigators were slowly but surely compelled to acknowledge the importance of the motivation of the individuals involved in the work process (see especially Roethlisberger, 1952, ch. II: 'The road back to sanity'). In the so-called 'relay assembly test room' where small telephone relays were assembled by hand (about 500 units per day, per person), were registered for five girls over five years: performance (quality, quantity), working conditions (humidity, hours worked, and so forth), personal circumstances (hours of sleep, meals, physical condition). During the first one and a half year of the experiment, performance improved continually; as a result, thought the investigators, of the experimental changes—until they re-introduced the old (less favorable) working conditions as a control measure. To their and our amazement, however, performance remained at the same high level. An analysis of exactly what the investigators had done yielded the insight that they had fundamentally changed the work situation along totally other lines than intended: the 'operators' were consulted about changes, which were not effectuated if the operators had serious objections to them; they were asked about their reactions to and feelings about the changes; their health and sense of well-being were a topic of considerable interest; in short, the normal leadership style was suddenly drastically changed. This made the investigators realize that the point at issue was the significance accorded to events in the organization by those involved, and the feelings which were developed by the participants concerning these events.

The picture of the economic individual who operates logically and rationally in his own interest, must apparently be supplemented by a picture of the individual who also has feelings and emotions with respect to his work situation. Other investigations in the Hawthorne series have illuminated other elements (the role of norms, for example; see Homans, 1951, ch. III–VI). The conclusions from these investigations can be summarized as follows:

a. An organization is a system. A change in one element cannot take place in isolation. When the element in question changes, the whole organization changes.

b. The organization not only produces goods or services, but it also distributes outputs and revenues (both material and non-material) among its members, who attach a certain significance to this distribution.

c. A continuous process of social evaluation takes place within the organization. Changes in the organization are evaluated for their social consequences, and in particular for their consequences for the status of the individual and of the group.

d. The behavior of individuals in organizations is not guided by economic motives alone. Values, opinions, and emotions all play an important role.

e. The personal relationships in an organization cause an informal structure to be formed alongside the formal structure; this informal structure has considerable influence upon the behavior of individuals.

The Hawthorne investigations have been subjected to a great deal of criticism. Carey's article 'The Hawthorne studies: a radical criticism' (1967), for example, is a devastating attack upon the various analyses upon which the conclusions of the Hawthorne studies are based. Carey makes it plausible that the production results of the relay assembly room were not achieved as a result of participation, consultation and so forth, but were due rather to a new system of compensation. He also makes plausible that it is more likely that a high level of performance, exacted by means of discipline, leads to a new form of leadership, than that the reverse process takes place. An aspect totally absent in the Hawthorne studies is consideration of task and work content, an aspect upon which the scientific management school, for example, places so much emphasis.

It has been pointed out from a sociologists' standpoint that although the Hawthorne investigations did succeed in bringing into relief the human aspects of organizations, they unfortunately succeeded at the same time in totally neglecting the institutional and structural components (Silverman, 1970, pp. 73–77). The human relations approach has been unable to provide any significant insight into the phenomenon of the organization as such (Perrow, 1972, p. 104). The approach does succeed in laying bare the problem of the *integration of individual and organization*, but provides no tools for finding a solution.

2.5. The scientific administration approach

The scientific administration approach is characterized on the one hand by a concentration upon the problem of grouping tasks into jobs, jobs into departments, and departments into the total organization; it is characterized on the other hand by the search for principles which will guide the management of the organization resulting from this process. The approach confines itself to the formal relationships within organizations; it makes virtually no use of 'theory' in the true sense of the word. It consists largely in a summing up of organizational activities and points which deserve the attention of the manager of an organization. Gulick (Gulick and Urwick, 1937, p. 13), for example, deliniates the seven functions of the manager as: 'planning, organizing, staffing, directing, coordination reporting and budgeting (POSDCORB).' The most important prescriptive principles of the scientific administration approach are (see Massie, 1965, p. 396 ff. Simon, 1957, ch. 2):

a. Scalar principle: authority relationships must run in a continuous hierarchical line from the top to the bottom levels of the organization.

b. Unity of command: each member of an organization must receive instructions and orders from only one other member of the organization.

c. Exception principle: all routine decisions must be reduced to procedures and then delegated. Only exceptions are referred back to the direct superior.

d. Span-of-control: the number of subordinates for each boss must be limited because individuals have a limited capacity for handling complicated relationships.

e. Specialization and departmentalization: distribution of work is a basic principle. The distributed work must be re-grouped in departments. This grouping can take place on the basis of (a) goal, (b) process, (c) customer, market or material, (d) location. The underlying idea is to combine homogeneous units and to separate heterogeneous units.

These principles comprise as it were a pragmatic complement to the abstract principles formulated by Weber. The assumptions upon which these principles are founded can be summarized as follows (Massie, 1965, p. 404):

a. Efficiency is measured in terms of productivity. Individuals are primarily motivated by material needs (loyalty for remuneration).

b. Human beings act rationally. To make this possible, tasks and competencies must be circumscribed as precisely as possible, and relationships must be laid down in a fixed pattern (Weber's rules and regulations).

c. People prefer the predictability and safety of a task which is described in detail; they prefer not to have to solve problems themselves. Simple tasks also lead to greater productivity (Weber's specialization and differentiation principle).

d. People often have an aversion to work, and they must therefore work within a framework of clearly determined responsibilities and under strict supervision. Management should be objective and impersonal (Weber's 'sine ira et studio').

e. Authority originates at the top of the organization and is delegated downwards (Weber's principle of the hierarchical superstructure).

f. The manager's task has universal features—which means that it can be carried out in the same way, no matter what the particular circumstances (Weber's principle of interchangeability and exchangeability; the fact that management is a profession for which one is educated, means that a manager can function at any location).

The 'theory' attempts mainly to solve the problem of *how the work can be split up and then re-integrated*. The system of requirements and suppositions is primarily descriptive and prescriptive, and therefore virtually untestable (March and Simon, 1958, p. 30 ff.; Simon, 1957, p. 20 ff.). When practical applications of the principles are attempted, irreconcilable contradictions often appear, unless it can clearly be indicated which criteria are considered most important (see Simon, 1957, p. 41 ff.). Implicit in this approach, as in the bureaucratic theories, is that the situation is more or less stable, and that the means-goals relationships are known. In this approach an even more pronounced emphasis than in the bureaucratic one has been placed on structuring the organization internally in the interest of efficiency.

2.6. Summary and conclusions

The four classical approaches put forward a number of problems which the organization must solve, and for which the approaches propose what is in principle a solution:

—The scientific management approach emphasizes the problem of how the individuals' working capacity can be utilized in the most efficient way possible, and how people can themselves be allowed to reap the benefits of this efficiency. The solution for this problem is sought in maximalization of the structuring and instrumentalization of the task, and in remuneration in accordance with work done.

—The bureaucratic approach puts forward the problem of how the organization can be protected against internal and external disturbances. Control and coordination of organizational operations is realized by means of a hierarchical structure and a system of rules.

—The scientific administration approach consists primarily of a pragmatic development of the bureaucratic idea, and gives directions for how to manage an organization efficiently. As in the bureaucratic approach, the emphasis lies upon internal efficiency.

—The human relations approach directs its attention to how the needs of people can be reconciled with organizational goals.

The achievement of a sufficient degree of efficiency, control, stability, structure, and motivation is the problem which unfolds within the context of the field of tension between individual-organization-environment. The different approaches demonstrate that the organization must navigate among a number of reefs to arrive at a solution for this problem. It must control the behavior of its members, and steer it in the direction most favorable for the organization as a whole, but must at the same time take care that these individuals remain sufficiently motivated. The organization must combine internal efficiency with flexibility, and adaptive capacity to changing circumstances. The more general statement can be made that the most basic problem for an organization is that it must meet the demands of both its members and its environment, while maintaining its own identity and cohesion.

3. THE FIELD OF TENSION BETWEEN INDIVIDUAL-ORGANIZATION-ENVIRONMENT

3.1. Introduction

The four classical approaches concentrate upon the tension between individual and organization. One aspect of this relationship is often emphasized and solutions proposed, based upon implicit assumptions and theories. The realization that a number of contradictory demands must be satisfied simultaneously in the search for solutions is often present somewhere in the background, but seldom receives the emphasis it deserves. A number of other approaches are considered below in which these contradictions are brought into the foreground, and in which an initial attempt is made to reduce the problem of reconciling these contradictions to manageable proportions.

3.2. The structural-functionalist approach

The structural-functionalist approach builds upon both the bureaucratic and the scientific administration approaches. The functionalists proceed from the assumption that organizations have a function in their environment—for example, an electricity company which provides electricity for homes and industry. As long as this function is fulfilled adequately, the organization retains its right of existence. It then receives the necessary support and contributions. One of the criteria for this adequate fulfillment of function is that fulfillment takes place at an acceptable cost. A good structure can help to control these costs. Thus a form of organization which makes it possible to act quickly without unnecessary controls, can help to cut costs.

The function which is fulfilled is the goal of the organization, and the '... *primacy of orientation to the attainment of a specific goal* is used as the defining characteristic of an organization which distinguishes it from other types of social systems' (Parsons, 1969, p. 33; Parsons' italics). In Parsons' view, an organization derives its cohesion from its value system, which is part of the more comprehensive value system of the environment within which the organization functions. For the organization to be able to function, it is necessary that individuals and groups share the value system of the organization, this is made possible by the fact that they in turn are part of the broader society. By fulfilling its functions within the framework of existing norms and values, the organization legitimatizes its existence with regard to both the society as a whole and the individuals who comprise that society. According to this view of organizations of Parsons, the existence and maintenance of shared norms and values is a necessary condition for the social systems' ability to maintain an orderly and cohesive existence. The structural functionalists' thought is highly dependent upon ideas of equilibrium. They try to explain why social order and continuity exist in organizations in spite of fluctuations in particular circumstances and changes in personnel. Shifts in the existing equilibrium can be a result of tensions within the organization and of tensions existing between the organization and its environment. The tensions within the organization are primarily due to too much emphasis upon efficiency or upon stability (too much coordination and maintenance of the status quo). This leads to a disruption of the equilibrium within the internal exchange relationships, because, for example, employees are no longer motivated to strive toward optimal performance. Tensions will also ensue when external exchange relationships are disrupted (products are too expensive, or of poor quality, so that no customers can be found for them). The organization then attempts to restore the equilibrium (see Parsons, 1967).

The core of the functionalist view of organizations is the conception that they can be regarded as natural systems, which seek to survive through adaptation. This means that changes can only be explained in terms of adaptations of the organization to internal and external disruptions. It is inherent in this approach that the theory can give a plausible account in retrospect of why some organizations adapt successfully and others do not, but it can make no predictions of success or failure. In addition, such a theory cannot explain *why* some organizations manage to adapt and others do not. To provide such an explanation, the theory must be able to incorporate the idea that an organization actively forms and influences its own structure and environment.

Another point of criticism is that this approach devotes little attention to the opposing interests which can exist between the organization on the one hand and its members on the other, and between the organization and the society in which it functions. The structural-functionalists proceed from the assumption that an 'unseen hand of nature' ensures that power is distributed in correspondence with the importance of the function fulfilled by individuals within the organization, and by the organization in society as a whole (see Silverman, 1970, p. 59 ff.).

The hand is blind, as well as unseen, and is therefore just. The winner has adapted, the loser has not. Disfunctions are by definition temporary. Such an approach fails to take into account that members of organizations, unlike natural organisms, are not specially programmed to function within organizations, and therefore are not likely to succumb to their fate without a struggle. By asking for whom the disfunctions are disfunctional, it becomes clear what kind of problems the theory entails. The strongest is always right ... in retrospect. It is impossible to predict who will win and how a conflict will be resolved. It is not surprising that the theory is chiefly illustrated with case studies (Clark, 1960; Messinger, 1955; Selznick, 1949).

There have been different rejoinders to the above criticism. Merton (1957, p. 5 ff.), for example, attributes the non-specific, largely non-predictive nature of the theory to the fact that it is too abstract and too general. In consequence, the theory has virtually no foundation in empirical research, and is not used in carrying out this type of investigation. According to Merton, the function of a broad, general theory of this type is primarily to provide a single framework within which more specific theories, which only attempt to explain a limited number of phenomena, can be grouped. Empirical work, however, should be carried out from within the framework of these 'middle range' theories.

Katz and Kahn (1978, p. 38 ff.) defended the analogy with natural organisms. And they continue to defend this analogy in the face of contradictory arguments such as the fact that members of an organization—unlike ants in an anthill or muscles in the body—are not specially programmed to do their work within the organization. They argue that this only means that the role of the 'maintenance' sub-system must receive a stronger emphasis in the organization. This sub-system is designed to maintain the integrity and cohesion of an organization (it should be noted that this sub-system must not be considered as a thing but as a system of procedures). Its primary goal will be to integrate and control the human component of an organization. That is, an organization must continue to make sure that the needs of all the members of the organization are met. This is not something that happens by itself; temporary disturbances and internal conflicts always remain a potential threat, and even serve as useful signals that adaptation is necessary somewhere in the organization. As long as the organization operates within the framework of a social value system, and ensures that the role requirements, as well as the distribution of the outputs (delineations of tasks and functions, and indications of how they must be carried out), stay within this value system, the organization is viable. This does not mean in their view that all the partial interests of groups and individuals can be fully honored. The possibility remains that individuals will leave the organization. Serious disturbances ensue, however, if the organization does not succeed in replacing them (if, for example, a building contractor cannot find any carpenters). This should be a signal for the organization that something is wrong. It remains, however, the basic weakness of theories such as this one that they cannot indicate the conditions under which the organization will show enough wisdom to do something in response to such a signal. The question likewise remains unanswered whether organizations can continue to exist when there are unresolved conflicts, or whether members of organizations can function and conform to organizational authority, without sharing the central values.

As Gouldner (1959. 412) has pointed out, all the versions of the 'natural systems model' have neglected the rational components in organizations. As a result, the different interests and desires of actors in organizations, and the problems caused by them, are not afforded the attention which they deserve. Such models are incapable of explaining the differences in the degree of integration and the degree of success of organizations, without supplementary notions about the dynamics of the processes, and the role played in them by conflicts of interests.

3.3. The integration-motivation approach

A number of organizational psychologists, in adherence with the human relations approach, have made the integration between individual and organization their central problem. Just as the structural-functionalists consider the regulation of internal contradictions as a given, and concentrate upon the relationship between the organization and its environment, organizational psychologists consider the latter aspect as a given and concentrate primarily upon the integration of individual and organization; in addition, they emphasize the positive contribution which well-motivated individuals can make to the organization. For this reason the approach is also designated as the 'Human Resources' approach. Another designation is the 'Neo-Human Relations' approach.

Argyris (1957, 1959, 1964) in particular has worked out this approach in detail. He lays stress on the fact that the formal, bureaucratic organization demands passive, dependent behavior of adult individuals, especially those who function at the lower levels of the organization. This is extremely frustrating for the individuals, who will react in a number of ways (e.g., with aggression, apathy) which constitute a threat to the desired gains in organizational efficiency because of the diminished motivation of the organization's members. Thus it is important for the organization that it strive for greater congruence between the needs of its members and the various task and organization structures. Argyris seeks the solution for this problem in the highest degree of autonomy possible, combined with clear task requirements (1964, ch. VII and IX). He recognizes as well that structure, style of leadership and such can change along with the situation (1964, p. 211).

Likert's (1959, 1961) central concern is how individuals can be motivated in such a way that they perform optimally for the organization (1959, p. 186). Likert proposes that the organization's guiding principle should be that its structure should ensure that the members of the organization experience all their interactions as supportive and as contributive to their sense of personal worth (1959, p. 191). For this to be realized, every member of the organization must be part of one or more 'well-knit, effectively functioning work groups' (p. 191). The coordination of these groups takes place by means of 'linking pins'. These are individuals who belong to two groups. They function as a superior for one group, and represent this group at the next highest level. At this higher level they themselves then function in a subordinate position. Likert's linking-pin structure is, in this sense, no different from classical organization structures. The difference lies primarily in Likert's idea that the superior does not interact with each individual separately, but with the whole group as a 'team'. The reciprocal trust and loyalty which develop as a result help to make conflicts about goals and interests manageable. A necessary condition for this process is the presence of possibilities for exerting influence from both sides of the relationship; the influence of the superior on his superior plays an essential role (1961, p. 114).

Both Argyris and Likert work with a more complex image of man than is usual in the classical theories. The needs they ascribe to organization members are very similar to the need hierarchy postulated by Maslow (1954): physiological needs, need for safety, need for social contact and security, need for respect (self-respect and respect of others, often acquired by means of work performance) and the need for self-realization or self-expression. These needs are actualized in the order given above in the sense that first the physiological needs must be satisfied to a certain basic level before the need for economic security, for example, starts playing a role. McGregor (1960) has pointed out that the conventional management conception presumes that people in organizations only are motivated by the needs at the lower level of Maslow's hierarchy, and that for the rest they are lazy and recalcitrant, so that they must be kept under strict supervision (theory X). When, however, it is assumed that needs higher in the hierarchy also play a role (McGregor's theory Y; 1960) and the organization takes this into account, then there is a possibility that individuals and organization can become better attuned to one another.

The integration-motivation approach is, in a number of aspects, an improvement over both the classical management approach and the human relations approach. Compared to the classical management approach, it uses a considerably more differentiated image of man than the rational-economic one prevailing in the former approach. Compared to the human relations approach there is clearly a greater emphasis upon structural solutions for problems. Yet the integration-motivation approach can also be criticized on a number of counts.

a. It has already been pointed out that the goals of organizations and the relationship to the environment are considered as a given in the integration-motivation approach. Schein (1965, ch. 6 and 7) has attempted to close this gap by making use of functionalist insights. He suggests that an organization is effective if it adapts itself to the demands of the environment and grows, thus increasing its chances of survival. The organization accomplishes this by means of 'adaptive-coping cycles' (p. 98 ff.) which are aimed at observing and interpreting changes in the environment; adaptation of activities follows. The criteria of effectiveness are further specified in terms of this cycle as (1) the capability of obtaining valid and reliable information, and communicating it; (2) possessing the necessary creativity and flexibility for introducing changes; (3) members' integration and involvement with the goals of the organization, (4) the presence of a psychological climate of support and freedom (p. 103).

b. This group of organizational psychologists proceeds from the assumption (as do the structural functionalists) that all organizations are basically the same. This leads to Likert's developing 'one best way' for organizations to function — the participative method (1961, p. 222 ff.; called system 4 in his later work, 1967). While it is true that he admits that broad generalizations are involved, and that there are specific translations of the theory appropriate to each specific situation (1961, p. 24), the prevailing idea remains that ' ... the description of the forest is valid, even though many of the trees are not, perhaps, where they should be' (1961, p. 77). This idea is so strong that in spite of clear indications that different styles of leadership can have different effects in different situations (1961, p. 89 ff.; see also the so-called contingency theories of leadership, Fiedler, 1978), his final position is that the participative system exhibits the 'operating characteristics' which the organization in general must have (p. 236).

c. The integration-motivation approach also assumes that an organization is, in principle, populated by emotionally mature individuals, who will identify themselves with the organization (Likert, 1961, p. 236). The possibility that individuals may exist with an abiding divergent orientation towards themselves and the organization is not seriously considered (see Goldthorpe et al., 1968; Silverman, 1970, p. 55).

d. The most fundamental criticism, however, is directed toward the Achilles' heel of the integration-motivation approach: the concept of needs. In a review of Maslow's theory by Wahba and Bridwell (1976), it is demonstrated that very little evidence has been obtained from empirical research in support of the categorization of needs used by Maslow. The available empirical evidence points more in the direction of two categories (deficiency need versus need for growth) or three categories (existence-relationship-need for growth; see Alderfer, 1969, 1972) of needs. There is likewise little support found for the other assumption in Maslow's theory, i.e. that needs play a role in people's behavior in a certain given order. The evaluation of the existing research in this area of theory is hampered by theoretical, methodological and technical measurement problems connected to the interpretation of the theories and the operationalization of the concept of needs. In the words of Salancik and Pfeffer (1977) in their general review of 'need-satisfaction' theories: ' ... the fact that the concept of need is ambiguous on the points of the origin of needs, the development of needs, and even the meaning and measurement of needs, makes the possibility of empirical refutation remote, and the concept, in its present stage of development, of limited utility' (p. 443).

Another group of motivation theories (VIE = 'Valence Instrumentality-Expectancy' theories; see Andriessen, 1975; Campbell and Pritchard, 1976; Vroom, 1964, ch. 2 and 7) do not proceed from the concept of needs, but from the subjective expected value which individuals attach to the outcomes of actions. The assumption in these theories is that people are motivated to act in such a way that the expected positive outcomes of their behavior will be the best possible.

Unlike the need-theories, this approach makes no assumptions concerning people's fundamental needs, nor any prediction of the order in which the expected values are thought to play a role. The attractiveness (called valence or utility) of behavioral outcomes may fluctuate, depending upon the situation and the mood of the individual in question. Yet, these theories cannot avoid making assumptions either about how people's needs are structured, if they do not want to fall into the circular reasoning that people find attractive those things which they choose and that they choose those things which they find attractive (see Locke, 1975).

These theories also have problems with explaining why different events have a different expected value under different conditions and at different points in time. Finally, one of the most central problems of the theory is how the different outcomes can be compared along one dimension (Wahba and House, 1974). If a good, empirically-validated theory of needs were available, which could put forward propositions concerning these points, it would be an extremely welcome supplement to the VIE-theories (Alderfer, 1977).

e. The empirical support for their ideas which Likert and his assistants in particular have collected is extensive. Yet it cannot be denied that this investigator does tend to a somewhat optimistic interpretation of data and correlations. Perrow (1972, p. 131 ff.), for example, demonstrates that in Marrow et al.'s (1967) investigation in the Weldon company, where a dramatic increase in production took place following the introduction of Likert's participative system, this effect was primarily the result of classical management and efficiency measures.

Reviews considering other investigations of, for example, the relation between participation and motivation, also convincingly demonstrate that the supposed relations are not as unambiguous as Likert (1967) would have us believe (Lowin, 1968; Veen, 1973).

3.4. Open-system theory

A system can be defined as a collection of elements which can be isolated from the total reality. These elements have relationships with one another and possible relationships with other elements in the total reality (in 't Veld, 1975, p. 10).

The first part of this definition provides a static picture of the organization, consisting of people, positions, and tasks, along with their interrelationships, as it is often presented in organization schemes. Without further additions this is a *closed*, independently operating system. With the addition that the system can have relationships with elements outside the system, *open systems*, interacting with their environment, also come to be included in the definition. As a result, the system takes on a dynamic character. Organizations are open systems which on the surface appear reasonably stable. This stability is not achieved because all the elements and their interrelationships remain unchanged, but because changes in one element, or in a relationship among elements, are compensated by changes somewhere else in the organization.

The open system maintains a dynamic equilibrium. If two department heads have an argument, but it is in the vital interest of the organization that their two departments work in harmony with one another, then either the individuals in the two departments will find a way of bringing about some degree of co-ordination, or cooperation will be imposed from a higher position in the organizational hierarchy.

The open-system theory has originated in an attempt to develop a science which would be able to explain the principles of systems in general. The open-system theory is a generalization from the principles of closed systems (kinetics, thermodynamics) developed in physics, and is therefore also known as 'general systems theory' (GST) (see von Bertalanfly, 1950; Berrien, 1958, ch. 1).

The open-system theory attempts to develop principles for describing systems which are valid for every level of analysis (see Berrien, 1968, p. 11; Miller, 1965). This means that the system boundary can be arbitrarily defined, depending upon the perspective chosen. A change in perspective does not mean that other insights are needed to explain relationships. If an organization is defined as a system (and with it, individuals as sub-systems and the environment as a supra-system), virtually the same insights are needed as when the group is defined as a system (with individuals as sub-systems and the organization as a supra-system). It is characteristic of the open-system theory, as applied to organizations, that, in a single coherent approach, it attempts to deal with the problem of harmonization of the relationship individual-organization-environment (see especially Katz and Kahn, 1978). In this approach, the following assumptions are made concerning the organization as a system (see Silverman, 1970, p. 27):

a. The sub-units of an organization are dependent upon one another and contribute to the whole, in exchange for which they receive a contribution from the organization. The system model is an *exchange model*. How the sub-units are linked to one another (the structure comes into being) is one of the most important questions studied.

b. Organizations are guided by their needs. If these needs are not satisfied, the organization ceases to exist. Goals are articulated on the basis of these needs. If goals are not achieved, or if there is too great a discrepancy between needs and goals, the viability of the organization is diminished.

c. Organizations behave as a coherent whole. It is of course true that this organizational behavior is shaped by the human elements (sub-systems) in the organization. Yet the only way of understanding the processes involved is to regard the individuals in terms of their relationships (structures). A mere summing up of the behavior of the component elements yields insufficient insight into the whole.

d. The organization as a system is in its turn part of a supra-system. The exchange relationships with this supra-system must fulfill the needs of both the organization and the supra-system.

A number of questions are raised by this approach:

—What different types of relationship exist among the elements, sub-systems, and systems?

—What contributions do the various structures (different relationship patterns) make to satisfying the system needs? Two criteria in particular are employed in this connection (Etzioni, 1960): the criterion of survival and the criterion of effectiveness (the extent to which goals are achieved).

—How do changes take place? One answer to this question proceeds from the supposition that the system will gradually grow towards a situation in which it will be so consistently constructed internally that it is optimally suited to fulfill the needs existing in and outside the organization. As these needs change, in this view, the system adapts itself automatically. We have already seen in the structural-functionalist approach that this makes it very difficult to predict differences among organizations. Thus, the system model is primarily descriptive in character.

The merit of the system model lies in the fact that it makes clear that the exchange relationships between individuals and the organization, and between the organization and its environment, are developing simultaneously, and that therefore the criterion of effectiveness must be met simultaneously for both the environment and the individuals in the organization. The environment will only make new input available to the organization as long as the organization offers goods and services at a socially acceptable cost. The individual will only make his labor available as long as the balance between costs and benefits continues to tip in his favor. The open-system theory, if it abandons the idea of automatic adaptation (which is not even inherent in all the organisms in the evolutionary model, as the example of the dinosaur can testify) can provide suggestions of why some organizations survive (positive balance) and others do not. In this sense the system approach offers a descriptive-analytical potential. To be able to predict which organizations will survive and which will not, however, it is necessary to gain knowledge of the processes and factors which play a role in survival. It is, therefore, necessary to further elaborate the descriptive framework, in which indications are given of which structures contribute under what conditions to the effectiveness of or/and capacity for adaptation. Additions should also be made to the theory to increase the understanding of the role played in that balancing process by the actively interacting elements, sub-systems, and systems, each having its own interests. The picture of an organization as a passive entity is replaced by an interaction perspective in which the meanings attached to these processes by human actors play a central role.

3.5. Summary and conclusions

In discussing the classical approaches, it was observed that efficiency, control, and motivation are the problems existing in the field of tension between the organization, the individual and the environment, for which the organization must find a solution. The structural-functionalist approach, which concentrates on the relationship organization-environment, assumes that the parts are automatically subordinate to the whole system (the organization). The motivation of individuals and the achievement of a sufficient degree of efficiency are not the problems which this approach addresses. They are, at most, constraints within which the actual problem unfolds: the adaptation of the organization (by means of its structure) to the environment. The approach provides no explanation for why some organizations succeed in adapting and others do not.

The integration-motivation approach, however, makes exactly this adaptation of individual and organization its main concern. It concentrates on the problem of how individual needs can be combined with an organization's need for a high degree of efficiency (ratio standard costs/actual costs) and a high productivity level (ratio results/costs). The adaptation of an organization to the environment is the marginal condition within which this problem unfolds.

Both the structural-functionalist and the integration-motivation approaches proceed from the assumption that organizations are comparable and that, under certain given conditions, there is one best way of organizing. The structural-functionalists emphasize the relationship between an organization and its environment, while the relationship individual-organization is taken as given. Just the opposite is the case in the integration-motivation approach: the relationship individual-organization is emphasized, while the relationship organization-environment is treated as a constant. This contrast graphically demonstrates that the reasoning process in the two approaches is applicable at two different system levels.

In the open-system theory it is made clear that the boundary between sub-system (group or individual), system (organization), and supra-system (environment) is an arbitrary one, and that the problems at each boundary are in fact the same. Not only must the organization be alert to changes in the environment—which, for example, lead to setting new requirements for production—the individuals functioning within the organization must also adapt to the changing requirements of the organization (for example, a different type of or more highly developed expertise). But the reverse is also true: an organization must take into account the desires of individuals; and the environment (society) cannot afford to ignore the desires of organizations (support, protection from competition) either. From this perspective, internal efficiency cannot be looked upon as a constraint within which problems of adaptation are somehow being solved (or vice versa). Since one of the vital elements in the survival of organizations is keeping costs at a socially acceptable level, and since internal efficiency plays an important role in this cost control, the achievement of a sufficient degree of efficiency is an essential part of the set of problems relating to adaptation. Thus, the open system approach makes clear that both at the boundary individual-organization, and at the boundary organization-environment, the same kind of problems must be solved; it also demonstrates that the structural-functionalist and the integration-motivation approaches supplement one another in this problem area. The problem of stability versus flexibility and adaptation must be solved at both levels. The same exchange relationship exists between individuals and organizations as between organizations and environment. In its structure, the organization tries to coordinate the various individual sub-goals with the goals it has with respect to the environment. The structure also fulfills a function in the control and harmonization of the elements of the organization. Because the stability acquired in this way is too rigid to guarantee survival in a changing environment, continuous adaptation to internal and external conditions is effectuated by means of decision-making processes. In a decision-making process, the different contradictory demands must be weighed against one another in an attempt to achieve a balance between stability and flexibility.

Theories on structure and decision-making are therefore a necessary complement to the approaches toward the phenomenon 'organization' as sketched in this section. These theories will be presented in the following section.

4. CONTROL AND DECISION-MAKING

4.1. Introduction

In the following section a short review is given of existing ideas in the area of structure and decision-making; an attempt is then made to arrive at a number of conclusions after consideration of the problems this analysis of ideas brings forth.

4.2. Control and structure

The topic of 'structure of an organization' (relationships among elements) may be divided into two parts:
a. What are the determinants of structure? How can divergent structural arrangements be explained?
b. What are the effects of the different structural arrangements upon efficiency and the chances of survival of the organization?

4.2.1. DETERMINANTS OF STRUCTURE

On the basis of empirical studies, the following findings can be formulated:
—A structure is determined by the size of the organization, the technology, the uncertainty in the relevant environment of the organization, and the values of the managers (see Veen, this Handbook, ch. 4.1). Such a summary naturally does not describe what the relationships described look like or how they can be explained. Thus, this approach typically concentrated on collecting empirical evidence, emphasizing the variables that play a role in the tradition of both bureaucratic and scientific administration. A number of research groups have had considerable influence on this development. In England, the Aston group has done a large number of comparative studies, in which attention was directed primarily to the development of measurement tools and to conceptual clarification (for a review of this material see Pugh and Hickson, 1976; Pugh and Hinings, 1976; Pugh and Payne, 1977).

The Comparative Organization Research Group of Blau and his associates has primarily studied the characteristics of bureaucracies and the connection between technology and structure (Blau, 1968, 1970; Blau and Schoenherr, 1971; Blau et al., 1976).

The theoretical ideas developed in this area are often connected in some way with the concept of uncertainty. Thompson (1967), whose theoretical position is worked out in greater detail than that of other theoreticians, says, for example: ' ... *we will conceive of complex organizations as open systems, hence indeterminate and faced with uncertainty, but at the same time as subject to criteria of rationality and hence needing determinateness and certainty*' (p. 10; Thompson's italics). 'With this conception the central problem for complex organizations is one of coping with uncertainty' (p. 13). In this view, structure is a precipitate of, among other factors, the attempts of organizations to control uncertainty.

A structure is ultimately determined by (a) more or less unchanging constraints to which the organization must adapt; (b) contingencies: changeable constraints, which do not lie within the control of the organization, and (c) factors which the organization can control.

Factors which an organization can partially control include the technology and individuals in the organization. This control, however, is incomplete, as a result of internal and external factors. An organization will strive for control which is as complete as possible. It attempts to screen the technological process from, or render it insusceptible to, external influences as much as possible, using mechanisms such as buffering (build-up of stocks), leveling (smoothing the path of sales by, for example, offering favorable rates outside peak hours), rationing, and making predictions and plans based on these predictions. Such measures have consequences for the organizational structure. On top of this, characteristics of the production process itself determine how an organizational structure will look. Such an approach elevates the organization to an independently reasoning organism (reification). 'But of course they do nothing except as individual members within them act. We must therefore consider the behavior of people in and around organization if we are to understand the behavior of organizations' (Thompson, 1967, p. 99).

One of the greatest uncertainties facing an organization is the unpredictability of the behavior of individuals in the organization. In this respect, the organization is faced with a two-fold task: to persuade individuals to behave in a certain way, and to coordinate these individual behaviors in such a way that organizational activities continue to display a certain unity. The organizational structure, consisting (among other elements) of a system of behavioral codes (rules and regulations), combined with a reward structure, must see to it that this is accomplished. Child (1972, 1973) mentions two control strategies to indicate that an organization emphasizes *either* a system of hierarchically ranked positions with accompanying decision-making authority (decision-making structure), *or* a system of formalized and standardized rules (bureaucratic structure). In addition to screening out external disturbances and controlling internal disturbances, an organization will attempt to obtain maximum control and power over contingencies in the environment, and will try to eliminate as many restrictions as possible. This leads, for example, to a tendency for organizations to incorporate activities comprising essential contingencies for their continued existence, and to strive for territorial expansion. If, for example, an oil company were to start worrying about the sales of its product, gasoline, because gas stations are owned by competitors, or by a single distributor, it could attempt to solve the problem by buying enough gas stations to ensure the sale of its products, and thus its continued existence. The more gas stations it owns, the more secure it will feel. Of course, such interventions have their own consequences for the structure of the organization.

The size of an organization is one of the most important determinants of structure (see Veen, this Handbook, ch. 4.1). As an organization expands, a process of specialization and differentiation takes place. The uncertainties and impending disintegration which ensue must be removed by making use of structural arrangements, along with other measures. Thus an important function of structure is to make possible processes of coordination which are needed to harmonize tasks and positions with one another. At the same time, the organization tries to keep costs at a minimum by combining interdependent positions and then making them relatively autonomous, and also by grouping homogeneous positions, thus promoting standardization.

However, a structure must also guarantee harmonization with the environment and in particular with the contingencies found in it. To achieve this end, the organization structures itself in such a way that special departments are concerned with homogeneous segments of the environment. For example: an organization which has to deal with both professional buyers (of advanced video and hi-fi equipment) and average consumers (who buy a kind of similar equipment for normal home use) will divide its sales department in two, so that it is not left to a single department to deal with the totally divergent problems connected with sales on the professional and consumer markets. By separating these boundary-crossing activities, the organization can react more effectively to the environment. If the technological and the boundary-crossing components can be separated from one another, an organization results that has a centralistic structure. If the technological components and the components directed toward the environment are not independent, combinations will be formed which are relatively autonomous (divisions).

To summarize: a structure is aimed at bringing about a 'coalignment' of individuals, tasks, and positions, so that the uncertainties caused by internal and external factors can be reduced at an acceptable cost and retaining sufficient flexibility.

4.2.2. Effects of the structure

The central idea developed within the structural approach is that the better a structure is adapted to the demands resulting from internal and external uncertainties, and the slighter the inconsistencies in the structure, the greater the effectiveness of the organization. This so-called contingency approach has become the dominant trend in the structurally oriented organization approaches (Child, 1977, p. 165; Galbraith, 1977, ch. 3; Lawrence and Lorsch, 1967; Hazewinkel, this Handbook, ch. 4.3). The basic notion of this approach is that as the uncertainties facing an organization increase, both the degree of differentiation (breaking down into sub-units) and of integration (cohesion) must rise. If an organization does not sufficiently succeed in absorbing these demands into its organizational structure, the following effects will be observed to a greater or lesser extent (Child, 1977, p. 10):

—decreased motivation and lower morale of individuals in the organization,
—delayed and qualitatively poor decision-making,
—conflicts and defective coordination,
—insufficient innovative reactions to changed conditions,
—rapidly increasing costs, especially in the administrative sector.

4.2.2. PROBLEMS CONNECTED WITH THE CONTINGENCY APPROACH

Although simplified presentations of the contingency approach suggest that it rests on solid empirical and theoretical foundations, there are myriad problems connected with the approach. The fact that the theory introduces specifications which were absent in the other theories likewise makes it possible to differentiate the problems which flow from this theory:

a. Neither the concept of structure, nor the concept of uncertainty are one-dimensional (see Veen, this Handbook, ch. 4.1, for an extensive discussion).

b. Uncertainty is caused, both internally and externally, by a large number of factors (Veen, this Handbook, ch. 4.1). The nature and scope of these uncertainties can differ considerably, and can therefore subject the organization to highly divergent demands.

c. The causality presumed in the assumption that structure is determined by the internal and external factors with which the organization must deal, has never been substantiated. A good case can be made for the assertion that the structure determines which uncertainties are perceived (see also under e).

d. The contingency approach is strongly colored by the assumption that all those involved (the organization) are in agreement with the goals and interpret the situation in the same way. This is far from being the case, which is in itself a source of uncertainties.

e. We have thus arrived at one of the most essential questions formulated within the framework of the theory: how can an organization know what are the best reactions to uncertainties? The theoretical model which has been worked out in the greatest detail, that of Weick (1979), proceeds from the assumption that organizing consists of reducing uncertainty by means of social interaction (p. 3). All kinds of criteria (assembly rules, p. 113) play a role in this social interaction; these criteria determine which behavioral possibilities are created and selected by the organization.

Weick, in accordance with Ashby's law of 'requisite variety', assumes that a large measure of the uncertainty outside the organization must be met with a large measure of variability within the organization. This means that, when an organization is faced with a great deal of uncertainty, the criteria determining which behavior the organization should select must be such that a wide array of behavioral possibilities can be taken into consideration. The chance will then be greater that one of the approaches is a successful one. In Weick's theory this is achieved by assuming that, when the level of uncertainty is high, very few criteria will be used to select behavior, so that many possibilities will be considered. An example: if certain machines have numerous breakdowns, with a great deal of uncertainty for production ensuing, and if the only rule used by the organization for choosing from the possible actions is 'Do whatever causes the least amount of disturbance in the organization,' then the possibilities open to the organization would include: do nothing, service the machines, form extra stand-by repair teams, carry out sharper control on servicing. Adding the rule 'Do whatever can be done without using any employees who are already busy doing something else,' would mean that the extra repair teams alternative would have to be dropped. With each new criterion, the chance becomes greater that an effective possibility for curing the evil will be lost (Weick, p. 114). Of course, trying out many of these possibilities involves costs.

The theory does not answer the question of how an organization can determine when the uncertainty is pronounced enough to make it worth the cost of investigating many possibilities. This problem is intertwined with another problem which has been lucidly formulated by Weick (p. 135): 'Under what conditions does adaptation preclude adaptability?' Each time an organization succeeds in reducing uncertainty has the consequence that this successful experience, exactly because it has been successful, thwarts adaptations in the future, which call for entirely different behavior. In addition, whenever the equilibrium is disturbed, the organization is faced with the dilemma noted earlier of short-term efficiency versus long-term effectiveness. A characteristic of this dilemma is that it is often clear enough what the *costs* are of certain actions in the short run, but not what the benefits are in the long run. Thus the choice will usually be made for 'efficiency in the short run'. This is usually not such a bad choice, since there are a number of indications in the literature that organizations that opt for a strict limitation of internal inconsistencies, even when it involves sacrificing the variability which makes long-term adaptation possible, can still be extremely successful (Khandwalla, 1973; Pennings, 1975). A possible explanation for this phenomenon is that short-term efficiency creates 'slack resources' (reserves) with which information systems can be set up, which can help making better predictions of uncertainties and which provide a measure of 'survival time' in case of a radical change in circumstances, thus allowing for effectuation of the necessary adaptations. Internal consistency is less essential for systems which can function satisfactorily with only loose connections among the sub-systems (see Weick, 1976). Such systems will also be able to adapt at a local level. Of course, up to a certain point, organizations are themselves capable of ensuring that they are composed of loosely coupled sub-units (using, for example, a divisional structure in which the divisions are as independent as possible).

f. Although the merit of the contingency theories, as compared to the structural-functionalist approach, is that they have imparted a considerable degree of specification and empirical underpinnings to the largely evolutionist insights, the fundamental problem remains that the approach is based upon the assumption that the organizations' long-term aim is survival.

Although this assumption is plausible enough in itself, there being plenty of examples of how organizations go to any lengths in order to continue its existence, the criterion for determining what 'survival' is has never been specified. The implicit assumption apparently is that an organization will continue to exist in its present form. There are, however, a great number of aspects connected with the organization: its name, capital, and location, the people working in it, its legal status, and so forth. When does organization X stop being itself? When its capital has been used up, when its name changes, when all the members have been replaced, if it moves, when it is bought by, or itself buys, another organization? What is the relationship between survival and adaptation? It is not an extremely adaptive reaction for an organization to dissolve itself if it no longer has any justification for its existence? The contingency approach has provided no answers to these questions.

The contingency approach has found a method for dealing with one of the objections which can be made against the functionalist approach. It has made it possible to specify the conditions determining which organizations survive and which do not. The relationship between short- and long-term strategies, however, remains obscure. This means that it also remains essentially unclear how decisions on these matters are made, and how the different sub-unit interests present in the organization are combined. Thus, although this theory does succeed in developing a perspective which can handle both fields of tension, individual-organization and organization-environment, it does not succeed in dealing with the efficiency versus effectiveness dilemma (adaptation) or the motivation versus efficiency dilemma. In order to understand the problems inherent in these shortcomings, it is necessary to illuminate the decision-making processes which play a part in the process as a whole.

4.3. Decision-making theories

The process of weighing alternatives sketched in 4.2.3 is accomplished by individuals within the organization. They decide what eventually is going to happen. A structure is the result of a number of such choices. Yet there is always considerable latitude for interpretation in this structure, even in highly bureaucratic organizations. Changing circumstances will also compel adaptations and readjustments. The equilibrium at one point in time will by definition be temporary and unstable. The decision-making process is thus a continuous process. Explanations of this process may contribute to an understanding of the phenomenon 'organization' (see also Koopman et al., this Handbook, ch. 4.6).

The classical decision-making model proceeds from the assumption that decisions are made rationally. Rationality in this model is defined as choosing among alternatives, in such a way that the expected outcome represents a maximizing of the values held by the decision-maker (individual, group, or organization; March and Olsen, 1976, p. 69; Simon, 1957, p. 75).

Such a model is based on a number of different assumptions (March and Simon, 1958, p. 138):

a. Rational behavior presumes knowledge of all the alternatives.

b. Rational behavior presumes knowledge of all the consequences.

c. Rational behavior presumes the working out in complete detail of an order of preferences.

These assumptions will seldom be found to be justified in the real world. Thus Simon states (1957, p. 79): 'It is impossible for the behavior of a single isolated individual to reach any high degree of rationality.' By radically simplifying the situation and by searching for satisfactory outcomes (satisficing), rather than for optimal, or even maximal, ones, an approximate form of rationality may be attained. 'Because of the limits of human intellective capacities in comparison with the complexities of the problems that individuals and organizations face, rational behavior calls for simplified models that capture the main features of a problem without capturing all its complexities' (March and Simon, 1958, p. 169).

The concrete consequence for the organization is that the behavior and attention of organization members can be channeled by means of a system of behavioral codes (role constraints) and that reactions to events occurring in the organization and in its environment can be precoded by means of formalized rules. The organization has a structure, in the sense that certain elements can be regarded as fixed, so that behavior is placed within boundaries, and thus made rational. The most stable characteristics of the structure are the procedures according to which programs are developed, expanded, and revised. The rules indicating when a switch must be made from one program to another are somewhat less stable; least stable are the programs themselves (March and Simon, p. 170). By means of this limited rationality ('bounded rationality') the organization, on the surface, manages to achieve a semblance of rationality. This semblance of rationality soon disappears, however, when we realize that rules and procedures are also framed by individuals in the organization, who themselves are hindered by the same limitations on their capacity to act rationally. In addition, it is necessary for the achievement of organizational rationality that individuals accept the definition of the situation as it is presented by the system of organizational rules. If this is not the case, then the model of bounded rationality will have to be replaced or supplemented by models dealing with conflict (e.g., coalition formation, negotiations; see March and Olsen, 1976, p. 82 ff.; Veen and van Haren, 1980).

March and Olsen (1976, ch. I-V) have pointed to a number of other problems which come to the fore when an attempt is made to explain organizational behavior on the basis of models of rationality. In their view, rational, intelligent action is based on two fundamental processes. The first is the process of rational calculation, as expounded above. The second is the process of learning from experience (feedback). The limitations for the organization inherent in the latter process have received little or no attention. Most theories implicitly assume that an organization is capable of distinguishing success from failure, and that the causes and effects of success or failure can be clearly comprehended. This is often not the case. Individuals in organizations must interpret events. The learning process assumed to be involved may be sketched as in figure 1, representing a chain of processes. Disturbances may occur in every link in this chain.

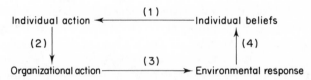

Figure 1. The learning process in organizations (March and Olsen, 1976, p. 57).

(1) Changes in opinion do not necessarily lead to changes in individual behavior—because, for example, the role constraints of the organization do not permit it. One of the collateral effects of organizational rules is that they hamper the transmission of innovative learning experiences.

(2) The link between individual behavior and the action finally taken by the organization as a whole is often far from clearly defined. Many influential factors are present simultaneously. The interests—and the coalition structures derived from them, along with the individual's own position in that coalition—determine the extent to which individual actions, based on changed insights, have a chance of having an effect upon the behavior of organizations.

(3) The connection between the behavior of an organization and the reaction of the external environment is far from clear. One of the biggest problems for an organization is to determine whether there is a causal link between a certain action (advertising campaign for example) and the reaction of the

environment (buying pattern). This means that the organization runs the risk of learning 'superstitiously'. Changes which take place immediately following an organizational action are considered effects of that action, although this may not be the true state of affairs.

(4) It is often unclear what exactly is happening in the environment. The signals received are often highly ambiguous. They are difficult to interpret; their meaning is hidden.

This state of affairs, in combination with the earlier observations with respect to the bounded rationality of decision-making, has as its most extreme consequence that all attempts at understanding the behavior of organizations are abandoned. If the process determining the composition of an organizational structure and organizational behavior is so irrational and so sensitive to all kinds of disturbances, it will by definition be impossible to explain the organization by rational representations. A chaotic mixture of new metaphors has been used in an attempt to break out of this impasse. Cohen *et al.* (1972) have described decision-making as 'a garbage can process in which answers are looking for a problem'; March and Olsen (1976, p. 69 ff.) talk about the technology of foolishness and draw up a set of rules to make it possible; Hedberg *et al.* (1976) recommend that organization structures be regarded in terms of 'camping on the seesaw'; Weick (1977b, p. 193 ff.) suggests that effective organizations be defined as garrulous, clumsy, superstitious, hypocritical, octopoid, organized anarchy, wandering, and grouchy. These images have led to amusing descriptions and to new categories and ways of understanding organizations. They primarily emphasize that organizing is a process which attempts to reconcile the irreconcilable. It would be more fruitful, however, to consider these metaphors as a first step towards formulating a meta-theory (a theory about theories, and thus a way of looking at problems which crop up in the course of theory formation) of organizations rather than as systematic attempts to construct a theory of organizations themselves (see Weick, 1979, p. 235).

4.4. Summary and conclusions

The structural approach has concerned itself with two questions:
a. Which factors determine a structure?
b. What are the effects of different structures?
The answer to the first question demonstrated that the most important function of structure is the reduction of uncertainty. The answer to the second question demonstrated that every reduction of uncertainty creates new uncertainties. The theories of decision-making, then, demonstrated that this web of shifting uncertainties is so complicated, that rational explanatory models must be divested of their rationality step-by-step to preserve their connection with empirical observations. The construction of a representative image of orga-

nizations begins to take on the character of an attempt, eternally doomed to failure, to steer a course between Scylla and Charybdis, in search of the promised land—rationality. The insistent question forced upon us in this respect is whether one of the constituent elements in this description of organizations— goal-directedness—can still be retained.

5. GOALS AND DIALECTICS

5.1. Introduction

The goal concept will be analyzed below, its central question being to what degree the rational elements can be retained. We will then consider the fundamental field of tension between rationality and irrationality in organizations.

5.2. Goals

The most distinctive characteristic of the definition of organizations is that of striving toward goals. 'Few discussions of organization theory manage to get along without introducing some concept of organizational goal' (Simon, 1964, p. 1). Two branches of this approach can be distinguished (see, e.g., Campbell, 1977, p. 20 ff.; Etzioni, 1960; Georgiou, 1973; Gouldner, 1959):
a. The so-called 'goal-centered' approach, which proceeds from the assumption that an organization is run by rational decision-makers, who visualize a set of goals which they are trying to achieve.
b. The natural systems approach, which assumes that an organization adopts as its overall goal 'survival'.

The second approach assumes that the demands made upon an organization are so changeable and complex that it is impossible to isolate a limited number of sharply defined goals of the organization. The organization therefore concentrates upon the goal of ensuring its continued existence. This continued existence is assured as long as the organization fulfills a function, at an acceptable cost, in the supra-system of which it is a part, and as long as it ensures that the vital components it needs from the environment as input (e.g., raw materials) do not run out. The objections most often made against this approach have been considered in our treatment of the system theory and the structural-functionalist theories. As we saw earlier, Gouldner (1959) alleged that the natural system theories neglect the rational component. The discussion of the decision theories showed, however, that the rationality of the behavior of individuals in organizations must be regarded with some critical reservations. At the same time, the question can be posed as to what extent we may expect organizational behavior to be explainable on the basis of shared goals, if it is virtually impossible to explain behavior at the individual level rationally. It is clearly not open to doubt that 'the' organizational goal does not exist.

Almost everyone agrees that organizations strive after a number of goals. The problem lies in determining what they are. Perrow (1961) proposes a pragmatic solution to this problem: to consider as goals of the organization the policy line it lays down (the so-called operative goals). This evokes the following questions: how do these goals come into being? When the various individual perspectives must be bundled, how is this done?

Cyert and March (1959, 1963, ch. 3) consider an organization as a coalition, within which different sub-coalitions operate. This view is based on the following assumptions: (a) an organization is composed of individuals having potentially extremely divergent interests, and therefore preferences; (b) coalitions are formed by means of negotiations; each coalition represents a shared order of preference (= objective = goal) for certain outcomes; (c) the coalition can then be seen as one actor (1959, p. 78). The last point does not mean that the goals of organizations have thus automatically been clearly defined. There is at most agreement on vaguely formulated primary goals, and there remains considerable uncertainty concerning secondary goals (1959, p. 79).

The determination of the compensations (side-payments) offered to the various members of the coalition is the main process by means of which the goals are specified. It is at the same time an indication of the value of the contribution of individuals in relation to a specified goals. This means that there must be at least minimal agreement with respect to the goals for someone to become a member of the coalition. In any case, for an individual who considers becoming a member of an organization, this means that the organization comprises a fully-formed reality in which certain activities take place. He will go to work in the organization if these activities are not completely unacceptable to him, and if the recompensation is adequate. On the other hand, the organization will only offer this compensation if the contribution of the new coalition member is needed. The coalitions are not stable. Continuous, small adaptations are introduced under the pressure of circumstances.

The underlying model is a mixture of a negotiation and a decision-making model. The outcomes of the negotiations comprise the data on which further organizational decisions are based, just as the outcomes of these decisions in their turn form the data used in the negotiating process.

Although this conceptualization at first glance appears to provide an answer to the question of how individual goals are combined in the organization, on further consideration very little new understanding has been generated, because the processes involved have not been specified. Simon (1964) has reformulated the problem in terms of the organization's (individuals in the organization) having to try to meet a large number of demands simultaneously for each decision which is made. One of these 'constraints' sometimes receives extra emphasis and is then promoted to being a goal. It is clear, for example, that organizations would want to use the best qualified manpower at the lowest possible cost. When cost minimalization is declared to be a goal, the danger arises that quality demands cannot be met. The demand for quality is a 'constraint' on the achievement of the lowest possible costs. When the demand for quality is elevated to the status of goal, the cost factor becomes a constraint on the achievement of that goal. If we add to this the fact that highly qualified workers only want to take on a job if it is challenging and motivating, then yet another constraint is introduced, which can, in addition, serve as a 'side-payment', so that the cost factor can be diminished. Each decision made with respect to one of the factors, serves as a constraint on the other decisions. In other words, the totality of goals and/or constraints behaves as a system. Certain decisions and the actions flowing from them are determined primarily by the relationships among the different demands present in the system. In order to understand the genesis of organizational goals (read: set of constraints), it is of primary importance to understand the interrelationships among these goals. Simon continues along this line of reasoning (p. 21): 'In view of the hierarchical structure that is typical of most formal organizations, it is a reasonable use of language to employ organizational goal to refer particularly to the constraint sets and criteria of search that defines roles at the upper levels.' The problem of what happens if the different sub-coalitions formulate a system of mutually exclusive demands remains unsolved—in this approach as well as in the others.

Pennings and Goodman (1977, p. 152 ff.) use Thompson's (1967, p. 128 ff.) concept of 'dominant coalition' to show that those having the most power exert more influence in determining the criteria used in decision-making. Their negotiating position is stronger. Their demands are more effective in determining the boundaries of what is possible in the organization than are the demands of others. Their demands take on more of the character of an organizational goal than do other constraints. Pennings and Goodman supplement Simon's definition of organizational goals when they call them ' . . . desired end states specified by the dominant coalition' (p. 161). The distinction between goals and constraints is specified further in the sense that goals have the special attention of the dominant coalition and are measured against a certain standard, while constraints have the properties of necessary conditions (lowest levels, minima) which must be met by the organization in the long term in order for it to be able to survive. For Pennings and Goodman, as for Simon, the dominant coalition is localized at the top levels of the organization.

Although it is plausible and defensible enough in itself that the top levels exert a greater influence on the determination of goals, looking at the situation from this angle may cause the observer to disregard the important circumstance that a number of other interested parties in and *outside* the organization make demands which can weigh so heavily that they must be elevated to a goal by the dominant coalition (employment opportunities by the unions; environmental protection demands by pressure groups). The so-called 'stake-holders' approach (Snellen, 1975, pp. 80 ff., 217ff.) attempts to map out the various interested parties and their interests. In this way an organization is conceived of as '... an arena within which participants can engage in behavior they perceive as instrumental to their goals' (Cummings, 1977, p. 59–60). This view of the nature of an organization's goals is closely connected with the various different interactionist perspectives on organizations which will be treated below. A consequence of this way of looking at organizations is that organizational goals are no longer clearly defined and stable, but must be considered as the ever shifting result of an implicit and explicit process of negotiation centered around a more or less constant set of tasks and activities (the organization). This means that the definition of rationality is in constant transition. Even if an organization did manage to resolve the dilemma inherent in steering a course between the Scylla of efficiency and the Charybdis of flexibility, there still would be no guarantee for the organization that its goal is closer to being fulfilled. In the bustle of maneuvering and negotiating, the chance is great that in the meantime another goal has been set.

5.3. The dialectic of organizing versus organizations (process and structure)

In his 'The social psychology of organizing' (1979), Karl Weick adopted the position that every organization is the result of a process of organizing, described as a '... *consensually validated grammar for reducing equivocality by means of sensible interlocked behaviors*' (p. 3, Weick's italics). This view envisions a reality that is created by the behavior of individuals in an organization; within the bounds of this created reality, the participants must manage to arrive at agreements on how to manipulate it, and these agreements must be constructed in such a way that they entail satisfactory outcomes for all those involved. While it is true for most of the actors that they experience the organization as an encountered reality, they do not accept this reality as a matter of course, and are always trying to influence and shape it (see Veen and van Haren, 1980). This phenomenon, combined with external influences, ensures that the organizations are in constant flux. The organizing process is always continuing. Parts of an organization may be static, but there is always movement somewhere in the organization. 'Any changes that impinge upon this order, whether something ordinary like a new staff member, a disrupting event, a betrayed contract; or whether unusual, like the introduction of a new technology or a new theory, will call for renegotiation or reappraisal, with consequent changes in the organizational order' (Strauss *et al.*, 1963, p. 165). This so-called 'negotiated order' perspective (see Day and Day, 1977) emphasizes the active role played by individuals in shaping organizational reality. The approach puts the emphasis on the ever self-changing network of interactions. This is in contrast to many of the preceding approaches, which emphasize either the stability of structures (structural functionalists; rational-bureaucratic approach), or the established nature of goals at organizational or individual levels (decision-making, integration-motivation approaches). The 'negotiated order' approach emphasizes the dialectical relationship between the (temporary) stable relationships (structure) and the actions of individuals and groups inside and outside this structure (see also Benson, 1977).

In this view, rationality is considered as a process of rationalization, which retrospectively gives meaning to behavior which, when seen from a perspective outside the actor, seems irrational and chaotic (Brown, 1978). Weick (1979, p. 152) states: '... People in organizations need to act to find out what they have done' and '... people act out and realize their ideas' (Weick, 1977a, p. 287). The orientations and opinions which people bring with them to the organization, as well as the interactions among all these orientations and opinions, determine what the organizational reality is. The disturbing element in this viewpoint, from a theoretical point of view, is that just as many images of an organization will result as there are people and groups. Thus the socio-psychological and sociological perspectives try to indicate what the stable elements in the process are and how a collective structure and a shared reality are formed from them. If such a perspective is to be useful, then a description must be given of how the orientations and perceptions of the individuals (actors) in an organization initiate a process in which essentially all variables play a role, and which reacts upon the environment.

The variables in such a model can be classified according to the concepts environment-process-value-structure-reaction/adaptation (feelings and opinions with respect to the situation). The elements represented by the last four concepts are constantly in interaction with one another within the organization and tend to be congruent with one another to a certain extent (Nightingale and Toulouse, 1977). This means that an organization will begin to crack if too great discrepancies begin to appear between the underlying values of those involved, their opinions and feelings about the situation, on the one hand, and the processes and structures on the other. The continued existence of the organization is endangered from within just as it is endangered from without if too great a discrepancy develops between the demands of the environment and the products or services provided by the organization. This means that for every organization the binding element is a system of formal and/or informal rules, about which agreements are reached as a result of 'negotiations'. An analysis of organizational events from such an action perspective will be directed toward the following areas (Silverman, 1970, p. 154):

a. The nature of the role system and pattern of interactions, and the way in which they have developed; the extent to which the values of the different actors are actually expressed.

b. The nature of the involvement of the ideal-typical actors and the characteristic hierarchy of goals.

c. The definition of the situation by those involved and their expectations with respect to the behavior of others, in particular insofar as this behavior has consequences for strategic resources.

d. The typical actions of the different actors, and the meaning they attach to these actions.

e. The nature and source of the intentional and unintentional effects of actions, especially in view of their effects on the involvement and institutionalization of expectations within the role system.

f. Changes in the commitment and goals of the actors and the reasons for these changes.

The action approach concentrates simultaneously on the attitudes, orientations, and behavior, and on the pattern of relationships that comes into being as a result of their interaction (Silverman, p. 22). The frequent use of case studies demonstrates the usefulness of the approach for composing penetrative portraits of organizational situations, but has not led to the formulation of theories from which testable predictions can be derived. Like the metaphors of the organization, this approach can more fruitfully be considered as a metatheory than as a theory.

Reasoning from this type of perspective, Benson (1977) makes clear that a dialectical approach, implicit in the 'negotiated order' perspective, must study an organization as a whole, with its multiplicity of levels and sectors which are connected with one another in various ways. Two levels of organizational reality are differentiated in this connection: the *morphological* level and the level of the *substructure*. The morphological level refers to the organization as it is abstracted from concrete reality; the shape which the organization has come to have, and the effects of this shape. The classical approach concentrates in this area on classifying the types of shapes and measuring the aspects of shape. The dialectical perspective concentrates on the processes by means of which a structure has come into being. The emphasis lies strongly upon rational aspects. The substructure perspective, on the other hand, concentrates on the more irrational aspects—on the interactions which act as catalysts of changes in the formal structure.

In this approach as well, an organization is seen as a producer of contradictions. In contrast to many other explanations of organizational behavior, these contradictions are not explained away, but are acknowledged as a fundamental property of social processes. Because contradictions are continually being generated, possibilities keep being created for reconstructing organizational reality (compare Weick, 1979, p. 147 ff.). 'The most basic generic contradiction is that between the constructed social world and the ongoing process of social construction' (Benson, 1977, p. 16). In this view, the contradiction between rationality and irrationality must not be eliminated, but must be seen as an essential element in the complex of organizational events, which means that this field of tension must be represented in the theories.

Theories which address themselves only to either one or the other aspect are by definition doomed to have only limited explanatory value. This does not mean that these partial theories can be set aside without further ado. It does mean that they must be supplemented by their counterparts.

Seen from the perspective of the rational (morphological) aspect, this means, for example, that it must be made clear what the irrational (in terms of the organization) aspects are of rational solutions. The emphasis is placed primarily on the interests which are linked to certain solutions. Thus, the influence and power processes occupy a central position in this type of analysis of the phenomenon 'organization' (see for example also: Brown, 1978; Veen and van Haren, 1980). The extremely complicated influencing processes within the organization lead to structural solutions and the formulation of rules of the game which are declared by the winner to be 'rational'. Those who feel that their interests receive lower priority, will continue to strive toward a larger share of the benefits. And according to the extent to which they succeed, the definition of rationality and effectiveness changes. Thus the fundamental problem for organizations is to find workable solutions for dealing with the power fields and conflicts of interests with which it is faced. These solutions by definition have the nature of a multiplicity of fragile equilibriums: constructed rationalities, which are constantly subject to discussion.

5.4. Summary and conclusions

In our discussion of the development of the concept of goal, it soon became apparent that organizations are faced with a constantly shifting reality, towards which new approaches must be found repeatedly. It appeared in this connection to be characteristic of an organization that its definition of rationality is constantly changing. Consideration of the actionist 'negotiated order' perspective finally proved to result in a dialectical point of view, whose consequence is that the emphasis comes to lie strongly on power relationships and influencing processes, with the inherent implicit viewpoint that 'rationality' and 'irrationality' must primarily be considered as labels for the opinions of the winners and losers, respectively, in the influencing process. As such, this type of concepts should be one component of theories of organizations. Such theories are not available at this time.

6. CONCLUSION

We started out with the observation, based on the classical approaches to organization theory, that an organization attempts to solve a number of problems—problems which are characterized by the fact that the solution of one partial problem aggravates another partial problem. We ended by observing that this is unavoidable and inherent in the phenomenon 'organization' when it is seen as an 'arena of interests.' We also ended with a perspective (way of looking) and not with a theoretical model. This may at first glance be ascribed to the fact that this perspective has only recently become an object of interest. However, this seems less probable when we realize that the intellectual roots of the dialectical perspective and of the 'negotiated order' perspective can be traced a long way back, and have never led to theories which make testable predictions possible. As a consequence, the question is raised whether or not it makes sense to strive after an organization theory. Such a theory would comprise an attempt to construct a general theory of social order, which for the time being remains beyond our reach. Considering this state of affairs, we adopt Merton's conclusion that it would be best to strive, in the foreseeable future, after theories of the 'middle range'. A phenomenon which is so complex as that of organizations probably can never be explained by just one theory. If we ask ourselves what it is about organizations that actually needs to be explained, it immediately becomes clear why this is so. Such a large number of component aspects present themselves that any theory which seeks to explain all of them will be so general and so abstract, that it is impossible to derive concrete predictions from it. In this sense it would be fruitful to consider the formulation of valid partial theories as a goal in itself, with the comforting thought that it may one day be possible to order the partial theories into a descriptive model. Reflections upon the perspective within which organizations can be regarded the most effectively can then help in choosing the most fruitful partial theories and can draw attention to those main processes which are worthy of further study.

REFERENCES

Alderfer, C. P. (1969), An empirical test of a new theory of human needs. *Organizational Behavior and Human Performance*, **4**, 142–175.

Alderfer, C. P. (1972), *Existence, relatedness and growth: Human needs in organizational settings*. New York: Free Press.

Alderfer, C. P. (1977), A critique of Salancik and Pfeffer's examination of need-satisfaction theories. *Administrative Science Quarterly*, **22**, 658–669.

Andriessen, J. H. T. H. (1975), De verwachtingstheorie voor werk motivatie [The expectancy theory of work motivation]. *Nederlands Tijdschrift voor de Psychologie*, **30**, 453–492.

Argyris, Ch. (1957), *Personality and organization*. New York: Harper.

Argyris, Ch. (1959), Understanding human behavior in organizations: One viewpoint. In: Haire, M. (Ed.), *Modern organization theory*. New York: Wiley, 115–154.

Argyris, Ch. (1964), *Integrating the individual and the organization*. New York: Wiley.

Benson, J. K. (1977), Organizations: A dialectical view. *Administrative Science Quarterly*, **22**, 1–21.

Berrien, F. K. (1968), *General and social systems*. New Brunswick (N.J.): Rutgers University Press.

Bertalanffy, L. von (1950), The theory of open systems in physics and biology. *Science*, **111**, 23–29.

Blau, P. M. (1956), *Bureaucracy in modern society*. New York: Random House.

Blau, P. M. (1968), The hierarchy of authority in organizations. *American Journal of Sociology*, **73**, 453–467.

Blau, P. M. (1970), A formal theory of differentiation in organizations. *American Sociological Review*, **35**, 201–219.

Blau, P. M., Schoenherr, R. A. (1971), *The structure of organizations*. New York: Basic Books.

Blau, P. M., McHugh Falbe, C., McKinely, W., Tracey, Ph.K. (1976), Technology and organization in manufacturing. *Administrative Science Quarterly*, **21**, 20–40.

Brown, R. H. (1978), Bureaucracy as praxis: Toward a political phenomenology of formal organizations. *Administrative Science Quarterly*, **23**, 365–382.

Campbell, J. P. (1977), On the nature of organizational effectiveness. In: Goodman, P. S., Pennings, J. M., and associates, *New perspectives on organizational effectiveness*. San Francisco: Jossey-Bass, 13–55.

Campbell, J. P., Pritchard, R. D. (1976), Motivation theory in industrial and organizational psychology. In: Dunnette, M. D. (Ed.), *Handbook of industrial and organizational psychology*. Chicago: Rand McNally, 63–130.

Carey, A., (1967), The Hawthorne studies: A radical criticism. *American Sociological Review*, **32**, 403–416.

Child, J. (1972), Organization structure and strategies of control. *Administrative Science Quarterly*, **17**, 163–177.

Child, J. (1973), Strategies of control and organization behavior. *Administrative Science Quarterly*, **18**, 1–17.

Child, J. (1977), *Organization: A guide to problems and practice*. London: Harper and Row.

Clark, B. R. (1960), *The open door college: A case study*. New York: McGraw-Hill.

Cohen, M. D., March, J. G., Olsen, J. P. (1972), A garbage can model of organizational choice. *Administrative Science Quarterly*, **17**, 1–25.

Cummings, L. L. (1977), Emergence of the instrumental organization. In: Goodman, P. S., Pennings, J. M. and associates, *New perspectives on organizational effectiveness*. San Francisco: Jossey-Bass, 56–62.

Cyert, R. M., March, J. G. (1959), A behavioral theory of organizational objectives. In: Haire M. (Ed.), *Modern organization theories*. New York: Wiley, 76–90.

Cyert, R. M., March, J. G. (1963), A behavioral theory of the firm. Englewood Cliffs (N.J.): Prentice-Hall.

Day, R., Day, J. V. (1977), A review of the current state of negotiated order theory: An appreciation and a critique. In: Benson J. K. (Ed.), *Organizational analyses: Critique and innovation*. Beverley Hills: Sage Publications, 128–144.

Etzioni, A. (1960), Two approaches to organizational analysis: A critique and a suggestion. *Administrative Science Quarterly*, **5**, 257–278.

Fiedler, F. E. (1978), The contingency model and the dynamics of the leadership process. In: Berkowitz, L. (Ed.), *Advances in experimental social psychology*, vol. 11. New York: Academic Press, 60–112.

Galbraith, J. R. (1977), *Organization design*. Reading (Mass.): Addison-Wesley.

Georgiou, P. (1973), The goal paradigm and notes towards a counter paradigm. *Administrative Science Quarterly*, **18**, 291–310.

Goldthorpe, J. H., Lockwood, D., Bechhofer, F., Platt, J. (1968), *The affluent worker: Industrial attitudes and behavior*. Cambridge: Cambridge University Press.

Gouldner, A. W. (1954), *Patterns of industrial democracy*. Glencoe (Ill.): Free Press.

Gouldner, A. W. (1959), Organizational analysis. In: Merton R. K., Broom, L., Cottrell Jr., L. S. (Eds.), *Sociology today*. New York: Basic Books.

Gulick, L., Urwick L. (Eds.) (1937), *Papers on the science of administration*. New York: Columbia University, Institute of Public Administration.

Hall, R. H. (1972), *Organizations: Structure and process.* Englewood Cliffs (N.J.): Prentice-Hall.

Hedberg, B. L. T., Nystrom, P., Starbuck, W. H. (1976), Camping on seesaws: Prescription for a self-designing organization. *Administrative Science Quarterly,* **21**, 41–65.

Homans, G. G. (1951), *The human group.* London: Routledge & Kegan Paul.

Katz, D., Kahn, R. L. (1978), *The social psychology of organizations.* 2nd ed. New York: Wiley.

Khandwalla, P. N. (1973), Viable and effective organizational design of firms. *Academy of Management Journal,* **16**, 481–495.

Lawrence, P. R., Lorsch, J. W. (1967), *Organization and environment: Managing differentiation and integration.* Boston: Division of research, Graduate School of Business and Administration Harvard University.

Likert, R. (1959), A motivation approach to a modified theory of organization and management. In: Haire M. (Ed.), *Modern organization theory.* New York: Wiley, 184–217.

Likert, R. (1961), *New patterns of management.* New York: McGraw-Hill.

Likert, R. (1967), *The human organization: Its management and values.* New York: McGraw-Hill.

Locke, E. A. (1975), Personal attitudes and motivation. In: Rosenzweig, M. R., Porter, L. W. (Eds.), *Annual Review of Psychology,* **26**, 457–480. Palo Alto (Cal.): Annual Reviews Inc.

Lowin, A. (1968), Participative decision making: A model, literature, critique and prescriptions for research. *Organizational Behavior and Human Performance,* **3**, 68–106.

McGregor, D. (1960), *The human side of enterprise.* New York: McGraw-Hill.

March, J. G., Olsen, J. P. (1976), *Ambiguity and choice in organizations.* Bergen (Norway:) Universitetsforlaget.

March, J. G., Simon, H. A. (1958), *Organizations.* New York: Wiley.

Marrow, A. J., Bowers, D. G., Seashore, S. E. (1967), *Management by participation: Creating a climate for personal and organizational development.* New York: Harper and Row.

Maslow, A. (1954), *Motivation and personality.* New York: Harper and Row.

Massie, J. L. (1965), Management theory. In: March J. G. (Ed.), *Handbook of organizations.* Chicago: Rand McNally, 387–422.

Mayo, E. (1975), *The social problems of an industrial civilisation.* London: Routledge & Kegan Paul.

Merton, R. K. (1957), *Social theory and social structure.* 2nd ed. Glencoe (Ill.): Free Press.

Messinger, S. L. (1955), Organizational transformation: A case study of declining social movement. *American Sociological Review,* **20**, 3–10.

Miller, J. G. (1965), Living systems: Basic concepts. *Behavioral Science,* **10**, 193–237.

Nederlands Tijdschrift voor de Psychologie [Dutch Journal of Psychology]. Deventer: Van Loghum Slaterus.

Nightingale, D. V., Toulouse, J. M. (1977), Toward a multi-level congruence theory of organization. *Administrative Science Quarterly,* **22**, 264–280.

Parsons, T. (1967), A paradigm for the analyses of social systems and change. In: Demerath, N. J., Peterson, R. A. (Eds.), *System, change and conflict.* New York: Free Press, 189–212.

Parsons, T. (1969), Suggestions for a sociological approach to the theory of organizations. In: Etzioni, A. (Ed.), *A sociological reader on complex organizations.* 2nd ed. New York: Holt, Rinehart & Winston, 32–46.

Pennings, J. M. (1975), The relevance of the structural-contingency model for organizational effectiveness. *Administrative Science Quarterly,* **20**, 393–410.

Pennings, J. M., Goodman, P. S. (1977), Toward a workable framework. In: Goodman,

P. S., Pennings, J. M., and associates, *New perspectives on organizational effectiveness*. San Francisco: Jossey-Bass, 146–184.

Perrow, C. (1961), The analysis of goals in complex organizations. *American Sociological Review*, 26, 584–865.

Perrow, C. (1970), *Organizational analysis: A sociological view*. Belmont (Cal.): Brooks-Cole.

Perrow, C. (1972), *Complex organizations: A critical essay*. Glenview (Ill.): Scott-Foresman.

Porter, L. W., Lawler III E. E., Hackman, J. R. (1975), *Behavior in organizations*. New York: McGraw-Hill.

Pugh, D. S., Hickson, D. J. (1976), *Organizational structure in its context: The Aston programme I*. Westmead: Saxon House.

Pugh, D. S., Hinings, C. R. (1976), *Organizational structure: Extensions and replications. The Aston programme II*. Westmead: Saxon House.

Pugh, D. S., Payne, R. L. (1977), *Organizational behavior in its context. The Aston programme III*. Westmead: Saxon House.

Roethlisberger, F. J. (1952), *Management and morale*. Cambridge (Mass.): Harvard University Press.

Roethlisberger, F. J., Dickson, W. J. (1939), *Management and the worker*. Cambridge (Mass): Harvard University Press.

Salancik, G. R., Pfeffer, J. (1977), An examination of need-satisfaction models of job-attitudes. *Administrative Science Quarterly*, 22, 427–456.

Schein, E. H. (1965), *Organizational psychology*. Englewood Cliffs (N.J.): Prentice-Hall.

Selznick, P. (1943), An approach to a theory of bureaucracy. *American Sociological Review*, 8, 47–54.

Selznick, P. (1949), *TVA and the grass roots*. Berkeley: University of California Press.

Silverman, D. (1970), *The theory of organizations*. London: Heinemann.

Simon, H. A. (1957), *Administrative behavior*. 2nd ed. New York: MacMillan.

Simon, H. A. (1964), On the concept of organizational goal. *Administrative Science Quarterly*, 9, 1–22.

Snellen, I. Th. M. (1975), *Benaderingen in de strategieformulering* [Approaches in formulating strategies]. Alphen a/d Rijn: Samsom.

Sofer, C. (1972), *Organizations in theory and practice*. New York: Basic Books.

Strauss, A., Schatzman, L., Bucher, R., Ehrlich, D., Sabshin, M. (1963), The hospital and its negotiated order. In: Freidson, E. (Ed.), *The hospital in modern society*. New York: Free Press, 148–169.

Taylor, F. W. (1911), The principles of scientific management. New York: Harper.

Thompson, J. D. (1967), *Organizations in action*. New York: McGraw-Hill.

Veen, P. (1973), Participatie: Een poging tot synthese [Participation: An attempt at synthesis]. In: Drenth, P. J. D., Willems, P. J., Wolff, Ch. J. de (Eds.), *Arbeids- en organisatiepsychologie* [Work- and organizational psychology]. Deventer: Kluwer.

Veen, P., Haren, Th. van (1980), Gedrag in organisaties [Behaviour in organizations]. In: Jaspars, J., Vlist, R. van de (Eds.), *Sociale psychologie in Nederland* [Social psychology in The Netherlands], *III*. Deventer: Van Loghum Slaterus.

Veld, J. in't (1975), *Analyse van organisatieproblemen* [An analysis of organizational problems]. Amsterdam: Agon/Elsevier.

Vroom, V. H. (1964), *Work and motivation*. New York: Wiley.

Wahba, M. A., Bridwell, L. G. (1976), Maslow reconsidered: A review of research on the need hierarchy theory. *Organizational Behavior and Human Performance*, 15, 212–240.

Wahba, M., House, R. J. (1974), Expectancy theory in work and motivation: Some logical and methodological issues. *Human Relations*, **27**, 121–147.

Weber, Max (1946), Types of authority. In: Gerth, H. H., Mills, C. W. (Eds.), *From Max Weber: Essays in sociology*. New York: Oxford University Press, 224–229.

Weber, Max (1947), *The theory of social and economic organization*. Transl. by A. M. Henderson and T. Parsons. Glencoe (Ill.): Free Press.

Weick, K. E. (1976), Educational organizations as loosely coupled systems. *Administrative Science Quarterly*, **21**, 1–19.

Weick, K. E. (1977a), Enactment processes in organizations. In: Staw, B. M., Salancik, G. R. (Eds.), *New directions in organizational behavior*. Chicago: St. Clair Press, 267–300.

Weick, K. E. (1977b), Re-punctuating the problem. In: Goodman, P. S., Pennings, J. M. and associates, *New perspectives on organizational effectiveness*. San Francisco: Jossey-Bass, 193–225.

Weick, K. E. (1979), *The social psychology of organizing*. 2nd ed. Reading (Mass.): Addison-Wesley.

Handbook of Work and Organizational Psychology
Edited by P. J. D. Drenth, H. Thierry, P. J. Willems and C. J. de Wolff
© 1984, John Wiley & Sons, Ltd.

4.3. Organizational structure and contingency theory

Aart Hazewinkel

1. INTRODUCTION[1]

1.1. What is a contingency theory?

Let us compare two secondary schools: the one a Montessori school where the emphasis is on the students learning to work independently, the other a more conventional school, whose central features are the academic achievements as expressed in the frequency of repeating classes and in the final-examination scores. The goal of a Montessori school requires a high degree of freedom for the students with respect to the amount of attention paid to each subject, the extent to which they gather information on their own, and the extent to which they themselves combine the information on various subjects into, for example, projects or papers.

This freedom for the students creates a high degree of uncertainty for the teachers. Often, they do not know in advance when and on what they will be called upon for information, explanation or help regarding planning problems or other difficulties of the work at school. Also, it depends on the individual student's requirements when tests are to take place. This has important consequences. Firstly, it is difficult for the teachers to plan their work ahead. Therefore, heads of sections or the school management are hardly in a position

Prof. Dr. Aart Hazewinkel, Instituut voor Sociale Psychologie, St. Jacobsstraat 14, 3511 BS UTRECHT.

[1]This chapter could not have been accomplished without the long and through discussions I had with dr. J. L. Knip. His views have greatly contributed to a clarification of the problems involved and to its form. I also thank dr. M. G. Boekholdt and drs. W. Polet for their critical remarks on one of the last versions.

to prescribe how a teacher should do his work, they can only provide general statements of principle. Secondly, the coordination of subject sections cannot be organized by means of agreements and procedures, because it is unpredictable in which subjects or—within the framework of projects and papers—in which combinations of subjects the students will be interested. Thus, in order to cope flexibly with the ever-changing questions and problems of students, continued consultations among the different sections are necessary. Finally, some teachers will have to fulfil the function of adviser to help the students along.

The traditional school represents almost the opposite. The teachers' working methods can be planned ahead. Their role with respect to the students is more clearly established. Problems of coordination—e.g. who tests when—can be solved by means of rules and because the students' freedom is limited, the function of adviser is superfluous.

These differences between two educational organizations occur in various other types of organization as well. We chose this example because most people are familiar with school organizations. Any generalization, however, requires a description with the aid of a number of abstract concepts. One was mentioned already: *goals*. One tries to attain some goal by doing something with or to raw materials, things, symbols, or people. The working method applied is called *technology*, also in those cases where, as in schools, few or no technical means are being used (Perrow, 1970). Thus, according to this terminology, differences in teaching methods—a lot of individualized education, use of projects, stimulating the independent use of libraries versus classroom education, clearly structured instructions, and homework—represent differences in technology.

We also discussed the various roles fulfilled in the school (school management, teachers of specific subjects, advisers), how these roles are coordinated, and the degree to which role behavior is fixed, specified. In this case, we speak of the characteristics of the *structure* of an organization. Below, we shall also encounter the concept of *environment*. The nature of a school's population, the presence of other schools, and characteristics of national educational policy are its important environmental characteristics.

It has turned out useful to speak of a structure that 'fits' a certain technology. A traditional school may function by means of clear-cut, formally established agreements and few consultations. Since the students all have the same tasks, to be completed at a fixed time, teachers are seldom confronted with anything unforeseen requiring consultations and joint resolution of problems.

In a Montessori school, however, the coordination and the working methods of the teachers cannot be established ahead—for now and ever—in the form of task descriptions, teaching schedules, and programs. The teachers have to improvise and consult more often and therefore should have more freedom to make their own decisions. Here, the structure is less stringent than in traditional schools. If a structure fits the technology we speak of a *congruence* between structure and technology.

This holds not only for educational organizations, but also for other types of organization. Burns and Stalker (1961) compared a rayon mill to, among others, an electronic plant. It appeared that the former utilized a well controllable, albeit complicated technology, where most events were reasonably predictable and where one was familiar with the correct reactions to exceptional events. The same held for the demand of its consumers. Thus, its technology and environment were characterized by certainty and predictability. In such cases, the behavior of the members of an organization may be preprogrammed to a large extent; there is no need for them to have a great deal of freedom in making decisions. Unexpected events can easily be dealt with by the top of the hierarchy. From a purely economic cost-benefit point of view these possibilities should obviously be utilized. Such an organizational structure Burns and Stalker call highly *mechanistic*. In many respects, the electronic plant represented quite the opposite. Its production process contained many uncertainties and its market was turbulent. This meant that problems always had to be solved at all levels of the organization, often in cooperation with researchers, production people, and sales staff. This required a structure Burns and Stalker call *organic*: less formal authority, more freedom in shaping one's function, consulting informally—not along hierarchical lines—and making decisions according to the situation.

The concepts of *organic* and *mechanistic structure* should not be understood as types, but as extremes on a continuum, just as the closely related concept of *degree of bureaucracy* indicates a dimension (even more than one, as we shall see below). A higher degree of bureaucracy, then, coincides with 'more mechanistic', a lower degree of bureaucracy with 'more organic'. Burns and Stalker point out that both forms of organization have their disadvantages: a strongly formalized, hierarchical 'mechanistic' structure leaves the members of the organization little freedom and initiative, whereas the 'organic' form of organization creates much uncertainty and requires a lot of consultation. But under their specific technological and environmental circumstances each of these two forms represents the best one—again: in terms of efficiency! This is the simplest description of what today we generally call a contingency theory of organizations: it depends on the situation which form of organization is the best one. 'There is no one best way to organize'.

'To organize' here stands for 'choosing a structure, giving form to an organization'. This implies that one would do well to have one's choice of structure dictated by an evaluation of the prevailing situation. In this case, important characteristics of the situation are size of the organization, technology, and environment. In many cases, the environment will be described in terms of economy, but also occasionally in terms of the labor market: the kind of personnel available. All these situational characteristics are comprised in the general term 'context'.

It is clear that, from the start, the contingency theory was of a strongly prescriptive nature: working methods should be adapted to the prevailing situation; the structure of an organization is, essentially, a working method, a system of rules, procedures, and agreements regarding the distribution of work and authority. This may seem obvious. Yet, it was a long time before this view appeared to be generally accepted in the theory of organizations. A summary of the as yet relatively short history of the scientific approach to organizations will illustrate this (for a more extensive survey, see this Handbook, ch. 4.1).

1.2. Theories of organizations: a brief survey of the history previous to the contingency approach

March (1965) mentions three books that, according to him, mark the beginnings of scientific work in the field of organization theory:
—Barnard, *The functions of the executive*, 1938.
—Roethlisberger and Dickson, *Management and the worker*, 1939.
—Simon, *Administrative behavior*, 1947.
Other authors (e.g. March and Simon, 1958; Massie, 1965; Perrow, 1972) associate the birth of the discipline with the publications of the sociologist Max Weber, particularly with the publication in 1921 of *Wirtschaft und Gesellschaft* (Economy and society), describing the model of a bureaucratic organization (for the different translations see Perrow, 1979, p. 3, fn. 4) and with observations of a number of managers and teachers at American business schools, who had developed the so-called 'scientific' or 'classical management theory'.

The theories of Max Weber and the classical management theories did not directly influence one another (Perrow, 1972). They were challenged by the so-called 'Human Relations School' and by the closely allied 'Human Resources School'. Both schools were based on empirical and experimental research of industrial and social psychologists. The exclusive interest of Weber and the management theorists in formal structures in particular was criticized. They emphasized not only the importance of group processes (leadership, communication, atmosphere in the working groups) for various organizational phenomena, but also the significance of the influence of people other than those at the hierarchical top of the organization (see e.g., Roethlisberger and Dickson, 1939; Marrow et al., 1967; Likert, 1967; and many other publications). For the present chapter it is of special importance, that both the classical theories and the succeeding Human Relations School and Human Resources School searched for a theory of organization, or rather rules and principles, that would be valid for all kinds of organization. These rules and principles were concerned with such divergent topics as the optimal number of subordinates a superior should directly control ('the optimal span of control'), the best way to supervise, the form of the organization—many or few hierarchical levels, many or few different departments, the basis on which departments are set up—, the distribution of influence and power within the organization, and the like.

A pivotal and controversial question was: to what extent should an organization be structured, or: how specifically should functions and activities be prescribed, the authority to make decisions and power relations be laid down, and to what extent should power be concentrated at the top? Or, using the terminology of Burns and Stalker: how mechanistic or organic should an organization be?

The publications of researchers such as Burns and Stalker (1961) mentioned above and also, among others, Woodward (1958, 1965), Thompson (1967), Lawrence and Lorsch (1969), and Perrow (1970) initiated an important new phase in organizational research and theory development. They demonstrated that the controversy among the defenders of the bureaucratic or mechanistic organization and those of the organic organization was a senseless one, because it depends on a variety of factors which form of organization is the best one. Above, this view was designated by the term 'contingency theory'. The term was first used in this sense by Lawrence and Lorsch, who, by using 'contingency', wished to indicate that the structure of an organization is dependent on the environment. 'Contingency' means dependence. It is not a very happy choice, since 'contingency' also means 'chance event', that is 'uncertainty': 'on the other hand, contingency expresses the uncertainty as to whether there are or can be premises for individual behavior at all' (Luhmann, 1976). Moreover, this second meaning is at variance with the deterministic nature of most contingency theories, which characteristic has given rise to much criticism, as we shall see below.

2. A CONTINGENCY APPROACH TO ORGANIZATIONAL STRUCTURES

2.1. The contingency approach: a confusing picture

The literature on contingency may sometimes strike the unprepared reader as being somewhat chaotic. That is because there are so many different emphases. Sometimes, the emphasis is on describing the nature of the relations between aspects of structure and context. It is explained why a certain structure fits—is congruent with—a given situation. Examples are our comparison of school types, the studies of Burns and Stalker mentioned above, and Khandwalla's (1974) description. (For an interesting attempt to relate five structural types—in Weber's sense of ideal or pure types—to the context of organizations, see Mintzberg, 1979.)

Sometimes, only statistical correlations between context and structure are noted, the context variables often having the status of independent variables (van der Zwaan, 1972). This summons up the picture of what, in the case of technology, some call 'technological determinism': the context variable 'techno-logy' is thought to determine the development of a structure. Some authors also point out that in successful organizations context–structure congruence is greater than in unsuccessful ones (Woodward, 1958, 1965; Lawrence and Lorsch, 1969), which will easily lead to prescriptive models. In that case, the prescriptions are concerned with the pursuit of congruence, that is, with developing structures that 'fit' the nature of the environment or technology (see above, section 1.1). Perrow (1970, ch. 3) presents a clear example of such a prescriptive model.

Finally, for some theoreticians determinism—context determines structure— is accounted for by the relationship between congruence and success. This implies a natural selection model: if congruence of context and structure is necessary for success, then organizations in which this relationship is insufficiently present will have less chance of survival, so that in the long run the context will determine the structure.

If we add to this the many seemingly contradictory research results, we begin to understand why the situation appears, to say the least, so opaque. That in many cases these research results are not really contradictory, because they concern different variables for no justifiable reason named the same, will be the the subject of section 3.1. In the following sections, we shall first look briefly into the different approaches and emphases.

2.1.1. THE CONCEPT OF CONGRUENCE

Important elements of the descriptions of context-structure congruence are the concepts of problem-solving, decision making, and uncertainty or unpredictability. Here, the influence of organizational decision-making models with their computer-derived terminology is unmistakable (March and Simon, 1958; Cyert and March, 1963; see also Koopman et al., this Handbook, ch. 4.6). An organization is a means of attaining goals as efficiently as possible. That can be done, if one 'programmes' as many tasks as possible, lays them down—once and for all—in formal procedures and fixed structures. Just as in everyday life an individual saves time and energy by developing and applying habits so an organization develops a structure.

Just as an individual can manage with these habits as long as his environment is stable (the bath- and diningroom situation at home, the familiar route to the office, driving his own car), so a great deal of organizational behavior may be preprogrammed in formal procedures and structures, if the environment is stable and therefore predictable, if the nature of the material to be processed is known and of a constant quality (Perrow, 1970). In this organizational model, efficiency in realizing clearly described goals is a value in itself:

'There is a norm of rationality in organizations, a tendency to try to increase stability and decrease uncertainty. Therefore, when technology allows, patterns of authority and communication will be made definite and orderly:

but when the task itself cannot be programmed, possessors of various kinds of individual expertise must play decision-making roles, usually in less predictable patterns and with less predictable results' (Mohr, 1971).

Or, in more everyday language: programming tasks and coordination with the aid of rules is, if the situation is suitable, the most efficient way of organizing. To incorporate more than the necessary flexibility in an organization is a luxury most organizations cannot afford (cf. Perrow, 1972). It is, moreover, not 'rational' to do so as long as there are no clear indications that this luxury will eventually pay off, for example by bringing about a decrease of dissatisfaction and, thus, of absenteeism and personnel turnover. Here, rational behavior presumes clearly described, mostly economic goals, which are pursued by means of methods involving no more uncertainty or costs than are acceptable. Thus, congruence may be defined in terms of efficiency in the pursuit of well-described goals: 'a certain structure fits a given context' then means 'the structure is the most efficient form of organization in the light of all known contextual factors and given the choice of certain well-described goals'. Clearly, in this view the problem of ambiguity, or at least diversity, of organizational goals does not come into the picture at all. That is, the definition of efficiency and thus congruence would cease to be unequivocal if the goals are not unequivocally defined or if it is not clear which of a range of divergent goals are the most important.

2.1.2. CONTEXTUAL DETERMINISM

As Van der Zwaan (1972) rightly notes, many publications about context-structure correlations at least suggest that their authors consider context factors the cause of structural characteristics. However, the nature of the research results—often correlations between simultaneously gathered measurements—hardly allows for such conclusions. Sometimes, closer analyses, for example by means of path analysis, even render the opposite hypothesis more likely. Thus Glisson (1978) concludes that a number of structural variables in his sample has consequences for the technology, and the research results of Leifer and Huber (1977) seem to indicate that the structure influences the perceived environmental uncertainty. On grounds of more qualitative analyses of environment–structure relationships, too, some researchers conclude that it is, to say the least, unlikely that the environment only determines the structure and not the other way around (Baker, 1974; Knip, 1975).

What holds for the deterministic explanation of structure from context, *mutatis mutandis* holds for the hypothesis that congruence leads to success. The research results barely allow any conclusions about cause-effect relationships. Here too, almost no longitudinal research is available.

2.1.3. THE NATURAL SELECTION MODEL

The natural selection model of the relationship between organizations and their environments in fact constitutes an application of Darwinian thought to organizations. Only those organizational structures, which sufficiently adapt to the requirements of their environment, survive. Thus, congruence is needed in order to survive.

There exists a less extreme model that has the characteristics of a learning model in the Skinnerian tradition: chance variations in structure lead to more or less favorable results. Those possessing the power to change or to maintain structural forms will learn something from this and later apply this knowledge when making structural decisions (Aldrich and Pfeffer, 1976). A statement such as Perrow's about the realization of environment structure congruence is in keeping with this: 'We must assume here that, in the interest of efficiency, organizations wittingly or unwittingly attempt to maximize the congruence between their technology and their structure' (1970, p. 80). One could, with some exaggeration, conclude that according to the natural selection model an organization is at the mercy of environmental influences.

2.2. Contingency theory at the departmental level: differentiation and integration

Lawrence and Lorsch's (1969) influential research was mentioned above in passing. In the literature on contingency theory they occupy an important if not unique place. Not only did they pay attention to the occurrence of congruence between structure and context in each separate department, but they also pointed out the congruence between the attitudes and orientations of their managers on the one hand, and the contexts of the departments on the other. What is more, they did research on its consequences for cooperation and conflict between the departments concerned.

Ever since the first publications about the possible relationship between technology and structure, there has been the question of such a relationship at the level of an organization's subdivisions. Hall (1962) found that organization departments with uniform routine tasks were more 'bureaucratized' than were departments with work that could not so easily be turned into a routine. Hickson et al. (1969) found a clear relation between the technology and structure of an organization if it was small and if its production department constituted a relatively large part of the organization. In bigger organizations, this relation was found only in those departments involved directly with production technology.

Thus, structure-technology relations will show up most clearly at the level of departments which are homogeneous with respect to technology. This idea has been elaborated in more detail by Lawrence and Lorsch (1969). Moreover, they point out that departments differ with respect to their environments: each department has its own specific environmental sector. Thus, a production department has to deal with suppliers of apparatus and raw materials and with a labor market, whereas a research and development department deals with the state of scientific knowledge and its applications, and a sales department with a consumer market.

Their most important contribution is, however, that they have made plausible that these differences in technology and environment (they comprise both context factors under the term 'environment'!) have important consequences, not only for the structure of the departments concerned, but also for the ways of working and the orientation and attitudes of their managers and thus for their mutual cooperation.

In their terminology: the more the environmental sectors of the separate departments differ in certainty and predictability, the greater the *differentiation* between the departments will be. The degree of differentiation between pairs of departments and thus the degree of differentiation within the organization as a whole is defined in terms of the extent to which departments differ on four characteristics. These characteristics are: the extent of bureaucratization of the departmental structure, the orientation of the department managers both with regard to goals and with regard to time, and their interpersonal orientation. These orientations were made operational by asking each manager what criteria he used for evaluating new ideas (technical-economic, scientific, or commercial criteria) and whether he spent more time on activities with short-term or on those with long-term financial consequences, and by having him answer Fiedler's LPC-questionnaire, which is supposed to measure personal preference for a certain style of leadership (more person-oriented or more task-oriented). It may be doubted, however, whether the LPC was such a fortunate choice for this purpose. There is quite some literature criticizing the interpretation of the LPC as a measure of style of leadership (see Porter *et al.*, 1975, p. 423; Schriesheim and Kerr, 1977; and, especially for his critical views, Vos, 1976).

Thus, a high degree of differentiation means that managers, or other personnel, of different departments have different priorities: to the manager of a production unit the quality of the product is important, while for the manager of a sales department it is its saleability, meaning that, for example, the product's price will be first on his list.

Also, in situations where decisions must be made jointly, they will display different styles of negotiating: the sales people will be more extrovert, the research and development people more task-oriented, and the managers of highly bureaucratized departments will typically behave more formally. Time orientation, too, plays an important role. The shorter it is, the more the manager concerned will be interested in short-term needs and tend to look for quick resolutions.

All these differences may lead to conflicts, the more so when, because of mutual task dependence, cooperation is needed most.

As the degree of differentiation increases, *integration*, being, in Lawrence and

Lorsch's terminology, the quality of cooperation, will require more attention. 'Because the members of each department develop different interests and different points of view, they often find it difficult to reach agreement on integrated programs of action' (1969, p. 11).

In spite of the fact that a high degree of differentiation in organizations may cause problems, it is not true that highly differentiated organizations could not function as efficiently as those with fewer differences in structure and orientation. In fact, these differences are necessary when organizations are faced with a very heterogeneous environment, or rather context (environment, technology, personnel). In that case, the differentiation-integration approach of Lawrence and Lorsch prescribes that such organizations be divided up into departments (for which they use the term 'differentiation' also) in such a way that each department has its own specific environmental sector, its own specific task, and its own kind of personnel. Thus, for each department, the context factors will be homogeneous; the departmental structure and the managers' orientation can and must be adapted to these context variables. The result is an organization with a high degree of differentiation and each of its subdivisions having the characteristics suitable to its particular context. A heterogeneous environment, Lawrence and Lorsch say, requires a highly differentiated organization. The fact that this may cause problems in cooperation should never be a reason for decreasing differentiation. Rather, explicit attention should be paid to promoting cooperation by, among other things, taking structural measures, appointing functionaries, or setting up commissions or even departments whose task is: to promote integration. For a discussion of the characteristics of such integrators as required by different types of organization, the reader is referred to Lawrence and Lorsch (1969, ch. III). Here, our summary of the contingency theory from the perspective of differentiation-integration may suffice. Organizations should adapt their degree of differentiation to the nature of their environment or context. The more heterogeneous the latter is, the more differentiated the organization should be. The higher the degree of differentiation, the greater the need of formal integration mechanisms in order to promote cooperation and solve the inevitable conflicts. With a low degree of differentiation, however, formal integration mechanisms not only are redundant, but may even be harmful (pp. 110, 117, and 122).

3. CRITIQUE

3.1. Defining and measuring the variables

The picture of a contingency theory of organizational structure one obtains from reading just one study is often a misleadingly simple one. Having reviewed a number of important contingency studies, Lawrence and Lorsch conclude: 'Of particular importance are some of the apparent differences our review highlights in the way the "external" conditions have been conceptualized and made operational in each study. While there are differences in terminology, our review suggests that these are referring to the same underlying phenomenon' (Lawrence and Lorsch, 1969, pp. 202–203).

This way of presenting the matter is a bit too optimistic. It is precisely these big differences in the definitions and measurements of theoretical variables that contributed to the above-mentioned confusion.

There are, first of all, context variables that, in statistical models, are considered as given and therefore are assigned the status of independent variables. 'They are contextual or external only to the extent that the organization itself has limited control over the degree and extent of their impact' (Porter *et al.*, 1975, p. 225).

Their definition and measurement is no easy matter (Pennings, 1975). In the case of environmental certainty, Lawrence and Lorsch wittingly chose for the managers' perception. It may well be asked, however, whether that perception is related to any actual certainty in the environment (Child, 1972; Starbuck, 1976, p. 1080 ff.).

Defining and measuring the concept of technology may be even more problematic. Woodward, for example, uses the term 'technical complexity', designating a variable that in no way resembles Lawrence and Lorsch's technology dimension. While Woodward (1958) distinguishes three different forms of production—the so-called 'small batch and unit production', 'large batch and mass production', and 'continuous process production' (e.g. chemical and oil industries)—, Lawrence and Lorsch emphasize the necessity of keeping up with new technological developments, the unpredictability of these developments, and the uncertainty of scientific knowledge as applied in production techniques. Others (Perrow, 1970; Hage and Aiken, 1969) work with a technology dimension defined by the extent of routine in the job. For a survey of definitions of technology variables, the reader is referred to Andriessen and Van Baren (1976), Porter *et al.*, (1975), or Van der Zwaan (1972).

The general concept of 'technology' has been analysed by the so-called Aston-group. They distinguish three dimensions of technology: the nature of the production process (operations technology), the nature of the materials (materials technology; cf. Perrow, 1970), and the nature of the knowledge used (knowledge technology; see Hickson *et al.*, 1969). Taylor (1971) also devised a three-dimensional classification system for production technologies. The total number of technology definitions used in the literature, however, amounts to at least five (Stanfield, 1976; Dewar and Hage, 1978). The apparent difficulties in making a conceptually and operationally satisfactory distinction between independent technology variables and 'dependent' structure variables cause additional complications. The more technology is defined as 'a working method' and not as 'technical means utilized' (Perrow, 1970), the more difficult it is to distinguish this behavioral aspect from other behavioral aspects as described under the heading of 'structure' (Perrow, 1972, p. 168; van der Zwaan, 1972; Stanfield, 1976). If, in addition, a technology definition is based also on the nature of the material to be processed and on the presuppositions about the properties of that material (Perrow, 1970), then technology and structure will increasingly and considerably come to overlap (Stanfield, 1976), especially so in those organizations or subdivisions of organizations where human material is involved ('people processing' or 'human services organizations'). This led Knip (1978, 1979) to speak of an intrinsic relationship between context and structure.

The characteristics of structure are not easily defined either. It can be shown that at least one often used dimension, 'mechanistic-organic' or degree of bureaucratization, can be divided into at least three independent dimensions. Thus, by means of correlation analyses, the researchers of the Aston-group found that three mutually independent dimensions of bureaucracy could be distinguished: (1) *structuring of activities*, the degree to which the behavior of employees is overtly defined, (2) *concentration of authority*, and (3) *line control of work-flow*, the degree to which control is exercised by line-personnel as against its exercise through impersonal procedures (Pugh *et al.*, 1969). Earlier, in 1963 and 1966, Hall had written about the multidimensionality of structure (Hall, 1972, p. 67).

Most contingency theories put forth statements about the consequences of structure-context relations for the success or efficiency of an organization, and all that has been said up to now about the quality and multidimensionality of structure and context variables holds at least as much for these so-called success variables. The literature on organizations abounds with discourses on the problems surrounding the definition of organizational goals and, in close connection therewith, on the large variety of goals of, or pursued within, organizations. Obviously, the content of concepts such as success, effectiveness, but certainly also efficiency, is highly dependent on the goals one has set oneself and the values assigned to the different goals. It is, moreover, important to know whose goals we are talking about, those of owners, managers, customers (Pfeffer, 1978), or employees. Thus, defining the success variable or variables is also problematic. (See also Perrow, 1979, pp. 152–153; this Handbook, ch. 4.1.)

In the light of the above it will come as no surprise that some researchers find clear relations between context and structure variables (Aldrich, 1972; Khandwalla, 1973, 1974; Blau *et al.*, 1976; DuBick, 1978) and others reach the opposite conclusion (among others, Mohr, 1971; Pennings, 1975). According to Stanfield (1976), the worst mistake is not the possibly idiosyncratic choice of variables and their operationalization, but to formulate conclusions in terms like technology, structure, or environment. Usually it is assumed, that these concepts cover a relatively heterogeneous set of variables rather than that each concept may be represented by one one-dimensional variable. Still, there is a wide-spread tendency to generalize conclusions regarding some specific variables to the whole complex aggregate (on this, see also this Handbook, ch. 4.2).

3.2. Structure-context congruence as a factor in strategic decision making

In the above paragraph we made some critical remarks regarding the somewhat optimistic and simplistic viewpoints of some contingency theorists. These, however, did not yet entail any fundamental criticism of the different aspects of the contingency theory, such as the concepts of congruence and determinism, or the natural selection model. On the contrary, by noting the confusion about the use of concepts and definitions as well as the undue identification of specific variables with general concepts such as technology and structure, one may come to view seemingly contradictory research results as non-contradictory, as simply concerning different kinds of organization-environment relations. Apparently, in terms of the contingency approach, some relations are important and others are not. One thing certainly has become clear: from the contingency perspective, many different variables must be taken into account when making structural decisions. It is, therefore, not surprising that this gave rise to the following question: what if these different variables lead to contradictory conclusions regarding the question as to which structural characteristics are to be desired?

Writing about possibly incompatible context requirements, Child (1976) stresses the fact that, in many cases, the absence of optimal congruence has only a limited influence on the success or failure of organizations. A too obsequious adherence to contingency prescriptions, however, might well lead to inconsistencies within an organization that may be more disastrous than an, according to contingency norms, non-ideal structure. These two assumptions were supported by a study of five airline companies. This modifies the significance of congruence for the effectiveness of organizations. Many organizations have much wider margins for choosing structures according to their preference than contingency theorists would have us believe. Even if the significance of congruence for the efficient functioning of organizations were irrefutable and relatively great—which is doubtful (Child, 1972, 1976)—there still is the fact that many organizations can afford a fairly high degree of inefficient functioning, without any real threat to their survival. One could think of commercial organizations in a mild market situation with little competition, or of various types of nonprofit organizations, where efficiency may become an important factor only in times of scarcity.

In two important articles, Child (1972) and Aldrich and Pfeffer (1976), determinism and the closely related natural selection model are critically reviewed. The important conclusions are that the organizational context—size of the organization, environment, technology, and personnel—are much less 'given' than the contingency approach implies. To a certain extent, most organizations can determine the character of their environment themselves by means of selection, most large organizations even by exertion of direct influence (cf. Schreyögg, 1980 and Perrow, 1972, ch. 5).

If changes in the environment influence decisions concerning the structure, they must first be perceived and, moreover, be judged important enough to justify structural changes. Many uncertainties in the environment are wittingly ignored. Standard procedures are applied in variable situations. Thus, for examples, teachers at all educational levels teach as if all students start from the same levels of knowledge and intelligence.

Technology especially is never completely given: what Trist *et al.* (1963) call 'organizational choice' is possible to a large extent. On grounds of such considerations, Child reaches the as yet empirically not wholly verified conclusion, that 'With respect to internal variables, strategic action will involve an attempt, within the limits of availabilities and indivisibilities, to establish a configuration of manpower, technology and structural arrangements which is both internally consistent and consistent with the scale and nature of operations planned' (Child, 1972, p. 17).

The central concept here is 'strategic choice', which indeed sharply distinguishes this view of organization from the natural selection model. In the latter model, we are concerned with an almost powerless organization, that can do little but meet the requirements of environmental and other contextual factors as well as they can. In the alternative model, which Pfeffer calls the 'resource dependence model', it is still necessary to take account of the environment, certainly to the extent that one depends on it for the much needed resources; but this dependence may, in principle, be influenced and the organization may take advantage of environmental possibilities. The organization, or rather, those in power in the organization, actively go to meet the environment. 'Administrators manage their environments as well as their organizations; and the former activity may be as important, or even more important, than the latter' (Aldrich and Pfeffer, 1976).

In this view, the distribution of power within the organization and the relation between this distribution and the environment receive much more attention than in most contingency theories, especially those based on the natural selection view.

A practical example, again borrowed from an educational organization, illustrates this relation. A recently founded school of medicine has great ambitions. They wish to do advanced medical-biological research and, simultaneously, to teach according to the most modern methods. The school's dependence on the environment is greater than may appear at first sight. For academic ambitions, it is dependent on the influx of young, ambitious researchers. For realizing its educational goals, the school depends on information from an environmental section not easily accessible to most of its staff members: the social sciences.

The structure is adapted to the situation: an educational psychologist is appointed and a separate department set up to do research and to advise the mainly medically trained teachers. Because of his specialized knowledge, the psychologist is able to reduce the school's uncertainty about the developments in the social sciences relevant to teaching. Knowledge and the ability to reduce uncertainties important to the organization are frequently mentioned as a source of power (Crozier and Friedberg, 1977; Pfeffer, 1978). This also happened in our case. Not only was the psychologist able to hold his own, in spite of being alone among a biologically and medically trained staff, he even managed to effect a structural change: his department was recognized as a department in its own right and he was promoted to the position of associate professor.

Thus, the environment, with its values and rapid, unforeseen developments, can influence the social structure of an organization. Aldrich and Pfeffer (1976) describe such a process of influence as follows:

'1. The environment provides many of the constraints, uncertainties and contingencies because of the necessity for transacting with the environment.

2. These contingencies affect the distribution of power and influence within organizations, providing some sub-units with more power and others with less.

3. Power is used in determining organizational social structures, particularly to the extent that there is uncertainty and the decisions concern critical issues.'

Aldrich and Pfeffer further distinguish between models emphasizing primarily the significance of perceiving the environment as the basis of strategic choices, and models paying more attention to the dependence on resources present in the environment (resource dependence!). This distinction becomes more relevant as the environment becomes less friendly. In this way, they modify to a certain extent the significance of environmental perception and of the leeway for strategic policy decisions in organizations having to operate in a more hostile environment and thus running a greater risk of failure. In that case, even natural selection models will be able to explain the environmental influences on structure.

In our practical example, the significance of the perception of the environment was obvious. The school of medicine perceived norms and uncertainties in the environment: a modern school should provide an education using the latest methods; which methods are considered the best is not clear and is subject to rapid change. The school could have ignored these norms and uncertainties. It could have been satisfied with a less prominent reputation and the ensuing consequences regarding the student population. It was, therefore, the perceived environment that was important for the decision. The second model may be illustrated by the fate of some small seminar groups of radical academic teachers and students that vainly sought recognition as a separate department. Existing in a more hostile environment and having fewer resources of power than the medical school, their actual dependence on resources in the environment is decisive. Ignoring that dependence may mean the end of such a group.

The notion of congruence is still valid: in terms of efficiency, some combinations of structure and context factors are more favorable than others. The relative importance of those congruences for efficiency and the importance of efficiency itself, however, are strongly qualified, and determinism, implying natural selection or at least the necessity to adapt to the peremptory contextual requirements, is considered applicable only in a very limited way. What we have here is, in fact, contingency of a higher order. A strict contingency theory with its deterministic character is applicable to small organizations fighting for their life in a very competitive market. If the situation is less threatening and less hostile, the strategic choice or 'resource dependence' model becomes more relevant.

3.3. Contingency theory and organizational models

In this chapter we were made familiar with so-called contingency thinking and its emphasis on the relative nature of many statements about organizations. Questions from managers as to the best kinds of leadership or the best way to design an organization were answered by more and more organizational experts with: 'It depends'. Subsequently, research was directed towards the factors on which it depends: the nature of the situation, the environment, the technology would determine what the manager could do best. In the last paragraph, we saw that this too led to qualifications: big, powerful organizations need not concern themselves with these context factors as much as small organizations threatened by competition.

This, plus other considerations, led Child (1972) to develop a strategic-choice model, where a dominant coalition develops a policy based on an evaluation of the possibilities in the environment.

In establishing a policy, a number of considerations play a role:—structure-context congruence influences efficient and effective functioning of an organization;
—the significance of an internally consistent structure of the whole organization sometimes exceeds the importance of maximal congruence;
—other criteria, such as personal preferences, taking into account the interests of others who are not part of the dominant coalition, and the like, must and can play a role.

The first consideration is crucial to the contingency approach and is based on a number of assumptions that are increasingly being questioned. One implicit point of departure of the contingency approach was that arguments of efficiency should determine structural decisions. No, Child says, generally that is not necessary. There is a wide enough margin; usually one can afford to pursue less than maximal efficiency.

Moreover, the pursuit of efficiency may be defined as the attempt to maximize the realization of some goal at the lowest possible cost. That is, efficiency always presupposes clearcut goals. The problem is, however, that organizations have multiple, sometimes contradictory, goals and that these goals are far from operational, i.e. put into too general terms or open to many a concrete explanation. Also, it is often difficult, if not impossible, to find the right balance between the importance of one goal and that of another (see Perrow, 1979, ch. 4).

One of Cyert and March's most influential views is that in practice this leads to sometimes contradictory goals being pursued simultaneously or successively within organizations and that, in organizations, there is a continued battle about the importance of various goals and about the actual realization of the generally formulated, non-operational goals. One's interpretation will be strongly influenced by one's position in the organizational structure: managers of production departments will present another interpretation than will managers of sales departments, the way a university's educational research unit formulates educational goals will differ from that of the members of the teaching staff.

Apart from the different interpretations of general organizational goals, disagreements at a more fundamental level play a role too. This led Pfeffer to say that ' . . . The issue of increasing organizational effectiveness begs the all-important question of effectiveness for whom—the owners, the managers, the clients or customers?' (Pfeffer, 1978, p. 175), or, elsewhere in the same book (p. 223): ' . . . the critical question becomes not how organizations should be designed to maximize effectiveness, but rather, whose preferences and interests are to be served by the organization'.

The outcome of this battle over goal interpretations and priorities also influences structural decisions. But, as we saw in the Child-model, other arguments play a role as well. An interesting new development in the literature on organizations is the attention paid to factors determining which criteria are considered important by whom and how much they count in the final decision making. Which criteria a person will apply is determined by his task in the organization, but also by his personal capacities: a personnel officer will put considerations of industrial peace ahead of everything else, whereas the head of a research and development department will use the possible application of an advanced technological invention as an argument in favor of some structural change. Both will, if necessary, try to relate these criteria to officially accepted organizational goals, but this might be an *ex post facto* justification hiding the the actual motivation for the choice of particular decision criteria. According to some theorists, this behavior is based on the need of influence and power (Crozier and Friedberg, 1977).

In any case, the need of influence and autonomy is an important factor in many decision-making processes in organizations. 'The contest for influence', Pfeffer states, 'is the most fundamental of all issues faced in organizations'. He justifies this by pointing to the great variety of interests, goals, and values among the members of organizations. Therefore, much attention is being paid now to the distribution of power.

The ability to deal with uncertainties on behalf of an organization, in other words, the possession of information and specialized knowledge and skills, relations, etc. not in the possession of others, is mentioned again and again as an extremely important factor in the realization of the distribution of power

(Hickson *et al.*, 1971; Crozier and Friedberg, 1977; Aldrich and Pfeffer, 1976; Pfeffer, 1978).

3.4. Summary and conclusion

In fact, no-one challenges the point of departure of the contingency theory, i.e. that there exists something like congruence between structure and context and that congruence enables organizations to function more effectively and more efficiently. The relative importance of congruence as a determinant of efficiency and effectiveness is, however, qualified, and the pursuit of congruence is no longer considered the most important factor in decision-making processes with regard to structures.

The battle for power is mentioned as an important factor, because structural decisions are always decisions influencing positions of power; therefore, existing power differences largely determine the possibilities for structural change. This also explains why drastic structural changes are not so easy to carry out: they evoke enormous opposition (Crozier and Friedberg, 1977). This does not mean that important structural changes, especially in cases of a great concentration of power at the top of big organizations (Perrow, 1979, ch. 6) or national systems—higher education in The Netherlands—are impossible to enforce.

3.5. Some closing remarks; the rational decision-making model

In all discourses to date it was assumed that managers, members of a dominant coalition, or other members of organizations act rationally. 'Acting rationally' here means choosing behaviors on the grounds of the expectation that they will bring the goal closer. March and Simon's concept of 'bounded rationality' comes under this heading: on the grounds of a simplified picture of the situation one looks for means to attain some state that satisfies certain criteria; they speak of 'satisficing' instead of 'optimizing' (March and Simon, 1958, p. 141; Koopman *et al.*, this Handbook, ch. 4.6).

According to this definition, all goal-directed behavior which involves the weighing of alternatives is rational (cf. Weick, 1979, p. 19: 'intended, thought about, planned, calculated, or designed for a purpose'). Thus, it does not cover Crozier and Friedberg's concept of rationality, which, although it does involve goal-directed behavior, does not necessarily constitute conscious choice. So, according to them, the strategy of a schizophrenic, too, constitutes rational behavior. That is why they conclude that, in fact, irrational behavior does not exist (p. 48). This is not a logically necessary conclusion. In recent literature on organizations (see also this Handbook, ch. 4.1) one encounters ever more frequently the opinion that at least part of human behavior is unpredictable, not because it is irrational in the sense used here, but because it cannot even be explained on the grounds of such unconscious strategies as meant by Crozier and Friedberg.

According to this view, behavior should sometimes be explained through the occurrence of chance, often trivial, events that do not involve any conscious or unconscious pursuit of goals. The goals are formulated afterwards and then used to explain the behavior. This is not a rationalization in the Freudian sense: that is, that representing as reasonable acts that are in fact 'unreasonable' is to be explained only from unconscious motives. The goals are used in an attempt at explaining psychologically a completely incidental, unmotivated act, because we are not able to accept the fact that some behavior cannot be explained, not even by unconscious anxieties or desires. Perrow (1979), a master in thinking up clear examples, illustrates this by the following incident: accidentally, through a misunderstanding or for some other reason, a book he always used in his lectures had not been ordered and later he explained that behavior by saying that he preferred some series of articles instead, either for didactic reasons or because it would take the students too much time to read the book. This psychological explanation holds good, while the 'explanation' of chance is not accepted. It is not because he is trying to hide something, but because we have a need to find explanations for everything. Chance is not a satisfactory explanation.

For the theory of organizations this means that many organizational processes are reconstructed by us in such a way as to make them look orderly and comprehensible. This can be done, for example, by connecting them with the goals of the organization or dominant coalition, or, also, with the goals of department managers or other interest- or power-groups. The idea that they might be purely accidental and therefore inexplicable and unpredictable seems difficult to accept.

Essentially this argument is based on the fact, that the goals encountered in organizational research do not necessarily precede the action explained through them, but may just as well follow that action and only serve to give them meaning afterwards. Weick (1969, p. 64), following Schutz, goes even further: 'All knowing and meaning arise from reflection, from a backward glance'. The logical conclusion, then, is that goals, being one of the most important sources of meaning for actions, can only be defined afterwards. So, in connection with the theory of dissonance, Weick remarks: 'Rationality makes sense of what has been, not what will be' (p. 38). In the second revised edition of his book he puts it even more concisely: 'Behavior isn't goal-directed, it's goal-interpreted' (Weick, 1979).

There are other, related, opinions qualifying the meaning of goals as a guide for our actions. Thus, Cyert and March assume that people have a large number of goals, which are not clearly organized and from which they choose when the situation seems to favor their realization. Crozier and Friedberg (1977, p. 369) put it in their own way, as follows: 'it should be confirmed that man has the right (sic!) of not knowing what he wants, of changing his desires according to his possibilities or to what he believes to be his interest'.

Much later, March elaborated his old idea into what he calls the garbage-can model of organization (Cohen *et al.*, 1972; March and Olsen, 1976). Some organizations are characterized by the absence of clearcut goals, by an equivocally defined technology, and by a lack of clarity as to who exactly their members are. Universities are a good example of such 'organized anarchies'. In such organizations, one finds many solutions not yet belonging to a problem, goals not yet clearly defined, and problems no-one does anything about. What happens then barely resembles the models of rational behavior, which hold that formulating a goal leads to problems for which one tries to find a solution. Here, the various components of the customary decision-making models are, so to speak, thrown together into a garbage can and people are looking for problems to apply their solutions to and afterwards try to justify that combination by formulating goals.

These closing remarks are intended especially to qualify somewhat the discussion on contingency theories. We do not intend to suggest that all rational models of human behavior and organizational processes should be thrown out as being fiction. But it seems sensible to keep an eye open to the limitations of many of our theories and approaches. This holds for classical management theories, the 'human relations school' and the 'human resources school', contingency theories and the political models of Pfeffer, Crozier, and others, as well as for such irrational models as the garbage-can model described above.

' . . . [R]ecent work in cognitive processes', Perrow writes (1979), 'has led me to emphasize accident, random choice, and poorly ordered preferences much more than I did in the past, but without assuming that most of life is like that. This should enable me to recognize these processes when they do occur, but not bend every occurrence to either fit them or exclude them'.

Let us close with a variation on a statement much used in contingency theory: 'There is no one best way of theorizing'.

REFERENCES

Aldrich, H. E. (1972), Technology and organizational structure: A re-examination of the findings of the Aston group. *Administrative Science Quarterly*, **17**, 26–43.
Aldrich, H. E., Pfeffer, J. (1976), Environments of organizations. *Annual Review of Sociology*, **2**, 79–105.
Andriessen, J. H. T. H. Baren, C. van (1976), *Technologie: Een inventarisatie van enkele betekenissen, problemen en meetinstrumenten* [Technology: An inventory of some of its meanings, problems and measuring instruments]. Amsterdam: University of Amsterdam, Dept. of Industrial and Organizational Psychology.
Baker, F. (1974), The living human service organization: Application of general systems theory and research. In: Demone, H. W., Harshbarger, D. (Eds.), *A handbook of human service organizations*. New York: Behavioral Publications.

Blau, P. M., McHugh Falbe, C., McKinley, W., Tracy, P. K. (1976), Technology and organization in manufacturing. *Administrative Science Quarterly*, **21**, 20–40.

Burns, T., Stalker, G. M. (1961), *The management of innovation*. London: Tavistock.

Child, J. (1972), Organizational structure, environment and performance: The role of strategic choice. *Sociology*, **6**, 1–22.

Child, J. (1976), *Organizational design and performance: Contingency theory and beyond*. The University of Aston Management Centre, Working Paper Series no. 53.

Cohen, M. D., March, J. G., Olsen, J. P. (1972), A garbage can model of organizational choice. *Administrative Science Quarterly*, **17**, 1–25.

Crozier, M., Friedberg, E. (1977), *L'acteur et le systemè*. Paris: Editions du Seuil.

Cyert, R. M., March, J. G. (1963), *A behavioral theory of the firm*. Englewood Cliffs (N.J.): Prentice-Hall.

Dewar, R., Hage, J. (1978), Size, technology, complexity and structural differentiation: Toward a theoretical synthesis. *Administrative Science Quarterly*, **23**, 111–136.

DuBick, M. A. (1978), The organizational structure of newspapers in relation to their metropolitan environment. *Administrative Science Quarterly*, **23**, 418–433.

Glisson, C. A. (1978), Dependence of technological routinization on structural variables in human service organizations. *Administrative Science Quarterly*, **23**, 383–395.

Hage, J., Aiken, M. (1969), Routine technology, social structure and organizational goals. *Administrative Science Quarterly*, **14**, 366–376.

Hall, R. H. (1962), Intra-organizational structural variation: Application of the bureaucratic model. *Administrative Science Quarterly*, **7**, 295–308.

Hall, R. H. (1972), *Organizations: Structure and process*. Englewood Cliffs (N.J.): Prentice-Hall.

Hickson, D. J., Hinings, C. R., Lee, C. A., Schneck, R. E., Pennings, J. M. (1971), A strategic contingencies theory of intraorganizational power. *Administrative Science Quarterly*, **16**, 216–229.

Hickson, D. J., D. S. Pugh, D. C. Pheysey (1969), Operations technology and organizational structure: An empirical reappraisal. *Administrative Science Quarterly*, **14**, 378–397.

Khandwalla, P. N. (1973), Viable and effective organizational designs of firms. *Academy of Management Journal*, **16**, 481–495.

Khandwalla, P. N. (1974), Mass output orientation of operations technology and organizational structure. *Administrative Science Quarterly*, **19**, 74–97.

Knip, J. L. (1975), Differentiatie en integratie in onderwijsorganisaties [Differentiation and integration in educational organizations]. *Tijdschrift voor Agologie* [Journal of Planned Change], **4**, 80–99.

Knip, J. L. (1978), *Differentation and integration in organisations*. Paper read at the Occupational Psychology Conference, Cambridge U.K., January 1978.

Knip, J. L. (1979), *Adventures with an American organization theory in Dutch education*. Paper presented at the workshop on European perspective in the Application of Social Psychology, Cartmel, U.K., January 1979.

Lawrence, P. R., Lorsch, J. W. (1969), *Organization and environment: Managing differentiation and integration*. Homewood (Ill.): R.D. Irwin.

Leifer, R., Huber, G. P. (1977), Relations among perceived environmental uncertainty, organization structure and boundary spanning behavior. *Administrative Science Quarterly*, **22**, 235–247.

Likert, R. (1967), *The human organization: Its management and value*. New York: McGraw-Hill.

Luhmann, N. (1976), A general theory of organized social systems. In: Hofstede, G., Kassem, M. S. (Eds.), *European contributions to organization theory*. Assen: Van Gorcum.

March, J. G. (1965), Introduction. In: March, J. G. (Ed.), *Handbook of organizations.* Chicago: Rand McNally.

March, J. G., J. P. Olsen (1976), *Ambiguity and choice in organizations.* Bergen, (Norway): Universitetsforlaget.

March, J. G., Simon, H. A. (1958), *Organizations.* New York: John Wiley.

Marrow, A. J., Bowers, D. G., Seashore, S. E. (1967), *Management by participation.* New York: Harper and Row.

Massie, J. L. (1965), Management theory. In: March, J. G. (Ed.), *Handbook of organizations.* Chicago: Rand McNally.

Mintzberg, H. (1979), *The structuring of organizations.* Englewood Cliffs (N.J.): Prentice-Hall.

Moch, M. J., Pondy, L. R. (1977), The structure of chaos: Organized anarchy as a response to ambiguity (Book review). *Administrative Science Quarterly,* **22**, 351–362.

Mohr, L. B. (1971), Organizational technology and organizational structure. *Administrative Science Quarterly,* **16**, 444–459.

Pennings, J. M. (1975), The relevance of the structural-contingency model for organizational effectiveness. *Administrative Science Quarterly,* **20**, 393–410.

Perrow, C. (1970), *Organizational analysis: A sociological view.* Belmont (Cal.): Wadsworth.

Perrow, C. (1972), *Complex organizations: A critical essay.* Glenview (Ill): Scott, Foresman.

Perrow, C. (1979), *Complex organizations: A critical essay.* 2nd edition. Glenview (Ill.): Scott, Foresman.

Pfeffer, J. (1978), *Organizational design.* Arlington Heights (Ill.): AHM Publishing Corp.

Porter, L. W., Lawler III, E. E., Hackman, J. R. (1975), *Behavior in organizations.* New York: McGraw-Hill.

Pugh, D. S., Hickson, D. J., Hinings, C. R. (1969), An empirical taxonomy of structures of work organizations. *Administrative Science Quarterly,* **14**, 115–126.

Roethlisberger, F. J., Dickson, W. J. (1939), *Management and the worker.* Cambridge (Mass.): Harvard University Press.

Schreyögg, G. (1980), Contingency and choice in organization theory. *Organization Studies,* **1**, 305–326.

Schriesheim, C. A., Kerr, S. (1977), Theories and measures of leadership: A critical appraisal of current and future directions. In: Hunt, J. G., Larson, L. L. (Eds.), *Leadership: The cutting edge.* Carbondale: Southern Illinois University Press.

Stanfield, G. G. (1976), Technology and organization structure as theoretical categories. *Administrative Science Quarterly,* **21**, 489–493.

Starbuck, W. H. (1976), Organizations and their environments. In: Dunnette, M. D. (Ed.), *Handbook of industrial and organizational psychology.* Chicago: Rand McNally.

Taylor, J. C. (1971), *Technology and planned organizational change.* Ann Arbor (Mich.): Institute for Social Research.

Thompson, J. D. (1967), *Organizations in action.* New York: McGraw-Hill.

Trist, E. L., Higgin, G. W., Murray, H., Pollock, A. B. (1963), *Organizational choice.* London: Tavistock.

Vos, J. T. F. (1976), Enkele contingentie-hypothesen over effektief leiderschap [Some contingency hypotheses on effective leadership]. In: Doerbecker, C. L., Vos, J. T. F., *Taakgroepen in een bedreigende situatie* [Task groups in a threatening situation]. Amsterdam, Free University (doctoral dissertation).

Weick, K. E. (1969), *The social psychology of organizing.* Reading (Mass.): Addison-Wesley.

Weick, K. E. (1979), *The social psychology of organizing.* 2nd edition. Reading (Mass.): Addison-Wesley.

Woodward, J. (1958), *Management and technology*. London: H. M. Stationary Office.
Woodward, J. (1965), *Industrial organization: Theory and practice*. London: Oxford University Press.
Zwaan, A. H. van der (1972), Organisatiesociologie; Technologie binnen de organisatiesociologie: Een literatuurstudie [Organizational sociology; Technology in organizational sociology: A study of the literature]. *Mens en Maatschappij* [Man and Society], **47**, 35–153.

4.4. A theoretical approach to organizational change

Hans Sopar

1. INTRODUCTION

The subject of organizational change comes up for discussion twice in this handbook. In chapter 4.9 Bruining and Allegro focus on organization development, an approach which has grown increasingly prominent during the last 15 years. The approach offered in this chapter is of a more general, theoretical nature. It is divided into five sections.

In section 2 the notion 'organizational change' is defined. The fact that this definition cannot claim to reflect a general consensus is due to the lack of a sufficiently coherent theoretical model. The want of a universally valid definition, however, does not release us from the obligation to define the notion 'organizational change' as it features in this chapter.

Section 3, 4, and 5 together from an interrelated whole. Section 3 describes the framework for planning, decision-making and action, which comprises processes of organizational change. From this it becomes evident that there are two sides to the strategies of change, an internal and an external one. The external side aims at the development of the relation between an organization and its environment. The internal side affects the manner in which the processes directed towards that aim are shaped and managed on the level of the organization's system.

These notions are both further expanded upon in the two subsequent sections. Section 4 focusses on a number of aspects which are inherent to the development of organizations and which are closely related to their role within society,

Drs. Ph. J. M. Sopar, Universiteit van Amsterdam, Vakgroep A & O psychologie, Weesperplein 8, 1018 XA AMSTERDAM particularly from an economic and social point of view. Section 5 deals with the strategy and method of organizational change as its central issue. Moreover, it includes several general observations on the research done in this field.

2. A DEFINITION OF ORGANIZATIONAL CHANGE

There are many different opinions and views on the concept of organizational change. The variety in them is probably closely related to the developmental stage in which this field of study finds itself. It is relatively young and it lacks an elaborate theoretical basis. Bekke (1976) restates the claim of This (in: Lippit, This and Bidwell, 1971) that concepts such as organizational change develop in a cycle of five stages. At first there is a concept—grown out of research or practical experience—which is published for colleagues. Thus, it may draw the attention of practical workers who, simplifying it for the sake of saleability and applicability, make commercial use of it. In the third stage the 'concept' takes root on the market and gradually saturates it. The product takes on fashionable assets. Its use raises questions about its actual effects. In the fourth stage it is subject to attacks from researchers. Moreover, this stage marks the beginning of a discussion on the semantics. Finally, the concept is rejected for being either too demanding or superfluous, only to be brought back to attention again after 10 to 15 years. In 1971, This estimated this development in the U.S. to have advanced to a point somewhere between the third and fourth stage. This estimate appears to us a close approximation of the current Dutch development.

Differences in opinion about organizational change are often to a certain extent determined by different conceptions of 'good' or 'healthy' organizations. Thus, ideas differ as to the aims the changes should be directed at.

Although our definition does not involve such differences, we do not underestimate the importance of assumptions regarding the aims of changes (which can be interwoven with particular methods). We do consider them important and will therefore deal with them in the ensuing sections. In so far as methods of organizational change are related to standards as to the structure and functioning of organizations, these different views often form a characteristic element of the method involved. A definition, however, should first and foremost comprise the aspects shared by the different approaches, and should indicate the framework within which they are applied.

In this chapter the general term 'organizational change' refers to 'directed, systematic organizational change'. An explanation of key-notions: the designation 'directed' indicates that the organizational change aims at the realization of a particular situation. This situation is a projection on the future, an image of a situation which is as yet non-extent for the organization involved.

This image, however, is not always equally clearly defined. Often only abstract criteria are available to give a more or less exact indication of the requirements which the 'target situation' should meet. Examples of such requirements are: 'a more flexible organization', 'reduction of absenteeism' or 'an organization which is more capable of standing up against the problems of the eighties'. Besides, those involved do not always agree on the criteria so that an attempt to define the target situation and, if possible, to reach a consensus on it becomes part of the process of organizational change.

The notion of 'change' emphasizes the fact that the target situation differs from the organization's present situation. It should be noted here that the changes involved need not be structural. Some approaches, among which that of process-consultation and the method of Argyris, are primarily aimed at increasing the organizations's problem-solving ability, and structural changes are not always relevant in this respect.

Organizational change comprises those changes which relate to the social system referred to as 'organization'. Thus it excludes purely technical changes but includes changes, such as processes of job design, in which technique is the main means of change and the social system is the actual object of change.

Between those two extremes there is an area of transition from primarily social changes with technical implication and primarily technical changes which also require organizational and psychological adjustment of employees and management, a requirement which, though very essential, is often sadly neglected. Examples of this are numerous in the fields of mechanization and automation.

Moreover, the key-word 'organization' indicates that changes, when affecting individuals, are not directed at their person, but at their function as members of an organization. The criterion of a change is to be found in role-behaviour and in the effects this may have on the organization.

Finally, 'systematic' means that the change is planned and executed accordingly. There is a wide variety in kinds of planning and we would like to specify the possible differences in two respects. Firstly, the planning can be aimed at:
a. The situations which have to be realized in the successive stages.
b. The development of criteria which those situations must meet.
c. Aspects of procedure.
Of course, in reality we come across a variety of combinations and gradations of a, b, and c. In both a and b the planning relates to aspects inherent in the change. In this respect a and b distinguish themselves from c.

The latter case does not state *what* the target situation should comprise, but *how* it should be realized. The planning is aimed at steering the process which leads to this realization and thus relates to the formal aspects of change. Anglo-Saxon literature on the subject refers to this distinction as the difference between 'theories of change' and 'theories of changing' (Chin, 1969). In other fields of study, a similar distinction is made, for instance in regional and urban planning (Hightower, 1969; Faludi, 1973). A second qualification of the key-term 'systematic' is the variable flexibility and range of the planning. At one extreme of the dimension involved one finds a situation in which the schedule of change is determined upon entirely or almost entirely beforehand, in terms of procedure, timing and intermediary target situations of the organization. One could apply the term 'blue print change' here. The situation at the other extreme is characterized by the fact that the initiated change process includes, within itself, the planning and decision-making which determine its nature and development. If we allow for a slight proportional distortion of theory as opposed to practice, this distinction can be described as follows: in the first case the change process originates from planning, in the second case planning originates from the change process.

3. PLANNING, DECISION-MAKING AND ACTION IN ORGANIZATIONAL CHANGE

3.1. The relation to the environment

With respect to the context within which organizations determine their goals and activities, Snellen (1975) and Mohr (1973) make a distinction between a transitive and a reflexive level. The *transitive* level refers to the maintenance of a certain level of supplying goods and/or services by the organization to its environment. The *reflexive* level refers to the internal system of the organization as the unit which supports the transitive function. Gross (1969) identifies the goals of the organization at the different levels as output goals and support goals. What is important here is their relationship.

Activities of organizational change do not occur in a policy vacuum, but can be seen as intended and goal-oriented. In a direct sense, this refers to the goal of bringing about changes on the reflexive level. However, such a goal is not isolated because the organization itself is not isolated. Its functioning is legitimized by society at the transitive level, namely, in transactions between the organization and its environment (Lawrence and Lorsch, 1969), and is seen ultimately in that context. Part of its policy, summarized in a general phrase, is concerned with optimizing its relationship with the environment according to the criterion of the usefulness—however defined—of those transactions. Ultimately, such policy aims form the background—whether explicit or not—of activities in the area of organizational change. This can be indicated as *the external aspect of the strategy of organizational change*. The way in which the resulting changes are induced at the level of the system of the organization is related to the *internal aspect* of that strategy.

In the next section we will first present a formal framework of planning, decision making and implementation activities related to that strategy. This will clarify which differences and which relationships there are between the external and the internal aspects of the strategy. In the two succeeding paragraphs, we will discuss the content of both aspects.

3.2. The framework of organizational change

Viewed as an ideal type, activities of organizational change are part of a comprehensive framework of planning, decision-making and implementation. In this framework, certain relationships between aims and means can be identified on various levels. What such a framework looks like can perhaps initially best be illustrated by an example. Suppose we are dealing with a production organization whose sales have increased rapidly in the course of a number of years. At a certain stage of this growth, the delivery time of products has become a problem. The organization is used to producing by order, and experience over the years has enabled it to anticipate the general rate of orders, so that there are no lags. However, the growth makes this increasingly difficult because the expected order rate has become more difficult to understand and predict. This makes an adequate planning of production impossible. The result is, that from time to time for some products, an uncontrolled accumulation of stock exists which ties up too much capital, while for other products a production lag occurs which increases the time of delivery.

In order to improve this situation, the organization can choose a number of solutions. For example, it could increase its productive capacity, so that during 'peaks' it can continue to deliver rapidly on order. It could also increase its stock, so that it can deliver from stock, or it could gather more and better information in order to make a more adequate sales prognosis. Let us assume that the organization which we have taken as an example chooses for a stock system combined with making more adequate sales prognoses. This leads to changes in many aspects. Probably, automated information systems and stock-control systems will need to be instigated. Since the stock will increase, no doubt the warehouse will need to be more mechanized. Moreover—and this is the point to be made here—the organization will need to be adapted. A structural change will have to occur because there will need to be departments for sales prognosis, sales planning and stock control, probably the existing departments will have to be reorganized. Also, the functioning of people will have to change on a number of points. For example, due to automation, high-grade administrative tasks requiring additional training will be created. Management puts different demands on such trained personnel. In order to give form to the newly-desired situation, a plan is necessary which on general lines indicates what will need to take place. This could, for example, lead to combining certain decentralized planning departments to form one centralized department; and to forming committees to work on separate parts of the plan, such as reforming the organizational structure, managing personnel with respect to changes in tasks and positions, and so forth. Probably, a managing committee will be formed to coordinate the activities of the various committees and to bring them in line with general policies. Perhaps a training program will have to be developed to equip people with skills needed for new tasks. It could mean that the total change requires a certain time-planning and phasing. Finally, the realization of the plan requires further planning and implementation of parts, such as actually developing and giving training, actual management of changing functions, task development, and so forth.

The example illustrates, among other things, how levels of planning and decision-making can be distinguished, through which goals can lead to concrete plans, and plans to action.

Initially there was a development in the relationship between the organization and its environment, which manifested itself as a problem of uncontrolled stock and unacceptable delivery times. In response, the organization develops a policy directed towards rearranging that relationship so that the problems are reduced. In doing this, the organization is confronted with the necessity of matching goals and means. As we have seen, the means included several alternatives which can be assumed to have different advantages and disadvantages, benefits and costs (in the broadest sense). The consideration of pros and cons leads to a decision which also comprises activities in the area of organizational change. This instigates the next round of planning and decision-making in which form is given to a general plan concerning the course the organization will follow from the actually existing situation to the desired situation or goal. Finally an area of activities can be identified in which form is given in a directly operational way to separate parts of that plan; this is the bridge between planning and implementation.

A representation of this process is given in the model in table 1; we have assumed there that the transitive goal has been set.

Parenthetically: the example and its description may lead to the idea that processes of organizational change in reality form such a structured process in which the identified levels of planning, decision-making and implementation are actually and explicitly distinguished in the procedures and phases. Sometimes this is so, but this is certainly not always the case. Usually, the levels are not explicitly distinguished, and often the related activities are done simultaneously. The model presented below should be seen as a formal construction in which change activities have been distinguished analytically and systematized, and not as a chronological description of what actually takes place.

In table 1, three levels are distinguished, namely, *strategic policy formation*, *strategic structuring* and *direct, operational structuring*. At each of those levels, the planning takes a similar course: the point of departure is an aim, described as a reference goal, that provides direction. The planning consists of choosing means to achieve that goal, and determining how those means will be used. For this process, a body of knowledge, referred to in the table as 'theory about the use of the means', can sometimes be applied. The immediate result of such planned activities or of such decisions made, assuming that this is what was intended, is described as the operational goal. This can be seen as a more operational definition of the reference goal, which momentarily takes its place.

Table 1. Levels of planning, decision-making and action (adapted from Mensink, 1963).

	Reference goal	Means to achieve the goal	Theory about the use of the means	Operational goal
LEVEL A: strategic policy formation	POLICY AIM	ORGANIZATION STRATEGY	ORGANIZATION THEORY	TARGET ORGANIZATION
LEVEL B: strategic structuring	TARGET OR-GANIZATION	STRATEGY OF CHANGING; STRATEGIC ACTION	THEORY OF STRATEGY OF CHANGING	STRATEGIC GOAL
LEVEL C: direct operational structuring	STRATEGIC GOAL	TACTICS OF CHANGING; METHODICAL ACTION	METHODS OF CHANGING	DIRECT OPERATIONAL GOALS

When the operational goal is achieved, the effect—at least, this is what is intended—is that the situation changes in the sense specified by the reference goal.

The common factor in the planning process at each of the three levels described is, therefore, that the planning continually concerns the translation of a reference goal—which, except for a subsequent adjustment to the available means, is set and indicative of the direction to be taken—into a more operational action goal. Also, the three levels are related to each other according to a hierarchical system of goals, in the sense that the operational goal that is the result of the decision-making at a higher level returns as the reference goal at a lower level.

Let us now, for a further explanation, follow the table with the previous example in mind. Point of departure is the policy aim in which the organization formulates a certain desired relationship between itself and the environment (example: shorter delivery time, controlable stock formation).

In most cases, various kinds of means are possible for the organization to achieve its policy aims. This is not evident in table 1. There we have limited ourselves to the application of means in the area of organizational change, because this is our subject. It should be clear that other kinds of intervention can also be considered. In other words, what remains implicit in table 1 is that the process of strategic policy formation implies weighing ends and means, taking the limitations of reality into account. In our application, we are assuming that the weighing process results in an organization strategy, i.e. a strategy aimed at achieving the policy aim, based upon adaptation of the organization (example: a centralized department assigned to sales prognosis, stock planning and control, and distribution planning). This then leads—according to certain lines of thought, irrespective for the purposes of this explanation whether these are based on an organization theory or not—to the projection of a target organization (example: global structure and mode of functioning of the intended centralized department; its position and role in the context of the entire organization). As an operational goal, this target organization is a more operational explicitation of the aforementioned policy aim; it is also the reference goal for directed and planned organizational change.

What is indicated in the table as 'strategic structuring' can be distinguished from strategic policy formation in more than one respect. In the first place, strategic policy formation is the external side of the strategy of change, i.e. determination of strategy by means of which the organization chooses a position with respect to its relationship with the environment. Strategic structuring, in contrast, refers to the internal side of the strategy, which is aimed at changing the internal system of the organization.

In the second place, to the extent that strategic policy formation includes organizational change, the planning of a certain state of the organization is the central issue. It is a matter of *what* needs to be changed. On the level of strategic structuring, the issue is that of planning the change process that will achieve the desired state. It concerns the question of *how* the change can be achieved; and what we have indicated in the table as strategy of changing and methods of changing, is concerned with this question. In this context, strategy of changing refers to a comprehensive program of activities directed towards initiating and structuring the process of changing and channelling it.

The strategic goal is the instigation of the process of changing as described (in our example: combining the decentralized planning departments into one central department, the instigation of functioning committees, and so forth).

Finally, in order to achieve the strategic goal, further planning and implementation activities on the level of direct, operational structuring are required. This planning is not concerned with the change process and its ends in its totality, but with structuring and directing separate parts of the strategy of changing (example: task development, the development of trainings, determining and managing task and function changes, and so on).

3.3. Additional definitions

It may be worthwhile to pay closer attention to a number of principles on which the classification in table 1 is based, because a number of concepts having to do with organizational change can thus be further defined. Two characteristics of the classification have already been dealt with. They can be summarized as follows.

First there is the distinction between more content-related and more procedural aspects of the process of planning and decision-making, the former taking place more on the level of strategic policy formation and the latter more on both lower levels.

Also, there is the relationship between reference goals and operational goals; this relationship determines the planning at each level, but also the relationship between the levels distinguished.

A third characteristic requires explanation. That characteristic is the hierarchical system of aims and levels. Actually, this does not determine the procedure. One can imagine 'working backwards'; then—assuming there is a global a-priori view with respect to policy—the realizability of lower goals leads to working for higher goals. What you often see in reality is a continual readjustment in the planning of higher and lower goals using interchanging procedures of 'working forwards' and 'working backwards'.

Nevertheless, higher goals are principally determinants of the lower ones, because the various goals mentioned are of a different 'order'. Qualitative and quantitative differences play a role here, and further explanation of what that means requires some comment on each of the identified levels.

We have already pointed out that transitive goals can in a certain sense be seen as autonomous, whereas 'lower' goals are of an instrumental nature. The level of strategic policy formation lies somewhat in between. This can be seen as an area of interaction, situated between transitive goals on the one hand and the use of means on the other. It is the level on which the interdependence of determining goals and determining means can be readjusted. It is not purely a matter of determining an aim—in the sense of an autonomous goal—because what is desired is evaluated in terms of the possibilities of the moment, and can eventually be reformulated in other, more realizable terms. But for the same reason it is more than simply the application of technology, because goals formulated in principle on that level do indicate the direction but do not have the nature of an indisputable delimitation. It is the level on which transitive goals are given their actual, but modifiable features; as already indicated, these features are not identical to those of the transitive goal, but rather are the concrete and momentary expression of it.

The lower 'order' of goals of the levels of strategic structuring and direct operational structuring is determined by the fact that these do represent the application of technology, and are limited by the delimitation effected by policy.

Its becoming operational allies further procedures not only to policy, but also, to a great extent, to the methodological rules of the concomitant disciplines and to professional insight, whether it has to do with theory of changing, theory of organization, logistics, military science or whatever other technology.

Usually one can make a further hierarchical distinction between strategic structuring and direct operational structuring, but on other grounds. We will comment on that difference later, but here we wish to point out that strategic planning is the planning on general lines, whereas direct operational structuring has to do with the planning of parts of the total changing strategy, namely those parts which are related to direct, operational goals. In this way a bridge is built between parts of the strategic plan and actual activity. This difference signifies that strategic structuring has an integral nature, and operational planning a relative one.

This further explication of the levels distinguished in table 1 makes it possible to describe the concept of strategy[1] used here more precisely. This requires a demarcation on two sides, namely on both the hierarchical higher and lower levels.

On the higher side, the distinction is made between strategic policy formation and determining the transitive goal: strategies are aimed at achieving transitive goals, but determining the goal itself is beyond the scope of strategy. This means—and that is the point—that the strategy concept has the quality of instrumentality. On the lower side, the level of direct operational structuring is

[1] The concept of strategy has military origins and was first defined systematically in the context of military scinece by the Prussian general and military scientist Carl von Clausewitz. We have used his systematization of the political and military decision-making process, modified by some more recent explications, in our theory. Discussing differences and similarities in this matter is beyond the scope of this chapter. We refer the interested reader to Mensink (1963) and Burnhauser (1966).

the point of demarcation. This boundary is crossed when parts of the strategic plan are developed in such a manner that direct action can follow, or when concrete parts are effectuated.

It is apparent that Table 1 has to do primarily with strategy, namely both higher levels. In view of the differences between them, apparently there are different modalities of the concept of strategy. We were already acquainted with them; they can be seen as *external* and *internal* strategy on the one hand, and *what* and *how* strategies on the other. External strategies are aimed at the aspect of the relationship between the organization and its environment. Internal strategies are primarily aimed at the reflexive level.

'What strategies' have to do with the development of operationalizations of the policy aim as to content. In the case of organizational change, then, these are organization strategies. 'How strategies' are procedural. In the case of organizational change, they are aimed at inducing and channelling goal-directed processes of changing. To differentiate them from organization strategies in table 1, we have used the term 'strategies of changing'.

The distinction between external and internal strategy is interwoven with that between 'what' and 'how strategies'. Internal strategies are primarily 'how strategies', but also partly 'what strategies', namely, to the extent that having determined the target organization still leaves room for further choices.

Finally, to distinguish from what we mean by 'strategy of changing' we have called the planning and activities that have to do with direct operational structuring 'tactics of changing'. The characteristic difference between these is that strategy of changing is aimed at the totality of the changing process, whereas the tactics of changing are aimed at parts. To the extent to which there are systematic methods, we have used the term 'methods of changing'.

4. THE CONTENT OF ORGANIZATIONAL CHANGE

In the previous section we gave a formal analysis of the planning and decision-making process connected with organizational change. One of the points discussed was that there are two important, complementary areas: the first has to do with the content of developments in the relationship between organization and their environment, and the concomitant development of organizations. The second is primarily concerned with the procedural aspect: strategy of changing and tactics of changing.

We will take a closer look at both areas in the rest of this chapter. This section will deal with the first area; the next section will deal with the latter.

4.1. A further exploration of the concept of development

The development with which organizations are concerned is a complex process. A central issue is whether, behind the complex reality, a simple principle can be distilled which gives it structure.

The problem essentially contains the question of how development should be understood. In the area of organizational change, few authors have concerned themselves with this question, which is a rather remarkable omission when it comes to such an essential concept. One of the first authors who did, is Chin (1969). He attributes the omission, which he notes, as due to the manner in which the systems model is used in the theorizing about organizations. He contends that the emphasis lies on how stability is achieved, and that the question of how change occurs, as a consequence of inconsistencies and conflicts within the system, is merely a derived one.

Chin, however, presents a model of development with five characteristics: direction, identifiable state or stadia, form of progression, developmental forces and potentiality. By direction he means that the development is going somewhere. That can be described by indicating a goal, an existing process, or what has already been attained. The idea of stadia is probably evident without further explanation. The concept of progression refers to increase and improvement, but also to the fact that there are 'higher' and 'lower' states, and that normally speaking there are no relapses. Developmental forces are dynamic forces, which can be seen as the motor behind the development and which essentially remain intact, although they produce qualitatively different effects during the various stages of development. Finally, potentiality is the capacity for development the system initially possessed, which expresses itself in the actual development.

Some Dutch authors have paid further attention to the concept of development; most recent is Bekke (1976). He names Lievegoed (1969) and Teulings (1969) as authors who have made a contribution. For Lievegoed, the phenomenon of progress is central to his concept of development. Development is 'progressive change', a matter of qualitative alteration. This development can take the form of directed organizational change if active goal determination and structuring of the process and planning takes place. Teulings distinguishes between growth models, adaptive models and developmental models. Characteristic of the third is the possibility of the development of qualitatively new forms and in that case the possibility of choosing from various alternatives, each related to the different interests various parties in or outside the organization have. In Bekke's view, development is not a result of laws of the system, but of the confrontation between alternative goals.

Four elements mentioned above seem to us important for determining the essence of development. We will indicate them in the form of questions.

First of all, the concept of development is related to the idea of progress, but just exactly what is progress? What is the criterion that can be used to judge whether we have to do with not just change or continuation, but progress?

Secondly, Chin (op. cit.) makes the idea of developmental forces explicit. What exactly are they? What is their nature?

Thirdly, both quantitative growth and change in the sense of qualitative alteration have been mentioned above. What is the relationship between both these aspects of development?

Finally, in developmental processes there is in any case active goal determination by the parties involved in the development. Some say there is also a determining effect of 'system laws'. What is the role of each and in what way are they related?

4.2. Organizations as carriers of developmental forces

Various authors in and outside our field have concerned themselves with this question and others like it.

The first who comes to mind is Romein (1935), who wrote about the historical development concept in such a way that his insights are also important for social science in general.[2] He maintains that the only real quantitive increase is the development of the forces of production which enables man to increase his control of nature and which, under certain conditions, can cause an alteration which differs qualitatively from an earlier phase. However, progress is more complex than that. Besides the development of the forces of production, it is also necessary for people to control their social relations, otherwise 'the lack of the latter would make the former illusory'. In his elaboration of this point, Romein follows a dialectical materialistic line of thought, in which he sees the development of the production force as thesis which, in the non-control of the thus created production relations, brings forth its antithesis; the synthesis is expressed in the progress which occurs in actual history. It is insufficient to attribute the development solely to system laws or simply to human choice processes. In this context, Romein refers to Engels' aphorism: 'People make their own history, but in a determined and determining milieu on the basis of present, actual relations'. In other words, the development until now sets limits for the possibilities of future development and the influence that human policy can have, but not in a degree that denies the significance of the latter.

Organizations, and in particular industrial organizations, can be seen in industrial capitalism as the principal carriers of the societal productive force and therefore also as creators of production relations. The concept 'organization' therefore has a double meaning in which the poles Romein refers to with regard to the concept of development are also relevant. On the one hand it refers to the aspect of the production force, namely to the 'organization' as form of structuring of work behavior and technological processes. But it also refers to a social phenomenon, namely the 'organization' as the expression of human relationships, in particular their production relations.

[2]Romein's treatment of the concept of development is complex and has many nuances. The description of his view in this chapter is very incomplete. For a comprehensive view we refer the reader to Romein's essay.

A theory about the development of such organizations at the intersection of, on the one hand, the determining influence of a broader development of society and, on the other hand, the strategy by means of which organizations attempt to structure that development themselves, should pay attention to those developmental forces. One could view the development of organizations as the result of the strategic behavior of interested parties in and outside the organization, each from the position which is determined by the given historical development of the production force and the production relations, and directed towards their further development in relationship to the interests of each of the parties.

As to the given development: an important element of such is the contradiction in the relation by which capitalist organizations function, namely, the condition that fulfilling general interests is tied to satisfying private interests. The first implies fulfilling societal needs by means of increasing the productiveness of labor; the second implies the private appropriation of the surplus value of collective effort. This relation is further complicated by the circumstance that those private interests are on the one hand incompatible, which leads to competition, but on the other hand have something in common, namely the need to stabilize and legitimize the existing societal relations (Altmann and Bechtle, 1971; Christis *et al.*, 1979).

In this situation, organizations develop strategies to ensure their own interests. What interests us are those strategies which are related to activities in the area of organizational change. They are aimed, under the conditions and according to the relations described above, at continuing to fulfill a societal need. On the one hand this requires development of the productive force in order not to succumb to competition. On the other hand it requires the maintenance of a certain control of the production relations.

4.3. Certain strategic aspects of the development of organizations

What are strategies of enterprises aimed at in this situation?

First of all, in this context a general distinction can be made between *developmental policy* and *adaptive policy*. This distinction is also made by others, sometimes in a different terminology, and most recently by Hamaker (1979). He refers in turn to Van Zuthem (1973) and Teulings (1969), although the latter contrasts development with *control*, a distinction we will discuss further on.

To the extent that developmental strategies are aimed at the development of *forces of production*, they can be indicated as *innovation strategies*. 'Innovation' is often, certainly in recent times, seen in connection with technological development. Here we take a somewhat broader view. There are, in fact, three components of forces of production, namely labor power, technology and organizing power. By 'labor power' we mean the capacity and willingness of workers to meet the requirements of their job. This is connected with their physical and motivational condition and with their education and experience. 'Technology' can in a narrower sense be seen as identical to 'technique', but in a broader sense it is the application of knowledge to the production process. 'Organization power', as a component of the forces of production, can be described as a way of controlling work behavior and technology. Innovation strategies are aimed at innovations which can contribute to the development of those three components. Initially, the focus was on the development of labor power and its organization, for example by means of division of tasks, specialization, improvement of work methods, and so forth. After the production process was mechanized, made possible by the nature of the organization that had developed from specialized manufacture, technical innovation also became part of the development. Although this did not initially lead to a lessening attention for the development of labor methods and the organization, gradually the emphasis shifted. We estimate globally that in The Netherlands between 1955 and 1965 the point was reached, that the development of labor power had largely been settled, and that the strategic emphasis had come to lie on technological development.

For many organizations this also changed their view of their environment, which developed in the direction of what Emery and Trist (1970) call a 'turbulent field': a dynamic force field in which changes depend not only on the actions and reactions of the organizations active in that field, but also on forces in that field which seem autonomous. Keuning (1973) identifies three factors which lead to such environmental dynamics. First of all he mentions the growth of organizations, which is necessary to resist competition, but which can become so strong that the environment becomes unstable. Secondly, he points to the increasing interdependence of economic forces and social factors, which are expressed in government intervention and legislation in a growing number of areas. Finally, he notes the increasing necessity to innovate products and production techniques, and also the research and development on which innovation is based; this simultaneously identifies a continuous source of change in the environment which leads to continual change. The resulting environmental dynamics placed the perspective of organizational change as a permanent process in the foreground.

Adaptation strategies can lead to change processes which in the first instance seem similar, but they are based on a more passive position, on a reaction to rather than an active interaction with the environment. Van Zuthem (1967) speaks of policy 'characterized by the attempt to adapt internal relationships and aspects to altered external circumstances'. In the case of the forces of production, those external circumstances should be seen as new developments in the force of production or in the changed competitive relationships which are its result.

As the background of adaptation strategies, one can think of a somewhat passive strategic stance of the organization. On the other hand, it can also be the situation which leads to such a stance. Particularly in a turbulent field characterized by uncontrollability and unpredictability, adaptation strategies can easily become prominent.

In the context of production relations, a similar distinction can be made, but it can also be extended by a third kind of strategy. Policy can, in that respect, be aimed at *development*, at *adaptation and control*, or at *autonomy*.

What is typical of developmental strategies lies in the way the production relations are viewed. It is a matter of attempting to achieve equality between the parties involved in the production relations with respect to their relationship to the means of production. This includes equalizing the degree of power and control, of ownership, and of the possibility of meaningful and responsible work. In the next section we will become acquainted with methodological approaches which have a strong affinity with such a view of development. But we shall also point out that the large amount of attention paid to such strategies in the literature is not proportional to the chance they receive in practice.

In both other cases, the most important source of strategic problems lies in the interdependence of the parties involved, especially the dependence of employers on labor. In this context we can first of all note the importance of *autonomy strategies*, which are aimed at making the realization of one's interests independent of the other party. In concrete, these strategies are aimed at making the functioning of the organization (more) independent of labor power and work behavior. On the one hand they have an affinity with technological development, to the extent that they are in part based on the wish to make labor superfluous by means of mechanization and automation. But also, decreased dependence occurs by the division of intellectual and manual labor, a viewpoint taken both when structuring an organization and when choosing a production technique (ISF, 1972).

However, to the extent that the functioning of the organization remains largely dependent on labor power, the issue of adaptation and control is problematic: how can the organizational relations be adapted to reproduce existing class-relations?

What control strategies concretely consist of, depends on the production relations involved. In the case of exchange relations—the availability of labor in return for pay—the strategy takes the form of a *disposition strategy*. We will not further discuss labor market strategies as beyond the scope of our subject, but refer to two other areas.

Firstly, there are strategies concerned with accomplishing the most favourable ratio between actually realized and potentially available labor power. These kinds of strategies are aimed at reaching or maintaining an acceptable level of motivation to work, absenteeism, turnover, and so on.

Secondly, there are strategies concerned with adapting available or potentially available labor power to the quantitative or qualitative manpower requirements of the organization. Examples of these are strategies of 'manpower-planning' (Bryant and Niehaus, 1978) or of areas known as 'human resource utilization' and 'human resource development' (Singleton and Spurgeon, 1975; Flamholz, 1974; Schein, 1978). The latter involves education, training, career planning and career counseling, management development and its application in achieving goals of the organization.

To the extent that relations of production are connected with the relation between management and those who carry out the work, *stabilizing and legitimizing strategies* play a role in adaptation and control. These are strategies aimed at stabilizing and legitimizing existing relations or adapting them to accompanying changes in attitude which may have developed. These strategies contribute to the control of production relations by keeping the system of the organization controlable. Many approaches can be classified under this heading. A number of them are concerned with the participation of employees at various levels in the organization. Others are aimed at facilitating certain forms of co-operation and relevant attitudes, of communication methods and skills, of certain leadership styles and attitudes, and so on. Training is usually the method used.

5. METHODS OF ORGANIZATIONAL CHANGE

There are many methodical approaches to organizational change which vary in the degree to which they differ. They originated primarily in practical settings, independent of each other. Some of these approaches are characterized by a certain artistry, in the sense that they are strongly tied to the personality of the consultant who works with a certain method, which may be unsuccessful in the hands of others. A difficult problem in comparative research on methods of organizational change—which actually is rather scarce—is the question as to whether one is comparing methods or personal styles and skills.

A number of methodical approaches have been more systematically translated into theories of practice; thus they have attained a certain level of transferability. An important example in The Netherlands in the so-called NPI model (Zwart, 1978: Glasl and de la Houssaye, 1975), which gives a representation of the concepts and models on which the methodical interventions of the NPI (Pedagogical Institute of The Netherlands) are based. In the foreign literature, especially the Anglo-American, there are more examples. The most important are the 'grid-model' (Blake and Mouton, 1969), 'intervention theory' (Argyris, 1970), the model of 'process consultation' (Schein, 1969), the 'survey-feedback model' (Bowers and Franklin, 1975) and the 'contingency approach' (Lawrence and Lorsch, 1969); (see also this Handbook, ch. 4.3). Most of these cases are approaches in which both the strategic and tactical levels are represented. An approach which is rooted especially in Europe is the socio-technical approach (Emery and Trist, 1970), which has also been further developed in The Netherlands (Allegro, 1973; van Beinum *et al.*, 1968; and others; see this Handbook, ch. 4.5 and 4.8). In this section we will not discuss each of these approaches separately for two reasons. First of all, much that can be said can be found in other chapters of this Handbook, besides those already mentioned, in chapter 2.11 (Training) and 4.9 (Organization development). Also, such overviews are available elsewhere (e.g. French and Bell, 1973; Beer, 1976).

Here we wish to discuss some general characteristics according to which methods of organizational change can differ or be similar, in order to arrive at a more general classification.

There are two classifications in which such similarities and differences become apparent, written at an earlier date, and fairly established. They are the classifications of Chin and Benne (1969) and of Leavitt (1965).

The classification of Chin and Benne is of a general nature, since all forms of intended induction of individual and social change, including organizational change, can be accommodated in it. They distinguish between rational–empirical strategies, normative–re-educative strategies, and power–coercive strategies.

Rational–empirical strategies are based on two related assumptions concerning human behavior. The first is that people are rational; the second is that they will let themselves be guided by their interests if they know what these are. This leads to the supposition that persons or groups will change when it can be made clear at a rational level that the change will serve their interests. One of its elaborations is the strategy of innovation by means of applying the results of scientific research. Important representatives of this approach are Havelock and Benne (1969).

Normative–re-educative strategies are not based on a denial of the rational amount in human decision-making, but on a supplementary assumption about the role that normative attitudes play in it. Peoples' actions are in general supported by norms and their attachment to those norms. Therefore, a change in patterns of action requires more than information alone. It requires the development of a new and different normative orientation regarding action and, concomitantly, change in attitudes, values and skills. On the chart that Chin and Benne present, this strategy encompasses a very broad range.

Influences they recognize include the work of Lewin and Freud: Lewin because of his emphasis on action research as strategy of change and participation in groups as medium for re-education; Freud due to his discovery of the unconscious as basis of behavior and of the possibilities offered by the use of the co-operative relationship between the change agent and the client system for purposes of therapeutic change.

They describe the formation of the National Training Laboratories in 1947, the embodiment of Lewinian influence, as a milestone.

A parallel development took place in England. This was derived from a

Freudian line of thought, and in particular from the application of its therapeutic insights into industry. Elliot Jaques (1952) can be seen as a representative.

Other parallel developments can be seen, according to Chin and Benne, in the counseling approach of Carl Rogers and in the Human Relations movement and the work of Mayo, Roethlisberger and Dickson; and more recently in the Neo Human Relations (see ch. 4.2) as expressed in the work of authors such as McGregor and Argyris.

Finally, *power–coercive strategies* are based on applying primarily political and economic power. We will discuss these later.

Leavitt's classification is more directly concerned with organizational change, especially with industrial organizations. He distinguishes between *structural approaches* of the change issue, *technological approaches* and *people approaches*. This classification is based on a view of organizations as complex, interdependent systems in which four groups of variables interact, namely, task variables, structural variables, technological variables and human variables. In general, changes in the last three types of variables are ultimately aimed at influencing task variables. Those refer to the grounds of existence of industrial organizations, namely, the production of goods and services.

Because the organization is an interdependent system, changes in one of the subsystems soon lead to changes in the others. The basis of the distinction in different types of approaches does not lie in the exclusion of variables not belonging to that type, but in the focal point in the organization, the relative emphasis given by the approach, and the underlying pattern of values. The names given to the approaches refer to their content: changes in the organizational structure, in the technology and the work method, or in human behavior. Leavitt notes that the approaches distinguished also differ in view, in the sense that the two former emphasize the business administrative and management functioning of the organization, whereas the latter accentuates the reduction of differences in power, human resources development and self-actualization. He adds that since the sixties, the literature on organizational change is strongly 'people-oriented'. In this respect we have already mentioned that it is doubtful whether this emphasis to be found in the literature is also found in practical settings. Furthermore, Strauss (1976) maintains that theories of organizational change one-sidedly emphasize co-operation and problem-solving, and that too little attention is paid to the role of conflict and negotiation and of power–coercive strategies. He contends that it is a common pitfall to assume that all problems can be reduced to perceptions and can be solved by better understanding.

Some other, more theoretically inspired lines of thought can be found in the work of Bekke (*op. cit.*) and Van Dijck (1972).

Bekke distinguishes between two conceptions of the phenomenon 'organization', namely, 'organization as construction' and 'organization as action'.

These conceptions are linked with two different approaches to social reality, which Bekke calls *catascopic* and *anascopic*. In a catascopic approach, social reality is viewed apart from the individuals acting in it. 'Society and organization', according to Bekke, 'can be viewed as structural frameworks with their own systematization, having their own rules for construction and process. Human action processes can then, viewed from above, be studied from the viewpoint of the structures'. In an anascopic approach the view is from below: social structures are analysed from the viewpoint of human action processes. Human interaction is the central issue; and what it gives rise to, and how, is explored as to the meaning given to it by human action. The distinction leads Bekke to characterize organizational (change) theory as primarily catascopic.

One finds different, but comparable, views in the work of Van Dijck (*op. cit.*). He distinguishes between two ideal types: interventions based on an organization theory view, and interventions based on a social intervention view. The former strive for a stabilizing effect, an improvement in the effectiveness of the system's functioning, change in the organization as a system of tasks, creation of conditions which appeal to human needs for certainty, clarity, consistency and integration. The latter are aimed at something else on all points, and on some points the opposite. They pursue a dynamic effect, and are aimed at promoting psychological and social well-being and activating participation, at change of the organization as system of exchange of expectations, norms and values, and at the creation of conditions which appeal to human needs for growth, expansion and self-actualization.

The most radical difference in approach between the intervention methods linked to the systems way of thinking and the intervention methods allied with the action way of thinking, appears to lie in the priority given to different aims. In the former, the goals of the organization have priority: vigilant and effective technical and economic functioning, and a corresponding view of adequate social functioning. As regards the people, it is a matter of the development of necessary capacities, motivation, and acquiring co-operation. In the action approach, it is not so much the general goals of the organization which have priority, but the goals and interests of separate groups within the organization. It is initiated as a process of development concerned with becoming aware of and clarifying goals, and concerned with the choices as to the further development and adaptation of those goals.

To these modalities of organizational change we wish to add another one which has received little attention in the literature. We are referring to compulsory reorganizations, which are implemented by the top without or minimally informing or consulting those directly concerned. Some attention is paid to this mode by Janssen (1974). He does not attribute the lack of interest to the rarity of occurrence of this kind of reorganization. More plausible is that the cultural climate of our time, characterized by a positive evaluation of participation, self-realization of people and other such values, does not make the subject of compulsory reorganizations popular. What is emphasized in the literature is not so much an expression of what happens in the reality of reorganizations, but rather a reflection of the attitudes and ideals of social scientists. And these are especially sensitive to ethical considerations in this context, more so than the often pragmatically-minded people in practical settings, such as the management, who implement such reorganizations.

Furthermore, theoretically speaking, compulsory reorganizations are not good strategy. It is a well-known fact that these arouse resistance, which can be removed by participation (Coch and French, 1948). However, Janssen points out—and our own research findings, to be presented further on, confirm this—that this argument is not always valid. Compulsory reorganizations can be recommended when change meets great resistance and simultaneously the advantages cannot easily be made clear before the change has been tried. Moreover, there are cases in which the time needed for a participative approach is lacking. That could be the case, for example, when there are great external pressures. The characteristics of such situations have been described by Breuer and Luscuere (1974).

Recently we completed two simultaneous case studies, in which a compulsory reorganization was compared with a reorganization accompanied by more participative procedures.[3] Three reasons proved to explain why in one case, which we shall call case X, a compulsory reorganization was chosen and not in the other—case Y. Two of these reasons are connected with what Janssen notes. Firstly, in the case of X, acute external pressures played a role. Continuation of the existing situation was unacceptable in view of economic reasons. In case Y, those pressures were less.

In the second place, there was great resistance to the reorganization in case X. The necessity and advantages of reorganizing were recognized by most of those concerned later on; but this could not be made clear beforehand, for a number of reasons we will not describe now. In case Y, the 'willingness for change' was much greater, because the problems that the reorganization was to solve were experienced by many on all levels of the organization.

There was also a third difference, which may have a more general significance. In case X, a technical solution was available for the existing problems; this required a reorganization, but the solution had been successfully applied in other organizations. This was not the case for Y. General and global criteria that the changed situation would approximately need to meet did exist, but no-one could describe what that situation would look like concretely. Nor was there ready-made expertise on the issue outside the organization.

---

[3] 'We' in this case refers, besides to the author, to J. F. G. Wijman as co-researcher. A more systematic and complete report of that study will be given elsewhere.

The situation of case X had two effects. First, the management chose for the available solution, despite some resistance. Subsequently, technical experts implemented the reorganization; they paid little attention to the social aspects. In case Y, the organization was confronted with undertaking an independent organizational innovation. This also had two effects. First, good research on the difficulties in the existing organization was deemed necessary; many people were involved because they had relevant information. Subsequently, creative forces which could contribute to implementing the innovation were mobilized, over a much broader range than in case X.

Summarizing and generalizing this third point, one could surmise that compulsory reorganizations, besides the first two reasons, occur sooner when a proven technical solution supported by expertise is available; whereas a more open situation, characterized by undertaking organizational innovation, increases room for participation.

To conclude this section, and also this chapter, we wish to comment on the state of scientific research on the applicability of various methods of organizational changing in different situations. Do studies provide a basis on which more definite answers can be given to questions such as, 'do certain methods fit certain problems or situations better than others?' and 'which methods have which effects in which situations?'. (See also Handbook, ch. 4.9.).

Much has been written about organizational change, although the interest in the subject is fairly recent. Many explanations of methods have been written, but there are also a number of contributions based on practical experiences with various methods and empirical research. However, most of those are case studies or an evaluation of one particular strategic approach or method. A systematic comparison of methods is rare, and when that is done, it is usually ex post facto: sometimes by means of comparing reviews in the literature of a number of different strategies (for example, Frohmann and Sashkin, 1970), and sometimes by means of comparing cases. Direct comparative research is done infrequently (Bowers, 1969; van de Bunt, 1978).

In the field of interventions in organizations, little experimental work has been done; and where it exists, most experiments are done with one particular strategy (Coch and French, 1948; Morse and Reimer, 1956; Marrow et al., 1967). We know of only one experiment in which various strategies are directly compared with each other (Bowers, 1971).

Apparently, organizational change is primarily a practical terrain and to a much lesser extent a field of scientific research. How can this be explained?

Perhaps the work of This cited earlier (see section 2) sheds some light on the question; he estimates that this kind of research is immanent. The recent research activities of Van de Bunt (op. cit.), in which the question as we have just formulated it is central, appears to indicate this.

There is another reason, namely, that doing the kind of research psychologists generally conceive of as such, for example, comparative (quasi-)experimental research, is extremely difficult in this field.

First of all, the practical possibility of experimenting does not generally exist. Not only are a large number of organizations needed for an acceptable experiment, but also the researcher would need to have the freedom to apply a certain kind of intervention, as an experimental 'treatment', in each of the organizations and usually for a longer period of time. It is probably clear that this is an unpractical proposition—whose results moreover would be disproportional to the problems which might result for the organizations concerned—which can best be left untried.

Experimenting with a smalll number of organizations also has its problems. One of the problems is that most of the intervention methods, in comparison with what experimental manipulations usually mean, are of an especially complex nature. Moreover, they are often strongly determined by the situation, in the sense that not only do general strategic and methodological principles set a course, but also strategy takes a certain form in the situation in which it is applied. Added to the 'artistic' nature of many intervention methods noted earlier, the conclusion becomes evident that the standardization of experimental manipulations required in an experiment is extremely difficult to achieve.

It is therefore likely, that hope should be set on other forms of research, although experiments on a much smaller scale than comparing intervention strategies remain conceivable in this field. In this research, comparative studies can be done more often than at present; and it is to Van de Bunt's (*op. cit.*) credit, that he has clarified the practical possibilities and difficulties involved.

But the strongly creative process of organizational change, difficult to isolate from the societal reality and the practical application, does for the time being, and perhaps even in principle, leave room for other forms of acquiring knowledge, including systematizing practical experience, case studies, and action research.

REFERENCES

Allegro, J. T. (1973), *Socio-technische organisatie-ontwikkeling* [Sociotechnical organization development]. Leiden: Stenfert Kroese.

Altmann, N., Bechtle, G. (1971), *Betriebliche Herschaftsstrukturen und industrielle Gesellschaft*. Munich.

Argyris, C. (1969), *Intervention theory and method*. Reading (Mass.): Addison-Wesley.

Beer, M. (1976), The technology of organization development. In: Dunnette, M. (Ed.), *Handbook of organizational and industrial psychology*. Chicago: Rand McNally.

Beinum, H. J. J. van, Gils, M. R. van, Verhagen, E. J. (1968), *Taakontwerp en werkorganisatie: Een sociotechnisch veld-experiment* [Task design and work organization: A sociotechnical field experiment]. The Hague: COP.

Bekke, A. J. G. M. (1976), *Organisatie-ontwikkeling: Confrontatie van individu, organisatie en maatschappij* [Organization development: Confrontation of individual, organization and society]. Rotterdam: Universitaire Pers.

Blake, R. R., Mouton, J. S. (1969), *Building a dynamic corporation through grid organization development*. Reading (Mass.): Addison-Wesley.

Bowers, D. G. (1969), *Three studies in change: An account of data-based organizational development activities*. Alexandria (Va.): Defense Documentation Center, Cameron Station.

Bowers, D. G. (1971), *Development techniques and organizational change: An overview of results from the Michigan Inter-Company Longitudinal Study*. Alexandria (Va.): Defense Documentation Center, Cameron Station.

Bowers, D. G., Franklin, J. L. (1975), *Survey-guided development: Data-based organizational change*. Ann Arbor: Institute for Social Research.

Breuer, F. J. L. I., Luscuere, C. (Eds.) (1974), *Reorganiseren en saneren: Organisaties onder druk* [Reorganizing and reconstructing: Organizations under pressure]. Rotterdam: Universitaire Pers.

Bryant, D. T., Niehaus, R. J. (1978), *Manpower planning and organizational design*. London: Plenum Press.

Bunt, P. A. E. van de (1978), *Adviseur en client: Duel of samenspel?* [Consultant and client: Duel or cooperation?]. Alphen a/d Rijn: Samsom.

Burnhauser, A. (1966), Grundbegriffe der Strategie. Ein Versuch zu ihrer Erläuterung und Abgrenzung. *Wehrkunde*, **15**.

Chin, R. (1969), The utility of system models and developmental models for practitioners. In: Bennis, W. G., Benne, K. D., Chin, R., *The planning of change*. New York: Holt, Rinehart and Winston.

Chin, R., Benne, K. D. (1969), General strategies for effecting changes in human systems. In: Bennis, W. G., Benne, K. D., Chin, R., *The planning of change*. New York: Holt, Rinehart and Winston.

Christis, J., Dols, H., Doorewaard, H., Fruytier, B., Martens, W. (Project Group 'Technique, Organization, Labor Market') (1979), *Techniek, organisatie, arbeidsmarkt: Samenvattend rapport* [Technique, organization, labor market: Summarizing report]. Nijmegen: Catholic University.

Coch, L., French, J. R. P. (1948), Overcoming resistance to change. *Human Relations*, *1*, no. **4**, 512–533.

Dijck, J. J. J. van (1972), *Organisatie in verandering* [Organization in transition]. Rotterdam: Universitaire Pers.

Emery, F. E., Trist, E. L. (1970a), Socio-technical systems. In: Emery, F. E. (Ed.), *Systems thinking*. Harmondsworth: Penguin.

Emery, F. E., Trist, E. L. (1970b), The causal texture of organizational environments. In: Emery, F. E. (Ed.), *Systems thinking*. Harmondsworth: Penguin.

Faludi, A. (1973), *Planning theory*. Oxford: Pergamon Press.

Flamholz, E. (1974), *Human resource accounting*. Dickenson Publ. Co.

French, W. L., Bell, Jr., C. H. (1973), *Organization development; Behavioral science interventions for organization improvement*. Englewood Cliffs (N.J.): Prentice-Hall.

Frohmann, M. A., Sashkin, M. (1970), *The practice of organizational development: A selective review*. Alexandria (Va.): Defense Documentation Center, Cameron Station.

Glasl, F., Houssaye, L. de la (1975), *Organisatie-ontwikkeling in de praktijk* [Organization development in practice]. Amsterdam: Agon/Elsevier.

Gross, E. (1969), The definition of organizational goals. *The British Journal of Sociology*, **20**.

Hamaker, H. G. (1979), Typen personeelsbeleid in theory en onderzoek [Types of personnel policy in theory and research]. *M & O*, **5**, 403–421.

Havelock, R. G., Benne, K. D. (1969), An exploratory study of knowledge utilization. In: Bennis, W. G., Benne, K. D., Chin, R., *The planning of change*. New York: Holt, Rinehart and Winston.

Hertog, J. F. den (1977), *Werkstructurering* [Job design]. Groningen: Wolters-Noordhoff.

Hightower, H. C. (1969), Planning theory in contemporary professional education. *Journal of the American Institute of Planners*, 35, 326–329.

ISF (1972), *Einsatz numerisch gesteuerten Werkzeugmachinen*. Munich.

Janssen, W. (1974), *Organisatie-ontwikkeling als veranderingsmodel: Hersenschim of realiteit?* [Organization development as model of change: phantasy or reality?]. Nijmegen: Catholic University, Inst. of Sociology (doctoral paper).

Jaques, E. (1952), *The changing culture of a factory*. New York: Holt, Rinehart and Winston.

Keuning, D. (1973), *Algemene systeemtheorie, systeembenadering en organisatietheorie* [General systems theory, systems approach and organization theory]. Leiden: Stenfert Kroese.

Lawrence, P. R., Lorsch, J. W. (1969), *Developing organizations: Diagnosis and action*. Reading (Mass.): Addison-Wesley.

Leavitt, H. J. (1965), Applied organizational change in industry. In: March, J. G. (Ed.), *Handbook of organizations*. Chicago: Rand McNally, 1144–1170.

Lievegoed, B. C. J. (1969), *Organisaties in ontwikkeling: Zicht op de toekomst* [Developing organizations: A look at the future]. Rotterdam: Lemniscaat.

Lippitt, G. L., This, L. E., Bidwell, Jr., R. G. (1971), *Optimizing human resources: Reading in individual and organizational development*. Reading (Mass.): Addison-Wesley.

Marrow, A. J., Bowers, D. G., Seashore, S. E. (1967), *Management by participation*. New York: Harper and Row.

Mensink, G. (1963), Leer der operatiën [Theory of operations]. *Militaire Spectator* [Military Spectator] (The Hague), 12, 546–551.

Mohr, L. B. (1973), The concept of organizational goal. *The American Political Review*, 67, 470–481.

Morse, N., Reimer, E. (1956), The experimental change of a major organizational variable. *Journal of Abnormal and Social Psychology*, 52, 120–129.

Romein, J. (1935), De dialectiek van de vooruitgang: Bijdrage tot het ontwikkelingsbegrip in de geschiedenis [The dialectics of progress: A contribution towards the concept of development in history]. In: Romein, J., *Historische lijnen en patronen* [Historical lines and patterns]. Amsterdam: Querido (1970).

Schein, E. H. (1969), *Process consultation*. Reading (Mass.): Addison-Wesley.

Schein, E. H. (1978), *Career dynamics*. Reading (Mass.): Addison-Wesley.

Singleton, W. T., Spurgeon, P. (Eds.) (1975), *Measurement of human resources*. London: Taylor and Francis.

Snellen, J. Th. M. (1975), *Benaderingen in strategieformulering* [Approaches in strategy formulation]. Brussels: Samsom.

Strauss, G. (1976), Organization development. In: Dubin, R. (Ed.), *Handbook of work, organization and society*. Chicago: Rand McNally.

Teulings, A. W. M. (1969a), Groei en ontwikkeling van organisaties [Growth and development of organizations]. *Mens en Maatschappij* [Man and Society], 44, 215–232.

Teulings, A. W. M. (1969b), Ontwikkelings- en beheersingsregiems [Developmental and control regimes]. In: Marx, E. H. C., Teulings, A. W. M., *Samenspel van managers en specialisten* [Managers and experts working together]. Utrecht: Het Spectrum.

Wester, Ph. (1978), Werkstructurering als een criterium bij organisatievernieuwing [Job design as a criterion in organizational innovation]. *M. & O*, 32, no. 6, 397–419.

Zuthem, H. J. van (1967), *Arbeid en arbeidsbeleid in de onderneming* [Work and work policy in the firm]. Assen: Van Gorcum.

Zuthem, H. J. van (1973), *Inleiding in de economische sociologie* [Introduction to economic sociology]. Amsterdam: De Bussy.

Zwart, C. J. (1978), *Gericht veranderen van organisaties* [Planned change of organization], *Vol. 1*. Rotterdam: Lemniscaat.

Handbook of Work and Organizational Psychology
Edited by P. J. D. Drenth, H. Thierry, P. J. Willems and C. J. de Wolff
© 1984, John Wiley & Sons, Ltd.

4.5. The sociotechnical systems approach to organizations

Jules J. J. van Dijck

1. INTRODUCTION

During the fifties a number of pioneering industrial-sociological and -psychological studies were done under the name of 'Sociotechnical Systems by the Tavistock Institute in England. The research workers and organization advisers at this institute advocated an approach which is currently characterized often as 'organization development'. Here, the central point was the insight that technological (technical) and social factors both determine the organization's behavior. At attempt was made to analyze and (re)design as a system a production process (system of activities). This approach brought up for discussion the one-sidedness of Taylorism as well as that of Human Relations thought. The first school was based on the optimalization of the ordering and processing of human and technical means, in order to attain the highest degree of efficiency possible (the best cost-benefit relationship). The main principles were division of labor, routinization of tasks, and a sharp separation of planning, preparation and performance of the work. In Human Relations thought the formal organization of the work was considered as given. Satisfying relationships and interactions in work groups were seen as the most important conditions for realizing and optimizing the adaptation to the requirements of the production process. Therefore, a human and group-oriented management style was seen as the key instrument.

The specific problem handled in this chapter is that the connection between technological and social factors still constitutes an obstinate problem for

Prof. Dr. J. J. J. van Dijck, Katholieke Hogeschool Soc. Fac., Hogeschoollaan 225, 5037 GC TILBURG.

designing and changing organizations. This problem was clearly stated for the first time during the fifties. Due to continuous technological and social development, this problem has also stood in the forefront of a more application-oriented social science. In the years to come the question of the conflict relationship between technology and social control will demand again much attention, e.g. in the form of 'social implications of automation and computerization'. This will apply to many types of industrial organizations and to almost all levels of work and occupations.

It is meaningful, then, to outline the evolution in social science thought on the connection between technological and social factors within the concept organization.

During the fifties and early sixties the STS (sociotechnical systems approach) was still predominantly a theoretically weak based sub-division of organizational psychology. It was especially concerned with finding a 'best fit' between technical-economic requirements of a production process and the psycho-social characteristics of individuals and small groups. Postulations about human needs referred to a universal anthropological 'vision' as developed by A. Maslow (1947). Only later was an embedding possible in the motivation theories of Murray, McClelland, Vroom and others (Vroom, 1964; McClelland, 1961).

During the sixties and in the beginning of the seventies, the STS approach was further developed, especially in England, Sweden and The Netherlands. Simple, sometimes naïve, hypotheses from the initial period were corrected. Two theoretically 'strong' lines of thought within organization theory determined the setting: the maturing and closely related organization-psychology and -sociology, and general systems theory (de Sitter, 1974b).

At present, the need to speak of a 'sociotechnical systems approach' to organizations is felt less and less. One can say that after a process of coming into being, maturing and incorporation into the broader science of organization, STS as school or stream does not have an identity of its own any more. This is true of theorization in relation to the connection between technological and social factors. This is also true of applications in diverse variations of organization development. However, at present we prefer to base the design and development of 'systems of activities' (e.g. a production process) on task formation and work structure, and in general on organizational innovation, instead of on psycho-social criteria (e.g. job satisfaction, motivation, autonomy on the job).

In this chapter the STS approach will not be dealt with in a chronological-historical sense, as it has been presented in successive contributions by authors since the fifties, but in a (personal) reconstruction of the 'wrestling'—in this case following the sociotechnical line—of the multidisciplinary science of organization with the question of people, technology and work. This reconstruction begins with an outline of a *decor*: a few main lines in social science thought on people and work, technology and organization (section 2). Subsequently, the *innovation moment* of the STS is brought into focus: the Tavistock studies on the English coal mines (section 3). Then the characteristics of the STS approach are handled (section 4).

The incorporation of STS thought into organization theory and general systems theory leads to a summing up of the main lines of the scientific *discussion* of the themes people, work and organization (sections 5 and 6).

The elaboration of the STS approach as intervention theory in variants, such as organization development, job design and industrial democratization, deserves separate treatment (section 7). This elaboration is but summarily handled in this contribution (see further the contributions of Bruining, Allegro and Den Hertog in this Handbook).

Finally, there follows 'Balance and perspective', where the questions of the connection between technological and social factors in the new shape of themes in social policy, such as 'quality of the work' and social control of technological development (section 8).

2. A DECOR

2.1. American organizational psychology

Human Relations thought was dominant in industrial and organization psychology during the fifties and the early sixties. Within this thought great significance was given to optimization of social interaction and relationships in work groups. Interventions then relate to the key 'variables': the manager, management and the *style of leadership*.

This development in the U.S. can be pictured as follows (Gellerman, 1963). The work of Mayo (1945) prompted a long series of studies on the connection between mentality and behavior of managers, productivity of work groups, and aspects of work motivation of individuals. In this context the Michigan Tradition can be pointed to (Likert, 1958, 1959, 1961; Katz *et al.*, 1961; Kahn, 1960).

The Ohio State studies, with the central distinction between a leadership type 'consideration' and a type 'initiating structure', are worth reporting (Fleishman *et al.*, 1955). The distinction between a 'production-centered' and an 'employee-centered' style of management became popular later. In the Michigan tradition, much attention is paid to the behavior patterns of managers in work situations and the effectiveness of individuals and work groups. In addition, the question of under which circumstances do the 'authoritarian' and the 'democratic' style of leadership lead to the best results (productivity). It seems that the nature of the work as co-determined by technological factors (e.g. the level of mechanization) explains a large part of the variation in the effectiveness of management style. Vroom introduced important nuances, especially relativeness, in the Michigan approach by showing that the results of supervision could depend to a high degree upon the personal motivation structure of individuals (Vroom, 1960).

To his merit, Likert (1961, 1967) interpreted and synthesized the results of the Michigan studies in an organization theory (see this Handbook, ch. 4.2). He formulated an 'applied' theory of organization, which did not infringe upon the right of management to run the business (in contrast to later democratization in commerce and industry, especially in Europe). According to Likert, the point is to design an organizational structure, and a system of management and consultation, wherein interactions are experienced as supportive and contributive to one's personal worth. Further, individuals and work groups should control their own immediate work situation. To achieve this, it is necessary that each person in the organization be a 'genuine' member of one or more work groups which function as a team. Participation is, therefore, a key concept. This comes from Human Relations thought, but it is used by Likert in a less flat sense. On this concept he based an innovative organization model, popularized by the 'linking pin' model of organization. In contrast to classical theory Likert's conception is not based on the individual but on team-oriented management.

The Pittsburgh studies are also of interest for the organization-psychological approach to questions concerning integration of the individual and organization (Herzberg et al., 1959). The distinction made, following the line of Herzberg, between task-intrinsic and task-extrinsic variables in work situations must be considered as an important innovation. The central concept 'satisfaction on the job' was, partly on the grounds of Herzberg's findings, relegated to the status of 'side-effect' in relation to the more central concept of motivation (van Dijck, 1968). Substantial challenging work, possibilities for initiative, and personal growth are some of the factors which could make work an instrument for self development. Besides participative leadership, delegation and decentralization, task-enlargement and -enrichment especially emerge as objectives of personnel policy (see further this Handbook, ch. 2.2, 2.3 and 4.8).

Argyris (1957) especially focussed on conflict, disequilibrium, indeed the conflict between the capacities and needs of the psychic 'normal' adult and the characteristics of formal organizational rules. The psychic mature employee is motivationally predisposed to development. He becomes frustrated, apathetic or behaves aggressively; finally, either he does not participate or he does so at a minimum productive level. The appearance of these reaction types can be explained by a number of mechanisms which are connected to organizations.

In this connection, Argyris mentions the functional-hierarchical structure of organizations, the directive leadership, and organizational rules such as budgeting and incentive pay systems. These mechanisms at present are interweaved in many situations in one style or another of management.

Argyris attempted to find criteria for a 'healthy' organization. In this difficult area, he formulated solutions for conflict between the individual and the organization. He considers this conflict to be psycho-socially damaging and unproductive besides, seen from the viewpoint of organizational goals. The solutions for the conflict should be sought in the area of task enlargement, greater autonomy, decentralization and participative leadership. The lines of thought on problems of people, work and organization were strongly influenced by the views of McGregor (1960) in the fifties. He distinguished by style two management 'philosophies': Theory X and Theory Y. The first is an observation about the working man, who is primarily concerned with his own economic advantage, experiences the work as an exchange relationship, submits like a marionet to authoritarian management. Within the last observation, the working man is oriented towards expression, achievement and development of his capacities at work. It is especially of interest that McGregor attached great explanatory value to attitudes or strategies (according to later terminology) of management and managers.

The two attitudes or styles of management refer to social-cultural realities and specially to values and norms in relation to people and work. Theory Y is considered by McGregor as an invitation to innovation in the social and cultural orientation of management in force during his time. According to McGregor the social orientation or 'strategy', which is expressed in Theory X or Y of the working man, is an important factor 'behind' the decisions and behavior of managers. Decisions and behavior refer to the technological design of production processes, organizing and to the actual patterns of managing.

2.2. French industrial sociology

In an evaluation of the STS approach, the French industrial sociological tradition of the fifties (and sixties) may not be omitted. In this connection, the studies and essays of its founder Friedmann (1950, 1956) must be considered first of all. Subsequently, also the studies of Touraine (1955), Naville (1956), and others. These French industrial sociologists have carried out pioneering studies on the connection between technical, social, and organizational factors in industrial enterprises. Here the accent was especially on an historical approach: the connection of technological development stages—in terms of the ideal-types craft, mechanized and automated production—and the social and organizational characteristics of work. The tone was clearly set at an early stage by Friedmann. He saw mechanization especially in its destructive effect on the work of the 'professional' (the skilled worker, the craftsman). He noted that the 'milieu naturel' (skills and crafts) was replaced by the 'milieu technique' of mechanized and automated industrial processes. Friedmann's work rested on the cogent question of the future of 'le travail humain' and was a plea for humanizing industry.

In the light of the actualities of the 1980's, Friedmann's thesis that automation might bring with it new possibilities for humanization is of great interest. From a scientific and systematic viewpoint, the work of Touraine (1955) offers a number of important starting points for the question of the connection of technical and social factors which we are concerned with because of the STS approach.

In a period of rapid mechanization (the fifties in the U.S. and Europe) all attention is focussed on the decreasing requirement of knowledge and skillfulness with which the workers are confronted by industrial processes. The scientist as well as the man of practice judge this situation one-sidedly on the basis of norms which originated in a pre-industrial period (craft production). Herewith, one easily loses sight of the *technological evolution*: mechanization is a period of transition—characterized by the operation of machines without demands of knowledge or skills—to a phase of automation in which direct productive work by people is gradually eliminated.

It is of interest to see what changes in the structure of the work (division of labor) have occurred during technological development. During the transition from craft production to mechanization and automation, a system disappears wherein the worker, his job autonomy and his occupational role were dominant. It is replaced by a technical-organizational production system, where social processes become dominant. The social aspect of organization 'around' the new production technology appears much more in the foreground and becomes strongly determinative for the goal-oriented functioning of an enterprise.

The social aspect of craft labor is especially posited in the unit of the occupational group solidarity. In addition to disqualification—the most striking change—an atomization of the social work context appears during the mechanization phase, which becomes a mass-like collective. The work becomes disconnected from interaction and relationships between *workers*, who all together are called an 'informal organization'. During progressive mechanization and automation, formal labor organizations and 'informal' social activities again coincide. Therewith, the work acquires a new social-organizing unit (Touraine, 1962). This means above all that productivity and results become more and more dependent upon organizing and social factors, 'climate' in the company, and especially the attitudes (orientations) of workers in relation to their work.

The macro-sociological significance of French industrial sociology of the fifties and sixties cannot be handled here. Of interest for what follows, is the still to be made distinction between *job*-content (and *job*-enrichment) and *role*-content (and role enrichment). In a narrow sense, the job decreases in significance at a high level of production technology. Horizontal job-enlargement or -enrichment—whereby the worker does more in direct relation to the product—then makes less sense. His role can, nevertheless, become more complex in a social and organizational sense, so that vertical enlargement or enrichment becomes possible (Davis, 1972).

2.3. Group dynamics

In a genealogy of task design and job design, Davis correctly designates group dynamics as the foundation; the concept was developed by Lewin and his students in the forties and fifties (Davis, 1972). This seems of interest for the subject of the sociotechnical approach in two ways. The insights and findings of group dynamics research have deepened applied organization psychological thought, which was still very much in the grip of Human Relations thought in the fifties. Interpersonal relationships, cooperation (with complementary tasks) and group decisions (in varying degrees of decentralization) became key points in an 'adapted' organization theory (see further this Handbook, ch. 4.9).

The insights of the group dynamics school also laid the foundations to the 'planning of change' approach which was outlined in the fifties (Bennis et al., 1971). By studying the phenomenon of resistance to change, especially technical-organizational changes, attention shifts from 'empirical-rational' to re-educative strategies of change (Chin, 1971). Resistance to change is not based on a lack of knowledge and insight, but on a non-adaptive mentality and attitude. It is not so much information and transfer of knowledge but rather involvement with and participation in (the design of) the process of change which increase the chance of an alternation in behavior and attitude. This is an important germ cell for later thought on organizational development (see also this Handbook, ch. 4.4).

The themes handled in this paragraph are relevant for the central problem of this chapter: the development in social science thought on the connection of technological and social factors at organization level.

In the period around the fifties a number of red threads are outlined which—with all the shifts in concepts and terminology—are recognizable in present-day thought. These red threads are:
—the question of integration of person and organization. In other words, the 'joint optimization' of productivity, adaptive capacity etc., and personal development, is the chief theme;
—the organizational structure and the system of management and consultation are simultaneous and connected optimization key variables, because they determine the content and context of the work-task and -role;
—decisions on organizing the work are based on values and attitudes, with regard to the relationship people-work. Cultural variables are very important;
—technological development—mechanization and automation—means a line of fracture: the organization of the work becomes a complex system, wherein technological and social factors are interweaved and integrated.

3. SEEDS OF INNOVATION

Organizational psychologists and consultants of the Tavistock Institute encountered a predominantly pre-mechanization stage (hand-got system) in the English coal mines (Trist and Bamforth, 1951). They characterized this situation as an equilibrium, a consequence of the demands posed by technique and situation (underground coal-getting) and the psycho-social characteristics of the task-system. The task-system consisted of very small groups two to five men), working at the coal-face (relatively thick seams of one to two meters) and consisting of all-round miners who had mastered the full breadth of tasks (hewing, boring, propping etc.) through many years of experience.

Such a small work group performed the complete cycle of tasks on one shift. The group supervised itself. The group made a contract with management, concerning production goals, wages etc. The group selected its own workmates. The work tempo was determined by the group; this was possible because of the relatively short coal-faces worked by the groups. The important characteristics are: the wholeness of the work task, the multiplicity of the skills of the individual, and the self-selection of the group' (Trist and Bamforth, 1951). This characteristics formed a pattern which made possible a production organization on the basis of small responsible groups, who were employed in a 'joint undertaking' by a remote (above ground) aggregate management system. According to the researchers at Tavistock, this work structure was ideal because of the possibilities of adaptation to underground work situations (heavy physical work, effective communication in dangerous situations, variable production on account of unpredictability of barriers, impossibility of supervision on account of the many scattered small groups etc.).

With the introduction of mechanical cutters and transport systems (conveyors etc.), the technology of coal-getting increased very much in complexity. Mechanization made it possible to work very long coal-faces instead of a series of short ones. In addition, it became economically feasible to work very thin seams of coal. During the fifties the 'longwall method' was introduced in English coal mines on economic grounds (as elsewhere generally). During the pre-mechanized period, the mine as a legal-economic unit indeed was very large, but the production itself was carried out on a very small scale in loosely coordinated districts of small coal-faces.

The size of the primary production unit increases sharply with mechanization. A 'factory organization' arose underground around the 'longwall' technology. A group of 40–50 men is responsible for a total cycle: preparations for the extraction and cutting the face, positioning the transport system and propping, extraction, and hauling the coal away. These activities take place in three shifts, under a shift-supervisor who reports to a supervisor of underground operations, etc. Between the above-ground management and staff (which increases in functions and number) and the work groups per shift emerges an intermediate organization of management, technical staff (more maintenance) and a co-ordinating staff.

With mechanization extensive changes in the scale of the production system and in the time-rhythm-structure of the work occur: the work is done in large groups on a long face (without much possibility for direct communication and contact), in a cycle of three shifts per 24 hours with each shift performing a part of the production cycle.

More and more specialized and interdependent 'occupational roles' come into existence (borer, cutter, gummer, belt-breaker, belt-builder, ripper, filler) and the production process forms a whole spread over three shifts.

The task interdependence becomes such that the production system is vulnerable, because it is dependent upon faultless task performance per step. The researchers at the Tavistock Institute typed the new organization of work as segmented. The worker is trained in one of the seven occupational roles already mentioned. This specialization is mirrored in the various wage systems (criteria: number of holes, number of yards, cubic meters of coal, weight of the coal on the conveyor) and in status differences, despite the common traditional background of the 'underground craft'. Also the extension of the production cycle over three shifts reinforces this tendency: the three groups never meet each other at work.

The primary work groups wherein the functions listed above are performed vary in social quality: pairs for boring holes and setting up conveyor belts, pairs for the mechanical cutting, a group of eight to ten rippers, and an aggregate of appr. 20 men working along hundreds of meters to extract and haul the coal away.

Given the great interdependence of the tasks, the integration of the total cycle group was a first requirement in the eyes of the researchers. In a social sense this group was far from forming a whole. This contradiction of the 'longwall' technology originated because 'the social organization is a simple reflection of the "job break-down"'. Because this latter is reintegrated into a technological whole by the task sequence, it does not follow that the differentiated role-groups concerned are also and thereby reintegrated into a social whole' (Trist and Bamforth, 1951).

The large scale and mechanized underground mass production system functioned economically and socially unsatisfactory. The Tavistock researchers considered the extensive differentiation and segmentation of the work structure to be the main cause of this. This is expressed in an extensive task specialization and in spreading the production cycle over a longer period. The economically unsatisfactory situation seemed to be due to the decreased adaptation capacity in unpredictable, physical working conditions and to the occurrence of production stoppages and disturbances, which become magnified as they are carried forward through the production cycles. The differences in productivity between the work groups (shifts) were sometimes considerable. In general the climate of consultation and negotiation between the work groups and management hardened. The work groups applied themselves primarily to performing their *component*-task and rejected responsibility for the production cycle as a whole.

Finally, it seemed that 'a norm of low productivity (per *component*-task, per shift) . . . the only adaptive method of handling, in the contingencies of the underground situation, a complicated, rigid, and large scale work system borrowed with too little modification from an engineering culture appropriate to the radically different situation of the factory' (Trist and Bamforth, 1951, p. 367).

Extensive study of the production system as a technological system brought the Tavistock researchers to the insight that the technological and social-organizational system, as sub-divisions of a 'system of activities', *influence each other and that with the same technology diverse social-organizational forms are possible.* This aspect of choice has turned out to be a very important basic idea in the further development of thought on the design of sociotechnical or production systems (Trist *et al.*, 1963).

This induced the researchers to replace the existing system—a complex formal organizational super-structure with a base of simple fractionated occupational roles (the 'longwall system')—with a simple organization built on complex occupational roles at the base. In this 'composite system', the interdependency of the occupational roles within one group addressed to one group-task is restored. The superiority of the 'composite system' lies, according to the Tavistock researchers, first of all in its greater capacity to solve problems and to adapt in regard to unpredictability and change which characterize task-situations. Consequently, the personal and social needs of the workers are met more. In contrast to the assumptions of Human Relations theory, this does not primarily mean workers' needs for friendship on the job (Emery and Trist, 1960). *Group development* produces important psychological effects (motivation, among others), when this process leads to a *system of occupational roles* whereby the workers, as a result of task-interdependence, become involved with each other and need each other in order to perform the task.

The most important insights to which the Tavistock studies have led are given in italics. (For a short description of the well-known Ahmedabad experiment in India (Rice, 1958), see this Handbook, ch. 4.8, section 2.1.) These insights could be considered as seeds of innovation for the further development of a theory on the connection of technological and social-organizational factors within (production) organizations.

4. THE SOCIOTECHNICAL SYSTEMS APPROACH: AN INITIAL CONCEPTUALIZATION

In the preceding section, sociotechnical thought was sketched from the viewpoint of the organization researcher and consultant. He encounters problems and bottlenecks and attempts to resolve them by redesigning the production organization on new principles. According to the sketch given, the sociotechnical systems approach above all emanates from the reflection on problems in practice. The confrontation of empirical findings (the coal mine studies) and several general theoretical studies led to an initial formulation in the form of a theory or conceptual framework.

It is difficult to check exactly how the interplay of induction and deduction went off in the case of the Tavistock researchers.

The initial conceptualization of the STS approach was concerned with the micro-level: the relationship of individual, task, work group and production process. An organization is dependent upon 'persons to operate its technology' (Emergy and Trist, 1960). Technology refers to activities or processes whereby inputs are turned into outputs and whereby material aids are also used (apparatus etc.). For an adequate performance of tasks, one or more of the following psychological conditions is valid. The performance of the task can satisfy in itself certain needs of the individual, being simultaneously both means and end. It also can be that the performance of the task bestows no satisfaction of needs, but is only a way of satisfying needs outside of the work situation in the strict sense (economic and status needs). In the STS approach the emphasis is placed especially on motivational forces which emerge from the task and task-situation itself. Task performance then is based on a 'task orientation' (Asch, 1952). In the literature on work motivation and work satisfaction, the stated distinction is recognized as the distinction between intrinsic and extrinsic motivation (Bruijns, 1972).

In the fifties, management consultants and organization experts assumed all too easily that work at the production level could become a source of psychological satisfaction. In the first instance, to achieve this, one used wages and stimuli of a material nature. Later, there also appeared in the foreground stimuli of a social character (relationships at work, friendly relations with management).

Scientific research on the situation in 'factory work' reported that in many cases there were feelings of alienation, 'dull contentment' and a high degree of satisfaction in general about the work situation (measured according to the so-called morale scale) in workers with low aspirations. It seemed that a situation whereby no alternatives could be experienced in the area of work satisfaction (in a deeper sense) led to resignation in many cases (Blauner, 1964).

In the STS approach the development of an *active task-orientation in the person* is emphasized. Important conditions for this are:
—The person should be able to regulate and co-determine the work process to a certain extent.
—The structural characteristics should be such that they motivate the person to performance and especially to continue the performance.

The room for decisions offered to the person by the organization in a task is a very important structural characteristic. In the earlier and current literature one encounters this notion expressed in various terms: autonomy (van Hoof, 1963), freedom at work (Schouten, 1974), influence or power (Crozier, 1965), job control (Mok, 1980) and capacity to regulate (de Sitter, 1980).

The following is an important 'leap' forward made by sociotechnical organization thought: In many production processes, it is not possible on economic grounds to give the 'occupants' of *individual functions* greater task responsibility and autonomy. Enlargement and enrichment of individual functions are drastically hampered in situations of mass production (assembly line) and mechanization, because of the adherence to Tayloristic principles of task formation.

Following the ideas of the Tavistock researchers, desiderata such as an increase in autonomy, broadening of knowledge and proficiency etc. can be better realized on the *work group level*. Consequently, there is more elbow-room for the development of task orientation on the social or group level. *The production process* (or a part of it), *and not an individual task, and the group as basic module of the organization, and not the individual person, must be integrated in a new manner.*

The basic notions of the STS approach are: interdependent tasks (= production process) and interdependent persons (= work group). This means a 'leap' in thought in relation to classical organization theory. It was a breakthrough in the individualistic, technical and bureaucratic thought on task and organization design (Herbst, 1976). This shift in thought to a greater coherence of workers and tasks marks the transition to system concepts which were worked out later (Miller and Rice, 1967).

The next important step in sociotechnical thought was the attribution of a *problem-solving or -adaptation capacity* to social work structures.

A division of labor based on interdependence of tasks and persons within a more autonomous social or group context is 'superior' to a bureaucratic form of organization, based on the principles of individual task positions and individual knowledge and competence (Herbst, 1976).

An organization is a 'system of activities' wherein inputs and outputs are transformed. Here, the problem of internal and external *regulation* in relation to the environment is given (Miller and Rice, 1967). This is the idea, in a nutshell, of a work structure as an *open sociotechnical system.*

The explanation for the greater adaptation capacity of an open sociotechnical system (see section 3, the underground work group in the 'composite system') in relation to a closed bureaucratic system (see section 3, the organization of work in the Tayloristic 'longwall' situation) lies especially in the attribute of equifinality. The internal structure of the work organization mentioned first is flexible and possesses a greater capacity to react to changing circumstances, i.e. has more alternatives at its disposal with which to react to abnormal situations. In unpredictable changes in the environment (e.g. disturbances, geological barriers in the coal mine situation), there are alternative ways to continue output. This is because a work organization which is based on interdependence of tasks and persons, resp. production process and group, is technologically and socially more heterogeneous and complex than bureaucratic organizations.

It is very characteristic of the STS approach that two criteria of *effectiveness* are emphasized:
—the individual and social task-orientation (motivation) of the participants;
—the 'regulating capacity' of the work system in relation to internal (operational) and external (transformational) disturbances and changes (van der Zwaan, 1973).

The simultaneous optimizing of these two dimensions of effectiveness—the psychosocial and the organizational—still forms in both theoretical and practical senses the key problem of organization theory.

5. THE SYSTEM THEORY FOUNDATION OF SOCIOTECHNICAL THOUGHT

5.1. General

The STS approach, as originated and developed in the fifties and sixties, has in a theoretical sense received strong impulses from general system theory (von Bertalanffy, 1969; Miller, 1955).

This general system theory was formulated from the foundations of the biological sciences and cybernetics. It held the promise of integration of the various disciplines concerned with the phenomenon of organization. Much later—in the seventies—this general system theory expanded to a scientific system-*tenet* (no theory!) in the service of an integration-oriented organization- and administration-science (de Leeuw, 1974).

It is to the merit of Katz and Kahn that they centrally placed 'the tenet of open (living) systems in a behavioral-scientific study of organizational activities' (1978). Within sociology, which already used it 'own' concept of social system for a long time, this tenet of open systems was only later assimilated in a scientific-theoretical sense (Luhmann, 1970; Buckley, 1967).

Views of systems, as developed by Katz and Kahn, reflect the attempt to make the problem of attuning person, organization and environment analyzable by using one coherent approach (see also this Handbook, ch. 4.2).

There was always general discontent with the 'machine' or 'construct' models of organization, which were especially favored by classical technical-economic oriented organization experts (Meij, 1965). In such views the reasoning begins at the top, with the goals as perceived and formulated by founders and designers (the managing elite). These goals were subsequently translated into sub-goals and sub-sub-goals etc. (Brech, 1957). Organizing is, therefore, this process and directing the means (technical and human) to the goals (finalize). Herewith, organization comes into existence as a *result* of organizing: a functional whole of activities that are directed to goals by means of coordination (van Doorn, 1956).

Space does not permit handling the various elements that are necessary for a general definition of systems (input, output, transformation, environment etc.) (for this, see this Handbook, ch. 4.2). Also, no further consideration will be given to a number of principles which have dominated general system theory for a long time. These principles refer to the survival tendency, to the dynamic equilibrium of system-and-environment, to growth and differentiation processes (Lievegoed, 1969) and the 'requisite variety' (Ashby, 1956).

5.2. Elaboration in the STS approach

In the STS approach the concept system is defined as a collection of a number of elements which exhibit relations in common. These elements—tasks, people, groups etc.—have characteristics or properties (technical, psychic, social). According to the goal, relations between the system elements can be established. In a sociotechnical analysis (handled in section 3) these elements are related to each other in terms of contexts (causal, functional). An organization is considered as a dynamic and empirical system. Within the STS approach organizations are concrete (not abstract) systems which exhibit observable changes.

Two consequences of general system theory have been elaborated in the STS approach in a convincing manner.

The first elaboration refers to the dynamic interaction between system (organization) and environment, and to the central concept of problem-solving or -adaptation capacity. Herewith, the STS approach at an early stage broke through the 'closed' system theory of the organization sciences. The post-Weberian organization sociology was imprisoned for a long time in the study of organizations with a one-sided emphasis on internal function as a closed system (Mouzelis, 1967; Thompson, 1967). The same is true of the empirical organization experts of the fifties and sixties (e.g. Newman et al., 1961). They were all closed approaches to the phenomenon organization: the exchange relations between organization and environment were neglected.

The second elaboration refers to the principle of equifinality, coined by Ashby (1956) in the law of the 'requisite variety'. The same end-situation can be reached from different start-situations, along a variety of transformations and operations (i.e. technologies, forms of organization etc.). This general theoretical framework lays the foundations for the important discovery of the 'organizational choice' idea within the STS approach (see section 4). Organization theory in the fifties was still based on the idea of the 'one best way of organizing'. It was searching for 'the' principles of organizing human cooperation, whereby the tracks of bureaucratic theory, scientific management (Taylorism) and Fayolism were followed.

5.3. Several theoretical objections

The biologically and cybernetics based general system theory does not arrive at a correct interpretation of the 'highly' complex system level, on which organizations (as social systems) must be situated (Boulding, 1956; van der Zwaan, 1973).

General principles valid at a 'lower' system level are more and more related to 'valuable analogies'. A system theory of complex social systems (organization) is currently considered as impossible and undesirable.

The impossibility lies in the fact that social behavior, resp. handling of individuals and groups, must be understood as action and interaction, that are aimed at the realization of meaning and significance (among other things, motives, interests). Within a psychological and sociological handling paradigm characteristics of structure (e.g. forms of organization) are considered as 'created' (perpetuated, changed) by action and interaction. These characteristics of structure also offer possibilities for actors. General system theory can lead to an irresponsible reification of organizational activities, whereby they come into existence as it were of themselves and separated from the actors (Silverman, 1970; Weick, 1969; van Dijck, 1972; de Sitter, 1974a). Internal and external processes of 'defining the situation' by individuals and groups, whereby motives and interests play a role, are of paramount importance in explaining organizational behavior. This is why the holistic character of a system theory must be considered as undesirable.

One gets the impression that in the STS approach there is indeed a question of a holistic 'design engineer theory', like that in classical organization theory. But there is an important difference: the psychosocial component, rather than technology, forms the point of departure for the organization-design. This holism requires the organizational goals, and the therein value judgements, to be considered as exogenous. Consensus of the participants on this is assumed to be present.

The neglect of processes of 'meaningfull' interaction and negotiation hinders a good view of the larger learning capacity which social systems have with respect to 'lower' living systems.

6. TECHNOLOGY AND ORGANIZATIONAL STRUCTURE: CONTINGENCY AND CHOICE

6.1. General

Empirical organization research—initiated above all by the Human Relations movement—limited itself in the sixties to the systematic collection of quantitative data on the behavior of individuals and groups in individual organizations. The organizational structure, (production)-technology, characteristics of the organization-environment were considered as marginal conditions, as constants (Kieser and Kubicek, 1978).

The comparative organization research after 1965 constitutes an important breakthrough in this respect. It addressed itself to the causes of structural differences of organizations, for example, exhibiting or not exhibiting bureaucratic characteristics (specialization, formalism, centralization etc.). For that purpose a large number of organizations were sometimes researched with standardized measuring instruments. The basic assumption was this: structural characteristics of organizations depend on the conditions under which these organizations must function. These conditions are collectively called 'context' or 'situational dependent'. This approach in organization sociology (especially in the U.S. and England) of the sixties and seventies has become known under the name of 'contingency approach' (see this Handbook, ch. 4.3).

The studies of the seventies can be grouped according to the main factor to which an explanatory value in relation to structual differences of organizations is ascribed:

—size or scale of organizations (measured according to the number of persons employed in it);

—environmental characteristics, and especially the frequency and nature of changes in markets and products.

In this connection there are the now well-known studies of Burns and Stalker (1961) and Lawrence and Lorsch (1969) (see this Handbook ch. 4.1). The first study showed that a bureaucratic model or regime (of management and organization) was efficient only under stable environmental conditions. Under conditions of fast technological change and high intensity of competition, forms of organization are required which make quick adaptation to changing external circumstances possible and promote product- or technology-innovation.

This form of organization is called 'organic'. Its characteristics are: free unprogrammed communication, also along lateral and diagonal (next to hierarchical) lines, working with task-positions in the group (rather than in the individuals) and others.

In the second study the environment was especially studied from the viewpoint of uncertainty, a result of dynamics and complexity (the number and interrelatedness of relevant environmental fields or 'task environments').

Also in studies of this type, the question had to do with the optimum 'fit' of environmental characteristics and organizational structure. This question led to questions like: 'Is the organizational structure differentiated in the most effective way' (in functional sub-units) in order to be able to handle relevant external uncertainty? Is the organization integrated in the correct manner? In this respect, does the organization use alternatives: hierarchy (bureaucratic), integrating roles, project approach in the work, etc.

A final category of studies and researches focussed on 'technology' as an important contingency factor. A common finding from various authors was that organizations show a high degree of bureaucratic (structural) characteristics to the extent that primary production processes are based on a routine technology.

6.2. Technology or the continuum predictable-unpredictable

In comparative organizational research (mostly carried out by organization sociologists), the factor or variable 'technology' is becoming more and more the object of theoretical and practical (i.e. design)-oriented research.

Organizational behavior could be partly explained from the nature of the technology (characteristics of the production processes).

An enlightening literature study by Van der Zwaan (1972) shows how difficult it is to make the concept technology explicit and to develop a consistent observation around this concept. An inventory of approaches of and on technology-connected concepts yields an unclear picture. The various approaches are sometimes encountered in one and the same author (see also this Handbook, ch. 4.1, section 1.3).

The following approaches are, in any case, of interest within the framework of this contribution:

—*Technology: the nature of the product.* Harvey arranges organizations according to the degree of variety and changeableness of the product which they produce. In a comparative sense Woodward (1965) designed a 'scale of technical complexity'. This put her in a position to investigate how organizational characteristics such as span capacity of lower management, the relation direct-indirect personnel etc., vary with technical complexity, operationalized in types like unit, batch, mass and process production.

—*Technology: the nature of the material to be processed.* An important enlargement of the concept 'technology' at organizational level is given by Perrow (1967). He attempted to construct four technological types by using two characteristics: uniformity and stability of the material, and the insight in the nature of the material (the kind of knowledge needed to, etc.). In other words: the number of exceptions and manner in which the solution is sought (knowledge of the cause-effect type, knowledge of the trial-and-error type, etc.). The enlargement of the concept made it possible to start speaking of 'material-processing' and 'people-processing' technologies. Afterwards, the concept was applied to processes of service (Damen, 1972).

In observations on technology as an explanatory factor for organizational behavior—otherwise than in the first period of sociotechnical system studies—the question has to do with the study of interrelationships at the organizational level, and not at the level of individuals and (small) groups. The organization sociologist interprets 'sociotechnically' broader and expands the problem to that of the connection between 'technology' and 'organizational characteristics'.

With all the apparent differentiation in concept use relating to technology and organization, most authors do seem to think along one scale or continuum: at the one extreme there is a highly standardized, technically complicated, highly mechanized or automated production- or service process; at the other extreme there is production- or service-process in which diversity of products and flexible manufacture with 'multipurpose' machines or functionaries (in the case of service) are the rule.

Rationalization is not possible because of insufficient knowledge and/or great variety of the problem (van der Zwaan, 1972). In the organization sociological approach to the connection of technological and organizational characteristics, the following concepts of organizational structure play an important role: formalization, hierarchy, specialization and division of labor, influence- and power relationships, and size or scale. The findings of the diverse studies cannot be treated in detail here. A few connections are:

—An increase in technical complexity leads to a greater number of hierarchical levels.

—An increase in technical complexity is accompanied with an increase in specialization and division of labor.

—With a decrease in technical complexity (a more flexible technology), communication will occur more along diagonal and horizontal lines, and will have less of the character of orders and instructions.

—Size is an important intervening variable in the relation between structure and technology.

6.3. Technology and organizational structure: a tautology

If one evaluates theory formation in relation to the problem of technology and organizational structure, three conclusions seem of interest: Most authors generally ascribe great explanatory significance to technology as an independent variable. This variable should, as situational factor, explain relatively much of the variance of structure differences of organizations. This still does not mean that the question has to do with a deterministic theory model.

The literature briefly treated here has great significance for the pragmatic oriented literature on the design of organizations. The former enables advice concerning organizational design to be founded on a contingency observation. There are no universal organization principles, but in proportion to the technology various principles are valid in designing (changing) organizations. The optimum 'fit' of technological and organizational characteristics can be achieved in various ways—in orientation of the organization to manageableness and effectiveness.

The literature on organization comes, therefore, to the same conclusion at the organizational level as the micro-oriented sociotechnical analyses: the notion that an 'organizational choice' is possible, that there are alternatives (Child, 1973).

However, the tenor of the literature handled above and other literature of the comparative type is conservative. Technologies which are based on routinization 'require' a bureaucratic (production) organization, without consideration for possible psychosocial dysfunctions in the area of individual and group behavior (Argyris, 1970).

A second evaluation of a more theoretical nature refers to the *slight systematics in technology-'theory'*. The astute analyses of Hickson led to the conclusion that the underlying dimension in the technology-theory is the same as that which lays the foundations to many organization typologies. It has to do with the dimension or key notion 'degree of specificity of role prescription' (Hickson, 1966). Typology of the stiff formalized bureaucratic organization with a predictable and static environment in contrast to the flexible 'loosely structured' organization in a dynamic environment. This dichotomy is worked out very well in the mechanistic and organic types (Burns and Stalker, 1961).

The key question, therefore, is: is there contamination between the concepts 'technology' and 'organizational structure'? Can they indeed be analytically distinguished?

The characteristic features of sociotechnical system theory (section 4) offered and offers a way out. Therein, the concept technology is applied to the total collection of possible operations in one organization or production system (van der Zwaan, 1972).

Organizations (or organizational departments) can be technologically typed according to the production process (many/few alternative operations). In this manner a dynamic conception of technology comes into existence: the production process refers to elements (people, machines, techniques) and their relation to one another. *This concept of technology based on system theory includes, therefore, the features of organizational structure.* In the formulations of Miller and Rice (1967), Van der Zwaan (1973) and De Sitter (1974a), there is consequently no need anymore for the concept of technology. The question of how does environmental variability determine the production process (technology + structure) becomes much more important. Attention in organization science to the problem 'technology as a determinative factor of organizational structure' has definitively shifted to the problem 'organizational processes in a variety of environmental conditions'.

6.4. Organizing: a choice-perspective

One last conclusion regarding the organization-sociological study of the connection of technology and organization concerns the study in depth of the *'organizational choice'*-notion. The static study of connections between organizational characteristics and situation characteristics (technology, environment) (Pugh *et al.*, 1969) has led to the idea that in designing organizations a configuration of characteristics should be chosen which 'fits' the situation (technology, environment etc.). Organizational structures could or should be developed in 'a process of fine tuning' (Child, 1973).

Sociologically speaking, comparative organization research does not make use of the fact that 'decision-making about organizations is not simply a matter of accommodation to operational contingencies. It is equally a political process into which other considerations, particularly the expression of power holders' values, also enter' (Child, 1972; van Dijck, 1975). This idea of 'organizational choice', worked out by Rice (1958) and Trist *et al.* (1963), marks a turn to a so-called politics or action paradigm in organization theory. The actors, their values (perceptions of interest), and strategies (in order to achieve goals) come to the foreground therein.

There is scope for selection from alternatives both in respect to environment (markets, products etc.) and in respect to the internal organizational system.

The internal and external power relationships influence these choice processes. In other words, the degree to which social, economic and psychosocial criteria will be valid in decision-making and choice processes depends on the relative power or influence at the disposal of the different groups in management, and at the operational level.

In our time, 'organizational choice' occurs more and more as a political and social problem, particularly in the area of task and organization design. The current discussion on the quality of the work forms a proof for this.

The sociological elaboration of the idea of 'organizational choice' (Child, 1972) brings to light how little comparative organization research was historically and socially involved during the sixties and part of the seventies. Kudera (1977) correctly typed these studies as 'Soziologie ohne Gesellschaft'. The same is true of the role which personality- and power-variables play in organizational functions (Kudera, 1977; Child, 1972).

7. THE ELABORATION OF THE SOCIOTECHNICAL APPROACH IN THE SEVENTIES

In the seventies, the STS approach appears in various forms. First of all there are authors such as Emery, Herbst and others, who applied the open sociotechnical system thought to the interaction of the 'total' organization with the social environment. An advance was made from the theoretical framework that was developed for micro-situations (production systems) to a macro-social consideration of the adaptation in the area of organization-and-environment. More than ever the question has to do with the 'total' organization, seen from the viewpoint of its goals, strategies, value systems and culture.

Further, there is a stream wherein three lines of thought flow together: organization development, a personnel policy oriented to promotion of motivation and individual development, and the sociotechnical designing of tasks and organizations (den Hertog, 1975) (see also this Handbook, ch. 4.8 and 4.9). This stream was developed via field experiments and change-projects, which is beginning to be designated as 'work structuring' (sometimes also in combination with work consultation). Following naturally from this, the notion 'quality of the work' became a central point in the second half of the seventies. This is a central concept for industrial sociology (van Dijck *et al.*, 1980) but equally for industrial psychology (de Galan *et al.*, 1980). The dominant element is the social-political thought on 'quality of the work' and 'full employment' which became spearheads of company policy in the eighties.

An elaboration of STS thought is of great significance in countries as The Netherlands, Norway and Sweden, where change and innovation in task- and organizational structure is being purposely carried out at the operational level in the perspective of company democratization. Democratization of work relationships must be based on a learning process which occurs in the company, according to representatives of this line, such as Thorsud; this can be effected by enriched task situations and renovated forms of work.

For the handling of the last two elaborations of the STS approach—work structuring and 'democracy at work'—the reader is referred to chapters 4.8 and 4.9 in this handbook. Here, the theme of the seventies, 'organizations in the social context', is handled further.

The consideration of 'the causal texture of organizational environments' has greatly influenced the organization-theoretical thought on the relationship between organization and environment (Emery and Trist, 1965; Terreberry, 1967). The essence is constituted by a typology of environmental conditions which was developed on analogy from biological system theory (von Bertalanffy, 1969). It is of particular significance that the environment of many organizations in a highly industrialized society changes from a 'disturbed-reactive' pattern to a pattern of 'turbulence'. With respect to each other, organizations can no longer act and react in an independent and autonomously strategic (analysis, planning etc.) manner. The environment of modern organizations exhibits more and more an autonomous dynamic, becomes thereby more complex, less predictable, sometimes even 'unknown', while many kinds of organizations become more entwined (relations, networks). In the organization theory of the seventies, the viewpoints of rate of exchange and uncertainty of the environment and the viewpoints of increasing and differentiating influence (use of power) from the environment acquire the significance of axioms (Thompson, 1967; Thompson and McEwen, 1958; Lawrence and Lorsch, 1969). The connection of technological and social factors in this theory formation plays no role of importance. The key problem is adaptation and innovation in the light of turbulence: markets, pressure groups, culture and political change. This demands of organizations strategies and transactions which are addressed to uncertainty and dependence.

Open system thought in the line of the STS approach is bound up in the general and rather abstract system theory of 'the' organization theory of Anglo-Saxon cut (van Dijck, 1975).

Open system theory à la Emery, Trist and others emphasizes relations and networks between organizations (van Gils, 1978).

Environmental turbulence 'requires some relationship between dissimilar organizations whose fates are basically positively correlated. This means relationships that will maximize co-operation ...' (Emery and Trist, 1965). In fact this is a linkage with the line in the sociology of the organization which runs from Weber through Selznick, Gouldner and others to the present-day observations on 'organizational values', socialization of organizations, the politicizing of the environment of organizations (Rhenman, 1973).

For all of that, authors like Emery and Trist still remain 'faithful' to the original observations on 'internal' innovation of task-orientations, communication and forms of organization. This is apparent from normative and engaged observations which are addressed to cultural change (Emery, 1977).

In the pregnant study, as far as the title is concerned, 'Futures we are in' three nonadaptive strategies of organizations in a situation of turbulence are handled. The first nonadaptive response is 'superficiality': the priority of material, economic and consumptive values. The second inadequate response is called 'segmentation': the turbulent environment is 'cut up' into surveyable parts which can be reacted to (market, union, law etc.). A total and coherent adaptation is not attempted.

The last undesired strategy is 'dissociation': people and groups retreat to private life. Social relations at work and in other spheres of life are avoided. Massification and isolation, hand in hand with a consumption autarky, mean gradual disintegration in a social sense. In contrast to these undesirable strategies of organizations—of people and groups in organizations—Emery presents an active scenario of organizations as 'ideal seeking systems'. The original core of the STS approach, the humanization of work and forms of work, is here clearly recognizable. Organizations can be 'ideal seeking systems' on condition that internal culture and structure are drastically modified; i.e., that there are learning processes required whereby work relationships, the quality of interaction and communication, and democratization of decision-making in organizations are actively developed. Emery's 'plea' is addressed to 'new' unbureaucratic work in which cooperation processes are central (Emery, 1977).

In an evaluation sense, it can be stated that such 'socially open' observations on organizations are broadly in step with current thought on the development of organizations. This almost generally accepted 'social' model of organization can be very difficult to realize in obstinate organizations. The explanation for this is based on a paradigm in which values and interests of actors are important elements. The theory on adaptation and innovation—also a core of the original STS approach—has almost become 'empty' in the system-oriented organization theory, but it acquires again a recognizable 'filling' with observations on values and ideals in relation to work and cooperation, and on power relationships and democratization.

Open sociotechnical organization thought did indeed depart from a completely different point, but finally—with other streams—arrived at the same destination: a socially and culturally critical consideration of organization. Finally, it must be said that studies such as those of Emery, Thorsrud, Herbst and others evoke sympathy because of their ethical and idealistic tone, for example, where 'learning' and cultural innovation by interactive and cooperative processes are concerned. They are still one-sided and simplified analyses, in which power and interest relationships in and around organizations are neglected. These two elements do appear in the analyses of organization sociologists (Silverman, 1970; Pettigrew, 1973; Mintzberg, 1978).

8. BALANCE AND PERSPECTIVE

From the foregoing it has become clear that the STS approach as a scientific strand, as a school within the social and organization sciences is not recognizable as such anymore. Insights and findings of sociotechnical studies and field experiments in the past decades have been gradually incorporated into the sociological and psychological approach to the phenomenon organization. Applied organization thought has especially been impregnated in a successful manner by sociotechnical studies. At present these can be retrieved from the application sphere and then under a different name: in the structural approach to non-attendance due to sickness, i.e. combatting the causes by (drastic) work structuring; in automating (processing) work groups, that is to say to lift the separation between planning and processing and thereby to enlarge the 'regulatory capacity' of the group (de Sitter, 1980); in the enlargement of the problem-solving capacity of organizations by 'organization-development processes'.

Under the influence of the STS approach important ideas have become commonsense in modern organization science. Production and service systems are now considered as 'total' phenomena. This is valid for the analysis and interpretation phase and surely for that of intervention and directed change.

The viewpoints of 'organizational choice' and of technology and technique as manipulable factors are commonly accepted.

The break with technological determinism is of great importance as a starting point for a social policy that will be characterized by humanization or enlargement of the quality of the work in organizations during the eighties.

On the basis of studies and field experiments of the seventies, many of which were carried out within the STS approach, it should be possible to build a more effective labor policy in the eighties. The balance of the practice of sociotechnical applications in the seventies was not entirely favorable.

There are still relatively few work situations in the industrial and administrative sectors of business that have been restructured and humanized from psychosocial viewpoints.

The directed choice of psychosocially attractive technological and organizational alternatives (e.g. decentralization by utilizing the new possibilities of computerization) still encounters resistance at management level. A similar approach assumes a gradual decrease in centralized (and academized) staff activities; it also involves a decrease in the number of supervisory functions.

Sociotechnical organization development has been marginal in many cases, due to interest-related implications at higher organization levels. Work structuring in the perspective of genuine organization innovation occurs only in a few large industrial organizations and then only in a few 'laboratories'. It is certainly true that the theme of employee participation in the seventies has demanded the greater part of the attention of managers, consultants and researchers. The problem of the quality of the work is defined by many primarily as the development of employee participation in formal indirect forms (works council) and in the direct form of 'work consultation'.

The explanation of the slight improvement in the area of humanization of the work must then be sought in the predominantly social scientific, that is to say monodisciplinary, approach to projects in the area of work structuring and organization development.

The impression exists that technical and organization experts as a rule are not involved in such projects. The almost proverbial difficult interdisciplinary cooperation forms a great obstacle in this area. Further, it can be noted that, hand in hand with the realization of democratization in companies, a sphere of ideological polarization around work structuring and work has come into being.

Works councils, unions, and sometimes also social advisers approach work structuring and work consultation with the perspective of 'democratization at the base'. Managers resist this and place (too) strong emphasis on the improvement of effectiveness and organizational control ('tool of management').

The application of micro-electronics in industrial and administrative production processes means a new phase of technological development for the industrial and commercial-service sectors. Automation and computerization will come more to the foreground also in the area of professional service (e.g. hospitals). This means that the question of creation and distribution of jobs will remain a priority in the decision-making on investments and innovation, cutbacks and reconstruction. The demands in the area of the quality of the work will definitely not be less ardent. Consequently, there are large problems for researchers and consultants in the areas of task design and organizational innovation, seen from the psychosocial or if you will the 'sociotechnical' point of view. A number of developments will promote a more principal (and less marginal) and a multi-disciplinary (and less one-sided social-scientific) approach to restructuring our work and our organizations. A large number of physically inconvenient work situations could be eliminated by automation.

The gradual switch of industry from mass production to small-scale and high technology production processes creates new possibilities of improving the quality of industrial work and of organizational innovation.

Computerization of information processing can support the restructuring of organizations according to the principles of decentralization.

Finally, managers and policy advisers more and more realize that stagnation in the area of innovation—in areas of many kinds—is largely caused by adhering to traditional principles of bureaucratic and Tayloristic organizing. In addition to the psychosocial and societal necessity, the pursuit of organizational innovation is beginning to be discerned also as a technical-economic necessity. The field of tension of appropriateness and legitimacy will be gradually transcended.

REFERENCES

Argyris, Chr. (1957), *Personality and organization*. New York.
Argyris, Chr. (1970), *Intervention in theory and method*. Reading (Mass.): Addison Wesley.
Asch, S. (1952), *Social psychology*. Englewood Cliffs.
Ashby, W. R. (1956), *Introduction to cybernetics*. New York.
Bennis, W. G., Benne, K., Chin, T. (1971), *The planning of change*. London/New York.
Bertalanffy, L. von (1969), The theory of open systems in physics and biology. In: Emery, F. E. (Ed.), *Systems thinking*.
Blauner, R. (1964), *Alienation and freedom*.
Boulding, K. E. (1956), General systems theory: The skeleton of science. *Management Science*, **2**, 197–208.
Brech, E. F. L. (1957), *Organization: The framework of management*. London.
Bruijns, R. A. C. (1972), *De invloed van werk en milieu op arbeidsmotivatie* [The influence of work and environment on work motivation]. Assen.
Buckley, W. (1967), *Sociology and modern systems theory*. Englewood Cliffs: Prentice-Hall.
Burns, T., Stalker, A. (1961), *The management of innovation*. London: Tavistock.
Caplow, Th. (1964), *Principles of organization*.
Child, J. (1972), Organizational structure, environment and performance: The role of strategic choice. *Sociology*, **6**, 1–22.
Child, J. (1973), Organization: A choice for man. In: Child, J. (Ed.), *Man and organization*. London, 243–257.
Chin, R. (1971), General strategies for effecting change in human systems. In: Bennis *et al.* (1971), 32–60.
Crozier, M. (1965), *Le système bureaucratique français*. Paris.
Crozier, M., Friedberg, E. (1978), *L'acteur et le système*. Paris.
Damen, P. (1972), *Technologie en organisatie* [Technology and organization]. Lochem.
Davis, L. E. (1972), Job design. London.
Dijck, J. J. J. van (1968), Motieven en waarde-oriëntaties in de arbeid [Motives and value

orientations in work]. In: Berting, J., Sitter, L. U. de (Eds.), *Arbeidsvoldoening en arbeidsbeleid* [Work satisfaction and labour policy]. Utrecht.

Dijck, J. J. J. van (1972), *Organisatie in verandering* [Organization in transition]. Rotterdam.

Dijck, J. J. J. van (1975), *Vermaatschappelijking van organisaties* [Organizations in society]. Leiden.

Dijck, J. J. J. van, *et al.* (1980), *Kwaliteit van de arbeid* [The quality of work]. Leiden.

Doorn, J. A. A. van (1956), *Sociologie van de organisatie* [Sociology of organizations]. Leiden.

Emery, F. E. (1977), *Futures we are in.* Leiden.

Emery, F. E., Trist, E. L. (1960), Sociotechnical systems. In: Churchman, C. W. (Ed.), *Management, science, models and techniques. Vol. 2.* Oxford: Pergamon, 83–97.

Emery, F. E., Trist, E. L. (1965), The causal texture of organizational environments. *Human Relations*, **18**, 21–32.

Fleishman, E. A., *et al.* (1955), *Leadership and supervision in industry.* Columbus (Ohio).

Friedmann, G. (1950), *Où va le travail humain?* Paris.

Friedmann, G. (1956), *Le travail en miettes.* Paris.

Galan, C. de, *et al.* (1980), *Humanisering van de arbeid* [Humanizing work].

Gellerman, S. W. (1963), *Motivation and productivity.* New York.

Gils, M. van (1978), De organisatie van organisaties [The organization of organizations]. *M & O* [Journal of Organization Science and Social Policy], **32**, 9–31.

Herbst, Ph. G. (1976), *Alternatives to hierarchy.* Leiden.

Hertog, J. F. den (1975), *Werkstructurering* [Job design]. Eindhoven.

Herzeberg, Fr., *et al.* (1959), *The motivation to work.* New York.

Hickson, D. J. (1966), A convergence on organization theory. *Administrative Science Quarterly*, **11**, 224–337.

Hoof, J. A. P. van (1963), *Autonomie en motivatie van arbeiders in industriële bedrijven* [Autonomy and motivation of workers in industry]. Nijmegen.

Hoof, J. A. P. van (1980), Kwaliteit van de arbeid: Een nieuwe combinatie van doelmatigheid en legitimiteit [The quality of work: A new combination of effectiveness and legitimacy]. In: van Dijck *et al.* (1980).

Jacques, E. (1956), *Measurement of responsibility.* London: Tavistock.

Kahn, R. L. (1960), Productivity and job satisfaction. *Personnel Psychology* (autumn).

Katz, D., Kahn, R. L. (1978), *The social psychology of organization.* 2nd ed. New York.

Katz, D., Macoley, N., Morse, N. C. (1950), *Supervision and morals in an office situation.* Chicago.

Kieser, A., Kubicek, H. (1978), *Organisationstheorien, II.* Stuttgart: Kohlhammer.

Kudera, S. (1977), Organisationsstrukturen und Gesellschaftsstrukturen. *Soziale Welt*, **28**, 16–38.

Lawrence, P., Lorsch, J. (1969), *Organization and environment.* Homewood (Ill.).

Leeuw, A. C. J. de (1974), *Systeemleer* [Systems theory]. Rotterdam.

Lievegoed, B. C. J. (1969), Organisatie in ontwikkeling: Zicht op de toekomst [Developing organizations: A book at the future]. Rotterdam: Lemniscaat.

Likert, R. F. (1958), Measuring organizational performance. *Harvard Business Review*, March/April.

Likert, R. F. (1959), A motivational approach to a modified theory of organization and management. In: Mottaire, A. (Ed.), *Modern organizations theory.* New York.

Likert, R. F. (1961), *New patterns of management.*

Likert, R. F. (1967), *The human organization.* New York: McGraw-Hill.

Luhmann, N. (1970), *Soziologische Aufklärung: Aufsätze zur Theorie sozialen Systeme.*

McClelland, D., *et al.* (1961), *The achieving society.* Princeton.

McClelland, P., et al. (1953), The achievement motive. New York.
McGregor, D. (1960), The human side of enterprise. New York.
Maslow, A. H. (1947), A theory of motivation. Psychological Review, 50.
Mayo, E. (1945), The social problems of an industrial civilization. Boston.
Mey, J. L. (1965), Lijnen in de ontwikkeling van de organisatiekunde [Lines in the development of organization Science]. In: Management van de automatisering [Management of automation]. Utrecht, 46–67.
Miller, E. J. Rice, A. K. (1967), Systems of organization. London: Tavistock.
Miller, J. C. (1955), The theory of living systems.
Miller, J. G. (1955), Toward a general theory for the behavioral sciences. American Psychologist, 10, 513–531.
Mintzberg, H. (1978), The structuring of organizations. Englewood Cliffs: Prentice Hall.
Mok, A. L. (1980), Arbeidstaakbeheersing. Kwalificatie en beroep [Job control. Qualifications and profession]. In: van Dijck et al. (1980).
Mouzelis, N. (1967), Organizations and bureaucracy. London.
Naville, P. (1956), La qualification du travail. Paris.
Newman, W. H. et al. (1961), The process of management. Englewood Cliffs.
Perrow, C. H. (1967), A framework for the comparative analysis of organizations. In: March, A.S.R. (Ed.), Handbook of organizations. Chicago.
Pettigrew, A. M. (1973), The politics of decision making. London.
Pugh, D. S., et al. (1969), The context of organizational structures. Administrative Science Quarterly, 14, 91–114.
Rathenau, M. (1979), De Commissie Micro-electronica [The Commission on Micro-electronics]. The Hague.
Rhenman, E. (1973), Organization theory for long-range planning. London.
Rice, A. K. (1958), Productivity and social organization. London: Tavistock.
Silverman, D. (1970), The theory of organization. London.
Schouten, J. (1974), Vrijheid in het werk [Freedom on the job]. Meppel: Boom.
Sitter, L. U. de (1974a), Een systeemtheoretich paradigma van een interacnetwerk [A systems-theoretical paradigm of an interaction network]. Mens en Maatschappij [Man and Society], 49.
Sitter, L. U. de (1974b), Sociotechniek [Sociotechnics]. Mens en Onderneming [Man and Enterprise], 2.
Sitter, L. U. de (1980), Kenmerken en functies van de kwaliteit van de arbeid [Characteristics and functions of the quality of work]. In: van Dijck et al. (1980).
Terreberry, Sh. (1967), The evolution of organizational environments. Administrative Science Quarterly, 12, no. 4.
Thompson, J. D. (1967), Organization in action. New York: McGraw-Hill.
Thompson, J. D., McEwen, X. X. (1958), Organizational goals and environment. Am. Soc. Rev., 23, 23–31.
Touraine, A. (1955), L'évolution technologique aux usines Renault. Paris.
Touraine, A. (1962), An historical theory in the evolution of industrial skills. In: Walkers, C. R. (Ed.), Modern technology and civilization. London.
Trist, E. L., Bamforth, K. W. (1951), Some social and psychological consequences of the longwall method of coalgetting. Human Relations, 4, no. 1.
Trist, E. L., Higgin, G. W., Murrau, H., A. B. (1963), Organizational choice. London: Tavistock.
Vroom, V. H. (1960), Some personality determinants of the effects of participation. Englewood Cliffs.
Vroom, V. H. (1964), Work and motivation. New York.
Weick, K. E. (1969), The social psychology of organizing. Reading (Mass.).

Woodward, J. (1965), *Industrial organization: Theory and practice*. London: Oxford University Press.

Zwaan, A. H. van der (1972), Technologie binnen de organisatiesociologie, een literatuurstudie [Technology in organizational sociology: A study of the literature]. *Mens en Maatschappij* [Man and Society], **47**, 35–53.

Zwaan, A. H. van der (1973), *Leveren en laten leveren* [To deliver and to have delivered]. Rotterdam.

4.6. Complex decision making at the organizational level

P. L. Koopman, J. W. Broekhuysen, and O. M. Meijn

1. INTRODUCTION

In the social sciences, terms used to denote complex concepts have their own cumulation of definitions, and this is equally true of the concept of decision making (Thompson, 1964; Mintzberg *et al.*, 1976; Harrison, 1981). In this chapter, decision making will be understood to be the process of thinking and acting that begins with a stimulus to action and leads to a choice of a course of action. The motivation to act lies in the more or less consciously perceived discrepancy between the existing and the desired states.

Thus formulated, it is obvious that decision making has many interfaces with other topics in work- and organizational psychology. A decision making process underlies each act, however inconsequential it may seem, although many such processes are automatic and we are only partly aware of them. We will restrict ourselves here to complex decision making at the organizational level. By this we mean decisions that have an impact on the perpetuation and continuity of an organization (Steiner, 1970; Child, 1972); the issues are central to firm policy (Hövels and Nas, 1976), occur fairly infrequently, and are of long duration: the organizational top predominates in such issues (Heller *et al.*, 1977; Koopman, 1980).

In the literature, decision making processes are often set out on a continuum, variously termed 'programmed vs. non-programmed' or routine vs. non-routine

Dr. P. L. Koopman, Vrije Universiteit, Vakgroep Arbeids- en Organisatiepsychologie, De Boelelaan 1081, 1081 HV AMSTERDAM.
Drs. J. W. Broekhuysen Drs. O. M. Meijn, and Philips N. V., Psychologische Dienst, Willemsstraat 20a, 5611 HD Eindhoven.

(Simon, 1960, 1977; March and Simon, 1958; McMillan, 1980), 'structured vs. unstructured' (Mintzberg et al., 1976), and 'well-structured vs. ill-structured' (MacCrimmon and Taylor, 1976; Ungson et al., 1981).

The decisions covered in this chapter are complex and show little structure. They are typically somewhat open-ended: the course towards a solution is undefined and obscure. The laternatives are unclear and can be specified only with difficulty. Uncertainty, complexity, and conflict are the most important factors contributing to the unstructured character of decision making (MacCrimmon and Taylor, 1976; Axelrod, 1978; Hage, 1980; Pfeffer, 1981).

By restricting ourselves to complex decision making at the organizational level or empirical research on this, the following fields are neglected:

—The many normative models, chiefly mathematical-economic ones (Cooper et al., 1958; Wagner, 1969; Mack, 1971; MacCrimmon and Taylor, 1976, give a recent survey). Such models are based on operations research, advanced statistical techniques, computer technology, theories on conflict management and management theories. From the latter, several strategies and instruments have been developed (see e.g. Kepner and Tregoe, 1965; MacCrimmon and Taylor, 1976; Feldman and Kanter, 1965).

—Decision making at the individual level (see Newell and Simon, 1972; Edwards and Tversky, 1967) or group level (Davis, 1969; Collins and Guetzkow, 1964; Huber, 1980), as well as laboratory experiments and 'game' theories (Siegel and Fouraker, 1960; Cross, 1969).

—Public administration (Synder and Paige, 1959; Gore, 1956; Pfiffner, 1960; Steinbrunner, 1974).

Our survey of the literature is arranged chronologically, and we will mention primarily new ideas, the 'added value', of each important author. Section 2 covers the period up to 1970, section 3 the more recent literature, which is something of a breakthrough. Section 4 is an attempt to relate current theories on complex decision making to the opportunities to apply this knowledge.

2. DEVELOPMENTS UNTIL 1970

The literature on decision making and, more in particular, on complex decision making in uncertain situations, only really got a good start in the sixties. At the beginning of this century, there was nothing in the way of a clear-cut 'decision making approach'. Publications by Barnard, and especially Simon and March, changed all this. The theory of Simon and March gave rise to many investigations and case studies which were the foundation of later theories and research.

2.1. Decision making in classic organization theory

In classic organization theory, the processes that play a role in decision making are not yet really seen as problematic. Classic thinking on decision making is typically rational and normative. Making a decision is a rational process and the person making the decision is acquainted with all the possible alternatives. On the basis of a conscious preference, he reaches a decision that maximizes his yield (Shubik, 1958; Churchman, 1961). Classic thinking can be called normative because managers often translated their practical experience into rules and regulations.

Barnard (1938) may be regarded as a pioneer in the behavioural science approach to decision making. He examined the assumptions the classic theory makes about human behaviour. He posits that biological and environmental determinants allow people very little freedom of choice. To overcome such limitations, the individual must co-operate, that is, he must accept a superordinate group goal. The individual continues his co-operation when the yields are reasonably commensurate to his contributions. The decision to continue co-operation is the result of the individual's assessment of the available alternatives and their consequences, and his own values and goals (cf. the decision to participate, and to produce, in March and Simon, 1958).

2.2. March and Simon

Although Barnard did not formulate his organization theory as a decision-making theory, he greatly influenced Simon and March. Herbert A. Simon is often regarded as the founder of the 'decision making approach' (Butler *et al.*, 1979; Mohr, 1982) and in 1978 he received the Nobel prize for his work in this field. He started by elaborating the ideas of Barnard: he, too, draws attention to the assumptions, at the very best incomplete, of classic economists.

Simon posits the 'administrative man', in contrast to the 'economic man', who rationally selects the best alternative from all those open to him and who is well acquainted with all of them (see Taylor, 1965). The 'administrative man' has only a restricted view of the possible alternatives, and can only consider a few of them at a time. Instead of the 'objective rationality' of the classic decision making theories, Simon introduces 'bounded rationality' (Simon, 1947, 1957).[1] The 'administrative man' chooses the alternative which gives him just enough satisfaction for his level of aspiration ('satisficing' rather than 'maximizing' behaviour).

In *Organizations* (1958), March and Simon develop these ideas further. They summarize various organization theories and test to what extent they take into account 'man as a problem solver'. Here, for the first time, decision making is central to organization theory, although their approach is very individually and psychologically oriented. They state that classic organization

[1]Simon devotes a good deal of his later work (1960, 1977) to computer-assisted decision making processes, chiefly through laboratory studies of individual decision making processes (see also Newell and Simon, 1972). Simon himself feels the results of this study are revolutionary. Mintzberg (1977) is much more skeptical of the practical applicability in organizations.

theory is incomplete and thus starts out from imprecise assumptions about human motives. It does not take into account the abundance of stimuli to which an individual is exposed and for which his information processing capacity is too limited. Therefore, an individual will work with a simplified model of reality ('his' definition of the situation). The elements in this definition are not objectively given but are the product of social and psychological processes at work in the person who decides and his environment. If he encounters a problem in his environment, an individual may react with a routine behaviour pattern, or, at the other end of the continuum, with 'programme' developing activities aimed at problem solving. A programme is a series of clearly defined behaviour patterns. Innovation processes in an organization are set in motion when the existing set of programmes (problem-solving patterns) no longer provides satisfactory solutions. This will occur when there is a discrepancy between the level of aspiration of the person who decides and his actual performance. But in looking for new programmes, the old reliable routine ones will generally be tried out first.

2.3. Reactions to March and Simon: empirical testing and adaptation

The sixties, in turn, were characterized by reactions to the theory of March and Simon, and adaptations of it. A great deal of such research was done at the Carnegie Institute of Technology where, apart from Simon and March, Cyert, Newell, Dill, and Trow were working. The support which was found for March and Simon's theory primarily came from a long series of case studies (cf. Feldman and Kanter, 1965).

Cyert et al. (1956) studied a computer purchase and found that the economic model had several hiatuses. First, often the problem must be defined before it is clear what solution must be sought. The alternatives are not known at once, but must also be looked for, as must the information on the consequences of each alternative. Also, choices are not made based on the basis of one criterion, but of several. Finally, often not the best alternative, but the alternative providing just enough satisfaction, is chosen.

A study by Cert et al. (1958) showed that expectations are formulated to justify a certain decision rather than that the decision is based on these expectations. Dufty and Taylor (1962) also found support for March and Simon's ideas on satisficing' rather than 'maximizing' decisions in a case of personnel transfer in a transport organization. The studies of Lindblom (1959, 1968) and Braybrook and Lindblom (1963) also point out discrepancies between the actual decision making process and that described in the classic models. The lack of clear goals during the decision making process is stressed. Complex decision making, according to Lindblom, is a long succession of small steps, an uncertain and irregular process of 'muddling through'. The choices participants make during this process are mainly strategy-oriented; again and again 'successive limited comparions' are made between various alternatives. Thus the goal gradually comes closer (this method of decision making is known in the literature as 'incrementalism'; see e.g. MacCrimmon and Taylor, 1976). Sometimes the goal only becomes clear during the decision making process itself. Sometimes the participants have different goals, but they can still reach some agreement on a strategy in which each individual's goals are partially realized.

Cyert and March (1963) were the first authors to take a closer look at power and conflict. They see an organization as a coalition of participants, each of whom brings in his own specific store of demands; in their view, decision making is a political process. They analyse the decison making process in organizations by means of a very detailed set of concepts and relationships. The central concepts are organizational goals, expectations, and choices. Each of these concepts consists of a number of aspects which are influenced by certain variables. Goals have two aspects: level of aspiration and of dimension. The level of aspiration is determined by past organizational goals, past achievement, and achievements of like organizations.

In order to describe the dynamic process of decision making, the authors identify four basic elements. In the first place, conflicts, occurring in the organization as a result of the variety of interests and preferences of the coalition partners are not 'really' solved, but reduced to acceptable proportions through various procedures ('quasi-resolution of conflict'). To ensure some degree of interdependence among partial solution, the organization applies the technique of satisficing (rather than maximizing) results and strives to pay successive attention to reaching apparently conflicting goals, with time acting as a buffer.

In the second place, organizations avoid direct confrontation with uncertainty ('uncertainty avoidance'). They try to obtain as much control as possible over the environment through agreements, contracts, and traditions. And they are continually adjusting their decision making procedures to environmental reactions (cf. also Allan, 1966).

Organizations set out searching for solutions to specific problems ('problemistic search'); once a problem has been solved, the search stops. The search takes place according to three rules: search close to the problem, look close to known alternatives, and try to blame the problem on organizationally weak departments. Lastly, organizations are capable of learning; that is, in the course of time, they are able to adapt themselves to altered circumstances (see also Alexis and Wilson, 1967).

Cyert and March indeed acknowledge the irrational aspects of organizational behaviour; nonetheless, they start from the assumption that organizations work along rational lines. An organization has a clear-cut hierarchy of priorities, it has a number of rules for choosing (avoid uncertainty, stick to the rules, and keep the rules simple) and it chooses so as to attain a maximum yield (as measured by the priority hierarchy). But persons who decide appear to be led by 'satisficing' rather than 'maximizing' decisions: attaining the level of aspiration is more important than a maximum yield. The authors illustrate their theory with a large number of cases in the field of economics.

Ansoff (1965) critizises the authors for basing their conclusions too much on operational decisions, and too little on strategic decisions. Carter (1971), heeding this criticism, studied three investment decisions and three take-over decisions. He concludes that the model of Cyert and March yields a useful description, although he makes a few small changes.

Pettigrew (1973) analyses the political processes which often underlie decision making. In one organization, he studied the decision about the purchase of a computer, using several methods. With this case he illustrates his premise that the yield of a decision making process cannot be explained satisfactorily without including the past, because it is primarily changes in the status and power position of groups that affect the process (see also Staw and Ross, 1978). Pettigrew emphasizes the 'social process' nature of decision making. He criticizes March and Simon and Cyert and March because they include too few power variables in their analysis, and have too little regard for the structural elements in decision making processes. Decision making is not merely a thought process by which means and goals are assessed, or where the possible choices are largely determined by the environment, but also a political process that mobilizes and balances various power groups. This view was further developed in later studies (MacMillan, 1978; Salaman, 1979; Bacharach and Lawler, 1980).

The Carnegie School's criticism of the classic decision making theories and the new ideas which arose from the case studies of the fifties and sixties are concisely summarized by Butler *et al.* (1979). 'In short, decision making is an activity which muddles through incrementally within bounded rationalites to merely satisficing and transient ends in a manner that need not be at all consistent or logical'.

3. RECENT RESEARCH

Until the early seventies, research on complex decision making processes was almost exclusively in American hands. It chiefly concerned case studies in industrial organizations, a large proportion of which included decisions on investments in electronic information processing equipment. In the seventies, studies were published that had a wider scope—they considered different types of organization and various sorts of decision making processes. The trend was towards constructing models and more comparative research. Emphasis shifted from description to explanation and prediction (Butler *et al.*, 1979).

The three prevailing issues in the research of this period are:
1. How do complex decision making processes take place?
2. What are the most important determinants for the manner in which decision making processes take place?

3. Under what conditions are different decision making strategies most successful?

The first question was the central issue for the Carnegie School. The last two questions were added fairly recently by European research groups. Entirely in keeping with the 'European research tradition' (Bass, 1978), there has been an increasing interest in the structural power distribution in organizations and the conflicts resulting from it.

We will discuss the research of Cohen et al. (1972) and Mintzberg et al. (1976), whose chief concern is to answer question one. The second question is predominant in the work of Butler et al. (1979), the third question is treated in the study by Heller et al. (1977).

3.1. The organization as a garbage can

In 1972, Cohen March, and Olsen published an article entitled 'A Garbage Can Model of Organizational Choice'. In this model, organizations are seen as 'organized anarchies', characterized by unclear or inconsistent goals, a technology enigmatic and incomprehensible to those who use it, and a highly fluctuating individual participation. Cohen et al. based their study primarily on decision making processes in universities, which they consider the prototype of the garbage can model (see also Cohen and March, 1974; March and Olsen, 1976). In the authors' view, organizations can be regarded as collections of (1) issues, (2) solutions, (3) participants, and (4) decision situations (i.e. occasions where the participants are expected to relate a problem to a solution, and in doing so to make a decision). 'From this point of view, an organization is a collection of choices looking for problems, issues and feelings looking for decision situations in which they might be aired, solutions looking for issues to which they might be the answer, and decision makers looking for work' (Cohen et al., 1972, p. 2).

The four elements are mixed together more or less arbitrarily in a garbage can, giving rise to utterly unpredictable combinations. There is no a priori time sequence. Solutions may come before problems, or issues and answers wait for a suitable opportunity for a decison. It will be obvious that here the order which was long taken for granted—'identification and definition of the problem, seeking solutions, considering the alternatives, and selection' (see e.g. Simon, 1947; Calkins, 1959; Cyert and MacCrimmon, 1968; Witte, 1972)—is turned around. 'Although it may be convenient to imagine that choice opportunities lead first to the generation of decision alternatives, then to an examination of their consequences, then to an evaluation of those consequences in terms of objectives, and finally to a decision, this type of model is often a poor description of what actually happens (Cohen et al., 1972, p. 2).

But the question remains to what extent these results can be generalized to other kinds of organizations. To call universities 'organized anarchies', collections of free and autonomous groups, 'loosely coupled systems' (Glasman, 1973; Weick, 1976) which are bound only by a common budget, may hold some water with regard to universities, but they would hardly seem fair qualifications of many other organizations (cf. Baldrige, 1971; Hills and Mahoney, 1978).

Terms such as 'garbage can model' and 'anarchy' can be misleading. The authors surely do not intend to assert that there is nothing systematic in the decision making of organizations. On the contrary, the point March and Olsen make is that the apparent anarchy has a structure and organization which is a reasonable, albeit not optimal, answer to the great environmental uncertainty the participants are in. But it is essential to the progress of the decision making process that the organization manages to have the participants pay sufficient attention to the problems (see also Cyert and MacCrimmon, 1968, p. 578). The participants generally have other things on their minds. It happens quite often that decision making takes place without explicit attention to the problem, or by simply postponing the problem. The authors see it as the task of organization management to co-ordinate the necessary attention and to steer it in the direction desired by the organization. It goes without saying that the garbage can model is a very long way from the rational models Simon was so opposed to.

3.2. A phase model for decision making

Attempts to divide decision making processes into chronological steps are not new. As early as 1910, Dewey formulated five phases in reflexive thinking (Mintzberg et al., 1976, p. 251). In the management literature many other examples can be found (Witte, 1972; Harrison, 1981; Bass, 1983). A typical example is the phase model of Brim et al. (1962, p. 9), who distinguish six steps: (1) identifying the problem; (2) search for information; (3) producing possible solutions; (4) evaluating the alternatives; (5) selection; (6) actual implementation of the decision. Another model is that of Simon (1947) containing the steps 'intelligence-design-choice-review'.

But until recently, there was little or no empirical evidence for a phased structure in decision making processes. This started to change with the studies by Witte (1972) and especially Mintzberg et al. (1976). Through document analysis, Witte studied 233 decision making processes, all of which concerned a computer purchase. His object was to find out in how far the phase theorem was supported by facts. He took the model of Brim et al. as his starting point, and divided each decision making process into ten equal time periods. He investigated whether step 2 (information gathering), step 3 (development of the alternatives), and step 4 (evaluation of alternatives) took place in the order expected, or at least occurred most frequently in this order. This expectation was not confirmed. Witte found that processes of information gathering were, in fact, the dominant activity in each interval. There were also general peaks of activity at the beginning and end of the entire decision making process.

Witte concludes: 'We believe that human beings cannot gather information without in some way simultaneously developing alternatives. They cannot avoid evaluating these activities immediately, and in doing this they are forced to a decision. This is a package of operations and the succession of these packages over time constitutes the total decision making process' (1972, p. 180). It should be mentioned that the analysis is based on documents available in the files of the computer suppliers, while this actual decision making process largely took place in the client's organization. A part of the process may thus have escaped the researcher's notice.

The study by Mintzberg *et al.* (1976) was much more rigorous in this respect. With the aid of 50 research teams, 25 decision making processes were analysed over a period of five years, using interviews with persons directly involved and additional observation and document analysis. Each decision making process was studied for three to five months. Mintzberg *et al.* also avoided the drawbacks to other studies (one-sidedness of subject—Witte, and of organization—Cohen *et al.*). The issues varied from the purchase of a new airplane to the dismissal of a radio reporter, and from the introduction of a new method of treatment in a hospital to the development of a new kind of beer. Most decision making processes involved investments in new machinery or a new product. Both production organizations and service organizations took part in the study; they came not only from the private sector but also from the public sector (Mintzberg *et al.*, 1976, p. 250). A study of the 25 'unstructured' decision making processes led to the discovery of a basic structure, described in 12 elements: three main phases, three supportive processes, and six dynamic factors. The three main phases—identification, development, selection—also show distinct sub-processes (see figure 1).

The *identification phase* chiefly consists of two activities: the recognition of a problem situation and a tentative diagnosis of it. A decision making process usually begins when a discrepancy between an actual and a desired situation is perceived (see also MacCrimmon and Taylor, 1976, p. 1399; Shull *et al.*, 1970). Whether such perception will also lead to the resolve to do something

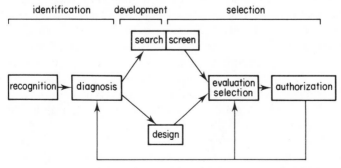

Figure 1. Simplified phase model of Mintzberg *et al.* (1976).

about it depends, partly, on the estimated likelihood of finding a satisfactory solution (Mintzberg *et al.*, 1976, p. 253; Cohen *et al.*, 1972). Then follows the diagnosis of the problem. This begins with an exploration of the usual information channels within the organization. The diagnosis is by no means always explicit; in a number of cases the official documents make no mention of it (Mintzberg *et al.*, 1976, p. 254). Other sources (e.g. Larson, 1962) also attach considerable importance to this phase for the further course of the decision making process. In connection with the decision making strategy to be followed an essential question is whether the issue should be viewed primarily as a 'logical' or as a 'political' problem (Thompson and Tuden, 1959; Thompson, 1964; Shull *et al.*, 1970; Veeren, 1978), in connection with the decision making strategy to be followed. Some authors emphasize the fact that values co-determine the definition of the issue (March and Simon, 1958; Koopman; 1980); the identification phase can in itself form a political process.

The *development phase*, which takes up the most time (see also Koopman, 1980), is described in terms of two basic processes: 'search' and 'design'. 'Search' applies to the exploration of already existing solutions. 'Design' refers to designing new solutions, or at least adjusting existing alternatives. The search takes place according to a hierarchy. First the most obvious, commonly recognized alternatives are considered. If this yields no satisfactory result, then more inaccessible alternatives are explored. This confirms what Cyert and March (1963, pp. 120–122) hypothesized on this point ('simple-mindedness' of the search process).

If no solutions are available, alternatives must be generated. Mostly this is approached in a very prosaic manner. Mintzberg *et al.* (1976, p. 256) report that usually only one solution is worked out, which would agree with the results of Snyder and Paige (1958). In a study involving decisions on foreign policy, these authors found that the person who had to make final decisions was faced with a lack of options. All he could do was affix his signature to a single suggestion. This information may throw new light on the actual distribution of power in complex decision making processes (Galbraith, 1967, pp. 67–70; Heller, 1976, p. 692). In Heller's terms: 'recommending decisions' sometimes offers more means to influence the process than 'deciding on recommendations'.

The *selection phase* in this model has three steps: 'screen', 'evaluation/choice', and 'authorization'. Screening is important if a large number of options is available. It is a rather superficial process whose main purpose is to rule out less acceptable alternatives. Later, after a more thorough evaluation, the most satisfactory one will be chosen. A similar step-by-step procedure is also described by Soelberg (1967). A good example is the procedure usually followed in personnel selection. The definitive choice is postponed as long as possible (Cyert and MacCrimmon, 1968, p. 580), but all kinds of sub-decisions are made. The evaluation/choice step can take three different forms:
—'judgment', that is, a choice made by one person;

—'bargaining', here a group of people with conflicting goals makes the choice;
—'analysis', evaluation on the basis of strictly factual information, done by specialists.

According to the study by Mintzberg *et al.* (1976), there is a general preference for judgment, probably because this is the quickest, easiest, and most relaxed way. The authors find little support for the analytical approach, so lauded in normative decision making literature (utility functions are drawn up on the grounds of pre-formulated criteria, maximum profitability determines the choice). The empirical studies of Soelberg (1967) and Carter (1971) had already pointed at this lack of evidence. Mintzberg *et al.* ascribe these results to two factors: (a) the use of several criteria which cannot really be compared, and (b) the vast amount of information to be processed (noted by Cyert *et al.* as early as 1956). The final step in the decision making process is official endorsement of the decision. With strategic decisions, this usually takes place in the top of the organization, or even outside it.

A number of supportive processes run parallel to the three main phases of decision making: decision making control processes, communication processes, and political processes (Mintzberg *et al.*, 1976, pp. 260–263). We mention them but cannot go into them here. The picture sketched so far is further complicated by a number of 'dynamic factors'. Interruptions, delays, and feedback circuits also regularly crop up in complex decision making processes. Strategic decison making is not a steady progression from one activity to the next, but a dynamic process with periods of acceleration and delay, 'comprehension cycles', in which the persons involved gradually get a better grasp of a complicated question, and 'failure cycles' in which they must return to previous phases if, for instance, conflicts stand in the way of an acceptable solution. The authors classify their 25 decision making processes into seven types, based on similar patterns in these interruptions and repetitions. A description of these types would go beyond the scope of this chapter.

3.3. Determinants of decision making

There is a growing amount of literature on the factors that determine the course of decision making processes, but most of it constitutes a normative approach (see MacCrimmon and Taylor, 1976). Only recently have more empirical studies become available. A few of the factors most frequently cited or studied are:
—traits of persons who make decisions (Taylor and Dunnette, 1974; MacCrimmon and Taylor, 1976);
—nature/content of the issue (Maier, 1963; Vroom and Yetton, 1973; Drenth *et al.*, 1979; Butler *et al.*, 1979; Hage, 1980);
—type of organization (Butler *et al.*, 1978; Abrahamson, 1977; Baldridge, 1971);

—power distribution within the organization and power influences from outside (Baumgartner *et al.*, 1976; Abell, 1975; Rus *et al.*, 1977; Pfeffer, 1978, 1981; Walsh *et al.*, 1981);

—amount of conflict among participants (Pettigrew, 1973; Stagner, 1969; Rus *et al.*, 1977; Hage, 1980; Bacharach and Lawler, 1980).

—type of environment (Duncan, 1972, 1973; Pfeffer *et al.*, 1976; Pfeffer and Salancik, 1978; Thompson, 1967; Galbraith, 1967; Axelsson and Rosenberg, 1978).

Below we will discuss the work of a group of researchers from the University of Bradford (England). Through interviews, content analysis of documents, and observation, they studied decision making processes in two very different organizations: a public utility and a university (Hickson *et al.*, 1978; Butler *et al.*, 1978). The authors assumed a systematic relationship between the method of decision making and certain environmental characteristics. This study, an extension of earlier work by the Aston group, was inspired by results of Burns and Stalker (1961) and Lawrence and Lorsch (1967), defining the relationship between organization structure and changes in the environment of the organization (Pugh *et al.*, 1968; Hickson *et al.*, 1971).

It will be obvious that the environments of two such organizations are very different. Decision making in the gas and electricity works is entirely dominated by the power of outside interest groups. Its prices are government-fixed, its sales area is established by law (monopoly in a defined region)—in short, the room for initiative is restricted. Company meetings are characterized by routine decisions, a 'calm placidity'; the authors even speak of a 'paralysed' decision making process. The situation at the university is different. Although it is also completely dependent on the government for funds and facilities, it has more freedom in allocating the money, within certain bounds. Decision making processes in this organization show more competition and conflict than those in the gas and electricity works (Butler *et al.*, 1978; Hickson *et al.*, 1978). These results agree with those of earlier studies by Baldridge (1971), Blau (1973), Pfeffer and Salancik (1974), and Weick (1976), in which universities are seen as 'loosely coupled systems' of interest groups. Baldridge distinguishes three types of organizations: the bureaucratic model (1), groups of professionals, organized on a corporate basis (2), and the political model (3). In the latter type, a coalition of interest groups, Baldrige places the university. Pfeffer and Salancik found that the power position of university departments (when controlled for research output, teaching load, etc.) correlated positively to the amount of the budget allocated to them.

The manner of decision making in the utility company fits better in the picture sketched by Pfeffer and Salancik in *The External Control of Organizations* (1978). The authors show that organizations are increasingly dependent on their environments for their resources. Organizational behaviour is controlled more and more by external power groups, which largely rules out risks and uncertainty in internal decision making. This view disagrees with that of Burns and Stalker (1961) and Lawrence and Lorsch (1967), who feel that it is the other way round: uncertainty and complexity more and more dominate the relationship to the environment, as a result of which participation and decentralization will increase.

On the basis of these results, the researchers developed a model to explain the differences between decision making processes both inside and outside organizations. They also indicated the most important variables and hypotheses (see figure 2).

The box 'process occurrence' contains the variables 'frequency' and 'regularity' of decision making processes. In the box 'process content' topics are ordered according to their consequences for the organization and according to the complexity and ambiguity of the required information. The box 'process action' contains the variables 'scrutiny' (to what extent is information sought during the decision making process) and 'centrality' (to what extent do lower levels in the organization participate in the process). 'Process performance' is the 'rapidity' and 'continuity' of the decison making process.

The 'routinization' hypotheses relate the frequency and regularity with which topics for decisions present themselves to the required behaviour patterns. The name is derived from the fact that frequency and regularity enable an organization to routinize, or organize, its activities. Frequent and regular topics lead to a more formalized search for information, and are taken care of at lower levels in the organization, because the top management cannot and must not always be concerned with routine issues. The 'efficiency' and 'participation' hypotheses relate the content of a decision to the required action. Subjects of import to the organization, for which the information to be collected is complex, ambiguous, and imprecise, must be thoroughly explored. They must be discussed and studied by all participants, and endorsed by the top of the organization. This is,

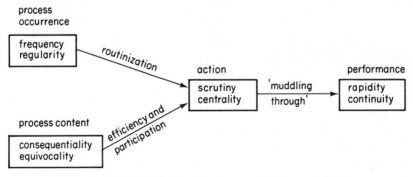

Figure 2. Model of the Bradford-group (Butler *et al.*, 1979).

according to the authors, the most efficient and participative method of decision making. The 'muddling through' hypotheses refer to the relationship between the method of decision making and the output criteria. The position of Butler *et al.* boils down to this: if (1) the search for information, needed to arrive at a decision, is insufficient and (2) the decision making process does not take place at all relevant hierarchical levels, then the decision making process will show slow progress and little continuity.

Applying this model to several well-known cases in the literature (Pettigrew, 1973; Olsen, 1976), Butler *et al.* (1979) found support for a few of these hypotheses. Another article by the Bradford group (Astley *et al.*, 1981) treats an amended version of the model, more particularly aimed at differences in decision making for different kinds of topics and in different kinds of organizations. A further discussion would go too far in this context. Moreover, the study has not yet been completed (see Wilson *et al.*, 1982).

3.4. A contingency model for decision making

To date, empirical studies of the conditions under which certain decision making strategies are most successful have been rare. As far as we know, Witte (1972) was one of the first to include a criterion (efficiency) in his study. Butler *et al.* (1979) included some output measures in their theoretical model, but so far this model has only been applied to a few cases.

The above question was studied much more extensively by the international research group 'Decision making in organizations' (DIO). The DIO project is a longitudinal field study of over 200 'strategic' and 'tactical' decision making processes in seven organisations in three different countries: England, Yugoslavia, and The Netherlands (Heller *et al.*, 1977; Rus *et al.*, 1977; Drenth *et al.*, 1979; Koopman, 1980; DIO, 1982; Koopman and Drenth, 1982). Figure 3 shows the search model and the most important variables.

Some assumptions at the outset of this project were:

—There is no such thing as 'one best way' in decision strategies; situational traits (contingency variables) helps to determine the relationship between the manner of decision making and the results of the decision making process.

—Decision making processes can be viewed as a flow of information, recommendations, tensions, etc.; various groups in the organization have access to this process at various points in time and in various ways, and can thus influence the outcome to a greater or lesser extent (Heller, 1976, pp. 650–695).

Partly following Mintzberg *et al.* (1976), four phases were distinguished in this project: starting-up, development, finalization, and implementation. For each phase a listing was made of the groups and organizational levels involved, and how decision making was realized (varying from receiving information to having complete control of a particular phase). This resulted in decision making profiles for each decision making process on an 'influence power continuum' (for the operationalizations of the variables, see Rus *et al.*, 1977, or—for the Dutch part of the study—Koopman, 1980). Several contingency variables were also included in the study, such as: influences from outside the organization ('meta power'), the formal internal power distribution ('status power'), conflicts and tensions during the decision making process, etc. (see figure 3). The most important criteria were: the extent to which the goals formulated were attained ('achievement'), the efficiency of the decision making process, and the satisfaction of the participants with the process and the outcome.

Analyses based on the 56 decision making processes studied in the Dutch part of the project showed that it is primarily the variables 'nature of the issue' (strategic vs. tactical), 'clarity of goals', and 'conflict' that affect the relationship between the power distribution in decision making and the dependent variables. 'Meta power' appears to have a more direct influence on the manner of decision making (Koopman, 1980; DIO, 1982). In an analysis based on 103 strategic decisions in the three countries, 'status power' appeared to be the primary determinant for the manner of decision making. The influence of each level varies greatly per phase of the decision making process (Drenth *et al.*, 1979; Koopman and Drenth, 1981). The phase model was reasonably workable, as it was for Mintzberg *et al.* The most frequent departures from the model were: (1) recurring interruptions, delays, and 'recycles', and (2) as a result, the somewhat obscure phase demarcations.

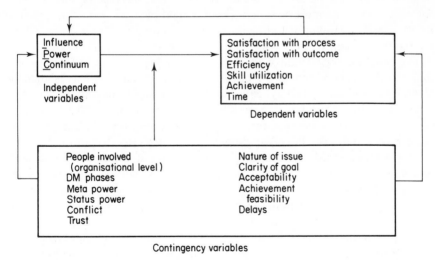

Figure 3. Model and variables in the DIO-project (Heller *et al.*, 1977).

4. FROM THEORY TO PRACTICE

In the previous sections we have seen how decision making theory has developed from a normative approach to an empirical phase theory or contingency theory. As we will briefly consider applications of the available knowledge, we wish to go into two points more thoroughly:
1. To what extent are we in a position to make normative statements on the basis of current research?
2. How can the means to participate in complex decision making processes be increased or improved and, at the same time, effectiveness be maintained or even improved?

As we will see, these questions are inextricably bound up with each other.

4.1. Are normative statements feasible?

A normative statement is one which precisely describes what mode of action must be followed under certain conditions in order to reach a certain goal. Converting empirical facts into normative statements is always risky: norms founded on actual practice are every bit as debatable as norms founded on a concept developed at a desk (Zeleny, 1981). This problem becomes the more pressing since the already scant empirical research has generally paid little or no attention to criteria. The course of decision making processes has been studied, but not a thought was given to their effects. Differences in the process itself can therefore not be systematically related to reasons for success.

Establishing a criterion is a problem in itself. Typical of the kind of decision making we are talking about is its uncertain course and results. The problems for which solutions must be sought can be called by many names and handled in many ways. Naming or coding problems or, rather, making a diagnosis, is a matter of some controversy. Two examples will make this clear.

The *first example* is in the field of product development. In order to survive, many firms must continually adapt their products to meet the clients' demand. Changes in legislation (safety, environment) also impel innovation. The development of new products is generally extremely expensive. The decision to do so is quite risky because future sales potentialities are highly uncertain: competitors' plans are largely unknown, trends are often hard to predict, etc.

This risk can be reduced considerably by splitting up the decision (of whether or not to develop a certain product) into a number of sub-decisions. For example, the process of development may be divided into the following phases: study, lay-out, construction, authorization, and production (Gründeman, 1977).

After each phase, using the additional information it has yielded, a decision is made as to whether or not to go on with the development. Such extra information could include: expected turnover figures, cost price, investments, initial costs, etc. The object of such a phased structure is to keep costs as low as possible during the first period of the project; the firm is only willing to make major investments when, on the basis of additional information, they are sufficiently sure about its profitability.

Generally the main participants are the top management, who decide after each phase whether to continue the project, plus a large number of various specialists, often brought together from several departments for the duration of the project.

Our *second example* is the decision to introduce a new system of consultation for an organization as a whole. Koopman (1980) studied the introduction of work consultation in three organizations. Some typical traits of such decision making processes are:

—Implementation depends strongly on the assent of those directly involved.
—The number of persons directly involved is very large: nearly everyone in the organization will be affected by the process.
—Not all groups involved are equally enthusiastic; some see existing rights and practices threatened, others feel uncertain because of different role expectations; all this can lead to internal tensions and boycott actions.
—Conflicts may occur in the relationship with the organized consultation of trade unions; there is apprehension that work consultation will disrupt the existing channels of consultation and negotiating; sometimes a trade union is not treated as a serious partner in discussions about organizing work consultation (see also van Gils, 1978).

Our first example (product development) can be characterized, in Veeren's (1978) terms, as a 'logical' issue, the second example (introducing work consultation) as a 'political' issue. With *logical* issues, the participants agree in general on the goals. The problem is how these goals can best be reached. 'Analytical processes' (March and Simon, 1958) are predominant in such decision making processes. The primary criterion here is the quality of the solution (Maier, 1963). Experts and specialists can do most of the work. With *political* issues, those involved disagree on the goals. Here the implementation of decisions requires a certain amount of commitment from those involved to the solution chosen. In this case, the primary criterion is acceptance of the solution (Maier, 1963). Such commitment can only be achieved if all parties are involved in the discussion at an early stage, and the solution chosen results from careful 'bargaining process' (March and Simon, 1958; Thompson, 1964).

We hope that these examples make clear that a decision making strategy must be geared to the *nature of the issue and the situation*. But they may be a little misleading, not only because it is unrealistic to make such a black-and-white division (most decision making processes have both 'logical' and 'political' aspects), but rather because of the tacit assumption that there are no differences of opinion on the diagnosis. The diagnostic phase itself is often a political process, precisely because its result will affect the choice of decision making strategy, in particular who will participate when, and how, in the decision

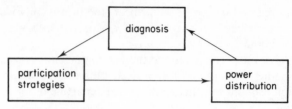

Figure 4. Relationship between power, diagnosis, and
participation strategies.

making process. So the existing power distribution in an organization indirectly
determines the choice of decision making strategy (see figure 4).

In this connection it is interesting to point out the 'traditions in problem
definition' cited in the literature. Already in 1958 March and Simon predicted
that top managers would tend to define nearly all problems cropping up in
organizations as logical problems which would simply have to be solved by
experts (specialists).

In many cases such a diagnosis is dubious. For instance, a businessman may
see a profitability problem as a logical issue, whereas workers may perceive it as
an issue of employment with a political nature (Veeren, 1978). The success of
initiatives towards co-determination in organizations may very well depend
largely on the extent to which employees succeed in bringing their viewpoint into
the bargaining process as early as the stage of problem definition. The fact that
the starting-up phase of complex decision making processes (where the diagnosis
takes place) takes much longer in Yugoslavian firms than in English and Dutch
organizations—the phase in which the influence of employees' representatives is
relatively high in Yugoslavia—lends credence to this (Rus et al., 1977).

What conclusions can we draw with regard to the question we posed at the start
of this section? Normative statements—as we have defined them—are not
possible, at least not yet. On the basis of empirical research, predictions can be
made as to what actions are likely to lead to certain results under certain
circumstances. But we have not yet progressed much further than illustrating the
complexity of decision making processes and describing some aspects and
relationships.

4.2. Complex decision making and participation

Another point to which we would like to direct our attention is how to increase
the means of participation in complex decision making, while maintaining its
effectiveness. We have already seen that the diagnosis of a problem (e.g. political
issues as logical issues; cf. the question of nuclear energy) may lead to the
exclusion of certain decision making strategies by the persons directly

responsible. But there are other points of tension between participation and complex decision making.

What are the possible means of formalization in the decision making process? An oft-heard objection to greater participation in complex decision making is that it causes delays and reduces efficacy. The underlying problems here are the factors 'time' and 'size of the organization' (Naschold, 1970, p. 62). Following Simon, Naschold distinguishes simultaneous and serial processes in decision making. All members of an organization can participate at the same time in simultaneous processes, such as voting; these take little time. Serial processes, however, such as group discussions, take a lot of time by comparison, and this alone puts serious restrictions on the nature and extent of participation by the members (p. 61). Or, translated into Mintzberg's phase model, the 'development phase' offers little latitude for participation by the many; opportunities are better in the 'finalization' phase if, for example, a vote were to be held on several alternatives. With a view to extending potential participation for the many, it would be interesting to know whether it is possible to conclude the starting-up phase, in which the diagnosis takes place, with some (little time-consuming) voting procedure. But here too it is primarily a question of political feasibility.

4.3. A last word

All in all, there is still a long way to go in research and theory formulation before we can effectively apply our knowledge to complex decision making in a well-founded manner. It is apparent from the literature that this field of research stands out for its complexity. The discussion on whether complex decision making processes do have a structure is a good illustration of this. Another example is the diagnosis of problems: when is something defined by whom as a problem, and how is that problem classed? It is, most of all, the research methods used since 1970 and the range of concepts developed in that period which put us in a better position to expose complex decision making processes through analytical description.

REFERENCES

Abell, P. (1975), *Organizations as bargaining and influence systems*. London: Heinemann.

Abrahamson, B. (1977), *Bureaucracy or participation: The logic of organization*. London: Sage Publications.

Alexis, M., Wilson, C. Z. (1967). *Organizational decision-making*. Englewood Cliffs: Prentice-Hall.

Allan, H. T. (1966), An empirical test of choice and decision postulates in the Cyert-March behavioral theory of the firm. *Adm. Sc. Quart.*, **11**, 405–413.

Ansoff, H. I. (1965), *Corporate strategy*. New York: McGraw-Hill.

Astley, W. G., Axelsson, R., Butler, R. J., Hickson, D. J., Wilson, D. C. (1981), *An arena theory of organizational decision processes*. Pre-publication draft.

Axelrod, R. (1978), *The structure of decision: The cognitive maps of political elites.* Princeton: Princeton University Press.

Axelsson, R., Rosenberg, L. (1978), Decision making and organizational turbulence. *Acta Sociologica*, **22**, 45–62.

Bacharach, S. B., Lawler, E. J. (1980), *Power and politics in organizations.* San Francisco: Jossey-Bass.

Baldridge, J. V. (1971), *Power and conflict in the university.* New York: Wiley.

Barnard, C. I. (1938), *Functions of the executive.* Cambridge: Harvard Univ. Press.

Bass, B. M. (1978), *Industrial democracy and participative management: U.S. and European perspectives.* 19th International Congress of Applied Psychology, Munich.

Bass, B. M. (1983), *Organizational decision making.* Homewood: Irwin.

Baumgartner, T., Burns, T., Buckley, W., Schuster, P. (1976), Meta power and the structuring of social hierarchies. In: Burns, T., Buckley, W., *Power and control.* London: Sage Publications.

Blau, P. M. (1973), *The organization of academic work.* New York: Wiley.

Braybrooke, D., Lindblom, C. (1963), *A strategy of decision: Policy evaluation as a social process.* New York: Free Press.

Brim, O. G., Glass, D. C., Larvin, D. E., Goodman, N. E. (1962), *Personality and decision processes.* Stanford, Calfornia.

Burns, T., Stalker, G. M. (1961), *The management of innovation.* London: Tavistock.

Butler, R. J., Astley, W. G., Hickson, D. J., Mallory, G., Wilson, D. C. (1979), Strategic decision making in organizations: Concepts of content and process. *International Studies of Management and Organization*, **9**, 5–36.

Butler, R. J., Hickson, D. J., Wilson, D. C., Axelsson, R. (1978), Organizational power, politicking, and paralysis. *Organization and Administrative Sciences*, **8**, 45–60.

Calkins, R. D. (1959), The decision process in administration. *Business Horizons*, **2**, 19–25.

Carter, E. E. (1971), The behavioral theory of the firm and top level corporate decisions. *Adm. Sc. Quart.*, **16**, 413–428.

Child, J. (1972), Organization structure and strategies of control: A replication of the Aston study. *Adm. Sc. Quart.*, **17**, 163–177.

Churchman, C. W. (1961), *Prediction and optimal decision.* Englewood Cliffs: Prentice-Hall.

Cohen, M. D., March, J. G. (1974), *Leadership and ambiguity: The American college president.* New York: McGraw-Hill.

Cohen, M. D., March, J. G., Olsen, J. P. (1972), A garbage can model of organizational choice. *Adm. Sc. Quart.*, **17**, 1–25.

Collins, B. E., Guetzkow, M. (1964), *A social psychology of group processes for decision making.* New York: Wiley.

Cooper, W. W., Hitch, C., Baumol, W. J., Shubik, M., Schelling, T. C., Valavanis, S., Elsberg, D. (1958), Economics and operations research: A symposium. *Review of Economics and Statistics*, **40**, 195–229.

Cross, J. E. (1969), *The economics of bargaining.* New York: Basic Books.

Cyert, R. M., MacCrimmon, K. R. (1968), Organizations. In: Lindzey, G., Aronson, E. (Eds.), *The handbook of social psychology*, **1**, Reading (Mass.): Addison-Wesley.

Cyert, R. M., March, J. G. (1963), *A behavioral theory of the firm.* Englewood Cliffs: Prentice-Hall.

Cyert, R. M., Simon, H. A., Trow, D. B. (1956), Observation of a business decision. *Journal of Business*, **29**, 237–248.

Cyert, R. M., Dill, W. R., March, J. G. (1958), The role of expectations in business decision-making. *Adm. Sc. Quart.*, **3**, 307–340.

Davis, J. H. (1969), *Group performance.* Reading (Mass.): Addison-Wesley.

DIO—International Research Group (1983), A contingency model of participative decision making. *Journal of Occupational Psychology*, 55.

Drenth P. J. D., Koopman, P. L., Rus, V., Odar, M., Heller, F. A., Brown, A. (1979), Participative decision making: A comparative study. *Industrial Relations*, 18, 295–309.

Dufty, N. F., Taylor, P. M. (1962), The implementation of a decision. *Adm. Sc. Quart.*, 7, 110–119.

Duncan, R. (1972), Characteristics of organizational environments and perceived uncertainty. *Adm. Sc. Quart.*, 17, 313–327.

Duncan, R. B. (1973), Multiple decision-making structures in adapting to environmental uncertainty. The impact on organizational effectiveness. *Human Relations*, 26, 273–292.

Edwards, W., Tversky, A. (Eds.) (1967), *Decision making*. Harmondsworth: Penguin Books.

Feldman, J., Kanter, H. E. (1965), Organizational decision making. In: March, J. G. (Ed.), *Handbook of organizations*. Chicago: Rand McNally.

Galbraith, K. (1967), *The new industrial state*. Boston: Houghton Mifflin.

Gils, M. R. van (1978), *Industriële demokratisering: Mythe of werkelijkheid?* [Industrial democracy: Myth or reality?]. Lunteren: NIP.

Glasman, R. B. (1973), Persistence and loose coupling in living systems. *Behavioral Science*, 18, 83–98.

Gore, W. J. (1956), Administrative decision making in federal field offices. *Public Administration Review*, 16, 281–291.

Gründeman, B. (1977), *Van idee tot produkt* [From idea to product]. Lecture held for DAF-Trucks, Eindhoven.

Hage, J. (1980), *Theories of organizations: Form, process and transformation*. New York: Wiley.

Harrison, E. F. (1981), *The managerial decision-making process*. Boston: Houghton Mifflin.

Heller, F. A. (1976), Decision processes: An analysis of power-sharing at senior organizational levels. In: Dubin, R. (Ed.), *Handbook of work, organization and society*. Chicago: Rand McNally.

Heller, F. A., Drenth, P. J. D., Koopman, P. L., Rus, V. (1977), A longitudinal study in participative decision-making. *Human Relations*, 30, 567–587.

Hickson, D. J., Butler, R. J., Axelsson, R., Wilson, D. (1978), Decisive coalitions. In: King, B. T., Streufert, S., Fiedler, F. E. (Eds.), *Managerial control and organizational democracy*. Washington: Winston, Wiley.

Hickson, D. J., Hinings. C. R., Lee, C. A. Schneck, R. E., Pennings, J. M. (1971), A strategic contingency theory of intra-organizational power. *Adm. Sc. Quart.*, 16, 216–229.

Hills, S., Mahoney, T. A. (1978), University budgets and organizational decision making. *Adm. Sc. Quart.*, 23, 454–465.

Hövels, B., Nas, P. (1976), *Ondernemingsraden en medezeggenschap* [Works councils and co-determination]. Nijmegen: Institute of Applied Psychology.

Huber, G. P. (1980), *Managerial decision making*. Glenview: Scott, Foresman and Company.

Kepner, C. H., Tregoe, B. B. (1965), *The rational manager; A systematic approach to problem solving and decision making*. New York: McGraw-Hill.

Kickert, W. J. M. (1979), *Organization of decision-making: A systems theoretical approach*. Amsterdam: North-Holland Publishing.

Koopman, P. L. (1980), *Besluitvorming in organisaties* [Decision-making in organizations]. Assen: Van Gorcum.

Koopman, P. L., Drenth, P. J. D. (1981), Conditions for successful participation. *Leadership and Organizational Development Journal*, 2, no. 4.

Koopman, P. L., Drenth, P. J. D. (1982), *Decision making and conflict management.* 20th Congress of Applied Psychology, Edinburgh.

Larson, R. L. (1962), How to define administrative problems. *Harvard Business Review,* **40**, 68–80.

Lawrence, P. R., Lorsch, J. W. (1967), *Organization and environment: Managing differentiation and integration.* Boston: Graduate School of Business, Harvard University.

Lindblom, Ch. E. (1959), The science of 'muddling through'. *Public Administration Review,* **19**, 79–99.

Lindblom, Ch. E. (1968), *The policy making process.* New York: Prentice Hall.

MacCrimmon, K. R., Taylor, R. N. (1976), Decision making and problem solving. In: Dunnette, M. D. (Ed.), *Handbook of industrial and organizational psychology.* Chicago: Rand McNally.

Mack, R. P. (1971), *Planning of uncertainty; Decision making in business and government administration.* New York: Wiley–Interscience.

McMillan, Ch. J. (1980), Qualitative models of organizational decision-making. *Journal of General Management,* **5**, 22–39.

MacMillan, I. C. (1978), *Strategy formulation: Political concepts.* New York: West Publishing.

Maier, N. R. F. (1963), *Problem-solving discussions and conferences.* New York, McGraw-Hill.

March, J. G., Olsen, J. P. (1976), *Ambiguity and choice in organizations.* Bergen, Norway: Universitetsforlaget.

March, J. G., Simon, H. A. (1958), *Organizations.* New York: Wiley.

Mintzberg, H. (1977), Review of 'The New Science of Management Decision' (H. A. Simon). *Adm. Sc. Quart.,* **22**, 342–351.

Mintzberg, H., Raisinghani, D., Théorêt, A. (1976), The structure of 'unstructured' decision processes. *Adm. Sc. Quart.,* **21**, 246–275.

Mohr, L. B. (1982), *Explaining organizational behavior.* San Francisco: Jossey-Bass.

Olsen, J. P. (1976), Choice in an organized anarchy. In: March, J. G., Olsen, J. P., *Ambiguity and choice in organizations.* Bergen, Norway: Universitetsforlaget.

Naschold, F. (1970), *Organisatie en demokratie* [Organization and democracy]. Utrecht: Het Spectrum.

Newell, A., Simon, H. A. (1972), *Human problem solving.* Englewood Cliffs, (N.J.): Prentice-Hall.

Pettigrew, A. M. (1973), *The politics of organizational decision-making.* London: Tavistock.

Pfeffer, J. (1978), *Organizational design.* Arlington Heights (Ill): AHM.

Pfeffer, J. (1981), *Power in organizations.* Boston: Pitman.

Pfeffer, J., Salancik, G. R. (1974), Organizational decision making as a political process: The case of a university budget. *Adm. Sc. Quart.,* **19**, 135–151.

Pfeffer, J., Salancik, G. R. (1978), *The external control of organizations.* New York: Harper and Row.

Pfeffer, J., Salancik, G. R., Leblebici, H. (1976), The effect of uncertainty on the use of social influence in organizational decision making. *Adm. Sc. Quart.,* **21**, 227–245.

Pfiffner, J. M. (1960), Administrative rationality. *Public Administration Review,* **20**, 125–132.

Pugh, D. S., Hickson, D. J., Hinings, C. R., Turner, C. (1968), Dimensions of organizational structure. *Adm. Sc. Quart.,* **13**, 65–105.

Rus, V., Odar, M., Heller, F. A., Brown, A., Drenth, P. J. D., Koopman, P. L., Wierdsma, A. F. M., Bus, F. B. M., Kruyswijk, A. J. (1977), *Participative decision making under conditions of uncertainty.* Second International Conference on Participation, Workers' Control and Self-Management, Paris, September 1977.

Salaman, G. (1979), *Work organizations: Resistance and control*. London: Longman.
Shubik, M. (1958), Studies and theories of decision-making. *Adm. Sc. Quart.*, **3**, 289–306.
Shull, F. A., Delbecq, A. L., Cummings, L. L. (1970), *Organizational decision making*. New York: McGraw-Hill.
Siegel, S., Fouraker, L. (1960), *Bargaining and group decision making*. New York: McMillan.
Simon, H. A. (1947), *Administrative behavior*. New York: Free Press.
Simon, H. A. (1957), *Models of man*. New York: Wiley.
Simon, H. A. (1960), *The new science of management decision*. New York: Harper and Row.
Simon, H. A. (1977), *The new science of management decision*. Rev. ed. Englewood Cliffs (N.J.): Prentice-Hall.
Synder, R. C., Paige, G. D. (1958), The United States decision to resist aggression in Korea: The application of an analytical scheme. *Adm. Sc. Quart.*, **3**, 341–378.
Soelberg, P. O. (1967), Unprogrammed decision making. *Industrial Management Review*, **00**, 19–29.
Stagner, R. (1969), Corporate decision making: An empirical study. *Journal of Applied Psychology*, **53**, 1–13.
Staw, B., Ross, J. (1978), Commitment to a policy decision: A multi-theoretical perspective. *Adm. Sc. Quart.*, **23**, 40–64.
Steinbruner, J. D. (1974), *The cybernetic theory of decision*. Princeton (N.J.): Princeton University Press.
Steiner, G. A. (1970), Strategic factors in business success. *Tijdschrift voor Efficiënt Directiebeleid* [Journal of Efficient Management], **40**, 434–441.
Taylor, D. (1965), Decision making and problem solving. In: March, J. G. (Ed.), *Handbook of organizations*. Chicago: Rand McNally.
Taylor, R. M., Dunnette, M. D. (1974), Relative contributions of decision-maker attributes to decision processes. *Org. Beh. and Hum. Perf.*, **12**, 286–298.
Thompson, J. D. (1964), Decision making, the firm, and the market. In: Cooper, W. W., Levitt, H. J., Shelly, II, M. W. (Eds.), *New perspectives in organizational research*. New York: Wiley, 334–348.
Thompson, J. D. (1967), *Organizations in action*. New York: McGraw-Hill.
Thompson, J. D., Tuden, A. (1959), Strategies, structures, and processes of organizational decision. In: Thompson, J. D., Hammond, P. B., Hawkes, R. W., Junker, B. H.,Tuden, A. (Eds.), *Comparative studies in administration*. Pittsburgh: University of Pittsburgh Press.
Ungson, G. R., Braunstein, D. N., Hall, P. D. (1981), Managerial information processing: A research review. *Adm. Sc. Quart.*, **26**, 116–134.
Veeren, H. (1978), *Influences of traditions in problem-typification on participative decision-making*. Paper to the Anglo-Dutch Conference on Occupational Psychology, Cambridge.
Vroom, V. H., Yetton, P. W. (1973), *Leadership and decision-making*. Pittsburgh: University of Pittsburgh Press.
Wagner, H. (1969), *Principles of operations research*. Englewood Cliffs (N.J.): Prentice-Hall.
Walsh, K., Hinings, B., Greenwood, R., Ranson, S. (1981), Power and advantage in organisations. *Organization Studies*, **2**, 131–152.
Weber, C. E., Peters, G. (1969), *Management action: Models of administrative decisions*. Scranton (Penn.): International Textbook Company.
Weick, K. E. (1976), Educational organizations as loosely coupled systems. *Adm. Sc. Quart.*, **21**, 1–19.
Wilson, D. C., Butler, R. J., Cray, D., Hickson, D. J., Mallory, G. R. (1982), The limits of trade union power in organisational decision making. *British Journal of Industrial Relations*, **20**, 322–341.

Witte, E. (1972), Field research on complex decision making processes: The phase theorem. *International Studies of Management and Organization*, **2**, 156–182.

Zeleny, M. (1981), Descriptive decision making and its applications. *Applications of Management Science*, **1**, 327–388.

Handbook of Work and Organizational Psychology
Edited by P. J. D. Drenth, H. Thierry, P. J. Willems and C. J. de Wolff
© 1984, John Wiley & Sons, Ltd.

4.7. The management of organizations

Paul M. Bagchus and Frans J. P. van Dooren

1. INTRODUCTION

In the foreword of this handbook the editors point out that the boundaries between work and organizational (W/O) psychology and other disciplines cannot always be clearly delineated. Some chapters in this handbook, therefore, have been provided by non-psychologists. Furthermore, the handbook includes several chapters about subjects that are not the exclusive province of organizational psychology. Indeed, the word 'management' does not even appear in many organizational psychology text-books, while most of the management text-books (and there are lots!) have been written by non-psychologists.

W/O psychology's contribution to the development of management theory is thus somewhat restricted. Nevertheless, a chapter on the subject has still been included in this handbook for two reasons. Firstly, because it is useful, and in fact essential, for anyone active in the field of W/O psychology to be aware of the problems involved in the management of organizations and of management principles and theories. Secondly, because the authors feel that W/O psychology can contribute to management theory.

Of both the phenomenon 'management' and the phenomenon 'organization' it can be said that they are complex and have many aspects. The choice of a satisfactory description of the concept *management* is complicated most of all by the fact that the term is used with a great many different meanings. Urwick

Prof. Dr. Paul M. Bagchus, Technische Hogeschool, Afdeling Bedrijfskunde, P.O. Box 513, 5600MB Eindhoven.
Prof. Dr. Frans J. P. van Dooren, Katholieke Hogeschool, Vakgroep Soc. en Org. Psychologie, Hogeschoollaan 225, 5037 GC TILBURG.

(1960), comparing some twenty definitions of management, noted that no less than 23 different meanings were associated with the concept. Becker (1968) differentiates four main groups of meanings of management, namely: (1) management as an activity, (2) management as a team in the enterprise, (3) management as a social category and (4) management as a body of knowledge.

Each of these main groups of meanings can be briefly elucidated as follows:

Management as an activity. In the classical literature on management, management activities are described in terms of functions. Various authors distinguish various management functions. Incidentally, the similarities between these function classifications are greater than the differences. Fayol (1916), for instance, singles out as functions: planning, organizing; commanding; coordinating and controlling. Gulick (1937) sums up the management activities in the acronym Posdcorb: Planning, Organizing; Staffing; Directing; Coordinating; Reporting; Budgeting. The essence of management as an activity is the execution and testing of policy.

Management as a team in the enterprise. According to this view the management-team is considered to consist of all those in their respective positions of authority. This description implies that the management category will exclude: specialists in an advisory function or those members of the organization who are higher up in the hierarchy but of whose functions managing is not a characteristic component. In practice this amounts to drawing a line at some level in the hierarchy. Office-holders above the line are considered to be managers, those below it are not. Although there are differences of opinion as to where, exactly, the line should be drawn, most authors tend to agree that the lowest level of command (that of the foreman) should not be classified as management. When 'management' is used in the truer sense of the word it refers to the highest level of command—top management.

Management as a social category. In this sense management is seen simply as a collection of practitioners of the same profession, which is typically exercised at the level of greatest responsibility for the directing of enterprises.

Management as a science. Management in this sense is seen as a body of knowledge, as the aggregate of normative principles and the sum total of scientific knowledge about management processes.

In this chapter, normative management principles and management theory will be given a critical review. Section 2 gives a brief overview of theories and approaches to management. In section 3 the basic functions of management are discussed. In section 4 attention is given to the actual activities of managers. Section 5 deals with the functional and interpersonal relationships between members of the most salient management team, namely, top management.

We shall now take a closer look at the relationship between management and organization and at the way in which the management of organizations is developing. Management and organization: the one cannot exist without the other. In every social structure displaying the characteristics of a work organization, management activities are being carried out. In fact, the phenomenon 'management' is localized in a formal organization. In many views of management a distinction is made between management and implementation. The manager is the one who plans and coordinates the implementation of tasks by others, but who does not, as a rule, undertake to actually carry out the task himself.

Within the management-as-a-team school various levels of management are often distinguished. Generally, three levels are differentiated: top-management, middle- and lower-management. The functions of management, already mentioned, are given a different emphasis at each of the three levels. For example: *planning* at top-management level consists of taking far-reaching strategic decisions about objectives, size and growth of the organization and the type of products or services it supplies. At middle-management level, planning amounts to drawing up budgets and schedules and developing procedures. At the lowest level of management planning means drawing up schedules and time-tables from a short-term perspective. In this chapter we shall restrict ourselves mainly to a discussion of the activities and relations of top management.

How does the management of organizations actually come into being? The division of work and hierarchy in organizations are closely linked. This linkage consists in the fact that the most radical form of division of labour—namely, that between design and direction on the one hand and implementation on the other—is interwoven with the hierarchic level. The general rule is: the higher up in the hierarchy the more direction and the less implementation.

The development of a work organization usually takes place along the following lines. Initially the work is split up, but each sub-task still contains both implementational and directional elements. The owner of a one-man carpenters/builders workshop hires an assistant; he himself continues to work alongside the other and they arrange for the execution of the work by mutual agreement. Before long they reach the stage of development that marks the beginning of the split between direction and implementation. The boss no longer accompanies his assistant on the job. He stays put, takes on new assignments, plans the activities, divides the labour and checks its execution. He allocates the work to his colleague who can then exercise relatively less influence on the way in which it is carried out.

This developmental process is denoted by the term 'vertical differentiation'; it is the process of division between directing and implementing along the vertical, hierarchical dimension of an organization. The very first developmental stage of an organization is almost invariably characterized by vertical differentiation. This development, however, very soon goes hand in hand with the process of horizontal differentiation. Within both the direction and the implementation of activities tasks are split up and joined together according to one or more principles. The best known and most widely applied principle of horizontal differentiation is that of division of labour according to function. As a firm develops, after some time, separate officers will start to occupy themselves with production, sales and finances, respectively. Officers performing activities within the same main function will be grouped together in one department. Besides by function, labour distribution (and hence the horizontal segmentation of organizations) can also be carried out by product, client, time or place.

This horizontal differentiation is not exclusive to implementation. Directing activities can also be split up according to one of these principles. Taylor (1911), for instance, had already developed the idea of 'functional foremanship': each implementational worker carried out his work under the supervision of several bosses, each of whom was responsible for different aspects of the same task. Horizontal differentiation leads to 'departmentalization': the splitting up of the organization into various sections or departments. In most cases, the departmental structure reflects horizontal differentiation according to function. For example, in a production firm separate departments can be found for design, purchasing, production, sales, research, finances and personnel.

This splitting up into functional departments often has dysfunctional consequences of varying degrees of severity. Each department develops its own objectives. These objectives may be so divergent that employees from the various departments are scarcely able to experience a sense of unity any longer. Still more serious is the situation in which the specific objectives of various departments clash with one another (as often happens in companies in the relations between the production and sales departments). Furthermore, differences in tasks and goals lead to differences in organizational structure and climate which, again, provide grounds for conflicts (Hazewinkel, this Handbook, ch. 4.3.).

In short, it is not only vertical differentiation but, especially, horizontal differentiation within organizations that can lead to problems of integration, that have to be solved by means of coordination. Coordination is one of the most important tasks of management. In the 'classical' form of organization, coordination occurs at the next level up in the hierarchy. In the product division of a large enterprise, composed of a number of functional departments, conflicts between, say, the sales manager and the production manager will have to be either anticipated and/or solved by the management of the product division. Where the organizational hierarchy proves to be inadequate to ensure integration and coordination, new organizational structures appear such as the matrix structure, which is essentially a fusion of product-based and function-based distribution of labour (see section 3.2.2).

Briefly summarized, a developing organization is characterized by vertical differentiation. It is the split between implementation and directing that arouses the need for a management to take charge of the directorial tasks. Horizontal differentiation creates the need for management with a (generally) functional specialization. Continuing horizontal differentiation leads to problems of integration and to the need for a management charged with primarily coordinating tasks.

2. MANAGEMENT THEORIES AND APPROACHES

The following is a brief summary of the different trends in management theory. The various approaches are so diverse, yet at the same time so mutually interwoven that certain authors (Koontz, 1961; Luthans, 1973) have, rightly, spoken of the 'jungle' of management theory.

CLASSICAL MANAGEMENT THEORY

At the beginning of this century a current of thinking developed that is now known as 'classical management theory' or 'Scientific Administration' (see Veen, this Handbook, ch. 4.2). The man considered to be the pioneer of this movement is Fayol (1916). It is characteristic of this trend that contributions to it almost invariably come from practising managers whose writings are based on their own experiences. Although the movement has been termed 'theory' it should be made clear that it completely lacks every characteristic of a scientific approach. A convergent set of guide-lines based on practical experience and laying claim to universal relevance—this is the most salient characteristic of the 'scientific administration' approach.

As regards content, two aspects can be differentiated within classical management theory. Firstly, various authors, following Fayol, have tried to identify the 'elements of administration', otherwise known as the functions of management. Section 1 has already listed the five functions distinguished by Fayol (1916) and the seven functions by Gulick (1937). Between the authors there are some differences of opinion concerning, for instance, the question of whether coordination is a basic function or rather the result of the correct fulfilment of other functions. The second aspect of the contribution is the formulation of a number of general guide-lines, usually referred to as 'management principles'. Fayol was the first to formulate, briefly and schematically, some 14 principles. The best known of these are the scalar principle (continuous hierarchical line from top to bottom), unity of command and subordination of individual interests to the general interest.

NEO-CLASSICAL APPROACHES

Classical theory persists in modern management literature in four different forms:

(a) A number of authors continues the traditional classical approach. Representatives of this are Davis (1951) and Urwick (1943). The latter is developing, on the basis of comparative study, a 'coherent and logical system' of 29 'principles of management'.

(b) Typical of the second form is the attempt to integrate the classical, analytical approach and empirical behavioural research. According to Newman and Summer (1961) empirical behavioural research is needed to test the assumptions of the classical theory. Within this approach, management literature is being expanded by new subjects such as participation, communication and motivation. This current opinion, however, continues to have a hybrid character; there is no question of a successful integration.

(c) Another branch is known as the comparative approach (cf. Dale, 1952, 1960). The universal guide-lines of the classical approach are rejected. Typical here is that comparative empirical research is carried out. In this research, various types of organization or organizations in different stages of development are compared with one another in order to obtain, in this way, a more precise insight into the major problems of management.

(d) Furthermore, Massie (1965) also distinguishes the so-called 'challenge-and-response' approach. Drucker (1954) is considered to be the main exponent of this. This movement is not concerned with developing a coherent theory but, rather, with emphasizing the fact that management is a 'practice'. Classical concepts are still used, but there is a highly pragmatic concentration on the search for answers to specific problems that habitually confront managers. 'Management by objectives' (MBO) is a good example of this approach.

QUANTITATIVE APPROACH

The term 'Management Science' refers to an approach to management that is mainly of an instrumental/methodological type. This approach, also called 'Operations Research', is not concerned with theory development or the formulation of practical principles for management but is characterized by its development of quantitative methods for solving the complex problems with which management is confronted.

The quantitative approach is almost exclusively the domain of mathematically trained engineers and economists. As there is scarcely any relation between 'Operations Research' and organizational psychology we have confined ourselves here to this brief description of the approach.

THE BEHAVIOURAL APPROACH

The behavioural approach to management problems was developed in the United States; its beginning can be traced back to the nineteen-thirties. Luthans (1976) points out that the economic depression and the rise of trade-unionism were responsible for the fact that human problems in the organization began to receive more attention.

It was the famous Hawthorne study (see Veen, this Handbook, ch. 4.2), in particular, that provided the real impetus to the development of behavioural insights into management. New ground was gained for the realization that informal patterns of relations occur, beside the formal organizational structure, and that the informal social relationships have considerable impact on the motivation and behaviour of the members of the organization. The current behavioural approach to management shows a great deal of overlap with the subject-matter of organizational psychology. It is often difficult, on the basis of content, to distinguish between a text-book with a typically behavioural approach to management and a text-book of organizational psychology.

THE SYSTEMS APPROACH

The application of the systems approach to management problems is relatively recent (e.g. Cleland and King, 1972). A general characteristic of the systems approach is the emphasis on the interconnections and mutual dependence between the parts in relation to the whole. The systems approach sees the organization as a conglomeration of interconnected and mutually dependent parts. No single subsystem can function effectively without the others. Actions taken within a given subsystem have repercussions for the environment of the organization. Changes in any one subsystem spill over in a chain of effects throughout the entire organization.

THE CONTINGENCY APPROACH

A special edition of the *Academy of Management Journal* (December, 1972) was devoted entirely to the application of systems theory to management. The majority of the authors underlined the positive aspects and possibilities of the systems approach, but also added a few critical marginal notes concerning, in particular, the highly abstract character of the systems approach. 'Everything is related to everything else, but how?' wrote Kast and Rosenzweig (1972). What these authors advocate is a 'new midrange level of analysis that falls somewhere between simplistic specific principles and complex, vague notions'. They use the term 'contingency view' to refer to this approach.

Contingency management specifies which management techniques will yield optimum results under which environmental conditions. Thus, a contingency relationship is always a functional relationship (in the form of 'if...then...') between environmental variables and management activities. For instance, *if* one is dealing with a mass production technology *then* a bureaucratic form of organization will produce the best results. The contingency way of thinking has been most clearly elaborated in 'contingency planning' (planning that takes unexpected events into account), in contingency models of leadership (Fiedler, 1967) and especially in contingency models of organizational structure (Burns and Stalker, 1961; Lawrence and Lorsch, 1967). Even such a confirmed advocate of the contingency approach as Luthans (1976) is forced to admit that 'there simply are very few clearly identifiable contingent relationships that have been empirically verified' (p. 53).

3. BASIC FUNCTIONS OF MANAGEMENT

Mintzberg (1980) mentions a number of different approaches to the description of the task of managers. The 'classical school' describes the activities of managers in terms of composite functions. Mintzberg (p. 10) expresses grave doubts as to the value of this approach. His main objection being that it is difficult, if not impossible, to fit the concrete, observed activities of managers into one of these categories of functions. Of all the other approaches the 'work activity school' is the one that (still according to Mintzberg) differs most in methodology from the classical approach. The method of this school consists of analyzing the manager's task by means of empirical methods. The techniques most used are the diary method, questionnaires, structured observation and 'activity sampling' (i.e. recording managers' activities at variable intervals). In our opinion Mintzberg is only partially correct. There is no question of having to select one particular approach at the cost of all the others. In fact, to gain insight into management processes it is even perfectly feasible to combine both types of approach. This is the line that will be taken in this chapter. The 'function' approach is an analytical one, while the 'activity sampling' method is empirical. The empirical method, however, has two disadvantages which can be compensated, to a certain extent, by the function approach. Firstly, it lacks a basis for grouping managers' activities into broader categories; secondly, although the method provides insight into how individual managers spend their time, it says nothing of management as a whole.

In this section the total management process is divided into four main functions: planning, organizing, directing and controlling. Planning means establishing objectives. Organizing is required to ensure that the work needed to achieve the objectives is carried out. Directing is necessary to stimulate the members of the organization into achieving the objectives. In the controlling phase the results actually achieved are compared with the objectives. A discussion of the content of these four functions gives some idea—albeit at a relatively high level of abstraction—of the total management task that must be carried out within the organization. In the next section the other approach will be followed: here we are concerned with—mainly on the basis of empirical research—which activity managers are engaged in and at what frequency.

3.1. Planning

3.1.1. GOALS

The entire management process is founded on goal-setting. Goals constitute an essential characteristic of every formal organization. March and Simon (1958) draw a distinction between 'operational' and 'non-operational' goals. Perrow (1969) makes a similar distinction between 'operative' and 'official' goals. An organization's official goals are usually set down in deliberately vague terms. These official goals say nothing about the priorities in the case of multiple goals nor about the unofficial goals being pursued by various groups in the organization. 'Operative' goals are those realized in practice by actual organizational behaviour.

The goals of an organization are not simply determined once and for all. As time goes by both the operative and the official organization goals may be subject to changes. In fact, within the organization there are a great many goals which, in many cases, may not be consistent with one another. These objectives range from the official, communal organizational goal to the concrete, specific objectives of the individual member of the organization. The various goals can be classified, by content, into four categories:

(a) *The provision of products or services.* Every organization creates an economic value in the form of products or services.

(b) *The survival and growth of the organization.* A much observed phenomenon is that the organization substitutes new goals for its original ones, in order to safeguard its continued existence. One could even go as far as to say that the goal of continued existence is of greater importance than the economic goal.

(c) *Goals of the organization's members.* Individuals and groups in the organization have their own goals which they attempt to realize through or in their activities within the organization. The need for promotion or for security are personal goals that must be respected by the organization in order to ensure its member's cooperation. This is one of the ways in which personal goals can influence the goals of the organization.

(d) *Social goals.* Much is heard about the increasing influence of the government on organizations. Legislation and government stipulations are largely responsible for the increasing degree to which social objectives are becoming interwoven with the objectives of the organization. A good example is the increasing importance attached to creating and preserving opportunities for work as an organizational goal.

The goals of organizations are always complex and multiple. This inevitably creates the problem of setting priorities among the goals. What relative importance should a police organization, for instance, attach to maintaining public law and order and tracking down criminals? The vaguer the formulation of a goal, the greater the risk that it will be distorted or 'adapted'. For goals that are more quantitatively determined this risk is smaller.

3.1.2. DECISION-MAKING

Decision-making is the keystone of every management theory. In classical management theory it is regarded as a rational process. Furthermore, decision-making theory is, like the entire body of classical management theory, highly normative. Kepner and Tregoe (1976) define a problem as a 'deviation from a standard of performance'. The 'standard of performance' can be seen as an objective of a department of the organization or of the total organization. So a decision can be viewed as making a choice from various possibilities in order to remove a deviation.

In the rational view of decision-making a number of phases are always distinguished. The first phase is that in which the decider becomes aware of a problem. The second phase is the establishment of criteria which the various methods of solving the problem will have to meet. The next phase is the generating of possible alternative solutions that meet the criteria. Immediately afterwards comes the assessment of the likely outcomes of each of these alternatives. The final step consists of making a choice from the alternatives. Simon (1957) criticized this principle of complete rationality. In his opinion it is impossible for deciders to consider all possible alternatives. According to him, deciders choose the alternative that satisfies them to a sufficient degree. Several studies confirmed the absence of strict rationality in decision-making. Decision-making is often a process of laborious searching and tiny steps forward (Lindblom, 1959) and often the objective only becomes clear in the course of the decision-making process (see also: Koopman *et al.*, this Handbook, ch. 4.6).

3.1.3. MAKING CONCRETE PLANS

A plan can be seen as programmed decision-making. A plan establishes which steps are to be taken—with a particular objective in mind—if certain circumstances should occur. An important distinction is that between once-only plans and permanent plans. Once-only plans can be subdivided into strategic plans and programs. A strategic plan entails establishing long-term objectives and choosing the ways and allocating the means of reaching these goals. Rapid technological developments compel the management of organizations to develop such long-term strategies. A program can be described as a phased series of planned activities within the bounds of the strategy envisaged. An example might be a program for product development on the basis of a new technology.

With respect to permanent plans, the following terms can be distinguished: (a) *Policies*. A policy is a principle or a series of mutually compatible principles with their associated prescriptions for action to provide for the attainment of specific organizational goals. An example of a policy is a ban on smoking in certain departments of a company. The policy principle formulated is that smoking is not allowed, plus a motivation of the ban. This policy is then worked out further in concrete pre- and proscriptions. (b) *Procedures*. A procedure is a series of steps to be taken in order to carry out a specific task. (c) *Norms*. A norm is considered here as a criterion against which actual performances are compared. Norms can be differentiated according to quality, quantity, time and costs.

3.2. Organizing

3.2.1. STATIC AND DYNAMIC ASPECTS OF ORGANIZATION

The implementation of plans at various levels calls for the next step in the management process: organizing. Organizing as a process is the establishment of work relationships between the organization's members. The designing of an organizational structure is an important instrument in the hands of the manager, and one by means of which he can influence the functioning of the organization. One often sees that change of management leads to alterations in the organization structure. When an organization has to react to different circumstances in the environment, adaptation is primarily sought by changing the organization's structure. The terms 'organizing as a process' and 'organizational structure' in the above, have been used indifferently. Some further explanation is now called for. What we are actually dealing with here is the difference between organizational structure, as a static characteristic of the organization, and organizing as a dynamic, in fact, a never-ending process within the organization. In the structure of the organization, horizontal and vertical relations between its members are established according to certain principles. Members of the organization encounter this organizational structure and are fitted into it on entry into the organization.

However, it would be wrong to assume that organizational structures are static and immutable. Certain authors (Weick, 1979, for instance) stress that members of the organization are continually influencing, changing and shaping organizational structures. Organizing is a dynamic and continuous process made possible by and at the same time making demands on the flexibility and creativity of the organization's members.

3.2.2. BASIC PRINCIPLES OF ORGANIZING

The design of organizations always boils down to the application of two principles. The first principle is the development of a hierarchy of functions. The second principle is the linking of these functions to one another in a number of formal, basic relationships.

A hierarchy of functions develops through the processes of vertical and horizontal differentiation. Vertical differentiation means the division of managerial and implementational work. Horizontal differentiation leads, at the top of the organization, to the grouping of tasks according to main functions (production, sales, finance). At lower levels functional splits take place in accordance with the principle that the most complex functions and those least resembling other functions should be separated from the rest. For example, within production product development and quality control both develop as independent functions. In this way a distinction arises between staff functions and line functions.

As a subsequent step, formal relationships must be established between the functions that have developed in this manner, namely relationships pertaining to responsibility, authority and accountability. Responsibility is the obligation laid on a member of the organization to fulfill a certain function, or carry out certain work. Responsibility is delegated by officials higher up in the hierarchy. If a boss delegates responsibility for certain tasks to a co-worker he creates between himself and that co-worker a relationship that is based on obligations. Delegation does not mean that the boss can 'liberate' himself from his original responsibility; it simply means that someone other than himself is doing the actual work. Delegation is a permanent dilemma and risk for the manager. Whatever he delegates, he still retains the final responsibility. So, in order to avoid running risks, he could try to delegate as little as possible. However, insufficient delegation may result in his becoming overworked. In many cases, lack of willingness or of courage to delegate may be interpreted as managerial incompetence.

Authority is derived from responsibility. Authority is the legal, institutionalized right to decide whether to commission others to do something or to do it oneself. Since it is derived from responsibility the distribution of responsibility and authority must follow the same general lines. It is not unusual to hear managers complaining that they have more responsibility than authority. Authority is essentially delegated in the same way as responsibility but many managers are less inclined to delegate authority than responsibility. In many cases, this lies at the root of the dilemma confronting bosses faced with the question of delegating responsibility.

Accountability is a logical sequel to authority. A person to whom authority has been delegated to fulfill obligations is accountable for the results of his actions.

3.2.3. ORGANIZING: RECENT DEVELOPMENTS

Organizational structures sometimes have dysfunctional consequences. As a rule these dysfunctions arise from three sources: (a) the dilemma between division of tasks and coordination; (b) lack of adaptation by the organization to its environment; (c) the organizational structure has caused the fundamental needs of the members to become frustrated. Each of these sources of dysfunction will be briefly explained below. Then an indication will be given of the answers that are being sought to these problems.

The dilemma between task-division and coordination. This dilemma is fundamental to the process of organizing. The processes of vertical and horizontal differentiation lead to an ever-increasing division of tasks within the organization. The more stringently this division of tasks is carried through, the more necessary, but also the more difficult it becomes to coordinate the efforts of the organization's members and departments and to ensure that they continue to direct their endeavours toward a common goal. There are four developments that may bring about a situation in which the various units of an organization find themselves in a situation of intergroup tension and conflicts which must be brought under control by means of coordination. First of all it is inherent in the nature of task division that different departments should have different objectives and that top management, moreover, expects the departments to attempt to achieve these divergent objectives. The sales manager aims for the greatest possible turnover while the works manager, particularly during an economic recession, will try to keep the level of costs as low as possible (Lorsch et al., 1978).

A second development is that the objectives of different departments may sometimes be in direct conflict with one another. The sales manager will be inclined to make considerable concessions to accommodate the specific demands of a major customer: the works manager will oppose this because conceding to these demands would mean higher costs.

A third development is that because of the difference in tasks performed in the various departments, their managers display a corresponding difference in time-perspective and in managerial style that can seriously hamper the effective integration and coordination of their contributions. The ways in which, for instance, a sales manager and the head of a research department see the same business problem can differ considerably (Lawrence and Lorsch, 1967). A recent development is that departments may come into conflict because they compete with one another to obtain scarce resources. In this way conflicts can arise between the departments of a university faculty about the distribution of research funds.

Increasing task-division, especially in the form of horizontal differentiation, makes increasing coordination necessary. How can the necessary coordination be achieved? According to Thompson (1967) and Galbraith (1973, 1977) the need for coordination is primarily determined by the need for information within and between departments. The more frequent the exchange of information between departments, the more extensive and complex is the coordination required. At least five different forms of coordination can be distinguished (Nadler et al., 1979). These forms differ from one another in the degree of comprehensiveness and intrusiveness of the coordination measures.

Coordination can be provided by: (a) rules and procedures, (b) hierarchic position, (c) communal planning, (d) formal information systems and (e) lateral relations, which provide coordination through, for example, special teams. Naturally these different forms can also occur in combination with one another. A combination of a and b occurs when the coordination between two departments required to collaborate closely (e.g. research and product development) is allocated to a special official in a position hierarchically higher than that of the heads of the two departments and when, furthermore, strict rules have been drawn up for the collaboration (for instance, the requirements to be met by plans and suggestions before research passes them on to product development). We shall not go into further detail here on the various forms of coordination, but shall restrict ourselves to the last two forms mentioned. If information can be formalized or is quantifiable then preference should be given to the development of management information systems. If information is informal, qualitative and difficult to quantify then lateral relations are the form of coordination. Management information systems, however, are mechanical by nature, while lateral relations are more organic (Tushman and Nadler, 1978).

Coordination by means of lateral relations can take very different forms. Coordination can be ensured by direct contact, whether formalized or not, between two members of different departments. A slightly more far-reaching solution is the creation of a coordination team consisting of representatives from the various departments. If coordination problems become greater, a solution often attempted is the appointment of an 'integrator' whose direct responsibility is the coordination of the activities of several departments. A product manager or a project manager are typical examples of this integrator's function. In highly complex organizations the most extreme form of coordination by lateral relations is chosen. This is the matrix structure solution (Davis and Lawrence, 1977). A simple example of a matrix structure is given in figure 1.

The matrix organization is a combination of two forms of horizontal differentiation: differentiation by function and by product. The managers at the intersection points of the matrix are always accountable to two bosses: a 'functional' boss and a 'product' boss. Integration of specialisms and strong lateral communication are typical characteristics of a matrix structure. The development of a matrix structure is the response to increasing complexity of the organization resulting from a very high degree of task division and thus a simultaneously increased need for coordination. We would like to point out, here, that an organizational form such as the matrix structure represents a possible solution to the dilemma of task division and coordination.

Poor adjustment of the organization to its environment. Two chapters of this Handbook (Veen: ch. 4.2; Hazewinkel, ch. 4.3) deal extensively with the so-

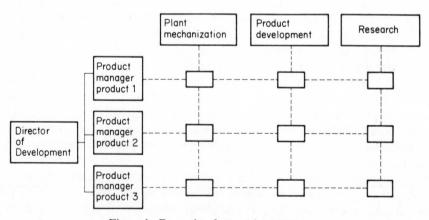

Figure 1. Example of a matrix structure.

called contingency theories. Underlying the contingency theories is the idea that the structure of the organization should be adapted to its particular type of environment. An environment with a high degree of uncertainty demands a pronounced degree of differentiation from the organization and, at the same time, strong integration (Lawrence and Lorsch, 1967). Newer versions of contingency theory do not confine themselves to environmental characteristics as determinants for the structure of the organization. By way of an example we would like to refer briefly to a model developed by Tushman and Nadler (1978). Their point of departure is that organizations can be seen as open, information-processing systems.

An organization's information-processing needs are determined by three groups of variables:
(a) Within each individual department: the degree of complexity and predictability and the degree of task-dependence of the members. The more complex the task and the greater the mutual task-dependence, the greater the uncertainty confronting the department and thus the greater the need for information.
(b) The degree to which the environment of a department can be described as being static or dynamic. The more dynamic the environment, the more uncertainty there is and thus, again, the greater the need for information.
(c) The degree of mutual dependence between departments. This inter-departmental dependence can take three different forms (Thompson, 1967): pooled dependence (each department provides its own contribution to the total result in a more or less autonomous fashion); sequential and reciprocal dependence. For a more detailed description of the various forms of dependence see Veen (this Handbook, ch. 4.1).

These forms of dependence are mentioned here in order of increasing complexity. The more complex the dependence relationship between departments, the greater the uncertainty that confronts them and the greater the need for information. Tushman and Nadler's proposition is that a certain level of information-processing requirement must correspond to a certain level of information-processing capacity. The organization's information-processing capacity can be influenced by the following variables:
(a) The way in which the departments are composed. Information exchange between members of the same department is easier than communication between departments. So the information-processing capacity can be enlarged by putting people who frequently have to communicate with one another in the same department.
(b) The type of relationships within departments. These can vary along the continuum mechanical-organic. An organic pattern of relationships is more capable of processing uncertainty than a mechanical one (van de Ven et al., 1976).
(c) Forms of coordination and control. As already mentioned, these can also be

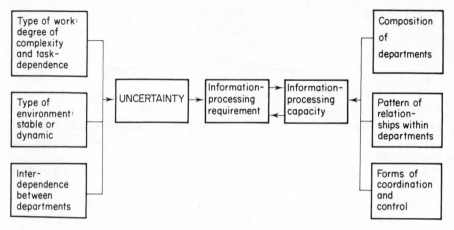

Figure 2. The contingency model of Tushman and Nadler (1978).

differentiated into more mechanical forms (management information systems) and more organic forms (several variations of lateral relations). Here again it is true to say that the information-processing capacity of the more organic forms is greater. Tushman and Nadler's model is reproduced in figure 2.

We have discussed this contingency model here because it is more comprehensive than the usual contingency models. It shows how dysfunctions in organizational structures can arise from several sources and hence be combated in various different ways.

The organizational structure has caused the members' fundamental needs to become frustrated. Even today our work organizations still display, to quite a considerable extent, the characteristics of the so-called 'classical' organization (van Assen and den Hertog, 1980). There is quite a large amount of work division. Implementation, thinking and deciding are strictly separated. Most organizational members have an implementing function which is designed in such a way that they only have a minimum of influence on the end result of their activities. The power structure is hierarchical and pyramidal in shape. Management is highly directive and controlling and leaves hardly any latitude for individual initiative and responsibility. Numerous authors (e.g. van Assen and den Hertog, 1980; de Sitter, 1980) already forcibly argued that the classical production-organization has negative consequences both for the effectiveness of the organization and for the well-being of its members. The fundamental human need for responsibility and self-actualization is simply not compatible with the robot structure of the traditional organization. If, nevertheless, people are compelled, for economic reasons, to work in such organizations it is inevitable that they should experience a sense of alienation (Blauner, 1969).

For a number of decades now attempts have been made to adapt the work in organizations to the needs and capacities of people. These attempts, often referred to by such terms as job enrichment, sociotechnical systems approach and job design are described in full elsewhere in this Handbook (van Assen and den Hertog, ch. 4.8). All of them aim to improve the quality of work. Gradually, however, a new realization has been gaining ground, namely, that improving the quality of work means changing the organization. Quality of work and quality of the organization are indissolubly linked (van Assen and den Hertod, 1980). The lesson to be learned from many job design experiments is that the content of the task is determined to a large degree by the type of manufacturing process, the systems of control within the organization and organizational design variables. Changing the task contents thus is only possible by changing these organizational variables. In fact, no task can be truly enriched if the traditional basic structures of the organization remain unchanged. Van Assen (1980) identifies three organization design variables that directly affect both the information and decision-making pattern and the task structure and hence, respectively, the latitude for joint consultation and participation and the latitude for work structuring. These organization design variables are: (a) the functional (or process-oriented) versus the product-oriented formation on the various aggregation levels of the organization; (b) the degree to which auxiliary and staff services are integrated with one another and with the production; and (c) the extent to which delegation of line authority occurs. The model developed by Van Assen is an example of the possibilities available for preventing the organizational structure from frustrating the fundamental needs of the organization's members.

3.3. Directing

When, in the planning process, goals have been established and when the organization necessary to attain those goals has been designed, the following step in the management cycle must be taken: directing. We have already defined directing as motivating and stimulating the members of the organization to make an effort to attain the organization's objectives.

The function of directing can be fulfilled, in principle, in three different ways:
(a) In the form of the exertion of personal influence by the manager; this is what is known as 'leadership'.
(b) In the form of formal systems within the organization designed to get employees involved in their work and raise the level of their work performance. Examples of such systems are: appraisal systems (see Drenth, this Handbook, (ch. 2.4); reward systems (see Thierry, this Handbook, ch. 4.11); training systems (see Coetsier, this Handbook, ch. 2.6); participation systems, such as joint consultation (see Koopman and Wierdsma, this Handbook, ch. 3.7).

(c) In the form of mainly group-orientated methods and techniques that are usually classed under the collective title 'Organization Development' (Bruining and Allegro, this Handbook, ch. 4.9).

From this brief overview of the various ways in which the management function 'directing' can be carried out it will be clear that this is the function that so intensively occupies the whole field of W/O psychology.

In this Handbook one or more chapters have been included on each of the methods listed for fulfilling this function (leadership, appraisal, reward, training, participation, organization development). Their inclusion is more or less a matter of course when one realizes that the essence of this particular management function is the stimulation of organizational members' motivation and performance. Since the various aspects mentioned will be dealt with in depth in other chapters of this Handbook we shall not go into them in any greater detail here.

3.4. Controlling

3.4.1. CONTROLLING AS A MANAGEMENT FUNCTION

Controlling is the last phase in the cycle of management functions. We can describe the management function of controlling as follows: the direction of organization activities in accordance with previously established plans with the aim of ensuring that organizational objectives are attained. The management of organizations is unthinkable without this control function: 'The barest essential of any organization is a control mechanism' (Boulding, 1963, p. 65).

3.4.2. ELEMENTS OF CONTROL SYSTEMS

Every control system must, of necessity, contain four particular elements (Porter *et al.*, 1975; Lawler, 1976; Thierauf *et al.*, 1977).

(a) *Norms*. In order to direct organizational activities it is necessary to be able to compare the results of these activities with previously determined norms. Norms may relate to quantity and quality of performance, to time and to costs.

(b) *Registration*. The behaviour of members of the organization must, in some way or another, be observed and registered if one is to be able to establish whether the result of their activities conforms to or deviates from the norms.

(c) *Comparison*. Registration is required so that, on completion of a cycle of activities, the results can actually be compared with the norms. A simple example is the comparison of an actual cycletime for assembly activities with the norm-times established on the basis of a time-and-motions study.

(d) *Corrective measures*. If, after comparison, deviations from the norm are diagnosed, there are basically two possible ways of taking corrective action. The first is that measures are taken to ensure that the result of activities conforms better to the norms. The second is that the norm itself is adjusted.

3.4.3. Typologies of control systems

There are a number of different ways in which control systems can be grouped together in categories.

(a) Control systems can be grouped on the basis of the type of norms being used. As already mentioned, norms of quality, quantity, time and costs can be distinguished.

(b) Control systems can also be differentiated according to the organizational function within which they are applied. Thus, financial, administrative and production control systems can be distinguished. An example of control within the financial function is a budget system; an example of control within the product function is a quality control system.

(c) Differentiation between control systems is also possible on the basis of the objectives for which the control system was created. At least two different objectives can be distinguished here: (1) the supply of information from the control system to management for the purpose of longer-term policy planning; and (2) the provision of direct performance-feedback to employees.

(d) A recent classification of control systems has been developed by Van de Ven (1979; van de Ven *et al.*, 1976). He distinguishes three different forms of control:

—*The systematized, impersonal form.* This form can be applied to relatively stable, unchanging tasks of a markedly routine nature. This form consists of: (1) a detailed description of the procedures to which the employee should adhere; (2) concrete and specific norms for each individual step in the cycle of task activities; and (3) built-in controls that allow for correction. An intensive care unit in a hospital is an example of systematized, impersonal control.

—*The discretionary form.* This form is found in connection with tasks that are relatively stable and unchanging but definitely not of a routine type. There are tasks in which variations and exceptions regularly crop up so that a variety of methods and procedures is required in order to solve the problems that occur in them. The discretionary form consists of: (1) a repertory of different strategies devised for the solution of the task problems most likely to occur; (2) a set of guide-lines for diagnosing situations and choosing the right strategy; and (3) a specification of the qualitative and quantitative output expected from the employee. A company salesman is a typical example of a function likely to be subject to discretionary control.

—*The developmental form.* This is seen in relation to tasks that are relatively new, difficult and complex and therefore require the opinion of a group and a group-search for solutions. This form consists of: (1) a global indication of objectives that must be attained within a certain period of time; (2) a number of norms and expectations about the behaviour and interaction between the members of the group. Tasks for which this form of control is seen are usually of short duration and call for intensive group collaboration in a shared process of creative problem-solving. Task groups drawn up to develop ideas for new products are an

HANDBOOK OF WORK AND ORGANIZATIONAL PSYCHOLOGY, VOLUME 2

example of this form of control. Van de Ven *et al.* (1976) show that the extent to which each of these forms of control is dominant depends on: (a) the degree of task uncertainty; (b) the degree of task dependence (that is, the degree to which employees are dependent on others for the execution of their task); and (c) the size of organizational units. The greater the task uncertainty and task dependence and the smaller the organizational units, the more the developmental form will dominate.

(e) Lawler and Rhode (1976) developed a typology of control systems that is based on the analogy between a control system and a cybernetic control loop (e.g. a thermostat). The typology classifies control systems according to the way in which the basic functions within the control process are carried out. The basic elements of a control system already mentioned are recognizable in this typology, which is reproduced in table 1.

A typology of control systems is important for two reasons. In the first place it is necessary to establish whether, and, if so, which independent variables affect the dominance of a certain type of control system. The type of technology, for instance, appears to be a powerful determinant of the type of control system (Rackham and Woodward, 1970; van de Ven *et al.*, 1976). In the second place, a typology is needed to establish the effects of a certain type of control system on the behaviour of the organization's members.

3.4.3. DYSFUNCTIONS OF CONTROL SYSTEMS

Controlling is a necessary management function. Nevertheless, it appears that control systems can, in themselves, lead to certain forms of dysfunctional behaviour among employees. Three types of dysfunction behaviour are usually mentioned in this connection (Lawler, 1976; Lawler and Rhode, 1976): (a) the

Table 1. Typology of control systems (from Lawler and Rhode, 1976).

REGISTRATION	A. complete—incomplete
	B. objective—subjective
	C. can be influenced by members of the organization—cannot be influenced
NORMS	D. who determines the norms?
	E. difficult—easy
COMPARISON	F. who compares what is registered with the norms?
COMMUNICATION	G. who gets the information (person concerned; boss?)
SPEED OF COMMUNICATION	H. immediate—delayed
FREQUENCY OF COMMUNICATION	I. at what intervals (hour, day, week?)
SORT OF ACTIVITY	J. important—unimportant
MOTIVATION	K. extrinsic—intrinsic

development of rigid, bureaucratic behaviour; (b) the provision of invalid data; and (c) direct opposition to the control system.

ad a) One speaks of rigid, bureaucratic behaviour whenever members of the organization to an extreme degree conform to certain controls, which means that although they succeed in satisfying the norm in question they do not succeed in making any contribution to the attainment of organizational goals. A good example of this is described by Blau (1955). Civil servants at an employment bureau had the job of acting as employment agency between companies and job-hunters. Management used certain statistical data (e.g. the number of interviews with job-hunters per civil servant) as control of their task performance. The result was that they tried to conduct as many interviews as possible, which led to wasting time and neglecting their real task as intermediary.

ad b) Two sorts of invalid data can be distinguished: data about what *can be done* and data about what *has been done*. An example of the first sort is the data provided by a group when it switches to 'restriction of output' (Coch and French, 1948; Whyte, 1955). Fearing that the rate will be cut, the group sets up an informal production norm that is lower than the company's official norm.

Majoration when estimates are being made is another example of providing incorrect information of the first type. For the provision of invalid information about what *has* been done employees may have different motives. One motive may be to conceal unsatisfactory performance. Sometimes a control system calls for historical data that are not available. This invites the provision of false information. When the system of reporting on research projects at university faculties calls for accounting afterwards, for the time spent on various research projects this amounts to little less than an open invitation to make unreliable and, often, false estimates.

ad c) The fact that members of the organization directly oppose a control system, a much observed phenomenon, may have various causes. In many cases, the introduction of (automated) control systems makes existing expertise superfluous. A good example here is the introduction of automated systems for the control of primary processes: production, stock-keeping and maintenance. This can be demonstrated even more clearly by the redundancy and reduction in content of functions resulting from the automation of control systems in the banking world. The introduction of (automated) control systems creates a new class of experts and disturbs the existing power relationships in an organization. This phenomenon is seen in all companies switching to automation. The automation department starts to constitute a new 'power' within the organization and one that often upsets the existing balance of power.

Control systems are often experienced as threatening because the result of activities is more fully and more accurately recorded. A good example is what is known as a 'human resources accounting system' (Likert and Bowers, 1969). The object of such a system is to record how a manager uses human resources. Naturally the introduction of a control system of this type will constitute a threat to managers who are little inclined to concern themselves with the personal interests of their staff, when they make decisions.

The degree to which the dysfunctions of control systems mentioned here occur depends on the way in which form is given to the basic characteristics (mentioned earlier) within a certain control system. Who establishes the norms, how data are recorded and how corrective measures are taken are all major determinants of the type and extent of any dysfunctional behaviour.

3.4.4. SELF-CONTROL AND INTRINSIC MOTIVATION

The idea underlying the so-called 'motivation-integration' approach (Veen, this Handbook, ch. 4.2) is that an attempt should be made to achieve greater congruence between the needs of people and the structure of the organization. According to McGregor's 'Theory Y' people in work situations are motivated by the need for responsibility and self-realization. The organization can comply with these needs by permitting as much autonomy as possible. Supervision and control, based on extrinsic motivation, are thus replaced by self-control based on intrinsic motivation. The sociotechnical systems approach (Susman, 1976), too, constantly advocates allowing as much autonomy as possible not, in this instance, to individuals but to groups. In those cases in which control based on extrinsic motivation is not feasible or would prove problematic, the alternative of self-control is worth considering.

4. ACTUAL ROLES AND TASKS OF MANAGERS

After describing management functions in the previous section we shall be concerned, in this section, with the question of what managers actually do, what their activities are and how they spend their time.

4.1. Methods for describing and analyzing managers' work

Studies of how managers spend their time are few and far between. Most of the existing research was carried out in the 50s and 60s. After 1970 practically no research of this kind was done anymore.

There are two possible reasons for this. Firstly, this type of work falls under the heading of 'descriptive research' and descriptive research simply does not have such a high status; it is less appealing to scientists than other forms of research such as hypothesis-testing (de Groot, 1961). A second possible explanation is suggested by Campbell et al. (1970). The results of those studies carried out are extremely complex. Complexity seldom arouses the interest of other researchers. 'The single elegant answer or simplified theory' (p. 97) would, paradoxically enough, be more likely to elicit further research.

Among the methods used to study the way in which managers spend their time, five different categories can be distinguished:

(a) *The diary method.* For this method, managers record all their activities during a certain period on precoded forms. On these they indicate how long the activity lasted, where it occurred and who participated, etc. Examples of the use of this method are the study by Carlson (1951) who had one French and nine Swedish managers record their activities for four weeks and that of Stewart (1967) who collected data on the activities of 160 British managers, again for a four-week period.

(b) *Activity-sampling.* This method requires no continuous recording but gets managers to record their activities at certain moments at varying intervals of time. In this way Kelly (1964) collected information about 1800 activities from four managers during a three-week period.

(c) *Observation.* The investigator observes and records the activities of the target managers. Ponder (1958) observed the activities of 24 managers for a total of 16 hours.

(d) *Questionnaire.* This method requires managers to fill out a questionnaire by indicating, for a number of activities, the degree to which these are an integral part of their task. An example of this method is the Executive Position Description Questionnaire (EPDQ), developed by Hemphill (1960) and consisting of 575 items.

(e) *Critical incidents.* This method, developed by Flanagan (1954), requires trained observers to provide more or less detailed descriptions of extremely appropriate *and* of extremely unappropriate task behaviour. Once a sufficiently large number of such 'incidents' has been collected this data base is used to obtain insight into the the essential characteristics of the function.

The methods listed here yield two kinds of results, which must be carefully distinguished from one another. The first category of results relates to more or less formal characteristics of the manager's work. Examples of such characteristics are: the number of hours per day and per week that a manager works, the people with whom he has contacts, the duration of the various activities and the type of communication channel(s) that he uses.

The second category of results relates to the content of the manager's work. These results provide an answer to the question of what a manager does (for example, solving a conflict between colleagues or negotiating with trade-unions about conditions of employment). The diary method yields relatively more results of the first category, the critical incidents and questionnaire methods yield relatively more information about the content of the managers' work. Both categories of results are discussed in the next two sections.

4.2. Characteristics of a manager's work

The typical characteristics of a manager's work can be grouped according to the following aspects (Mintzberg, 1980):

(a) *Amount of work and work tempo.* One of the most important characteristics of a manager's work is the demands that it makes on his time. Most managers have their minds almost constantly 'on the job', their working day is long and they also do a lot of work in the evenings. Their work is a continuous stream of activities that is seldom interrupted by a real break.

(b) *Pattern of activities.* Managers' activities are usually brief, fragmented and highly diversified. Important and less important activities alternate without any fixed pattern. Mintzberg (1968), in his study of five top managers, observed that fifty percent of all activities occupied less than nine minutes. Moreover, activities were characterized by frequent interruptions.

(c) *The relationship between action and reflection.* Managers appear to have a strong preference for action in their work; they prefer concrete, specific activities to 'vaguer' reflective ones and, furthermore, have an aversion to routine activities.

(d) *Communication.* Managers' work is characterized by frequent communication with others. The managers in Stewart's study (1967) spent almost 70% of their time on planned and impromptu discussions.

(e) *Network of contacts.* Managers almost invariably have at their disposal a complex network of relations outside their own organization. In the Mintzberg study managers appeared to spend 44% of their time on contacts outside the organization.

(f) *Managers' freedom to dispose of their own time.* From the various studies it appears that the manager himself only has a very limited say in how he spends his own time. Almost half of all the contacts in Mintzberg's study appeared not to have been initiated by the manager himself.

4.3. Content of the manager's work

It is mainly the investigators using the critical incidents method or the questionnaire method who have attempted to formulate the dimensions along which a manager's work can be described. There is one point on which the various studies all agree: the number of dimensions is still relatively large.

For instance, Flanagan (1954), on the basis of 3,000 critical incidents collected from Air Force officers, formulated no less than 54 descriptive categories, subdivided into some six main groups. Hemphill (1960) carried out a Q-factor analysis of the answers of 93 respondents to the 575 items of the EPDQ. He found ten different clusters each of which can be taken as a dimension on which to describe the work of the manager. Examples of the clusters are: 'supervision of work'; 'internal business control' and 'long-range planning'. The EPDQ can be used to determine the profile of a specific manager's function, on the basis of the ten dimensions. A disadvantage of such dimensional analyses is that there are so many dimensions and that the description of the dimensions is, in general, rather vague.

Another approach, that leads to more usable results, was followed by

Mintzberg (1980). Mintzberg observed the behaviour of managers and during the observation developed descriptive categories. The result of this is that Mintzberg describes the work of the manager in terms of ten roles, which can be grouped under three main headings: interpersonal roles, informational roles and decisional roles. Mintzberg's classification of roles is shown in figure 3.
The various roles can be briefly described as follows:

1. *Figurehead.* The manager, on the basis of his formal position, fulfils a number of mainly ceremonial and representative obligations. In Mintzberg's study (1975) managers appeared to spend an average of 12% of their time on activities of this kind.

2. *Leader.* In this role the manager is responsible for the work that the members of the organization carry out in his company or department. In this role he exerts personal influence on the members, determines the climate of the organization or department and motivates and stimulates his subordinates.

3. *Liaison.* In this role the manager is a link between organization and environment. Managers spend a large percentage of their time on contacts with colleagues outside the hierarchical line and usually have a network of contacts outside the organization.

4. *Monitor.* In this role the manager searches for and collects information about what is going on inside the organization and in the environment. He receives this information from very varied sources.

5. *Disseminator.* Much of the information he has collected he then disseminates within the organization.

6. *Spokesman.* In this role the manager disseminates information from the organization to the environment. This information can be given to those directly

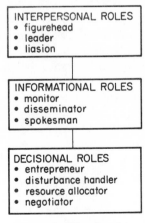

Figure 3. Mintzberg's classification of a manager's roles.

involved, such as shareholders or the Supervisory Board or to the general public.

7. *Entrepreneur*. In this role the manager initiates voluntary, controlled changes within the organization. He puts forward ideas and takes the initiative in setting up development projects.

8. *Disturbance handler*. This is the role in which the manager deals with non-voluntary, unplanned changes within the organization. These disturbances can be highly divergent in type. At one moment a conflict between co-workers or the loss of resources (withdrawal of subsidy, firing of subordinates), at another moment disturbances in the relationship between organization and environment (cancellation of an order by a major customer).

9. *Resource allocator*. The manager makes decisions about the allocation of resources. 'Resources' is used here in the broader sense of: time, money, equipment and manpower.

10. *Negotiator*. Managers spend a considerable amount of their time on negotiations with other organizations or with individuals.

Mintzberg emphasizes the fact that the various roles cannot be seen in isolation from one another. Together they constitute an integrated unit, a 'Gestalt'.

4.4. Typology of management functions

On the basis of the variations noted in the content of managers' work Mintzberg (1980) groups the various management functions rather loosely together in eight different types. The types are distinguishable from one another by the relative weight attached to one or more roles. Table 2 shows the eight types of managers as differentiated by Mintzberg with an indication of the principal role(s) associated with each type.

The *contact man* is a manager who spends a great deal of time outside the organization, who tries to obtain orders or exclusive information and spares no effort to promote his organization's reputation. The *political manager* also spends a lot of time outside the organization but his task mainly consists of

Table 2. Eight types of managerial function (according to Mintzberg, 1980).

Type	Principal role(s)
Contact man	Liaison, figurehead
Political manager	Spokesman, negotiator
Entrepreneur	Entrepreneur, negotiator
Insider	Resource allocator
Real-time manager	Disturbance handler
Team manager	Leader
Expert manager	Monitor, spokesman
New manager	Liaison, monitor

reconciling the various political forces affecting the organization. The *entrepreneur* spends his time principally searching for and scanning new possibilities and carrying through changes in the organization. The *insider* is a manager who is primarily occupied with running internal operations. The *real-time manager* is also mainly involved in the control of internal operations, but in doing so he directs his attention chiefly to dealing with disturbances and solving conflicts. The *team manager*, again, is primarily involved in internal operations but his main concern is the creation and maintenance of an effectively functioning team. The *expert* functions as specialist and adviser in a certain field. The term '*new manager*' is used for a manager who is new to his function and whose chief interests are therefore seeking and collecting information and building up a network of contacts.

In this section the tasks and roles of individual managers have been treated at some considerable length. The findings discussed here might, wrongly, give the impression that managers operate as lone wolves. On the contrary, they almost invariably work together, as a team, in management teams, Executive Committees and Boards of Directors.

5. MANAGEMENT TEAMWORK IN VARIOUS MODELS OF COMMITTEES

5.1. The development of management teams

When the size and complexity of an organization increase to such an extent that it becomes impossible for one person to attend adequately to all the aspects of management, the manager will delegate certain tasks to functionaries of the second rank. This brings about a change in the structure of responsibility. The cycle of planning, organizing, directing and, finally, controlling becomes, as a result of delegation, a chain in which functionaries other than the manager himself constitute a link. Thus, management becomes a process in which the manager, as delegator, involves the functionaries to whom he delegates important tasks in such a way that the correspondence between the various aspects of management remains sufficiently assured through special and frequent forms of communication such as staff meetings (Leavitt, 1978).

That component of planning usually referred to more specifically as policy-determination or -establishment is, as an activity, the most characteristic for the role of top manager. This task stamps him, most particularly, as the entrepreneur or policy-maker who, in selecting the objectives, holds himself, first and foremost, responsible for the realization of the assignments proceeding from them and formulated in his own policy planning. Because of the typical top manager's 'subjective' view of opportunities in the field and of his own capabilities and because of his (partly based on the foregoing) daring in taking decisions, this policy-determining activity will be the one that he experiences as being the most characteristic of himself (van Dooren, 1966). The fact that his decisions in this aspect of management may have far-reaching consequences for the organization intensifies his sense of bearing a responsibility from which he can seek no refuge elsewhere—in other words, the ultimate responsibility. For this reason policy determination is a top management task that cannot be delegated.

If the manager is no longer able to continue taking the final responsibility for the delegated tasks because, for instance, delegates are not conforming to the essential lines of the policy in the interpretation or execution of their tasks, the need arises to 'take back' these tasks to top management level. The production manager or chief accountant often moves up to the highest management level via the intermediate step of deputy director, or else qualified candidates from outside the organization are appointed in a top management function if none of the existing second-rank functionaries appears suitable to fulfil it. Management of the organization is now a task confronting a team instead of a single individual; the one-man board becomes a polyarchy, turns into an Executive Committee whose members jointly set out the policy for the organization and share the burden of final responsibility.

5.2. Models of task distribution within management teams

We shall now describe a few forms of task distribution within Executive Committees and the patterns of interpersonal relationships that these forms partly impose.

A management team, for example, can consist of three people who, together, constitute the directorate and, as such, are responsible for the determination of policy. Each of these directors, moreover, may have been allotted a particular area for which he alone is responsible. In a production plant, for example, such areas might be production or marketing or finance and economic affairs. When a strategy is being jointly set out for the organization each member of the Committee is expected—on the basis of his greater expertise in and extra responsibility for his own sector—to contribute arguments and criteria valid for this sector to the Committee's communal pool of insight. The unity of policy that leaders of the organization in the top management team ought to achieve is, however, greater than and different from the sum of the policy views of the separate sectors. This means that the double role in which the members of the team find themselves, and in which they are perceived by their fellow-members, can lead to intra-personal conflicts and interpersonal friction (van Dooren, 1962; Hodgson et al., 1965).

In order to guarantee effective team-work in the Committee and an equilibrium in the mutual relationship, one member is nearly always appointed Chairman. It is his particular task to attend to all matters concerning company planning and development when these require a coordinated effort from

Committee members. Since the various contributions should all converge at the top of the organization, the Chairman will give especial weight to the objectives of the team-as-a-whole, as collectively established assignments. The greater his success in reaching agreement as to the strategy to be collectively followed, the less risk there is of undesired conflicts within the team (Wilemon, 1973; Krouse, 1972).

Making a choice among the various models of possible task distribution in a Board of Directors, we would like, by way of illustration, to compare the distribution pattern characteristic of functional differentiation with that associated with product (groups) parallelization. The former involves allocating to each of the members of the Board, or top management team, a particular functional area that is complementary to the areas allotted to the other members, such as production, marketing, finance and economic affairs, personnel and organization, etc. Optimal promotion of a particular area's interests is only possible with the aid of and in harmony with the other functional areas. The notion of mutual dependence and responsibility and the sense of partnership as colleagues have already been assumed in the complementary structuring of tasks and roles and are thus enhanced by them (figure 4).

If one of these product-group directors should also fulfil the role of Chairman his colleagues would inevitably subject him to stringent scrutiny in his 'privileged' position, which would cramp the team's functional style because the experience of parity is so great that it is difficult to tolerate a primus (inter pares). This is because the synonymous positions of the policy-making directors offer, in a way quite different from that in a complementary task distribution, many points of direct comparison, on which to see how they measure up to one another. The competitive orientation that this stimulates can then lead to interpersonal rivalry that changes open discussion within the team into a tense negotiating climate with a competitive instead of a collegial tenor. If the risks just mentioned are

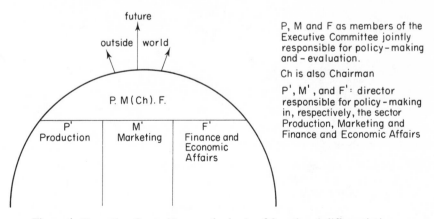

Figure 4. Executive Committee on the basis of functional differentiation.

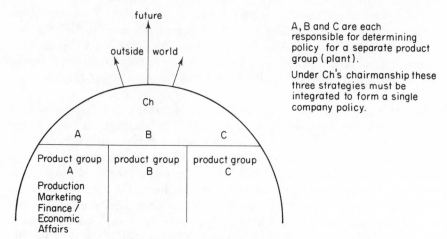

Figure 5. Executive Committee on the basis of product groups parallelization.

anticipated and if one wishes to avoid them the choice of the 'independent' chairman formula is the most common solution (figure 5).

If the organization in question has grown even larger, in terms of size, diversification of products/services and geographical distribution, one could say, in a manner of speaking, that the role of Chairman is being carried out by a 'committee' in the form of a Board of Directors (figure 6). None of the members of the Board of Directors has direct responsibility for a division or central service. Together, they constitute a policy-making Board that integrates the

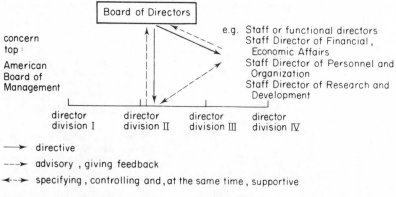

Figure 6. Top management polyarchy, showing different levels. First level, Board of Directors: policy-making and evaluation of the concern; second level structures on the basis of both functional differentiation and product groups parallelization (divisions).

policy plans of the divisions and the contributions of specialist know-how from the central service departments.

The fact that in a Board of this kind the individual tasks are not clearly delineated, that a regular overlap of action radii is inevitable and that the synonymity of the members, positions is very great, leads to the appearance of two undesirable tendencies in the mutual relationships.

The tendency towards rivalry mentioned earlier, can, in a competition to demonstrate personal prominence and to expand one's own sphere of influence, bring about more interpersonal tension than is desirable in this form of collaboration. Another tendency is that towards an exaggerated emphasis on the cohesive nature of the team so that, to the outsider, and particularly to the second level, it presents the appearance of a closed centre of power or as a 'clique', whose members form a mutual protection society (Adizes, 1979; Jay, 1969).

The foregoing was a brief indication of some of the frequently occurring basic patterns of task distribution within top management teams. The variations on the theme are numerous and their more detailed analysis would require consultation with other sciences able to provide information about factors by means of which top-level team work is conditioned and influenced, factors such as economic, legal, political and technological pressures.

Thus, views on management authority and responsibility can differ considerably, the differences being partly laid down in legal provisions and partly anchored in national traditions and/or company cultures. Both the functional formula and the mentality behind management team operations can be totally different on cardinal points in, for instance, The Netherlands, Japan and the United States. This is true, for instance, of the authorities or persons to whom top management is accountable or of those by whom the policy is tested or supported. The role of the 'Board of Directors' in a Dutch company with both a Supervisory Board (that keeps a watchful eye on management activities, should approve all major policy plans and may function in an advisory capacity) and a Works Council acting as consultative body with respect to social policy, in particular, is quite different from the role of executives in an American Executive Committee whose primary frame of reference are the reactions of stockholders to economic results. One expects a different kind of role behaviour from top management in a Japanese company, operating on the basis of such concepts as the family-system (seniority principle, life-time employment, etc.) and dominance of the group over the individual (a concept deeply rooted in the Japanese life-style) than from the directors of a Dutch organization in which thinking and acting proceed more in terms of a 'Gesellschaft' (association) mentality than of a 'Gemeinschaft' (community) mentality (Vogel, 1975; Brech, 1958).

Adopting a cross-cultural approach to the phenomenon 'management' is thus an important assignment for W/O psychology (Weinshall, 1979; Karsh, 1976;

Murayama, 1977; Barrett and Bass, 1972; Tannenbaum *et al.*, 1977). In this way one could avoid the pitfalls of making premature generalizations on the basis of findings in one particular context and comparative research could be carried out to extract essential factors and processes.

REFERENCES

Adizes, I. (1979), Organizational passages. *Organizational Dynamics*, **8**, 71.

Assen, A. van (1980), Organisatie-ontwerp, een analytisch model voor werkoverleg en werkstructurering [Organization design, an analytical model for work consultation and job design]. In: Assen, A. van, Hertog, J. F. den, Koopman, P. L. (Eds.), *Organiseren met een menselijke maat* [Human organization]. Alphen a/d Rijn: Samsom.

Assen, A. van, Hertog, J. F. den (1980), Werkbeleving en werkstructurering [The experience of work and job design]. In: Galan, C. de, Gils, H. R. van, Strien, P. J. van (Eds.), *Humanisering van de arbeid* [Humanizing work]. Assen: Van Gorcum.

Barrett, G., Bass, B. (1972), *Crosscultural issues in industrial and organizational psychology*. Rochester: University of Rochester, Management Research Center.

Becker, H. A. (1968), *Management als beroep* [Management as a profession]. The Hague: Nijhoff.

Blau, P. M. (1955), *The dynamics of bureaucracy*. Chicago: University of Chicago Press.

Blauner, R. (1964), *Alienation and freedom*. Chicago: University of Chicago Press.

Boulding, K. (1953), *The organizational revolution*, New York: Harper.

Brech, E. (1958), Human relations in the board room. In: Hugh-Jones, F. (Ed.), *Human relations and modern management*. Amsterdam: North-Holland Publ. Co.

Burns, T., Stalker, G. M. (1961), *The management of innovation*. London: Tavistock.

Campbell, J. P., Dunnette, M. D., Lawler, E. E., Weick, K. E. (1970), *Managerial behavior, performance and effectiveness*. New York: McGraw-Hill.

Carlson, S. (1951), *Executive behavior: a study of the work load and the working methods of managing directors*. Stockholm: Strombergs.

Cleland, D. I., King, W. R. (1972), *Management: A systems approach*. New York: McGraw-Hill.

Coch, L., French, J. P. (1948), Overcoming resistance to change. *Human Relations*, **11**, 512–532.

Dale, E. (1952), *Planning and developing the company organization structure*. New York: American Management Association.

Dale, E. (1960), *The great organizers*. New York: McGraw-Hill.

Davis, R. C. (1951), *The fundamentals of top management*. New York: Harper.

Davis, S. M., Lawrence, P. R. (1977), *Matrix*. Reading (Mass.): Addison-Wesley.

Dooren, F. J. P. van (1962), Spanning in de top [Stress in the top]. *Sociale Wetenschappen* [The Social Sciences], **5**.

Dooren, F. J. P. van (1966), De creativiteit van de ondernemer [The creativity of the businessman]. In: *De vrijheid van de ondernemer in verleden, heden en toekomst* [The freedom of the businessman, past, present and future]. Haarlem: Nederlandse Maatschappij voor Nijverheid en Handel.

Drucker, P. F. (1954), *The practice of management*. New York: Harper.

Fayol, H. (1916), *Administration industrielle et générale*. Paris.

Fiedler, F. E. (1967), *A theory of leadership effectiveness*. New York: McGraw-Hill.

Flanagan, J. C. (1954), The critical incident technique, *Psychol. Bull.* **51**, 327–358.

Galbraith, J. (1973), *Designing complex organizations*. Reading (Mass.): Addison-Wesley.

Galbraith, J. (1977), *Organizational design*. Reading (Mass.): Addison-Wesley.

Groot, A. D. de (1961), *Methodologie: Grondslagen van denken en onderzoeken in de gedragswetenschappen* (English tr. 1969: Methodology: Foundations of inference and research in the behavioural sciences). The Hague: Mouton.

Gulick, L. H. (1937), Notes on the theory of organization. In: Gulick, L. H., Urwick, L. F. (Eds.), *Papers on the science of administration.* New York: Columbia University Press.

Hemphill, J. K. (1960), *Dimensions of executive positions.* Columbus (Ohio): State University, Bureau of Business Research, Research Monograph no. 98.

Hodgson, R., Levinson, B., Zaleznick, A. (1965), *The executive role constellation; An analysis of personality and role relations in management.* Boston: Harvard University Press.

Jay, A. (1969), *Management and Machiavelli.* London: Hodder & Stroughton.

Karsh, B. (1976), Industrial relations in Japan. In: R. Dubin (Ed.), *Handbook of work, organization and society.* Chicago: Rand McNally.

Kast, F. E., Rosenzweig, J. E. (1972), General systems theory: applications for organization and management. *Academy of Management Journal,* December.

Kelly, J. (1964), The study of executive behaviour by activity sampling. *Human Relations,* **17**, 277–287.

Kepner, C. H., Tregoe, B. B. (1976), *The rational manager: A systematic approach to problem solving and decision making.* New York: McGraw-Hill.

Koontz, H. (1961), The management theory jungle. *Journal of the Academy of Management,* December, 174–188.

Krouse, C. (1972), Complex objectives, decentralization and the decision process in the organization. *Admin. Sci. Quart.,* **17**, 544.

Lawler, E. E. (1976), Control systems in organizations. In: Dunnette, M. D. (Ed.), *Handbook of industrial and organizational psychology.* Chicago: Rand McNally.

Lawler, E. E., Rhode, J. G. (1976), *Information and control in organizations.* Pacific Palisades (Cal.): Goodyear.

Lawrence, P. R., Lorsch, J. W. (1967), *Organizations and environment.* Boston: Harvard Business School, Division of Research.

Leavitt, H. (1978), *Managerial psychology.* Chicago: University of Chicago Press.

Likert, R., Bowers, P. G. (1969), Organizational theory and human resources accounting. *American Psychologist,* **24**, 585–592.

Lindblom, Ch. E. (1959), The science of 'muddling through'. *Public Administration Review,* **19**, 79–99.

Lorsch, J. W., Baughman, J. P., Reece, J., Mintzberg, H. (1978), *Understanding management.* New York: Harper.

Luthans, F. (1973), The contingency theory of management: A path out of the jungle. *Business Horizons,* **16**, 67–72.

Luthans, F. (1976), *Introduction to management: A contingency approach.* New York. McGraw-Hill.

March, J. G., Simon, H. A. (1958), *Organizations.* New York: Wiley.

Massie, J. L. (1965), Management theory. In: March, J. G. (Ed.), *Handbook of organizations.* Chicago: Rand McNally.

Mintzberg, H. (1968), *The manager at work—determining his activities, roles and programs by structured observation.* Cambridge (Mass.): MIT Sloan School of Management.

Mintzberg, H. (1975), The manager's job: Folklore and fact. *Harvard Business Review,* **53**, 49–61.

Mintzberg, H. (1980), *The nature of managerial work.* Englewood Cliffs (N.J.): Prentice-Hall.

Murayama, M. (1977), The oriental paradigm in business value systems. In: Poortinga, Y. (Ed.), *Basic problems in cross-cultural psychology.* Amsterdam: Swets & Zeitlinger.

Nadler, D. A., Hackman, J. R., Lawler, E. E. (1979), *Managing organizational behavior*. Boston: Little, Brown & Co.

Newman, W. H., Summer, C. E. (1961), *The process of management: Concepts, behavior, practice*. Englewood Cliffs (N.J.): Prentice-Hall.

Perrow, C. (1969), The analysis of goals in complex organizations. In: Etzioni, A. (Ed.), *Readings on modern organizations*. Englewood Cliffs (N.J.): Prentice-Hall.

Ponder, Q. D. (1958), *Supervisory practices of effective and ineffective foremen*. Unpublished doctoral dissertation, Columbia University.

Porter, L. W., Lawler, E. E., Hackman, J. R. (1975), *Behavior in organizations*. New York: McGraw-Hill.

Rackman, J., Woodward, J. (1970), The measurement of technical variables. In: Woodward, J. (Ed.), *Industrial organization: Behavior and control*. London: Oxford University Press.

Simon, H. A. (1957), *Models of man*. New York: Wiley.

Sitter, L. U. de (1980), Kenmerken en functies van de kwaliteit van de arbeid [Characteristics and functions of the quality of work]. In: Dijck, J. J. J. van, Hoof, J. P. A. van, Mok, A. L., Nijs, W. F. de (Eds.), *Kwaliteit van de arbeid* [The quality of work]. Leiden: Stenfert Kroese.

Stewart, R. (1967), *Managers and their jobs*. London: MacMillan.

Susman, G. I. (1976), *Autonomy at work*. New York: Praeger.

Tannenbaum, A. S., Kavčić, B., Rosner, M., et al. (1977), *Hierarchy in organizations*. San Francisco: Jossey-Bass.

Taylor, F. W. (1911), *The principles of scientific management*. New York: Harper.

Thierauf, R. J., Klekamp, R. C., Geeding, D. W. (1977), *Management principles and practices*. New York: Wiley.

Thompson, J. D. (1967), *Organizations in action*. New York: McGraw-Hill.

Tushman, M. L., Nadler, D. A. (1978), Information processing as an integrating concept in organizational design. *Academy of Management Review*, **3**, 613–624.

Urwick, L. F. (1943), *The elements of administration*. New York: Harper.

Urwick, L. F. (1960), The problem of management semantics. *California Management Review*, **2**, 3.

Ven, A. van de (1979), A revised framework for organizational assessment. In: E. Lawler, D. Nadler, C. Camman (Eds.), *Organizational assessment; Perspectives on the measurement of organizational behavior and the quality of working life*. New York: Wiley.

Ven, A. van de, Delbecq, A., Koenig, R. (1976), Determinants of coordination modes within organizations. *Amer. Sociol. Rev.*, **41**, 322–338.

Vogel, E. (1975), *Modern Japanese organizations and decision making*. Berkeley: University of California Press.

Weick, K. E. (1979), *The social psychology of organizing*. Reading (Mass.): Addison-Wesley.

Weinshall, Th. (1979), *Managerial communication*. London: Academic Press.

Whyte, W. F. (1955), *Money and motivation*. New York: Harper.

Willemon, D. L. (1973), Managing conflict in temporary systems. *Journal of Managerial Studies*, **10**, 281.

Handbook of Work and Organizational Psychology
Edited by P. J. D. Drenth, H. Thierry, P. J. Willems and C. J. de Wolff
© 1984, John Wiley & Sons, Ltd.

4.8. Job design: From job rotation to organizational design

A. van Assen, F. J. den Hertog

1. THE QUALITY OF WORK AND ORGANIZATION

Since the first experiments with job rotation which date from World War II, views on job design have gone through an evolution. This evolution has taught us, that isolated approaches in the laboratory only lead to marginal changes (Davis, 1976). Today, job design can no longer be considered a separate issue, but must be part of an integrated approach to organizational design. This development is the subject of the present chapter.

Job design may be generally described as the attempt to adapt work and work organization as much as possible to the desires and capabilities of man. As such, job design may be viewed as a potential remedy against the negative consequences of rationalization and bureaucratization in work organizations. The rationalization and bureaucratization of work concern processes which already started in the last century and were considerably accelerated by the rise of scientific management. Chapter 4.2 (this Handbook) presents the most important elements of the scientific management approach to organizations, which in our days still holds a strong position.

In our contemporary society, however, the conditions which made possible the development of scientific management have undergone essential changes. Here we shall briefly go into three of these conditions:
—the higher average level of education;

Dr. Albert van Assen, Katholieke Universiteit, Vakgroep A en O Psychologie, Montessorilaan 3, 6525 GG Nijmegen, Te.: 080–512641.
Dr. Friso J. den Hertog, Philips Gloeilampen Fbr. N.V. Sociale Zaken Afd. Onderzoek, Willemsstraat 20, 5611 HD EINDHOVEN (privé Franciscahoeve 17, Gouda).

—changing work ethics;
—changing task environments in industrial organizations.

1.1. The rise of the average level of education

The sweeping developments in education (*Nota inzake Werkgelegenheid*, 1975) have led to an increasingly wider gap between the qualities of the workers (knowledge and skills) and those of the work itself. Ever more people are working below their capacity. The first consequence of this is, that opportunities for personal growth are cut off. Workers become demotivated (*Onvrede en Klachten van Werknemers*, 1975). Studies on the industrial sector (e.g. Arends, 1974) indicate that workers, employed in production work that is clearly below their capacities, show a higher rate of turnover than do workers for whom no such imbalance exists.

The second consequence is that in organizations, a considerable part of the available human potential goes unused (see figure 1; Maher, 1972, p. 29). In the American literature on management such waste of human capital is called 'human resource waste'.

1.2. Changing work ethics

In the literature (for The Netherlands, e.g. van Strien, 1980) it is pointed out that in our society work ethics are changing. A large minority in our society no longer considers earning your living as something self-evident (Keniston, 1968; Roszak, 1968). They drop out and either end up in some alternative circuit or are receiving some kind of state benefit (Van Strien, 1980). The majority remaining in the industrial process has, in the past years, come to set higher standards for the quality of that part of their lives spent working (*Sociaal-cultureel Rapport*, 1976, p. 52). And those who, under pressure of economic developments, are forced out

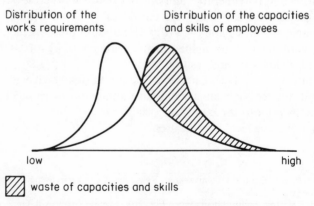

Figure 1. Human resource waste (Maher, 1972, p. 29).

of the industrial process also set high standards for possible new jobs. These standards particularly concern inconveniences (refusal to work in shifts or at an assembly line), pay rates, and the extent of participation as an opportunity for personal growth (*Sociaal-cultureel Rapport*, 1978, p. 49).

1.3. Changing task environments

Perrow (1970) indicates that production bureaucracies work well as long as they perform routine tasks in a stable environment. It is these conditions that are affected. Technologies and products succeed one another at an ever faster pace, while at the same time, too, consumer markets are rather turbulent. The quality of products delivered and services rendered is increasingly subject to criticism.

In such a situation, the industrial organization is faced with its own unwieldiness and rigidity and thus with its own incapability to adjust to changing requirements. In section 2 an eloquent example of this is presented. Under such circumstances, organizations are forced to invest in new strategies (Galbraith, 1973).

Among the possibilities for adjustment, two main directions can be distinguished (Emery, 1967). The first aims at extension and sophistication of the control system by, for example, extending hierarchical lines, formalizing and describing more narrowly tasks and procedures, and streamlining and automating information system. In other words: one tries to find a way out by means of further rationalization and bureaucratization.

The other goes exactly the opposite way. One tries to make the organization more flexible by reducing the bureaucratic nature of the organization. Decentralization, despecialization, deformalization, and deverticalization are utilized in an attempt to break down the rigidity and to have the members of the organization participate more in the functioning of the whole. Such a pursuit denotes (de Sitter, 1977) the improvement of the *quality of the organization*. De Sitter emphasizes that such an improvement bears a direct relation to that of the *quality of work*.

In this light, job design may be considered a condition for any improvement in the functioning of an organization as a whole (*Job Reform in Sweden*, 1975; den Hertog and Wester, 1979; de Sitter, 1977). In the present chapter we will first go into the first pioneering studies in the area of job design. Next, its content and its management will be discussed. Then, following an outline of the developments in various countries where the status of job design in existing industrial relations enjoys particular attention, the 'state of the art' will be considered. Finally, implications for the future are indicated.

2. EARLY AND MORE RECENT DEVELOPMENTS

In many areas of industrial and work psychology one pursues the integration of two goals: the well-being of the individual and the effectiveness of the organization. This is certainly true of job design. this pursuit is expressed in the title of Herzberg's latest book: *The managerial choice: to be efficient and to be human.* In this approach, the structure of the work itself (Ford, 1969) is viewed as the key to the integration of the above-mentioned goals.

Job design is an action-oriented approach. This means that the formation of ideas on this subject strongly relies on and, moreover, aims at practical applications in field projects. In this section, a number of pioneering studies and some fairly recent field projects are discussed. To be sure, the first attempts at job design, made fifteen to twenty years ago in various parts of the world, are not the first examples of job design. For these, one should go back to the fourties or even the thirties. The job enlargement experiments at IBM and the job rotation experiments in the English tobacco industry can be dated back to that period (Kuylaars, 1951). However, the pioneering studies to be described here may be considered the first attempts at setting up a 'school' for developing job design. Especially the description of more recent field projects will show this to be the case.

2.1. The Ahmedabad experiment in India

One of the first experiments in job design that was described extensively (Rice, 1958) was carried out in a textile mill of Calico Mills in Ahmedabad, India. The content and management of the experiment were determined to a great extent by the consultant and researcher whom the mill had hired to resolve its serious manufacturing problems: Rice, a staff member of the Tavistock Institute of Human Relations. His approach was based in particular on the experience in the English coal mining industry of his colleague at Tavistock, Trist (Trist and Bamforth, 1951). Both Trist and Rice may be considered early representatives of the sociotechnical school of job design.

The problems the Calico mills had on introducing automated looms occasioned these experiments. When this new technology was introduced, the work process was divided into small partial tasks—on the basis of industrial studies. As a result, in this new situation, the work was done by a number of isolated individuals: the weaver's trade disintegrated into partial tasks that were barely interrelated. Tasks and role relations had become obscure and there was no recognizable group structure.

This led to the new mill functioning worse than the old one. Efficiency and quality became serious problems. Rice's proposal was to make groups of workers responsible for the whole weaving process around a fixed number of machines. The management and the workers agreeing to this, the proposal was carried out in March 1953. Besides task integration and group formation, individual piece rate payments were replaced by a form of group wages. The first seven months of this new system, the textile mill worked well. Then the groups' results began to decline. The variety of materials to be weaved turned out to be too great and there were too few replacements available to keep the process going. Both the training of new workers and the training on behalf of the introduction of new products were neglected. the group leaders were allowed too little time to get used to their leadership and the foremen passed them over. A series of measures was sufficient to readjust the experiment: introduction of basic flat wages, separation of training tasks and production, and restoring the variety of products in the group. Recovery came fast—which led Rice (1958, p. 110) to the following conclusion:

'It was concluded that the first spontaneous acceptance of the new system and the subsequent determination to make it work were due primarily to the workers' intuitive acceptance of it as one which would provide them with the security and protection of small group membership which they had lost by leaving their villages and their families to enter industry. At the same time the new system allowed them to perform their primary task effectively and thus provided them with an important source of satisfaction'.

In 1954, a comparable experiment was carried out in the non-automated weaving mill. Here, each weaver worked at two looms, formally as an independent, isolated individual. In practice, however, they cooperated closely informally. But they had problems with the existing organization of their work. Formally, responsibility for the whole work process lay with three different functional departments, but in actuality the weavers were held responsible for the quality and quantity of the whole work process. Again, in the new system, small work groups were conceptualized and entrusted with all tasks related to the weaving itself and to the maintenance of the equipment. The groups were arranged according to the kind of material to be woven. This was done to prevent a too great variety in products. Basic flat wages were raised and a system of group bonusses for quality and productivity was introduced. Informal meetings of the group leader and his group, where all kinds of technical, organizational, and social topics could be discussed, proved to be an important element in maintaining the social system. This could be called a kind of work consultation. The new system made it possible to work in three instead of two shifts.

The experiment led to remarkable results. The weavers' average income was raised by 55%. The output rose by 21%. Flaws in quality decreased by 50%. This is what Rice says about the results:

'The experimental system has established new forms of performance and earnings for non-automatic weaving. The conclusion was reached that the acceptance of the new system and the determination to make it work were due to its providing more opportunities for effective task performance and for the building of stable and secure small work-group relationships than those existing in the conventional system with which the traditional norms of performance and wages were associated'.

In a follow-up study. Miller (1975) noted, that 16 years later only the second experiment still functioned reasonably well. In the automated weaving mill, clear task differentiation had returned and thereby a deterioration of team coherence and cooperation.

According to Miller, the main reason was that the management was unable to cope adequately with the great pressure from the market for new products against lower prices. It translated this pressure into short-term efficiency-measures. Thus, boundary management, which guards the relation between grouptask and organizational environment, received too little attention and the groups' effectiveness declined. In the non-automated weaving mill fewer problems arose. However, they produced materials that were much less subject to external pressure and change (Miller, 1975, p. 382).

2.2. Developments in the United States

The roots of job design lie mainly in the United States. In the sixties, at AT & T and particularly its daughter-company Bell—nearly one million employees, mainly in the telephone company—much experience was obtained with an American equivalent of job design: job enrichment. Ford (1969) presents a detailed report on 19 such projects. Below, we will take a closer look at one of these pioneering studies.

JOB ENRICHMENT AT AT & T: THE TREASURY DEPARTMENT

The project was carried out in AT & T's treasury department. This department comprised a special group charged with the correspondence concerning complaints from shareholders. The problems the correspondents were confronted with and the information they had to obtain often were of a very complicated and specialized nature and made enormous intellectual demands on the correspondents. Therefore, personnel for this department was recruited by the company especially from among college graduates. However, in this category of young, well-educated women turnover was very high. The personnel department had already informed the department management that 'You don't deserve the people we send you' (Ford, 1969, p. 16). Measures in the area of compensation and work environment had had little effect. In the organization, one began to realize that something had to change drastically.

Solution of the problems was sought in Herzberg's job enrichment theory. Herzberg (1968) had pointed out that only the work itself motivates man. To his thinking, the factors surrounding work (such as working conditions, social contacts, remuneration, leadership climate, etc.) do not influence the positive input of the worker. They do, however, lead to dissatisfaction if something goes wrong with them.

Job satisfaction and a positive input are realized only if the task itself allows for personal growth (for this see this Handbook ch. 2.2). Job enrichment aims at the integration of executive work and task elements of a qualitatively higher level, the vertical load of a job. Thus, Herzberg rejects job enlargement, which only integrates executive tasks into a larger whole, whereas the quality level of the work remains the same.

The experiment took the shape of a controlled experiment with measurements before and after and with control groups. Herzberg's theory was introduced to the managers at the third and fourth levels above the executive one. Next they were invited to brainstorm about the elements by which the correspondents' tasks could be enriched. The ensuing list of elements was then cleared from those with horizontal loading. These activities led to a series of measures aiming to increase the independence and responsibility of the tasks of the correspondents.

The changes were effected very gradually in an experimental group of twenty correspondents. The changes were received well. This became clear at the evaluation: personnel turnover and labor costs had declined considerably, while job satisfaction and the quality of the service had improved appreciably. In the further development of American job design Herzberg's orthodox job enrichment approach was adopted by many companies as a point of departure. The initiative for such projects was almost exclusively with the management. Motivating the employees was the most important goal.

In some companies, job enrichment was used as a strategy to keep the unions away from their doorstep (Scott Myers, 1970). In a limited number of companies (AT & T and Texas Instruments) it became an essential aspect of personnel policy (Ford, 1969; Myers, 1970).

Mills (1978) points out, that in the United States both unions and employers were, until recently, almost exclusively oriented towards 'the economic man' ('human beings perceived and valued by their purely economic worth and potential, Mills, 1978, p. 147).

William Winsipinger (Sapulkas, 1974, p. 116), a top functionary in the powerful AFL-CIO, makes clear what this means for job enrichment: 'If you want to enrich a job, enrich the pay check. There is no better cure for the blue collar blues'.

It is remarkable, that these last years the tide seems to be turning. Important to this development are the strikes and sabotage actions that occurred in the beginning of the seventies, shortly after GM opened its super-efficient automobile plant in Lordstown. The incidents in Lordstown were one of the reasons for the QWL (Quality of Working Life) investigation by a senate commission headed by Edward Kennedy. This eventually resulted in a gradually increasing willingness on the part of both company managements and trade organizations to jointly negotiate about QWL programs, be it a QWL approach 'made in USA' (Mills, 1978, p. 151). This means that the approach is not characterized by ideological differences between employers and unions, but is directed towards the 'operational and functional concern for feelings of self-worth, human dignity and the life space of every individual in work organizations'. Mills adds that '... this pursuit is fully congruent with that organization's pragmatic, bottom-line goals, and its effectiveness as the profitmaking institutions its stockholders expect'.

Since the mid-seventies, the number of institutes concerned with research and promotion in the field of QWL also has greatly increased. Important institutes are the National Center for Productivity and QWL, the Work in America Institute, and the Center for QWL. The latter is managed by one of the founders of job design, Louis Davis, and is typically oriented towards sociotechnics (cf. Davis, 1976).

A NEW PLANT IN TOPEKA

General Foods Corporation, a giant in the American food industry, had already for a long time been producing dehydrated pet food at their Illinois plants. Both the plants and the production technology were very antiquated, while internal relations and the workers' motivation were not very good either. Its top management saw the only solution for this situation—which was felt to be badly deteriorated—in carrying out their 1968 decision to build a brand new plant at a totally different site: in rural Topeka. One of the most important criteria presented to the project team charged with its design was: 'the human involvement in work' (Walton, 1972, 1977).

The plant, opened in 1971, was described in the American press as a major breakthrough in the search for solutions to the 'blue collar blues'. To contemporary standards too, the changes in traditional plant design, as implemented in Topeka, may be called radical. The plant is organized according to the principle of autonomous groups. These groups each comprise seven to fourteen persons and are big enough to be able to handle a coherent and meaningful series of tasks and small enough to be able to influence, in the form of direct work consultation, the decision making and coordination. The tasks were designed in such a way as to '. . . include functions requiring mental abilities, such as planning, diagnosing mechanical problems and liaison work' (Walton, 1977, p. 422).

In the Topeka plant, numerous activities, that in a traditional plant are carried out by staff functionaries, are integrated into the tasks of independent groups (maintenance, quality control, calculation, but also, for example, selection of applicants for jobs in the group!).

Each group is assigned a team leader, whose main instruction is to stimulate team formation and decision making within the group. The groups are supplied with sufficient information and directions to allow for self-management. The compensation system, the architecture, and the technology were adapted as much as possible to the new approach and most external status differences in the plant were eliminated.

Especially during the first years the results were very positive, both techno-economically and socially. In these first years, there was at all levels of the organization a strong sense of pride of what had been achieved. The Topeka plant was an excellent place to work.

A follow-up study (Walton, 1977) shows that further developments were not free from problems. Six years later, the original design philosophy was still in force and economic results were still excellent, but the QWL seemed to have 'eroded' somewhat. Too little attention was being paid to social maintenance. At the plant, the attitude had become defensive in order to hold on to what was achieved. This attitude, however, did not lead to new impulses to further expand the plant design. In this situation, Walton blames the lack of support from the top management of the locally responsible managers.

2.3 Developments in The Netherlands

In The Netherlands, the development of job design was mainly supported by initiatives of individual companies and work done by a small group of academic social scientists. Trade organizations have long been watching these developments in job design with suspicion (van Beinum and van der Vlist, 1979) and did not become actively involved. Contrary to the Scandinavian unions, they were only to a limited extent oriented towards problems occurring in the immediate work situation at the bottom of organizations. This is due partly to their originally centralistic character (Windmuller and de Galan, 1978) and partly to the low rate of union membership (a mere 40%) among the Dutch working population. Nevertheless, in the past years a 'return-to-the-basis-movement' is unmistakably taking place in the trade unions (Windmuller and de Galan, 1978, p. 188) as well as an increasing interest in the quality of work, which is influenced particularly by the consequences of automation and mechanization. But at the same time, developments in the quantity of work (volume of employment) are so alarming, that in practice trade organizations pay relatively little attention to its quality.

Since World War II, the government has been very influential in industrial relations. From the early seventies on, the government has been assuming more and more responsibility for the quality of industrial social policy. The government takes upon itself the task both of stimulating improvements in the quality of work (subsidies for experiments with job design, work consultation, and participation) and of formulating its norms through legislation. The Act on Working Conditions, under discussion in 1980 and containing numerous elements directly related to job design and work environment, may be viewed in this light (de Gier, 1978).

Since the early sixties, ideas about job design have been put forth by the academic world, especially by the sociotechnical school. One of the pioneers of that school was Van Beinum (van Beinum et al., 1968), whose project in the 'giro' division of the PTT (i.e. the state banking system) gained wide renown. A more recent project originating from this school is that of Allegro at Centraal Beheer (Allegro and de Vries, 1979).

As for the initiatives of individual companies towards job design, the Philips company assumes a special position in the Netherlands (den Hertog, 1977). This company's history in job design is about 20 years old. The first projects involved experiments with job rotation, extension of time cycles, group formation, and buffer supplies. These occurred on the occasion of the stormy growth of the company in that period, of increasing difficulties in finding personnel for the monotonous work in mass production and keeping them, and of the vulnerability of the highly rationalized production systems. One of the first—not only in The Netherlands, but also in western Europe—pioneering studies was carried out at the Eindhoven television factory in 1962 (van Beek, 1964). Van Beek's study presents an analysis of the assembly line as a work system. The approach displays distinct similarities to that of sociotechnics, although at the time there was no question of any substantial influence from that school.

THE ASSEMBLY LINE OF THE EINDHOVEN TV-FACTORY UNDER DISCUSSION

When in western Europe, towards the end of the fifties, television came very much into vogue and sales figures soared, the television factory was confronted with increasing delivery problems. These gave the definitive push towards a fundamental discussion on the assembly line system. In those days, television sets were assembled on a long shifting line, along which every $1\frac{1}{2}$ minute, at the signal of a lamp or a buzzer, panels were moved on from one working place to the next. The problems with this production procedure were waiting time, hitches, bad quality, and dissatisfaction of the workers. A preliminary study led to the design of an experiment, in which the basic structure of the assembly line was retained. The line was subdivided into five groups (see figure 2) in between which there was room for buffer supplies, where the production of one hour was stored. Thus, waiting times due to hitches in the supply of materials could be reduced by 55%. In the old system, the quality controllers had been put at the end of the line. Now, they were distributed over the five groups. The much faster feedback in this new set-up had a major effect upon the quality of the end-product. The number of mistakes made in welding and assembling was much reduced. Moreover, an opinion survey showed that in the system with buffer supplies the work was experienced more positively than at the old assembly line.

In another respect too, the experiment signified an important breakthrough within the company, i.e., thorough insight was obtained into efficiency problems inherent in any assembly line system. A lot of time is lost in 'adjustment losses' (losses as a consequence of the variations in mean work speed among employees) and in 'system losses' (variations across time in the work speed of individual employees). Computer simulation has shown, that the use of buffer supplies may

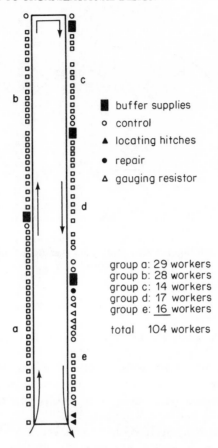

■ buffer supplies
o control
▲ locating hitches
● repair
Δ gauging resistor

group a: 29 workers
group b: 28 workers
group c: 14 workers
group d: 17 workers
group e: 16 workers

total   104 workers

Figure 2. Lay-out of the experimental
assembly line (van Beek, 1964, p. 162).

reduce system losses (see figure 3). Simulation has also produced an outline of the
relation between adjustment losses and the length of the line. If at a line with five
men such losses amount to 10% then, according to Van Beek, at a line with
twenty men adjustment losses of 20% should be expected. Van Beek reached the
conclusion (1964, p. 164), that the classic problem of 'how to balance the line' is
not so much a matter of adjusting and organizing tasks, but rather is connected
with differences in work speed among workers. This problem is inherent in the
long line without buffers. Apparently, the classic assembly line did not have such
a standard recipe for efficiency as industrial technicians had been thinking for
years. Thus, the first crack in the bastion of the classic study of work became
visible, one that later on could not be mended anymore. These first experiments,
of which the above is one example, all had the following characteristics:

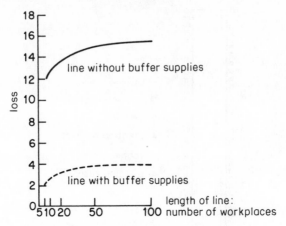

Figure 3. The relation between system losses, lay-
out and length of the assembly line (van Beek, 1964,
p. 165).

—the experiments were limited in size and often carried out in a 'secluded corner'
of the plant;
—the initiative came from an individual production manager and/or staff
functionary;
—only a limited number of job design elements were experimented with;
—little attention was paid to research or to theoretical support;
—the workers concerned were hardly ever involve in designing the experiment.

Although these first experiments of the first phase (1960–1965) were limited in
size and content, they have had an important function. They brought the
effectiveness of the classis approaches under critical discussion and demonstrated
that alternatives were available. The great importance of the human task to an
effective functioning of industrial systems—and, thus, the relevance of contributions from behavioral scientists to their design—became very conspicuous.

In the next phase (1965–1972) the importance of job design was formally
recognized at corporate level. The goal was described as follows
(*Werkstructurering*, 1968, p. 4): 'To organize the work, the work situation and
the working conditions in such a way that the tasks will correspond as much as
possible to the capacities and ambitions of the employees, while maintaining or
improving the profits'.

However, the initiative and responsibility for its execution remained the
concern of local management, supported by the guidance, training, and research
from central staff divisions.

During that period, the number of experiments increased considerably.
Changes were made to include still more elements of job design. However, as yet

little attention was paid to the strategy of these changes and, also, the workers became involved only gradually. Roughly, the projects can be divided into three categories:

1. Designing *'single places'* in manual assemblage. In this case, a worker assembles the complete product or a major part of it. He is disengaged from the production line and may set his own pace.

2. Composing relatively *independent, product-oriented* assembly groups. A small group of workers is responsible for assembling the complete product. Within the group, moreover, tasks are performed that previously were the domain of the lower echelons and of employees of staff and service departments (division of work, quality control, supply of materials, etc.).

3. *Function integration* in machine-bound work. This particularly concerns the integration of maintenance and adjustment operations that are part of the tasks of machine service operators.

An extensive description of such projects can be found in Den Hertog (1977). An evaluation of the state of affairs in job design by a special commission, instituted by the Central Works Council (Centrale Ondernemingsraad) of the Philips company, provided a none too bright picture. It was established that, in spite of the mutiplicity of projects, in the whole company only a limited group ($\pm$ 3100) had had any dealings with job design. Experiments apparently did not diffuse, but remained isolated within small 'experimental gardens'.

The commission reached three main conclusions, which were firmly supported by the research carried out within the company (den Hertog, 1977; den Hertog and de Vries, 1979; den Hertog and Vossen, 1974):

1. In most projects, the persons involved are allowed to participate in the designs only to a limited extent.

2. Often, job design is applied in 'crystallized industrial systems', but it should in fact begin to play a role as soon as an industrial system or a machine is being designed ('preventive job design').

3. Mostly, its introduction follows the prescriptions too closely. Not enough attention is paid to the process of change.

Within the company, this *phase of criticism* (1973–1978) has raised doubts as to the value of job design. A new direction was plotted, but not without problems. In the past few years, its outlines gradually became clearer and it may be designated the 'phase of organizational innovation', in which the emphasis is on:

—an integral approach to organizations;

—the system design;

—greater involvement of the workers in designing the companies' projects;

—local responsibility for the organizational innovation policy.

In practice, this new approach is materializing only very slowly. An important factor here is, that for the organization the consequences are much more drastic than those of the small, delimited experiments. The experiences in Philips' main machine plant clearly have been a stimulus in these developments (see den Hertog and Wester, 1979; Alink and Wester, 1980).

2.4 The Scandinavian countries

In Norway and Sweden job design was developed from a very different background—especially as to its ideological color—than in the United States or The Netherlands. In both countries, the political climate was determined mainly by the social-democrats. There are strong links with the labor unions which are jointly organized in the L.O. (Landsorganisasjonen) and which have a high membership rate (about 90%). The two employers' organizations (Arbeidsgiver Forening) in Norway and Sweden (NAF and SAF, respectively) also have a high membership rate.

Scandinavian industrial relations were characterized by cooperation at the central level, which was making itself felt again and again in the joint consultation groups at the lower levels. For the sake of good cooperation, a balance of power relations was pursued. Since the early sixties, industrial democratization and the QWL have been important topics, for which, in the aforementioned consultation groups, both employers and trade unions have accepted responsibility. At the national level, this joint responsibility is found in the Norwegian Industrial Democracy Project. This project was begun in 1962, under the supervision of a 'cooperation board' composed on the basis of parity. At the time, projects aiming at changing the immediate work situation fell on fertile ground. An important catalyst in that process was the charismatic personality of Thorsrud, then director of the Institute for Industrial Social Research in Trondheim.

In 1962, the Cooperation Board mentioned above commissioned Thorsrud's group to evaluate first of all the existing formal consultation structures—whose extension was cogently argued for by the trade unions. From that study (Emery and Thorsrud, 1969) it appeared that the formal measures regarding democratization were of little significance for the way in which workers at the bottom experienced their work situation. The researchers emphasized the necessity of participation at the shop floor. They pointed out the importance of task content and of meaningful changes therein: changes oriented towards job design and work consultation. The result of the cooperation between Thorsrud and the Tavistock Institute was that the proposed approach contained clearly discernible elements from sociotechnics.

In 1964, the next phase was started with selecting four companies, where experiments in job design were to be carried out. The conditions under which the experiments should take place were discussed extensively. An important element was, that projects at the lower levels would be supervised by groups composed on the basis of parity. Both workers and management would be allowed to stop the experiments if they thought there were reasons to do so. The four experiments are described *in extenso* by Emery and Thorsrud (1976). Below, attention will be paid to one of these experiments.

The program of the Swedish Cooperation Board was started in 1970. Initially, this program was greatly inspired by what had happened in Norway in the previous years. This means, that in the first experiments the notion of semi-autonomous groups received the most attention. A clear difference with the Norwegian situation is that in Sweden, in parallel to the experiments supervised by the Cooperation Board, a separate series of projects was developed. Numerous individual employers took steps towards job design in their own companies.

Thus, job design in Sweden became a decentralized process (Dundelach and Mortensen, 1979). The projects are not centrally coordinated. The committee on personnel policy of the Swedish employers union (SAF) does stimulate this process, but does not steer it. Trade unions and social scientists play a much less dominant role than they do in Norway. In Sweden, there is more emphasis on integrating job design and work consultation in the everyday practice of management (*Job Reform in Sweden*, 1975). Experiments in secluded experimental gardens are considered less important, because of the risk of hobbyism and isolation of projects.

Another remarkable difference with the Norwegian approach is that in Sweden interest is strongly focused on designing new technologies and production organizations. It is these elements that render the developments in Sweden so interesting. The idea (Katz and Kahn, 1978) is that, in view of the high investment costs, the margin for job design in existing, crystallized organizations is extremely narrow. The development of new technologies and the design of new plants provide the opportunity, at an early stage, for taking into account social criteria and for developing, on that basis, feasible alternatives.

A project group is presently studying the alternatives in the various main areas of organizational design (Lindholm, 1979):
—process technology
—transport systems
—industrial architecture
—arrangement of individual workplaces
—product design
—manufacture lay-out.
A recent SAF publication presents a summary of the work of this project group (Agurén and Edgren, 1980).

The much discussed project of Volvo's new site in Kalmar is distinctly representative of this approach (see Agurén *et al.*, 1976).

Below, attention will be paid to one of the four projects described by Emery and Thorsrud (1976), which have had an exemplary function in Norwegian developments.

THE NOBØ PROJECT

The experiment was started in a daughter factory of the Nobø corporation. In this small factory, providing jobs for 100 men and women, electric panel heaters were manufactured. The production process was divided into three stages:
1. mechanical operations (pressing, welding, and grinding);
2. surface treatments (cleaning, spray-painting, and drying);
3. assembling and packing.

The organization of the work was modelled along Taylorian lines. This means that the tasks, especially those in the assembly department, were rather strictly separated. Thus, the duration of apprenticeship varied from a few days to a few weeks at most. For the experiment, a department was selected where mainly women (30) were working. They were paid according to an individual piece rate system. The norms for this were established on the basis of Method Time Measurements. In the factory, there were no complaints about the quality of the product, the productivity, or the attitude of the workers.

The research team introduced its ideas to the management and the shop stewards as well as to the workers of the experimental department. The management and the shop stewards were much in favor of the ideas presented. On the basis of a sociotechnical analysis of the work system, a proposal for changes therein was made. These proposals were accepted by all parties and resulted in:
—the establishment of semi-autonomous groups;
—re-training the workers for five tasks instead of one;
—appointing liaison persons per group, so that adjustments between the groups could be regulated;
—the introduction of flat rate payments;
—decentralizing service and maintenance jobs towards the groups;
—introducing a signalling system for the quality and production control within the groups.

After ten weeks of gaining experience with this new method of working, it was decided to proceed and to extend the experiment to other departments of the plant. During the experimental phase, productivity rose by 20% and during the following two years by 10%. The quality of the product remained stable, as did the rate of personnel turnover and absenteeism, which at the start of the experiment was already below the national norm. For the workers, the project meant an increase of the time span by $2\frac{1}{2}$ days to $2\frac{1}{2}$ months.

A survey among 68 workers (Table 1) demonstrated, that the majority was markedly content with the new set-up. For a long time, the new approach remained confined to the daughter factory. Only when this small factory was incorporated into a newly designed, larger plant, was the experiment extended. The workers of the small daughter-factory were only prepared to work in the new factory, if the latter would also be organized according to the principle of semi-

Table 1. How the changes in the tasks were experienced (Emery and Thorsrud, 1976, p. 96).

	Better now	Could not judge%	No change	Worse
Responsibility taken	77	4	19	0 = 100%
Participation in decisions	64	3	33	0
Learning on the job	47	13	34	6
Variety in the work	55	20	22	3
Mutual support on job	67	23	6	4
Meaningfulness of job	51	7	42	0
Relations to Management	60	32	4	4

autonomous groups. Subsequently, the 400 new jobs in the new factory were structured on this model.

Thorsrud himself (1977, p. 411) indicates that in the sixties such demonstration projects were necessary in order to prove that there existed real alternatives to the classic organization models. The positive results of these projects did not automatically lead to new initiatives or to a wide diffusion of the new design philosophy. According to him, one of the most important reasons for this is, that in most companies planning and control systems were not adjusted, so that new forms of working were absorbed by the existing bureaucratic procedures and structures. Another reason, says Thorsrud says, is the fact that often the negotiations with the trade unions about the projects were conducted too centrally and too far from the shop floor. In the early seventies it became clear, that new strategies were needed for shaping the QWL in Norwegian industry. This process led to a reorientation, particularly towards the democratization of the design process itself. Thorsrud (1977, p. 411) describes the results as follows: 'Perhaps most important are not the specific things done, like re-design of jobs, improved training, information and so on, but the way things are done, that changes are done by the people in their own work situations and not for the people, that organizations are changed from the inside and not from the outside'.

Elden (1979) designates this phase in the Norwegian democratization process as phase C. The people themselves, not any contributions from the researchers, are the prime movers of projects.

An important means for setting the process going are the 'do it yourself workshops'. These are meetings supervised by Thorsrud's institute, the trade organizations, and the employers' organizations, at which different groups from an organization learn to analyze their own situation and to formulate plans that allow for joint discussions and decisions by those concerned at all levels of the organization.

3 ELEMENTS AND INTERVENTIONS

By means of job design the industrial content of tasks is changed in such a way that the result is a more meaningful task for the performer. Each of the approaches discussed in the previous section has made its contribution to the whole of *substantial elements* of job design.

The strategy followed, too, plays an important role in the course the process of change takes. The nature of the interventions of the various approaches also deserve attention.

3.1. Elements of job design

In the course of time, various schools in the development of job design could be distinguished. Above, sociotechnics, job enrichment, and the practice-approach at Philips were discussed. Reverting our attention to the content of job design, it appears that each approach has produced its list of criteria that a meaningful task should meet (see table 2).

Besides similarities (e.g. concerning feedback), distinct differences may be noted. Strikingly, job enrichment lacks criteria regarding horizontal job loading, group formation, and work consultation. It is group formation in particular, which received so much emphasis in the other two approaches. The resulting aspects of job design may be described according to the elements each different approach has contributed.

Horizontal loading, job enlargement

The work cycle is extended when more activities of the same quality level are combined into one task. In automobile assemblage, for example, this means that instead of lining only the left door, one takes care of the lining of the whole car. One performs a larger part of the total number of operations. Thus the work may become more of a unity. The contribution of individual production workers acquires a recognizable character.

Herzberg (1968, p. 59) rejects job design, because according to him it does not bring about qualitative improvements in the work. But in practice (den Hertog, 1977), job enlargement or cycle extension obtains its value especially from the conditions it creates: smaller work groups, more insight into the manufacturing process, reduced dependence on the work pace of others, greater freedom of movement. This element, sometimes also labelled 'horizontal loading', clears the ground for the introduction of other elements.

Job rotation

In this case, the work system remains intact, but the group members regularly rotate either according to a fixed schedule or spontaneously according to mutual

Table 2. Criteria for a meaningful task.

Herzberg (1974)	Thorsrud (1972)	Den Hertog (1977)
	• optimal alternation of tasks and movements • task should be a self-contained and meaningful unit • optimal length of task cycle • the work should make a perceptible, useful contribution to the total product • couple tasks as much as possible and promote rotation	• horizontal job loading or extension of time cycle • job rotation
• individual responsibility for product	• creating working groups with group task, feedback on group production and influence on activities in immediate environment of group (autonomous group)	• establishing small product-oriented working groups
• direct relation with consumer within or outside the organization • possibilities for self-development as new elements are added to the work from a higher level (by delegation from above) • delegating responsibility for control of costs • freedom to directly contact colleagues in other departments, as required by one's work	• integration of work and work preparations and final operations • utilizing knowledge and skills	• job enrichment: adding elements of a qualitatively higher level • deverticalization by delegating tasks and responsibilities downward
• direct feedback on performance in non-judging terms	• good feedback on performance	• feedback of information on quality and quantity
		• work consultation: in this approach being both element of and condition for job design

agreements. Greater variation in the work and increased flexibility of the members are considered to be among the advantages.

Herzberg rejects this form of job design also: 'This means washing dishes for a while, then washing silverware' (1968, p. 59). In Sweden experiences (*Job Reform in Sweden*, 1975, p. 62) with job rotation on a fixed schedule are not positive either. However, positive experience was gained from a systematic horizontal training for more jobs, which was in operation for a limited period. Such preparation enables members of a work group to replace one another in cases of illness, changes in the production, etc. Spontaneous job rotation, i.e. when necessitated by the work in the group, is considered the best form of job rotation.

VERTICAL LOADING, JOB ENRICHMENT

Job enrichment is concerned with the qualitative changes occurring in the work. Tasks previously performed by a sub-foreman or by employees of service departments are now performed by the employees themselves. Examples of such tasks are work preparation, work control, administration, taking samples, adjustment work, and minor repair and maintenance operations, writing out orders, division of work. Meyers (1970) points out that each work process may be divided into three stages:
1. planning and preparation;
2. production;
3. control and servicing.

To him, the essence of job enrichment is that elements of planning and control are again incorporated into the production task.

Often, job enrichment is possible only when the traditional barriers between groups and departments are removed.

FEEDBACK OF DATA ON QUALITY AND QUANTITY

In order to enable a system to learn to regulate itself and to control a number of environmental variables, good feedback of its functioning is practically indispensable. Setting up fast and accurate signalling systems plays an especially important part in job design projects. Chances that the project will get out of hand increase when there are too many links and filters between the place where the mistake was made and the place where the mistake is noticed. If within the group, there is insufficient insight into the course and the result of the work process, it will soon become dependent on outside agencies. Both sociotechnics and job enrichment emphasize the importance of this element.

SEMI-AUTONOMOUS GROUPS

Formation of semi-autonomous groups is propagated especially in sociotechnics. Here, the group is considered a unit that, within a larger unit, is made responsible either for a part of the production process (process-oriented group) or for a specific range of customers (customer-oriented group). The group is charged with especially those tasks, that are necessary to keep the work process going (e.g. maintenance) or to redirect it (e.g. adjustments and quality control). Thus, small independent and orderly organized work units come into existence, whose members can themselves assign work, redirect, establish stable work contacts and survey the whole process.

Production-oriented groups have the advantage that their work has more identity. Everybody has a clearer view of what he is doing.

With very complex products, it is often difficult to limit the size of production-oriented groups. One may look for the middle road and divide the product into self-contained parts.

It is again Herzberg (1974) who sees no good to be gained from this approach. Two arguments are put forth: the fact that it may get individuals into predicaments because of *group pressure* and the thesis that social contacts within groups do not act as satisfiers.

WORK CONSULTATION

Within the approach of job design, work consultation is a central element. Such changes involve not only changes in structure but also changes in culture and in mutual relations. Work consultation can then be an important support of the project.

Either on the regular basis of some schedule or incidentally at the request of executives or the group, meetings are held where problems of the previous period are discussed, information is passed on from higher to lower levels, and arrangements are made for the next period. Work consultation is a most meaningful and self-evident matter in small production units that, in social-psychological respect, form a group. There, consultation takes place directly and with all members of the group present. Work consultation is not only inherent in job design but also a means towards it: it is both an element and a condition (*Job Reform in Sweden*, 1975).

DEVERTICALIZATION

Contracting the hierarchical lines clears the way for delegating tasks and responsibilities downward. The resulting 'flat' organization may constitute a basis for more open and more democratic organizational relations and for more direct contact between employees and management (Buitendam, 1968). In the orthodox approach of job enrichment (Herzberg, 1974) there is no room either for work consultation or for deverticalization. Both elements are expected to have only temporary effects. However, experiences in Sweden (*Job Reform in Sweden*, 1975) and in companies like Philips (den Hertog, 1977) point in another direction.

3.2. The strategy of the process of change

The course of the process of organizational change is not only determined by the content of the changes. The direction they take in practice plays a part at least as great. The job enrichment school has from the start always been very outspoken about the strategy of job design.

This approach is characterized by its approach from *above*. In the organization, one of the members of higher management assumes the role of the key figure (Ford, 1969), who is charged with controlling the progress of the plan. The actual elaboration is left to the immediate superiors of those whose tasks are involved.

The realization of job enrichment runs its course following a standard procedure. In the first phase, the immediate superiors are given an exposé about Herzberg's theory. It is pointed out, that together they should look for satisfiers, for changes contributing to the personal growth of the employees. This is followed by a brainstorming session ('greenlight session'). Their task then is to list as many motivating changes as possible, without paying attention to their feasibility. In the third phase, the list of ideas is carefully scrutinized ('redlight session'). Finally, the changes are introduced into the tasks and the employees are instructed as to how to perform their new tasks.

Herzberg (1968) points out that, with direct participation of the workers, job enrichment is doomed to fail. They would tend to be too strongly oriented towards matters that have nothing to do with the work itself. And anyway, participation would only temporarily provide a sense of involvement. It is remarkable, that the approach of the orthodox version of job enrichment has not evolved at all in those 15 year of gaining experience with it (see Herzberg, 1976).

Representatives of sociotechnics do, however, show signs of evolvement. This is reflected in the pursuit to increase the involvement of those concerned (see also this Handbook, ch. 4.9). This pursuit represents a distinct difference between American and European industrial relations.

In the first experiments (Rice, 1958; van Beinum et al., 1968) the approach to the process was hardly ever given a thought. One operated from a doctor-patient-model. Management was or was being convinced of the necessity of change. Researchers analyzed the system and, according to their model, made a proposal. This proposal was carried out when approved by the management and discussed, or not, with the people concerned. In other words: the projects were strongly dominated by the researchers. In the next phase, the emphasis on active involvement of those concerned gradually gained force.

A good illustration is the development in Norway, as outlined by Elden (1979). The researcher continues to play a very important part. Gradually, however, this part was being limited to the diagnostic phase. More room is coming available for those concerned to participate in formulating proposals for change, while the function of the researcher is rather an advisory one. In the last phase, the role of the researcher is limited to a supportive one. During the whole course of the process, the initiative lies with the management and the workers themselves.

An identical tendency may be observed in the course of the experiences at the Philips company (den Hertog, 1977, p. 97) and in Sweden (*Job Reform in Sweden*, 1975, p. 14): 'It is only common sense that a workplace can be best designed using the contributions of those who know most about the work—those who do it'. In this connection, Allegro (1973) points out the necessity of linking job design and organization development.

4. THE STATE OF THE ACT

The sociology of science informs us (Crane, 1972) that for every developing discipline there comes a point where the ideas and models of the classic pioneering studies need to be reformulated, because they no longer cover reality. New possibilities must be found for further expansion and in order to prevent erosion.

Considering the large number of critical studies on job design, which has been growing ever since the mid-seventies job design seems to have reached this point. In 1976, Davis indicated that, 20 years after the introduction of job design, ideas and theories on this subject have spread extremely slowly. According to him, there is a discrepancy between the attention paid to job design in professional literature and mass media, and the way in which job design is carried out in practice. The promises of the pioneering studies have hardly been honored. Experiments do not diffuse and get stuck in the 'experimental garden' stage. Davis does not stand alone with his conclusion. Researching the effects of the job design projects at Philips, Den Hertog (1977, p. 168) concluded that the good and convincing results, obtained occasionally at micro-level, had hardly ever found their way to the meso-level of the organization.

Similarly, Ackoff (1974) notes that until 1974 at most 3000 workers in the United States had been involved in experiments to 'humanize' work. Asked how ideas on job design may be successfully disseminated throughout whole companies, even Bob Ford, AT & T's Grand Old Man in job enrichment, could not but reply: 'I don't know; as yet I have never seen anybody do it' (1971, p. 211). Thus, Ackoff predicts that future historians will look back on this as a pursuit which was put into practice too little and too late (1974, p. 53).

4.1. Elements for a new strategy

In the past years, it has become clear that job design is at a critical state and that re-orientation is necessary. There is a need for a new strategy, which should make possible the large-scale application of the valuable ideas of the pioneering studies. A strategy which can be used to make job design an integrated part of the social-organizational policy of industrial organization. The construction of such a strategy requires a thorough analysis of the impasse which job design as an intervention has arrived at. A large number of studies is concerned with just that task. Below, the most important elements for a new strategy, as presented in such studies, are summarized.

A PROBLEM-ORIENTED DIAGNOSIS

The literature on organizational change makes it unequivocally clear that attempts at change should be directed towards the problem and not its solution. Often, the diagnosis of specific problems is an important spring-board for action (Lawrence and Lorsch, 1969). According to Birchall, in job design the initial diagnosis should bring to light possible weaknesses of the operational system, policy, and manning, and should, moreover, provide indications concerning the relations among these basic variables of the system. Once the problem is defined, the definition will often determine which subsystem of the organization will be dealt with. If, at the beginning of a project, attention is paid only to the social aspects of an organization, the proposed solutions will also be in that area. (For an illustration see Den Hertog and Wester, 1979). Any job design approach which starts from a diagnosis oriented towards social aspects only, will remain an isolated social phenomenon within the organization. The development of approaches that are successful and have a lasting effect requires an approach to and analysis of the organization as a whole, while as much attention should be paid to economic and technical aspects as to social aspects of the system.

A HIGHER LEVEL OF INTERVENTION

Most experiments are characterized by interventions at micro-level: the level of individual tasks. However, the content of these tasks is to a great extent determined by the design of the systems at the higher level. The technology of the production process (Davis, 1971, 1976) often strongly marks the nature of both the work and what is expected from the individual and from the organization. The same holds for information and control systems (den Hertog, 1978; Thorsrud, 1977; Mumford and Henshall, 1979). Often, when these systems are left out of the discussion, there is only very little room for essential changes in the relation between man and work. One could say, that the structure of an individual task is a dependent variable, determined by systems at a higher aggregation level. The product, the technology with its control systems, and the organization of the whole (see figure 4) determine the amount of room available for creating tasks with a human design.

Designing production systems implies choosing from among alternatives. Alternatives in the area of production apparatus, lay-out, routing, materials management, planning systems, etc. these alternatives may have divergent consequences for the tasks of individuals and groups. This is the appropriate

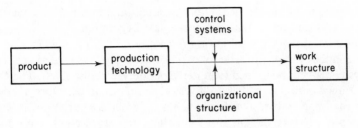

Figure 4. Job design as a derivative.

level for dealing with the organization of work (Davis, 1976; den Hertog, 1977; Gulowsen, 1973; van Assen, 1980). Actually, the message is that in job design we should direct our attention towards the design of the organization as a totality.

THE NATURE OF INTERVENTION SHOULD BE PREVENTIVE

Most job design projects bear the mark of a cure rather than of prevention. This means that managements take action only when the rusty systems begin to crack and clearly identifiable problems in the relation between worker and production system come to light. This is illustrated in figure 5, where the course of three job design projects is plotted against the time axis. The projects were started a few years after the installation of a production system.

After that, the introduction of job design takes one or two years. A few years

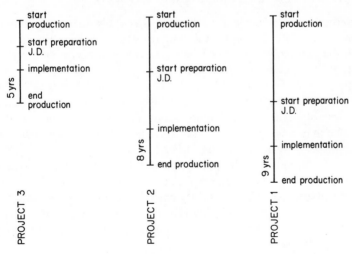

Figure 5. Job design and the product's life cycle (den Hertog, 1977, p. 172).

later, production is discontinued. Other products and means of production are introduced and one starts again from the very beginning.

Job design and work consultation (*Job Reform in Sweden*, 1975) should be embedded in the everyday practice of management. They become topical as soon as the system is being designed (van der Does de Willebois, 1968). The Central Works Council of Philips makes itself very clear on this point: 'Once it is decided to apply job design, job design should be taken into account right from the start (for example, product design, mechanization, factory lay-out, etc.) and not belatedly at the last minute, as if it were a kind of sauce to give whatever is being served more flavor. We may call this aspect integration in time or also preventive job design' (*Wat doet Philips...*, 1973, p. 22).

THE QUALITY OF WORK AS A JOINT RESPONSIBILITY

The experiences in Sweden (*Job Reform in Sweden*, 1975) may teach us, that when the initiative of staff functionaries is the mainstay of a project, chances of its survival are minimal. In that case, management will have its doubts from the beginning. On the other hand, projects often appear to rely too much on the efforts of an individual department manager. It is suggested that the quality of work should be an integrated part of company policy (ford, 1971; den Hertog, 1977). A policy based on involvement of the top management and smooth cooperation between staff and line personnel. The quality of work requires a joint responsibility.

PARTICIPATION IN DESIGNING AND PLANNING INTERVENTIONS

In the Netherlands in particular, there is a steadily increasing number of publications, critically discussing the way in which workers are made participants in the planning of work consultation and job design (Kuipers, 1972; Ramondt, 1974; Looise, 1976). Scandinavian studies (*Job Reform in Sweden*, 1975; Emery and Thorsrud, 1969; Gulowsen, 1973; Thorsrud, 1977) state clearly that the workers' participation and involvement are essential conditions for any form of organizational innovation. The Dutch studies cited show, however, that in practice participation in deciding how one's own work situation is to be changed is wishful thinking rather than reality.

Ramondt (1974) indicates, that participation should be institutionalized in a clear-cut way. According to him, the modern Dutch institutionalized forms of consultation (works councils and parity consultations) are at present not very appropriate for this purpose. Günther (1974) supposes that, in Germany, trade organizations especially are wanting in good strategic models for getting a better hold on the quality of work.

From the developments outlined in section 2.4 it may be inferred that the conditions for institutionalization are to a large extent determined by the system of industrial relations in the country concerned. It is not surprising, therefore, that in the Scandinavian countries such conditions have reached a more advanced stage of development than elsewhere.

THE POSSIBILITY TO LEARN FROM INTERVENTION

From many sides it is being emphasized that job design should be considered a learning process (Allegro, 1973; Thorsrud, 1972; Davis, 1976; this Handbook, ch. 4.9). Most projects require a process of change which should create the opportunity to gain experience.

In reality, however, goals often shift in the course of a project. The experiment is then no longer considered as an intervention in the context of a broader process of change but as a goal in itself. It is like an admission exam: if the candidate fails, the door remains closed to him.

However, more may be learnt from mistakes and failures in less successful experiments than from glib success stories. But in that case, it is prerequisite that success and failure may be discussed freely. Or in the words of Van Beinum (1973): 'Self-innovation means learning and learning hurts'.

4.2. A look into the future

It may be expected that, in future, the pressure on industrial organizations to adapt to new developments will continue or even increase. Also, the gap between the quality of the employees and those of the work offered will grow wider (*Nota inzake Werkgelegenheid*, 1975). Nor is it conceivable that in the years to come the demotivation tendency (Cools, 1979) will diminish. The concern of legislators and various interest groups regarding the quality of work is as yet only in its initial phase. In the fields of technology and organization, too, developments keep presenting themselves that make it necessary to pay attention to this issue. Developments in technology render the technological systems ever more dependent on the human factor.

This increasing dependence implies that, for these systems to work well, ever more attention must be paid to adapting the work to the worker (Davis, 1971). Therefore, in designing work systems and organization structures, the quality of work should more frequently count as an equally valuable design criterion, besides technical and economic criteria (Wester, 1978). Such an approach of job design will show up two important developments. In the first place, in the technical and organizational sciences alternative will be developed and selected that are in better agreement with social criteria. Above we have seen that in various countries the first steps have already been taken. Thus, one may take a look at developments in the field of production technology in Sweden, where, for example, alternatives to internal transportation were developed that offer more possibilities for designing industrial systems according to the criteria of job design (Agurén and Edgren, 1980). In The Netherlands, ideas about the relation between job design and organizational design are worked out in detail in the model of Van Assen (1980).

Noteworthy in the field of information technology is the work of systems analysts at Rolls Royce, who, under the guidance of Mumford (1979), have worked on the development of new systems. Mumford describes how in the company these alternatives were weighted on task-content criteria, in cooperation with those who would have to work with them. Another example is the tendency to design information systems in terms of system flexibility (den Hertog et al., 1980), so that they can always be adapted to changing work systems.

Finally, the relation between industrial architecture and the experiences and needs of its users is an object of study at the French institute for the quality of work, ANACT (Grenier, 1979).

Another development concerns the strategy of change. Thorsrud (see section 2.4 above) indicates, that the involvement of workers in designing work systems may possibly be more important than the content of the changes.

However, participative consultations will not be realized on the basis of intentions only. Concrete strategies should be worked out. Mumford's ETHICS method for participative design and Thorsrud's 'do it yourself workshops' (Thorsrud, 1977) represent steps in that direction.

An industrial and organizational psychologist will be able to contribute to both developments. Firstly, by mapping out the problems of the organization and weighting alternative solutions on their work-content aspect, in cooperation with system designers and system consumers.

Secondly, by working, in supervising and researching, on strategies for the participative design of technical and organizational systems. According to the present authors, both fields are practically unexplored.

It will be clear, that a work and organizational psychologist does not function like an evangelist who, from his limited perspective on technology and organization, preaches the gospel of job design.

The consequence of such a development is that job design will be less delimited and restricted. It no longer concerns experimental gardens demarcated by flower pots, on view in a corner of the organization, but rather continuous changes, melting into the everyday practice of the industrial organization (*Job Reform in Sweden*, 1975).

REFERENCES

Ackhoff, R. L. (1974), *Redesigning the future. A systems approach to societal problems.* New York: Wiley and Sons.

Agurén, S., Edgren, J. (1980), *New factories. Job design through factory planning in Sweden.* Stockholm: SAF.

Agurén, S., Hansson, R., Karlsson, K. G. (1976), *The impact of new design on work organization.* Stockholm: Rationalization Council SAF-LO.

Alink, J. B., Wester, Ph. (1980), Organisatieverandering in een gereedschapmakerij [Organizational change in a tool factory]. In: van Assen et al. (1980).

Allegro, J. T. (1973), Sociotechnische organiatie-ontwikkeling [Sociotechnical organization development]. Leiden: Stenfert Kroese.

Allegro, J. T., Vries, E. de (1979), Project: Humanization and participation in Centraal Beheer. Working on the quality of working life: Developments in Europe. Boston: Nijhoff.

Arends, G. (1974), Labour turnover. Summary of findings in the Philips-concern. Eindhoven: Philips.

Assen, A. Van (1980), Organisatie-ontwerp, een analytisch model vour werkoverleg en werkstructurering [Organization design, an analytical model for work consultation and job design]. In: van Assen et al. (1980).

Assen, A. van, Hertog, J. F. den, Koopman, P. L. (1980), Organiseren met een menselijke matt [Human organization]. Alphen a/d Rijn: Samsom.

Beek, H. G. van (1964), The influence of assembly line organization on output, quality and morale. Occupational Psychology, 38, no. 3 + 4, 161–172.

Beinum, H. J. J. van, Gils, M. R. van, Verhagen, E. J. (1968), Taakontwerp en werkorganisatie. Een sociotechnisch veldexperiment [Task design and work organization. A sociotechnical field experiment]. The Hague: COP.

Beinum, H. J. J. van (1973), Personal communication.

Beinum, H. J. J. van, Vlist, R. van der (1979), QWL developments in Holland: An overview. In: Working on the quality of working life: Developments in Europe. Boston: Nijhoff.

Birchall, D. (1975), Job design, a planning and implementation guide for managers. Epping: Gower Press.

Buitendam, A. (1968), Deverticalization in production departments. Eindhoven: Philips.

Cools, E. (1979), Demotivatie [Demotivation]. Sociale Kroniek [Social Reports], Philips, Vol. 1, no. 2, p. 2–6.

Crane, D. (1972), Invisible colleges: Diffusion of knowledge in scientific communities. Chicago: University of Chicago Press.

Davis, L. E. (1971), The coming crisis for production management: Technology and organization. In: Davis, L. E., Taylor, J. C. (1972), Designs of jobs. Harmondsworth: Penguin Books.

Davis, L. E. (1976), Developments in job design. In: Warr, P. (1976), Personal goals and work design. London: Wiley and Sons.

Does de Willebois, J. L. J. M. van der (1968), Werkstructurering als organisatie-ontwikkeling [Job design as organization development]. Eindhoven: Philips.

Dundelach, P., Mortensen, N. (1979), Denmark, Norway and Sweden. In: New forms of work organization. Part 1. Geneva: ILO.

Elden, M. (1979), Three generations of work-democracy experiments in Norway: Beyond classical socio-technical systems analysis. In: Cooper, C. L., Mumford, E. (Eds.), The quality of working life in Western and Eastern Europe. London: ABP.

Emery, F. E. (1967), The next thirty years: Concepts, methods and anticipations. Human Relations, 20, 3, 199–237.

Emery, F. E., Thorsrud, E. L. (1969), Form and content of industrial democracy. London: Tavistock.

Emery, F. E., Thorsrud, E. L. (1976), Democracy at work. The report of the Norwegian industrial democracy program. Leiden: Nijhoff.

Ford, R. N. (1969), Motivation through work itself. New York: American Management Association.

Ford, R. N. (1971), A prescription for job enrichment success. In: Maher, J. R. (Ed.), New perspectives in job enrichment. London: Van Nostrand Reinhold.

Galbraith, J. (1973), Designing complex organizations. London: Addison-Wesley.

Gier, H. G. de (1978), Making work more human. Een beschouwing over de betekenis en achtergronden van het wetsontwerp arbeidsomstandigheden [Considerations concerning the significance and background of the draft bill on working conditions]. *Beleid en Maatschappij* [Policy and Society], **5**, 10, 263–273.

Grenier, V. (1979), *L'architecture industrielle et les conditions de travail*. Paris: ANACT.

Gulowsen, J. (1973), Organizational design in industry. Towards a democratic, sociotechnical approach. *Personnel Review*, **2**, 2, 30–37.

Günther, H. (1974), Labour oriented approaches to the humanization of work. *International Institute for Labour Studies Bulletin*, no. 11, 21–24.

Hackmann, J. R. (1974), *On the coming demise of job enrichment. Technical report no. 9.* Yale: University, Dept. of Administrative Sciences.

Hertog, J. F. den (1977), *Werkstructurering* [Job design]. Alphen a/d Rijn: Samsom.

Hertog, J. F. den (1978), The role of information and accountancy systems in the process of organizational renewal. *Accountancy, Organizations and Society*, **3**, 1, 29–47.

Hertog, J. F. den, Vossen, H. P. (1974), *Organisatievernieuwing speciale miniatuur Terneuzen* [Organizational innovation special miniature Terneuzen]. Eindhoven: Philips.

Hertog, J. F. den, Vries, H. J. J. de (1979), Breaking the deadlock: The search for new strategies for QWL. In: *Working on the quality of working life: developments in Europe* (1979). Boston: Nijhoff.

Hertog, J. F. den, Wester, Ph. (1979), Organizational renewal in engineering works: A comparative process analysis. In: Cooper, C. L., Mumford, E. (1979), *The quality of working life in Western and Eastern Europe*. London: ABP.

Hertog, J. F. den, Wielinga, C., Heine, P. (1980), The integration of a computer system in the task environment of process operators. A case of action research. In: Mowshowitz, A. (1980), *Human choice and computers, 2*. Amsterdam: North-Holland Publishing Company.

Herzberg, F. (1968), One more time: How do you motivate employees? *Harvard Business Review*, **46**, 1, 53–62.

Herzberg, F. (1974), The wise old turk. *Harvard Business Review*, **52**, 5, 70–81.

Herzberg, F. (1976), *The managerial choice: To be efficient and to be human*. New York: Dow Jones-Irvin.

Job Reform in Sweden (1975). Stockholm: SAF.

Katz, D., Kahn, R. L. (1978), *The social psychology of organizations*. 2nd ed. New York: John Wiley.

Keniston, K. (1968), *Young radicals notes on committed youth*. New York: Harcourt.

Kuipers, J. H. (1972), *Verantwoordelijkheidsverruiming in de directe werksituatie* [Expanding responsibility on the shop floor]. The Hague: COP/SWI.

Kuylaars, A. M. (1951), *Werk en leven van de industriële arbeider als object van een sociale ondernemingspolitiek* [The work and life of the industrial worker as the object of a social management policy]. Leiden: Stenfert Kroese.

Lawrence, P. R., Lorsch, J. W. (1969), *Developing organizations: Diagnosis and action*. Reading: Addison-Wesley.

Lindholm, R. (1979), Towards a new world of work. Swedish development of work organizations, production engineering and co-determination. *International Journal on Production Research*, **17**, 5, 433–443.

Looise, J. C. (1976), *De proef op de som* [The proof of the pudding]. Utrecht: SWOV.

Maher, J. R. (1971), *New perspectives in job enrichment*. London: Van Nostrand Reinhold.

Miller, E. J. (1975), Socio-technical systems in weaving, 1953–1970: A follow-up study. *Human Relations, Vol. 28*, no. 4, p. 349–386.

Mills, T. (1978), Europe's industrial democracy: An American response. *Harvard Business Review*, **56**, 6, 143–152.

Mumford, E., Henshall, D. (1979), *A participative approach to computer systems design.* London: ABP.

Myers, M. S. (1970), *Every employee a manager.* London: McGraw-Hill.

Nota inzake werkgelegenheid [Memorandum on the volume of work] (1975). The Hague: Ministry of Social Affairs.

Onvrede en Klachten van Werknemers [Dissatisfaction and complaints of employees] (1975). Utrecht/Nijmegen: ITS & SWOV.

Perrow, C. (1970), *Organizational analysis.* London: Tavistock Publications.

Ramondt, J. (1974), *Bedrijfsdemocratisering zonder arbeiders* [Industrial democratization without workers]. Alphen a/d Rijn/Brussels: Samsom.

Rice, A. K. (1958), *Productivity and social organization: The Ahmedabad experiment.* London: Tavistock.

Roszak, T. (1968), *The making of a counter culture.* New York: Doubleday.

Sapulkas, A. (1974), Unions: A new role? In: Rosow, J. M. (Ed.) (1974), *The worker and the job.* Englewood Cliffs: Prentice-Hall.

Sitter, L. U. de (1977), *Produktie-organisatie en arbeidsorganisatie in sociaal-economisch perspectief* [A socio-economic perspective on production organization and industrial organization]. The Hague: NIVE.

Sociaal en Cultureel Rapport 1976 [Social and Cultural report 1976] (1976). The Hague: Social and Cultural Planning Bureau.

Sociaal en Cultureel rapport 1978 [Social and Cultural report 1978] (1978). The Hague: Social and Cultural Planning Bureau.

Strien, P. J. van (1980), Wat betekent humanisering van de arbeid? [What does 'humanizing work' mean?]. In: Galan, C. de, Gils, M. R. van, Strien, P. J. van (1980), *Humanisering van de arbeid* [Humanizing work]. Assen: Van Gorcum.

Thorsrud, E. L. (1972), Job design in the wider context. In: Davis, L. E., Taylor, J. C. (1972). *Design of jobs.* Harmondsworth: Penguin Books.

Thorsrud, E. L. (1977), Democracy at work: Norwegian experiences with nonbureaucratic forms of organization. *Journal of Applied Behavioral Science,* **13**, 3, 410–422.

Trist, E. L., Bamforth, K. W. (1951), Some social and psychological consequences of the longwall method of coal-getting. *Human Relations,* **4**, 1, 3–38.

Walton, R. E. (1972), How to counter alienation in the plant? *Harvard Business Review,* **50**, 6, 70–81.

Walton, R. E. (1977), Work innovations at Topeka: After six years. *Journal of Applied Behavioral Science,* **13**, 3, 422–434.

Wat doet Philips in Nederland aan werkstructurering, gezien van onderaf? [What does Philips do in The Netherlands about job design, as seen from below?]. COR a.i. Eindhoven: Philips.

Werkoverleg en werkstructurering in Zweden [Work consultation and job design in Sweden] (1975). The Hague: NIVE.

Werkstructurering, een samenvatting van experimenten bij Philips 1963–1968 [Job design, a summary of experiments at Philips 1963–1968] (1968). Eindhoven: Philips.

Wester, Ph. (1978), Werkstructurering als criterium voor organisatievernieuwing [Job design as a criterion for organizational innovation]. *Mens en Onderneming* [Man and Enterprise], **32**, 6, 397–420.

Windmuller, J. P., Galan, C. de (1970), *Arbeidsverhoudingen in Nederland* [Industrial relations in The Netherlands], 2. Utrecht: Spectrum.

Handbook of Work and Organizational Psychology
Edited by P. J. D. Drenth, H. Thierry, P. J. Willems and C. J. de Wolff
© 1984, John Wiley & Sons, Ltd.

4.9. Organization Development: an umbrella for two approaches

Georg R. P. Bruining and Jacques T. Allegro

PREFACE

This chapter is a survey of approaches to Organization Development (OD), to be conceived of as deliberately planned, purposeful activities directed at organization-wide or sub-system change. We hope this survey will stimulate our readers to acquaint themselves more thoroughly with this field.

At the same time we have tried to connect two different approaches, each having its own history. After a brief historical outline, a few specific methods of each approach are presented (section 1). Section 2 presents the results of research. We conclude (section 3) by indicating in what direction the desired integration may be achieved.

1. ORGANIZATION DEVELOPMENT: A BRIEF HISTORY

1.1. Introduction

During the 1950s two comparatively autonomous approaches were developed, both intended to improve the functioning of organizations. These two approaches, the *process*- and the *task-structural* approach, each have their own specific characteristics.

The *process approach* is concerned on the one hand with changes in or effects of influence upon the worker (opinions, attitudes, behavior) and, on the other hand, with organizational processes (communication, policy formulation and decision

Drs. G. Bruining, Vakgroep voon Sociale Pedagogiek en Andragogiek Katholicke Universiteit, Erasmusplein 1–18, Nijmegen.
Dr. Jacques T. Allegro, Fokke Simonzstraat 61, Stichting CCOZ (p.b. 5665), 1017 TE Amsterdam, Tel. 020–233769.

making processes, problem and conflict resolving). This approach is based on the assumption that development or growth of the members of an organization and improvement of interrelational processes will lead to an organization which functions more adequately. Ideas with respect to how this can be promoted are primarily derived from the insights and experiences drawn from group dynamics.

The process techniques and interventions thus developed aim to influence interpersonal relations with a view to effecting an open communication that enables the development of alternative structures and processes within the organization. The underlying idea is, that it is necessary to create an organizational climate in which the members of the organization establish their own conditions towards an effective functioning of both themselves and the organization.

A fundamental factor in the process approach is the nature of the relation between consultant and members of the organization. In this respect the members involved can, for instance, be given a chance to participate in the analysis of problems and the development of solutions.

So the shape of the relationship (e.g. giving the client the power to exercise influence) may help to mobilize human potential and engender processes that will lead to more opportunities for self-realization of the workers within the (structure of the) organization. This means that the emphasis is on *how* to bring about changes in an organization. In fact, this can be labelled an indirect approach.

The client is taught how to find a solution himself and how to give effect to it. The consultant's professional knowledge and skills are employed to engender a learning process towards the development of solutions.

The methods applied in this approach are often used as synonyms for Organization Development (OD). In our opinion, this view is too limited. We will discuss this in more detailed in section 3.

The first reports on and evaluations of these attempts at organization development date from the early 1960s.

The consultative activities of McGregor at Union Carbide and the events in the space-travel industry (TRW Systems) are considered milestones in the development of the above method (Davis, 1967; Marrow *et al.*, 1967). In the following years a number of consultants gained recognition through their publications, e.g. Argyris, Beckhard, Blake, Miles, Mouton, Schein, Shepard and, in The Netherlands, though from a different background, Hutte and Lievegoed.

Noteworthy in the last decade is the increased interest in this approach and its subsequent expansion. Its course can be traced in the successive volumes of the *Journal of Applied Behavioral Science* and of the *Harvard Business Review*. Even to-day these publications play an important role in articles on approaches to OD and their related theories and research. A good deal of representative material from those volumes was included in readers (Dalton *et al.*, 1970; Burke and Hornstein, 1972; Burke, 1975, 1977; Adams, 1975).

All these publications give a good impression of the methodical variations and refinements that resulted in the presently available ample supply of intervention techniques, modifications of strategy, research reports on more or less successful attempts at OD, as well as discussions about the values which form the basis of this approach.

In spite of the fact that in these volumes the subjects are categorized, no consistent and comprehensive picture of this approach to OD does emerge. Obviously, it was hardly a matter of a carefully considered, well-planned development supported by research-based theoretical evaluation. The approach seems to consist merely of an amorphous mass of techniques and models, which in a few cases only are backed up by a dash of theory.

It will be clear that the authors, as regards the aspects of this approach, chiefly engaged in theories on how influence is exercised and on the phases of change processes, interventions, the consultant's role, and other planned-change related issues. Moreover, most of these authors have one main aspect in common: their attention is focused on attitudes, behavior, and interpersonal and intergroup processes.

This is at variance with the viewpoints of those representing the *task-structural* approach. Publications in this field are more of an organization-theoretical nature and mainly concern diagnostic aspects and descriptions of solutions to organizational problems, i.e. the end state takes precedence over the process of development, strategies, or questions of implementation. This task-structural approach focuses on changes in task- and organizational structures, and on structural aspects such as role relations. In their opinion, changes in task-design and procedure will influence the attitudes, the behavior of the workers in the organization and their work relations.

This approach partly derives from the so-called 'classic' consultancy (scientific management and industrial engineering), whose procedure for dealing with organizational problems is as follows. Experts analyze the functioning of the organization and recommend changes to ensure improvement. The consultant's role is centered on designing a solution. Schein (1969) illustrates this by means of the so-called doctor-patient model: the consultant examines the client as if he were a doctor. A diagnosis is made, after which the consultant gives directions for treatment in the form of a report, which contains recommendations for changes, like in a prescription.

Apart from its deriving from classic consultancy, the task-structural approach can also be viewed as a reaction against it, considering the fact that it incorporates the lessons of the Human Relations Movement. This movement drew attention to the aspect of man, with his personal needs (satisfaction in his work) and social relations, as functioning within a network of techniques and structures. In analyzing and solving organizational problems not only the relation between social and structural aspects is considered, but, at a later stage, there is also a gradual increase in the attention given to, for instance, the importance of participation of those involved in the processes of change.

The first projects and resulting reports appeared at the beginning of the 1950s. In this respect a pioneering role was played by the researchers from the Tavistock Institute for Human Relations, who conceptualized the open socio-technological system approach (Trist and Bamforth, 1951; Trist *et al.*, 1963; Emery, 1959, 1963; Rice, 1958; Herbst, 1962, 1974). Emery and Thorsrud (1976) published their findings on the so-called Industrial Democracy project in Norway. In The Netherlands there appeared publications by Hutte (1966) and Van Beinum *et al.* (1967), Allegro (1973), and Allegro and De Vries (1979). (See this Handbook, ch. 4.5 and 4.8).

At the beginning of the 1950s, descriptions of projects intended to achieve changes in the technological system and task structure of organizations appeared elsewhere too. See Alderfer (1969) on job enlargement, and Davis and Canter (1956) on job design.

Towards the end of the 1950s concepts of job enrichment began to take shape (Herzberg *et al.*, 1959; Ford, 1969; Paul *et al.*, 1969). Journals that played an important part in furthering the knowledge of these approaches are *Human Relations, Harvard Business Review* and later on, though to a lesser extent, the *Journal of Applied Behavioral Science*. In The Netherlands there were contributions from *Mens en Onderneming*.

In recent years collections of articles have appeared, containing a selection of older and more recent publications on processes of change. See Davis and Taylor (1972); Davis and Cherns (1975). Moreover, a number of so-called Trend Studies appeared, describing the developments of this approach in various countries, such as: *Work in America* (1973); Van Beinum and Van der Vlist (1977); Van Gils and Van der Moolen (1980); Allegro (1980).

1.2. Some trends

It is as yet difficult to distinguish more detailedly between the essences of the two approaches, which both are still in the process of being developed and apparently tend to increasingly influence one another. The following survey of books published over the past years and the themes discussed therein, only means to throw some light on the specifics of the methods applied. The survey outlines the direction these views took and is as such mainly intended to be a guide to the reader.

1.2.1. THE HUMAN PROCESS APPROACH

The early phase of the so-called Human Process approach is characterized by efforts to establish the identity of this new approach to organizational change and to construct its conceptual framework. As regards defining the field, an important contribution was made by the Addison-Wesley series on organization development edited by Schein, Bennis, and Beckhard. The various publications contain a wide survey of OD in history and practice (Bennis, 1969), a description of strategies and interventions, as well as their diagnosis (Beckhard, 1969), organizational-diagnostic contributions (Lawrence and Lorsch, 1969; Blake and Mouton, 1969), and discussions on subtechniques in relation to specific problem areas (Walton, 1969; Schein, 1969).

In all these publications the two main sources of OD, as specified later on by French and Bell (1973), are evident: the laboratory method of training (T-group method) and the survey feedback method, which evolved from the former. Both these methods applied principles of learning, such as feedback, learning by experience, and learning by doing.

Characteristic of the laboratory method of training is the feature that the participants in an initially non-structured group (there are neither agenda, rules, procedures, nor is there a chairman) turn their own interactions and the group dynamics into the object of their studies. During a period of training, usually three to five days, and mostly guided by two staff members, the members of the group can learn from the discussions about their joint experiences and from the feedback they give each other. Learning themes are, for example, leadership, functions of group members, communication, decision-making, problem-solving, group development, and group norms.

The increase of interpersonal competence not only aims at more insight into that aspect, but also at experimenting with a more adequate behavior (learning by experience and learning by doing).

An essential feature of the survey feedback method is the use of survey and feedback sessions. With the help of a questionnaire, data on the organization are collected systematically. These data concern the individual perceptions of the organization's members of the various aspects of its functioning which affect satisfaction, motivation, and the results of the (members of the) organization. The information thus obtained is reported back to the related (or all) levels of the organization.

Next, during group sessions, the respondents are assigned the task to analyze the data, to interpret and to compare them with a situation thought to be desirable (diagnoses). Finally, plans (action plans) are designed to achieve improvements in the functioning of the organization.

Application of the laboratory method of training or of the principles derived from this important educational method, were, at its earlier stage, considered an important vehicle for changing organizational culture (feelings, informal behavior and interactions, group norms and group values). Authors like Schein and Bennis (1965) and Bennis (1966) have contributed much to the construction of a theory on this method for intervention in social processes and its applications.

This was followed by the development of new methods and refinement of the existing ones. In this respect, the emphasis was especially on attempts to overcome an important shortcoming of the T-group method: the minimal or insufficient transfer of what was learned to the work situation.

Reviews of the new process techniques thus developed and manuals on their application were published by Fordyce and Weil (1971), French and Bell (1973, 1978), and Margulies and Wallace (1973). These publications also show that the principles of the data survey feedback method, which had meanwhile developed independently, are widely applied in, for instance, group and intergroup interventions. Another example can be found in a publication by Dyer (1977) about methods for team building.

Team development

Team interventions may be focused on group processes (e.g. interrelations, communication, decision processes) or on the tasks of a work unit (for instance, its reallocation). In most cases both aspects will be taken into account.

Although the nature of the problem in question and the specific activities in a team-building conference may vary, there is a basic procedure which is generally followed in such meetings. As a rule a meeting will cover two to five days, with a procedure as follows:

—Step 1. Establishing the goals of the meeting.

—Step 2. Collecting the data. Views on problem-areas, interrelations, and suggestions for improvement are collected from the team members. The information thus acquired is then categorized by the consultant in a manner meaningful to the team.

—Step 3. Planning the meeting. The structure the consultant gives the meeting (with the help of a preparatory group) includes the procedure in general, the outline of the successive activities or exercises, theoretical input, and the definition of the roles and responsibilities of those involved.

—Step 4. Conducting the meeting. The information collected is submitted in a categorized form. After checking whether the rendering is correct, usually four sub-steps will follow:

—the themes are listed by the team according to their priority (agenda);

—the dynamics or structural aspects at the root of the respective problems are investigated;

—solutions and ways of implementation are designed;

—decisions, responsibilities as to implementation, and a planning in time are decided upon.

Lastly, a date will be set for a follow-up meeting.

—Step 5. Follow-up. This meeting is to check on the degree of implementation of the action plans. The problems encountered and the results achieved will be examined too. If necessary, the plans are adjusted or new ones designed.

Intergroup intervention

This intervention is appropriate when the diagnosis is that between work groups that have to cooperate, there exists, for example, insufficient or inadequate communication, a misunderstanding, rivalry, negative stereotypes, or hostility. A procedure often applied is the design for two groups made by Blake, Shepard, and Mouton. (See also French and Bell, 1978.)

—Step 1. Promoting commitment. The leaders of the two groups, helped by the consultant, assess whether the groups are able and willing to tackle the existing tension. The hour, duration, and place of the meeting are agreed upon.

—Step 2. Collecting the information. The two groups meet separately (in two different rooms) and receive each a different set of assignments. To start with, the opinions and feelings existing within the group about the functioning and activities of the other group are listed. Then, reversely, it is predicted what items will rank first on the other group's list (how does the other group see us?).

—Step 3. Sharing the information. The two groups assemble. First group A reports its views of group B. Next, group B reads out its list of how it sees group A. Then the respective 'prediction'-lists are exchanged. Discussion is not allowed during this session.

—Step 4. Diagnosing the problems. Each group returns to its own room to comment on the information obtained (what did we learn about ourselves and about the other group?). At this stage one usually finds out that many of the difficulties spring from misinterpretations. Consequently many of the remarks on the first list are crossed out, which leaves them with the more relevant items requiring adjustment. A new list is made of problems to be solved.

—Step 5. Action planning. The two groups assemble again and compare their respective lists. Next, one joint list is made of problems agreed upon and items to be resolved. Further procedures are similar to those in team-building intervention (see step 4 and 5 under team development).

The special attention given to data feedback and action research mainly started with the publications of Mann (1957), and Miles et al. (1969, 1970). This survey feedback technique was also published later in the form of a practical handbook (Hauser et al., 1977; Bowers and Franklin, 1977; Franklin et al., 1977). Nadler (1977) presented an eclectic survey of the techniques that can be applied in collecting data and their feedback to the client. These recent developments towards a market of practical, specific material reflect the increasing interest in and wider application of these techniques. Attempts have even been made to dispense with the consultant by drafting programmed lists of instructions for team development (Rubin et al., 1978) and for organization development (Francis and Woodcock, 1975).

In The Netherlands and Belgium the development of the techniques outlined above was closely observed from the start. This has, however, only recently become evident from the publication of books on organization development. It must be said, though, that the number of publications does not yet equal the amount of attention given.

Also, the majority of publications contain case-histories and reflections upon them. The themes are similar to those mentioned before, such as defining the identity of the method, defining the concepts, views on strategies, and value issues. Worthy of note are Glasl and De la Houssaye (1975), Van Dijck and Van

Hoof (1976), Feltman (1976), Verhallen (1979) and De Cock (1976). Other contributions from Dutch researchers will be discussed in section 3.1.

Expansion of the area of application

Besides the increase of the intervention methods available, the area of application is also expanded. The methods and techniques of OD were developed within industrial organizations. And although so far, they were applied the most frequently in that field, there soon came a tendency to adapt the existing approach to organizations of a different type, particularly to the so-called 'non-profit' sector. And, within this sector, most distinctly so to the fields of education and health care.

1. Schools

As pointed out by Fullan and Miles (1978), the first OD projects in schools were carried out in the US as early as 1963. Although, on the basis of two empirical studies, they found that OD developed more slowly in the field of education than in any other field, the number of publications by American authors has been steadily on the increase since then. In these publications a similar development from definition of identity to specific handbooks can be traced.

Miles (1964), Schmuck and Miles (1971), and Baldrige et al. (1975) compiled a series of articles in which they pay attention to characteristics typical of school organizations, the related relevant goals of change, and the required adjustments of interventions. In this respect, implicit and explicit comparisons with industrial organizations are involved. Furthermore, a remarkable aspect is the link established with the so-called innovation theory, which supports the introduction of new working methods into educational organizations. Experience and insights obtained in OD are used to enlarge upon this theory.

In this way the limiting aspect, i.e. the one-sided attention given to technological aspects of school organizations, is removed. Thus a relation is established between teaching and the organizational structure of schools. Finally, there are publications containing instructions about how to put theory into practice, among them a planning model by Zaltman et al. (1977) with specific directives for the implementation of innovations. Schmuck et al. (1977) work out a considerable number of intervention methods intended to influence process factors within school organizations.

2. Primary health care systems

A stimulus for applying OD in primary health care in recent years were the activities of a number of researchers at the Massachusetts Institute of Technology (MIT), in the department of Beckhard. Apart from case material, discussions on diagnostic and strategic viewpoints (Wise *et al.*, 1974; Rubin *et al.*, 1977), they also developed programmed instructions for planned change in primary health care systems (Rubin *et al.*, 1975).

Here also, the experiences gained from consultative activities in industrial organizations are used as frames of reference to point out in what respects this type of organization is different. In this context attention is called to its end product 'health', which is very hard to define, and to its less well-defined working methods (uncertain technology), i.e. the hard-to-define characteristics of 'good treatment' as well as the autonomy of professionals. All these aspects generate more uncertainty in this field than in any other system, which has its consequences as regards strategy and methods of change.

Summarizing, in all the above-mentioned publications relatively much attention is paid to the description of strategies and methods of change. Each one of them is often used as a synonym of OD and is, moreover, scarcely based on any coherent model or systematic theory. The attempts to establish an integrated theory or a frame of reference have more or less lagged behind. The number of authors engaged in this field of work is limited. Attempts have been made, though, by Argyris (1970) and Golembiewski (1972). An important contribution towards promoting a critical analysis of the applications (amongst which also the analysis of the task-structural approach) was made by Hornstein *et al.* (1971) in their analysis of strategies for organizational change. They thus laid the foundations for theory formation. Rothman (1974) made a noteworthy attempt at supporting his work by empirical evidence. He translated social-science research into useful practical knowledge for workers in the field.

1.2.2. TASK-STRUCTURAL APPROACH

Four methods can be distinguished:
—the open socio-technical system approach;
—job design;
—job enlargement;
—job enrichment.

As regards its contents, the tradition of job design (Davis) may be looked upon as a branch of the open socio-technical system approach, a branch mostly directed towards the individual. As such it will not be discussed separately here.

As to job enlargement: this form of change in task structures aims to join various tasks belonging to the same (low) level. In principle, the only change lies in the increased number of tasks to be performed. Therefore this method must be clearly distinguished from job enrichment and from the socio-technical system approach. The latter two are different in that they appeal to a large number of basic needs. Job enlargement was only a minor contribution, with regard to both its contents and its theory. Many authors have criticized its throwing together of all the small chores into one big chore (de Sitter, 1974; Herzberg, 1968; den Hertog, 1977). It turns out, however, that job enlargement in that particular form is hardly ever found in practice.

In the reviews of Beer (1976), Friedländer and Brown (1974), and Katz and Kahn (1978), examples are given of job enlargement projects, which on closer analysis, prove to contain some elements of job enrichment as well. It would therefore be more correct to speak of horizontal job enlargement if only an increased number of the same type of little tasks is involved. From a theoretical viewpoint, the foundation of horizontal job enlargement proves to be rather insubstantial, because it appears to have no links with current motivation-theories. Contrary to job enrichment and the open socio-technical system approach, job enlargement does not have any theoretically supportive literature. This is one of the reasons why no example of horizontal job enlargement will be given here. The emphasis in our chapter will be on the open socio-technical system approach and on the tradition of job enrichment. Moreover, we will enlarge upon the approach to industrial democracy, a notable Dutch tradition which has recently categorized itself under organization development. The reader is referred to chapter 4.5 of this Handbook (van Dijck) and to chapter 4.8 (den Hertog and van Assen) on the related tradition of work structuring at Philips. In contrast to these authors, who are mainly concerned with the contents of the task-structural approach, we will, apart from discussing more general themes, put foremost emphasis on aspects of implementation.

The open socio-technical system approach

This approach proceeds from the view that behavior within the organization can only be understood from and changed by the interaction between the social system (the individuals and their material, social, and psychological needs) and the technical system (machinery and production process). This whole system can only exist thanks to its ever open relationship with the environment in all its dimensions. Considering this, it has proved feasible, by means of socio-technical analysis and a related process of change, to realize work situations in which individuals feel more involved and function more adequately.

A concrete action program, in which the researcher's role is progressively made subordinate to the role of those concerned, will contain the following steps.

Phase I: general orientation (two to three months).—After obtaining permission from trade unions, works council,[4] and board of directors to carry out the project, the (action) researchers acquaint themselves with the organization. Ample attention is paid to the production-technical system as well as to the social system. A supportive steering committee comprising representatives from all levels is installed to advise the board of directors and the works council. The results of this

---

[1]A works council consists of members elected by the workers and, recently, also a chairman from among the workers. The elections are free. The trade unions take an active part. The council's decision-making power is limited.

introductory phase are reported to this steering committee. Mainly on the basis of this report further steps are taken: a) selection of a department in which an experiment could possibly take place, and b) investigation of which general problems in personnel and organizational policy should be tackled.

Phase IIa: socio-technical analysis of a department (appr. six weeks).—During this phase an analysis is made of the most prominent problem areas in the department selected and of how these are to be controlled. Besides, attention is paid to the formal and organizational structure in that department, to the policy as regards wages and salaries, and to how the employees experience their work situation. The basic principle of such an analysis is, that it is made in close cooperation with employees and management, preferably in some formal framework such as, for example, a work committee at departmental level.

Phase IIb: solving personnel and organizational problems (two weeks to two years).—During the general orientation a number of problems pertaining to the greater part of the organization will have emerged, concerning for instance, function classifications, wages and/or physical working conditions. The steering committee lists these according to their priority and advises the board of directors and the works council, after which solutions will have to be worked out as soon as possible (see also phase III).

Phase III: design and implementation of an action program (appr. two years).—On the basis of the information obtained during phase II and primarily in consultation with the work committee, a new task- and organizational structure is developed in which the creation of relatively autonomous groups is the central issue. It is advisable to start these activities simultaneously in various departments. The activities aimed at solving the personnel and organizational problems should meanwhile be continued, both at the departmental and at the organizational level via the steering committee.

Phase IV: evaluation of the project.—Evaluation takes place by means of various measuring instruments, preferably over a certain period of time. Those directly concerned should play a major part in this evaluation.

Job enrichment

The basic idea of Herzberg *et al.* (1959) is, that the factors affecting work satisfaction and motivation in a positive way are those factors that concern the work itself: the so-called motivators, such as growth, recognition, and responsibility.

Dissatisfaction is mainly attributed to factors outside the work itself, the so-called hygienic factors, such as supervision, wages, and working conditions. In this approach certain activities pertaining to higher and staff levels are shifted to and integrated into individual tasks at lower levels.

Steps to be taken in job-enrichment projects are the following (a free adaptation from Herzberg, 1968):

The program is supervised by one of the top managers, who controls the proceedings and leaves the executive part to the direct supervisors of those concerned.

1. Select a number of tasks, keeping in mind that motivation is a very important aspect of their performance and that the necessary investment for changes should not be too high.

2. Proceed from the view that tasks can be changed. Managers often assume that such a thing is impossible.

3. Do some brainstorming on all possible enrichments, emphasizing motivators—definitely no job enlargement—without taking into account whether they are feasible.

4. Do by no means allow the employees directly involved to participate; after all, the subject is task content and not the participation process. (Myers, 1970, who partly proceeds from this approach, does leave room for participation.)

5. Carry out a controlled experiment in which the hygienic factors remain constant. Achievements and attitudes must be measured before and after the experiment.

6. Allow for an initial drop in production

7. Allow for fear and hostility on the part of the supervisor concerning the adjustments that are made. Only later will he recognize that shifting part of his work to the employees enables him to turn his attention to tasks that have so far been neglected.

Industrial democracy

This concerns efforts towards linking policy-making in work organizations to the opinions and approval of those groups for which the policy is intended, and to the possibilities for the employees to achieve and expand their goals (Ramondt, 1974).

We will confine ourselves to Walravens (1977), who is from the same school as Ramondt, i.e. the department of Industrial Sociology of the Free University, Amsterdam (van Zuthem, Ramondt, Walravens, Kuipers, and Scholten). Walravens describes his approach as democratizing organization development.

In contrast to the other approaches, the researcher does not focus solely on the shop floor as the best perspective from which to set the democratization process in motion. There are more perspectives, such as the board of directors, the works council, or trade unions. A very important aspect in Walravens' approach is the emphasis on the socio-political dimension of changes. Moreover, considerable attention is paid to maintaining continuity by means of formal procedures and association with institutional frameworks. The following phases are distinguished:

Phase 1: Introductory phase, in which the project is introduced via consultations between works council, board of directors, and trade unions. Agreements are reached on the contents and conditions of the project, such as:

—approval of all persons involved;

—explicit agreements on time and money;

—possibilities of training and schooling;

—ultimate responsibility for the project rests with the works council, executive responsibility with the steering committee;

—involvement of trade unions, particularly in supervising and controlling the changes;

—possibility of supervising the board of directors with a view to continuity.

All employees are informed verbally and/or in writing and requested to give their opinions on the desirability, nature, and contents of the project.

Phase 2: Orientation phase: the researchers study the organization and its relevant environment by way of a systematic study of its history and a description of the current situation. At this stage also, a survey is held among the employees to gain insight into the individual characteristics and attitudes of the members of the organization at the start of the project.

Phase 3: Goal-integration phase, in which it is attempted to clarify and specify the goals of the project via concrete problems, for example by involving an employees' representative when appointing a personnel manager.

Phase 4: Organization phase, in which the final selection from the various disciplines for the research team is made. Agreements are reached on task-assignment as regards the guidance of the activities within the framework of the project. A steering committee is installed which has executive responsibility for the experiment. In this committee, the representatives of the production workers constitute the majority (three out of five). The decision process and the control of the project's continuity are settled, as well as the relation with the trade unions. An experimental program is designed in which the topics of the project are defined, for instance the election of a new works council with more responsibilities, and the starting of work consultation on current problems. Work consultation takes the form of regular discussions in the work situation between the supervisor and the workers on matters related to work. The conditions are fulfilled.

Phase 5: Phase of development; the organization now functions on the basis of the experimental project and the fulfilled conditions. The current policy is systematically adjusted to the new objective.

Phase 6: Phase of continuity, in which the conditions for the continuity of the democratization process are realized in cooperation between researchers, members of the organization, and other persons involved. The results of the process of change are evaluated at regular intervals and laid down in procedures and regulations to form a basis for the functioning of the organization and a starting point for future developments.

Phase 7: Evaluation; the project is mapped out by means of an extensive case description and of a number of quantitative and qualitative measurements.

When taking a closer look at the more general themes of the task-structural approach, the following characteristics may be noted:

—As in the process approach, the theoretical foundations of the task-structural approach turn out to be rather deficient. For criticism on the open socio-technical system approach see, for instance, De Sitter (1974) and Van der Zwaan (1973). They point to the absence of explicit definitions, to the assumed distinctiveness and equality of the social and technical subsystems, to the deficient analysis of norms, values, and structures, to the incomplete research methodology, and to the insufficient attention paid to its open-system character. An exception is Herzberg's theoretical work, which forms the basis of the job-enrichment approach. It must be said, however, that his work has also frequently been criticized.

Particularly Hackman and Oldham (1976) have criticized the deficient theoretical support of the task-structural approach and subsequently developed a model themselves. In this context, we will not discuss the merits of that model, but we think that efforts should be made to establish clear connections between the practice theories which developed out of this approach and the motivation theories which developed for instance out of experimental-theoretical psychology. For a method to measure task dimensions see Algera (1980).

—In most projects based on this approach, the differences between individuals were insufficiently considered, whereas various investigations have shown this aspect to play an important part (Blood and Hulin, 1967; Schouten, 1974).

—Often, the projects are carried out in an isolated department. This diminishes the possibility of an overall process of change, i.e. a change encompassing the whole organization. The assumption that a successful experiment in one isolated department will, to a certain extent, spread to other parts of the organization, is hardly supported. In particular Walravens (1977) pays ample attention to this question and focuses on the total organization, although the representatives of the open socio-technical system approach are also increasingly paying attention to the organization as a whole.

Another isolating aspect is the too exclusive attention for task-directed (intrinsic) factors in most experiments. Owing to this, the developments regarding the culture of organizations lag behind. There are some attempts at integration through a more process-oriented approach, specifically so in the open socio-technical system approach (see e.g. Allegro and de Vries, 1979).

—Particularly in the earlier projects, insufficient attention is paid to the many processes of learning and development. Sometimes also too little thought is given to involving those directly concerned. In some instances even, they are excluded on principle (Herzberg, 1968). However, attention for other roles besides of experts is increasing (den Hertog, 1977; Emery and Thorsrud, 1976; Elden, 1978). Thus it may be said that there is an increasing tendency to make use of the results and principles of the process-approach. Particular reference may be made to the importance of participation as a means to effect in those involved 'ownership' of the intended changes, as well as to the importance of data feedback, action research, and the use of groups to effect changes.

However, the use of representative steering committees and work committees often results in tension between these representatives and those represented. The latter do not feel involved and assume a passive attitude, which might be improved by well-functioning work consultation.

When problem solving concerns a change of organizational policy, developments are usually very slow, due to the emphasis put on consistent policy. Experimental departments often have but limited possibilities. Especially experiments with other ways of delegating responsibilities raise many problems.

—As with the process approach, there is an expansion of the area of application. The original socio-technical projects were carried out in the industrial sector (coal mines, textile factories), but attention later gradually shifted to service organizations, among them administrative organizations (van Beinum et al., 1967; Mumford, 1975; Allegro and de Vries, 1979), hospitals (Boekholdt and Allegro, 1975; Boekholdt, 1979), shipping companies, and education (Herbst, 1974). A remarkable feature is that, contrary to the process-approach, many of these projects are carried out at the lower levels of organizations (the primary work group), although there is a tendency towards projects at higher levels and projects for the total organization (Hill, 1971; *Job Reform in Sweden*, 1975, Allegro and de Vries, 1979).

As regards the tradition of job enrichment, it could be said that this tradition is more strongly directed to the middle level of organizations.

—Most projects, with the exception of Walravens (1977), have only limited significance for industrial democratization in a broader sense, although they are occasionally presented as such. This is particularly the case with the open socio-technical system approach.

2. RESEARCH ON THE EFFECTS OF APPROACHES TO ORGANIZATION DEVELOPMENT

2.1. Introduction

In section 1, it was shown that publications on the process approach mainly contain descriptions of strategies and interventions. The tendency seems to be to first develop the practice and then to direct attention to providing the theoretical and, especially, empirical foundations.

In his evaluation of 'the state of the art', Kahn (1974, p. 491), for example, shows himself rather unfavorably impressed when he remarks: 'Scientific research and explanation, however, require concepts that get beneath convenient labels and represent explicitly defined and observable events and behaviors. The literature of organization development is disappointing in this respect; it is tied closely to the labels in terms of which the varied services of organizational development are packaged and marketed'.

One often hears the opinion expressed, that empirical evaluations really deserving the predicate 'scientific' are hard to find in the field of OD. The reports on the efforts at change are often anecdotal and of the autobiographical type (Franklin, 1973; Friedlander and Brown, 1974; Margulies *et al.*, 1977). On the other hand, Porras and Berg (1978) are more positively inclined. They observe that, especially in recent years, more effective evaluation research has been carried out that will stand the test of methodological criticism. However, it is not surprising that a great deal of the research in the field of organization development is as yet little refined or barely valid. Evaluative research to investigate the effects of a treatment, is difficult.

Practical and methodological questions will, as Rabbie and Van der Vegt (1970) and Van der Vegt (1974) indicated in their studies on the measurement of training effects, play an equally important role in the field of organization development. The type of research approach necessary for investigating the differential effectivity of various OD-interventions, is complex and troublesome, if only because such investigations generally have to be carried out in actual organizations. It is extremely difficult to create research conditions with stringent possibilities for methodological control. In this respect, a quasi-experimental design will definitely ensure the best possible results (see this Handbook, ch. 1.2).

The investigations reported by us, were chiefly set up according to that model. Secondly, the treatment or (intervention) method, cannot yet be adequately described and this will remain so for some time to come. According to Kahn (1974), the independent variable is often a package rather than a scientific concept. Thus one and the same method may be labelled differently.

Nevertheless, despite all the difficulties described here, research results are beginning to appear which provide insight into the question as to which OD-approach or method produces what effects in what specific situations.

2.2. Research data on effects and conditions

Considering the limited scope of this article we will not give a complete survey of all the research done in the field of organization development. We only intend to provide an introduction. There have already been various attempts to summarize and evaluate the present empirical studies. For these, we refer the reader to the reviews of Sashkin (1972), Franklin (1974), Strauss (1973), Alderfer (1976), Friedlander and Brown (1974), Srivastva et al. (1975), Beer (1976), and Margulies et al. (1977). Here we will present summaries of only some research results and of the most cited and most instructive reviews. A number of comparative studies, which have contributed to the development and support of so-called contingency thinking in consultation, will also be discussed (see section 3). In that context, other recent empirical research will be mentioned as well.

To begin with, research data concerning the leading methods in the process approach will be discussed, followed by those of the task-structural approach. Next, information will be given about the relative effectiveness of the two approaches. In indicating the conditions under which the respective methods can be applied most successfully, Beer (1976) will be our main source.

THE PROCESS APPROACH

Review articles show that, all in all, the methods of the process approach, such as team development, data survey feedback, and intergroup interventions, have a number of positive effects on the attitudes, satisfaction, and morale of those concerned, as well as on organizational climate in general (Friedlander and Brown, 1974; Beer, 1976; Margulies et al., 1977). On the whole, there are no grounds for stating that the actual organizational processes change nor that either effectiveness or productivity changes. Only in a few cases, an effect on the quantity and quality of work is mentioned, be it cautiously (Margulies et al., 1977). Recent empirical studies also confirm that the human process approach contributes to a more positive attitude towards work and organization, while at the same time a decrease in personnel turnover, absenteeism, and role stress is noted (Hautuluoma and Gavin, 1975; Gavin and McPhail, 1978).

Research on the most frequently applied methods within the process approach, i.e. those of group development, showed up considerable evidence of short-term changes in attitudes. As regards the effects on attitude and behavior, it remains unclear whether the effects in question reach beyond the developed team itself. Nor is it clear, what mechanisms contribute to successful group development activities, what conditions have to be met for the learning outcomes to be transferred beyond the functioning of the team, or what the effects are on task performance.

T-group training seems an important instrument in cases when there is no commitment to change in the organization. Such training has softening effects and can pave the way for the desired change. However, such a training is by itself not sufficient to effect actual changes in the organization. To realize that change, T-group training will have to be followed by other interventions (Beer, 1976; see also Rabbie and Van der Vegt, 1970).

Team-building would be adequate to apply in case of diagnoses like: the group is incapable of solving problems, the power to influence is not well distributed, the relationship with the teamleader is bad, or the individual involvement of the team members is inadequate (Beer, 1976).

It cannot be shown conclusively that application of data survey feedback by itself leads to changes in individual behavior or in the achievements of the organization. The conclusion that short-term attitude changes occur, does seem justified (Friedlander and Brown, 1974; Margulies *et al.*, 1977; Hand *et al.*, 1975).

In the search for specific conditions under which the application of this method is appropriate, two studies are worth mentioning. Hand *et al.* (1975) suggest, as a result of their research on the effectiveness of the data survey feedback method in a laboratory-setting, that as a process-approach OD would be more relevant under uncertain conditions, when innovative behavior is required, than under routine-task conditions. This would imply that this method is chiefly relevant at higher levels in the organization. Hautaluoma and Gavin (1975), however, using a 'one-group pre-test/post-test design', conclude on the basis of the observed effects that the method might also be used as an alternative to 'job-re-design' for blue-collar workers.

To conclude with, the *intergroup methods*. Little systematic research has been done on their effectiveness. The present case-studies leave many questions open (Friedlander and Brown, 1974).

The reports on the effectiveness of these methods are merely subjective opinions. In this connection, Beer (1976) observes that success seems highly dependent upon (as yet unknown) characteristics of the organization in which the intergroup problems occur, upon the nature and causes of the conflict between the groups, upon the willingness of the respective team leaders to solve the problems, and upon the agenda for the meeting. As to the diagnosis, it appears to be important that the (intervention) methods in question not only influence issues and feelings from the past, but even more so new problems.

There is hardly any information available on the relative effectiveness of the respective methods mentioned so far (which method accomplishes most?). Here we should mention the pioneering study of Bowers (1973) on OD techniques and their results, based on the data of over 14,000 respondents in 23 industrial organizations. By means of a questionnaire the respondents were asked to indicate whether an organizational development treatment resulted in improved organizational climate and attitudes. The scores before and after application of the (intervention) methods are reported (raw gain scores). The effects of four 'experimental' treatments were investigated: Survey Feedback, Interpersonal Process Consultation, Task Process Consultation, Laboratory Training (T-group), as well as those of two control treatments: Data Handback and No Treatment.

In Interpersonal Process Consultation, the consultant's purpose is to increase his client's ability to develop and give effect to his own change program. Those concerned are mainly assisted in examining their feelings, attitudes and needs, and the informal group processes themselves.

The Task-Process consultant focuses on the task objectives and the associated specific, interpersonal processes. A characteristic of this approach is, that the consultant analyzes the work-task situation of a subsystem and at a later stage stimulates discussion about data selected by him.

Data Handback is limited to solely sending the tabulated research data to the supervisors in the organization. Problem-solving discussions in groups are not encouraged. The remaining treatments are in accordance with the descriptions given earlier in this chapter.

Comparing the various methods, to determine their relative association with an improved functioning of the organization, Bowers concludes that: 'Survey Feedback was associated with statistically significant improvement on a majority of measures, that Interpersonal Process Consultation was associated with improvement on a majority of measures, that Task Process Consultation was associated with little or no change, and that Laboratory Training and No Treatment were associated with declines' (p. 21). Finally, he is of the opinion that the mediating factor of 'organizational climate' has considerable influence on these results and that only Survey Feedback results in a substantial improvement of the variables in that domain (e.g. in the form of support and interaction facilitation by the management).

These findings were not presented by Bowers as conclusive results, although the alternative hypothesis has been put to the test, i.e. whether the results mainly indicate a 'regression toward the mean!' A problem still is, that data are lacking as to the question whether the groups compared were similar on one or more significant variable. Other shortcomings are the but sketchy description of the (intervention) methods, the lack of diagnostic data on the organization before treatment, and the lack of stringent criteria for organizational change (i.e. as regards productivity, absenteeism due to illness). Further research is therefore required.

THE TASK-STRUCTURAL APPROACH

Research on the effects of the methods of the task-structural approach—that is: the open socio-technical system approach, job enlargement, and job enrichment—shows that there is evidence of lasting effects on the organization, particularly with regard to the first method. There are, moreover, signs of increased satisfaction and improved morale and work climate.

The effects on quality and productivity can be more clearly demonstrated than is the case with the methods of the process-approach (Friedlander and Brown, 1974; Beer, 1976; Margulies et al., 1977).

In the experiments with the socio-technical system approach, brought into notice by Friedlander and Brown, the objective of the change was to improve the fit between the social and the technical aspects of the work-organization. Both aspects of the organization showed improvement. Even more extensive changes could be pointed out besides: effects not only on productivity but also on the 'alienation' of the employees. Job design and job enlargement[2] as well as job enrichment also show significant improvements in performance, productivity, and work satisfaction. In comparison with the socio-technical system approach, however, these results are less obvious and more research is needed. The socio-technical system approach most clearly displays its effects on performance.

Again, little information is available on the conditions under which these methods can best be applied. Beer does report on a large number of research data concerning the conditions, but these concern job design. Particularly important are the data on the interaction of individual differences among employees and characteristics of the job. Furthermore, relations are shown to exist between the proposed effect and urban or small town employees, and the values held by the employees with respect to work and achievement. Finally, attention is drawn to the role of organizational variables in the attempts to attain the proposed result: culture, social processes, technology, relations with trade unions, and re-muneration system. A diagnosis should be made before deciding on job design.

The same applies to job enrichment, which is feasible only if there is a reasonable degree of trust between the organization's employees and manage-ment. Another important aspect appears to be whether, as a consequence of such a method, it is possible for the employees to get more pay when their responsibilities increase. One more aspect is: good relations with the trade unions. And finally, the nature of the production technology is an important determinant of the success of the method. Characteristics such as autonomy, task variation, task identity, and feedback cannot be created in just any type of

---

[2]In our view, these methods cannot be considered as separate methods.

organization. Therefore, the interaction of technology and intervention method should be investigated in advance.

Several authors (Looise, 1976; Allegro, 1980) have pointed out that the as yet scarce Dutch projects in industrial democracy (Walravens, 1977) convey a moderately positive impression in the sense that increased participation of employees is effected.

3. ORGANIZATION DEVELOPMENT AS AN UMBRELLA FOR THE TWO APPROACHES

3.1. Introduction

More and more often, it is argued that the two approaches should be integrated to a certain extent (see e.g. Burke, 1977).

Process-consultants are becoming ever more convinced that they should not merely facilitate (inter-)group processes, but that in some situations a more directive approach is required and their expert knowledge regarding social, structural, and technological aspects should be brought in.

At the same time, those engaged in the task-structural approach are becoming more responsive to the idea that, under certain conditions, it is necessary to assist the members of the organization in solving their own problems or to have them participate (for instance, in the open socio-technical system approach).

It is interesting that the distinction between the two approaches, as made in the Anglo-Saxon literature, is less strictly made in The Netherlands. Implicit as well as explicit attempts to connect the two approaches are made from two view points.

The first view proceeds in a way that is not exclusively restricted to either the process approach, based on planned-change theory, or to the task-structural approach. Typically, in a number of publications these two approaches are linked. Already as early as 1966 Hutte's 'Sociatrics of work' was published, the first part of which contains a diagnostic framework concerning growth disturbances in organizations that resembles the socio-technical system thinking of the Tavistock group. In the second part, strategic principles and tactics are discussed.

Lievegoed (1972), proceeding from a change-oriented concept, also gives a description of the functioning of organizations. Particularly interesting is his contribution to organization-diagnostics in his description of developmental phases of the organization. He attracted attention with his description of the pioneering, differentiation, and integration phases which indicate in what direction change can be effected.

The dissertations of Zwart (1972) and Bekke (1976) are partly a follow-up of this study. They try to establish a connection between organization theory and planned change theory in general and the strategies of OD in particular.

And, lastly, in the work of Marx (1975) we come across an interest in both aspects. In aid of the development of comprehensive schools, he designed a diagnostic frame of reference, outlining five combinations of educational and organizational models.

The second view proceeds in a way that focuses on the consultant's role as the object of study. By means of a case history of consultative activities in an educational institution, Knip *et al.* (1975) deal with the question which consultant role (i.e. that of process-consultant, expert, or politician, respectively) is appropriate under what conditions (or phase of the project). The view that, depending on the situation, a choice must be made between three possible ways of influencing behavior, leads to the concept of the 'umbrella' mentioned in the title of this section. The first kind of choice is to effect changes in the task structure. The second is to improve relationships or to stimulate cooperation. And lastly, the third is to combine the methods of both approaches. The idea of alternative options joins the approaches under one umbrella, which we call: Organization Development.

Research data also contribute to breaking down the exclusive confinement to a single approach and promote their coming together within organizational change projects. They show the consultant that he has a choice and that it is possible to establish a better connection between the diagnosed need of change and the choice he makes from the variety of methods in response to those needs. In short, not only the many options for solving the diagnosed problems, but also, and even more so, the increased knowledge of the effects of the interventions in question contribute to a more satisfactory answer to the question as to what approach and what intervention are adequate under what conditions.

In section 3.2 we will present research data that may be considered a plea for integration. In section 3.3, a model for a more integrated organization development will be outlined. And, to conclude with, we will introduce some theoretical points of view regarding the development of a contingency approach in consulting (section 3.4).

3.2. Combining the two approaches: some research data

The preceding research survey shows that, in terms of improving attitudes, it hardly makes any difference what intervention method is applied, whereas in terms of productivity, the choice of intervention method seems to be crucial. However, this conclusion requires some modification.

Beer (1976), for instance, states that task-structural changes appear to be effective at lower levels in the organization, whereas process or educational interventions are more appropriate at the higher levels. Task-structural interventions appear relevant at the lower levels in the organization, because particularly at those levels problems arise from the organizational structure, technology, and (administrative) control.

These problems take the form of obstructed or restricted participation of the employees, frustrated adulthood, and various other psychological problems. In such cases, changes in the formal structure, procedures, and financial remuneration are important means of inducement at that level and may lead to self-realization and individual 'growth'. However, to say that changes in the structure of the organization, task content, formal procedures etc., are more effective at the organization's lower levels than process interventions, and that the reverse applies to the higher levels, is possible only when both approaches have been put to the test at both levels.

Another critical remark concerns the effects of the two approaches. The fact that no or hardly any influence on, for instance, the quality and quantity of production was observed when applying methods of the process approach, does not necessarily mean that such effects are actually absent. We would like to point out that production criteria, that can be established at lower levels in the organization, are impossible or far more difficult to establish at the higher levels. This means that the question of the comparative effectiveness will remain unanswered for the time being. This also appears from a Dutch contribution to the contingency approach of consultation, supported by empirical research (see section 3.4).

Van de Bunt (1978) made a systematic study of the effects of the expert (or content) consultation approach[3] and process consultation. In particular, he examined the conditions under which these two approaches are successful. The results of his investigation are as follows. First of all, empirical evidence is supplied on the differences between both the two consultation approaches and the two different types of organization (i.e. normative and utilitarian).

The hypothesis that the expert consultation approach will (in general) be more satisfactory than process consultation could not be confirmed. Such a conclusion is in accordance with contingency thinking as regards consulting, since, as we have seen previously, according to the latter differences in success may be determined by different conditions.

None of the hypotheses concerning the success of combining the approaches and types of organization or of combining the approaches and types of problems, could be confirmed. On the basis of a closer examination of the data, Van de Bunt nevertheless draws the conclusion that there are indications that the type of problem is a more important determinant of the result than the type of organization.

Instead of getting involved in a conflict about methods, we prefer to pursue a different course and advise to investigate which elements of the two approaches could be valuable in a particular change project. A number of research results already point to the relevance of such a course. These results concern a project in which a method from one approach is 'added' to a method from the other approach or in which a combination of methods is applied (subsequently).

---

[3]To avoid confusion in the context of this article, the term 'method' is here substituted by 'approach'.

The first and foremost method to be mentioned is that of involving the employees in finding solutions to organizational problems (an essential element of the process approach), which is followed by task-structural methods.

Methods from the task-structural approach are generally described as solutions or, rather, end-stages. Thus, French (1976) has the impression that certain forms of job enrichment are introduced, without a precise diagnosis having been made in advance and without participation of the employees concerned. In short, there appears to be a minimal interest in the question of development or implementation.

A number of fairly recent studies shows the positive effects of combining interventions of the two approaches. Thus, doing research in support of a job-redesign activity, Seeborg (1978) found that a procedure leaving room for participation leads to more job satisfaction and that identical changes are perceived as 'better' by those employees who participated in their own task design. Greiner (1967) and Dunn and Swierczek (1977) also confirm that procedures offering possibilities for the client's cooperation and participation in the change process, appear to be more successful than those without these possibilities. Particularly in structural interventions, the problem of willingness is thought to be more important than in the other approach (McMillan, 1975) and there is the necessity to involve, at an early stage, the employees concerned in the planning process (Frank and Hackman, 1975).

Golembiewski et al. (1974) speak in more general terms about the favorable effect of applying process methods prior to a task-structural intervention. With reference to a longitudinal effect study, they remark that the introduction of a flexible work-hours program proved successful due to the organizational culture. This particular organization had gone through a great many activities based on the OD-values of the process approach (see section 1.1). A large number of the employees took part in human processual methods, under the supervision of Golembiewski et al.

The researchers are of the opinion that the effect also resulted from the fact that the client accepted the OD-values (among which autonomy of the employees) as expressed in the work-hours design itself (i.e. their own decision on their work-hours) and in the dynamics of the implementation of the design. They point out that they were accepted within the organization and had established a basis of trust.

It appears that a more far-reaching, planned connection, particularly by means of combining methods of the two approaches within one consultation project, are worth the effort.

In a quasi-experimental design Pasmore and King (1978) investigated the differential impacts of a socio-technical system approach, of job re-design, and of survey feedback on a wide range of attitudinal and performance measures in comparable units of an organization. They conclude that the effects of the respective interventions on attitudes are quite similar. The combination of task-structural and survey feedback methods resulted in more positive effects on attitudes than the sole application of survey feedback. Only the socio-technical method brought about considerable improvements in productivity and cost savings. The limited effects of a process approach on productivity, however, should not give rise to a partial preference of the other approach.

The authors conclude that the task-structural methods, owing to their threatening aspects (fear of being dismissed, transferred etc.), could not have been used if they had not been preceded by the survey feedback method. Therefore, a combination of the two methods is considered necessary.

However, there is more to it than just drawing upon the variety of methods available in the two approaches, as is shown by Nadler and Pecorella (1975). They point out how important it is to establish a good integration of the methods of the two approaches. With reference to a re-examination of an organization development effort over a number of years in one organization, they observe that the various activities have had different effects on different groups in the organization. The various process and task-structural methods resulted in more autonomy in the task-performance of employees at the higher levels. At the level of production workers, participation in decision-making processes had increased. However, the lack of integration of the various methods caused role-ambiguity and dissatisfaction with decision-making processes among supervisors and technical employees.

On account of these observations the conclusion seems justified, that methods have to be integrated to prevent unplanned or differential effects that were not anticipated.

In connection with the integration of consulting approaches advocated by us, it is interesting that there is a number of trends, reported by Van de Bunt (1978), indicating that, in practice, the consultation approaches are already coming together. Representatives of each approach are applying elements of the other's approach. As a consequence, it turns out to be difficult to find a pure type of either consultation approach. Process consultants no longer hesitate to provide task-structural support, if necessary, and task-structural consultants increasingly involve their clients in their search for solutions to organizational problems.

In our opinion, the research data mentioned so far, support our view that integration of the two approaches is relevant. Moreover, that view is supported by the fact that an individual change by itself is not sufficient, no more so than an exclusive change of structure or jobs. The following model serves to illustrate the choices available in an integrated Organization Development.

3.3. A model for organization development

In view of the above-mentioned desirability of joining the two approaches, it is necessary to take a closer look at the dimensions contained in the approaches outlined so far. To suppose that integration merely consists in shuttling between

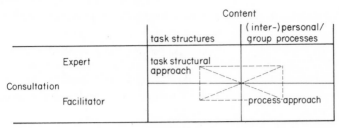

Figure 1.

the two approaches in the course of the change project will not do.

Agreeing with Van de Bunt (1978), we think it necessary to distinguish analytically between the content towards which an approach is directed, i.e. task structures or (inter-)group processes, and the consultation roles, i.e. those of expert and/or facilitator. This analysis is represented in the matrix of figure 1.

Up till now, we have mainly found certain specific combinations of roles and content in the OD-literature. The combinations given in our matrix occur most frequently: the so-called task-structural (1) and process (4) approaches. The dotted lines indicate what other combinations are possible, for instance that of focusing on task-structure (1) with a facilitator role (3). This implies the creation of conditions on behalf of those involved so that they can themselves design tasks and organizational structures. Examples may be found in the projects of Allegro and De Vries (1979), Seeborg (1978), and others. The last possibility (2) concerns focusing on (inter-)group processes from the viewpoint of an expert-role. An example is the teacher in a management-course, who demonstrates the theory presented by him by means of exercises.

A more dynamic elaboration of an integration-directed approach is given below.

Often, in the course of a change process, varying situations may occur, which require corresponding approaches. Thus, at a certain stage, a lack of knowledge may occur with regard to social, technical, economical, or structural aspects, which makes it necessary to bring in the relevant professional knowledge. Such an input may subsequently lead to a more group-directed consultation (group facilitation), so that its consequences can be examined in an open atmosphere and those involved can be stimulated to implement the corresponding, 'taught' organization principles in their own work situation.

Conversely, knowing that change often gives rise to resistance if it is brought about by external advice (e.g. purchase of expert information or service), a consultant may decide to let those involved participate first in the analysis of the organizational problem. On the basis of this analysis the consultant can then make a proposal for improvement and finally try to find ways to put these into practice in cooperation with the client. Such an intermediate form is described by Albrecht and Schierz (1971) in a cooperation model. In this model, knowledge regarding solutions is linked with a procedure in which the client participates in collecting the data, in the analysis and diagnosis, and finally in introducing the change (solution).

Thus, Organization Development is characterized by attempts to employ these roles alternatively (contingently), depending on situations or needs. The emphasis is mainly on stimulating the learning process of the members of the organization. Attention is alternately turned to task-structural and/or process factors.

For a theoretical support of this integration, we feel that a link can be established with so-called contingency thinking as it has been developed in various areas of organizational psychology. Thus, Leavitt (1951) shows the connection between task characteristics and their related communication structure, which influences group performance. Fiedler (1964, 1967) rejects the notion that someone who acts as leader in one situation, would, as a matter of course, be as suitable a leader in all other situations. His contingency theory gives insight into the question what type of leadership behavior is adequate under what circumstances. These aspects concern the nature of the relationship between the leader and the members of the group, the position of authority of the leader and the structure of the task concerned.

Lawrence and Lorsch (1969, 1972) (see also this Handbook, ch. 4.3) formulated a contingency theory for organizations. They note that 'There is not one best way of organizing'. They show, among other things, that an organization will function more effectively the more the nature of various characteristics of a unit corresponds with the stability (certainty of information) of the environment towards which it is oriented. Thus, with a stable environment, the related unit can be structured formally, a short time-orientation is adequate, and task-oriented interpersonal relations are appropriate. The reverse applies to a unit directed towards an unstable environment.

3.4. Towards a contingency approach in consulting

Following the above approaches, a contingency theory for organization development could be realized, proceeding from the view that there is 'not one best approach' to be applied in all situations. A conceptual model should be developed enabling the consultant to establish a rational matching between his consulting behavior (or interventions) and the nature of the problems diagnosed, the objectives defined and the conditions (e.g. characteristics of the organization), which all influence change possibilities. The first steps towards the development of such a frame of reference have already been taken. These concern formulations, chiefly based on the study of the literature and consulting experiences. We already referred to the contribution of Knip et al. (section 3.1).

Harrison (1970) makes an attempt at differentiation by proceeding from differences in the extent to which the client's (emotional) involvement is required in order to solve the organizational problem. This way, the different intervention methods, having different in-depth effects, may vary.

Clark (1972a, 1972b) discusses the matching between change strategies (or the consultant's role) and the variables to be influenced (foci) and characteristics of the organizational context. He distinguishes four role models and their appropriateness. As regards, for example, the so-called collaborative/dialogic strategy, he states: ... this role model is most appropriately utilized when the focus is solely upon the social system variables of improving interpersonal relations and authenticity, and when the context is characterised by a confident client with ample resources of time and money, with a commitment to deep penetration of attitudes, and occupying an integer power centre' (1972a, abstract).

To conclude with there is the frame of reference concerning the matching of interventions with problem causes (precursors) of Bowers *et al.* (1975). The authors distinguish three conditions or causes of problematic functioning in the organization: the presence, absence, or quality of the information, skills, and situational aspects, respectively. Subsequently, the types of intervention are classified according to the three precursors. These are classified according to the conditions on which their impact will be strongest.

The above-mentioned models are provisional, preliminary profiles. More research data than are presently available regarding the differential effects of approaches are required to support them empirically.

REFERENCES

Adams, J. D. (Ed.) (1975), *New Technologies in organization development, 2.* La Jolla (Cal.): University Associates Inc.

Albrecht, H. K., Schierz, J. (1971), De verhouding adviseur-bedrijf: Drie modellen [The relationship consultant-firm: Three models]. *Tijdschrift Efficient Directiebeleid* [Journal of Efficient Management], *6.*

Alderfer, C. P. (1969), Job enlargement and the organizational context. *Personnel Psychology*, **22**, 418–426.

Alderfer, C. P. (1976), Change processes in organizations. In: Dunette, M. D., (Ed.), *Handbook of industrial and organizational psychology.* Chicago: Rand McNally, 1591–1639.

Algera, B. (1980), *Kenmerken van werk* [Characteristics of work]. Meppel: Krips Repro.

Allegro, J. T. (1973), Sociotechnische organisatie-ontwikkeling [Sociotechnical organization development]. Leiden: Stenfert Kroese.

Allegro, J. T. (1980), Humanisering in de werk situatie [Humanization in the work situation]. In: Jaspars, J., Vlist, R. van der (Eds.), *Sociale psychologie in Nederland, III: De organisatie* [Social psychology in The Netherlands, III: The organization], 151–199.

Allegro, J. T., Vries, E. de (1979), *Project humanisering en medezeggenschap Centraal Beheer.* The Hague: COB/SER [English transl.: Project: Humanization and participation in Centraal Beheer, in: *Working on the quality of working life: Developments in Europe* (1979). Boston: Nijhoff].

Argyris, Ch. (1970), *Intervention theory and method: A behavioral science view.* Reading (Mass.): Addison-Wesley.

Baldridge, J. V., Deal, T. E., Ancell, M. Z. (Eds.) (1975), *Managing change in educational organizations.* Berkely (Cal.): McCutchan Publishing Corporation.

Beckhard, R. (1969), *Strategies of organizational development.* Reading (Mass.): Addison-Wesley.

Beer, M. (1976), The technology of organization development. In: Dunette, M. D. (Ed.), *Handbook of industrial and organizational psychology.* Chicago: Rand McNally, 937–994.

Beinum, H. J. J. van, Vlist, R. van der (1977), *Trends and developments with respect to the quality of working life in The Netherlands.* ILO brochure.

Beinum, H. J. J. van, Gils. M. van, Verhagen, E. J. (1967), *Taakontwerp en werkorganisatie in een socio-technisch veldexperiment* [Task design and work organization in a socio-technical field experiment]. London/Leiden: Tavistock/NIPG.

Bekke, A. J. G. M. (1976), Organisatie-ontwikkeling: Confrontatie van individu, organisatie en maatschappij [Organization development: Confrontation of individual, organization and society]. Rotterdam: Universitaire Pers.

Bennis, W. G. (1966), *Changing organizations. Essays on the development and evolution of human organization.* New York: McGraw-Hill Book Company.

Bennis, W. G. (1969), *Organization development: Its nature, origins and prospects.* Reading (Mass.): Addison-Wesley.

Blake, R. R., Mouton, J. S. (1969), *Building a dynamic corporation through grid organization development* (Mass.): Addison-Wesley.

Blood, M. R., Hulin, C. L. (1967), Alienation, environmental characteristics and worker responses. *Journal of Applied Psychology,* **3**, 284–289.

Boekholdt, M., Allegro, J. T. (1975), Organisatieverandering op de verpleegafdeling [Organizational change in the nursing department]. *Tijdschrift voor Ziekenverpleging* [Journal of Hospital Nursing], **20**, 949–957.

Bowers, D. (1973), O. D. techniques and their results in 23 organizations: The Michigan ICL Study. *Journal of Applied Behavioral Science,* **1**, 21–43.

Bowers, D. G., Franklin, J. L. (1977), *Survey-guided development I: Data-based organizational change.* La Jolla (Cal.): University Associates Inc.

Bowers, D. G., Franklin, J. L., Pecorella, P. A. (1975), Matching problems, precursors, and interventions in OD: A systemic approach. *Journal of Applied Behavioral Science,* **4**, 391–410.

Bruining, G. R. P. (1979), Over de begeleiding van samenwerkingsverbanden [On guiding cooperation networks]. In: Beugen, M. van (Ed.), *Hulpverlenen in de eerste lijn.* Assen: Van Gorcum, 93–120.

Bunt, P. A. E. van de (1978), *De organisatie-adviseur: Begeleider of expert?* [The organization consultant: Guide or expert?]. Alphen a/d Rijn: Samsom.

Burke, W. W. (Ed.) (1975), *New technologies in organization development: 1.* La Jolla (Cal.): University Associates Inc.

Burke, W. W. (Ed.) (1977), *Current issues and strategies in organization development.* New York: Human Sciences Press.

Burke, W. W., Hornstein, H. A. (1972), *The social technology of organization development.* NTL Learning Resources Corp.; Virginia: Inc. Farfax.

Clark, P. A. (1972a), *Intervention theory: Matching role, focus and context.* Paper delivered to the International Conference on the Quality of Working Life. New York.

Clark, P. A. (1972b), *Action research and organizational change.* London: Harper & Row.

Cock, G. de (1976), *Er hapert iets. Praktijk en theorie van organisatie-ontwikkeling* [Something is wrong. Practice and theory of organization development]. Antwerp/Amsterdam: De Nederlandse Boekhandel.

Dalton, G. W., Lawrence, P. R., Greiner, L. E. (Eds.) (1970), *Organizational change and development*. Homewood: R. D. Irwin, Inc. & The Dorsey Press.

Davis, L. E., Canter, R. R. (1956), Job design research. *J. Ind. Eng.*, 7, 275.

Davis, L. E., Cherns, A. B. (1975), *The quality of working life I, II*. New York: The Free Press.

Davis, L. E., Taylor, J. C. (1972), *Design of jobs*. Harmondsworth: Penguin Books.

Davis, S. A. (1967), An organic problem-solving method of organizational change. *Journal of Applied Behavioral Science*, 3, 3–21.

Dijck, J. J. J. van, Hoof, J. A. P. van (Eds.) (1976), *Organisaties in ontwikkeling* [Developing organizations]. Rotterdam: Universitaire Pers.

Dunn, W. N., Swierczek, F. W. (1977), Planned organizational change: Toward grounded theory. *Journal of Applied Behavioral Science*, 2, 135–159.

Dyer, W. G. (1977), *Team building: Issues and alternatives*. Reading (Mass.): Addison-Wesley.

Elden, M. (1978), *Three generations of work democracy experiments in Norway. Beyond classical socio-technical systems analyses*. Trondheim: IFIM.

Emery, F. E. (1959), *Characteristics of socio-technical systems*. London: Tavistock Doc. T. 42.

Emery, F. E. (1963), *Second progress report on conceptualization*. London: Tavistock Doc. T. 125.

Emery, F. E., Thorsrud, E. (1976), *Democracy at work: The report of the Norwegian industrial democracy program*. Leiden: Stenfert Kroese.

Feltman, E. (1976), *Een oog over OO. Een organisatiepsychologische bijdrage over en aan organisatie-ontwikkeling* [Running an eye over OD. An organizational-psychological contribution on and to organization development]. Deventer: Kluwer.

Fiedler, F. E. (1964), A contingency model of leadership effectiveness. In: Berkowitz, L. (Ed.), *Advances in experimental social psychology*. New York: Academic Press, Vol. I, 149–190.

Fiedler, F. E. (1967), *A theory of leadership effectiveness*. New York: McGraw-Hill Book Company.

Ford, R. N. (1969), *Motivation through the work itself*. New York: American Management Association.

Fordyce, J. K., Weil, R. (1971), *Managing with people*. Reading (Mass.): Addison-Wesley.

Francis, A., Woodcock, D. M. (1975), *People at work: A practical guide to organizational change*. La Jolla (Cal.): University Associates, Inc.

Frank, L. L., Hackman, J. R. (1975), A failure of job enrichment: The case of the change that wasn't. *Journal of Applied Behavioral Science*, 4, 413–437.

Franklin, J. L. (1973), *Organizational development: An annotated bibliography*. Ann Arbor (Mich.): Center for Research on the Utilization of Scientific Knowledge, Institute for Social Research, University of Michigan.

Franklin, J. L., Wissler, A. L., Spencer, G. J. (1977), *Survey-guided development III: A manual for concepts training*. La Jolla (Cal.): University Associates, Inc.

French, W. (1976), Extending directions and family for OD. *Journal of Applied Behavioral Science*, 1, 51–59.

French, W. L., Bell, C. H. (1978), *Organization development*. Englewood Cliffs (N.J.): Prentice-Hall Inc.

Friedlander, F. S., Brown, L. D. (1974), Organization development. *Annual Review of Psychology*, 25, 313–341.

Fullan, M., Miles, M. B. (1978), *OD in schools: The state of the art. Vol. I. Final report.* Ontario Institute for Studies in Education.

Gavin, J. F., McPhail, S. M. (1978), Intervention and evaluation: A proactive team approach to OD. *Journal of Applied Behavioral Science*, **2**, 175–195.

Gils, M. R. van, Moolen, R. A. J. van der (1980), *Nieuwe modellen van werkorganisatie* [New models of work organization]. The Hague: COB/European Foundation for the Improvement of Working conditions.

Glasl, F., Houssaye, L. de la (Eds.) (1975), *Organisatie-ontwikkeling in de praktijk* [Organization development in practice]. Amsterdam: Agon Elsevier.

Golembiewski, R. T. (1972), *Renewing organizations.* Itasca: Peacock Publ. Inc.

Golembiewski, R. T., Hilles, R., Kagno, M. S. (1974), A longitudinal study of flexi-time effects: Some consequences of an OD structural intervention. *Journal of Applied Behavioral Science*, **4**, 503–533.

Greiner, L. E. (1967), Patterns of organization change. *Harvard Business Review*, **3**, 119–130.

Hackman, J. K., Oldham, J. K. (1976), Motivation through the design of work. *Org. Beh. and Hum. Perf.*, **16**, 250–279.

Hand, H. H., Estafen, B. D., Sims, H. P. (1975), How effective is data survey and feedback as a technique of organization development? An experiment. *Journal of Applied Behavioral Science*, **4**, 333–348.

Harrison, R. (1970), Choosing the depth of organizational intervention. *Journal of Applied Behavioral Science*, **2**, 181–203.

Hausser, D. L., Pecorella, P. A., Wissler, A. L. (1977), *Survey-guided development II: A manual for consultants.* La Jolla (Cal.): University Associates, Inc.

Hautaluoma, J. E., Gavin, J. F. (1975), Effects of organizational diagnosis and intervention on Blue-Collar 'Blues'. *Journal of Applied Behavioral Science*, **4**, 475–497.

Herbst, Ph. G. (1962), *Autonomous group functioning.* London: Tavistock Publications.

Herbst, Ph. G. (1974), *Socio-technical design, strategies in multidisciplinary research.* London: Tavistock Publications.

Hertog, J. F. den (1977), *Werkstructurering* [Job design]. Alphen a/d Rijn: Samsom.

Herzberg, F. (1968), One more time: How do you motivate employees? *Harvard Business Review*, **46**, 53–62.

Hill, P., (1971), *Towards a new philosophy of management.* New York: Barnes and Noble.

Hornstein, H. A., Bunker, B. B., Burke, W. W., Gindes, M., Lewicki, R. J. (Eds.) (1971), *Social intervention, a behavioral science approach.* New York: The Free Press.

Hutte, H. A. (1966), Sociatrie van de arbeid [Sociatrics of work]. Assen: Van Gorcum.

Job Reform in Sweden (1975), Stockholm: Swedish Employers Federation.

Kahn, R. L. (1974), Organizational development: Some problems and proposals. *Journal of Applied Behavioral Science*, **4**, 485–503.

Katz, D., Kahn, R. L. (1978), *The social psychology of organizations.* New York: Wiley.

Knip, H., Speijer, D., Woerden, W. van (1975), Veranderingsstrategieën en onderwijsvernieuwing. Een case-studie over de invoering van project onderwijs [Strategies of change and educational innovation. A case study on the introduction of project teaching]. Delft: Delftse Universitaire Pers.

Kuipers, J. H. (1972), *Verantwoordelijkheidsverruiming in de directe werksituatie* [Expanding responsibility on the shop floor]. Amsterdam: Free University.

Kuipers, J. H. (1974), *Beleidsvoering door werkoverleg* [Management by work consultation]. Alphen a/d Rijn: Samsom.

Lawrence, P. R., Lorsch, J. W. (1969), *Developing organizations: Diagnosis and action.* Reading (Mass.): Addison-Wesley.

Lawrence, P. R., Lorsch, J. W. (1972), *Het verbeteren van organisaties* [Improving organizations]. Alphen a/d Rijn: Samsom.

Leavitt, H. J. (1951), Some effects of certain communication patterns on group performance. *Journal of Abnormal and Social Psychology*, **46**, 38–50.

Leavitt, H. J. (1965), Applied organizational change in industry: Structural, technological and humanistic. In: March, J. G. (Ed.), *Handbook of organizations*. Chicago: Rand McNally.

Lievegoed, B. C. J. (1972), *Organisaties in ontwikkeling* [Developing organizations]. Rotterdam: Lemniscaat.

Looise, J. C. (1976), *De proef op de som* [The proof of the pudding]. Utrecht: SWOV.

McMillan, C. B. (1975), Organizational change in schools: Bedford-Stuyvesant. *Journal of Applied Behavioral Science*, **4**, 437–454.

Mann, F. C. (1957), Studying and creating change: A means to understand social organization. In: Arsenberg, C. M., *et al.* (Eds.), *Research in industrial human relations*. New York: Harper, 157–167.

Mann, F. C. (1961), Studying and creating change. In: Bennis, W. G., *et al.* (Eds.), *The planning of change*. New York: Holt, Rinehart & Winston, 605–615.

Margulies, N., Wallace, J. (1973), Organizational change: Techniques and applications. Glenview: Scott, Foresman & Comp.

Margulies, N., Wright, P. L., Scholl, R. W. (1977), Organization development techniques: Their impact on change. *Group and Organization Studies*, **6**, 428–448.

Marrow, A. J., Bowers, D. G., Seashore, S. E. (1967), *Management by participation*. New York: Harper & Row.

Marx, E. C. H. (1975), *De organisatie van scholengemeenschappen in onderwijskundige optiek* [An educational theoretical view on the organization of compound schools]. Groningen: Tjeenk Willink.

Miles, M. B. (Ed.) (1964), *Innovation in education*. New York: Teachers College Press, Columbia University.

Miles, M. B., Calder, P. H., Hornstein, H. A., Callahan, D. M., Schiavo, R. S. (1970), Data feedback and organizational change in a school system. In: Golembiewsky, R. I., Blumberg, A. (Eds.), *Sensitivity training and the laboratory approach*. Itasca (Ill.): Peacock Publ. Inc., 352–361.

Miles, M. B., Hornstein, A. H., Callahan, D. M., Calder, P. H., Schiavo, R. S. (1969), The consequence of survey feedback: Theory and evaluation. In: Bennis, W. G., *et al.* (Eds.), *The planning of change*. 2nd ed. New York: Holt, Rinehart & Winston, 457–468.

Mumford, E. (1976), *Industrial democracy and system design*. Manchester.

Myers, M. S. (1970), *Every employee a manager*. New York: McGraw-Hill.

Nadler, D. A. (1977), *Feedback and organization development: Using data based methods*. Reading (Mass.): Addison-Wesley.

Nadler, D. A., Pecorella, P. A. (1975), Differential effects of multiple interventions in an organization. *Journal of Applied Behavioral Science*, **3**, 348–366.

Pasmore, W. A., King, D. C. (1978), Understanding organizational change: A comparative study of multifaceted interventions. *Journal of Applied Behavioral Science*, **4**, 455–469.

Paul, W. J., Robertson, K. B., Herzberg, F. (1969), Job enrichment pays off. *Harvard Business Review*, **47**, 61–78.

Porras, J. I. (1979), The comparative impact of different OD-techniques and intervention intensities. *Journal of Applied Behavioral Science*, **2**, 156–179.

Porras, J. I., Berg, P. O. (1978), Evaluation methodology in organization development: An analysis and critique. *Journal of Applied Behavioral Science*, **2**, 151–173.

Rabbie, J. M., Vegt, R. van der (1970), Over de laboratoriummethode van training: Variatie en evaluatie [On the laboratory method of training: Variation and evaluation]. In: Drenth, P. J. D., Willems, P. J., Wolff, Ch. J. de (Eds.), *Bedrijfspsychologie: Onderzoek en evaluatie* [Industrial psychology: Research and evaluation]. Deventer: Kluwer/Van Loghum Slaterus.

Ramondt, J. (1968), *Verantwoordelijkheid in het werk* [Responsibility on the job]. Alphen a/d Rijn: Samsom.
Ramondt, J. (1974), *Bedrijfsdemocratisering zonder arbeiders* [Industrial democratization without workers]. Alphen a/d Rijn: Samsom.
Rice, A. K. (1958), *Productivity and social organization: The Ahmedabad Experiment.* London: Tavistock Publications.
Rothman, J. (1974), *Planning and organizing for social change: Action principles from social science research.* New York: Columbia University Press.
Rubin, I. M., Plovnick, M. S., Fry, R. E. (1975), *Improving the coordination of care: A program for health team development.* Cambridge, Mass.: Ballinger Publ. Comp.
Rubin, I. M., Plovnick, M. S., Fry, R. E. (1977), The role of the consultant in initiating planned change: A case study in health care systems. In: Burke, W. W. (ed.), *Current issues and strategies in organization development.* New York: Human Science Press.
Rubin, I. M., Plovnick, M. S., Fry, R. E. (1978), *Task-oriented team development.* New York: McGraw-Hill.
Sashkin, M. (1972), Organization development practices. *Professional Psychology*, **00**, 187–192.
Schein, E. H. (1969), *Process consultation: Its role in organization development.* Reading (Mass.): Addison-Wesley.
Schein, E. H., Bennis, W. (1965), *Personal and organizational change through group methods: The laboratory approach.* New York: John Wiley & Sons, Inc.
Schouten, J. (1974), *Vrijheid in het werk* [Freedom on the job]. Meppel: Boom.
Schmuck, R. A., Miles, M. B. (1971). *Organizational development in schools.* Palo Alto (Cal.): National Press Books.
Schmuck, R. A., Runkel, P. J., Arends, J. H., Arends, R. I. (1977), *The second handbook of organization development on schools.* Oregon: Mayfield Publ. Co.
Scholten, G. (1975), *Medezeggenschap en organisatieverandering* [Co-determination and organization change]. The Hague: COP/SER.
Seeborg, I. S. (1978), The influence of employee participation in job redesign. *Journal of Applied Behavioral Science*, **1**, 87–99.
Sitter, L. U. de (1974), Socio-techniek [Sociotechnics]. *Mens en Onderneming* [Man and Enterprise], **28**, (2), 65–83.
Srivastva, S., Salipante, P., Cummings, J., Notz, W., Bigelow, I., Waters, J. (1975), *Job satisfaction and productivity.* Cleveland: Case Western Reserve University.
Strauss, G. (1973), Organization development. In: Rubin, R. (Ed.), *Handbook of organization in society.* Chicago: Rand McNally.
Trist, E. L., Bamforth, K. W. (1951), Some social and psychological consequences of the longwall method of coal getting. *Hum. Relat.*, **4**, 3–38.
Trist, E. L., Higgin, G. W., Murray, H., Pollock, A. B. (1963), *Organizational choice.* London: Tavistock.
Vegt, R. van der (1974), *Opleiden en evalueren. Een veldexperimentele studie naar uitkomsten van een bedrijfsopleiding* [Training and evaluation. A field-experimental study of the outcomes of training on the job]. Meppel: Boom.
Verhallen, H. J. G. (Ed.) (1979), *Veranderaars veranderen: Organisatie-adviseurs over hun werk* [Changers change: Organization consultants talk about their work]. Alphen a/d Rijn: Samsom.
Walravens, A. H. C. B. (1977), *Veldexperimenten met industriële democratie* [Field experiments with industrial democracy]. Assen: Van Gorcum.
Walton, R. E. (1969), *Interpersonal peacemaking: Confrontation and third-party consultation.* Reading (Mass.): Addison-Wesley.

Wise, H., Beckhard, R., Rubin, I., Kyte, A. L. (1974), *Making health teams work.* Cambridge (Mass.): Ballinger Publ. Comp.

Work in America, 1973. Report of the special task force to the secretary of Health, Education and Welfare. Cambridge (Mass.).

Zaltman, G., Florio, D. H., Sikorski, L. A. (1977), *Dynamic educational change: Models, strategies, tactics and management.* New York: The Free Press.

Zuthem, H. J. van (1973), *Macht en democratie binnen de onderneming* [Power and democracy in the firm]. Amsterdam: De Buooy.

Zwaan, A. H. van der (1973), Een kritische evaluatie van socio-technisch systeem-onderzoek [A critical evaluation of sociotechnical system research]. In: Drenth, P. J. D., *et al.* (Eds.), *Arbeids- en organisatiepsychologie* [Work- and organizational psychology]. Deventer: Kluwer.

Zwart, C. J. (1972), *Gericht veranderen van organisaties* [Planned change of organizations]. Rotterdam: Lemniscaat.

Handbook of Work and Organizational Psychology
Edited by P. J. D. Drenth, H. Thierry, P. J. Willems and C. J. de Wolff
© 1984, John Wiley & Sons, Ltd.

4.10. Industrial democratization

Erik J. H. Andriessen and Pol L. Coetsier

1. INTRODUCTION

Democratization, co-determination, participation and so on are concepts with different meanings, sharing however a common core: people's involvement in the decision making of their organization or their environment. In many organizations attempts are being made in order to increase this involvement, though the enthusiasm of the sixties has frequently turned into disappointment.

It has become clear that democratization processes can be realized in many different ways, but also that there are many conditions to be fulfilled for a given form of democratization to function successfully. The aim of this chapter is to pass in review different forms of institutionalized processes of industrial democratization, and to discuss experiences with their present functioning as well as conditions for improvements.

For our definition of industrial democratization we refer to the IDE-group (1980a). In industrial democratization the following principles are at stake:
1. All the members of an organization have equal rights to participate in all the decisions concerning the organization.
2. The members have the right to delegate decision making to elected representatives in representative bodies, who are accountable to their constituency.
3. Various factors can limit the permanent application of principle 1. The most important are the following:
a. the expertise required for some decisions;

Dr. Erik J. H. T. H. Andriessen, IVA-Instituut voor Sociaal Wetenschappelijk Onderzoek, Tilburg University, Tilburg.
Prof. Dr. Pol L. Coetsier (R. U. Gent—Lab. v. Toegep. Psychol.), Meersstraat 7, 9830 Sint–Martens Latem, België, (pasteurlaan 2), (9000 Gent—België).

b. the demand of efficiency in connection with the organization's aims;
c. the rights of individuals and minorities.
4. Decisions to delegate certain decisions to certain persons or groups should be made according to principle 1.

The pivotal dilemma of industrial democracy consists in finding a balance between principles 1 and 3.

This definition refers to an end stage of a dynamic development. In view of the human possibilities, the issue of how close one can get to that end stage is still hotly debated. Therefore, we shall not be dealing with industrial democracy itself, but with the processes of industrial democratization. This term designates processes by which those who are less powerful in an organization directly or indirectly get more opportunities to assert their own definition of a situation (Scholten, 1975) and thus to influence the organizational processes. This implies influence not only on specific decision making processes, but also on the structuring of decision making, i.e. on the rules of the game, the bodies and the procedures within which decisions are made. The ultimate aim of increasing the influence of those less powerful is to see they have equal rights to participate in decisions, as formulated in principle 1.

Democratization processes take place at various levels: in work-groups, in an organization's top management, in industrial sectors, or at a national level. More specifically the concept of industrial democratization concerns the institutionalized forms of democratization in work organizations. The notion does not only include industrial organizations, but also other profit and non-profit organizations such as hospitals, government agencies and welfare organizations. As a matter of fact, the democratization processes in organizations of the latter kind have hardly been studied.

In the context of participation and democratization (see also Lammers, 1965; van Zuthem, 1978), three aspects may be distinguished:
1. the ideologically and anthropologically determined motives for the pursuit of democratization;
2. the specific and sometimes legally founded form democratization takes at a given time;
3. the actual functioning of the processes of decision making and influence; in these processes, the behaviour of individuals is determined by their own capacities and ideas as well as by the legal structure of which they are part, the organization characteristics, and the socio-economic, political, and cultural contexts (see figure 1).

It is these three aspects that will be discussed in this chapter. In section 2 we will deal with the forces underlying democratization movements. In section 3 the forms and models as they have been developed in various countries are discussed. The remainder of the chapter will be devoted to the actual functioning of some of these forms and to the conditions required for this to be successful.

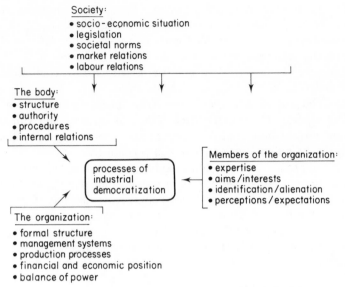

Figure 1. Determinants of industrial democratization.

2. GOALS AND STRATEGIES OF DEMOCRATIZATION

Democratization may be pursued with a view to goals at different levels: micro, meso and macro levels, i.e. the goals may concern individuals, organizations or society.

2.1. Goals at the individual level

In this approach democratization is put at the service of human growth. In our western society this implies both autonomy and participation in decision making. Tannenbaum (1969) considers participation as a source of satisfaction because it can prevent frustration connected with lower rank positions. An entirely different approach, which is, however, still at the level of the individual, considers man as a responsible being who is accountable for his deeds. The aim, then, of democratization is to give working man the opportunity to fulfill this responsibility. People must participate, not because they want to, but because it is, first and foremost, a condition for maturity.

2.2. Goals at the organizational level

At this level, there are two entirely different approaches to be distinguished. On the one hand, the idea that democratization could contribute to an organization's productivity and efficiency. Democratic decision making is believed to be of a higher quality because it uses all available human knowledge ('human resources'). Moreover, participation stimulates motivation and identification with the organization.

Consequently, democratization may be used to realize traditional organizational aims. In this approach, democratization is a new management technique. The use of democratization as an instrument has been strongly criticized. Kuipers (1975) calls it a 'trick of the management' and Ramsay (1978) argues that present industrial democratization in most cases consolidates the system and even reduces the employees' independence.

The other approach at the organizational level considers democratization as a process serving not individual growth or organizational efficiency ('functional' democratization), but rather the fundamental redistribution of power in the organization ('structural' democratization; Lammers, 1970). According to this approach, the often opposite interests of the different parties can, as a result of such a power shift, be resolved not only into harmony and satisfaction, but also into conflict.

2.3. Goals at the societal level

Because productive life is so prominent in the organization of work, social reformers find industrial democratization very important. To the marxist view, and in certain christian conceptions as well, work is so central that industrial democracy cannot but be the core of the entire social democratization process.

Pateman (1970) argues that participation in a democratic work situation has an educative effect. People learn how to influence their environment and this training may contribute to the ongoing democratization of society. In this approach the shift of power in society is realized in an indirect way.

On closer examination, it appears that there are different perspectives on organizations and society underlying the various goals of and subsequent strategies for democratization. A major distinction can be made between, on the one hand, the perspective by which an organization is an integrated social system and, on the other, the perspective whose starting point is the different parties in an organization (see e.g. Lammers, 1980).

The first perspective's starting point is the organization as a whole with its specific, socially functional goals. The different individuals and groups in the organization work together in order to attain these goals. Such an approach emphasizes concepts such as integration and efficiency. In the light of involvement and motivation the terms 'participation' and 'co-determination' are preferred and much attention is paid to the question as to whether democratization can be reconciled with efficiency and productivity.

In the second perspective the interests and goals of the different individuals and parties come to the fore. The term 'democratization' is preferred and heavy stress is laid on the possibilities for those less powerful to assert their own wishes

	Degree of unanimity on goals	Presence of conflict	Conflict resolving mechanisms
Harmony model	high	few and non-intensive conflicts	consultation (partly negotiation)
Confrontation model	medium	occasional conflicts	divergent
Conflict model	low	many and/or intensive conflicts	battle (partly negotiation)

Figure 2. Models of industrial relations.

and their 'situation definition'. Such possibilities, moreover, imply a certain degree of independence and power of the different parties and consequently a greater chance of conflict. Advocates of this approach are rather anxious about whether participation within the existing systems might make employees less independent and even encapsulate them (Ramsay, 1978).

In figure 2 some elements of these two approaches are presented. In practice, their goals turn out sometimes to run parallel and sometimes to be contrary to each other. Conflict and co-operation can and must alternate in some cases. This implies the existence of an intermediate model.

In practice, it strongly depends on more general (party) political opinions and principles, whether one of these models or the intermediate model is advocated. In Belgium the choice of the model is connected with the opposition between the two major trade-unions and thus indirectly with the language boundary: in Wallonia, as in France, the conflict model is widely adhered to; in Flanders, as in The Netherlands, the harmony model is (and was) generally favoured.

Mainly ideological, but also historical and other causes have often led the different parties in the industrial relations system to choose very different ways to realize their ideas about democratization. The following democratization strategies can thus be distinguished:
1. the further development of consultations among representatives of both employers and employees concerning working conditions (Collective Bargaining Agreements etc.). Such consultation may be organized at a national or sector level, but also (as in England) in individual organizations or even in subdivisions of organizations. In England and the United States this has long been considered the only legitimate form of employees' co-determination.
2. resistance: strikes or occupation of a plant or building.
3. changes in ownership relations: employees as shareholders, production co-operatives etc.
4. the introduction of (co-)determination by employees in the organization's management: worker-directors, the Yugoslav workers' council.
5. creating or strengthening institutionalized forms of consultation: works councils, health and safety committees.

6. restructuring the work process and the work distribution connected with it: work structuring, job enrichment, autonomous groups.
7. changing the climate: change of leadership style, group consultations.

In this chapter most attention will be paid to the institutionalized forms of consultation.

3. DIMENSIONS AND MODELS OF DEMOCRATIZATION PROCESSES

The different ways in which industrial democratization has been realized can be distinguished according to a number of dimensions (see also Bolweg, 1976; Dachler and Wilpert, 1978; Thierry et al., 1979). These dimensions concern:
a. *the structure of the decision-making process*, i.e. form (directly or indirectly, personally or impersonally), degree of institutionalization and formalization, degree of involvement and organizational level.
b. *the nature of the decisions*, i.e. domain, centrality to the organizational processes and phase.

Form: directly or indirectly, personally or impersonally
In the direct forms all members of a group are involved. In indirect participation the persons concerned are represented by a few from their own number. Regular work consultation is, in most cases, a direct form, whereas works councils represent the indirect form. Both cases, however, concern specific bodies in which various persons meet.

There are also more impersonal forms to involve people in decision making, such as polls and suggestion boxes.

Degree of institutionalization and formalization
Institutionalization means that the decision-making process is a highly structured one. A board, fixed meeting dates, and agendas are aspects of such institutionalization. Formalization concerns the extent to which the consultation conditions are laid down in rules, agreements, or even laws. Highly institutionalized consultation is not necessarily laid down in all sorts of written regulations, but in practice there will often be a connection between both aspects.

Degree of involvement
This concept refers to the degree to which a group is involved in consultations. A traditional distinction is that between shared knowledge, joint discussion and co-determination. There are, however, many intermediate forms. A more complete series is the following: the opportunity to ask for information, the right to certain information, the opportunity to give one's opinion, the possibility to give formal advice, the obligation to give advice, joint decision-making, veto-right, autonomy.

A certain degree of involvement does not necessarily include a higher degree of actual influence on decision-making.

Organizational level

The level in the organization at which consultation takes place has, in most cases, consequences for the number of persons or groups participating in the decision making: one or a few individuals (as in work structuring), a work group (direct participation in the work), a department (departmental consultation), an organization (works council, board of directors), a sector of industry or the national industrial relations system

Domain

The potential role of a body depends on the domains in which it is involved. Various classifications of domains have been proposed. Most of these classifications deal with the following issues:
—the organization of work and working conditions;
—personnel policy (conditions of employment);
—technology and means of production;
—economic, financial and commercial aspects.
The system of consultative bodies, such as works councils, is often criticized because such bodies have only limited control over decisions on important economic and organizational topics.

Centrality

In each of the above-mentioned domains, decisions are hierarchically structured: there are *strategic* decisions concerning the general goals of the organization and the resulting policy in a certain domain (as to, e.g., opportunities of growth for employees). *Structuring* decisions translate the general policy into concrete procedures (concerning, e.g., the internal advertising of vacancies). The latter then find their concrete shape in *operational* decisions (e.g., the appointment of a functionary). It is evident that participation in strategic decisions implies more power than does participation in decisions at the level of concrete procedures or ad hoc decisions.

Phase

The last dimension is that of the phase of the decision-making process in which participation takes place: identification of the problem, investigation and assessment of the possible choices and decisions, ultimate choice or decision, implementation and control. Many existing forms of industrial democratization are criticized because they only leave room for participation in choosing between alternatives at the level of procedures and routines which have been preselected and preprogrammed by others.

In the above we have distinguished between various dimensions along which concrete forms of industrial democratization can differ from each other. As a result of various circumstances, a limited number of structures have developed in the course of the 19th and 20th centuries.

There is a high degree of diversity in the developments as they occurred in the various European countries where, in most cases, the emphasis was on institutionalization and formalization, but where at the same time the need to create bodies for consultation and participation was much stronger than in, for example, the United States (IDE, 1980b).

What specific form was developed in each country depended on, inter alia, the following factors:

1. the political and socio-economic situation: centrally planned systems (e.g. Eastern Europe) vs. the free enterprise system (Western Europe);

2. the prevailing value systems of the trade-unions: emphasis on 'keeping aloof' and control afterwards (Southern Europe) or on participation in decision- and policy-making (Northern Europe);

3. the emphasis of the industrial relation system: decentralized, in the enterprise (as in England) or strongly centralized at the national level (The Netherlands). Belgium occupies an intermediate position: participation takes place alternately, centrally and peripherally;

4. the juridical tradition; does one attach great importance to general formal rules and laws such as the Dutch and Belgian works council acts or rather to agreements between different parties (such as the Norwegian and Swedish agreements between trade unions and employers' organizations);

5. the corporate structure: are there two levels, i.e. a supervising board of directors and an executive committee (e.g. Germany, The Netherlands), is there one top level, or is it a mixed structure (e.g. Belgium and France)?

All these factors have influenced the development of a series of specific participation structures in organizations. The most frequently occurring are the following:

Consultative and advisory bodies. Elected employee representatives consult with top management or its representatives. The best-known example is the works council which exists in many countries, but lower level committees such as the Belgian health and safety committees belong to this category as well. The Dutch works council and the German 'Betriebsrat' are reckoned among this category, but strictly speaking they do not belong to it, because they consist of elected employee representatives only. However, in addition to their own meetings these councils also meet with management. Committees and councils of this category greatly differ in the extent to which their rights and authority are elaborated and laid down.

Employee representatives in boards of directors. The best-known example of this kind of structure is to be found in Germany, more specifically in the mining, iron and steel industries. In these firms, one half of the board of directors consists of shareholders' representatives, the other of employees' representatives and, in addition, one neutral member. The German system, called 'Mittbestimmung', also includes a work manager (and the works council mentioned above). In other German organizations as well as in other countries the amount of employee representation in boards is rather low. In The Netherlands they are by no means compulsory by law, though some organizations haven appointed an employee director.

Workers' Council. In 1948, the system of 'self-government' was introduced in Yugoslavia as part of the national policy to avoid a stalinist centralization of power. The core of this model is the workers' council, whose members are all elected representatives of the workers. This council is the most powerful body in the organization. The director is employed by the council and can also be fired by it. An executive board, consisting of a small number of council members, together with the director, has the day-to-day supervision of the implementation of the workers' council's decisions.

The Yugoslav 'self-government' system was introduced in all kinds of organizations and levels. It is the most extreme system of industrial democratization. In various countries there are companies which can to some extent be compared with the Yugoslav companies. The best-known example is that of production co-operatives, as are also found in The Netherlands. Their most typical characteristic is that they are managed by a co-operative association, whose members all work in the company itself. The association's board has the day-to-day supervision of the director, who is employed by the association.

Trade-union representation. In many countries, there is some form or other of trade-union representation in the companies. The best-known form is the British 'shop steward', a representative elected by the trade-union members of a certain firm, whose main task is to negotiate working conditions and to look after the employees' interests. In larger firms there can be several shop stewards. The underlying principle of this model is not the idea of consultation and joint decision making, but rather the confrontation and conflict model, though in practice a thorough mutual understanding may come about between shop stewards and top management.

In other countries they have similar officials, as in, for example, the Scandinavian countries, where they play a part along with the consultative bodies and councils. The Belgian syndicate delegation is yet another example of this model. The Dutch 'bedrijfscontactman' also is a representative elected by the trade-union members. His task, however, is not (yet) to negotiate but, among other things, to mobilize the union members and to maintain relations between them and the trade-union.

Supplying information. An important element in various participation structures are the regulations concerning the information to be provided. In several countries there are legalized regulations regarding the supply of company information to employee representatives in works councils, trade unions, councils or committees (Jain, 1979). The new Dutch works council act mentions some specific issues on which the councils must receive accounts regularly. Trade unions tend to put more and more emphasis on increase in the number of such regulations.

Reporting to the entire personnel is by no means compulsory. During the last fifteen years, however, the development in this respect has clearly been one from strictly financial annual reporting to the shareholders, to more extensive reporting—social reporting—which addresses the employees also. A survey carried out in 1976 in The Netherlands shows that this form of reporting leaves much to be desired (van Hoorn and Dekker, 1977; see also Eisses et al., 1980).

The systems in the various countries not only differ as to whether the bodies mentioned exist or not, but also as to their complexity and the authority asigned to such bodies and their representatives. To date, countries such as England and The Netherlands in fact know only one system: trade-union representation or works councils, respectively. The new Dutch act on working conditions contains stipulations for consultative bodies in matter of safety and working. Belgium has for a long time now known various bodies: works councils, safety and health committees and trade-union delegations. The German 'Mittbestimmung' system has, as mentioned above, three levels of co-determination. And in Norway and Sweden there is, apart from these three levels, also trade-union representation in the firms. The position of the works council is not as strong as it is in Germany, however.

From a formal point of view, workers in Yugoslav firms have the highest amount of control, compared with other European countries. The German system, inasfar as formal regulations are concerned, takes a good second place (King and van der Vall, 1978; IDE, 1980a).

Obviously, our list of models is incomplete; there are more current models, based on more and other dimensions than those we mentioned.

4. THE SITUATION IN THE NETHERLANDS AND BELGIUM

Both The Netherlands and Belgium are acquainted with workers' participation at various organizational levels. In The Netherlands, relatively large companies have to comply to certain rules. These rules state that the works council (cf. below) is entitled to nominate candidates for the Board of directors. Although the Board does the actual appointing, the works council has the right of veto. It is widely debated whether part of the Board should be appointed by the employees.

The works council is known also in Belgium, where it is proportionally composed of employee representatives (nominated by the unions, elected by the employees) and the employer's representatives (nominated by the management). Since the 1979 Act, the Dutch councils are composed of elected employee representatives only. Candidates can be nominated by the unions or by independent groups of employees.

In both countries, there are works council acts, specifying the issues on which a council must be informed, the issues it must be consulted about, and those on which it has right of veto.

The two countries are also acquainted with union representatives in the companies. Unlike in England, they are not union people, but company employees. The Belgian union delegation is more institutionalized than it is in The Netherlands. It is the most important channel through which workers can communicate problems and complaints, and as a body it can negotiate directly with the management on certain internal issues (i.e. not about wages).

The Dutch 'bondswerk in de bedrijven' (union presence in the enterprise) is less far developed. It was set up in order to reduce the distance between the centrally operating trade unions and the union members. The task of the union executives involved can be a varying one, for example mobilizing union members for actions, communicating complaints to the union, organizing the works council's constituency, preparing the consultations on Collective Bargaining Agreements.

Finally, there are the Belgian health and safety committees. Such a committee's responsibility involves the safety measures in the organization and the improvement of working conditions. Its authority is merely advisory. Similar committees might be set up in Holland as well, in view of the regulations of the new work environment act.

It will be clear that the system used in both Belgium and The Netherlands is entirely different from that used in most English-speaking countries. It does not provide for real collective bargaining within companies, nor does it have a shop steward system. The French system is very similar to that of the Benelux countries.

5. THE FUNCTIONING OF REPRESENTATIVE BODIES

In the preceding sections, the various forms and structures that came into being in the framework of industrial democratization were described. How do these structures operate in practice? In this section we wish to discuss some important problems, more in particular those connected with works councils. One of these problems is the fact that in many cases works councils have only limited actual influence on decision making and that they operate as an additional co-ordinating body for the management. A second problem is the relations they have with their constituency.

Many studies have shown that, in most cases, workers' representatives have very little actual influence. Emery *et al.* (1969) established this for workers' commissioners in Norwegian companies.

According to Coetsier (1966) and Gevers (1973), until recently only few Belgian works councils have succeeded in arriving at a reasonable level of problem formulation. Hövels and Nas (1976, 1978) painted a slightly more favourable picture of Dutch works councils. They studied approximately 100 works councils. Data were collected via analysis of minutes and interviews with key persons. They found four major types of works council:[1]

—marginal works councils (appr. 20%); these are practically inactive;

—works councils as an extension of management ($\pm$ 20%); all activities (agenda formulation, discussions etc.) are entirely dominated by the chairman (managing director);

—works councils as bodies of employee members ($\pm$ 16%): the members act fully independently and, as a party, are the managing director's opponents. It may happen, however, that they achieve but little, because the management ignores them, e.g. by withholding relevant information;

—works councils as consultative bodies ($\pm$ 43%): elected members act independently, but issues are dealt with by means of compromises or negotiations.

The study suggests that there is a considerable number of works councils potentially having influence on the company's decision-making processes. Although influence was not measured directly in this study, the authors conclude, on the basis of indirect indications, that in most cases this influence is rather limited.

The results of the IDE-project support this scepticism (IDE, 1980a). Some of the works councils studied appeared to have quite some influence only on a few decisions, like for example, drafting a working hours schedule. Decisions regarding appointments, investments, reorganizations or changes in or, as the case may be, expansion of production, apparently were scarcely or not at all influenced by works councils (Andriessen *et al.*, 1983). On the one hand, the weakness of the works council's position emerges from the fact that in many cases it has little to say about the issues discussed at its meetings. On the other hand, it turns out that various—including important—decisions are never dealt with by the works council. In some instances, this concerns issues which the works council itself had referred to other consultative bodies (e.g. the negotiations between trade unions and employer). In other cases, issues are kept out of the works council by the chairman (Hövels and Nas, 1976).

Given the fact that works councils have so little impact on policy decisions, it is not surprising that they have assumed all kinds of unintended functions. Lammers (1965) described various kinds of these 'malfunctions', such as the works council as a passer on of complaints, as an appeasement agency, as an advisory body, or as a suggestion box. In all these cases the works council is taking over functions from line management, which as a consequence often feels passed over by the works council.

The results of this study seem to indicate that works councils often function as an instrument of co-ordination and information to management, instead of as a body serving to funnel the employees' contributions and interests. According to the Hövels and Nas (1976) study, only 12% of the directors/chairman interviewed and 20% of the works-council members believed their works council

---

[1] This study was done when works councils still had a company director as chairman.

to have achieved more for the employees than for the management. And the IDE survey (IDE, 1980a) showed that most informants (from all levels) believed that their works council had contributed to people being better informed about what goes on in their organization and that decisions were more easily accepted if they had been discussed in the works council. The number of informants believing that the works council had contributed to an equalization of power, was, however, much smaller.

The last problem connected with works councils (and other representative bodies) is the problem of their constituency. All surveys show the relation between works-council members and the other employees to be a rather feeble one. There is, moreover, no regulation whatsoever prescribing the works-council members to justify themselves before their constituency. Studies as carried out by Hövels and Nas (1976) in firms, or in hospitals (Lammers *et al.*, 1980), show that such contacts are rather limited and, at the same time, that a constituency disposes of only few facilities and possibilities.

Works-council meetings are rarely open to the public (in 8% of the firms studied and 5% of the hospitals) and although, in most cases, their agenda is announced to the employees, their minutes are fully publicized in only 45% and 35% of the cases, respectively. Elected members have consulting hours in 29% and 15% of the organizations, respectively. And only 40% of the works-council members claims to have more than incidental contact with groups or employees or their representatives.

In the last section of this chapter we will go further into the matter of the employees' attitude towards this phenomenon and of their wishes and preferences concerning representative participation.

6. PREREQUISITES FOR SUCCESSFUL DEMOCRATIZATION

In the preceding section we could not but conclude that, on the whole, representatives have only little influence on an organization's decision making. What are the reasons for this and what are the conditions to be fulfilled in order to increase their influence? Knowledge of the processes of power in general could possibly clarify the situation.

The extent to which one has influence on decision making strongly depends on one's position of power. The power of a group or person is, among other things, determined by their 'power basis' and their 'sources of reward', i.e. by factors controlled by them and desired by others.

Traditionally, five power bases are distinguished (French and Raven, 1960):
a. the legitimate, formal position in the organization; this is an important power basis for executives;
b. having disposal of negative sanctions, e.g. punishment, coercive measures;
c. having disposal of material or immaterial rewards;
d. personal attraction, charisma;
e. expertise, information.

Some authors mention more power bases. Laaksonen (1877), for example, mentions adherence to ideology as a power basis of executives in a country like China. More important is how the power basis principle works out in actual organizational situations. What sanctions and rewards do certain positions have at their disposal? What kinds of expertise give certain persons or groups more power? Answers to these questions are important in order to deal with the problem of what factors stimulate or obstruct democratization processes.

One of the most important bases for power in an organization is, as mentioned above, a person's or group's formal position in the hierarchy. In the literature, the notion of hierarchy has various meanings. Mostly it is a strongly negative notion, linked to lack of freedom and rigid supervision.

A hierarchical structure develops with increasing division of labour. Such a structure can have several functions. An important one is co-ordination. As the number of different tasks in an organization grows, there is a greater need of co-ordination. In complex organizations a hierarchical structure is, under certain conditions, a very useful way to reach certain goals. In the framework of industrial democratization the most important question is whether hierarchical structures are incompatible with the goals of participation and redistribution of power. Indeed, in practice, hierarchical structures appear to have not only a co-ordinating function, but also one of controlling and restraining behaviors, of exercising and maintaining power. If more democratization is to be pursued, should then all hierarchy be wiped out or would it be possible to create such conditions as to prevent hierarchical structures to become an instrument of unnecessary power maintenance?

The position of power of certain persons or groups in an organization is also determined by their position in the production process, in the communication structure, or in the network of relations with the environment. The more important and the more difficult to replace a certain person's or department's expertise and experience with respect to the organization's main processing system and its need for raw materials, people, technical knowledge, funds and sales markets, the stronger their position of power (Hickson et al., 1971).

This leads us to a major source of power differences, i.e. expertise and information. In Mulder's (1977) power-distance reduction theory, differences in expertise play an important part. His most debated thesis with regard to industrial democratization is: if the power-distance is too great, participation will lead to an increase instead of a decrease of this distance.

This is explained by the fact that, often, power-distance is based particularly on differences in the information available, in experience and expertise. These differences are so great that those less powerful are entirely overcome by the expertise of those more powerful, but their presence puts a semblance of democracy on the unilateral decision-making and increases the acceptance of decisions. Consequently, those more powerful get still more power. According to Mulder, this phenomenon frequently occurs in works councils.

This assumed lack of expertise of members of representative bodies, which is reported by other authors as well, can, however, not be taken at face value: it should be carefully examined as to why this should be so. Apparent differences in expertise may be traced to various sources (Lammers, 1965; de Jong, 1978):

a. the available information is dispensed selectively to certain participants only;

b. management and staff are too inexpert (or unwilling) to explain complex issues clearly and succinctly;

c. differences in social skills, e.g. verbal skills;

d. differences in problem-solving skills associate with capacities and experience.

Only the latter category concerns the differences in expertise in the sense meant above. These differences certainly do occur, especially when financial, economic or legal issues are involved. Or, according to De Jong's study (1978), this is at least how works-council members see it. The respondents were, however, not convinced of there being differences in expertise in other fields.

In Mulder's view the differences in expertise are so important that he advocates a programme for the step-by-step learning of how to participate, starting in the work situation, where the expertise and motivation of those less powerful is usually greater.

It is clear that the existing systems of the division of work in organizations assigns more power to certain groups, such as higher management and staff experts, than to the employees. If true democratization is to be pursued, then something must be done about the reasons of these differences. In other words, power equalization is not automatically the result of democratization processes, but democratization is possible only when the power differences are not too extreme. What factors can contribute to such an equalization of power, i.e. what are the concrete conditions for democratization processes to operate successfully?

In the first place, the factors reducing such power differences as mentioned above need to be changed, e.g. the division of labour and control procedures. Apart from this, a number of other conditions may be mentioned, such as improving the conspicuity of the power structure and increasing the powers and responsibilities in the organization. In order to attain the organization's goals, co-ordination and power differences are essential. Control on how the power is exercised, however, is necessary.

This control is possible only if the decision-making criteria and rules are conspicuous. Only then can the way in which a person or group exercises its power be controlled. Many so-called democratized organizations turn out to be very undemocratic. The actual decision making has become very obscure and takes place in committees and councils where the exercise of power by some is obscured by the presence and so-called co-responsibility of many.

Another series of prerequisites has to do with improving the employees' position and that of their bodies, e.g. by supplying information. In his study on the functioning of organizations with an advanced form of industrial democracy, Bernstein (1977) concluded that the following conditions should be met:

—availability of organizational information as well as training in how to deal with that kind of information;

—protection of the people involved by means of private ballots, immunity from discharge or transfer, the right of meeting;

—possibility of appeal, independent of management.

A further condition is the extension of the formal authority of employees and their representatives. Although this condition is sometimes judged negatively, many people are convinced that legal powers may reinforce the position and thus the influence of the works council. For this reason, the new Dutch Works Council Act (1979) confers more authority on the works council than the previous one. The rightness of this measure is supported by research such as that of Looise (1976) and the IDE-group (1980). Looise evaluated a number of experiments with institutional consultation at the organizational level and with joint ownership. According to him, the success of these experiments depended on the existence of legal regulations for laying down the powers of co-determinating bodies and for restricting the influence of those traditionally in power (managing directors, shareholders, advisory directors). The IDE-research showed that the actual influence of representative bodies was connected, on the one hand, with the amount of authority these bodies had and, on the other, with the extent of union membership among the employees (IDE, 1980a).

The next group of conditions has to do with the employees' and management's attitudes and motivation. To Bernstein (1977), for example, important conditions are the financial advantages for the people involved, but also the presence of certain value systems and attitudes among those less powerful (initiative, resistance against manipulation, etc.) and among those more powerful (openness, equality, confidence, etc.).

A last group of conditions is revealed by some studies evaluating Dutch experiments (Scholten, 1975; Ramondt, 1975; Looise, 1976) to wit:

—a differentiated, but at the same time integrated structure of bodies and processes of democratization at various levels, i.e. there should be various channels, well attuned to each another, through which individuals and groups can air their wishes and opinions.

—active involvement of the employees and trade unions from the start of the first development of new democratization structures onwards.

In summary, we can say that the success or failure of democratization processes depends, on the one hand, on the existing power differences, resulting from the division of work, production process, organizational structure and external relations, and, on the other, on the extent to which the position of minority groups is reinforced by:

—the transparency of the power structure;

—Clear regulations concerning the powers of the bodies, the supply of information, and the protection of those involved;
—the existence of a certain pattern of attitudes and a certain degree of mutual trust;
—a differentiated negotiation structure;
—a strong position of the unions.

7. ALIENATION, SATISFACTION AND THE WISH TO DEMOCRATIZE

As was pointed out in the beginning of this chapter, it has often been tried to put industrial democratization at the service of the struggle against individual alienation of employees. In the USA, for example, a bill was proposed by the Senate in 1973, which aimed to provide solutions for the problems of alienation among American workers. One of its recommendations was that work be designed, so that its potential for democracy would be optimal (Wall and Lischeron, 1977, p. 2).

The question remains as to what extent industrial democratization is able to remove alienation. Blumberg (1968) draws a rather optimistic picture of the positive effects of introducing participative structures. We have already pointed out that in order to reach the intended goals, certain preconditions should be fulfilled. The positive relationships found between participation and job satisfaction are linked mainly with the degree of participation in the direct work situation. Wall and Lischeron (1977) have their doubts about this as well.

As far as indirect participation is concerned, the research on its relation with job satisfaction is altogether unconvincing. (The concepts 'alienation' and 'dissatisfaction' are not entirely identical. In most studies, however, only the effect on job satisfaction is measured.)

The Yugoslav participation structure has been much studied, because in that country the workers' self-government has aroused quite some scientific interest. Most studies point out that these indirect forms of participation have no or only little influence on job satisfaction (Rus, 1979). Obradovic (1970) concluded that the degree of representative participation did not result in job satisfaction among workers in highly automated work situations, but that it did among workers in less automated working situations. In general this effect should not be overemphasized.

In Germany too, direct links between job satisfaction and representative participation have rarely been found. Although most studies exhibit a rather positive attitude towards participatory structures, it remains a fact that they have no or only little influence on job satisfaction. The study by Tannenbaum et al. (1974) was not able either to show up any relationship between the degree of participation and job satisfaction in Yugoslavia, Israel the USA or Italy.

It is obvious that a relationship between the functioning of (representative) participation and job satisfaction will occur only if such (representative) participation plays an important part in the employee's life. The first question, then, should be how employees feel about the various forms of industrial democratization. How strongly do employees want to participate in their company's decision-making processes and how do they think should this participation be organized? Various studies have shown that, mostly, employees are more interested in decisions concerning their own job than in decisions about general management.

Wall and Lischeron (1977), in their review of the relevant literature, draw the following conclusions:
—many employees consider the participation of executive personnel in general management decisions too limited;
—there is almost never a desire for the power of veto in these decisions, but there is a desire for discussion opportunities;
—there are important differences between individuals and groups as to their desires concerning the types of decisions in which employees, or their representatives, should be involved.

The findings of the IDE-group (1980) concur with the latter remark. One of their conclusions is that skilled workers and employees in the service industries have a strong preference for direct participation in various decisions, whereas metal workers—more specifically unskilled workers and union members— mainly claim influence for the representative bodies.

This shows that many employees really want their representatives to be involved in their firm's top level decisions. It does not mean, however, that in practice they have a positive view of how democratization bodies operate.

Various Dutch studies (e.g. Drenth and van der Pijl, 1966) have demonstrated that only few employees are truly interested in the functioning of industrial democratization bodies. In the IDE-project (1980) only 39% of the employees interviewed seem to be personally interested in works-council activities, a figure that is probably even flattered because of the social desirability of the answer. (Moreover, the IDE-research took place in metal industries and insurance companies only.) Only 15% would be willing to run for works-council membership. And only few indicate that they occasionally communicate a question or complaint to the works council.

According to the complaint survey by Schmitz et al. (1975) employees communicate their complaints to the works council in 16% of the cases. The IDE-research reports that 38% of the metal workers and 13% of the insurance employees occasionally submit a question or complaint to a works-council member.

This problem of the constituency apparently occurs in many countries (cf. e.g., Wall and Lischeron, 1977). Moreover, the IDE-research shows up rather important differences. A question concerning the employees' interest in the work of the representative bodies was answered positively by only a limited number of respondents: between 19% (Italy) and 58% (Israel). The number of employees willing to become a member of a representative body varies from 14% (Denmark) to 28% (Belgium). In this matter, Yugoslavia towers above the other countries with 55%.

The problem of constituencies seems to be greater as the psychological distance between the bodies and the employees is greater. Some studies (e.g. Emery et al., 1969; Engelstad and Quale, 1977) reveal that the employees' interest in their representatives in the Boards (as in Germany and the Scandinavian countries) is even less than their interest in works councils. Here one of the dilemmas of industrial democratization reveals itself. Potentially, the power of workers' representatives in Boards is often greater than the power of works-council members, but, at the same time, the distance to the employees is greater and as a result their involvement is less.

How can the employees' involvement in this kind of processes be increased? This question can only be answered if we know why the involvement and interest are so low. Various answers can be given to this question. Wall and Lischeron (1977) think that the cause can be found in the origin and in the kind of representative bodies. According to these authors, systems of representative participation have, in most cases, been set up by the management or by law. The lack of interest may be due to the fact that these systems are not adapted to the true concerns of the employees. Moreover, the structures and rules of de-mocratization are sometimes instruments in the hands of experts and therefore may have an alienating effect (de Corte, 1979). An example is the—sometimes purposely—complicated presentation of financial information.

Another reason concerns the actual functioning of the bodies. In general, they turn out to have little real influence on the decision making within the organization. According to this line of thought, the employees are very much aware of this and therefore are not particularly interested in its activities. This notion is supported by the results of the IDE-project (1980). According to that study there appears to be, in many countries, a positive relationship between the influence of representative bodies and the employees' interest in such bodies.

A third line of reasoning looks for the cause among the employees themselves. Because of education, training, experience, or whatever other reason, only relatively few people would be interested in issues that are beyond their own immediate situation. The finding that active involvement in and outside the job are often correlated (Elden, 1977) seems to support this hypothesis.

Each of these explanations probably contains its grain of truth. More research is needed to find out which explanation applies to which situation.

The views of members of representative bodies

A big problem for representatives is the role conflict in which they often find themselves. When the opposition between management and employees is clear-cut, representatives will have no difficulty to come to an understanding with their constituency. In a typical consultation situation, however, there is every chance that the representatives—together with top management—make decisions that their constituency may find hard to accept. A Belgian study (Coetsier, 1966) showed that a representative's popularity, after a period of initial growth, may often drop perceptibly. Thus, representatives will often find themselves in a role conflict. This kind of conflict was found in works-council members (Drenth and van der Pijl, 1966), shop stewards and workers' representatives in Boards (Brannen *et al.*, 1976).

The role conflict described above may be coupled with a feeling of helplessness and alienation. Obradovic (1970) and Arzensek (1977) concluded that the alienation of Yugoslav workers-council members was greater than that of the employees taken together. This seemingly contradicts the finding that representatives are often more interested and involved in the functioning of representative bodies. In the IDE-project, 45% of the Dutch works-council members interviewed, said they would run again (as opposed to 15% of the remaining employees). These differences are found in other countries as well.

There are various theories trying to explain this phenomenon. The theory of cognitive dissonance argues that representatives assume a positive attitude because a negative one cannot be combined with their investments in the bodies. Mulder's (1977) power-distance reduction theory starts from the assumption that the exercise of power acts as a drug.

A third explanation could perhaps be found in the fact that membership of a representative body seems to grow into a new profession or to become part of a certain kind of career. In large Dutch firms, for example, works-council membership can be a step towards an executive job in the organization or be a stage in a trade-union career. Membership of central works-councils (a controlling council for an entire group of firms) is in many cases a part-time and sometimes a full-time job, which stimulates its further professionalization.

8. CONCLUSION

Especially during the sixties certain groups had great expectations with respect to societal and industrial democratization. The Yugoslav model was often the example to be followed. Workers' self-government seemed to be a realistic or, at any rate, valuable ideal.

It has since become clear that real industrial democratization implies thorough changes in the organization of work and decision making, and therefore gives rise to many problems. It is also clear that, when democratization processes are restricted to certain levels only—e.g., only work consultation or only representation in boards of advisory directors—these processes remain isolated and are practically doomed to fail. Other prerequisites for the success of democratization processes have been discussed above. Research on the present functioning of different bodies in different situations, but first of all experiments with new forms of organization, will have to show how and to what extent these conditions can be fulfilled. Work and organizational psychologists could play an important part in this issue.

REFERENCES

Abell, P. (1975), *Organizations as bargaining and influence systems.* London: Heinemann.

Andriessen, J. H. T. H., Drenth, P. J. D., Lammers, G. J. (1983), *Medezeggenschap in Nederlandse bedrijven. Verslag van een onderzoek naar participatie en invloedsver-houdingen* [Co-determination in Dutch firms. Report on an investigation of participation and influence relations]. Amsterdam: North Holland Publ. Co.

Arzensek, V. (1977), *Alienation and self-management.* Paper for the 2nd International Conference on Participation, Workers' Control and Self-Management, Paris.

Bachratz, P., Baratz, M. S. (1963), Decisions and non-decisions: An analytical framework. *American Political Science Review*, **16**.

Bernstein, P. (1976), *Workplace democratization: Its internal dynamics.* Kent (Ohio): Kent State University.

Blumberg, P. (1968), *Democratie in het bedrijfsleven* [Industrial democracy]. Utrecht: Het Spectrum.

Bolweg, J. F. (1976), *Job design and industrial democracy.* Leiden: Nijhoff.

Boonzajer Flaes, R., Ramondt, J. J. (1974), *Autoriteit en democratie. Arbeiderszelfbe stuur in rijke en arme Joegoslavische ondernemingen* [Authority and democracy. Workers' self-management in rich and poor Yugoslavian enterprises]. Rotterdam: Universitaire Pers.

Brannen, P., Batstone, E., Fatchett, D. J., White, P. (1976), *The worker directors: A sociology of participation.* London: Hutchinson.

Buckley, W., Burns, T. R. (1974), *Power and metapower. Relational control and development of hierarchical control systems.* Paper for the 8th World Congress of Sociology, Toronto.

Coetsier, P. (1966), *Organismen voor medezeggenschap in de onderneming* [Organisms for industrial co-determination]. Antwerp: Standaard Wetenschappelijke Uitgeverij.

Corte, W. de (1979), Realiteitswaarde van de notie feitelijke participatie: Een studie in de variante taal van het sociopsychologisch onderzoek [The reality value of the notion of actual participation: A study of the variant language of sociopsychological research]. *Psychologica Belgica*, **19**, 33–360.

Dachler, H. P., Wilpert, B. (1978), Conceptual dimensions and boundaries of participations: A critical evaluation. *Administrative Science Quarterly*, **23**, 1–39.

Dongen, H. J. van (1970), Over gebieden van medezeggenschap [On areas of co-determination]. *Mens en Onderneming* [Man and Enterprise], **24**, 217–232.

Drenth, P. J. D., Pijl, J. van der (1966), *De onderemingsraad in Nederland* [The works council in The Netherlands]. The Hague: COP/SER.

Eissen, A., Gelderen, A., van, Kerkhof, W. H. C., Thierry, Hk. (1980), *Sociale informatie en sociaal verslag* [Social information and social reporting]. Amsterdam: University of Amsterdam.

Elden, J. M. (1977), *Political efficiency at work: More autonomous forms of workplace organization; link to more participatory politics.* Paper for Seminar on Social Change, Dubrovnik.

Emery, F. E., Thorsrud, E., Trist, E. (1969), *Form and context in industrial democracy.* Assen: Van Gorcum.

Engelstad, P. H., Quale, T. V. (1977), *Innsyn og innflytelse.* Oslo: Tiden.

Etzioni, A. (1971/75), *A comparative analysis of complex organizations*. New York: The Free Press.

FNV (Federatie Nederlandse Vakbeweging [Federation of the Dutch Union Movement]) (1976), *Open boek. Een nota over de behoefte van werknemers aan informatie over hun onderneming* [Open book. Memorandum on the employees' need for information about their firm]. Amsterdam: FNV.

French, J. R. P., Raven, B. H. (1959), The basis of social power. In: Cartwright, D. (Ed.), *Studies in social power*. Ann Arbor: Michigan Institute for Social Research.

Gevers, P. (1972), *Ondernemingsraden, randverschijnsel in de Belgische industriële demo-cratiseringsbeweging?* [Are works councils a marginal phenomenon in the Belgian democratization movement?]. Louvain: Catholic University Louvain, Dept. of Social Science.

Hickson, B. J., Hinings, C. A., Lee, C. A., Schneck. R. E., Pennings, J. M. (1971), A strategic contingencies theory of intra-organizational power. *Administrative Science Quarterly*, **16**, 216–229.

Hoorn, T. P. van, Dekker, H. C. 1977), Sociale verslaggeving op een tweesprong [Social reporting at a crossroads]. *M & O*, **31**, 167 ff.

Hövels, B., Nas, P. (1976), *Ondernemingsraden en medezeggenschap* [Works councils and co-determination]. Nijmegen: Busser.

Hövels, B., Nas, P. (1978), Ondernemingsraden: Enkele conclusies op ground van een onderzoek [Works councils: Some conclusions based on a study]. *M & O*, **32**, 330–347.

IDE—International Research Group (1980a), *Industrial democracy in Europe*. London: Oxford University Press.

IDE—International Research Group (1980b), *European industrial relations*. London: Oxford University Press.

Instituut voor Toegepaste Sociologie/Sociologisch Instituut [Inst. of Applied Sociology/Sociological Inst.] (1973), *Het functioneren van de ondernemingsraad. Literatuurstudie en onderzoeksopzet* [The functioning of works councils. A study of the literature and a research design]. Nijmegen: Catholic University.

Janin, H. C. (1977), *Prerequisites for effective participation (information and training)*. Working Paper, December 1977, European Institute for Advanced Studies in Management, Brussels.

Jong, E. de (1977), *Macht, deskundigheid en onderemingsraden* [Power, expertise and works councils]. Delft: University of Technology.

King, C. D., Vall, M. van der (1978), *Models of industrial democracy. Consultation, co-determination and workers' management*. The Hague: Mouton.

Kuipers, J. H. (1975), *Beleidsvoering door werkoverleg* [Management by work consultation]. Alphen a/d Rijn: Samsom.

Laaksonen, O. J. (1977), The power structure of Chinese enterprises. *International Studies of Management and Organization*, **7**, 47–70.

Lammers, C. J. (Ed.), (1965), *Medezeggenschap en overleg in het bedrijf* [Co-determination and consultation in the firm]. Utrecht: Het Spectrum.

Lammers, C. J. (1970), Democratisering van bedrijf en universiteit [Democratization of industry and university]. In: Braam, A. A. van (Ed.), *Actuele sociologie* [Contemporary sociology]. Assen: Van Gorcum.

Lammers, C. J. (1980), *Ontwikkeling en relevantie van de organisatie-sociologie* [Development and relevance of organizational sociology]. Utrecht: Het Spectrum.

Lammers, C. J., Andriessen, J. H. T. H., Meys, A. A., Meurs, P. L. (1980), Maakt de ondernemingsraad in het Nederlandse ziekenhuis een kans? [Does the works council have a chance in Dutch hospitals?]. *M & O*, **34**.

Lane, J. E. (1978), *Preliminary steps toward a new approach of the concept of power*. Paper for the 9th World Congress of Sociology, Uppsala.

Looise, J. C. (1976), *De proef op de som* [The proof of the pudding]. Utrecht: SWOV.

Mulder, M. (1977), *Omgaan met macht* [Managing power]. Amsterdam: Elsevier.

Obradovic, J. (1970), Participation and work attitudes. *Human Relations*, **23**, 459–471.

Pateman, C. (1970), *Participation and democratic theory*. London: Cambridge University Press.

Ramondt, J. J. (1974), *Bedrijfsdemocratisering zonder arbeiders* [Industrial democratization without workers]. Alphen a/d Rijn: Samsom.

Ramsay, H. (1978), *Phantom participation: Patterns of power and conflict*. Paper for the Conference on Participation, European Institute for Advanced Studies in Management, Brussels.

Rosenstein, E., Strauss, G. (1970), Workers' participation: A critical point of view. *Industrial Relations*, **90**, 197–214.

Rus, V. (1979), Limited effects of workers' participation and political power. In: Burns, T., *et al.* (Eds.), *Work and power*. London: Sage.

Schmitz, H. P. W., Laenen, G., Koekenbier, H. A. J. (1975), *Onvrede en klachten van werknemers* [Discontent and complaints of employees]. Nijmegen/Utrecht: ITS/SWOV.

Scholten, G. (1975), *Medezeggenschap en organisatieverandering* [Co-determination and organizational change]. The Hague: COP/SER.

Spit, W. J. L. (1978), Medezeggenschap: Een kwestie van democratie en humaniteit in de arbeidsorganisatie [Co-determination: A matter of domocracy and humaneness in the work organization]. In: Sitter, L. U. de, *et al.*, *Medezeggenschap in de onderneming* [Co-determination in the organization]. Nijkerk: Callenbach.

Tannenbaum, A. S. (1969), *Social psychology of the work organization*. London: Tavistock.

Tannenbaum, A. S., Kavcic, B., Rosner, M., Vianello, M., Wieser, G. (1974), *Hierarchy in organizations*. San Francisco.

Thierry, Hk. (1977), *Expectancy and the prediction of participative behavior*. Paper for the 2nd International Conference on Participation, Workers' Control and Self-Management, Paris.

Thierry, Hk., Jong, J. R. de, *et al.* (1979), *Naar participatie en toerekening Theorie en praktijk*. [Towards participation and imputation. Theory and practice]. Assen: Van Gorcum.

Veen, P. (1973), Participatie. Een poging tot synthese [Participation. An attempt at synthesis]. In: Drenth, P. J. D., Willems, P. J., Wolff, Ch. J. de (Eds.), *Arbeids- en organisatiepsychologie* [Work- and organizational psychology]. Deventer: Kluwer.

Vliet, G. E. van (1973), Het bedrijvenwerk en de veranderingen binnen de Nederlandse vakbewging [The shop steward system and changes within the Dutch trade union movement]. *Mens en Onderneming* [Man and Enterprise], **27**, 269–283.

Vliet, G. E. van (1979), *Bedrijvenwerk als vorm van belangenbehartiging* [The shop steward system as a form of interest promotion]. Alphen a/d Rijn: Samsom.

Wall, T. D., Lischeron, J. A. (1977), *Workers' participation*. London: McGraw-Hill.

Zuthem, H. J. van (1978), Sociologische aspecten van de medezeggenschap van werknemers [Sociological aspects of employees' co-determination]. In: Sitter, L. U. de, *et al.*, *Medezeggenschap in de onderneming* [Co-determination in the organization]. Nijkerk: Callenbach.

Zuthem, H. J. van, Wijnia, A. (1967), *Medezeggenschap* [Co-determination]. Noordwijk aan Zee.

Handbook of Work and Organizational Psychology
Edited by P. J. D. Drenth, H. Thierry, P. J. Willems and C. J. de Wolff
© 1984, John Wiley & Sons, Ltd.

4.11. Systems of remuneration

Henk Thierry

1. AN AREA UNEXPLORED

Work and organizational psychologists have never paid much attention to the issues and problems of remuneration and income. Only a few Dutch psychologists are, at this moment in the early eighties, engaged in research or are involved in advising companies or other work organizations on the practical problems and policy issues of remuneration. It should be said, however, firstly that this is not a recent development but is typical of the state of affairs, at least, since the Second World War (see the Appendix in Bunjes *et al.*, 1977). Secondly, it is not typical of The Netherlands alone. Relatively few (W and O) psychologists are active in this field in countries such as Belgium, West Germany, the U.K., Sweden or the United States. Thirdly, the psychologists are not alone in their lack of interest in this field, the same can be said of sociologists, political scientists and other social scientists. We will not, however, be going into this point in the context of this chapter.

How can this relative neglect by W and O psychologists and the relatively peripheral place occupied by this theme within W and O psychology be explained? Could it be—and we wish to concentrate our question on this issue in this chapter—that psychological points of view are hardly or not at all to be posed in research or in professional practice concerning the meaning of remuneration in all kinds of work and organizational issues and problems? We have in mind, for example, the role played by remuneration:

Prof. dr. Hk. Thierry, Universiteit van Amsterdam, Vakgroep Arbeidspsychologie, Weesperplein 8, 1018 XA AMSTERDAM.

—as one of the essential components of labour contracts between an individual employee and an organization;

—as a regular theme of conflict in collective bargaining between employers' organizations and unions with or without active government interference, and as an important part of every Collective Labour Agreement;

—as (for the foreseeable future) one of the most important points in the discussions—and policy—on the redistribution of power;

—as the medium through which labour conflicts often become manifest and are practically always regulated ('solved');

—as a component which is, as a rule, influenced by, and mostly itself influences, the degree of work motivation, work satisfaction and performance;

—as a means used to clarify one another's relative position in processes of social comparison, which in turn also determines the extent to which each individual can measure his societal recognition.

This question, in fact, contains two aspects: it points, on the one hand, to the 'translation' of questions of remuneration deriving from work, organization and societal relations, into terms of psychological problems which can be researched. On the other hand, there is the aspect of the 'application' of psychological theories and of the results gained from research to remuneration issues in the practice of work and organization. Both approaches will be dealt with in this chapter: our main theme is that the present state of affairs in work and organizational psychology—though there are many areas still to be explored—makes it possible to contribute more to the wide field of remuneration for work than has, till now, been the case.

To this end we shall first investigate, in section 2, which psychological theories are of particular importance in this context. In the two following sections, 3 and 4, we shall present, as examples, two important 'themes from the field': the link between performance and remuneration, and the relationship between participatory behaviour and remuneration.

It is, all the same, questionable whether lagging insight into the interaction between practical questions and psychological problems is the most important reason for the relative lack of attention paid by psychologists to the subject of remuneration. Seen in a wider context we have in mind the properties that Eisenga (1978) attributes to the industrial psychology phase of the developments in W and O psychology in our country. He found that most research in industrial psychology in the fifties and early sixties bore an exploratory and inventory-making character. In the process he questions whether the contributions made by psychologists towards a greater insight into work behaviour were sufficiently based on *psychological* theories and results. In so far as Dutch psychologists were actually involved in remuneration issues—to give our interpretation of Eisenga's ideas—the basis of their research was perhaps excessively dominated by the practical problems of the time. Consequently, not enough attention was paid to the specifically psychological aspects of such remuneration problems nor to the contributions that could be made based specially on psychology as a science.

More specifically, our criticism is directed toward the idea often to be found among psychologists (and other social scientists) that the remuneration of work is of little more than secondary significance. We shall limit ourselves to naming three aspects of this point here. In the first place, remuneration is often considered to be only a matter of 'labour politics', just one section of the terms of employment. 'Technically' this is, of course, correct. But, on the one hand, what is often meant is that decisions about the level and the components of wages are made by representatives of employers' organizations, unions and the government. The employees are at best spectators and, for this reason, remuneration is a matter which 'leaves them cold'. On the other hand, it indicates that remuneration is considered merely to be a condition, not the heart of the matter. This is closely connected with a second notion, held by many, that the content of work—such as the degree of working autonomy and mutual relations among employees—is of far greater importance to workers than the remuneration they receive for that work. Consequently, work content and work remuneration are mostly seen as issues bearing little or no relation to each other. In the third place it is frequently emphasized that remuneration is only intended as a means to control work behaviour, and particularly, besides the systems of incentive payment that are little used in The Netherlands these days, to 'buy off' labour conflicts, make dirty and unpleasant work financially 'attractive', 'compensate' for shift work, etc.

We already pointed out that these three ideas attach little value to remuneration. They often do so without sufficiently investigating whether such an interpretation is justified by the results of empirical research. But the most pressing question is whether the conclusion that wages are of minor significance has not been drawn too hastily and is perhaps insufficiently based on theory. In section 2, therefore, we wish, before discussing various psychological theories, to decide what place remuneration should be given in theory.

2. THEORY RECONNOITERED

2.1. Some concepts

Up till now we have used the concept *remuneration* in the sense of the material returns gained from work, in other words the gross earnings of an employee of a work organization. We will continue to do so in the rest of this chapter. However, the immaterial returns such as the degree of work autonomy, winning recognition, the exercising of influence on decision-making, etc., are also included in the concept of remuneration by some writers. Here and there we will point out a possible connection between the two 'categories' of returns.

The definition of remuneration in terms of a person's (gross) earnings means that the concepts *wages* and *salary* will not be differentiated. The original significance of this distinction was the differentiation between the terms of employment of manual and office workers. Manual workers were paid an hourly, daily or weekly wage, but office workers were paid a monthly salary. Apart from this a large number of other—and probably more fundamental—differences also existed between the two 'groups', for example, in the field of sick pay arrangements, provision of pensions, etc. The distinction between the terms wage and salary gradually disappeared as the terms of employment for manual and office workers were brought into line—a process known as harmonization in The Netherlands and which got under way here in the sixties.

As far as the concept *income* is concerned a distinction is usually made between primary, secondary and tertiary income. The *primary* incomes are decided by the prices for the use of the production factors labour and capital. Besides these, the incomes of the self-employed, interest, rent, profit and emoluments such as telephone and travel expenses also belong to this category.

The *secondary* incomes are created by re-distribution by the government of a part of the primary incomes. A system of social security is financed partly by levying insurance contributions and partly from direct taxation. This system allows the payment of benefits in cases of unemployment, illness, disablement, retirement, etc.

The *tertiary* incomes are those services made available by the government below the cost-price or even free. These include education, police and fire service, the use of roads, concert and theatre-going, health care, etc. The financing again is mainly from taxes.

Since we previously described the concept remuneration as earnings from work it is clear that we are limiting ourselves in this chapter to the field of the primary incomes, and within that category in particular to income from work.

The analysis of such incomes can of course be approached from different angles. The manner in which the earnings are *distributed* among the personnel of an organization or the members of professions, the inhabitants of a country, etc. could, for example, be emphasized. The relative positions of the incomes e.g. are then observed. A second approach emphasizes the function of remuneration in the context of a work organization's *policy*. Such an approach can concentrate, for example, on the degree to which the organization is made (more) attractive to potential employees, and to those already employed to continue working for the organization. The degree to which remuneration can stimulate a particular type of work behaviour etc. could be also investigated. We will touch on this approach briefly at several points later. A third angle of approach examines the *significance* an employee can attach to remuneration, especially in the context of work motivation and work satisfaction. We will pay considerable attention to this approach in sections 2.2 and 2.3. A fourth approach concentrates on the manner in which remuneration is *brought about*.

This fourth approach confronts us with another limitation. By far the greatest portion of an employee's income from work is usually composed of the remuneration awarded to the *rank* of his or her job. We shall not go into further details of the methods on which such job evaluation is based in this chapter (see this Handbook, ch. 2.10 for such details). In sections 3 and 4 we shall concentrate in particular on the *personal* remuneration, with particular attention for that portion of income that an employee receives on the grounds of his or her contribution to the production process. For a more detailed treatment of the concepts mentioned here see: Samuelson, 1968; Albeda and de Galan, 1970; Pen and Tinbergen, 1977; van Niekerk, 1979; de Galan, 1981; Thierry, 1983.

2.2. Determination

It is clear, as we saw in the previous paragraphs, that remuneration can be studied from different angles of approach, at different levels of analysis and in the context of different disciplines. Seen in the light of W and O psychology the essence of the matter is *the significance of remuneration in influencing an individual's behaviour.* Various theories as to *how* remuneration can attain significance will be discussed in section 2.3. Some of these point out the importance of learning processes, but most of them accentuate the role of motivational processes. The analysis of individual behaviour can be approached from various angles. Remuneration can be of significance (a few examples will have to suffice):

—in the search for, or an offer of, a suitable position via the labour market;
—in a decision to continue with the same job, in spite of onerous conditions;
—in the learning of new, for example, more participatory, behaviour;
—in achieving a particular level of performance;
—for the degree of job satisfaction;
—in the development, the progress and the settlement of a work conflict.

The heart of the 'object', mentioned above, of a W and O psychological approach is the question *what factors determine the manner in which remuneration acquires and maintains significance, and in which the significance becomes weaker or disappears.* This means we attach great importance to the changes in significance that may occur and the processes underlying such changes. In the following model a number of potential factors (determinants) that determine the significance of remuneration for the individual worker are worked out in greater detail. Seen from the angle of the researcher various levels of analysis appear. As we shall demonstrate in more detail later, we distinguish determinants related to the person, the group to which he belongs, the job, the working unit, the operational policy, the structure and context of the organization involved, and its environment.

Some determinants can exercise 'direct' influence on the significance of remuneration for the individual worker. We assume, for example, that the characteristics of the job—such as the variation in job content—can influence the significance of remuneration. Other determinants can only do that in an 'indirect' manner. We do not expect, for example, aspects of the organization's structure—in particular the character of the control systems—to have a direct 'effect' on the significance of remuneration, but they can be of influence by means of one or more 'intermediate stages'. Control systems can colour, for instance, the nature of operational policy; the main features of this policy can in turn influence the functioning of the working unit, consequently the significance of remuneration for all the members of that unit can be influenced through, for example, the nature of their mutual social relationships. Put briefly: each 'lower' level in the model can fulfil a moderating function.

If all the possible direct and indirect relationships were to be included then the presentation of this contingency model (figure 1) would become unnecessarily complicated. They have, for this reason, been left out. Only a few examples have been given in the explanation of each determinant. We then continue with some remarks on the ways in which this model can be used.

According to figure 1, there are eight determinants which can influence the significance of remuneration for the individual worker. One of these can, firstly, be the various characteristics of that person: besides biographic and demographic variables—such as composition of the family; relative income position—personality variables can also play a role (including the strength of the need for rivalry; see this Handbook, ch. 3.1). We then distinguish the contributions made by a person to the working process—taking the initiative; bearing responsibility; checking equipment, etc.—and the returns received from work. Since we concentrate on the ways in which remuneration could be significant, we consider other material returns (e.g. the number of days off), immaterial returns (e.g. freedom to arrange one's own work schedule) and the connections between the two. It is also important to realize what relationship exists, or should exist, between contribution and return according to the person himself.

In the second place the significance of remuneration can be determined by the characteristics of the *group* within the work organization which the employee considers he belongs to. We have both defining characteristics—which, essentially, demonstrate what a group is—and variation characteristics in mind: the latter accentuate differences between groups (see this Handbook, ch. 3.1). We would in particular like to point to the patterns of norms and values, the aims, and the number of people in the group.

In the third place the *job* can also play an important role. In addition to the length of the cycle, the variation in content and skills needed and the degree of autonomy are examples of characteristics which can determine the significance of remuneration. They influence, for example, motivation and/or performance; they can be treated as factors to be valued and rewarded, and so on. Of course, besides individual jobs group jobs can also be at stake, and the group can also exert influence on the way in which jobs are performed: for these reasons, boxes 2 and 3 in figure 1 are connected by arrows.

By *working unit* we understand the organization (section) or the technical

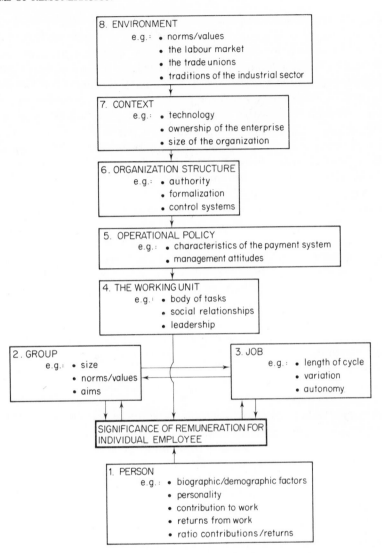

Figure 1. Potential determinants of the significance of remuneration for the individual employee.

'unit' (an assembly line, for example) to which the group or the tasks to be carried out can be considered to belong at the lowest level of planning, co-ordination and control. Its characteristics include the body of tasks (e.g. organization according to phase of production or according to product), the social relationships (such as co-operation or competition), and the nature of the leadership (e.g. participatory or directive). These characteristics partly can be of direct influence on the significance of remuneration for an employee—as, for instance, is the case when leadership is concerned—but can equally be of indirect influence.

In the case of determinants 5 to 8, potential indirect influence is of principal importance, although several direct relationships can appear. This applies in particular to *Operational Policy*: on the one hand we have in mind technical features of a remuneration system and procedures for their practical application. On the other hand we have the, often enduring, attitudes and convictions held by employees on, for example, the significance of remuneration (these are of an 'operative' nature: see Thierry and de Jong, 1979, section 3.6.2). As a rule, neither type of example allows any operational differentiation to be seen for each employee individually, but both mostly refer to all those who are considered as belonging to the working unit.

In the sixth place, characteristics of the *organization's structure* can be of influence. These are, on the one hand, characteristics such as authority, formalization, and so on (see this Handbook, ch. 4.1). Although these can indicate the degree and general manner in which control is effected, we wish, on the other hand, to lay particular emphasis on the properties of specific control systems. Several examples: budget, production progress and quality control. Norms for these controls can be based on work studies.

In the seventh place, we distinguish the characteristics of the *organizational context*. Technology should be considered here, seen, for example, in the light of the question as to the degree to which systems of incentive payment would be of use in (perhaps only a few parts of) the work organization (see further section 3). Other characteristics include: ownership (an independent enterprise as opposed to a subsidiary) and size.

Our eighth and last potential determinant is the *environment* to the extent in which this is of importance for the existence and future of the work organization. Firstly, 'social' norms and values can be of influence on, for example, acceptable differences in income, the desirability of a link between performance and remuneration, etc. Such factors could influence not only the views and policy-making within the organization on remuneration—and, therefore, its significance for the employee—but can also be of 'direct' influence on the way in which each employee values his or her remuneration, for example, if the perceived differences in income deviate from the normative ideas about that income. Other characteristics include the labour market, in particular where the scarcity of jobs as opposed to the scarcity of workers is concerned; the basic principles and policy of the unions, and traditions in that particular industrial sector, for example, in the field of incentive payment.

In the context of this chapter a short explanation without any further detail will have to suffice, both as far as the number of characteristics for each determinant and the availability of research results for each characteristic are concerned. In sections 3 and 4 we will, however, be giving some data on the last point in connection with the themes dealt with there.

This model could, in the first place, be used to make clear at which levels of analysis theories of remuneration—for example, those reviewed in section 2.3—can be applied. Greater insight could be gained into the degree to which a remuneration theory can be regarded as a full-bodied theory of work- and organizational psychology with the help of the dimensions and variables included at each level. We will return to this point in section 2.4.

We have, then, looked at the model from the bottom upwards, in other words, from the viewpoint of the individual employee. Depending on the problem in hand—and this points to a second potential use—a different route could be followed. Just suppose that a work organization has to choose from alternative remuneration systems and that particular attention is paid to the functions that remuneration of employees can have in the light of that organization's objectives. One could then start at box 5, and follow a path upwards or downwards. In the process, attention will have to be paid, on the one hand, to the important role played in this choice by processes of decision-making about the manner in which the remuneration system is adapted to the structural, contextual and environmental characteristics of the organization. On the other hand, we cannot ignore the weighing of the interests held by many parties in such remuneration questions (such as the individual employee, various working units in relation to each other, managers of different professions, work floor and office personnel, the trade unions, etc.). We refer here to the great significance of 'organizational choice' (for more detailed discussion see this Handbook, ch. 4.2, 4.3, and 4.5).

If the problem mentioned above—the choice of a remuneration system—were to be interpreted solely in terms of the question of which systems are applicable in a 'technical' sense, then boxes 7, 6, 4 and 3 should especially be considered. Should an attempt be made to map 'the functioning of an existing wage system', then a downward path—starting from box 5 with a characteristic of box 6 added—should be followed, etc.

2.3. Psychological theories of remuneration

Innumerable examples can be mentioned which demonstrate that remuneration *is* very important for the individual employee. But a far more complicated question is *why* remuneration acquires, keeps or loses significance. It is often said that material remuneration is valued by a person because the returns he can acquire are of 'use' to him. The well-known distinction between the 'consumptive' and the 'symbolic' significance of remuneration can be placed on this same line: in the case of the first the significance of satisfaction of—primary or non-primary—daily needs is alluded to. The second significance is also allusive but aimed at returns such as status, recognition, etc. According to another, fairly well-known opinion, a person's behaviour in relation to remuneration should be interpreted as a reflection of his or her up-bringing, education and present working and living conditions (for a more detailed discussion of the subject see:

Gouldner, 1954; Gellerman, 1963; Cofer and Appley, 1964; Thierry, 1969; Lawler, 1971).

Nevertheless there are more than just a few nuances in the differences between the two approaches named above. This becomes apparent, for example, from the importance attached to events and developments in a person's past or rather, on the contrary, to cognitions and preferences existing in the present. For this reason we wish to divide the theories about to be presented into two categories: the learning theory approaches as against the—a term used in the widest sense—cognitive-theory approaches.

2.3.1. LEARNING THEORY APPROACHES

2.3.1.1. An acquired drive

According to the concept of drive reduction, certain drives come into existence in the (human) organism when it experiences a deficiency in a basic need (sustenance, for example). These drives cause the organism to be 'attentive' to opportunities in the environment to satisfy that need. The more effectively these opportunities are used, the more the strength of the drives is reduced until in the end the deficiency is eliminated (the need is satisfied).

This train of thought would have it that money can often play an important role in reducing such drives. When this is in fact the case—and for a long period—then the organism gradually associated the appearance and the satisfaction of basic needs, together with the associated drives, with the factor money. Consequently, money assumes the significance of a drive (which has now been acquired): it causes behaviour, even when no deficiencies in basic needs exist.

Lawler (1971) pointed out that this approach closely resembles Allport's concept of functional autonomy. Although earning money is, in the first place, significant for the realization of primary motives, it gradually acquires its 'own' significance. The relationship with those primary motives does not play any further role in this process.

2.3.1.2. Reducing fear

This approach is in fact an extension of the line of thought dealt with in the section above. However, instead of reducing positive drives, emphasis is now laid on the association of money with reducing avoidance drives. One example is reducing fear (see Brown, 1961). Small children associate painful experiences—such as falling or having an accident—with frightened and anxious behaviour by their parents. If parents display the same behaviour when faced with financial problems, then children transfer their fear to the object money. The pursuit of money—in earning wages—then gains a strongly motivational significance, in particular in order to reduce fear. This can then gradually acquire an 'autonomous' character, without the fear itself playing a (direct) role.

2.3.1.3. A secondary, generalized reinforcer

If money is often connected in time and space to the primary satisfaction of an existing need (as occurs when someone allays hunger by eating), then money can acquire the significance of a *secondary* reinforcer. This means that money can influence behaviour without the aid of any primary reinforcer. This effect only appears, however, if there is indeed any question of deprivation of any particular need(s). This point distinguishes this approach from the conception of money in terms of an acquired drive (see 2.3.1.1), because the latter acts without any deprivation of (basic) needs. Now Skinner and others have, in fact, pointed out that *generalized* secondary reinforcers can develop. This type of reinforcer is then not tied down to one particular need but to all those needs to whose primary reinforcement it has ever been connected. In other words, money may have a reinforcing significance whenever a human lacks e.g. food, safety or recognition (we almost put: 'anything').

These approaches to the significance of money based on the learning theory satisfy the condition we posed earlier that they shed light on the manner in which changes may occur in that significance. In spite of this, these concepts have not led to much elaboration or application within the field of work- and organizational psychology. We cannot go into the reasons here; we would, however, like to point out that many consider that with the aid of these theories much of the significance of money can be made clear, if only with hindsight. These theories are, however, considered to be of little use in forecasting such significance (the reader can find a more detailed account of these theories in Opsahl and Dunnette, 1966 and Lawler, 1971).

2.3.2. COGNITIVE THEORY APPROACHES

2.3.2.1. Distributive justice

This theory as conceived by Homans (1961) can be applied to the behaviour of people involved in an exchange relationship, or who maintain an exchange relationship with a third party, such as an employer. Three concepts play a central role in this theory, namely investments, costs and returns. A person's investments are, for example, his training, age and experience. Costs include: the effort expended; the risks taken; the high tempo; onerous circumstances; the loss of returns that might have been earned in a different exchange relationship. Returns include: status; promotion; feeling competent; and remuneration.

Distributive justice can be said to have been achieved when each person's profit (i.e.: returns minus costs) is in correct ratio to the investments. This is illustrated by the following figure:

PERSON A   REFERENCE PERSON B

$$\frac{\text{returns minus costs}}{\text{investments}} = \frac{\text{returns minus costs}}{\text{investments}}$$

If the *ratio* between profit and investments is regarded as unequal, then both parties will experience a sense of injustice. The person for whom this ratio is smallest, will experience relative deprivation. The accompanying dissatisfaction will stimulate him to strive for change.

What, then, can we say about the significance of remuneration on the grounds of this theory? Taking person A as our example, this significance can be determined by:

—the number and the nature of his other returns. We assume that the significance of remuneration will increase as A receives a smaller number of and/or less important returns;

—the size of the remuneration, keeping costs in mind, in relation to his investments. An important factor is the manner in which person A translates his investments and his costs into preferences for the nature and number of returns to be received. We will return to this in the following section;

—the extent to which A experiences this relationship as unequal in comparison with B. Suppose A attempts to eliminate his relative deprivation. The question then arises which components of the three concepts are considered most amenable to change. The situation in which A and B are placed will undoubtedly play an important role. Various studies have made it clear, however, that—at least, when changes in returns are being considered—a high level of priority is given to remuneration.

Various authors have adopted the basic ideas of Homans' theory, but have also made changes in the components that a person relates to each other and evaluates when comparing himself to a referent. Patchen (1961), for example, states that employees operate in the following manner when comparing their wages:

$$\frac{\text{my wage}}{\text{his wage}} \text{ compared with } \frac{\text{my position in relevant dimensions}}{\text{his position in relevant dimensions}}$$

Adams (1965) criticized Homans for being insufficiently specific about the events which cause injustice to be experienced and their consequences. He elaborated on these two aspects in his well-known equity theory; see this Handbook, ch. 2.2. (Should the reader be interested in other detailed elaborations of Homans' theory and in critical studies of it, we would refer them to the literature mentioned at the end of this section).

Finally we wish to point out that great importance is attached to *balance* in the type of theories discussed here. People strive to achieve a balanced relationship between their contributions and their returns in order to maintain balanced relationships with those they compare themselves to. In the following section, however, we shall discuss several unbalanced factors which, according to the train of thought presented there, characterize the manner in which an employee and a work organization regulate the exchange of their contributions and returns by means of a labour contract.

2.3.2.2. The exchange of contributions and returns

According to Belcher and Atchison (1974, 1976) the economic model is exemplified by a type of labour contract in which the employee makes his labour (effort, knowledge, skill) available in exchange for wages or payment in kind, and the organization contributes money (income) and receives performance (output). However, besides being one-sided—common means for divergent or even conflicting aims—this model is above all inadequate: both parties expect far more of each other. The organization mostly expects its personnel to display a degree of responsibility, engagement, ability to adapt, etc. Employees mostly count on being able to enter into satisfactory social relationships in the organization, to acquire a certain status, to gain recognition, etc.

Although, according to the authors, such a wider concept of exchange processes is becoming increasingly usual, economic aspects are still specified in far greater detail in labour contracts than non-economic aspects. Moreover, the non-economic clauses are rarely tied to a firm commitment in time.

Belcher and Atchison assume that both parties make contributions—in Homans' terms: costs and investments—in exchange for returns, and that they expect things of each other that are only very briefly specified. When this is used in particular to analyse questions in the field of remuneration, the following problems become apparent:

—The 'units' on the contributions side are not the same as those on the side of the returns. To illustrate this point, the reader should think of taking the initiative as a contribution and of remuneration as a return. As far as remuneration is concerned the units can be easily and unambiguously defined: there is an obvious zero point, and each following unit expresses a particular figure, for example Dfl. 100.-; 150.-; 200.-. But how can taking the initiative be expressed? Should that be specified quantitatively (much-little), or in terms of frequency (often-seldom), or, for example, by referring to the importance of a theme (about investments or about a holiday scheme)? Which anchor points reflect a satisfactory grading between, for instance, much and little. And what should be understood by terms such as much, often, seldom, etc.? What can be accepted as the zero point?

Yet another problem is the lack of a common norm for establishing a fair relationship between contributions and returns.

—Too little is known about the contributions that employees expect to exchange.

—Too little is known about the contributions the organization expects employees to make.

—Organizations generally know exceptionally little about the employees' preferences for returns.

—Organizations are mostly hardly aware that they *do* in fact give employees

certain returns—intrinsic returns for example—or that they *could* give them. They mostly assume that only economic aspects play a role in the exchange.
—The characteristics of organizations and the qualifications of employees influence the exchange relationships.

We would like to mention as an 'aside' that the use of the Contributions-Returns Questionnaire developed by Tornow (1971) could shed some light on the ideas individual employees have on the matter (see von Grumbkov, 1980). To return then to the question of what in the context of this approach determines the significance of remuneration, we can refer in particular to the influence of the following aspects:
—the manner in which the individual or the organization 'translates' his or its contributions into preferences for particular returns (such as remuneration);
—the relationship between material and non-material—and between intrinsic and extrinsic—returns;
—the manner and the degree in which 'parties' manage to express their contribution-return preferences under common denominators.

2.3.2.3. Means-goal relationships: instrumentality

The next theory is derived directly from one of the most important work motivation theories that has been developed in the past 15 years. This instrumentality theory (also known by other names) is based on the principle that each individual is regularly confronted, in his work as well as in other fields, with the necessity to choose between various alternative ways of behaving. The attractiveness of an alternative is determined by the interaction between, on the one hand, the valence (attractiveness) of a person's long-term goals (gaining promotion, for example) and, on the other hand, the means (such as good performances) which he expects to lead to the realization of those goals (for a more detailed account, see this Handbook, ch. 2.2).

Lawler (1971) in particular has applied this theory to the question of how remuneration acquires significance. The central idea is exceedingly simple: the significance of remuneration is determined by the degree to which it is seen as a good means to realize motives that are important for that person. Lawler illustrates this with the aid of Maslow's needs scale:

Instrumentality	*Valence of Motives*	*Significance of remuneration*
Wages as a means for:		
●Physiological needs	$\otimes$ Physiological	$=$ (Wages $\rightarrow$ P) $\otimes$ Val. P
●Need of security	$\otimes$ Security	$=$ (Wages $\rightarrow$ S) $\otimes$ Val. S
●Social motives	$\otimes$ Social	$=$ (Wages $\rightarrow$ So) $\otimes$ Val. So
●Motives for recognition	$\otimes$ Recognition	$=$ (Wages $\rightarrow$ R) $\otimes$ Val. R
●Motives for autonomy	$\otimes$ Autonomy	$=$ (Wages $\rightarrow$ A) $\otimes$ Val. A
●Motives for self-realization	$\otimes$ Self-realization	$=$ (Wages $\rightarrow$ Se) $\otimes$ Val. Se

$\sum$: total significance
of remuneration.

The total significance of remuneration for an individual therefore consists of the sum of the various (in this example: six) components. Each component contains the importance of a particular motive for the person in relation to the degree in which the remuneration is seen as a means to realize that motive. Let us illustrate this with an example.

Let us suppose an individual strives for recognition. Let us further suppose that he expects a certain amount of remuneration to be a good means towards gaining that recognition (by the goods he can purchase, for example). The interaction between the two 'values' indicates the significance of the remuneration for this person, at least, as far as this motive is concerned. Should one of the two values equal 0, then the wages have no significance for him in this respect, but probably do in respect of other motives. (We have symbolized this interaction with a $\otimes$; the product of the two values, has, as a rule, been used for this purpose, which, however, is in most cases incorrect; see further Koopman-Iwema, 1980).

In the first place, this theory makes clear that when employees indicate (in a questionnaire, for example) that they consider remuneration to be very important, this fact has not in itself then been interpreted, at least not from a psychological point of view. Secondly, it is apparent—and this could be closely connected with the previous point—that should an individual think he has fewer alternative means at his disposal with which to realize his motives, then remuneration will become more important. Research has demonstrated that many kinds of biographic and demographic variables, such as the profession the person belongs to, can influence the significance of remuneration (namely, the valences of relevant motives and also the instrumental character of the wages) (see a.o. Wernimont and Fitzpatrick, 1972).

2.3.2.4. A hygiene variable?

Herzberg's two-factor theory (1959, 1966) has influenced practical policy in work organizations considerably (for a more detailed account see this Handbook, ch. 2.2). According to this theory, satisfaction and dissatisfaction relate to entirely independent dimensions. The characteristics that result in satisfaction likewise differ from those causing dissatisfaction. Intrinsic characteristics of work, in particular, such as bearing responsibility, result in satisfaction or motivation. On the other hand, extrinsic characteristics—particularly when they are lacking in some way—such as the physical working conditions or human relations, cause dissatisfaction. When intrinsic characteristics are lacking in some way, dissatisfaction does not result, while a 'satisfactory' work environment does not cause satisfaction: in both cases a neutral, indifferent feeling appears. According to Herzberg, satisfaction and motivation—both concepts are used by him in the same vein—produce results that differ from those caused by dissatisfaction.

What is of great importance for our subject is that Herzberg places remuneration in the category of extrinsic variables. This implies that sufficient remuneration could, at most, lead to the employee feeling he has *not* been unfairly treated and that his reward is *not* inadequate, economically speaking. Remuneration, then, could never lead to satisfaction or motivation. It just has to be fulfilled without further ado: it is a 'hygiene variable'.

Herzberg's advocacy of concentrating on the content of work has aroused a wide response. In the United States particularly it has led to all kinds of job enrichment programmes (see this Handbook, ch. 4.8). It has also lent weight to the opinion that remuneration is of little significance as a return for work behaviour. However, a large number of studies have demonstrated that this theory is untenable. This does not refer to the distinction between intrinsic and extrinsic variables, but to the proposition that work content cannot give rise to dissatisfaction and that the work environment—which includes remuneration—cannot be a source of motivation.

Besides the works already mentioned in this section, we refer the reader to March and Simon (1958), Weick (1966), Thierry and Drenth (1971), Thierry (1968, 1969, 1975), Mahoney (1979) and Metsch (1980).

2.4. Evaluation

Each of the theories discussed in the last two sections helps, in its own way, to cast light on the manner in which remuneration can acquire, keep and lose significance. If, however, we examine whether—using the model depicted in figure 1—any attention has been paid to the influence that could be exerted by various types of determinants, a far more negative picture emerges. Every theory, of course, distinguishes various characteristics of individuals. But in some theories extremely implicit assumptions, or none at all, are made in relation to the role of other levels of determinants. Though Herzberg's approach cannot, in certain vital respects, be vindicated, it does clearly demonstrate the significance of several determinants. The instrumentality theory undoubtedly offers many *touching-points* to which the theoretical significance of the eight determinants can be attached, but this significance has not, till now, been examined in the sense meant here, as far as remuneration is concerned. We must, therefore, conclude that many important theoretical notions on the significance of remuneration for individual behaviour at work are available, but that we still lack a proper W and O psychological theory of remuneration which provides a satisfactory theoretical expression of the influence of the determinants mentioned. Far more attention will have to be paid to this in the future.

It would not be too venturesome to presume that the lack of such a theory constitutes an important reason for the paucity of attention that has been and is being paid in most organization theories to the possible significance of remuneration as a factor influencing work behaviour (see this Handbook, ch. 4.2). It cannot be deemed impossible that these factors have become locked in a vicious circle. A brief sketch will have to suffice: partly caused by Taylor's principles, partly as a result of their elaboration by others within the scientific management movement, remuneration of work has been placed in a light which can at best be called dubious. During the 'human relations' period the quality of relationships between people was emphasized; work content, remuneration and other dimensions were supposed to be of secondary importance. Remuneration was placed at the 'lower' end of Maslow's scale of needs. Herzberg completed the circle as it were by stating that remuneration could never motivate. A psychologist who paid little attention to the possible significance of remuneration seemed, for this reason, to be acting in an 'historically' responsible manner, and might even have been considered 'modern'.

3. PERFORMANCE AND PAYMENT

In practice, however, the behaviour of employees at work demonstrates that remuneration most certainly plays an important role. Results of empirical research, both in the past and more recently, generally point in the same direction. Even though managers often overrate the significance attached to remuneration by employees (Lawler, 1971; Hoolwerf *et al.*, 1974; Whitmore and Ibbetson, 1979), remuneration plays often a role in cases of mistrust, friction, conflicts and even strikes. It can also, in many cases, be closely related to the way in which other aspects of work and working relationships are experienced. This has been proved to be the case by studies of incentive payment schemes.

In this section we will examine this subject more closely. We will begin by reviewing the main characteristics of incentive payment and the extent to which such systems are applied in The Netherlands (section 3.1). This will be followed by a discussion of the results of empirical research into the functioning of incentive payment (section 3.2). We will put forward various considerations that may be important when choosing a payment system (section 3.3). We shall also pause to reflect on the benefit that could be derived from some of the remuneration theories dealt with in section 2. We also intend, quite apart from the importance of devoting a separate section to incentive payment, to demonstrate (cf. section 1) that greater insight into the problems of remuneration and, in particular, incentive payment may be expected of a W and O psychological approach.

3.1. The uses of incentive payment

It is characteristic of *incentive payment* that performance or output is linked, in one way or another, to a premium or bonus mostly expressed as a percentage of the basic wage. Such incentives can be awarded for results achieved by an individual employee, a group, a department, or by a work organization as a whole. Though a large number of different incentive systems exist, they have at least two things in common:

(1) *Norms* or *standards* which employees' output has to meet. In most cases these are based on the results of work study. They are included—often linked with instructions on the working methods to be followed—in the setting of tasks for each worker or group of workers, etc.

(2) The *linking* of the (measured or assessed) performance or output to a (small) portion of the income earned.

Sub 1: Norms can be expressed in terms of the time set for performing a task (in normal circumstances), but also in terms of the product to be produced or service to be rendered, such as the quantity, quality, number of rejects, etc. Although systems with a single remuneration factor—quantity—are the most common, changes in the content of tasks has stimulated the introduction of systems with two or more (multi-) factors (for a more detailed account of work study and norm fixing see: ILO, 1979; Koopman-Iwema and Thierry, 1981a).

Sub 2: The performance or output can be linked proportionately to payment, but this can also be done in a less than proportionate way: the latter is often referred to as a 'degressive' link. A more than proportionate ratio, or 'progressive' link, can, of course, be made, but is rarely used. Both degressive and progressive links, moreover, can take the form of a stepped or curvi-linear relationship between performance and payment (for a more detailed account of incentive systems see: Thierry, 1969; Marriott, 1971; Bowey and Lupton, 1975; Whitmore and Ibbetson, 1979; Koopman-Iwema and Thierry, 1981a).

Although we have only mentioned the most important distinctions in the previous paragraphs, it will be clear that not only do many different incentive payment systems exist, but also quite a few variations within each system. The latter is particularly true of the *bonus* and *merit rating* systems much used in earlier years. The main feature of the bonus system (such as measured rates) is that the amount to be paid for a specific task or service is made known beforehand. A first variant is related to the way in which time standards are fixed. If these are based on systematic time study and work method analysis, this is known as measured rates. If, however, norms are derived from the experience of similar work gained in the past, this is known as experience rates. A second variant is related to the number of payment factors: although in most cases the quantity of production was the only factor, cases have been known of rating systems with two or more payment factors. A third variant is related to the manner in which the bonus is linked to performance (see sub 2 above), and a fourth variant links the rate to individual employees, to a group, a department or even a whole enterprise. In the case of merit rating—the assessment of the degree to which an employee merits extra payment—many variations can occur depending on the method of assessment (ranking, for example), the frequency of assessment, the number of aspects to be assessed, the linking of assessment results to bonuses, and whether it is applied individually or to a group.

The size of and variation in the bonus can, further, be strongly influenced by the period for which it is paid. Weekly payment gives a different result than when a progressive averaging method is used. The latter involves the basing of bonus calculations on the results achieved during a, for example, four- or thirteen-week period, in which the results of the last week are always included and those of the first are left out. A contract can also be drawn up for production and bonus levels during a half-year period. The longer the period in which bonuses remain unchanged, the less we can really refer to them as real incentives. When bonuses can in principle only be changed once a year, then we refer to them as a *fixed wage*.

Incentive payment was widely used in Dutch industry till late in the sixties. How has the situation developed since then? The Wage Administration Control Department (Loontechnische Dienst) of the Ministry of Social Affairs publishes statistics annually (see, among others, LTD, 1980).

It should be mentioned that the 1970 statistics were related to a large reference group, but those of 1979 are representative of companies and institutions with more than 50 employees. Table 1 shows that 86% of employees in 1979 enjoyed a fixed wage: 75% of these were on a time-wage, and 11% were subject to a system of personal assessment. Data on 1980 are very similar. Study of the statistics on the years in between reveals that the fairly drastic decline in the use of incentive payment occurred step by step through the years. However, the percentage of employees on incentive payment stayed at a fairly constant level between 1976 and 1979. The decline in this country has been, both relatively and absolutely, far greater than in other countries of the European Community. We should add that wide differences exist between the various industries, and that no exact statistics exist showing the extent to which the (assessment of) performance by middle and higher management is linked to a part of their salary (see further: van Dam *et al.*, 1973).

3.2. The functioning of incentive payment

What led to the large scale abolition of incentive payment? We shall only mention the most important points here (for a more detailed account see: Koopman-Iwema and Thierry, 1981a, b).

To begin with, the coordination of terms of employment of 'manual' and

Table 1. The use of incentive payment and of fixed payment for employees in The Netherlands in 1970 and 1979.

Method of remuneration	1970	1979
Incentive payment systems:		
● objective system	30% ⎫	
● less objective system	4% ⎬	2%
● personal assessment	25% ⎭	12%
Fixed wage	41%	86%

'office workers'—the 'harmonization'—meant that, if the use of incentive payment was to be continued, such a system should be relevant to clerical and managerial work as well as to production line work. This caused problems; consequently, in many cases a change was made to a system of personal assessment which in the course of time acquired the character of fixed payments. Secondly, increasing mechanization and automation complicated the fixing of appropriate standards of performance, especially as incentive payment demands that employees' influence on performance and output results can be made tangible. Thirdly, new, mostly team-oriented forms of work organization, such as work structuring, semi-autonomous groups, project or matrix groups, etc., created not only specific problems in fixing norms, but often new ideas about how differences in payment ought to be based too.

Our impression, however, is that one of the most important causes has been *the manner in which incentive payment has functioned in practice*. We begin by discussing the main points of studies related to various incentive systems and then pass on to the results of research, comparing fixed and variable remuneration. There are not many of these studies and those that do exist are dated, in part because incentive systems have been little used in recent years. We should add that the majority of these studies was of an exploratory character and was not generally based on a specified, theoretically defined, problem of the significance of remuneration and the role of potential determinants. (This brief review is based on data derived from the following studies: ILO, 1951; Whyte, 1955; van der Graaf, 1957; Hickson, 1963; de Jong, 1964; Ydo, 1965; Bolle de Bal, 1965; Buiter, 1968; Marriott, 1971; Lindholm, 1972; Thierry and Wesseling, 1973; van Ginneken et al., 1974; LTD, 1975; Lawler, 1976, 1981; Lundgren, 1976; Drenth and van Dam, 1976; Farr, 1976; Thierry, 1966, 1968, 1969, 1977; Terborg and Miller, 1978; Whitmore and Ibbetson, 1979; Bowey, 1980; Metsch, 1980; Koopman-Iwema and Thierry, 1981b; von Grumbkov, 1980, 1982).

The use of an incentive system cannot be seen as an isolated activity; on the contrary, it touches many aspects of (operational) policy and the way work is experienced. This is made quite clear by the intensive work analysis needed for the setting of norms and tasks and by the degree in which the immediate management itself plays a role in the daily operation of a system. This means that little can be said with any certainty about the causes of the advantages and disadvantages that research reveals. Time and again the question presents itself whether the incentive system as such is at stake, or rather the—often improved—organization of the production process, or the manner in which the system is applied.

Many complaints have been made about *norms*: they were incorrectly fixed (too high or too low), they became less and less relevant (because the work gradually changed), and they were screwed up higher and higher: when the bonuses earned were systematically higher than had been expected, workers became afraid that the targets would—for the same level of earnings—be set higher. This caused a climate of mistrust: when the level of a 'normal' performance was to be established, experienced workers would attempt to mislead the work analyst by, for instance, adding extra movements. The analyst, in turn, was well aware of what was going on and tightened up the norms a little extra; teams of workers reacted by putting a relatively low ceiling on production levels to make sure that norms were not tightened any further, and so on. Systems using only one payment factor (mostly quantity) were, in particular, the cause of complaints about a 'narrowing down' of work behaviour: employees neglected work that was not included in the norms set, such as care for the quality of the product. This narrowing down of the work was reflected in workers' complaints that they felt confined in a strait jacket, the work was far too prescribed, the tempo too hurried, 'you don't bother about anything except money'.

All the same, it does have favourable consequences. The *analysis* of work and working methods quite often resulted in the improvement of order and work flow planning, better control of the work process, the cutting of costs, and higher productivity, etc. Workers' incomes rose temporarily or permanently. Provided relations among workers—and with the supervisor—were good, the setting of tasks could be a stimulating influence on work behaviour.

In cases where incentive payment was felt to be stimulating excessive individualism among workers, a change-over sometimes was made to group incentives. (It should be said that group incentives were regularly used for group tasks.) This gave extremely mixed results: one disadvantage often brought up was that workers no longer really understood exactly how their bonuses were determined. Their *insight* had never really been very great in any case: systems that made use of several payment factors or which were based on a complicated relationship between performance and payment presented problems, which, in turn, affected workers' attitudes to their work. The supervisor could also influence the degree of insight, by, for example, the frequency with which he informed his workers of their productivity results: the more frequent the information, the greater the insight workers had. However, management, and especially higher management, all too often assumed that incentives would 'automatically' produce the desired effect and make little or no further claim on the supervisor's attention. This meant they were blind to a number of things, such as the supervisor's responsibility for the 'normal conditions' in which standards, norms and the linking of performance to earnings were supposed to function, for the quality of the goods produced, for the assessment of performance, etc.

An important motive for higher management to go ahead with the introduction of incentive payment was their expectation that it would increase *productivity*. Studies have produced contradictory results—no change, reduction, increase (sometimes of short duration, sometimes not)—and, again, there is little agreement on the causes. Neither do the few studies of the consequences of the change from the one system to the other allow any unambiguous conclusions.

In this connection we shall now examine in slightly more detail the main results of a considerable piece of research undertaken by Bowey (1980). She investigated the consequences of the recent introduction of incentive payment systems in 63 British work organizations. More than a 1,000 questionnaires were filled in by managers, shop stewards and shop floor workers, and a large number of interviews (427) were held. In addition, 28 companies recorded specified data for 12 months, and detailed case studies were made of two organizations. There were, naturally, quite a few differences in the character of the various incentive systems used; it is, however, striking that in 38 organizations the bonus was based on collective performance (in 33 cases the bonus varied) and in 15 companies bonuses varied according to individual performance.

The first notable result to emerge is that the consequences of the introduction of the incentive systems—as reflected in, for example, costs per unit product, quality, number of workers employed, earnings, team-work, etc. — display little relation to the characteristics of these systems. These are, for example, the question whether work study is necessary, the time norms, the remuneration factors, the individual, group or collective application, etc. It turned out—and this is our second point—that those consequences were in fact related to characteristics of the organization and its environment, such as the (assessed) degree to which the market made an increase in production desirable, the time needed between receiving and delivering the order, the importance of standards governing quality, the introduction of new technology, etc. Bowey concluded from a large number of analyses, not referred to here, that, above all, the way in which a system was introduced determined what results it would give. The time and effort spent by management on *consulting* the employees and *planning* the changes were of paramount importance. The process itself reveals the shortcomings in the organization that have to be solved before the incentive system can be introduced. The results of this research support what was said earlier about the (positive) consequences of work analysis and study of methods.

Turning our attention now to the issue of fixed or variable payment, we must conclude yet again that little can be said with any certainty about the opinions and experience of employees on the grounds of the empirical research carried out to date. People often express a preference for a system they do not have; work motivation seems mostly to have become more positive after a change to fixed payment; after experiencing fixed payment for a while many begin to yearn for some variation again. It could be said that, in the course of the years, opinion is *subject to the swing of the pendulum*. For a while feelings of 'solidarity' dominate: equal pay for those working at the same job, or for those dependent on teamwork to get a job done. Then again voices are heard suggesting that some variation in payment is justified, provided this is based on actual differences in performance. Each swing should be kept within limits, according to the findings of several more recent studies. Those aspects that workers consider to be very important in their own work should be reflected in higher rates of pay—provided those workers are able to influence them sufficiently. The clearer the relationship between a worker's effort, performance, assessment and remuneration is to him, the more he has been found to be satisfied. Important evidence in this respect—and Lawler (1976, 1981) in particular has pointed this out—has demonstrated that employees sometimes prefer incentive payment because it provides them with a certain degree of *control*. Resistance to an incentive scheme could, therefore, indicate a lack of trust in management's will to apply the system fairly, and reflect employees' anxiety that they will not be able to exert sufficient influence on it (for further reference, see White, 1975; Thierry, 1977). Researchers have, at various times, suggested that variable payment could be attractive if work is experienced as monotonous and routine. What might well be of greater importance is the suggestion that in the long run employees on a fixed wage lose interest in acting on their own initiative.

3.3. Choosing a system

The research results discussed in the previous section which, apart from a couple of exceptions, only refer to factory workers leave hardly any room for doubt as to whether one can speak of 'the' consequences of the application of a payment system. The answer is negative, whether it is a question of incentive payment or the distinction between fixed and variable payment. One need only study the *methodological* demands that must be made of a research study if one wishes to be able to make such general statements for this to be quite clear. For example, in most cases a very great number of factors would have to be kept constant, and, at the very least, a longitudinal research design would be needed. It would also be necessary to investigate the functioning of the same system under different conditions, or the functioning of differing systems under (practically) the same circumstances, etc.

However, we wish in this section to go into the *substance* of the question at issue—the consequences of the use of incentives. We pointed out in the previous section that so many—often necessary—changes occur previous to and at the time of the introduction of a remuneration system that a considerable degree of uncertainty remains about the causes to which the various advantages and disadvantages can be attributed. In most cases the functioning of an (incentive) payment system is influenced by the care taken in analysing working methods, carrying out time studies etc., which by itself may bring about improvements in production processes. As time goes by, changes—smaller or larger—are continually occurring in the content of the work, in the type of raw materials used and in the manner in which the work is carried out. Consequently, a second factor influencing the functioning of a system is the degree to which such changes are reflected in a systematic adjustment of the norms. A third factor is the 'procedural' side of a payment system. By this we mean the manner in which the characteristic rules of a system are applied from day to day. Let us suppose that one of the features of a system is the proportional linking of the bonus to performance for consecutive four-week periods. It will make quite some difference if each employee receives information on his performance *often* (daily? every fortnight?), *when* it is given (next day? the following month?), in *what form* the information is put (number of units? a cumulative percentage?), *how many people* the information refers to, etc.

A fourth, and very important, factor is the quality of the social climate in which the payment system is planned and put into action. We have in mind the extent to which the motives of (groups of) employees and the objectives of (categories of) management are taken into account, and the conflicts that can occur between them. It is also a matter of the quality of leadership in each department and—to sum up—the quality of operational and social policy.

Since it is impossible to talk of 'the' consequences of a payment system, it is just as difficult to say that any one system of (fixed or variable) payment is 'ideal'. It may certainly not be concluded, however, that the actual content and characteristics of a payment system are of no further importance, and to act as if they could be considered 'neutral'. But it does make us question whether the correct conclusion was drawn when trying to avoid the negative aspects involved in the functioning of (incentive) payment systems discussed in section 3.2, namely the wide-scale abolition of incentive payment.

Which factors, then, should be taken into account when choosing a new payment system or evaluating an existing system? We should once again point to what was said in section 2.2 on 'Organizational choice' and, in particular, to our emphasis on the importance of adjusting the system properly to the characteristics of the organization and its environment. More specifically, these factors are, in the first place, related to the *preconditions for the use of a system* which can indicate what choices could be made. These can be derived from boxes 2 to 5 of figure 1 (section 2): to what degree can tasks be standardized? To what extent can individuals or groups of employees influence their performance or output results? Is that influence really relevant, both for the employee and for the work organization? Is there sufficient trust in the performance assessment? Are the assessors sufficiently competent? Etc., etc.

Secondly, we must consider *the motives of both management and employees for introducing or continuing* a system. It is our impression that many researchers working on this theme have not really quite got hold of the right point. They often asked employees all kinds of questions about their opinions or preferences, for example, the relative importance of particular remuneration factors, fixed or variable income, the portion that should be variable, about individual, group of collective application, or particular systems. The answers to such questions undoubtedly yield useful material. But greater insight could be gained into such motives if the questions were based on a statement of problems derived from viewpoints founded on theory. However, this research is directed in most cases toward the issues as they occur or have occurred in practice, and hardly at all toward the theoretical background. This relatively superficial approach has quite possibly contributed to the swings between fixed and variable payment mentioned earlier.

In the light of the theoretical ideas about the significance of remuneration dealt with in section 2, we believe that greater insight into this problem can be gained by approaching it from the angle of W and O psychology. A systematic analysis (with or without a reference group) could be made, for the benefit of both the employee and the work organization, to see which contributions are thought or expected to be important, which returns are, or are expected to be, essential, and what relationships are desired, or are possible, between contributions and returns (see further: Metsch, 1980; Wijn, 1982). This last aspect in particular—the possible relationships—draws our attention yet again to the role of the various determinants in figure 1. This would also be the case if the instrumentality model were to be taken as a starting point: after all, the prediction that motivation and performance will improve if the relationship between performance and returns (remuneration is but one part of them) is visible can only be made if such a relationship really exists. Many determinants can influence the construction of this relationship and its further continuation, such as—see figure 1—control systems, management attitudes, leadership behaviour, length of job cycle, and the size of the group.

A responsible choice (or construction) of a remuneration system would seem possible with the help of this type of research. If data is collected systematically on (changes in) the various determinants mentioned earlier, a strategy of decision-making is made possible which could decide on the remuneration system to be used to achieve the greatest significance of payment for the individual employee. It is, for example, quite conceivable that the use of *incentive payment* will not lead to a narrowing of behaviour but will do the opposite, stimulate employees—for example, if payment is related to the degree of participatory behaviour—to augment their repertoire of behaviour (see also: Nash and Carroll, 1975; White, 1975; Marshall, 1978; Henderson, 1979; Lawler, 1981).

4. PARTICIPATORY BEHAVIOUR AND REMUNERATION

The title of this section encompasses two themes: participation *in* (the settlement of) the remuneration, and participatory behaviour *as* a factor which can be remunerated. We shall be brief about the first theme. The second theme is actually a special form of the subject of the previous section. We shall devote a separate section to the relationship between participatory behaviour and remuneration because it involves several special problems. Just as we did in the case of the topic 'performance and payment', we shall also pay attention to the question what can be contributed from the perspective of W and O psychology.

4.1. Participation in remuneration

It may be considered quite remarkable that exceptionally few cases are known in which employees are involved in one way or another in (parts of) the decision-making process about their payment, for example, on the relevant payment factors, the level of remuneration, the reasons for payment differences, the system as such, etc. Several studies have shown that quite a few employees would like to have more influence on these aspects (see, for example, van Ginneken *et al.*, 1974; Thierry *et al.*, 1979). One of the very few examples of employees being allowed to design their system themselves was an experiment with groups of window cleaners in the United States (Lawler and Hackman, 1969; Scheflen *et al.*, 1970; Lawler, 1981). Most of the workers belonged to a minority group and had had little education. Under the guidance of the research workers various groups constructed their 'own' system; other groups had a system imposed on them, or could talk once to the research workers, or were not involved in any change. The system developed with the participation of the workers gave the best results in terms of motivation, involvement, etc., as well as productivity. This was still the case when the researchers returned a year later.

Quite a different manner of participating in remuneration is related to the involvement of employees in the *design* of (a part of) their income, the form in which they wish to receive it. This is known as the Cafeteria Plan in which no changes occur when the income is being formed, or in the level of remuneration, etc. Employees may choose periodically (each year, for example), from various alternatives, such as: a shorter working week; a shorter working day; longer holidays; a bigger cash salary; educational leave; supplementary insurance policies, etc. These 'income components' supplement, just as in the case of an 'ordinary' salary, the usual social security and the provisions laid down in the (collective) labour agreement. The maximum amount which may be spent by each person on alternatives can, for example, be determined by the annual (real or nominal) increase in salary, but it can also be provided for—especially if there is no increase in income—by assigning a part of the existing salary for 're-allocation'. It can also be used in the case of promotion, when adjusting job content and terms of employment for older employees, etc. The central conception of the plan is to fit the range of income components as well as possible to employees' preferences; the latter vary not only from one individual to another but also change with the passing of time (age, marital status, type of work, etc.; for a more detailed account see: Thierry, 1977).

There are practically no examples to be found of the systematic use of the Cafeteria Plan in The Netherlands; however, it has been used in the United

States. An initial study has been made by Croonen (1979; also Thierry and Croonen, 1980), using a sample of more than 200 members of middle and higher management in a large organization, as to which behaviour determinants play a role when choosing alternative options of expenditure. Since the Plan is not actually in use—its introduction is being seriously considered—the questions were related to employees' concrete preferences *if* the Cafetaria Plan were to be introduced. Each participant could put together his or her own package from the following alternatives (several variants of each alternative were available, such as 3, 6, 11 or 16 extra days off): shorter working week; longer holidays; saving up days off with a view to early retirement; saving up days off for educational leave; normal raising of salary. The average costs of each variant were indicated for each salary group from which participants had been drawn.

The first thing to emerge was that the method used for employees to make their choice can make quite some difference. The relative value of five different methods was investigated in this study. They were, for example, paired comparisons; rating of attractiveness (on a five-point scale); and the 'Game Board'. In the last method the respondent is asked how he or she wishes to divide up a certain sum among different alternatives. It could then be seen that quite a number of variables are related to the choices made, such as: biographic and demographic characteristics (including length of service; level of financial obligations); the targets employees set themselves (for example, having challenging work; time for the family); aspects which are especially important for the employee (such as: following training courses with an eye to acquiring better qualifications), etc. To sum up, the results demonstrate, in the first place, that there is quite a wide variety in the choices made. A second point is that it is probably quite possible to predict the general lines along which the choices will run by means of the variables mentioned (and several others; see also Vinke, 1982). Repeated measurement and the actual use of the Plan are, of course, necessary to be able to test the validity of this statement.

It is clear that research into the theme of participation in remuneration is still in its infancy. Greater involvement of W/O psychologists is highly desirable for at least three reasons: firstly, it is a subject that in itself can be of great value. Secondly, it can be significantly related to the use of participation in other fields (see this Handbook, ch. 3.7, 4.8, 4.9, and 4.10). And thirdly it could form an important *starting-point* for the process of change in an organization (see, for example, Lawler, 1974, 1981).

4.2. Participatory behaviour as a remuneration factor

In the case of the second theme we are thinking of the remuneration, financial and otherwise, of the activities of employees who are involved in the structuring of work, in semi-autonomous working groups, in job consultation, special project groups, and the Works Council. Few examples are to be found in practice; we will return to this presently.

Many writers on this theme refer to the Scanlon Plan. In the thirties, the American union leader, Joseph Scanlon, developed a strategy of a surprisingly simple nature in a company threatened by bankruptcy. Firstly, the development and stimulation of participatory behaviour among all the employees was encouraged. A system of committees was designed to this end: committees in each department were to encourage employees to think about the work, to assess the ideas put forward and, if possible, put them into practice; a central committee assessed proposals that involved more than one department and co-ordinated the whole process. Secondly, a 'formula' was drawn up by which all employees could benefit collectively from the financial results of their participatory behaviour. Scanlon thought the ratio between the labour costs and the sales value of a year's production would form a good yardstick: if this was determined by the production of several years previous to the introduction of the Plan, then the alterations made in it after introduction of the Plan would reflect how 'effective' participation had been (for more detail, see: Lesieur, 1958; Frost et al., 1974). The company concerned was soon out of the red. Other companies in the United States then followed its example. The Plan became popular in the 70s, although the results were certainly not always successful.

A study, of a more exploratory character, was carried out in our country in the late 60s (de Jong et al., 1970). More recently, research has been carried out in several companies on the introduction of the Scanlon Plan, christened 'Participation and Gain Sharing' (P and GS) in The Netherlands (Thierry et al., 1979; de Jong et al., 1979). This research investigated, among other things, the effectiveness of several types of gain sharing, the significance of providing regular information and the development of participatory behaviour. The research revealed the existence of clear differences in ideas on the relationship between participatory behaviour and remuneration. For the sake of clarity we will give these differences as two points of view.

According to the first—held by most members of the Works Council and several of the managing staff and of the employees—(a possibly provisional form of) gain sharing should be introduced as soon as possible after a P and GS system has been started. This 'coupling' of the two is an essential part of the employees' learning process and can, therefore, be regarded, to a certain degree, as a condition for the further development of participatory behaviour. The gain sharing can, firstly, indicate how seriously management takes the aims of this system. It becomes clear what type of information on what subject at what moment should be available, and, moreover, management and employees learn to use this information through the practical experience of the periodic calculation of results and the sharing of gains. Employees quickly learn what consequences can result from (more) participatory activities by having to discuss them regularly. They then learn what value and significance participation can have. The above can mean that initially especially the material significance of participation is accentuated, but that this accent will gradually shift to both material and immaterial returns of participation. The nature of these returns will, quite simply, be determined both by what the employees find attractive and valuable and by what the organization is able in practice to attach to participatory behaviour.

The second point of view was more often to be found among management staff, some production workers and among the external advisers. Their main theme was that *if* the coupling with remuneration—the gain sharing in this case—is introduced, it can only be permitted as a *final conclusion* to the development of participatory structures and a climate of participation. The swift introduction of allocation would be, as it were, a strategy to catch everyone unawares. But the development of participation could, on the other hand, be of great value as a process in itself, in which norms, values and attitudes gradually develop, the characteristics of groups undergo changes as time passes, the hierarchic distribution of power and authority are ultimately made the subject of discussion, the decision-making process and the objectives of the organization exposed to criticism, etc. Once participation had become 'sufficiently' developed, the question can be raised *whether* a coupling of remuneration to participatory behaviour is desirable. In contrast to the first point of view, the returns on participation are mainly immaterial, at least, in the short run; they could, in the long run, become material too.

Actually, the issue here is one of the 'returns of participation'. Although participation can have both intrinsic and instrumental significance for employees (see, for example, Koopman-Iwema, 1980), both points of view would seem to exclude the other during the phases in which a participation system is planned, introduced and goes through its teething troubles.

We have now come up against a far greater problem. We pointed out earlier that, among other things, the members of Works Councils and those who take part in job consultation do not for the most part receive any financial remuneration for their participatory activities (see also Koopman-Iwema, 1980). It can be concluded from an analysis of experiments in and outside The Netherlands carried out in the 70s in the field of work structuring, greater sharing of responsibility, job consultation, etc. that—apart from a couple of exceptions (for example, Allegro, 1973)—in general little attention has been paid to remuneration (van Overbeek, 1981). The most striking feature is that this neglect must be laid at the door of the views held by the research workers, advisers and higher management in the work organizations involved, because it was very often the employees who asked about the (financial) returns.

Little by little, sounds of protest against this 'subordination' of remuneration have begun to be heard in writings outside The Netherlands. Strauss (1975) states that in many organizations people think that more satisfaction and more interesting work 'ought to be rewarding enough'. Fein (1976) protests strongly against work structuring 'because it has to be done for nothing', in other words, without remuneration (the reader should compare this with Herzberg's ideas mentioned in section 2.2). Bernstein (1976) concludes after analysing a series of examples of 'workplace democratization' that at least six conditions should be fulfilled for the democratization and humanization of work. The second condition refers to regular payments, over and above the basic wage, which are directly related to work behaviour and given to all participating employees. In connection with work redesign', Hackman and Oldham (1980) also accentuate the significance of connecting financial returns (as well as others) to work behaviour, especially when employees can also participate in the *design* of the remuneration system (see for further detail, among others, Jenkins, 1975; Birchall, 1975).

4.3. Reward structures

The 'reserve' that often exists towards the connection of financial returns to participatory work behaviour is, besides what was said in section 1, often attributed to ethical considerations. Participation is seen as an ethically desirable or even necessary quality of a person's fulfilment of his job. We consider this a completely acceptable view. But should the conclusion be drawn—as is often enough the case—that this is (ought to be) the sources of his returns too, and that it cannot tolerate financial remuneration, then we object. In our opinion this is a confusion of the (ethical) motive for encouraging participation with the psychological problem of what actual, possible and desirable returns can be expected of participation and the significance employees attach to them.

The reserve we mentioned above also quite often has to do with the idea that intrinsic motivation is 'more important' than extrinsic or even—in emulation of Deci (1975)—that giving extrinsic returns will diminish the degree of intrinsic motivation. We refer the reader to Chapter 2.2 of this Handbook for further details; however, we would like to add here that no convincing evidence for such ideas is to be found in research data, which emphasize the significance of both 'kinds' of motivation.

We believe that more research by W and O psychologists is urgently needed: several of the theories mentioned in section 2 could be of use in this research. Special attention should be paid to what we would like to call the development of *'reward structures'*. This involves a systematic analysis:

—of *targets*, i.e. what returns the employees have in mind if they wish to co-operate in participation and the changes it is to bring about;

—Which *reward structures* are needed to this end, i.e. which behaviour variants can be coupled to certain returns, and how these relationships are to be 'organized' and gradually made permanent;

—how these behaviour-return relationships can best be *learnt* by employees.

Such an approach does not isolate remuneration in an overrated or underrated position, but allows the link between participatory behaviour and remuneration to be one of the (many) possible choices. It is the significance employees attach to remuneration and the factors derived from the organization that play a role in the process (see figure 1, Section 2), which should exercise a decisive influence. Secondly, we are stressing here the point that the creation of both more intrinsic and more extrinsic motivation requires a sound and systematically developed policy of organization (see also Lawler, 1976). Thirdly, such a development of reward structures could contribute to the creation of better *conditions* to stimulate the *broadening* and *renewal* of work behaviour.

5. CLOSE

In this chapter we have postulated that W and O psychology should primarily be concerned with the significance of remuneration for an individual employee's behaviour. The essence of the matter lies in investigating which determinants are responsible for the creation, maintenance and disappearance of that significance.

Having presented a model that could be suitable for use—which includes various kinds of determinants—and having discussed various segments of theory about remuneration, we concluded that W and O psychology has not, as yet, developed a proper theory of remuneration. We did postulate that the present state of affairs would allow of a considerably greater contribution by W and O psychologists than is at present the case.

We have attempted to demonstrate by means of two examples—performance and payment and participation and remuneration—that it should be a matter of two-way traffic: on the one hand the translation of remuneration issues taken from practice into terms of psychological problems which can be researched, and on the other hand the application of research results to the problems that arise in practice.

We hope that W and O psychologist will be able to find in this chapter various handles to come to grips with the issues raised in it. We would consider it just as important, though, if it were to lead to a well co-ordinated approach by W and O psychologists to themes that have been left untouched here, especially the redistribution of income, inconveniences at work, and discrepancies in the labour market.

REFERENCES

Adams, J. S. (1965), Inequity in social exchange. In: Berkowitz, L. (Ed.), *Advances in experimental psychology*. New York: Academic Press.
Albeda, W., Galan, C. de (1970), *Inkomen: Vorming, verdeling, belied* [Income: Creation, distribution, policy]. Groningen: Wolters-Noordhoff.

Allegro, J. T. (1973), *Sociotechnische organisatie-ontwikkeling* [Sociotechnical organization development]. Leiden: Stenfert Kroese.

Belcher, D. W. (1974), *Compensation administration*. 3rd ed. Englewood Cliffs: Prentice-Hall.

Belcher, D. W., Atchison, T. A. (1976), Compensation for work. In: Dubin, R. (Ed.), *Handbook of work, organization, and society*. Chicago: Rand McNally.

Bernstein, P. (1976), *Workplace democratization: Its internal dynamics*. Kent: Kent State University Press.

Birchall, D. (1975), Job design. In: Bowey, A. M. (Ed.), *Handbook of salary and wage systems*. Epping: Gower Press.

Bolle de Bal, M. (1965), *De menigvuldige functies van het produktieloon* [The many functions of payment by results]. *Synopsis*, **91**, 1–20.

Bowey, A. (1980), *The effects of recently introduced incentive payment systems in Britain. Management Decisions*, **18**, 295–303.

Brown, J. S. (1961), *The motivation of behavior*. New York: McGraw-Hill.

Buiter, J. H. (1968), *Modern salariaat in wording* [Modern 'salaried workers' on the move]. Rotterdam.

Bunjes, A. M., et al. (1977), *Inkomens op tafel. Persoonlijke meningen over eigen en andermans salaris* [Incomes in the open. Individual opinions about one's own salary and that of others]. Alphen a/d Rijn: Samsom.

Cofer, C. N., Appley, M. K. (1964), *Motivation: Theory and research*. New York: Wiley.

Croonen, J. J. F. (1979), *Zelfbediening in het arbeidsvoorwaarden pakket* [Self-service in the 'package' of working conditions]. Amsterdam: University of Amsterdam, Dept. of Work- and Organizational Psychology (research paper).

Dam, A. G. van, et al. (1973), *Salaris-inventaris* [Inventory of salaries]. Deventer: Kluwer.

Deci, E. L. (1975), *Intrinsic motivation*. New York: Plenum Press.

Drenth, P. J. D., Dam, A. G. van (1976), *Hoger beroep* [The professions]. The Hague: COP/VU.

Farr, J. L. (1976), Incentive schedules, productivity, and satisfaction in work groups: A laboratory study. *Organizational Behavior and Human Performance*, **17**, 159–170.

Fein, M. (1976), Motivation for work. In: Dubin, R. (Ed.), *Handbook of work, organization, and society*. Chicago: Rand McNally.

Frost, C. F., Wakeley, J. H., Ruh, R. A. (1974), *The Scanlon Plan for organization development*. East Lansing: MSU-Press.

Gellerman, S. (1963), *Motivation and productivity*. New York: American Management Association.

Ginneken, P. J. van, et al. (1974), *Verdiensten van hoger personeel* [Earnings of higher personnel]. Deventer: Kluwer.

Gouldner, A. (1954), *Patterns of industrial bureaucracy*. New York: The Free Press.

Graaf, M. H. K. van der (1957), Inspanning en beloning [Effort and reward]. *Mens en Onderneming* [Man and Enterprise], **11**, 12–23 and 81–94.

Grumbkov, J. von (1980), *Sociale vergelijking van salarissen* [Social comparison of salarises]. Tilburg: Van Spaendonck.

Grumbkov, J. van (1982), *Beloningen in organisaties* [Rewards in organizations]. Deventere: Van Loghum Slatekus.

Hackman, J. R., Oldham, G. R. (1980), *Work redesign*. Reading: Addison-Wesley.

Henderson, R. I. (1979), *Compensation management: Rewarding performance*. 2nd ed. Reston (Virginia).

Herzberg, F. (1966), *Work and the nature of man*. Cleveland: The World Publ. Cy.

Herzberg, F., Mausner, B., Snyderman, B. B. (1959), *The motivation to work*. New York: Wiley.

Hickson, D. J. (1963), Worker choice of payment system. *Occupational Psychology*, **37**, 93–101.

Homans, G. C. (1961), *Social behavior: Its elementary forms*. New York: Harcourt, Brace & World.

Hoolwerf, G., Thierry, Hk., Drenth, P. J. D. (1974), *Ploegenarbeid: Een bedrijfspsychologisch onderzoek* [Shiftwork: An industrial-psychological research study]. Leiden: Stenfert Kroese.

International Labor Organization (1951), *Payment by results*. Geneva.

International Labor Organization (1979), *Introduction to work study*. 3rd ed. Geneva.

Jenkins, D. (1975), *Job reform in Sweden*. Stockholm: SAF.

Jong, J. R. de (1964), De ontwikkeling op het gebied van de beloning [The development in the field of remuneration]. In: *Prestatie en beloning* [Performance and remuneration]. 2nd ed. Utrecht: RBB, 3–15.

Jong, J. R. de, Levisson, K. S., Thierry, Hk. (1970), *Produktiviteitstoerekening: Ervaringen en mogelijkheden* [Productivity sharing systems: Experiences and opportunities]. The Hague: COP/NIVE.

Jong, J. R. de, Thierry, Hk., et al. (1979), *Zeggenschap en beloning* [Co-determination and remuneration]. Assen: Van Gorcum.

Koopman-Iwema, A. M. (1980), *Macht, motivatie, medezeggenschap* [Power, motivation, co-determination]. Assen: Van Gorcum.

Koopman-Iwema, A. M., Thierry, H. K. (1981), *Incentive payment in The Netherlands*. Dublin: European Foundation for the Improvement of Living and Working Conditions.

Lawler, E. E. (1966), Managers' attitudes towards how their pay is and should be determined. *Journal of Applied Psychology*, **50**, 273–279.

Lawler, E. E. (1971), *Pay and organizational effectiveness*. New York: McGraw-Hill.

Lawler, E. E. (1974), *Participation and pay*. Paper 3rd EFPS/EAPM Conference on Work and Pay, Amsterdam, 1974.

Lawler, E. E. (1976), Control systems in organizations. In: Dunnette, M. (Ed.), *Handbook of industrial and organizational psychology*. Chicago: Rand McNally.

Lawler, E. E. (1981), *Pay and organization development*. London: Addison Wesley.

Lawler, E. E., Hackman, E. R. (1969), Impact of employee participation in the development of pay incentive plans: A field experiment. *Journal of Applied Psychology*, **53**, 467–471.

Lesieur, F. G. (1958), *The Scanlon Plan: Frontier in labor management cooperation*. Cambridge: MIT Press.

Lindholm, R., et al. (1972), *The condemned piecework*. Stockholm: SAF.

Loontechnische Dienst (1975), *Beloningsmethoden in 1974* [Methods of remuneration in 1974]. The Hague.

Loontechnische Dienst (1980), *Beloningsmethoden in Nederland* [Methods of remuneration in The Netherlands], 1979. The Hague.

Lundgren, H. (1976), *Instead of piece rate. Report on new payment systems*. EFPS/EAPM, Research Conference on Pay Methods, Noordwijkerhout, 1976.

Mahoney, Th. A. (1979), *Compensation and reward perspectives*. Homewood: Irwin.

March, J. G., Simon, H. A. (1958), *Organizations*. New York: Wiley.

Marriott, R. (1971), *Incentive payment systems*. 4th ed. London: Staples Press.

Marshall, D. R. (1978), *Successful techniques for solving employee compensation problems*. New York: Wiley.

Metsch, J. C. (1980), *Loonsatisfactie en variabele beloning* [Pay satisfaction and variable payment]. Amsterdam: University of Amsterdam, Dept. of Work- and Organizational Psychology (research paper).

Nash, A. N., Carroll, S. J. (1975), *The management of compensation*. Monterey: Brooks/Cole.

Niekerk, N. C. M. van (Ed.) (1979), *Tertiaire inkomensverdeling* [Tertiary income distribution]. The Hague: Institute for Research on Government Expenditures.

Opsahl, R. L., Dunnette, M. D. (1966), The role of financial compensation in industrial motivation. *Psychological Bulletin*, **66**, 94–118.

Overbeek, R. van (1981), *Mede-deelzaamheid* [Fair sharing]. Amsterdam: University of Amsterdam (research paper).

Pen, J., Tinbergen, J. (1977), *Naar een rechtvaardiger inkomensverdeling* [Towards a fairer income distribution]. Amsterdam: Elsevier.

Samuelson, P. A. (1967), *Economics*. New York: McGraw-Hill.

Scheflen, K. C., Lawler, E. E., Hackman, J. R. (1970), The long-term impact of employee participation in the development of pay incentive plans: A field experiment revisited. *Experimental Publication System* (APA), no. 154A.

Strauss, G. (1975), Job satisfaction, motivation, and job redesign. In: Strauss, G., *et al.* (Eds.), *Organizational behavior: Research and issues*. Madison: Industrial Relations Research Association.

Terborg, J. R., Miller, H. E. (1978), Motivation, behavior, and performance: A closer examination of goal setting and monetary incentive. *Journal of Applied Psychology*, **63**, 29–39.

Thierry, Hk. (1966), *Beloningsmethodieken*. [Reward methods]. Noordwijk aan Zee: Steering Group Social-Science Research.

Thierry, Hk. (1968), *Loont de prestatiebeloning?* [Does incentive payment pay off?] Assen: Van Gorcum.

Thierry, Hk. (1969), *Arbeidsinstelling en prestatiebeloning* [Job attitude and incentive payment]. Utrecht: Het Spectrum. (Rev. ed. in preparation.)

Thierry, Hk. (1975), Nivellering en arbeidsmotivatie [Equalization of income and work motivation]. In: *Inkomensnivellering in de arbeidsorganisatie* [Income equalization in the work organization]. The Hague: NIVE/NVP.

Thierry, Hk. (1977), Zeggenschap in de opbouw van het inkomen [Codetermination in the design of one's income]. *Economisch-Statistische Berichten* [Economic-Statistical Reports], **62**, 1045–1052.

Thierry, Hk. (1983), Humanisering van arbeid en beloning [Humanizing work and remuneration]. In: Galan, C. de, Gils, M. J. van, Strien, J. P. van (Eds.), *Humanisering van de arbeid* [Humanizing work]. 2nd ed. Assen: Van Gorcum.

Thierry, Hk., Croonen, J. J. F. (1980), Does the cafetaria-plan pay off? An empirical research study. *Management Decisions*, **18**, 303–312.

Thierry, Hk., Drenth, P. J. D. (1971), De toetsing van Herzberg's 'two-factor' theorie [Testing Herzberg's 'two-factor' theory]. In: Drenth, P. J. D., Willems, P. J., Wolff, Ch. J. de (Eds.), *Bedrijfspsychologie: Onderzoek en evaluatie* [Industrial psychology: Research and evaluation]. Deventer: Kluwer.

Thierry, Hk., Wesseling, P. L. J. (1973), Participatie en arbeids- en loonattitudes [Participation and attitudes towards work and pay]. In: Drenth, P. J. D., Willems, P. J., Wolff, Ch. J. de (Eds.), *Arbeids- en organisatiepsychologie* [Work- and organizational psychology]. Deventer: Kluwer/NIVE.

Thierry, Hk., Jong, J. R. de, *et al.* (1979), *Naar participatie en toerekening* [Towards participation and gain sharing]. Assen: Van Gorcum.

Tornow, W. W. (1975), The development and application of an input-outcome moderator test in the perception and reduction of inequity. *Organizational Behavior and Human Performance*, **6**, 614–638.

Vinke, R. H. W. (1982), *Naar een persoonlijk inkomenspakket* [Towards a personal income package]. Amsterdam: University of Amsterdam, Dept. of Work- and Organizational Psychology (research paper).

Weick, K. E. (1966), The concept of equity in the perception of pay. *Administrative Science Quarterly*, **11**, 414–439.

Wernimont, P. F., Fitzpatrick, S. (1972), The meaning of money. *Journal of Applied Psychology*, **56**, 218–226.

White, M. (1975a), Incentive bonus schemes for managers. In: Bowey, A. M. (Ed.), *Handbook of salary and wage systems*. Epping: Gower Press.

White, M. (1975b), *Employees' attitudes towards pay methods*. EFPS/EAPM Pay Methods Research Conference, Noordwijkerhout, 1975.

Whitmore, D. A., Ibbetson, J. (1979), *The management of motivation and remuneration*. London: Business Books.

Whyte, W. F. (1957), *Money and motivation*. New York: Wiley.

Ydo, M. G. (1965), *Prestatie en beloning in een nieuw licht* [Performance and payment in a new light]. Alphen a/d Rijn: Samsom.

4.12. Women and work

E. Marlies Ott

INTRODUCTION

To devote a separate chapter to women and work is not to imply that all the other chapters are exclusively about men. Why then, one might ask, a separate chapter at all?

In the first place, because the analyses presented in the other chapters are not automatically valid for women. In some respects working women are different from working men, and there are a number of characteristics about organizations which will have different effects on men and women. A great many studies hardly take these differences into account. Moreover, analysis of these differences has led to a discussion on dividing up work according to sex, a phrase which refers to the division between men's jobs and women's jobs. As a result of this discussion, the objective of 'the re-distribution of work among men and women' has received growing attention over the last few years. With respect to this objective, many questions have been raised.

The purpose of this chapter is to call attention to differences between two types of relationships: that between men and work and that between women and work. The questions mentioned above will be dealt with within this respective. The range of this chapter is limited, nor does it claim to be complete. Such a claim would be impossible, since in this field various disciplines, such as sociology and economics, may contribute knowledge.

For a survey of the differences between working men and working women one needs first of all to go into the differences in the *content* of the work. This chapter therefore begins with the question: what sort of work is done by women? The

Drs. E. M. Ott, Universiteit van Amsterdam, Vakgroep Arbeidspsychologie, Weesperplein 8, 1018 XA AMSTERDAM.

answer is supported by statistical data. The next question discussed is: are there any differences between men and women as to the *individual characteristics* usually considered to be determinants of working behaviour? Subsequently, the *situational* characteristics which may have different effects on men and women are considered as well as the interaction between personal characteristics of the individual worker and situational characteristics. After that, it will be illustrated how research may lead to erroneous interpretations, when the above-mentioned differences are not taken into account.

Section 3 discusses the present-day division of work and presents a number of questions this discussion raises. The chapter concludes with a definition of what is and what could be the task of work- and organizational psychology.

1. WHAT SORT OF WORK IS DONE BY WOMEN?

In The Netherlands, women engaged full-time in household work, i.e. housewives, form the majority. Off all women between 15 and 64 years of age, 58.1% are full-time housewives. According to 1979 data, 77% of all married women with children are full-time housewives. In 1980 only 29.1% of the women had a job outside the home (CBS, 1981).

Before defining the occupation practised by most women, namely that of housewife, two points need to be made:
1) Women with a full-time job also do the household chores. Women living with a partner, and working full-time, average 17.5 hours a week on household chores. This amounts to a 57.5-hour working week. For men living with partners, the figure is 8.5 hours a week, which amounts to a total of 48.5 hours (Meyer, 1977). These figures include gardening and other outdoor chores.
2) Any individual woman's activities can vary widely in the course of her lifetime. She may, for example, find herself in each of the following situations consecutively.

Example: A girl takes up nursing (at 17). She is still living at home. At 21 she moves into rooms of her own and does her own housework. She becomes a head-nurse (at 23). Her hospital work changes. She gets married (23). Apart from her job, she does the housework for both of them. She starts getting children (25) and quits her job to become a full-time housewife. At 40 she starts to work as a volunteer (visiting old people). Her daily task still consists of housekeeping. Five years later (45) the children start to leave home. She applies for a part-time job at a hospital, which engages her. She is no longer eligible for promotion; she stays at the hospital till the age of 60. Housekeeping is still a considerable part of her daily work.

1.1. Housewives

The housewife is a familiar figure to us all. She may be our mother, wife, sister or daughter, and you may be it yourself. At the same time, housewives form an almost forgotten group. They are seldom taken into consideration or studied as a subject of research. This probably has to do with the fact that being a housewife is not regarded as an occupation; when asked to indicate her occupation, for example when filling out a form, a Dutch housewife will often answer 'none'. What is the reason for this?

In the first place, women rarely consciously choose to become a housewife. You automatically become one, along with getting married and having children. The image people generally have of a housewife, is that of someone who does her work out of love for her family. The underlying idea seems to be that this is a 'natural' situation, a result of the biological differences between men and women. 'After all, there are two kinds of people'. Since only women can breastfeed children, it is considered 'natural' for them to provide the family with the basic necessities. One is a housewife by nature, it seems. There is no professional training for it, nor does it have the reward of a pension.

Another important reason why being a housewife is not regarded as an occupation, is that there is neither an employment contract, nor an independent income for a housewife. For a family unit the income of a 40-hour working week is considered sufficient (after tax deduction and including special family allowances). Husband and wife are taken to be an economic unit, the husband being the breadwinner and the wife looking after the home. This situation is very different from an 'ordinary' job, which is characterized by a formal training, a contract and an income.

Although it is quite understandable that being a housewife is not usually considered to be an occupation, this nevertheless has some negative effects. Housekeeping is not regarded as 'real' work, and there is little interest in the organization of housekeeping or in the required skills. Work- and organizational psychologists have so far paid little attention to housewives and housekeeping. One exception in the research on working is the ergonomist Grandjean (1973), who studied the requirements a house, a kitchen etc. should meet in order to satisfy a housewife's needs.

Research tells us little about the position and the work of housewives. Obviously, the situations of housewives will differ, depending on income, the number of children, their ages, the relationship between husband and wife, the husband's work, as well as on the influence of all kinds of individual variables of the members of the family concerned. De Monchy (1981) provides a survey of the available literature, which will be summarized below.

Because of the fact that everyone has some image of a housewife's work and therefore claims to know what housekeeping involves, it is necessary to formulate a definition. There are many definitions current. We will use the definition given by Van Houten and Spaander (1980). Household work involves the following tasks:

—cleaning the home, taking care of meals, clothes, the pets, and the garden;
—the organization and planning of these activities;
—raising the children and taking care of the partner.

In general, it is particularly the last two categories which are underestimated. The amount of time spent on housekeeping is considerable. According to research on the spending of time, women with small children work 41.4 to 71 hours a week on average. Due to the different definitions used in the studies on housekeeping, the figures vary. But one can doubtless speak of a full-time working week, comparable to a working week outside the home or an occupation performed at home.

Housekeeping has the following *positive* aspects:

—*Autonomy*; this is a quality of professional work, which many housewives also feel to be characteristic of their work. They feel that they are free from the daily obligation of going out to work and that they are independent.

—*Competence*; the planning and organization of a household is at least as demanding as the planning and organization of a small business. The input consists of the family to be taken care of, the throughput of housekeeping, and the output of the fact that the breadwinner, the housewife, and the children are taken care of, not only in a material, but also in a psychological sense.

—*Responsibility*; the responsibility for those we care about can be very great especially at times when extra care is called for because of illness, children's learning problems, or a breadwinner's problems at work.

Housework also has *negative* qualities:

—*Monotony*; cleaning the home, taking care of food and clothing are ever recurring and absolutely predictable activities.

—*Social isolation*; housewives experience a great deal of loneliness and isolation in their work.

—*Invisibility*; a great many chores involved in housekeeping are invisible. They become visible only when they are not done.

—*Little appreciation*; this aspect is related to invisibility. Housekeeping is not regarded as 'real' work and it is undervalued.

—*Lack of career perspectives*; for a number of years, while the children are growing up, the work keeps changing. As soon as the children leave home, both the work and the responsibility decrease.

—*No separation of work and leisure time*; housewives rarely really have a day off, because housekeeping remains a necessity during weekends and holidays too.

Friedan was the first to do extensive research on the experiences of housewives. Her study exposed the myth of the contented housewife. Her book *The Feminine Mystique* (1963) became a bestseller. According to Friedan, housewives feel left out, useless and not taken seriously. What they need, she says, is work which involves a challenge and calls for their human capacities. They need an occupation which gives them their own identity, not the derived identity of 'professor X's wife' or 'Y's mother'.

In Germany, Pross (1974) studied the experiences of housewives from a different viewpoint. The research was prompted by the irritation caused by feminists maintaining that being a housewife constitutes a situation of oppression which must be changed. According to Pross, it cannot be concluded that all housewives have a hard time, merely on the basis of such subjective experiences of housewives as feeling houseproud, feeling isolated, complaints about financial dependence, an unfulfilled longing for an occupation. The picture shown by Pross is ambivalent. Housewives are content with many things, but simultaneously dissatisfied with the very same things: for example, many women feel content with their husbands' social superiority to themselves, but they are also dissatisfied with it. This becomes evident in their dissatisfaction with the feeling of their standing in their husbands' shadow: his name is her name, his occupation is the measure of her status, his income is decisive for her standard of living. Most women, Pross says, are content. They do not want to change roles with their husbands, or share both roles, or change the family structure (e.g. an extended family, community living, etc.). But there are dark sides too. One of the symptoms is, for example, that 50% of the women say they would rather pursue an occupation if they could choose again. Medical research in particular has introduced the term housewife-syndrome. In The Netherlands it was first used by a medical doctor, Van de Velden (1971). He was intrigued by women coming to consult him about vague complaints and evidently needing to have someone to talk to. Further research led him to conclude that the use of the term 'housewife-syndrome' is justified for such complaints as depression, restlessness, irritability, lack of energy, insomnia, fatigue.

1.2. The activities of women working outside the home

This section will deal with the following subjects: participation in the labour market, level of work, occupational sectors, part-time work and unemployment figures, and clandestine work.

1.2.1. PARTICIPATION IN THE LABOUR MARKET

According to the Central Bureau of Statistics, the Dutch working population amounted to approx. five million in 1980. Thirty per cent of the working population were women (CBS, 1981). Of all women working, 36% was under 25 years of age (17% for men). Of all EEC-countries, The Netherlands scored lowest on this point. Why The Netherlands has such a remarkably low percentage of women working is unknown. The reasons sometimes given are that the rate of individual pay in The Netherlands is in accordance with the needs of a family, or that the social security system functions in such a way that the need for women to go out and work is not as strong as in the surrounding countries. In the light of the labour participation among Swedish women, who live under similar circumstances, these explanations are, however, not wholly convincing. In Sweden, 55.2% of the women work outside the home (Cottin,-Bogriëbin, 1981).

Another explanation sometimes given is the negative attitudes in the past of the political parties, both denominational and progressive, and the unions. Whereas the denominational parties did not accept women manifesting themselves in public life on religious grounds, the progressive parties and the trade unions based their objections primarily on the deplorable conditions of working-class families at the end of the 19th century, when child-labour and women's labour were widespread phenomena.

1.2.2. LEVEL OF WORK

In its study of the levels of work, the Wage Administration Control Department of the Dutch Ministry of Social Affairs and Employment applied eight job levels. Very simple activities, so-called unskilled work, are classed under level 1; management of a large business firms or of an equivalent part of a company or institute is classed under level 8.

Table 1 shows women to be over-represented at the lower levels and under-represented at the higher levels. The turning point lies between levels 3 and 4. This situation is reflected in the rates of pay. In October 1977 the average gross hourly rate was:
—men over 21: Dfl. 14.34;
—women over 21: Dfl. 10.78.

1.2.3. OCCUPATIONS

In The Netherlands, there are virtually no women holding a post in 171 of the 293 occupations listed (see table 2). Only 13 occupations are almost exclusively pursued by women (90–100%; see table 3). All in all, 25.9% of women workers are engaged in typically 'female' occupations. In this respect, secretaries, typists

Table 1. Rates of full-time workers—men as well as women—in percentage per job level.

Level	Men	Women
1	2.5	10.5
2	33.0	43.3
3	29.5	32.2
4	21.9	13.2
5	7.6	1.4
6	4.0	0.4
7	1.3	0.05
8	0.3	0.02
Total	100%	100%
(abs.)	136,824	25,586

Source: Loontechnische Dienst, 1978.

Table 2. Occurrence of women in occupations, according to the percentages of women in those occupations (1979).

Percentages of women among the total number of workers in any occupation	Number of occupations	Percentages of working women out of the total number of working women
0–10	171	3.5
10–20	40	5.2
20–30	20	7.2
30–40	16	10.0
40–50	8	10.4
50–60	11	7.4
60–70	5	4.9
70–80	5	16.8
80–90	4	8.6
90–100	13	25.5
Total	293	100.0

Source: Van Mourik and Siegers, 1982.

Table 3. Occupations in which 90% and upwards of the workers are women (working population in the strict sense, 1979).

Name of occupation	Percentage of women in each occupation	Percentage of women in each occupation, out of the total number of working women
Dental hygienists	100	0.0
Chemist's assistants	96.5	0.7
Dieticians	90.9	0.1
Midwives	100	0.1
Maternity nurses	100	0.4
Nursery school teachers	99.5	1.7
Secretaries, typists, telexists	96.6	9.5
Keyboard operators	98.2	0.8
Domestic servants, etc.	89.7	3.5
Medical welfare workers (not mentioned above): child (welfare) workers, mother's aids, geriatric nurses and assistants	97.9	6.8
Doctor's assistants, dental assistants, veterinary assistants	97.7	1.0
Milliners	100	0.0
Dressmakers	95.5	1.3

Source: Van Mourik and Siegers, 1982.

and telexists form the largest category. Nurses are not included in table 3 because at present more than ten per cent of the nurses are male.

1.2.4. PART-TIME WORK, UNEMPLOYMENT FIGURES AND UNREGISTERED WORKING WOMEN

The chapter on work and working time in the present Handbook (3.6) includes data on part-time work and points to the problems in interpreting the statistics on part-time work. It should be added that, in 1977, 19% of the female working population and 1.5% of the male working population was engaged in part-time work, part-time work being defined as a 16–30 hour working week (CBS, 1981). Table 4 shows that the percentage of women in part-time work decreases as the number of working hours increases.

It is common knowledge that the number of unemployed is growing. By the end of June 1982, there were 521.600 registered unemployed, among them 164.100 women, i.e. 14.5% of the female population, as against 11.0% of the male working population (see table 5.). The percentage among women not only is higher, it also increases at a greater rate.

Table 4. Active working population* according to sex and weekly working hours, March–May, 1977.

	Less than 15 hours	15–24 hours	25–34 hours	35 hours and more	Total
× 1000					
Total	205	305	243	3939	4759
Women	179	249	142	731	1322
	(89%)	(83%)	(58%)	(19%)	

Source: CBS, 1981.
* Not including the active working population residing in institutions and homes, nor the population living on the road or on the water.

Table 5. Registered unemployed individuals, yearly average percentages of the employed working population* (Social Monthly Statistics, February 1982, published by CBS, vol. 30, no. 2).

Unemployed	1965	1970	1975	1978	1979	1980	1981	June 1982
Men	0.8	1.2	5.0	4.3	4.1	4.9	8.2	11.0
Women	0.4	0.9	5.0	7.5	8.2	8.9	11.4	14.5
Men and women	0.7	1.1	5.0	5.0	5.1	5.8	9.0	11.9

* The term 'employed working population' refers to the entire working population with the exception of the self-employed. The registered unemployed group consists of all those who are available for paid work in full-time service, i.e. with a minimum of 25 hours a week. Until January 1978 the minimum was 30 hours a week.

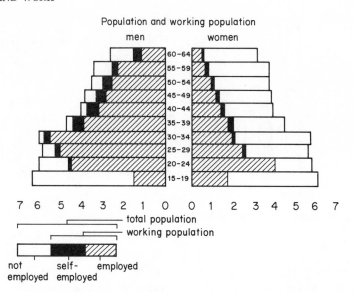

Figure 1. Population, working population and registered unemployed of 15–64 years of age, 1 January 1980 (Source: CBS, 1981).

Moreover, these are biased figures, because women who are not bread-winners frequently do not register at the Employment Office after 26 weeks of unemployment, since their unemployment benefits cease then anyway. 66% of the registered unemployed women are under 24 years of age (CBS, 1981).

Figure 1, representing the size of the working population, shows that the decline of the female working population begins in the age-group of 25–29. The male working population still grows in that age-group. Figure 2 shows that the particularly high unemployment rate among women is caused especially by the unemployment among women of 15–18 years of age.

The figures do not tell us everything about working women. Domestics and charwomen, for example, who work less than three days a week, are not registered anywhere, so that their number is unknown. The same is true of home-workers, i.e. those who are employed by companies to work at home on an average rate of Dfl. 3 to Dfl. 4 an hour. Hundt (1981a, 1981b; see also this Handbook, ch. 3.6) claims that paid work at home is increasing, particularly as a result of the economic decline. However, no data are available on this matter.

2. DETERMINANTS OF WORKING BEHAVIOUR

With respect to the determinants of working behaviour the following distinction is usually made: individual characteristics and situational characteristics. One must bear in mind that these characteristics may be correlated, having mutual influence, and rarely have independent effects on working behaviour. The

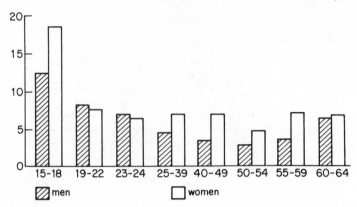

Figure 2. Registered unemployed individuals in percentages of the employed working population (source: CBS, 1981).

following questions are essential for work- and organizational psychologists:
1. Are the individual characteristics different for men and women?
2. Are the situational characteristics different for men and women?
These questions will be dealt with below, the emphasis being on the importance of raising the questions. An elaborate answer is beyond the scope of this chapter, as it would involve many areas of psychology. The questions form a framework for discussing a number of interesting research results.

2.1. Individual characteristics

Questions about the differences in individual characteristics of men and women have interested a great many psychologists. In their book *The Psychology of Sex Differences*, now a classic, Maccoby and Jacklin (1975) survey the research results up to 1975. After 1975 this type of research has become less frequent. The question of sex differences is considered somewhat taboo. This is understandable, though not very sensible. It is understandable because data on sex differences have more than once been abused to legitimatize the existing role division between men and women, with total disregard for the complicated and largely unknown interactions between situation and person. It is not sensible because strategies of change need to be based on insight into these interactions.

The question of possible differences in individual characteristics has gained additional importance because of the American anti-discrimination act (Roe, 1983), prohibiting both direct and indirect discrimination in the selection of applicants. Discrimination is direct when the selection is made on grounds of sex differences which are irrelevant to the work to be done. It is indirect when, although the characteristic of sex as such plays no role in the selection decisions, the result of the decisions is that applicants are placed at a disadvantage because of this characteristic. Such a paradoxical phenomenon can occur when the characteristic of sex affects the relationships between predictors and criteria, in other words, when it has a moderator effect.

We will deal with the question of individual characteristics on the basis of the distinctions made by Roe in chapter 2.2. He mentions three categories: dispositional characteristics, habitual characteristics and motivational characteristics. These categories can be distinguished according to the degree of assumed stability. Dispositional characteristics, also called traits, are considered to be the most constant. They originate in hereditary factors and/or past experiences. Examples: various intellectual abilities and styles.

It is assumed that habitual characteristics are acquired through environmental influences, namely through learning, practice and habituation. Examples: various kinds of knowledge, skills, attitudes, expectations and habits.

Motivational characteristics refer to temporary or more permanent conditions of (or in) any individual, which cause a particular level of activity and a specific directedness of behaviour. Examples: needs such as hunger and thirst, but also the level of ambition, cognitive dissonance, etc.

These three categories of individual characteristics have no clear borderlines, and may, therefore, overlap.

Obviously, there are differences between men and women with respect to the motivational characteristics. They are the most unstable and depend on the situation. Since women as a rule find themselves in different situations and do work which is different from men's work, differences are bound to occur in this respect. We shall illustrate this by an example of the levels of ambition among male and female employees. These levels are influenced partly by the expected career opportunities. The greater the chance of promotion, the more likely one will develop a high level of ambition. The fact that women are mainly employed in jobs providing limited career opportunities, makes a relatively low level of ambition more probable (Kanter, 1977). Such phenomena are discussed extensively in reflections on female achievement (see O'Leary, 1977; Frieze et al., 1978).

Differences are also likely to be found among the habitual characteristics, because up-bringing and learning experiences play an important role. We have often been made aware of the influence of the expectation that women will, in due course, become housewives and mothers (see section 1), and the complex system of up-bringing, education and choice of a career, has often been referred to. In a girl's upbringing there is more emphasis on housekeeping, on motherhood and on the personal qualities required for such a position, than on how to raise one's chance of survival in an organization. This difference of career intentions is very likely to influence men and women in the development of their respective interests, values, knowledge and skills.

Hennig and Jardim (1977), two American researchers, have given many courses for personnel in trade and industry, aimed at developing awareness of the effects differences in upbringing have on working behaviour. The participants were asked what they had learned, when engaged in team sports in childhood. They answered as follows: you learned to compete and to cooperate with boys (girls) you would not choose as friends; you learned what losing is like; you learned to take criticism from the coach, from fellow players and from spectators; you learned that you had to make plans, you learned that others refused to help you if you put yourself in the limelight too often; you learned that it is essential to know the rules thoroughly, if you wish to influence the referee's decisions; you learned that some people are better than others, but that they nevertheless need each other; you noticed that the coach was important for the group's morale.

According to Hennig and Jardim it is due to women's lack of experience with team sports that they are insufficiently aware of the importance of the informal system of relationships, shared information, loyalties, dependence, mutual advantage and protection. Hennig and Jardim's approach aims to adapt women to the existing situation. Nowadays, we realize that the specific skills which women acquire through their upbringing can be equally effective and efficient in an organization. However, it is necessary to stay alert for the confusion which may result when women participate in their own way in organizations in which the rules-of-the-game have previously been determined primarily by men.

One of Henley's studies (1977) shows that a difference in upbringing can directly cause a difference in working behaviour. This study was mainly concerned with non-verbal behaviour. The fact that men and women learn, and also apply, different forms of non-verbal communication, apparently has a great influence on the positions men and women are able to attain in society. Most of the studies on non-verbal communication do no more than establish the differences between men and women. According to Henley, however, there is a highly important intermediating variable, namely power. Her study shows that much of the behaviour between a subordinate and his superior resembles the behaviour between husband and wife. According to Henley, this behaviour not only is caused by the difference in power; it emphasizes and even increases the difference. Moreover, she is convinced that from early childhood on, women are taught to exhibit this feminine, i.e. subordinate behaviour. As soon as women start behaving as superiors, it is regarded as male conduct, or it is ignored, punished or interpreted sexually. For a woman supervisor, this implies that either she cannot really behave as a supervisor, that is, show behaviour connected with coordinating, delegating, criticizing, etc., or she will be looked upon as unfeminine.

Fewest differences were found among the dispositional characteristics, which are considered to be the most constant. As a group, boys have higher scores on spatial insight and physical agression. Women score higher on verbal skills; this difference, however, is not found among children (Maccoby and Jacklin, 1975).

2.2. Situational characteristics.

The central question in this section will be: are the situational characteristics different for men and women? In a material sense, one could consider the place where one works, the machinery, the tempo of work; in an immaterial sense there are such factors as the existence of other people and their expectations. Earlier in this chapter it was mentioned that there are considerable differences in the kinds of work and in the conditions under which work is done. There are other differences in situational characteristics, examples of which follow here. The first one is a characteristic which as such is not different for men and women, yet has different *effects* on men and women. As a rule, organizations are based on a 40-hour working week, the assumption being that the employees all have someone to take care of them at home. This is not true for all male employees. However, for women this is almost never true. Since women employees are in charge of the greater part of household work, a 40-hour working week will more often cause them strain.

Another situational characteristic concerns staffing policy. Those who create such a policy may use stereotyped images of men and women, and so develop different policies for men and women. Many personnel managers take for granted the stereotype that women will continue to work until the birth of their first child and then leave the organization. This idea is supported by the considerable turnover of women personnel. Organizations have several ways of taking this into account. One is that frequently women are employed exclusively in jobs characterized by monotony and a lack of career opportunities, for example as typists and keyboard operators. There are also organizations which take into account the turnover of women and deliberately engage a number of women in order to prevent stagnation for men at the higher levels. Sometimes, however, women are not a useful group for an organization. High training costs seem wasted on women, and the desire for part-time work, which exists virtually only among women, causes organizations a great many practical problems. The views held by those in charge of personnel policy can also play a role when it comes to chances for promotion. To illustrate this, table 6 contains the answers to the following question: 'Suppose there are two employees, who differ in one respect only. They are equal in all other respects. If one of them were to be eligible for promotion, who should it be?'

It appears that 33.6% of the respondents favour men for the promotion, against 2.4% who favour women. Sixty-four per cent feel that it should not make any difference. Hennig and Jardim's case studies (1977) show that women with successful careers usually either are unmarried or were married at a later age. Thus, the figures on promotional preference show women to be at a disadvantage as compared to employees with a family: 41.6% prefer employees with families, 2.3% prefer employees without one, while 58.1% feel it should not make any

Table 6. Views on different treatment of certain population groups (1978) in percentages (N = 1015, representative sample).

Preference for promotion		(1) should be promoted	(2) should be promoted	Should make no difference
(1)	(2)			
Employee with a family	Unmarried employee	41.6	2.3	56.1
foreigner	Dutchman	1.5	30.1	68.4
man	woman	33.6	2.4	64.0
Surinamese	Dutchman	1.4	23.8	74.8
younger person	older person	21.5	23.5	54.7
white person	coloured person	14.7	2.0	83.0

Source: Study of Cultural Change in The Netherlands 1975–1978, from: Sociaal en Cultureel Rapport, 1978.

difference. This means that both being a woman and being single are disadvantages for possible promotion.

Finally, an important situational characteristic is that the majority of organizations consists primarily of men. This characteristic also has different effects for men and for women. One of the effects is that women in men's occupations or in higher-level positions often find themselves on their own. This can instigate processes as described by Kanter (1977) in her study of an American company. The lives of these women in the middle and the top of organizations are determined by the fact that there are so few of them. To some of the women it has the advantage of being conspicuous. This is important in a system in which success is connected with being known. Usually, however, they feel lonely and left out, like strangers placed in a different culture, and alienated by the process of assimilation. In any case, turnover and non-attendance due to illness was twice as high as for their male colleagues.

Kanter also observed that a group of men, who were used to associating with each other in a certain way were disturbed by the arrival of one female colleague. Suddenly the men realized that they had particular ways of associating with each other, and they started wondering to what extent this could remain that way. The arrival of the woman usually caused distinctly masculine behavior. Dirty jokes, stories about chasing women and memories of their time in the army would be told especially in front of her. The woman would be unable to take an active part in such conversations, which would result in her being isolated. This was often emphasized by a well-meant: 'gentlemen, there is a lady among us!'. On such occasions the men would feel less relaxed than when they were among themselves. It was then that they would talk about more neutral affairs, such as the prices of houses, motorcars, etc. In time, they began to meet separately,

without inviting the woman. On the basis of these and other observations, Kanter concluded that the ratio of the sexes in a group is a vital factor. In this respect she distinguishes four groups:
—uniform groups: groups with a ratio of 100:0;
—skewed groups: groups with a ratio between 99:1 and 85:15;
—tilted groups: groups with a ratio between 85:15 and 65:35;
—balanced groups: groups with a ratio between 65:35 and 50:50.

Kanter refers to the tiny minority in the skewed groups as 'tokens': these people are frequently regarded as representatives of their category rather than as individuals. From what is known about the social psychology of perception it can be predicted that the relatively rare occurrence of 'tokens' will cause them to be more conspicuous; it will accentuate the difference between them and the majority, and it will increase the assimilation of the few existing 'tokens'. According to Kanter, this means that 'tokens' will be under close observation, that the characteristics will be perceived as being consistent with the stereotypes generally held of the minority group concerned. These effects will lead to great psychic pressure, and hence to lower achievement. On the basis of the afore-mentioned observations, Kanter formulates a number of concrete hypotheses, e.g.: that 'tokens' are more conspicuous; that they experience greater pressure and are more anxious about making mistakes because of this; that they will try to attract the least possible attention; that the stereotyping of the feminine role will mean extra interference with their work; and that they will be excluded from the informal system.

Another effect of the fact that organizations primarily consist of men, is that women are frequently confronted with 'womanizing' behaviour. This may seem trivial at first, but it can be embarrassing for women, particularly because they are usually the womanizers' inferiors. Farley (1978) has meticulously assembled data on sexual abuse at work. It is evident from her account that sexual blackmail, even rape, occurs more often at work than one would be willing to believe.

The more enjoyable results of amorous feelings, the 'affairs', unfortunately also affect women more negatively. Led by the observation that amorous relationships are not appreciated at work and that they affect personnel policy with regard to women, Quinn (1977) made a study of romance on the job. One remarkable conclusion in his study is that, in cases of affairs, women are dismissed twice as often as men.

2.3. Interaction

It is an established fact that the structure of an organization influences individual characteristics. Thus, career opportunities affect the ways people regard themselves and their jobs: possibilities of promotion influence the attitude towards work, the level of ambition and the sense of responsibility. Conversely, people who have 'fallen behind' behave differently than people with successful careers, which further limits their possibilities.

When examining the problem of why women in particular hold lower positions in organizations, one is hampered by the question to what extent this could be explained by either situational characteristics or rather by individual characteristics such as the motivation of women. The study of De Jong et al. (1982) shows that women employees view the problem as resulting from unequal treatment, and that the management attributes it to women's lack of motivation. Both viewpoints appear to be supported by the results of preliminary research. Information on the relative influence can be gained only from longitudinal studies, which, unfortunately, are rare due to practical difficulties.

2.4. Erroneous interpretations

Frieze et al. (1978) provide a survey of the one-sided approaches in psychological research which may lead to erroneous conclusions. Three types of errors are mentioned here:
1. The use of concepts which have been applied with respect to male employees only.
2. Ascribing the differences found among employees to the situation in an organization, without taking into account the differences between male and female employees, which may have been caused by the differences in role attitudes with regard to men and women.
3. Ascribing the differences between male and female employees to their respective sexes, regardless of the differences of the positions they hold in an organization.

Re: 1. The 'reality shock' (Hall, 1976) may serve as an example of the first type of error. Someone who begins at his first job will have a number of expectations, e.g. intrinsically satisfying work, an anti-authoritarian employer, good pay and possibilities of promotion. When these expectations turn out to be unrealistic, he will have to adjust his expectations. The company, too, has expectations regarding the new employee, such as competence, acceptance of the standards of the organization and its informal power system, loyalty, etc. During the first period the socializing influence of the company will be strongest and most frustrating for the new employee.

There is no certainty as to whether this 'reality shock' also happens to women. In a case study, in which 25 women at the levels of vice-president or president of an organization were extensively interviewed, Hennig and Jardim (1977) found that none of the 25 women appeared to have suffered such a reality shock. They were extremely pleased with their first jobs, and their expectations had not run high. To the women, the starting period had really been the reverse of a reality shock. They found the work enjoyable, and realized that they were doing better than most of their colleagues. This example demonstrates that having high hopes is an essential condition for a reality shock to occur. Owing to the fact that women generally do not prepare themselves for a long career in an organization, their expectations, as a rule, will not be high.

Re: 2. The second type of error can be illustrated by an imaginary study on satisfaction concerning career opportunities. If research were to be done among male and female police constables, it might turn out that those receiving reports and those working on the vice-squad are more satisfied with their career opportunities. This might be attributed to the actual career opportunities for these positions. However, closer investigations might show that women are over-represented in those jobs and that they are more satisfied because they make lower demands with respect to career opportunities, because they only intend to work for a few years.

Re: 3. The following will serve as an example of the third type of error. One frequently finds, in organizations, a preference for male managers, among men as well as women. Often this is attributed to the difference in management styles between men and women. Kanter (1977) reports of studies which demonstrate that styles of management may vary according to the manager's power and career opportunities, and that there is a general preference for those management styles which prevail in positions offering a great deal of power and many career opportunities. Such positions however, are held relatively more often by men. This might imply that it is not so much a question of preference for men, as for managers with power and career opportunities.

3. THE DIVISION OF WORK ACCORDING TO SEX

The previous sections have clearly shown that, in The Netherlands, there is a strict division of work, namely into household work and occupational work; and that this division corresponds to a division of work according to sex. Housekeeping is women's work. But also in paid work, there is a segregation between 'men's jobs' and 'women's jobs'. By the term 'division of work according to sex' we mean both segregational phenomena.

The division of work according to sex is part of a single dualistic system, in which men's work and women's work are defined as complementary (therefore interdependent) and diametrical (therefore mutually exclusive). The family is the cornerstone of this dualistic system. The structure of the organization, its 40-hour working week, its standards and values, maintain this system.

This division of work according to sex has far-reaching consequences for the role attitudes of men and women and for the personal characteristics they may develop. It affects the mutual (power) relationships between the sexes, as well as the relationships men/society/family and women/society/family.

The following negative aspects of this situation can be pointed out:
—Women are under-represented in those key-positions from which our society is

formed. Consequently, especially the experiences of women are insufficiently included in this process. An example taken from the field of housing: because architects generally work away from home for over 40 hours a week, they are often not fully aware of what it means to spend the entire day as a housewife in a suburb. They tend not to take into account the possible wishes regarding such matters as the location of a kitchen in the house, or the location of schools in a residential district.

—Husband and wife are mutually dependent. He depends on her for his basic needs; her standard of living depends on his income. This may easily cause conflicts. Moreover, when a relationship is not clearly defined because there is no contract, conflicts are hard to deal with.

—When, in case of a conflict, a family is confronted with officials, they are mostly men. The odds are that such an official will sooner identify with the man and fail to see the woman's problems in the right perspective.

—The media pay little attention to the views of women. Usually women are described and filmed by men, which puts them into the position of 'the other'. It is especially this aspect that Simone de Beauvoir dealt with in her famous book *The Second Sex*.

—Whenever women leave the traditional role and take, for example, a man's job, they remain dependent on men's acceptance.

—Cumulation of all these aspects in particular increases women's liability to become alienated.

During the last few years awareness that the division of work according to sex promotes these negative aspects has been growing. Initially this was pointed out by women who, in spite of a good education, ended up as housewives (Smit, 1967). Later they were joined by men who realized the one-sidedness of their existence and/or condemned the relatively powerless position of women in our society.

An increasing number of people are urging a re-distribution of household work and work outside the home, i.e. men ought to take their share of housekeeping and women should be able to have their share of all jobs on *all* levels. At present, in our culture, the discussion has become so widespread that even the government has expressed the intention to promote a re-distribution of work among the sexes.

It has become a generally acknowledged objective to put a stop to the division of work according to sex. Although there seems to be some movement in that direction, it will take many years before this has been achieved. The movement can be found at the levels of action groups, trade unions and political parties, but also at a scientific level. In the past few years, various disciplines have concerned themselves, directly or indirectly, with the consequences of the division of work. Naturally, the social sciences are among them, but also economics, law and the study of history. There is hardly any field of learning or science which is not involved in this discussion, not even philosophy, medical science, architecture, literature or theology.

Book reviews and articles on this subject are published in special periodicals. A specific circuit of information has been developed. The International Records of the Women's Movement (I.A.V.) in The Netherlands issues a survey of new publications every three months. The Provisional Supervisory Committee on the Study of Emancipation includes representatives of the government, the world of science and women's organizations. There is frequent contact between this committee and the Emancipation Council, a body which advises the government. Apart from these, there are two institutions enabling scientific researchers to contact each other: Women's Studies and the Emancipation Study Group which belongs to a foundation operating as a liaison between the various social science departments at Dutch universities.

4. TASKS FOR WORK- AND ORGANIZATIONAL PSYCHOLOGY

The problem of the unequal division of work between men and women has been mentioned above. Some of the solutions offered are the reduction of working time and the abolition of what, in this country, is called the bread-winner principle, so that net wages will be based on individuals (plus children's allowances) and not on families. The expectation is that this will not be sufficient. We are often reminded, in this context, of the existing resistance to change, such as men's aversion to household work, women's fear of sacrificing 'their domain', and unfamiliarity with women in management and/or men's jobs.

Because of these problems the following questions need to be answered:
—How can an organization introduce reduction of working time (see also this Handbook, ch. 3.6)?
—How can the resistance to a re-distribution of household work be diminished?
—How can a policy of selection and promotion without discrimination be instigated?
—How can equal treatment be ensured? For instance, what possibilities are offered by the various systems of job evaluation? (See also this Handbook, ch. 2.11.)
—How can an organization help remove the resistance to women in high positions and men's occupations?
—Under what conditions can women be introduced into men's occupations, such as the navy, the fire brigade and the police force?
—How can women be assisted when resuming paid work after having raised children for a number of years?
  more general questions are:
—How has the division of work come into being?

—How do prejudice and discrimination arise?
—How are differences in power maintained?

So far, work- and organizational psychology has not contributed a great deal in this field, which is unfortunate. Work- and organizational psychology, preeminently, could serve the purpose of emancipation. It could apply the theories of social psychology, which has become a source of information on sex role stereotypes and discrimination, and also those of sociology, whose researchers have been trying, for quite some time, to explain the origins of segregational phenomena and the family's position in society. Finally, work- and organizational psychology has access to and experience with policies of change in organizations. Undoubtedly a great deal of information provided by this Handbook, even if it is not specifically applied to the re-distribution of work, can be useful in this context. Consequently, we may justifiably expect that work and organizational psychology can prove to be of use in this new and challenging field of study.

REFERENCES

Bruyn- Hundt, M. (1981a), Huisindustrie [Home industry]. *Economisch-Statistische Berichten* [Economic-Statistical Reports], **66**.

Bruyn-Hundt, M. (1981b), Voor jou tien anderen [Ten others for your job]. *Intermediair*, **17**, no. 38, 47–53.

CBS [Central Bureau of Statistics] (1981), *Statistisch zakboek* [Statistics pocket book] *1981*. The Hague: Staatsuitgeverij.

Cottin-Bogriëbin, L. (1981), Feminists in Sweden have seen the future and it (almost) works. *M & S*, April.

Farley, L. (1978), *Sexual shakedown: The sexual harassment of women on the job*. New York: McGraw-Hill.

Friedan, B. (1963), *The feminine mystique*. 5th pr. New York: Dell.

Frieze, I. H., Parsons, J. E., Johnson, P. B., Ruble, D. N. Zellman, G. L. (1978), *Psychological perspective*. New York: Norton.

Grandjean, E. (1973), *Ergonomics of the home*. London: Taylor & Francis Ltd.

Hall, D. T. (1976), *Careers in organizations*. Pacific Pallisades (Cal.): Goodyear.

Henley, N. M. (1977), *Body politics: Power, sex and nonverbal communication*. Englewood Cliffs: Prentice-Hall.

Hennig, M., Jardim, A. (1977), *The managerial woman*. New York: Anchor Press/Doubleday.

Houten, M. van, Spaander, G. (1980), Beroep huisvrouw [Profession housewife]. In: de Monchy (1981).

Jong, A. de, *et al.* (1982), Banking on women managers. *Management Today*, February.

Kanter, R. M. (1977), *Men and women of the caperation*. New York: Basic Books.

Klooster-'t Wingerden, C. M. van (1981), De vrouw in Nederland [Women in The Netherlands]. *Vrouw en Samenleving* [Women and Society]. Assen: Van Gorcum.

Knulst, W. R. (1975), *Een week tijd* [A week's time]. The Hague: Staatsuitgeverij.

Loontechnische Dienst [Wage Administration and Control Dept.], Ministry of Social Affairs (1978), *Rapport gelijke kansen voor vrouwen en mannen* [Report on equal opportunities for women and men]. The Hague.

Maccoby, X., Jacklin, X. (1975), *The psychology of sex differences.* London: Oxford University Press.

Meyer, J. L. (1977), *Sociale atlas van de vrouw* [Social atlas of women]. The Hague: Staatsuitgeverij.

Monchy, C. de (1981), *Gedeelde smart is halve smart (huisvrouw, huishouden en A & O psychologie)* [A sorrow shared is a sorrow halved (housewife, household and work- and organizational psychology)]. University of Amsterdam, Dept. of Work- and Organizational Psychology.

Mourik, A. van, Siegers, J. J. (1982), *Ontwikkelingen in de beroepssegregatie tussen mannen en vrouwen in Nederland* [Developments in job segregation between man and women in The Netherlands] *1973–1979.* Research report. University of Utrecht, Economics Institute.

O'Leary, V. E. (1977), *Toward understanding women.* Monterey: Brooks/Cole Publ. Co.

Pross, H. (1974), Die Wirklichkeit der Hausfrau. In: de Monchy (1981).

Quinn, R. E. (1977), Coping with Cupid: The formation, impact and management of romantic relationships in organizations. *Administrative Science Quarterly,* **22,** 30–45.

Roe, R. A. (1983), *Grondslagen der personeelsselectie* [Foundations of personnel selection]. Assen: Van Gorcum.

Smit, J. (1967), Het onbehagen bij de vrouw [Women's discontent]. *De Gids,* no. 9/10.

Sociaal en cultureel rapport [Social and cultural report] *1978.* The Hague: Staatsuitgeverij.

Velden, H. G. M. van de (1981), Huisvrouw, huisarts, huisgezin [Housewife, general practitioner, family household]. In: de Monchy (1981).

Handbook of Work and Organizational Psychology
Edited by P. J. D. Drenth, H. Thierry, P. J. Willems and C. J. de Wolff
© 1984, John Wiley & Sons, Ltd.

4.13. Automation: design process and implementation

Jen A. Algera and Paul L. Koopman

1. INTRODUCTION

Automation, robotization, information society are key words referring to developments which will drastically alter our society in the coming years. Automation is not new; it first made its appearance several decades ago. But new technological developments in the field of micro-electronics have led many people to believe that automation has since been revolutionized and that in the near future truly explosive changes can be expected. For our purposes we can define automation as the use of advanced technical resources in entirely or largely self-regulating processes or subprocesses, thus eliminating to a large extent the human intervention in the direct production process (SER, 1968; van Hoof, 1980). This classical definition originally referred to the automation of industrial production systems, but in recent years it has also come to refer to computerized information processing systems, particularly in the administrative sector (Tissen and Zanders, 1982). We will elaborate the definition and the different types of automation in section 2.

Leyder (1979) distinguishes a 'first round' and a 'second round' in the influence of automation on society, particularly on the quantity and the quality of employment opportunity. During the first round—until the early 1970s—the introduction of automation was quite gradual. The use of computers was limited to an élite: it was chiefly large organizations that decided to invest in one (see e.g.

Dr. Jen A. Algera and Dr. P. L. Koopman, Vrije Universiteit, Vakgroep Arbeids—en Organisatiepsychologie, De Boelelaan 1081, 1081 HV AMSTERDAM.

Nora and Minc, 1978). One very important circumstance during the first round is that automation took place in a period of economic growth. This means that the increased productivity led to an increase in the gross national product, but not to an increase in unemployment at a national level. Of course, certain jobs became redundant, but on the other hand new jobs were created, while the service sector and civil service, both still growing, were able to absorb many who had lost their jobs as a result of automation.

The second round is characterized by several fundamental technological and socio-economic changes. Spectacular *technological developments* in the field of micro-electronics removed technical and economic obstacles to further automation. Thanks to micro-electronics, it is possible to build computers for a very low price with a very large capacity on a very small surface. The reduction in size, the increase in capacity, and the decrease in costs, as well as the feasibility of mass production, have made possible a nearly universal use of the computer. It is therefore to be expected that employment will undergo drastic changes in the near future, not only in quality (structure) but also in quantity.

The *socio-economic context* in which the second round is taking place is fundamentally different from that of the first round. Economic growth had slumped in the second half of the 70s, the profits of commercial enterprises had fallen, and few new investments were made which could alleviate the loss in employment. It is precisely the service sector, which was an area of growth for employment in the recent past, that is expected to feel the pinch of labor-saving automation (Briefs, 1980; Leyder, 1979) in a time when the growth of the civil sector as come to a stop and is declining as well.

It would seem that the use of robots in industrial production will have a less dramatic effect on employment than the expected effects of automation on the service sector. In a recent report (SER, 1982) about the effects of micro-electronics on employment, the rate of introduction of micro-electronics in industrial production is judged to be the highest for process control. The introduction of robots gets a comparatively low score. Van der Auwera (1981) mentions several economic and social obstacles on the robot revolution. Although, in purely technological terms, 10% to 15% of the jobs in certain sectors could now be robotized, it is estimated that by the turn of the century a maximum of 5% of the jobs will be filled by robots. One reason for this comparatively low figure is the fact that, in the entire industrial sector, the number of persons who actually carry out production is less than 50% of all those involved in production (Rathenau, 1980). The figures mentioned here refer to the industrial sector as a whole. Obviously, the percentage of jobs that will be lost in specific areas where robots are introduced can turn out to be considerably higher, as illustrated by examples from the automobile industry (SOFI, 1981; van der Auwera, 1981) where 80% of the jobs were eliminated when robot systems were applied.

Of course, the automation industry itself also creates jobs, but it is highly questionable whether this will outweigh the loss in jobs elsewhere. Leyder (1979) expects that the growth in computer personnel will decrease, corresponding to a saturation of the market for general purpose computers which can be used for simple data processing. An increasing population of users, he says, will make interactive computer use an integrated part of their users' tasks, thus yielding increased productivity.

Prognoses on the expected effects of automation on *employment* are widely divergent. It is important here to distinguish between short- and long-term effects (Leyder, 1979; Verkerk, 1981). Against the background of the present economic situation, the introduction of automation would seem to lead to higher unemployment in the near future, aggravated in some countries (e.g. The Netherlands, see SER, 1983) by the increase of the working population, while in the far future economic growth would again be possible.

The effects on the volume of employment will also be greatly dependent on the rate of introduction of micro-electronics. In its report to the Dutch government the 'Rathenau advisory group' (1980) remarks that technological development need not be an autonomous process. The government must adopt an active attitude and steer developments. The advisory group also found widely divergent opinions about the development of employment in the next 20 to 30 years. According to the most pessimistic prognoses (Schaff, 1979; Friedrichs and Schaff, 1982), nearly all human work will become redundant through auto-mation. The advisory group itself is less pessimistic if government and industry would actively take advantage of the opportunities afforded by the use of micro-electronics. The group therefore feels that, in general, to put restraints on the use of micro-electronics is not a sensible strategy for The Netherlands. This would be detrimental to the country's competitive position and would endanger employ-ment more than would taking effective advantage of the possibilities offered by technological development.

To counter a drastic decline in employment opportunity, as is expected to happen in the banking and insurance branch, some political circles suggest studying the feasibility of levying 'automation tax'. This tax, it is expected, would slow down the loss of jobs and would only apply to firms which are not exposed to foreign competition. The service sector of the Dutch federation of trade unions has also suggested taxing automation (van Gelder, 1979; Huppes, 1980). Their suggestion is more specifically aimed at 'faulty' rationalizations which omit personnel costs such as unemployment benefits and additional training from the calculations. But not all the member unions of the Dutch federation are in favor of the idea of a tax on automation (Industriebond FNV, 1980). Unions in the industrial sector, rather than hoping simply to retard automation, are concerned with setting conditions regarding the quality of the work, for instance. They are also hesitant about the practicability of such a tax.

Prognoses concerning the effects of automation on the volume of employment are clearly widely divergent. This is true as well for the effects automation is expected to have on the *quality of work*. The 'Rathenau group' remarks that the introduction of micro-electronics will mean that many people will be required to perform at another level of knowledge and skill, generally a higher one. The expectations of 100 experts in this field in The Netherlands, collected using the Delphi method (SER, 1982), also are generally positive. This is primarily true for working conditions; the optimism is somewhat tempered for task content, but still clearly predominant. Van Hoof (1980), on the other hand, concludes that the optimistic expectations of the effects of automation on the quality of jobs (primarily in industry) are unfounded. He feels there will definitely not be a general rise of job qualifications nor will there be a gradual elimination of burdensome work situations. For jobs in the administrative and service sectors, Van Hoof also concludes that they will not reach a higher level. Kern and Schumann (1970) and Briefs (1980) expect a 'polarization' of job qualifications. This would create a comparatively small élite of specialists who are constantly obliged to expand their knowledge, and a large mass of semi-skilled workers who perform marginal routine tasks without having any insight into the systems in which they operate. Unions in the industrial sector (e.g. Industriebond FNV, 1980) also expect that, as to employment, jobs at the middle level will be worst hit, such as skilled manual labor and administrative jobs which require a fair amount of education and training.

One of the difficulties in discussing the effects of automation on the quality of work is that this concept has not been clearly delineated and the use of this term can easily lead to misunderstandings (Evans, 1982; Roe, 1982). De Galan *et al.* (1980) approach improvements in the quality of work from very different angles, such as the physical working conditions, the task content, and participation of employees in the decision making processes of the organization. It is very well possible for automation to have a positive effect on one of the aspects of the quality of work (for instance, the elimination of unpleasant and hazardous work through remote control) and at the same time to have a negative effect on another aspect (programming decisions into the machinery so that an operator has little else to do but supervise).

Regarding the structure of the organization in which the work is performed, decentralization of decisions through micro-electronics is theoretically possible (see e.g. Ekkers *et al.*, 1980; Wentink, 1981a). But in actual practice this alternative is often omitted, and automation leads to centralization of the decision making (Rathenau, 1980; Mickler *et al.*, 1976; SER, 1982). It is also possible that information systems are needed to bring about decentralization, but that this makes data available which can serve to strengthen central control. Hedberg (1975) describes how information systems had to be greatly expanded in order to allow a Volvo automobile works in Sweden to operate on the basis of semi-autonomous groups of production workers. A set of computer systems was installed which made available information necessary for the semi-autonomous group to be able to control the process, production, and quality. Hedberg remarks that these computer systems bring about decentralization of responsibilities (i.e. to the work group), but that also detailed information on mistakes, work pace, etc. becomes available which may strengthen complete control by the management.

The emphasis of this chapter will be on the design process and implementation of automation projects. We will see that an automation project can be viewed as a complex decision making process involving various groups of participants. In such a process there are several points at which choices are made that have implications for task content and for the structure of the organization.

Section 2 will consider the question whether the new technology theoretically allows for different solutions (for task content and organization structure) in order to reach the system's goal. In sections 3 and 4 the nature and the course of the decision making process in automation projects will be discussed. This will primarily concern the feasibility and the limitations of user participation in the design and implementation of automated systems.

2. THE IMPACT OF TECHNOLOGY

2.1. Technological determinism

In the past, technological developments such as the invention of the electric motor have exercised great influence on the design of work tasks and the structure of the organization in which the work takes place. It is expected that this effect will be even stronger with an accelerated introduction of automation. The study of the influence of technology on organzations has led to much debate in the literature (Porter *et al.*, 1975). One important reason of the differences in opinion is, according to Katz and Kahn (1978), the fact that many authors make no distinction between the 'internal' technology already used by the organization and the 'external' technology potentially available in the environment. They use the term 'technological environment' for the knowledge of technical processes and design of installations which exists outside of the organization itself. In this view, an organization can purchase this knowledge either in its original form or in an altered version. Katz and Kahn (1978) remark that companies tend to take a positive attitude towards the introduction of new technology, particularly in competitive situations and when their competitors also encourage or implement technological innovations (see also Poeth, 1980). In a market economy, the choice of a technical system will therefore generally be determined by economic criteria, as is also substantiated in a recent report by the socio-economic advisory council to the Dutch government (SER, 1982). According to this report, economic factors (lowering production costs, improving the competitive position) are the most important motives for the continued introduction of microelectronics.

In considering the question what influence technology has on the design of work tasks and organization structure, it is important to take note of the idea of 'technological determinism' as it has been developed in the literature. Technological determinism comprises three basic elements (Davis and Taylor, 1976). In the first place, it asserts that technology develops according to its own laws, independent of its social and cultural environment. A second premise is that, for an effective use which will benefit society, the development of technology ought not to be impeded by considerations other than those of the engineers and technicians who are directly involved in the development. In the third place, it asserts that the structure of an organization is dictated by its technology. Particularly this last assertion is important in light of the question how much latitude the introduction of new technology (i.e. automation) allows in task design and in determining the organization structure, so that the quality of the work can be taken into consideration in the design of systems.

A classic study in this area is that of Woodward (1965) (see also this Handbook, ch. 4.1). In a sample of 100 English manufacturing companies, she studied the relationship between technology and several organization structural indices in relation to the economic success of the organization. The companies were divided into three categories of increasing technical complexity: unit production, mass production, and process production. She found several linear and curvilinear relationships between her technology scale and the organization structure (such as number of supervisory levels, ratio of supervisory to non-supervisory personnel, span of control of the first supervisory level) and concluded that the technology was of decisive importance for the most suitable organization structure.

2.2. Reactions to technological determinism

Woodward's study was criticized on a number of points, for instance the interpretation of the technology scale. Some authors (e.g. Starbuck, 1965; Mintzberg, 1979) regard Woodward's categories as a scale for increasing smoothness of production rather than increasing technological complexity. Another point is the composition of the sample of manufacturing companies. In a later study by Hickson et al. (1969) in 46 organizations, Woodward's conclusions were not confirmed. The relationships between technology and a number of organization structure indices turned out to be weak. These authors used a different measure for the technology than did Woodward. The scale they developed reflected the degree of work flow integration (such as the degree of interdependence of the production subprocesses). The explanation for the contrasting findings of Woodward's study and their own was sought in the different composition of the two samples. Woodward's sample contained a larger percentage of small companies than the sample of Hickson et al. They feel that the relationship between technology and structural variables will manifest itself at the production level. The smaller the organization, the better observable are these relationships; in larger organizations such relationships will not be so strong because of their administrative and hierarchical structure which is not directly involved in production. This explanation implies that the relationship between technology and organization structural indices is modified by the size of the organization. Porter *et al.* (1975) conclude that, although relationships have been found between technology and structural indices, it is extremely difficult to established to what extent technology can be regarded as a *causal* factor. In their view, technology can also be treated as a dependent variable, and thus as susceptible to change and adaptation based on human needs.

The concept of technological determinism is rejected also in a series of studies specifically concerning automation. These studies are part of an international research project involving a total of 15 countries with both market economies and planned economies. Based on the preliminary results from four participating countries where both types of economy are represented, Forslin *et al.* (1979) conclude: '...although seen from different angles, an almost unanimous conclusion in these reports is the rejection of the idea of technological determinism, i.e. that automation is a blind force both independent of its social context and unaffected by its actors'.

In a comparative study of England and West Germany involving the application of computer numerical control (CNC) of machine tools, Sorge *et al.* (1982) find CNC technology to be extremely 'malleable'. This is shown by the applications of CNC technology which have been adapted to existing organization structures, existing personnel management strategies, etc. In smaller plants, the programming function, for instance, is much less concentrated in specialized departments, away from the work place, than it is in larger ones. Differences between England and West Germany in management, training, etc. remained after the introduction of CNC technology. The empirical findings of Sorge *et al.* (1982) illustrate that, given a certain technology, there is still leeway for organization design. Systems designers often say that in the technical design process there are options which differ little in their technical and economic respects, but which have entirely different organizational consequences (Van Assen, 1981).

These empirical findings challenge the principles of technological determinism, but the concept has been criticized from a more theoretical viewpoint as well. For instance, according to the socio-technical systems approach (see also this Handbook, ch. 4.5), production systems consist of two components, a technical system and a social system. The technical system is the installations, machinery, and work methods needed to transform input into output—products and services. The social system refers to the relationship between task performers and the technology and that between the task performers themselves. The socio-technical systems approach is based on the idea that there generally is a certain amount of leeway in the design of an effective production system (Cooper and

Foster, 1971). The goals of a system are best reached not by optimizing the technical system and then adjusting the social system to it, but through 'joint optimization' of the technical and social components. Of course, here, too, economic criteria will be important in determining what is optimal. Insufficient integration of the social and technical aspects of a production system can result in absenteeism, high turnover, poor group cohesion, etc. Fundamental to the socio-technical systems approach is the autonomy of the unit (individual or group) which leads to self-regulation; that is, the unit is capable of solving the problems that come up. This approach runs counter to technological determinism, which assumes that organization design is dictated by the technology.

Ekkers et al. (1980) use the term 'design philosophy' for the general idea underlying the design of work situations. Application of the principles of scientific management (see also this Handbook, ch. 2.3 and 4.2) led to repetitive tasks which were very quickly learned. Experiments based on the views of the socio-technical approach to systems design have also been carried out, but this does not imply that the principles of scientific management belong to the past. More specifically, in relation to jobs in automated systems (control and supervisory tasks) Ekkers et al. remark that, until recently, considerations such as the task's meaningfulness and attractiveness for the operator were of very little importance in the design process. The allocation of tasks between men and machine was primarily based on the differences in skills people or machines were said to possess. These authors see a gradual development in design philosophy, starting with the view that man should function as an extension of the machine (supplementary function), through the idea that man and machine must be regarded as equal system components (supplementory skills), to the present view that machines must be designed to serve human capabilities and needs, without losing sight of technical and economic effectiveness. They also feel that modern technology is highly flexible, and that there are in fact more design alternatives available than the designer actually considers.

Van Hoof (1980) points out that, in addition to the role of designers, the management also has a role in determining the way in which work is organized. Management strategies should not only be understood from a viewpoint of economic considerations, but also, to a certain extent, from a 'political' viewpoint: the necessity to maintain their own supremacy. Noble (1978) also feels that technology allows for various alternatives and states that in the past the choices that can be made in this respect were too often left to management. Marxist literature in the field of industrial sociology (Projektgroep 'Techniek, organisatie, arbeidsmarkt', 1980) proposes several hypotheses which also put strong emphasis on the influence of management on the design of work and of the organization. Two types of strategic behavior are distinguished which management uses to confirm the existing balance of power. The strategy of autonomy destruction (Taylorism) keeps the planning, conception, and control of the work strictly separate from its performance. Therefore, there can be little autonomy in the performance of work because the planning, conception, and control are management-dominated. The second strategy, primarily applied to a few key positions, is autonomy regulation (neo-Taylorism); that is, management attempts to bring autonomous behavior by the workers in line with the criteria of management. These hypotheses also imply a rejection of the idea of technological determinism.

The sources cited above supply arguments for rejecting the idea of technological determinism in its strict sense. As a starting point, we may state that technology leaves room for variation in organization design, but that there is a limit to the variation. Theoretically, more than one organization design is possible, but economic criteria and limitations inherent in the technology restrict the set of designs. Which of the possible designs is ultimately chosen will also depend on the existing value systems and interests in the organization (see also Briefs, 1975; Hedberg, 1975; Gallouédec-Genuys, 1975; Camman and Nadler, 1976; Mickler et al., 1976).

A recent study (Ekkers et al., 1980) on the nature and the quality of human work in highly automated systems is interesting, because of its expectation that, in view of the development of micro-electronics, in the near future the work of many people will consist of controlling automated technical systems. Twenty-four man-machine systems of varying degrees of automation and complexity in different branches of industry were studied. A distinction was made between two types of technical system: process control systems (to control industrial production systems, traffic systems, etc.) and administrative computer systems. The technological developments of these two types are generally the same, but their effects on the automation level are different. The term 'automation level', or stage of automation, in this study refers to the task division between man and the technical system, and it is an indication of the extent to which control of the system is left to the operator or to the machine. *Three levels* (*stages*) *of automation* are distinguished: (1) manual control (the operator is an integrated component of a closed control circuit), (2) introduction of information processing systems (certain control acts are performed by the operator, but other interventions are carried out by a machine), (3) supervisory control (here the technical system is entirely controlled by the machine and the operator monitors it).

The authors remark that technology offers possibilities which could result in a very high level of automation. In the task of the operator, there is a general trend from manual control in the 50s to supervisory control in the 70s. But the use of more advanced apparatus (for instance, process computers) does not necessarily imply a higher level of automation. The choice of the structure of the man-machine system, and along with it the level of automation, is equally determined by technical production and process characteristics and by economic characteristics of each individual situation in a plant (Ekkers *et al.*, 1980). The 24 cases studied show a wide range of levels of automation. In contrast to process control systems, the task of the operator in administrative computer systems has shown relatively little change over the past decades, because these types of technical systems, despite great technical differences between the successive generations, has remained at the same stage of automation (stage 2, introduction of information processing systems).

For task content, this study showed that less time is generally spent on operating at higher levels of automation, while the percentage of time spent 'resting' shows a large increase. At lower levels of automation, operating tasks are more routine, and monitoring tasks less passive (watching the meters) than at higher levels of automation (sitting back and waiting for breakdowns to occur).

It was expected that more integrated large-scale production processes would show more latitude for autonomous work groups as described by the socio-technical systems theory. But in none of the plants studied were there any experiments with other organizational forms than the traditional hierarchical model: there were no different organizational forms for different stages of automation. The administrative computer systems show a different picture. These systems are in the same (second) stage of automation. For task content, Ekkers *et al.* conclude that in process control systems with a high level of automation, the operator has few substantial duties to perform. He serves merely as a monitor waiting for irregularities in the functioning of the system. In contrast, in administrative computer systems the operator is quite active, but he performs very routine duties which must be carried out in accordance with strict procedures. These drawbacks to highly automated process control systems and administrative computer systems find expression in this study in the frequent absenteeism and the very low job satisfaction among the workers. The highly automated process control systems do show some differences between work situations in their effects on task content. The supervisory control tasks generally found in these systems show some variation in level of activity.

Then there is the question what effects administrative automation has on the centralization or decentralization of decision making in the organization. Van Weenen (1980) notes that originally a strong trend towards centralization was predicted. But, based on an evaluation of nine studies, he comes to the conclusion that, although several organizations show centralist tendencies in the decision making, in many other cases no substantial influence was found. Apparently, computers make possible both centralized and decentralized decision making processes.

Going on the basic assumption that technology in principle allows leeway for various tasks and organization structures, an important question is whether it is possible to obtain a better view of the nature and the course of decision making processes which occur in automation projects. This question will be considered in the next section.

3. AUTOMATION PROJECTS IN PRACTICE

3.1. 'Blueprints'

An automation project may be regarded as a complex decision making process. The number of persons involved is often considerable, the material is complicated and largely very technical. The costs can be very high. In addition, at the start of the project it is not always clear whether automation is the best solution to the organization's problem.

These characteristics make the control and management of automation projects difficult. Therefore, the 'blueprints' (manuals) generally used divide up the project into separate phases. Each phase comprises various activities and concludes with a report containing the information necessary for the decision whether to start on the next phase. Table 1 shows the phases given in the manuals employed by several large companies in The Netherlands. SDM (System Development Methodology) is used by the Dutch post office and telephone company, AFA (a phased approach to automation) is used by the Dutch railway company, PRODOSTA (PROject control and DOcumentation STAndards) by the Dutch multinational Philips, WEGWIJZER by a Dutch steel company. PARAET (Project Approach RAET) has been adopted by thirty firms (Roeleveld, 1981). More such 'blueprints' can be found in the literature (Mumford and Henshall, 1979; Ekkers *et al.*, 1980; Gelper, 1981; Laagland and Schaddelee, 1982). We will now discuss the primary activities per phase. Emphasis will be put on the automation of information processing systems.

As is often the case with complex decision making processes, it is difficult to pinpoint the beginning of an automation project. Sometimes an *exploratory* or *preliminary study* of a concrete company problem is the first step. This could involve inventory control, supply times, cost management, or quality control. In other cases, this phase is an integrated part of medium-term plans which are made periodically and in which department heads can indicate their wishes regarding developments in information supply. Their wishes might be prompted by a lack of efficiency which is correctly or incorrectly believed to exist in the work or in the department, by a feeling they are lagging behind others who have already computerized, or by an attempt of top management to look 'modern'. Also, the computer department, whose very existence is justified by automation, will sometimes take initiatives. There may also be pressure from suppliers of hardware and software. Once implemented in certain parts of the organization, automation may turn out to be efficient only if other parts are also computerized. A computer of the next generation increases the possibilities for application, etc. (Verhallen, 1982a). From a recently published report on the effects of micro-electronics on employment (SER, 1982) it appears that economic factors (decreasing production costs, improving the competitive position) were the major stimuli for introducing automation, followed by technical considerations

Table 1. Phases in automation projects according to various manuals.

SDM	AFA	PRODOSTA	WEGWIJZER	PARAET
0. Exploratory study	0. Preliminary study	1. Preliminary survey	1. Departmental study	1. Preliminary study • definition of the problem • feasibility study
1. Definition study	1. Feasibility study	2. Application analysis	2. Laying down automation plan	2. System study • logical design • technical design
2. Preliminary design	2. Basic design	3. System specification	3. Study phase	
3. Detail design	3. Procedures and computer-oriented systems analysis	4. System definition	4. Project preparation phase	3. System construction • programming • system test
4. Program and human job development	4. Programming	5. System development	5. Project finalization phase	
5. Testing	5. System and acceptability tests			4. Introduction • acceptability • implementation
6. Conversion and system implementation	6. Conversion and implementation	6. Operational phase	6. Implementation and control of system	
7. System operation and maintenance	7. Project evaluation			5. Production • production • evaluation

relating to the production (better handling of the production process, improving the quality of the products). In the third place come considerations relating to internal organization (improvement of the information flow and the organization of work).

Some authors point to the risks of thinking in terms of solutions in this phase. It may lead to an over-emphasis on the technical aspects of information and to an incomplete diagnosis of the firm's problem (Mumford and Weir, 1979; Huber, 1980; Argelo, 1982). Especially when the computer department is involved in the problem at a very early stage, chances are that the firm's problem is defined as an automation issue. In that case, the direction of the solution has been established before the problem itself has been sufficiently clarified. In this connection, Verhallen (1982a) remarks that a firm as such has no problem. It is persons or groups in or outside of the firm who define a situation as troublesome. Thanks to its position, management is able to issue its definition of a problem along with the request to solve it. Of great importance in this case is that the person making this request also assumes responsibility for the final result.

The main objective of the *feasibility study* is to ascertain whether and to what extent automation forms a solution to the firm's problem. According to some sources (Argelo, 1982) this is the most difficult and most important phase. Alternative solutions must be worked out and from the alternatives the best solution must emerge. This solution should not only solve the firm's problem at least partly, it also should not contrast too much with other policy criteria (often, one solution creates another, even bigger, problem). Verhallen (1982a) gives a fictitious example. Through computerization, payments to an electricity company can be made in equal monthly installments, and the meter checked only once a year. This may make the processing of payments more efficient, but it runs counter to the policy of energy conservation, since the consumer no longer gets any direct feedback on his consumption pattern. Automation often leads to unintended side effects. These must be taken into consideration in the assessment of the proposed solution.

An important question at this stage is who has a voice in determining policy criteria. The final result of this phase is an automation plan or a recommendation that the issue can better be solved in another way. The project structure is part of this plan (for this, see section 3.2). For it is here that the actual project management starts. The earlier phases basically took place in the normal organization structure. (The manuals differ on this point. PRODOSTA, for example, starts earlier with project management.) An overall cost-benefit analysis and a schedule for the following phases are also part of the automation plan. All too often a good project structure is neglected. The budget, it later turns out, was estimated very inaccurately.

The *basic design* builds on the results of the feasibility study in order to establish the system requirements and to convert them into exact system specifications.

These specifications cover the design of the entire system, including the required hardware and software, up to the point where programs and manual procedures must be determined. Here, specifications of the user-system interface must undergo a tentative test for usability. Requirements are also formulated for the acceptability test which will be given later. The consequences for the organization and the personnel must be determined.

Most manuals emphasize that, with a view to cost management, it is better to design the entire system in general terms before working out parts of it in detail. Technical details can only be worked out on the basis of the report which terminates the basic design phase. This report contains an estimate of the total project costs.

The *detail design*, as the name indicates, works out the subsystems in detail. In automation projects on a limited scale, the distinction between basic and detail design can become somewhat vague. And there is another difference in scope between the two designs. Where the basic design primarily covers the 'logical design', the emphasis in the detail design lies on the 'technical design'. As will be discussed later, this distinction is of great importance with a view to the possibilities of user participation in the design process.

The detail design leads to a concrete project proposal. This forms the transition from the preparatory phase to the finalization phase. The project proposal contains the requirements for the systems and acceptability tests, the schedule for the introduction phase, and a cost-benefit analysis.

The *finalization phase* comprises the following main activities: programming and determining manual tasks, systems and acceptability tests, conversion and implementation. Some manuals (SDM, AFA, and PARAET) treat these activities as phases in themselves. The goal of the finalization phase is to convert the now completed design into manual tasks and computer programs. Especially SDM (see Hice *et al.*, 1978) pays a great deal of attention to manual tasks. The reason for this is that, according to this manual, most mistakes in automated systems are made when information is exchanged between man and machine. The most important aspect of programming is to write a program which is as efficient and also as complete as possible.

After this come the systems and the acceptability tests. The former is a technical test of programs and of the system as a whole. The latter is a test by the users based on previously formulated requirements. Some manuals also mention the importance of instruction to the users in this phase.

If the system satisfies the requirements, conversion of data files and implementation of the new system can be taken in hand. Contrary to the activities of the earlier phases, the activities to be carried out in this phase have direct influence on the functioning of the organization. This will generally mean a drastic reorganization in user departments. Depending on the circumstances, there are three ways of implementing the new system: immediate and total conversion from the old to the new situation, phased implementation, or shadow operation. In the last case, both the old and the new systems are employed for a time. Finally the new system is turned over to the user organization, the computer department, and the maintainance department. This is the finalization of the project organization.

During the *operational phase* there must be attention to the control and thus to the effectiveness of the new system. This is a phase which is often forgotten (Argelo, 1982). Examples of topics for evaluation in this phase would be: have the system goals been reached? have the bottlenecks been eliminated? how do the actual costs relate to the estimated costs? how is the system accepted by the users? did the reorganization go well? are there any unintended side effects? (Hice *et al.*, 1978).

3.2. Groups involved

In automation projects, generally three main categories of people involved can be distinguished: the future users, the designers, and the management. Often a more modest role is played by the works council (advisory power) and by staff officials from the personnel and organization departments.

Figure 1 gives a very rough indication of the changing amount of involvement of the various groups during the phases of the automation process according to one of the manuals (PRODOSTA, 1977). Clearly the role of the designers expands as the process goes on and becomes more technical. The users are active primarily in the early phases. After that they more or less vanish and will not reappear until the operational phase. Other manuals (SDM, AFA) specifically provide for an acceptability test by the users before the actual implementation (see table 1). As we will discuss later, this is an important point with a view to the ultimate acceptance of the system by the users, and as a result of this, the effectiveness of the system in the operational phase.

Figure 1 gives only a very rough sketch of the involvement of the main categories in automation projects. A more precise analysis will show that the group of *users* in fact consists of several subgroups. We might mention the operational user, who is in direct contact with the new system (word processor, terminal) and whose job can change considerably as a result of automation, and the department heads who make use of the information which the new system provides them. This is also true of the concern management. But for practical reasons we will not extend the meaning of the word 'user' to include the concern management in this context.

The term *management* also requires more explanation. First of all, this of course

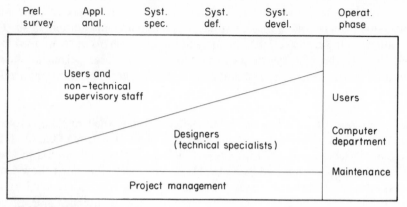

Figure 1. Changing involvement of the various groups during PRODOSTA

involves the concern management who must make available time, money, and manpower to carry out an automation project. After each phase the management makes an evaluation of whether or not to continue the project. But the concern management generally does not do this personally. This responsibility is usually delegated to a steering committee, from the basic design up to and including the introduction. The project structure varies slightly per manual and per phase. Generally, besides the steering committee there are also a project team and several work groups (den Hertog and van der Wee, 1982). A few important points here are: is the project manager, who is the real driving force, a manager or a technical specialist? what possibilities does the project structure provide for the future users (or for the personnel department) to make their wishes known?

The third main category, the *designers*, consists of technically trained specialists, including systems analysts and programmers. They are indispensable in automation because of their specific knowledge and they play a dominant role in a large part of the project.

Most manuals allow some unspecified leeway for advice and recommendations from a personnel and organizational viewpoint, in reference to the foreseeable consequences of automation for task content and organization structure. Finally, in The Netherlands, the works council is also involved in larger automation projects. According to article 25 of the works council act of 1979, the works council has advisory powers in large reorganizations. And a new act on working conditions, which has been in force since 1983, gives the works council the responsibility to promote the welfare of the employees by ensuring that jobs are created which make use of the knowledge and professional skill of the user. The involvement of the Dutch trade union movement in automation has thus far only been slight. But there are signs that the unions want to become more involved in these issues in the future by means of collective bargaining (van Gelder, 1979).

3.3. Discrepancies between 'blueprint' and actual practice

The picture of automation projects as described here makes a very logical and rational impression. But from the literature on complex decision making in organizations it is known that such processes often take an entirely different course in actual practice (see Braybrooke and Lindblom, 1963; Cohen *et al.*, 1972; Kickert, 1979; Mohr, 1982; Koopman *et al.*, this Handbook, ch. 4.6). The complexity of the information and the conflicts of interests between the groups involved often make the project less orderly and sometimes even chaotic. To what extent does this happen with automation as well?

To start with, the role of the technical specialists (the designers), especially in the more complex projects, is much more predominant than the blueprint would lead us to believe. The role of management often turns out to be much more modest than the blueprint would indicate (Argelo, 1982; Vossenaar, 1983). The interest of the management is often limited to the economic aspects: what is it all going to cost, what will it yield, and will we get it on time? They have less interest in the technical information aspects. Being at a great disadvantage as to knowledge compared to the designers and being fairly ignorant of the jargon, management wrongly tends to delegate a large part of its responsibility to this groups. The management sees automation as a 'technical' problem that must be solved by an expert. Whether or not the expert also has much experience in work coordination and planning is a different matter entirely. Whether he has any idea of how to negotiate or act as a process consultant is a question which is often not asked. The management, even though it is responsible, makes only partial use of the means it has available to regulate and to control the process. It has the power to divide the project into phases, to spread out the phases in time, and, after each phase, to give its approval for the next one to start (including budget and time management). These possibilities are generally poorly utilized. Especially the first two phases, in which the diagnosis and the feasibility study take place, are often neglected, which has a bad effect on the quality and acceptance of the choices made. At later stages, management contributes only via the steering committee. The management, although primarily responsible, has no time for complete control of the project. The steering committee becomes a bickering bunch of department heads who are involved in the project, with the specialist/project manager as the neutral expert. So he takes over the actual management and he tells the steering committee what to do instead of it telling him (Argelo, 1982).

The future users are also usually much less involved than the blueprint indicates. Just like the management, the users have a tremendous lack of technical knowledge, especially compared to the designers. This power distance is sometimes also carefully cultivated by the specialists through the use of jargon and rather incomprehensible documents (the baseline documents which give the rationalization for the steps taken). The users regard the blueprint employed in the very last place as an instrument for themselves. Lack of knowledge, inhibition, and indolence lead the users to brush off all responsibility and to leave it to the technical specialists. The specialists have not the slightest objection, since they already felt that automation issues were their territory anyway (Argelo, 1982). In section 4 we will discuss extensively the consequences such a limited contribution by the users may have.

Automation often brings about great changes in the task content and working conditions of the users. If, in the course of the change process, the management does not build up a sort of foothold for the changes among those directly involved, a smooth introduction phase cannot be guaranteed (Koopman and Drenth, 1981; DIO, 1983). A common reaction of the user is to make only partial use of a new information system or even to boycott it (Eason et al., 1975). The greater efficiency which was to be achieved through automation is thus lost entirely. The problem of limited user participation becomes the more urgent when the socio-organizational role of the staff is also neglected. Contributions from this side are often negligible or else they are brought into the process much too late (den Hertog et al., 1980). Projects which systematically include social and organizational criteria as early as the design phase are rare (Ekkers et al., 1980; for a good exception see van Assen, 1982. To date, the role of the works council has also been marginal, because automation projects are seldom seen and reported as important organizational changes.

4. USER PARTICIPATION

4.1. Problems around automated systems

According to the literature, in automation projects the goals set are sometimes only reached to a very small degree; the effectiveness of the system leaves a great deal to be desired. This is caused by two chief problems: the system is not really based on the wishes, difficulties, and capabilities of the user organization, and no foothold for the system is created among the users during the preparation and the design, with the result that the system meets with inadequate acceptance (Mumford and Henshall, 1979; Blokdijk, 1981; de Maio, 1980; Faddegon et al., 1981 den Hertog and van der Wee, 1982). Some authors blame this on the predominant position of the designers in automation projects. In answer to this, generally some kind of the socio-technical systems approach is advocated. It is essential that social and personnel aspects be included in the design from the very beginning (Hedberg and Mumford, 1975; de Maio, 1980; Courbon and Bourgeois, 1980; van Dijck, this Handbook, ch. 4.5). Other authors feel that it is not only a question of too much emphasis on the technical aspects, but that a systematic management philosophy is responsible for the creation of tasks which have been divested of as much brain work as possible, and where the knowledge about the work process is centralized in the concern management. In this connection, the introduction of Taylor (scientific management) in the office is often mentioned (Cooley, 1980; Briefs, 1980; Bjørn-Andersen and Eason, 1980; Galjaard, 1982).

In the literature, various *arguments* are put forward in favour of involving the future users in automation projects. First of all, in order for the new system to function well, its acceptance by the user organization is necessary. From several studies it has appeared that the way in which the users are involved in preparation, development, and introduction might quite possibly be of great influence on the degree of acceptance and thus on the effectiveness of the new system (Koopman, 1980; Oppelland and Kolf, 1980; Land et al., 1980; Argelo, 1982).

Another argument for user participation is that the user often has available specific knowledge and experience which can be great importance to the project. His motivation to 'hand over' this knowledge will be highly dependent on the way in which he is informed and consulted during the project (Lawler and Rhode, 1976; Sääksjärvi, 1980; den Hertog and van der Wee, 1982). Lastly, user participation is sometimes employed because legal regulations or collective labour agreements stipulate it: participation is a right. Nowadays, such regulations are mostly found in the Scandinavian countries and in West Germany, but they will probably soon find broader acceptance in The Netherlands as well (van Gelder, 1979; Höyer, 1980; Jonasson, 1980).

4.2. Possibilities of and limitations to user participation

There is a rapidly growing body of literature in which some form of user participation is propagated as a means of alleviating the problems mentioned above. On the other hand, research is bringing to light more and more bottlenecks which limit the scope of user participation. In this section we will first go into the possibilities. Important questions here are: does it involve direct or indirect participation? in what phases of the automation project does the participation take place? at what subproblems and subactivities is the participation aimed?

Most authors agree that participation can only be meaningful if it takes place at a point when there is still something to be decided (Edström, 1977). This means that participation must not be restricted to the introduction phase, as actually quite often happens. User participation must primarily be aimed at the preparation and the design. More in detail, the future users (as far as they are known) can be involved in defining the problem, determining the goals and criteria, exploring alternatives, evaluating the final design with respect to the requirements set, and evaluating the system in operation (Mumford and Weir, 1979). In terms of table 1, user participation can be considered from the exploratory study up to and including the basic design, and from the acceptability test up to and including the evaluation. It is generally felt that the technical phases in between lend themselves much less to contributions by the users. What can be done very profitably is to enlist users in problems around the implementation related to information and re-training.

Mumford's ETHICS method—short for Effective Technical and Human Implementation of Computer Systems—is based on the principles of the socio-technical system approach (see van Dijck, this Handbook, ch. 4.5). The social aspects of the requirements are shaped as much as possible by the users. This is done by their representatives in a design committee. This group also includes a few systems analysts and an internal as well as an external management consultant. The method is as follows: first of all, using questionnaires and group discussions, an attempt is made to get a picture of the problems and the wishes of the user organization. The future task characteristics are one of the points of discussion. On the basis of this and other information, the design committee formulates the test criteria by which the new system will be evaluated at a later point in time. The criteria include technical, economic, and socio-organizational aspects. Then the designers in the group are asked to prepare design alternatives. The alternatives can be presented to all employees so they can express their views, and are then assessed in the design committee. The alternative emerging as the best one is worked out in more detail by the designers and evaluated again by the representatives of the user organization against the criteria.

What is noteworthy in the approach described here is the strong position of the users in the design committee. In the case described by Mumford and Henshall (1979) there were six representatives of the user organization and two systems analysts in the group. More important still is that the design committee had been delegated extensive powers by the management. Finally, it is important that the design committee assisted in and was consulted throughout the entire automation process. The authors describe this case explicitly as a success story and conclude that user participation is an important means to obtain a better fit between the social and the technical systems.

The recent literature gives more examples of automation projects which attempted an integrated involvement of the human factor in the preparation and introduction of new systems (e.g. Oppelland and Kolf, 1980; Land et al., 1980 Shneiderman, 1980). Not all researchers report success. Hedberg, in a very well-known article (1975), describes two positions in which representatives of the user organization often wind up. The first is termed the 'hostage situation'. Having scant knowledge of information technology, a representative wants to avoid at all costs asking what he considers to be stupid questions. He does not take a very active part in the discussions, he takes no risks. The result is that he has hardly any influence on the course of events. The second situation is known as the 'indoctrination alternative'. In this case the representative does ask 'stupid' questions. If the designers take him seriously, gradually a learning process takes place. The communications between designers and user representatives are thus improved. But this leads straight to a new problem: communications with the people they represent, who can no longer identify with representatives who think and talk more and more in the terminology of the designers.

The problems involved here are familiar to us from other situations of representative consultation, for example in the works council (IDE, 1981). The expertise here is specifically technical. From the outset, the designers have a great advantage in knowledge over the users. Often this advantage is consciously cultivated by the use of technical jargon. For, here too, knowledge is power (Crozier, 1964; Mintzberg, 1979; Pfeffer, 1978, 1981). The impression that technical specialists will adopt a cooperative attitude and direct their efforts at satisfying the wishes of the users—an impression somewhat aroused by the publications of Mumford *et al.*—is, in general, not confirmed. Various researchers report tensions in the relationship between designers and users. Part of this can be ascribed to different orientations and/or views on work. An example will clarify this. Generally, designers are primarily interested in a sound technical system, preferably with many innovations, which can do a lot and in which little can go wrong (for instance, through improper use). Investments in system flexibility are but frugal, because in this view flexibility can only be achieved at the expense of optimum performance. But flexibility is the very thing the user needs if he is to create meaningful tasks (Argelo, 1982).

This example illustrates that automation involves the question of power. Ideologies and management views are two determinants of the form new jobs will take and of whether the decision making will be centralized or decentralized (Mickler *et al.*, 1976; Höyer, 1980; Docherty, 1980). As was shown by the study of Hedberg (1975), there is little to be gained for the user either way. These results are entirely in line with the conclusions of Mulder (1971): when there are great differences in expertise, participation only leads to indoctrination. It is even dubious if the management can always be considered an equal match for the designers. Faced with the dilemma of the hostage versus the indoctrination situation, Hedberg looks for a way out through influence via the 'meta system' of the organization. Decision making processes are controlled *indirectly* by means of the meta system in that it lays down rules and preliminary conditions (Kickert, 1979). What Hedberg advocates boils down to this: employee representatives, using the available consultative bodies (works council, bargaining with unions) should try to convert their interests and goals into guidelines to serve as the foundation for automation projects. In this way, influence is exercised on the conditions designers have to stick to before and not during the process. Other authors also emphasize the great importance of values and management philosophy in automation. If employees could effectively influence it, automation could make a contribution to greater democratization and more meaningful tasks (Briefs, 1975 Manor, 1975; Argyris, 1977).

But reality is often not like this. On the basis of recent experiences in the Scandinavian countries, Nygaard (1980) concludes that advance influence (via the meta system) is not enough to obtain a firm grasp on the course of the automation project. Formulating requirements in terms of system characteristics in an abstract sense turns out to be no guarantee for the desired result, for example in terms of job characteristics. The author therefore concludes that user participation is necessary in all phases (but not in technical details), from the initial exploration of the possibilities up to and including the ultimate implementation.

4.3. User participation in the eighties

Not yet so long ago, the introduction of technological innovations lay entirely in the hands of technical specialists. In the past decades changes have started to come about (Höyer, 1980, 130; Wentink, 1981b; Zanders, 1982). Below we will take a look at the motives underlying these changes and to see what perspective can be sketched for user participation in the eighties. Looking back, three points seem to have been of great importance. First of all, there was the growing insight that mechanization or automation involves not only a system fit but also a process fit (Oppelland and Kolf, 1980). This means that the effectiveness of the system is determined not only by intrinsic qualitative aspects of the system (consistency, completeness, etc.), but also by the way in which the users appreciate these aspects (Blokdijk, 1980). This is why it is vital to involve the user organization in the project and to pay timely attention to foreseeable problems and conflicts between parties. The project manager must be experienced in process consultation. In this connection it is sometimes advocated not to put the project into the hands of a technical specialist, but rather into those of an experienced manager (den Hertog and van der Wee, 1982).

The second point of importance is that the dominant management or organization philosophy greatly influences the manner in which mechanization or automation is effected (Boland, 1979; Cooley, 1980). Most authors agree that there is no such thing as an absolute 'technological determinism'. On the contrary, recent technological developments theoretically provide the necessary flexibility to be able to make policy decisions. The extent to which this latitude can be utilized is closely intertwined with the question whether the wishes and interests of operational users are compatible with the dominant organization philosophy. Here we might think of views about task content and control in the organization (Mickler et al., 1976; Briefs, 1980; de Maio, 1980; Galjaard, 1982).

A third motive for user participation in automation was undoubtedly the democratization movement of the late sixties and early seventies. This factor has led to changes in legislation and in agreements between employers and employees in several countries. Little has remained of this 'cultural optimism'. The economic recession has confronted us with new problems. Many companies struggle with stagnating sales markets and the resulting diminished production. The social climate seems to be characterized by a 'new functionalism' (Heemstra, 1982). What implications does this have for the possibilities of user participation in the eighties? What conditions are important here? We will distinguish between practical organizational conditions and more fundamental conditions and start with the latter.

As is the case with other forms of consultation (see Koopman and Wierdsma, this Handbook, ch. 3.7), we assume that participation in decision making only 'works' if (1) the persons involved see the usefulness of it and (2) there is sufficient latitude for participation. In automation, this means that the management will only stimulate user participation if the users have essential information which is not available anywhere else, or if the management has little confidence in successful implementation of the new system without participation (Vroom and Yetton, 1973). The expected greater *effectiveness* will have to be the basis for user participation. More ideological motives which were popular in the sixties and seventies, such as participation as a goal in itself and as a means to greater work satisfaction, will be relegated to the background (temporarily?). Of course, employee representatives will sometimes be able to make use of participation rights as laid down in legislation and in agreements. This brings us back to the discussion about the meta system. But, as we saw, the possibilities of exercising indirect influence are fairly limited. To start with, consultative bodies such as the works council often get only involved in a problem when several decisions have already been made (Ahlin and Svensson, 1980). Furthermore, formulation of general points of policy in no way ensures a firm grasp on the rest of the process. So, from the point of view of the user, direct participation in the automation project is an important demand. All this is based on the assumption that the user organization is interested. There can also be circumstances in which participation becomes an issue: for instance, when automation will mean that many of the personnel will lose their jobs.

A second condition for effective user participation was that there be sufficient latitude. This implies early involvement, at a point when most decisions still have to be made. Another factor which greatly influences the amount of latitude is the choice between buying a ready-made package (hardware and software) and making software yourself (Van der Poel, 1981). In the latter case, there is obviously more opportunity for making choices. A third factor involves the size of the automation project and the nature and size of the organization. Especially in large, bureaucratic organizations with many plants and a strong emphasis on standardization, user participation very soon begins to resemble manipulation.

Apart from such fundamental conditions, some practical organizational conditions are important in the choice of the actual participation strategy. As was discussed in section 4.2, there are several variants which can also be used jointly. One must keep in mind that each variant has specific advantages but also a price tag. Costs and benefits must be considered. None of the variants are ideal. Participation in the design committee via group representatives brings us to the dilemma of Hedberg (hostage versus indoctrination alternatives). Conditions are that the representatives have certain amount of expertise and motivation and that they have a good relationship with the people they represent (Rajkovič, 1980). This variant assumes that the representatives have a vivid imagination. They will have to form a fairly abstract picture of a future situation (Blokdijk, 1980). In entirely new and complex automation projects, this leads to almost insurmountable problems. If those involved have had some experience with automation, or if the project is an expansion of an earlier one, then the problems can be more easily managed (Vossenaar, 1983). If the variant of direct participation, such as the 'consensus participation' of Mumford and Weir (1979), is chosen, then there are other conditions, such as a large investment in time and money and intensive process support and assistance from management consultants, not to mention the fact that this variant is only possible in very small-scale projects (Winkelhage and Marock, 1980). Participation through the meta system has various limitations which have already been discussed.

The choice will have to be made for each individual situation depending on local conditions. Often a combination of several variants will emerge. But in many cases, the help of third parties will have to be called in. Here we are thinking primarily of socio-organizational assistance, which is the last topic of this chapter.

4.4. The socio-organizational contribution

Socio-organizational departments can contribute to an automation project in various ways, differing both in the nature of the advisory work and in the position from which they advise. A primary distinction here is internal or external advice. The management can seek external advice (examples are given in Mumford's publications), but this is also increasingly being done by employees representatives, in The Netherlands by the works council. This generally involves professionals from the trade-union movement. Experience with this type of consultancy indicates that the trade-union movement has little influence on automation projects (van Gelder, 1979; Ahlin and Svensson, 1980). Usually a firm will want to enlist internal expertise from a socio-organizational viewpoint, although even this is not yet common practice (Verhallen, 1982b; van Kesteren, 1982). Here, too, in what phases of the process this is done is a decisive factor. In order to take serious account of social and organizational criteria, they must be taken into consideration from the outset.

We would like to class the socio-organizational contribution into four categories:

—socio-psychological and ergonomic advice geared to task content and the man-machine interface;

—professional organizational advice regarding the adaptation of the new information system to relevant organization characteristics;

—process consultation;

—advice and assistance in retraining, transfers, etc.

Section 2 discussed the results of scientific research on task characteristics. They stress the importance of variation, social contact, feedback on results, opportunities for training, etc. The Working Conditions Act which recently came into effect in The Netherlands officially underlines the importance of these points. The literature gives many suggestions for translating these and similar requirements into concrete job characteristics in automation projects (Landeweerd, 1978; Shneiderman, 1980; Ekkers et al., 1980; Faddegon et al., 1981; Algera, 1981).

Sound advice about man-machine combinations presumes expert knowledge of the strong and the weak aspects of both components, the man and the machine. Knowledge of the system goal is also necessary, as it is decisive for an optimal synchronization of the human and the non-human components.

A contribution from social scientists may also be expected at a meso-organizational level. This primarily involves synchronizing the new system with existing organization characteristics (Mintzberg, 1979; Ginzberg, 1980; Macintosh, 1981; de Sitter, 1981; van Dee and Mens, 1982). This was discussed in section 2. We call to mind the issue of centralization versus decentralization and, more in general, the way in which the organization handles its control problems.

A social advisor can contribute not only to the content but to the process as well. Above we have seen that it is often difficult for the user organization to obtain an effective grasp on the automation project. The complex and difficult material can easily obscure the view of the whole. If conflicts of interest between the participants also occur, the project may quickly become uncontrollable. In such a situation, process consultation by a consultant with experience in the fields of decision making and conflict managment can be beneficial.

Lastly, socio-organizational departments can be expected to cooperate and assist in the introduction of the new system. This involves instruction, additional training or retraining, as well as transfers and hiring new personnel (Tissen, 1981; Rodenburg, 1982).

REFERENCES

Aanpak en Fasering Automatisering [Approach of and phasing automation]. (AFA) (1976). Utrecht: Dutch Railways.

Ahlin, J. E., Svensson, L. J. P. (1980), New technology in mechanical engineering industry: How can workers gain control? *Economic and Industrial Democracy*, **1**, 487–521.

Algera, J. A. (1981), *Kenmerken van werk* [Characteristics of work]. Lisse: Swets & Zeitlinger.

Argelo, S. M. (1982), Valkuilen bij automatieprojecten [Traps in automation projects]. *Informatie*, **24**, 133–140.

Argyris, C. (1977), Organizational learning and management information systems. *Accounting, Organizations and Society*, **2**, 113–123.

Assen, A. van (1981), Het rijke effect van semi-autonome groepen [The fruitful effect of semi-autonomous groups]. *Management Total*, June, 44–46.

Assen, A. van (1983), *Kwaliteit van de arbeid en mechanisatie/automatisering in de produktie* [The quality of work and mechanization/automation in production]. Eindhoven: Philips.

Auwera, F. van der (1981), Toekomstperspectieven van de industriële robot [The future of the industrial robot]. *Informatie* [Information], **23**, 456–465.

Bjørn-Andersen, N., Eason, K. D. (1980), Myths and realities of information systems contributing to organizational rationality. In: Mowshowitz, A. (Ed.), *Human choice and computers*, 2. Amsterdam: North-Holland.

Blokdijk, P. (1980), A participative approach to systems design. In: Lucas, H. C., Land, F. F., Lincoln, T., Supper, K. (Eds.), *The information systems environment*. Amsterdam: North-Holland.

Blokdijk, P. (1981), Systeemontwikkelingsmethodiek SASO [The SASO method of systems development]. *Informatie* [Information], **23**, 222–237.

Boland, R. J. (1979), Control, causality and information system requirements. *Accounting, Organizations and Society*, **4**, 259–272.

Braybrooke, D., Lindblom, C. (1963), *A strategy of decision: policy evaluation as a social process*. New York: Free Press.

Briefs, U. (1975), The role of information processing systems in employee participation in managerial decision making. In: Mumford, E., Sackman, H. (Eds), *Human choice and computers*. Amsterdam: North-Holland.

Briefs, U. (1980), The effects of computerization on human work. In: Mowshowitz, A. (Ed.), *Human choice and computers*, 2. Amsterdam, North-Holland.

Camman, C., Nadler, D. A. (1976), Fit control systems to your managerial style. *Harvard Business Review*, **54**, 65–72.

Cohen, M. D. March, J. G., Olsen, J. P. (1972), A garbage can model of organizational choice. *Administrative Science Quarterly*, **17**, 1–25.

Cooley, M. (1980), Computerization: Taylor's latest disguise. *Economic and Industrial Democracy*, **1**, 523–539.

Cooper, R., Foster, M. (1971), Sociotechnical systems. *American Psychologist*, **26**, 467–474.

Courbon, J. C., Bourgeois, M. (1980), The information system designer as a nurturing agent of a socio-technical process. In: Lucas, H. C., Land, F. F., Lincoln, T., Supper, K. (Eds.), *The information systems environment*. Amsterdam: North-Holland.

Crozier, M. (1964), *The bureaucratic phenomenon*. London: Tavistock.

Davis, L. E., Taylor, J. C. (1976), Technology, organization and job structure. In: Dubin, R. (Ed.), *Handbook of work, organization and society*. Chicago: Rand McNally.

Dee, G. M. van, Mens, G. F. M. (1982), Kwaliteit van de arbeid en arbeidsomstandigheden [The quality of work and working conditions]. In: Verhallen (1982c).

DIO—International Research Team (1983), A contingency model of participative decision making: An analysis of 56 decisions in three Dutch organisations. *Journal of Occupational Psychology*, **56**, 1–18.

Docherty, P. H. G. (1980), Some mismatches constraining user choice in systems development. In: Mowshowitz, A. (Ed.), *Human choice and computers*, 2. Amsterdam: North-Holland.

Eason, K. D., Damodaran, L., Stewart, T. F. M. (1975), Interface problems in man-computer interaction. In: Mumford, E., Sackman, H. (Eds.), *Human choice and computers*. Amsterdam: North-Holland.

Edström, A. (1977), User influence and the success of MIS-projects: A contingency approach. *Human Relations*, **30**, 589–607.

Ekkers, C. L., Brouwers, A. A. F., Pasmooij, C. K., Vlaming, P. M. de (1980), *Menselijke stuur- en regeltaken.* [Human control tasks]. Leiden, NIPG/TNO.

Evans, J. (1982), Arbeitsnehmer und Arbeitsplatz. In: Friedrichs, G., Schaff, A. (Eds.), *Auf Gedeih und Verderb: Mikroelektronik und Gesellschaft.* Wien: Europaverlag.

Faddegon, J., Maathuis, P. G. M., Vrins, A. G. M. (1981), Aanbevelingen voor het ontwerp van mens-machine-dialogen [Recommendations for the design of man-machine dialogues]. *Informatie* [Information], **23**, 476–482.

Forslin, J., Sarapata, A., Whitehill, A. M. (1979), *Automation and industrial workers.* Oxford: Pergamon Press.

Friedrichs, G., Schaff, A. (1982), Microelectronics and society. Oxford: Pergamon Press.

Galan, C. de, Gils, M. R. van, Strien, P. J. van (Eds.) (1980), *Humanisering van de arbeid* [Humanizing work]. Assen: Van Gorcum.

Galjaard, J. (1982), Wetenschap, technologie en kwaliteit van de arbeid [Science, technology and the quality of work]. *Tijdschrift voor Organisatiekunde en Sociaal Beleid* [Journal of Organization Science and Social Policy], (*M & O*), **36**, 208–219.

Gallouédec-Genuys, F. (1975), The computer and democracy. In: Mumford, E., Sackman, H. (Eds.), *Human choice and computers.* Amsterdam: North-Holland.

Gelder, W. van (1979), *Automatisering en werkgelegenheid, een vakbondsvisie.* [Automation and employment, a trade union's view]. Woerden: FNV.

Gelper, R. P. E. (1981), METHOD/1. *Informatie* [Information], **23**, 597–607.

Ginzberg, M. J. (1980), An organizational contingencies view of accounting and information systems implementation. *Accounting, Organizations and Society*, **5**, 369–382.

Hedberg, B. (1975), Computer systems to support industrial democracy. In: Mumford, E., Sackmann. H. (Eds.), *Human choice and computers.* Amsterdam: North-Holland.

Hedberg, B., Mumford, E. (1975), The design of computer systems; Man's vision of man as an integral part of the system design process. In: Mumford, E., Sackman, H. (Eds.), *Human choice and computers.* Amsterdam: North-Holland.

Heemstra, J. M. R. (1982), Nieuwe zakelijkheid en sociaal beleid [New functionalism and social policy]. *Gids voor Personeelsbeleid, Arbeidsvraagstukken en Sociale Verzekering* [Guide to Personnel Policy, Labour Issues and Social Insurance], **62**, no. 17.

Hertog, J. F. den, Wee, E. van der (1982), Gebruikersparticipatie: Uitgangspunten bij het inschakelen van gebruikers in automatiseringsprojekten [Users' participation: Principles in involving users in automation projects]. *Informatie* [Information], **24**, 141–151.

Hertog, J. F. den, Wielenga, C., Heine, P. (1980), The integration of a computer system in the task environment of process operators: A case of action research. In: Mowshowitz, A. (Ed.), *Human choice and computers, 2.* Amsterdam: North-Holland.

Hice, G. F., Turner, W. S., Cashwell, L. F. (1978), *System development methodology.* Rev. ed. Amsterdam: North-Holland.

Hickson, D. J., Pugh, D. S., Pheysey, D. (1969), Operations, technology and organization structure: An empirical reappraisal. *Administrative Science Quarterly*, **14**, 378–397.

Hoof, J. J. van (1980), Op weg naar humanere arbeid? [Towards more humane work?]. In: de Galan *et al.* (1980).

Höyer, R. (1980), User participation—why is development so slow? In: Lucas, H. C., Land, F. F., Lincoln, T., Supper, K. (Eds.), *The information systems environment.* Amsterdam: North-Holland.

Huber, G. P. (1980), *Managerial decision making.* Glenview: Scott, Foresman.

Huppes, T. (1980), *Maatschappelijke gevolgen van de 'chip'-technologie* [Consequences of chip technology for society]. Leiden: Stenfert Kroese.

IDE—International Research Group (1981), *Industrial democracy in Europe.* Oxford: Oxford University press.

Industriebond FNV (1980), 'Chip Ahoy'. *Kader*, no. 2.

Jonasson, S. (1980), Computerisation and social requirements. In: Mowshowitz, A. (Ed.), *Human choice and computers, 2*. Amsterdam: North-Holland.

Katz, D., Kahn, R. L. (1978), *The social psychology of organizations*. 2nd ed. New York: Wiley.

Kern, H., Schumann, M. (1970), *Industriearbeit und Arbeiterbewustsein*. Frankfurt: E. V. A.

Kesteren, R. A. van (1982), De inbreng van de sociale discipline [The contribution of social discipline]. In: Verhallen, (1982c).

Kickert, W. J. M. (1979), *Organisation of decision-making: A systems-theoretical approach*. Amsterdam: North-Holland.

Koopman, P. L. (1980), *Besluitvorming in organisaties* [Decision making in organizations]. Assen: Van Gorcum.

Koopman, P. L., Drenth, P. J. D. (1981), Conditions for successful participation. *Leadership and Organization Development Journal*, **2**, no. 4.

Laagland, P. T. M., Schaddelee, C. (1982), PRISMA:Een methode voor informatie-systeemplanning en systeemontwikkeling [A method for information systems planning and systems development]. *Informatie* [Information], **24**, 17–30.

Land, F., Mumford, E., Hawgood, J. (1980), Training the system analyst of the 1980s: Four analytical procedures to assign the design process. In: Lucas, H. C., Land, F. F., Lincoln, T., Supper, K. (Eds.), *The information systems environment*. Amsterdam: North-Holland.

Landeweerd, J. A. (1978), Systeemergonomie: Ergonomisch ontwerpen van mens-machine-systemen [Systems ergonomics: The ergonomic design of man-machine-systems]. *Intermediair*, **14**, no. 44, 55–59.

Lawler, E. E., Rhode, J. G. (1976), *Information and control in organizations*. Pacific Palisades: Goodyear.

Leyder, R. (1979), De computer, de werkgelegenheid en de krisis: Een beschavingszorg? [The computer, employment and the crisis: the care of civilization?]. *Informatie*, **21**, 408–426.

Macintosh, N. B. (1981), A contextual model of information systems. *Accounting, Organizations and Society*, **6**, 39–53.

Maio, A. de (1980), Socio-technical methods for information systems design. In: Lucas, H. C., Land, F. F., Lincoln, T., Supper, K. (Eds.), *The information systems environment*. Amsterdam: North-Holland.

Manor, Y. (1975), The contribution of computers to participatory democracy. In: Mumford, E., Sackman, H. (Eds.), *Human choice and computers*. Amsterdam: North-Holland.

Mickler, O., Ditrich, E., Neuman, U. (1976), *Technik, Arbeitsorganisation und Arbeit. Eine empirische Untersuchung in der automatisierten Produktion*. Frankfurt a/Main: Aspekte.

Mintzberg, H. (1979), *The structuring of organizations*. Englewood Cliffs: Prentice-Hall.

Mohr, L. B. (1982), *Explaining organization behavior*. San Francisco: Jossey-Bass.

Mulder, M. (1971), Power equalization through participation? *Administrative Science Quarterly*, **16**, 31–38.

Mumford, E., Henshall, D. (1979), *A participative approach to computer systems design*. London: Associated Business Press.

Mumford, E., Weir, M. (1979), *Computer systems in work design: The ETHICS method*. London: Associated Business Press.

Noble, D. F. (1978), Social choice in machine design: The case of automatically controlled machine tools, and a challenge for labor. *Politics and Society*, **8**, 3–4, 313–347.

Nora, S., Minc, A. (1978), *L'information de la société*. Paris: La Documentation française.

Nygaard, K. (1980), Workers' participation in system development. In: Mowshowitz, A. (Ed.), *Human choice and computers, 2*. Amsterdam: North-Holland.

Oppelland, H. J., Kolf, F. (1980), Participative development of information systems: Methodological aspects and empirical experiences. In: Lucas H. C., Land, F. F., Lincoln, T., Supper, K. (Eds.), *The information systems environment*. Amsterdam: North-Holland.

Pfeffer, J. (1978), *Organizational design*. Arlington Heights (Ill.): AHM.

Pfeffer, J. (1981), *Power in organizations*. Boston: Pitman.

Poel, K. G. van der (1981), Programmatuur: Maken of kopen [To make or to buy software]. *Informatie* [Information], **23**, 545–550.

Poeth, G. G. J. H. (1980), *Technology assessment en economische rationaliteit* [...and economic rationality]. Delft: Interuniversitair Instituut Bedrijfskunde.

Porter, L. W., Lawler, III, E. E., Hackman, J. R. (1975), *Behavior in organizations*. New York: McGraw-Hill.

PROject control and DOcumentation STAndards (PRODOSTA) (1977). Eindhoven: Philips/CSD-ISA.

Projectgroep Techniek, Organisatie, Arbeidsmarkt (1980), *Techniek, organisatie, arbeidsmarkt* [Technology, organization, labour market]. National Programme for the Study of the Labour Market, Publication no. 6.

Rajkovič, V. (1980), Development of an information system in a self-management environment. In: Lucas, H. C., Land, F. F., Lincoln, T., Supper, K. (Eds.), *The information systems environment*. Amsterdam: North-Holland.

Rathenau, G. (1980), *Rapport van de adviesgroep 'Maatschappelijke gevolgen van de micro-electronica'* [Report on 'Societal consequences of micro-electronics']. The Hague: Staatsuitgeverij.

Rodenburg, K. J. (1982), Opleidingsplanning. [Planning of education]. In: Verhallen (1982c).

Roe, R. A. (1982), *Kwaliteit van arbeid en het onderzoek van arbeid en gevolgen* [The quality of work and the study of work and consequences].Delft: University of Technology.

Roeleveld, C. L. G. (1981), PARAET: Projekt Aanpak RAET [Project Approach RAET]. *Informatie* [Information], **23**, 608–615.

Sääksjärvi, M. (1980), Framework for participative systems long range planning. In: Lucas, H. C., Land, F. F., Lincoln, T., Supper, K. (Eds.), *The information systems environment*. Amsterdam: North-Holland.

Schaff, A. (1979), *Conferentie 'Social-economic problems and potentials of the applications of micro-electronics at work'*, Zandvoort.

Shneiderman, B. (1980), *Software psychology: Human factors in computer and information systems*. Cambridge (Mass.): Winthrop.

Sitter, L. U. de (1981), *Op weg naar nieuwe fabrieken en kantoren* [Towards new factories and offices]. Deventer: Kluwer.

SER = Sociaal Economische Raad [Social Economic Council].

SER (1968), Rapport over de automatisering [Report on automation].

SER (1982), Rapport werkgelegenheidseffecten micro-electronica [Report on the effects of micro-electronics on employment].

SER (1983), Ontwerp-rapport arbeidsmarktverkenning [Draft report reconnoitring the labour market].

Sorge, A., Hartmann, G., Warner, M., Nicholas, I. (1982), *Mikroelektronik und Arbeit in der Industrie*. Frankfurt/New York: Campus Verlag.

SOFI (Soziologisches Forschungsinstitut Göttingen) (1981), *Industrieroboter: Bedingungen und soziale Folgen des Einsatzes neuer Technologien in der Automobilproduktion*. Frankfurt/New York, Campus Verlag.

Starbuck, W. H. (1965), Organizational growth and development. In: March, J. G. (Ed.), *Handbook of organizations*. Chicago: Rand McNally.

Tissen, R. J. (1981), Personeelsbeleid en automatisering [Personnel policy and automation]. *Intermediair*, 17, no. 3.

Tissen, R. J., Zanders, H. L. G. (1982), Begripsbepaling: wat is automatisering? [What is understood by automation?]. In: Verhallen (1982c).

Verhallen, H. J. G. (1982a), Automatisering als gestuurd proces [Automation as a planned process]. In: Verhallen, (1982c).

Verhallen, H. J. G. (1982b), Wat is er te doen en voor wie? [What is there to do and for whom?]. In: Verhallen (1982c).

Verhallen, H. J. G. (Ed.), (1982c), *Automatisering, de sociale dimensie* [Automation, the social dimension]. Alphen a/d Rijn: Samsom.

Verkerk, J. (1981), *De chip en haar consequenties voor de arbeidsverhoudingen* [The chip and its consequences for industrial relations]. Rotterdam: Erasmus University.

Vossenaar, C. (1983), *Automatisering en de rol van de gebruikers* [Automation and the role of its users]. Amsterdam: Free University.

Vroom, V. H., Yetton, P. W. (1973), *Leadership and decision making*. Pittsburgh: Pittsburgh University Press.

Weenen, B. van (1980), *Computer, arbeid en organisatie* [Computer, work and organization]. Alphen a/d Rijn: Samsom.

Wegwijzer voor de organisatie van de automatisering [Guidelines for the organization of automation] (1981), Ijmuiden: Hoogovens-Estel.

Wentink, A. A. (1981a), *Gevolgen van kantoorautomatisering voor de organisatie, management en arbeid* [Consequences of office automation for organization, management and work]. Waalre: Dataplus Benelux B.V.

Wentink, A. A. (1981b), *Kantoorautomatisering en de gevolgen voor de kwaliteit van de arbeid* [Office automation and its consequences for the quality of work]. Conference on 'Automation, administration and ergonomics'. Eindhoven: NVE.

Winkelhage, F., Marock, J. (1980), Problems of consensus design in cooperative information system design projects. In: Lucas, H. C., Land, F. F., Lincoln, T., Supper, K. (Eds.), *The information systems environment*. Amsterdam: North-Holland.

Woodward, J. (1975), *Industrial organization: Theory and practice*. London: Oxford University Press.

Zanders, H. (1982), *Automatisering en kwaliteit van arbeid* [Automation and the quality of work]. The Hague: VIFKA.

Part 5

The interaction between organization and environment

Handbook of Work and Organizational Psychology
Edited by P. J. D. Drenth, H. Thierry, P. J. Willems and C. J. de Wolff
© 1984, John Wiley & Sons, Ltd.

Introduction

Pieter J. D. Drenth

This last part of the Handbook contains a series of contributions on subjects that are not usually found in handbooks on W/O psychology. Early Industrial Psychology, but later Work- and Organizational Psychology too, used to be confined to what happened within organizations; only on rare occasions was any attention paid to the relationships between organization and external environment. This seems to us an unjustified restriction of the domain. The boundaries of the system in which interesting interactions between individual people and/or groups take place and to which W/O psychologists should turn their attention in research, do not coincide with the factory gate or the hospital's revolving door. Much is happening beyond these boundaries that influences events within organizations and in which they are directly involved. The organization itself as well as its various departments, groups, or even individuals are in continuous communication with what goes on beyond the gates.

In this Handbook, an increasing number of levels was distinguished with regard to the system within whose framework the processes and interactions are studied. Part 2 was concerned with the interaction between a person and his task, part 3 with the interaction between a person and the groups of which he or she is part, and part 4 with the interaction between person or group and organization. This fifth and last part in fact continues this line and is concerned with the interaction between organizations and their environment. It did not seem opportune, however, to retain the division into A- and B-parts. The distinction between fundamental concepts and processes on the one hand and applications on the other turned out not to be a very fruitful basis for structuring the present part. So the distinction was dropped, the chapters here covering those different aspects or dimensions of the organization's environment with which it has some relation or other.

The first chapter focuses on the organization as part of a network of organizations and discusses the various models that made it possible to study such a network. In the same way as departments and divisions form a network within an organization, within which various forms of cooperation and competition, dependence and independence, complementarity and overlap occur, this pattern is found also at a supra-organizational level in situations involving other organizations. An analysis of the rules of the game and of the strategies and forms of cooperation, depending, of course, on the nature and objective of the network of which an organization is part, may widen the perspective from which organizations and behaviour in organizations are to be studied.

The second chapter, too, views an organization or firm as part of a societal system. For a long time, purely economic models and variables—covering especially the cost of wages, capital costs, the price of raw materials—were used to assess the quality of this societal system. Since the sixties, and particularly since the seventies, more attention has been paid also to immaterial aspects and social developments. This required these aspects to be made measurable in a quantitative way, which goal is pursued in the so-called 'social indicators' movement. The framework of thought on social indicators puts the work organization in a societal context. A major part of these social indicators concerns the rate of employment and the quality of the work. Thus, not only the availability of work is involved, but also its quality and the workers' satisfaction with the tasks and working conditions. Such notions have always been important research topics for W/O psychology.

The contribution from architectural psychology focuses on the physical environment of the organization: the organization's coat, as it were. Architectural psychology is an essential chapter in environmental psychology, in which the interaction of man and (built) environment are more closely examined. Clearly, one can quite correctly speak of interaction. The built environment does make an impact on man and his behaviour. Conversely, man structures, changes, and builds, wherever possible, his own environment. This is not exclusively a matter of individual-psychological interaction; a group- and social-psychological analysis of this interaction, too, offers worthwhile perspectives. Such an analysis provides concepts like privacy, personal space, territorial behaviour, and crowding with an interesting content.

The domain of industrial relations has traditionally attracted little attention from W/O psychology. It is first and foremost the province of organizational sociology, as it concerns social processes at meso- and even macro-levels. It is, however, difficult to see how organizational-psychological phenomena and developments—such as participative leadership, representative participation, work consultation, and shop steward systems—can be at all understood without their being considered in relation to the more general societal processes in the area of industrial relations. In this case too, it is true that the interrelations do not stop at the factory gate: their lines are continued to trade unions and trade associations, to employers' associations, to the government and its formal and legal provisions, in short: to the whole interplay of forces among employers' and employees' associations and the government. Thus, a discussion of these industrial relations—particularly if viewed in the light of present macro-economic developments—appears indispensable if one is to understand the 'industrial relations' within organizations. One can, then, not really raise the objection that a discussion of such phenomena at certain points exceeds the field of psychology as such. Relevant societal phenomena do not cluster according to the lines demarcating the scientific disciplines.

The fifth chapter focuses on phenomena and processes in another dimension of the external environment: traffic and mobility. If W/O psychology were to confine itself exclusively to phenomena and processes within work organizations, traffic psychology, being oriented towards a much broader social system, would not in the first place belong to this field. But the fact that traffic psychology faces numerous problems that are closely related to W/O psychology justifies the inclusion of this field of attention. One could think of problems such as appraisal and selection, training and education, task and criterion analysis or ergonomic optimalization of traffic environment. There are also points of affinity in the analysis of (causes of) accidents and accident prevention, of the traffic system—including the motives for taking part in it—, of means and objectives or the choice of the most adequate behaviour, and so on. The chapter on traffic and mobility presents a survey of psychological approaches to such problems and it shows how, on certain points, there are distinct overlaps with the field of classical W/O psychology.

Finally, the last chapter proceeds from the premise that an organization is subject to influences from the cultural environment; the study of organizations from this viewpoint may be an interesting and enriching approach. Cultures can vary greatly and it is interesting to see to what extent and in what form these cultural environments leave their stamp on organizations or on the behaviour of an organization's members. Thus, organizational psychology is put in a cross-cultural perspective. By means of international and cross-cultural comparisons, taking so to speak the world as a natural laboratory and national and cultural differences as independent variables, organizational psychology may acquire important insights with regard to the generalizability or culture-specificity of organizational behaviour and characteristics as identified in the research.

We have attempted, in this last part of the Handbook, to protect W/O psychology from the dangers of isolation: spatial isolation if only those phenomena were studied that occur 'within the gates', social isolation in the case of insufficient recognition of the fact that events and processes within an organization are part of a larger complex of societal phenomena and processes, and national or cultural isolation which could mean having too little insight into the culture dependency of one's findings and which could lead to unwarranted generalizations to another cultural context.

Handbook of Work and Organizational Psychology
Edited by P. J. D. Drenth, H. Thierry, P. J. Willems and C. J. de Wolff
© 1984, John Wiley & Sons, Ltd.

5.1. Interorganizational relations and networks

Maarten R. van Gils

1. INTRODUCTION

For the last two decades, there has been an ever-increasing interest in the subject of organization and environment. Partly owing to the influence of studies by, *among others*, Woodward (1965), Burns and Stalker (1961), Lawrence and Lorsch (1969), there has been a break-through in closed-system thinking, so characteristic of the classical doctrine of management and the so-called 'human-relations' approaches.

In closed-system thinking the environment of an organization is often looked upon as a given fact or as a predictable force that influences the organization. The goals of the organizations are considered to be known and the technology is regarded as fully understood; there are also means available to support the organization in its functioning. The underlying premise of closed-system thinking is that it is possible to design an organization on the basis of a rational balancing process.

The above-mentioned studies have contributed greatly to the break-through in closed-system thinking. This has led to a flood of research and publications in which, in some way or other, the interplay between organization and environment takes up a central position.

The field of organization-environment theories is characterized by a great heterogeneousness in approach and by conceptual confusion. In this contribution, an attempt will be made to describe a number of the main schools of thought. For this, the following classification will be used as a starting-point.

Contingency approaches (2.1)—Here, the central points are the influence of the environment on the structuring of organizations and the explanation of the differences in structure between organizations.

Interorganizational approaches (2.2)—These can be divided into two categories:

—Interorganizational field (2.2.1): the object of analysis is a set or field of strategically interdependent organizations. It is not the individual organization that takes up a central position but the totality of organizations which are part of this set.

—Interorganizational networks (2.2.2): an interorganizational network is a form of co-operation between two or more organizations, directed towards the realization of goals which each organization separately could achieve only at greater expense, or not at all. In such a case, a network can act as an organizational unity, and can make decisions as such.—Examples of networks are hospital associations, the (Dutch) Academic Council,[1] the Socio-Economic Council, cartels, umbrella organizations in the field of social welfare, public health, and education. A network is concerned with a set of partly dependent and partly independent organizations, which have partly conflicting and partly corresponding interests, and which arrive at forms of collective decision-making and collective activities.

In the analysis of an interorganizational field as well as of an interorganizational network, structure and behaviour are central concepts. How does the structure of an interorganizational field or network develop? To what extent does this structure influence the behaviour of each individual organization and *vice versa*? What patterns of conduct do the organizations exhibit to influence the dependence of other organizations? What is, in such a case, the effect on the efficiency and effectiveness of a network?

The differences between these two interorganizational approaches, field analysis and network analysis, are, especially from a theoretical point of view, not great. In both approaches, frequent use is made of the theory of exchange and of the power dependence theory. The central question in network analysis is how co-operation is set up, how organizations arrive at collective action. Field analysis is primarily directed towards the forms of interaction of mutually dependent organizations.

The point of view of the contingency approaches differs from that of the interorganizational approaches in that, in the former case, the emphasis is on the explanation of the differences in structure between organizations, while the individual organization and not the entire field or network is the object of analysis.

Particularly the problem of interorganizational networks has received much

---

[1] The Academic Council is a national advisory body in which all Dutch universities are represented.

attention in The Netherlands. This interest is nourished partly by the necessity, felt by the national government, to reorganize complex fields that consist of a large number of organizations and to make visible the interactions between these organizations. Examples of this can be found in the fields of industrial politics, public health and welfare work, educational and cultural policy. The interorganizational problem also plays a part, particularly for the national government, in dealing with new developments in which a large number of organizations are involved.

It is a characteristic of these developments that the problems which arise here can manifest themselves at different levels, namely the macro-level the meso-level and the micro-level. The macro-level is concerned with the problems of policy fields, which i.a. find expression in government policy. At this level, the problems are greatly influenced by normative and political accents. The meso-level is concerned with systems of organizations that, in some way or other, are connected with each other (questions of co-ordination and attuning exchange, joint activities between organizations, joint strategy). The micro-level, finally, is concerned with the individual organizations themselves (size, growth, strategy, structure, dependence position, relations to the meso-level and the macro-level; de Bakker and Kruyt, 1980, p. 417). Examples of complex reorganizations in this field are the reorganization of the civil service, the reorganization of municipal territories, the reorganization of national umbrella organizations in social welfare work, the regionalization of public health, the restructuring of branches of industry, the reorganization of the organizational system of social security.

As was already said before, characteristic of these projects is the large number of organizations involved, the interaction between macro-level, meso-level and micro-level, the tension between co-operation and the preservation of autonomy, the lack of unequivocal goals, as well as the lack of a powerful directing body. The initiation of projects in this field is often based on dissatisfaction with the functioning of these systems and on the notion that in a number of social sectors the developments ought to proceed more systematically. It is notable that the national government in particular, under strong political pressure, often plays an initiating part in this.

Problems in this field make high demands on researchers and consultants. De Bakker and Kruyt (1980), who have collaborated in investigating the functioning of the national welfare organizations as part of the reorganization of private initiative in this field, are of the opinion that for these problem fields the set of tools of the management consultant or the researcher are not sufficient. In their opinion, the tools now available are based particularly on the individual organization and not on systems of interdependent organizations.

Furthermore, they hold the view that an adequate approach to this problem requires a careful analysis before recommendations can be made and a change strategy can be pointed out. This last conclusion seems fairly self-evident, but must above all be seen against the background of the fact that it applies to systems of comparatively autonomous organizations which have aims that are certainly not unequivocal (de Bakker and Kruyt, 1980).

Intraorganizational relations and interorganizational relations differ from each other only in degree. Two differences in emphasis can be mentioned.

a) The intraorganizational relations are for an important part created consciously (hierarchy) and are tied up in rules and procedures. The interorganizational relations, on the other hand, have a more organic character and are very much determined by the need for interaction of the individual organizations and by their position of power.

b) The intraorganizational relations are partly visible (organization scheme, rules, procedures, etc.). The structure of the interorganizational level is often scarcely defined, if at all, unless a clear and recognizable pattern of interaction has developed in the course of time.

In the following sections, the schools of thought mentioned earlier will be discussed in detail. Special attention will be paid to a few prevailing theoretical approaches. Subsequently, the theme of interorganizational relations will be considered from the point of view of the organization consultant, especially with regard to the change aspects. Since chapter 4.3 of this handbook deals extensively with the so-called contingency approaches, they will be considered only very briefly in this contribution.

2. ENVIRONMENT THEORIES

2.1. The contingency perspective

In this perspective, the environment is looked upon as an external constraining phenomenon for the organization. The contingency approach is based on the following two questions:

a) which situational factors explain the differences between organization structures;

b) what is the effect of situational factors and organization structures on the behaviour of the members of the organization and on the efficiency of the organization (Kieser and Kubicek, 1978).

Figure 1 represents the basic model of the contingency approach (Kieser and Kubicek, 1978, p. 112). The model's underlying assumptions will not be pursued further here. It is important, however, that this approach is strongly dominated by an 'information perspective'. It is the uncertainties in regard to the information about the environment that are employed as the most important factors in explaining the organization structure. Environmental characteristics are defined in abstract terms, such as stable versus dynamic, simple versus complex benevolent versus hostile, homogeneous versus heterogeneous (Mintzberg, 1979, p. 268). Consequently, this leads to hypotheses, such as:

a) a stable, simple and homogeneous environment induces a bureaucratic organization structure;

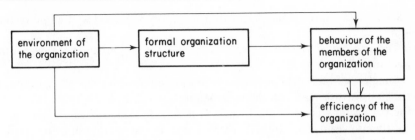

Figure 1. Model of the contingency approach. (Kieser and Kubicek, 1978).

b) hostility in the environment of an organization causes the organization to centralize its structure temporarily;

c) the more uncertain the environment is (less predictable) the longer the time orientation of the members of the organization will take.

The contingency approach suggests an 'objective' approach of the environment. Furthermore, it is suggested that there is a cause-effect relation: given certain environmental characteristics, the structure of the organization must be such and such.

Mintzberg (1979) and others have pointed out, however, that the management's perception of certain contingency factors is a crucial factor, and that this perception can determine what the structure will look like (figure 2). Furthermore, there are also other factors involved in the question of how managers react to environmental characteristics. One could think of the efficiency criteria employed, of the possible prospects of influencing the environment and of other aims, besides efficiency, that are pursued. Child (1972) speaks, in this connection, of the 'organizational choice' the management has at its disposal.

In view of the above, it is not surprising that the contingency approach has received much criticism. Attention may be drawn to, inter alia, the following:

a) its theory-deficient character;

b) its neglect of historical and social aspects;

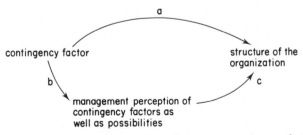

Figure 2. Interaction between contingency factors, perception, and structure (Mintzberg, 1979).

c) its neglect of interfering personality and power variables in organization design;

d) its being directed towards the environment of the present and not towards the environment of the future;

e) its neglect of multiple contingencies that conflict with each other in regard to the impact they make on the organization;

f) the passive character of the theory. It is suggested that organizations must adapt themselves to the external environment. However, organizations have a multitude of strategies at their disposal, with which this environment can be actively influenced (Breuer, 1982, p. 356).

Detailed criticism of this contingency approach may be found in, among others, Schreyögg (1978). Partly owing to the influence of this criticism, a kind of research has gradually developed that approaches the environment as a set of other organizations with which exchange relations ought to be maintained. The environment relevant to an organization ('focal organization') consists of other organizations with which the organization has a relation of direct or indirect dependency. Evan (1976) in particular has elaborated the concepts 'focal organization' and 'organizational set'.

Evan's points of departure are aimed at explaining intra-organizational characteristics. From this point of view, his aim differs only in degree from the above-mentioned contingency perspective. Yet, Evan presents a more concrete approach to the concept of environment by taking the environment as a set of organizations with certain structural and cultural properties.

It is through this that in the analysis of the environment the emphasis comes to lie on the actual interaction processes of the focal organization with other organizations. Attention will be paid to, inter alia, the nature of the interactions (information, resources), the intensity, frequency and reciprocity of the inter-actions, as well as the extent to which the aims of the focal organization correspond to the aims of other organizations that are part of the set. By starting from the notion that the environment consists of other organizations, more attention has come to be paid to the question of how an organization can influence the dependence relations that result from this, and to the question of what strategies are used to this end. This has broadened the contingency perspective considerably. It includes the question of how organizations adapt themselves to their external environment as well as the question of how organization try to influence and, if possible, to control this environment.

2.2. Interorganizational approaches

2.2.1 THE ENVIRONMENT AS AN INTERORGANIZATIONAL FIELD

In the preceding section, the emphasis was on the relation of the individual organization to its environment.

When 'interorganizational field' (Warren, 1967) is mentioned here, the matter at issue is not so much the behaviour of a single organization but rather the totality of interdependent organizations that maintain interactions with each other as part of their involvement in one and the same problem situation. An interorganizational field is, therefore, not a 'corporate body' of itself and cannot act as an organization (Aldrich, 1978, p. 281).

The analysis of an interorganizational field is based on the assumption that the totality of interdependent organizations in the field promotes or impedes, in a systematic way, the activities of individual organizations; activities that cannot be reduced to the properties of the individual organizations (Godfroy, 1981, p. 110).

Aldrich states that the analysis of an interorganizational field is directed towards the interactions of all the organizations in a particular set (Aldrich, 1979, p. 281).

Pennings (1981) confines himself to those particular relations between organizations that result from, what he calls, the strategic interdependences between organizations. By this he means the relations between organizations that compete with each other for scarce resources. On the whole, this analysis of an interorganizational field focusses on the following three points:
a) the structure of the field of strategically interdependent organizations;
b) the interorganizational patterns of conduct within a field;
c) the significance of strategic interdependence for the effectiveness and structure of organizations.

Pennings distinguishes three forms of interdependence, interdependence being defined as the organization's behaviour which has an effect on other organizations (Pennings, 1981, p. 434). The three forms are:
a) Horizontal interdependence;
b) vertical interdependence;
c) symbiotic interdependence.

Horizontal interdependence occurs if organizations compete with each other in order to obtain similar resources, or to sell similar products or services. Interorganizational behaviour in a field, dominated by horizontal interdependence, can be described as a function of the market structure in that field. This market structure, however, will often show oligopolistic characteristics. A perfect oligopoly refers to a market in which a restricted number of organizations compete with each other in the selling of homogeneous products or services and in which the activities of one organization influence the activities of the other organizations. The number of sellers and buyers in such a field is sufficiently small to enable them to react to each other.

Hospitals, for instance, or welfare organizations in a city or region may find themselves, in relation to each other, to be in a oligopolistic situation. Each organization within this oligopoly tries to respond immediately to changes in the strategic behaviour of the other organizations, but is at the same time aware of the fact that its own behaviour is being observed in the same measure by the other organizations. In The Netherlands, especially in the state-subsidized 'non-profit' sectors (health education, social welfare, culture), there is a considerable increase in market-oriented behaviour. During the period of virtually unrestricted economic growth, the strategic effects of horizontal dependence were hardly a problem. For, there was no obvious scarcity of resources and organizations could function in a way that left them comparatively independent of each other. Meanwhile, the scarcity of resources has increased to such an extent that a (often not open) battle of competition is fought also between organizations. This requires new forms of strategic behaviour from these organizations.

However, one of the problems here is that, in the past, strategic behaviour, directed towards the external environment, was hardly necessary, whereas now many organizations do not know how and with what instruments they should, in a strategic sense, approach the new environmental uncertainties. In many respects, these organizations lack a strategic orientation towards changing external circumstances.

Vertical interdependence exists between organizations that are in the various stages of a chain of production. This refers to a sequential relation. Examples are the relation between community and residential health organizations and the relations between educational organizations: from primary education up to and including higher education.

Many of these vertical relations have a formal and institutionalized character. However, there is more room for strategic behaviour in situations in which the rules of these sequential transactions are reconsidered. Government policy directed towards strengthening community health care at the expense of residential health organizations, is an example there of, especially because it affects existing relative power. The same applies to national umbrella organizations in social welfare work in their relation to executive welfare work.

The present decentralization policy of the national government leads to shifts in the interorganizational field of welfare. It affects existing positions and forces organizations into forms of strategic behaviour in order to control the uncertainties that arise from this.

Symbiotic interdependence, finally, exists between organizations that complement each other in a functional sense in rendering services to third parties. What benefits one organization also benefits the other.

To attain their aims organizations are dependent on external resources. When these sources are scarce, the main question for the organization is how to avoid or exploit the dependences (and therefore uncertainties) that result from this situation.

Yuchtman and Seashore (1967) express this accurately in their definition of the concept 'organizational effectiveness'. By this they mean 'the ability of an organization to exploit its environment in obtaining resources, while at the same time maintaining an autonomous bargaining position'. The chief question in the literature on interorganizational relations is, above all, what strategies organizations use to deal with strategic interdependences.

In the literature published by behavioural scientists, the analysis of the dependence relations occurs under various names. Most authors build on the theory of exchange (Blau, 1964). Well-known variants of this are the 'resource-dependency' model (Aldrich, 1979; Emerson, 1962; Pfeffer and Salancik, 1978) and the 'political economy' model (Benson, 1975; Wamsley and Zald, 1976).

In essence, the various theoretical approaches proceed from the following assumptions:

1) Organizations are confronted with situations characterized by resources that are of restricted (scarce) availability.

2) Organizations are dependent on other organizations for the acquisition of these resources. To acquire these resources organizations enter into exchange relations with other organizations in the field. The purpose of this is, among other things, to reduce the uncertainties and to make the availability of scarce resources more predictable.

3) The acquisition of scarce resources from outside the organization reduces the anatomy of an organization.

4) Organizations aim at preserving their autonomy and try to find that particular form of interaction which involves the lowest cost in terms of loss of autonomy and power.

5) Organizations develop strategies that are directed towards the prevention of unpredictable behaviour of other organizations, towards the prediction of other organizations' behaviour, as well as towards the interception of the effects of the behaviour of other organizations (Thompson, 1967; Pfeffer and Salancik, 1978).

The above propositions strongly emphasize the exchange character of the interactions between organizations in an interorganizational field. An exchange relation consists of a series of transactions that relate to the exchange of resources between two or more actors and which are of use to all parties involved. To put it differently, the exchange is arranged only if the parties expect that the relations will yield more than would have been the case if they had not been established. Exchange in an interorganizational field may be described as the situation in which each actor in the field offers the possibility of transactions to at least one other actor in the set (Cook, 1977, p. 70).

It is not surprising, therefore, that many studies in the field of interorganizational relations are directed particularly towards the analysis of exchange relations and the processes of power linked to them, as they occur between organizations, as well as towards the strategies that result from these relations and processes. 'Power and dependence' and 'Power and exchange' are concepts that are often used in these studies. Benson (1975) speaks of the importance of a 'political economy' perspective in the analysis of interorganizational relations. With this, he refers to the interrelations between a political (structure of rules) and an economic system (system for the production and exchange of goods and services).

In this view, the concept 'political' contains two components, namely (a) values and (b) power structure. Furthermore, this concept refers to aspects such as legitimacy, recognition of domains, and the aims of the dominant coalition in the respective organizations.

'Economic system' refers to the combination of factors of production, the division of labour, the allocation of resources to organizational tasks, and the maximization of efficiency (Wamsley and Zald, 1976, p. 15). The 'political economy model' represents the way in which organizations, by means of their political system, try to secure their domain and the way in which they try to intercept the influences that threaten to disturb the primary processes.

The development of theories in the fields of power and dependence has been greatly influenced by the work of, among others, Emerson (1962) and Blau (1964). Nearly every author who wants to explain the significance and influence of relative power in the analysis of interorganizational relations falls back on these authors. Emerson's starting-point is that power is based on somebody else's dependence. In an interorganizational analysis, power and dependence are always characteristics of the relation between two or more organizations.

The dependence that comes to exist with regard to an exchange relation is characterized by two dimensions: (a) the comparative importance of the resources that can be obtained and (b) the extent to which these resources are substitutable (figure 3).

Naturally, the importance of the resource should be determined in relation to the total number of resources that an organization needs to carry out its activities. Therefore, the power of an organization in an exchange relation will increase when the range of resources or the number of different resources that the organization possesses increases. For, then, the organization is able to operate in a multitude of markets', so that the vulnerability resulting from a lack of alternatives can be spread.

The second dimension in figure 3 is the degree of replaceability of resources. It implies that an organization which finds itself in a dependence position has alternative possibilities at its disposal. Giving up a resource may also be included among these possibilities. Two basic types of resource take up, a central position

importance of resource

		high	low
substitutability of resource	high	low dependence	independence
	low	high dependence	low dependence

Figure 3. Degree of dependence in exchange relations (source: Scharpf, 1978).

A's dependence on B

		high	low
B's dependence on A	high	mutual dependence	unilateral dependence
	low	unilateral dependence	mutual independence

Figure 4. Three types of dependence relation (source: Scharpf, 1978).

in the political economy of interorganizational fields: money and authority or recognition (Benson, 1975). The concept of authority refers to the right and the responsibility to exercise tasks and offices of a particular kind. It indicates that the domain covered is experienced as legitimate or that claims to certain tasks and offices are recognized as legitimate. In, for example, the practice of open-heart surgery or starting a new field of study, etc., legitimacy plays an important part, because it is by being legitimized that access is gained to the scarce funds and thus to resources in general.

Both dimensions, 'importance of the resource' as well as 'replaceability of the resource, are combined by Scharpf (1978), resulting in three types of dependence relation (figure 4).

From figure 4 two questions can be deduced that are important to the analysis and the advisory work in regard to interorganizational relations. Starting from these three conditions, one can ask oneself:
a) What strategies can be used by the organizations under these three conditions?
b) What possibilities of intervention are the most suitable under a certain condition?

Especially the demand for possibilities of intervention in a particular type of dependence relation has, strangely enough, hardly been investigated, although there is a need for better insight into this matter. In The Netherlands, Mastenbroek among others has concerned himself with this question (Mastenbroek, 1982).

Mutual dependence

When two or more organizations are mutually dependent, this implies that the resources acquired are important to all parties and that none of the parties has alternative possibilities at its immediate disposal. It is, therefore, attractive for the parties involved to continue the exchange relation and to prevent disturbances in this relation as much as possible. How this is done will for a large part be determined by the extent to which the goal orientations of the most important actors correspond to each other. If this is the case, there is a firm enough basis for co-operation. However, if the goal orientations run counter to each other, then the parties will try to bend the symmetry in dependence relations in the direction of a one-sided dependence relation, i.e., they will try to get the power to have their own view accepted or they will try to become independent. This symmetry in dependence relations is an important prerequisite for interorganizational co-operation. It prevents parties from manoeuvring each other into unattractive situations by means of threats. For, the parties can make reprisals against each other.

In a situation in which the preservation of this reciprocity is in the interest of the properties involved, rules will be developed to protect the relation and to prevent that one of the parties will manoeuvre itself into a strong position. The more the goal orientations of the actors diverge, the more important will be the position of these rules in the relation. The rules are particularly significant in regard to making the behaviour of the other party predictable. It may be expected that the rules get a more detailed character and also a broader range, as the importance of maintaining the relation is greater, the interests are more divergent, and confidence in the other(s) diminishes. The rules delimit the zone in which influence strategies are felt to be legitimate. Activities outside this zone are not accepted.

These rules can, at the same time, lead to a power vacuum. The parties keep each other in balance and as soon as a change is experienced as a threat to this balance of power, the parties will appeal to these rules. Then, the laboriously constructed rules may, through lack of flexibility, be an impediment to effective decision making. The rules themselves are no longer appropriate to the altered circumstances, but are still used to prevent disturbances in the balance of power.

The experiments in the National Productivity Centre may serve as an illustration. The 'National Productivity Centre' is a committee of the Socio-Economic Council (SEC). The Socio-Economic council is a tripartite network in which employers' organizations, trade unions, and independent members, nominated by the Crown, participate. Besides representatives of the government, employers and employees are the most important participants in this project. Within the setting of the productivity council, these parties—and the employers' and trade-unions' representatives in particular—need each other for new initiatives and, in this case, to get the series of experiments off the ground. The parties also have diverging interests as regards the results of these experiments. It is, as it were, a matter of a 'policy arena', in which parties participate with partly compatible, partly incompatible objectives. Furthermore, the parties are also partly independent and partly interdependent (network of actors). In such situations, it is very difficult to establish the rules needed to regulate the relations between the participants so as to guarantee the mutual dependence. For a considerable period of time, the rules themselves will be the stakes in a negotiation game. In the case of the 'Experiments in workers' participation', it took almost three years of laborious negotiating before the steering committee of the employers' and trade-unions' representatives published its plans, indicating the criteria the experiments have to meet. In fact, these plans, at the same time, established the most important rules to be used in the relation between employers' representatives and trade-union representatives.

The possibility unfavourable effect of these rules on the results of the projects themselves is of secondary importance in this discussion. In a different context, Segers points out that research should on no account be harmful to the good relations between the SEC partners (Segers, 1982, p. 69). In other words, the aim of maintaining a situation of mutual dependence receives priority and, therefore, become an aim to which research is made subordinate.

Mutual independence

In this situation, the dependence relation plays a subordinate part or is understood as such. The exchange relationship is not very important to the parties involved, or alternative resources are easily available. Interaction between organizations takes place only if it is felt to be mutually satisfactory. However, this is not to say that the activities of the one will not affect the other. When B1 and B2 supply the same products or render the same services to organization A, this may have consequences for B1 as well as for B2, e.g., an increase in the services rendered by B1 to A at the same time leads to a decrease in the services rendered by B2 to A (competitive relation; negative coupling).

When B1 and B2 each render different services to A, this may lead to a situation in which an increase in A's demand for B1's services could cause an increase in the demand for the (other) services rendered by B2. In such a case, we can speak of a symbiotic relation (Aldrich, 1979, p. 266) or of 'positive coupling' (Cook, 1977, p. 71).

Unilateral dependence

Unilateral dependence involves asymmetrical interests and therefore an asymmetry of process. Organizations in a dependence position will, when the dependence becomes too oppressive, try to bend the dependence towards a situation of mutual independence or mutual dependence. Scharpf (1978) points out that the conditions for co-ordination of policy between organizations seem to be best in situations of unilateral dependence, because the presence of a power centre seems to guarantee this. On the other hand, the weaker party will be motivated to change the nature of the relation in such a way that the dependence decreases, either in the direction of mutual dependence or in the direction of mutual independence.

The dimensions of dependence are not constant, but are, as Bacharach and Lawler state, under continuous tacit or explicit negotiation (Bacharach and Lawler, 1980, p. 154).

A power-dependence model as used here draws attention to the tactics and strategies involved in the interorganizational power struggle. What actions are taken to change the power relationship, what are the existing strategic options for changing the dependence relations between organizations, how do organizations attune their behaviour to each other?

In the literature on power, a number of schemes have been developed to classify the tactics used by actors to change a specific power-dependence relationship. (Bacharach and Lawler, 1980; Blau, 1964; Thompson, 1967; Aldrich, 1979). Bacharach and Lawler recognize four basic types of tactic:

a) Improving the quality of the bargainer's alternative. This tactic aims at avoiding to become subservient to elements in the task-environment by means of maintaining or seeking alternatives.

b) Decreasing the quality of the opponent's alternatives. This tactic aims at increasing the opponent's dependence on the bargainer. Coalition formation and the control of alternative and strategic resources are elements of this tactic.

c) Decreasing the value of what the opponent gives to the bargainer. This tactic tries to re-evaluate the outcomes obtained in the relationship. It may be that the less powerful party in a unilateral dependence more or less withdraws from the situation, or threatens to do so. This party then not only decreases the significance of the opponent's influence tactics, but may also be able to create conditions for a more realistic exchange.

d) Increasing the extent to which the opponent values what the bargainer provides. This tactic involves the ability of the bargainer to manipulate the opponent's key values or to manipulate the opponent's perception of the bargainer. This serves to increase the opponent's dependence on the bargainer (Bacharach and Lawler, 1980, p. 156).

Thompson states that organizations competing for support seek prestige, this being the 'cheapest' way to acquire power (Thompson, 1967, p. 33). Aldrich draws attention to the significance of being able to control innovation and the formation of ideologies.

In a more general sense, Benson identifies four strategies actors develop to effect changes in 'network-relations'. These four strategies are defined by the means employed to effect network changes.

a) *Cooperative strategies.* As dependence introduces constraints and contingencies, organizations will avoid having to anticipate environmental action by arranging negotiated environments. By using cooperation to gain power with respect to elements of the task environment, the organization, as Thompson states, 'must demonstrate its capacity to reduce uncertainty for that element and must make a commitment to exchange that capacity' (Thompson, 1967, p. 34). Because of these restrictions, the conditions for success of co-operative strategies are rather limited. The strategy will work as long as the parties involved have something that is of value to the other parties.

b) *Disruptive strategies.* These strategies involve, according to Benson, the purposive conduct of activities which threaten the resource-generating capacities of other actors. There are several ways in which this can be accomplished:

1. domain violations; the invasion of the domain of another organization by the construction of programmes clearly falling within the domain of that other organization;

2. fund diversion; the acquisition of funds that would otherwise have gone to other organizations involved;

3. programme circumvention; activities which interfere with the programme effectiveness of others and thereby diminish their capacity to compete for funds and authority.

c) *Manipulative strategies.* The purposeful alteration of environmental constraints affecting the flow of resources.

d) *Authoritative strategies.* This type of strategy involves the authoritative argument or realignment of network relations. Relations are then specified by an authoritative body that may also control the flow of resources.

From the above it appears that, in theory, organizations may have a wide range of possibilities at their disposal, either to reduce the power of other organizations in an exchange relation or to increase their control over other organizations.

An elaboration of the kinds of strategy organizations use to cope with the uncertainties resulting from dependence, can be found in Pennings (1981), Pfeffer and Salancik (1978), Thompson (1967), and others. Included among these strategies are horizontal as well as vertical integration, joint ventures, product differentiation, overlapping memberships (co-optation, 'inter-locking director-ates'), industrial espionage, etc.

Examples of the application of the theory of exchange or of the power-dependence theories in The Netherlands are, among others, Können (1980, public health, merger problems), De Zwaan (1980, public health), Lammers (1981, labour relations), Berg (1978, municipalities), Godfroy (1981, public health, social welfare work), Van Gils (1981, universities), Breuer (1982, consultancy), Wassenberg (1980, industry).

Above, attention was paid particularly to investigations that emphasize exchange and power dependence relations. However, fewer examples are to be found of analyses in which a 'process approach' is used (Hartman, 1982). In the process approach, attempts are made to characterize the field of inter-organizational relations as, what Hartman calls, 'a unit in time'. The approach is particularly concerned with a closer analysis of the process of growth of such a field. In the Dutch literature on this subject, two investigations that start from the process approach attract attention: an investigation into the closing-off of the Oosterschelde (ten Dam and Hillenius, 1982) and an investigation into co-operation processes between hospitals (*M & O*, 1980).

The 'Oosterschelde project'

The closing-off of the Oosterschelde-estuary is a complex affair in which a great number of organizations, institutions, and action groups were (and some still are) involved. It is a field of interacting organizations that, because of a varying composition and a highly dynamic structure, can hardly be defined. These organizations maintain relations with each other as part of their involvement in the same problem situation (Hartman, 1982). In the analysis, the following lines of approach are used:

a) *The analysis of the field itself*

a1) *The pattern of structural relations.* The structural analysis is concerned with establishing the aspects and qualities of the participants and pays attention to elements such as interests, ideology, prestige, availability of financial means, etc. The degree of institutionalization of the separate participants, the availability of professional managers, negotiations, etc. are of importance also. Ten Dam en Hillenius (1982) consider it particularly important to trace the existing ideological correspondences and differences and to examine whether and to what extent memberships overlap.

This structural analysis could provide information about the question of whether the participants have similar, complementary, or conflicting interests, and about the question of whether the perspective from which the participants work has a temporary, a permanent, or a greatly varying character.

a2) *The pattern of mutual interactions.* This line of approach is concerned with the way in which the interactions between the participants take place. Why are the contacts made? What is the nature of the contacts: bilateral or multilateral, formal or informal, who has taken the initiative, etc.? What is the function of the contacts (what do the parties involved wish to achieve)? What is the frequency, intensity, emotionality, urgency, involvement, importance of the contacts? To what extent are the interactions of the system's participants influenced by interactions within the organizations themselves and by interactions that take place via publicity.

a3) *Historical analysis of the developing and shifting relations.* Central to this analysis is, inter alia, the internal political history of the network, the formation and break-down of coalitions, the disappearance and appearance of participants, the extent to which subsystems of organizations are accessible, and the shift in influence positions within the network.

This first analysis leads to, among other things, the conclusion that the events surrounding the Oosterschelde are an example of a clash between, on the one hand, the formal executive network, i.e. the Delta Service, the Ministry of Public Works, the national political bodies, the administrative, more bureaucratic fractions of the national and local networks and, on the other hand, the informal network of action groups supplemented by sections of political and administrative subsystems. The formal network, with its procedures, hierarchy, positions, and planning, is confronted with spontaneous coalitions of interest groups, that not only use different arguments but also different influence techniques during the negotiations.

Ten Dam and Hillenius conclude that the informal network cannot be bureaucratically controlled, as a result of which there is uncertainty and powerlessness in the formal network. 'The formal system will then tend to formalize and integrate the informal system.' Thus, in connection with the Oosterschelde, tripartite negotiations have started in which also interest groups, if only the officially organized ones, take part (ten Dam and Hillenius, 1982, p. 37).

This formalization has the function of making these groups more easily accesssible and of making them fit in with the repertoire of the official bodies. Especially with regard to the interest groups that were formed spontaneously, it appears from this investigation that such a 'strategy of control' is less effective.

The ties within the informal network are formed by the common dissatisfaction with the functioning of the official bodies. The informal network operates on the basis of these ties and to a lesser extent on the basis of the allocation of tasks and the definition of responsibilities and qualifications. The network derives its force particularly from the spontaneous, the accidental, and the incidental.

2.2.2. INTERORGANIZATIONAL NETWORK

In the above, the emphasis was mainly on the interaction processes and dependence relations among strategically interdependent organizations. In this section, a more specialized treatment of this subject will be given, in that it will deal with the way in which organizations arrive at co-operation, concerted decision making, and action.

In the literature, there are various names for the way in which organizations arrive at co-operation. Warren speaks of 'concerted decision making', understanding this as '... a process in which the individual decisions of two or more units are made on a more inclusive systematic level which includes these units' (Warren, 1972, p. 21). This collective decision making is based on the consideration that concentration of forces produces a more satisfactory result than does individual decision making.

Van de Ven (1975) uses the concept 'interorganizational collectivity' (IC). The principal participants in an IC are two or more organizations. 'These organizations join together as an action system to attain a specific objective by performing a set or series of goal-directed behaviour acts ... as a collectivity, this role structure is such that the IC can act as a unit and make decisions to attain the goal of the system'.

In The Netherlands, Godfroy and Wassenberg among others use the concept 'network', by which is meant 'a concrete action system that is created and changed to regulate the interdependence problems between the organized groups involved' (Godfroy, 1981, p. 114).

Wassenberg uses the term 'network' in the sense of 'the objective structure of mutual relations (the structure) and the pattern of an existing understanding between dependent organizations (the culture)' (Wassenberg, 1980, p. 22). In itself, this description does not contain a form of collective action. However, Wassenberg continues by explicitly placing the networks that come to exist between organizations at, what he calls, the 'meso-level'.

Thus, these organizational networks are placed inbetween the micro-framework of individual organizations and the macro-perspective of external dependences. The meso-level has its own planning and control principles that cannot be reduced to an addition sum of individual organization strategies. Nor do these planning principles result from an order that has come or been imposed from outside, and to which organizations should adapt themselves.

At the meso-level, lasting forms of negotiation come about between organizations. From these forms, schemes develop for strategies at the meso-level instead of at the micro-level. Industry may serve as an example. Branches of industry, in De Feyter's (1981) opinion, develop from organizations that often share the same past and have a comparable technology. A branch of industry can function as a communicative framework that makes it possible to discuss future situations.

A similar approach to networks is presented by Rieken in his analysis of industrial and social security policy (Rieken, 1982). In his analysis, Rieken mentions the necessity to pay attention to the resolution of problems at a meso-organizational level. This implies attuning and co-ordination among mutually dependent organizations.

Network analysis is directed towards the questions of the why and the when of networks (Wassenberg, 1980, p. 17). The why-question refers to the conditions influencing the development of networks. The when-question refers to the strategic behaviour of networks. When do organizations use the possibility to form networks? Under what conditions are organizations willing to make decisions collectively? What are the circumstances that stimulate or impede interaction? What is the part that external coercion plays in this? In view of the above, it is characteristic of networks that, in spite of conflicting aims, interdependent organizations try to attune their activities to each other, seek to develop a joint strategy, and try to realize corresponding goals. A network strategy is a form of collective action directed towards control and change of the relevant environment.

An important, but certainly not the only condition for such a network is that organizations are confronted with uncertainties or changes with which they cannot deal independently, or that high costs are attached to the preservation of independence.

The realization of a network is often a conflictive event. For, the strategy of a network is the resultant of a process of balancing the partly compatible aims of organizations against the partly incompatible aims of organizations, which are partly interdependent and partly autonomous. The intensity of the conflict will depend partly on how the organizations weigh the advantages to be expected from co-operation in the future. Particularly in the public sector, these advantages cannot be indicated in quantitative terms. Moreover, in the public sector some quantities, e.g. increase of turnover, speeding-up of the production process, better service, sometimes play a minor part in the balancing process, in comparison with values such as preservation of an identity of one's own, preservation extension of one's own field of work.

It seems that, in the public sector, organizations decide upon network formation only when its positive results are perceptible within a short time. In general, it appears that co-operation is more easily established at the operational level of organizations than at the strategic level. Examples of co-operation at the operational level are communal bloodbanks for hospitals, communal training for nurses, a communal administrative system for the payment of salaries, etc.

Co-operation at the strategic level, which is concerned with the nature and level of the goals and objectives of organizations and with how these objectives can be realized, is considerably more problematic. Co-operation at this level is often experienced as a loss of autonomy and therefore as a decrease in scope for emphasizing one's own identity (as expressed in, inter alia, the working methods used). When, in addition, the results of co-operation do not appear to have concrete results, there will be relatively little willingness to combine forces.

In this respect, the private sector differs considerably from the public sector (the subsidized quatenary sector is considered to belong to this sector). In the private sector, there is a greater tendency towards co-operation at the strategic level, although it may take longer before its results become clear. Market considerations, and thus profit considerations, play a decisive part here.

Luscuere distinguishes three broad 'co-operation ideologies': the power ideology, the survival ideology and the symbiotic ideology (Luscuere, 1978, p. 52 f.).

The *power ideology* starts from the formation of a 'mass' confronting a recognizable and apparent opponent, for example, to change intended policies of other groups, such as the government.

In Dutch society, this co-operation, based on the formation of power, has acquired an institutional character. The national umbrella organizations in the fields of welfare and public health and co-operations of organizations active in the same field, for instance, derive their legitimacy to a great extent from their systematically exerting influence on government policy. This has proved to be so effective that it is also referred to as the 'fifth power', the iron ring surrounding the government.

The *survival ideology* starts from the notion that co-operation is a reaction to an uncertain environment, which forms a threat to the continuation of the organization.

In many instances, a co-operation based on the survival ideology is not established until there is much pressure from the environment. Particularly the national government and, increasingly so as a result of developments in decentralization, local authorities too use this pressure in the allocation of public funds. Funds for certain facilities, new tasks, investments, etc. will not be released until certain requirements are met. The co-operation established under such pressure will be comparatively unstable, since the exchange relation between organizations is of a forced character and the participating organizations will do their utmost to restore the former situation. For the participating organizations, the negotiations preceding this enforced co-operation are directed particularly towards the maximal preservation of the status quo.

Co-operation geared to a survival ideology can easily develop into a power ideology. If co-operation is enforced by means of sanctions and such, this can stimulate the development of a power block, because it is important to the participating organizations to oppose the authorities as much as possible. An enforced network will then be 'confronted' with contra-networks. Insofar as this phenomenon occurs, it seems likely that the authorities are worse off than they were before, certainly as regards the controllability of complex policy fields.

The *symbiotic ideology* starts from co-operation that is supposed to strengthen the position of each partner. This involves forms of co-operation in which there is an exchange relation that is evidently experienced as profitable. Joint ventures are an example of this.

When networks have already been formed, this does not necessarily imply that a structure of strategic possibilities has been established at the same time. An example of a network that does not sufficiently succeed in developing its own strategy is the Academic Council. As yet, Dutch universities have, at the administrative level, barely managed to effectively co-ordinate decision making among themselves or to develop rules for advancing the realization of collective decision-making and, with that, the realization of a joint strategy. In the present situation, the Academic Council cannot sufficiently use its potential power capacity, because, for the time being, its members expect more from their own individual actions. The result is, however, that, in the absence of a strong network, the power to shape and to control higher education has to increasingly passed into the hands of the Ministry of Education (van Gils, 1981).

In the literature on networks, the meso-level plays an important part. The meso-level is the starting-point from which organizations, by means of collective action, attempt to control and change the relevant environment.

The connections among organizations crystallize at a supra-organizational (meso-) level and can become independent (network formation) in such a way that micro-development and macro-development can be influenced (Wassenberg, 1981; Hartman, 1980, p. 370).

Edelman Bos (1980b) emphasizes the meso-level in connection with the increasing importance of network development. In his opinion, the social problems that result from scarcity and overcapacity both in the private and in the public sector will bring about a change in the relation between the macro-level (government) and the micro-level of individual organizations. Edelman Bos expects that neither the macro-level nor the micro-level of the individual organizations is able to solve these problems of scarcity and overcapacity. The chances are more favourable for the meso-level, especially when at this level network formation occurs in the fields of industrial policy, educational policy, cultural policy, welfare and public health policy.

It is not clear who, in Edelman Bos' opinion, should stimulate these developments of the meso-level. Is this the responsibility of the government or does Edelman Bos proceed from the idea that the initiative should come from voluntarily established networks, possibly in co-operation with the government? Till now, there are few indications that the impulses to network formation given by the government are successful. The decentralization policy in the fields of welfare and public health is stagnant. The reorganization of the system of social security, industrial policy, as well as the reorganization of the civil service itself are also examples of stagnating policies.

3. NETWORK CONSULTANCY AND NETWORK DEVELOPMENT

Very little has been written about network consultancy and network development. Given the complexity of the field of forces within a network, the relevant question is whether network consultancy requires a kind of approach from the advisors that is different from the approach used in the more 'traditional' organization consultancy work.

There is not a single reason for defending the need for a separate network consultant. A lot of the problems with which a consultant is confronted in an organization are identical to the problems involved in network consultancy. Moreover, the characteristics of an organization differ from those of an interorganizational network only in degree. Some organizations, e.g. universities, closely resemble networks. They are what Weick calls 'loosely coupled systems' (Weick, 1976).

Some networks have developed into firmly structured units and could, because of the way in which their decision making is organized and the way in which they exchange information, be looked upon as organizational units.

Yet, there is enough reason for dealing with the problems of network consultancy separately. Several aspects may be pointed out that need special attention.

a) In network consulting, the consultant is confronted with several clients. Moreover, it is sometimes not sufficiently clear to what extent these clients represent the network. An additional point is that the clients cannot always function as a power centre with hierarchical authority over the network. This is why, certainly in the initial phase, it is difficult for the consultant to find out to whom and in what way his activities are important, and how strong the clients' position is within the network itself. The latter is particularly important if the consultant has to work with people other than the clients themselves.

b) That some networks do not have an explicit hierarchical structure does not imply that relative power does not exist in a network. On the contrary, in a network

interactions take place almost continuously on the basis of the positions of power the organizations assume. A network has a 'political' character that is partly determined, on the one hand, by the attempt to preserve the autonomy of the organizations that participate in the network, and, on the other, by the atttempt to exert the greatest possible influence on the results the network is supposed to produce. The lack of a formal and legitimized power centre, which is a characteristic of many networks, strengthens their political character. The implication of this for the consultant is that he has to work in a political context, in which the fight over the distribution of scarce resources takes a central place.
c) The essence of network development is the realization of co-operation. In a network, co-operation is often a conflictive event. A conflict's intensity will increase in proportion to whether the co-operation has to be established under external pressure, the goals of the individual organizations diverge greatly, or the organizations display a heterogeneity from a cultural point of view.

The consultant, who has been asked to make a contribution in establishing co-operation, is usually not familiar with the turbulent phase that preceded the formulation of the assignment. The formulation of the assignment itself may already be a political compromise. The implication of this for the consultant is that he must be able to create enough room for putting its formulation up for discussion at a later date.
d) Organizations (or parts of organizations) operate in a multitude of networks. The implication of this for the consultant is that right from the start he must ask himself whether he is dealing with the proper network. A commission from an association of hospitals, for instance, suggests that the network consists of the associated hospitals. However, consulting physicians connected to these hospitals are also united in so-called interstaff boards and thus form their own network either inside or outside the framework of the association.
e) Network consulting should lead to certain results. The results may not be acceptable to all participants. If the process leads to results that affect the interests of one or more organizations, this may induce some of the participants to question the legitimacy of the consultant. In such a case, the consultant is reproached for not having taken a sufficiently independent position and for having supported the interests of certain organizations. Then, the power process within the network revolves around the position of the consultant by affecting his position, attempts are made to block and change developments that have already been set in motion. Because of this, the consultant is extremely vulnerable. It is important for the consultant to be accepted by all parties. This could lead to a limitation of the part he plays in the network.

Now, what are the elements that are important in network consulting? Hartman in particular, in connection with an analysis of the co-operation between a number of hospitals, has tried to answer this question (Hartman, 1980). He distinguishes three strategic positions for the consultant:
a) consulting from an overall-perspective;

b) consulting from a party-perspective;
c) consulting from a combined perspective at meso-level.

Advising from an overall-perspective starts from the assumption that the parties in the network as a whole have a uniform and common interest with regard to the environment; an interest that emphasizes the necessity for forms of co-operation. The consultant is expected to make a contribution towards the realization of this co-operation which is considered necessary. He will also be expected to make the 'why' of the co-operation manifest again and again.

Especially in places in the network where, from conflicting motives, attempts are made to find possibilities of co-operation, it is important to the advisor that he keeps the parties together by offering perspectives and workable models.

In addition to being an expert, the advisor is also a discussion leader in that he sees to it that the participants concentrate on that which unites them and that they do not develop a preoccupation with that which separates them. Within the framework of an overall-perspective, Hartman mentions, inter alia, the following consultancy activities (Hartman, 1980, p. 373):

—Establishing the 'objective' goals and motives in order to arrive at co-ordination in a network context.
—Designing a structure of control for the network, organizationally and legally.
—Designing a phased plan (procedure of decision-making) to attain such a structure.
—Assisting in filling in and manning management structures for the network.

From an overall-perspective, choice alternatives are put forth. The consultant assumes that the parties call on his expertise. He must offer something, especially because the parties themselves do not succeed in developing an acceptable solution. Naturally, it is important that the models to be offered by the advisor fit in with what is acceptable to the participants.

The advisor will have to link his expertise to insights into the political dynamics of the network. In cases in which he lacks knowledge of the internal and external political context of the network, co-operation with an internal consultant can be attractive.

The risk involved in the overall-perspective is that it abstracts away from the political reality of the network. For, a network consists of numerous parties with partly conflicting and partly corresponding interests. Hartman is of the opinion that the consultant will also be concerned with the *how-question*, i.e., how within a network such a decision power is attained that the designed structure and arrangements can also be realized (Hartman, 1980, p. 374).

Because of this, the consultant, besides working from the overall-perspective, may also opt for strategies that can be looked upon as belonging to the *party-perspective*. In addition to being concerned with the network in its totality, the consultant also pays attention to the individual organizations. The following are examples of activities undertaken from a party-perspective:
—working on internal conditions within an individual organization;

—helping to outline the party's own interests in relation to the interorganizational context;

—translating developments in the environment into organizational consequences.

Working from the party-perspective, some consultants tend to confront parties with the images and expectations that they have of each other. They expect this to lead to an increase in the parties' understanding for each other and to the removal of stereotyped prejudices so that a suitable climate for bargaining will be created leading in the direction of problem solving.

Such a strategy, which can be very useful in an intraorganizational context, seems to be less useful with regard to networks, because the parties in an interorganizational network are chiefly intent not on improving their relation with each other, but on structuring the co-operation with each other, preserving a maximal degree of autonomy for each individual participant. Especially in this paradoxical situation, there is a need for someone who will make the perspective of the co-operation evident, who will see to it that matters remain open to discussion, and who will give guidance by offering alternatives.

The use of strategies based on a party-perspective carries risks. The consultant may loose his independence and be absorbed by the multitude of partial and often conflicting interests present in the network. Furthermore, the consultant creates the expectation that he will meet the partial interests of the individual organizations, whereas this is virtually impossible.

The party-perspective proceeds from the acknowledgement that negotiations between the parties are of primary importance and that the parties have diverging interests. Nevertheless, it is questionable whether the advisor must choose a position in which he is mainly concerned with the 'how-question' in relation to decisions that have to be taken. If he chooses a position in which giving advice to one or more parties also stands in the forefront, it seems unwise, if not impossible, to advise from an overall-perspective as well.

However, Hartman feels that this is possible and calls it the combined perspective at the meso-level; an approach, therefore, in which the overall-perspective as well as the party-perspective appear to full advantage. Hartman recognizes, however, that it is virtually impossible to achieve this in any field of diverging interests. He points out that when the completion of such a consultancy-project takes a long time, it is almost inevitable that the consultant 'degenerates and becomes the umpteenth political factor in an already complex political field of forces' (Hartman, 1980, p. 376).

The picture presented above is hardly encouraging for consultants. Working from an overall-perspective seems to offer insufficient guarantee for the development of an effective decision-making system in the network. The approach is somewhat detached and directed especially towards spreading information that is developed by the participants in the network themselves or that is considered necessary by the consultant. The consultant pays comparatively little attention to the aspects connected with process developments in the network. He directs his energies towards structuring the decision making-around concrete subjects.

The party-perspective offers better prospects of improving the internal conditions for decision making. In the case of the party-perspective, however, the consultant is in danger of getting entangled in the multitude of partial interests and diverging expectations, which puts him in an extremely vulnerable position. When this happens, the consultant himself becomes a factor that contributes to the uncontrollability of the decision-making processes. The study of Hartman *et al.* of co-operation between hospitals gives an illustrative example of an unsuccessful consultancy project from the party-perspective (*M & O* 1980).

The combination of both approaches (the meso-perspective) is attractive on paper but seems to be difficult to realize in practice, not in the least because in a network the power usually does not move from the top downwards but from the bottom upwards. Moreover, experience in consulting from a meso-perspective has scarcely been committed to paper.

For the present, it seems justifiable to conclude that most consultants who deal with network problems start from the overall-perspective. It is not only the least vulnerable approach but it also seems to meet the expectations of the participants themselves most clearly: the participants expect that the consultant will try to get the participants together and keep them together as regards matters of content (Edelman Bos, 1980b, p. 222).

EPILOGUE

It may be expected that in the near future the interest in the problems involved in interorganizational relations and co-operation will increase. This interest is nourished by the problems that are connected with the control of complex, greatly differentiated policy fields.

The emphasis on control comes primarily from the government. But, partly because of the rapidly diminishing financial means, the organizations themselves, too, recognize, though on different grounds, the necessity of interorganizational co-ordination and co-operation.

There is as yet comparatively little knowledge and experience of the problems involved in interorganizational relations and co-operation, and the literature of this field is fragmentary and hardly systematic.

It seems necessary that the administrative sciences pay more attention to the problems involved in interorganizational co-operation. With regard to this, co-operation with those in the fields of economics and political science certainly appears desirable.

REFERENCES

Aldrich, H. E. (1976), Resource dependence and interorganizational relations: Relations between local employment service offices and social services sector organizations. *Administration and Society*, **8**, 419–453.

Aldrich, H. E. (1979), *Organizations and environments*. New York: Prentice Hall.

Aldrich, H. E., Midlin, S. (1978), Uncertainty and dependence: Two perspectives on environment. In: L. Karpik (Ed.), *Organization and environment*. London: Sage, 149–171.

Bacharach, S. B., Lawler, E. J. (1980), *Power and politics in organizations*. San Francisco: Jossey Bass.

Bakker, K. P. E. de, Kruyt, G. J. (1980), Versnipperd of synoptisch [Dispersed or synoptic]. *M & O*, **34**, 413–427.

Benson, J. K. (1975), The interorganizational network as a political economy. *Administrative Science Quarterly*, **20**, 229–249.

Berg, E. L. (1978), Omgangsvormen tussen organisaties [Manners among organizations]. *Bestuurswetenschappen* [Public Administration], **5**, 371–391.

Blau, P. (1964), *Exchange and power in social life*. New York: Wiley.

Boje, D. M., Whetten, D. A. (1981), Effects of organizational strategies and contextual constraints on centrality and attributions of influence in interorganizational networks. *Administrative Science Quarterly*, **26**, 378–395.

Breuer, F. (1978), De interorganisationele analyse [The interorganizational analysis]. *M & O*, **32**, 32–45.

Breuer, F. (1982), *De organisatie-adviseur en zijn netwerk* [The organization consultant and his network]. Alphen a/d Rijn: Samsom.

Burns, T., Stalker, G. M. (1966), *The management of innovation*. London: Tavistock.

Child, J. (1972), Organizational structure, environment and performances: The role of strategic choice. *Sociology*, **6**, 1–22.

Commissie Hoofdstructuur Rijksdienst [Government Commission Main Structure] (1980), *Elk kent de laan die derwaarts gaat* [Each knows the lane that leads there]. Report 3. The Hague: Ministry of the Interior.

Cook, K. S. (1977), Exchange and power in networks of interorganizational relations. In: Benson, J. K. (Ed.), *Organizational analysis: Critique and innovations*. London: Sage, 64–85.

Dam, H. W. ten, Hillenius, H. (1982), De afsluiting van de Oosterschelde: Een netwerkanalyse [The closing of the Oosterschelde: A network analysis]. *M & O*, **36**, 7–40.

Doorn, J. A. A. van (1980), Overvraging van beleid. Over oorzaken en gevolgen van groeiende bestuurlijke onmacht [Asking too much of policy. On the causes and effects of growing administrative impotence]. *Beleid en Maatschapij* [Policy and Society], **2**, 39–49.

Edelman Bos, J. B. M. (1980a), Netwerken: Functies en functioneren in strategisch perspectief [Networks: Functions and functioning in a strategic perspective]. In: Wassenberg (1980).

Edelman Bos, J. B. M. (1980b), In breder verband . . . over netweken en netwerkadvisering [In a wider context . . . on networks and network consultancy]. *M & O*, **34**, 215–224.

Emerson, R. M. (1962), Power-dependence relations. *American Sociological Review*, **27**, 31–40.

Evan, W. M. (1976), *Organization theory: Structures, systems and environments*. New York: Wiley.

Feyter, C. A. de (1980), Industriële herstructurering in het netwerkperspectief [Industrial re-structuring from the perspective of networks]. In: Wassenberg (1980).

Gils, M. R. van (1978), De organisatie van organisaties: Aspecten van interorganisationele samenwerking [The organization of organizations: Aspects of interorganizational cooperation]. *M & O*, **32**, 9–31.

Gils, M. R. van (1981), *Universitaire planning: Cui bono* [University planning: Cui bono]. Address at the start of the academic year 1981. University of Groningen.

Godfroy, A. (1981), *Netwerken van organisaties* [Networks of organization]. The Hague: Vuga.

Hartman, C. (1980), Netwerkadvisering: Strategische positie als invalshoek [Network consultancy: Strategic position as the angle]. *M & O*, **34**, 367–383.

Hartman, C. (1982), Het netwerk Oosterschelde. I: Inleiding: Naar een procesanalyse van netwerken [Network Oosterschelde. I: Introduction: Towards a process analysis of networks]. *M & O*, **36**, 7–12.

Heyink, W. G. (1980), Het verschijnsel 'fusiefuik' [The phenomenon of 'the trap of mergers']. *M & O*, **34**, 322–331.

Hickson, D. J., Hining, C. R., Lee, C. A., Schneck, R. E., Pennings, J. M. (1971), A strategic contingencies theory of intra-organizational power. *Administrative Science Quarterly*, **16**, 216–229.

Hinings, C. R. D., Hickson, J., Pennings, J. M., Schneck, R. E. (1974), Structural conditions of intra-organizational power. *Administrative Science Quarterly*, **19**, 22–24.

Idenburg, Ph. A. (1981), Het bestuurbaarheidsvraagstuk als probleem [The issue of public administration as problem]. *M & O*, **35**, 437–450.

Kieser, A., Kubicek, H. (1978), *Organisationstheorien I & II*. Stuttgart: Kohlhamme*!*.

Klonglan, G., Warren, R. D., Winkelpleck, J. M., Paulsen, St. K. (1976), Interorganizational measurement in the social services sector: Differences by hierarchical level. *Administrative Science Quarterly*, **21**, 674–699.

Können, E. (1980), Interorganisationele samenwerking in het licht van ruiltheorie en coalitietheorie [Interorganizational cooperation in the ligh of exchange theory and coalition theory]. In: Greve, W. B. de, Vrakking, W. J. (Eds.), *Strategie van samenwerking tussen organisaties in welzijns- en gezondheidswerk* [Strategy of cooperation in organizations in social welfare, mental-health care and medicare]. Lochem: De Tijdstroom.

Lammers, C. (1981), Arbeidsverhoudingen vanuit een interorganisationeel perspectief [Industrial relations from an interorganizational perspective]. *M & O*, **35**, 207–226.

Lawrence, P. R., Lorsch, J. W. (1977), *Organization and environment*. Irwin.

Levine, S., White, P. E. (1961), Exchange as a conceptual framework for the study of interorganizational relationships. *Administrative Science Quarterly*, **5**, 117–130.

Luscuere, C. (1978), Samenwerking tussen organisaties: Ideologieën en dilema's [Cooperation between organizations: Ideologies and dilemmas]. *M & O*, **32**, 49–61.

Marrett, C. B. (1971/72), On the specification of interorganizational dimensions. *Sociology and Social Research*, **56**, 77–92.

Mastenbroek, W. F. G. (1982), *Conflict hantering en organisatie-ontwikkeling* [Conflict management and organization development]. Alphen a/d Rijn: Samsom.

Mintzberg, H. (1979), *The structuring of organizations*. New York: Prentice Hall.

M & O, (1980), Samenwerkingsprocessen tussen ziekenhuizen [Cooperation processes between hospitals]. *M & O*, **34**, 270–279.

M & O, Tijdschrift voor Organisatiekunde en Sociaal Beleid [Journal of Organization Science and Social Policy].

Nationale Raad voor Maatschappelijk Welzijn [National Council of Social Welfare] (1980), *Kiezels of tegels: Kiezen of delen in welzijnsland* [Take it or leave it in welfare land]. The Hague.

Pennings, J. M. (1981), Strategically interdependent organizations. In: Nyström, P., Starbuck, W. H. (Eds.), *Handbook of organizational design*. London: Oxford University Press, 433–456.

Perrow, Ch. (1970), *Organizational analysis: A sociological view*. Belmont: Wadsworth.

Pfeffer, J., Salancik, G. R. (1978), *The external control of organizations: A resource dependence perspective*. London: Harper and Row.

Rieken, J., Baayens, J. (1982), *Effectiviteit en bestuur van organisaties* [Effectiveness and management of organizations]. The Hague: Vuga.

Scharpf, F. W. (1978), Interorganizational policy studies: Issues, concepts and perspectives. In: Hanf, K., Scharph, F. W. (Eds.), *Interorganizational policy making. Limits to coordination and central control.* London: Sage, 345–371.

Schreyögg, R. (1978), *Umwelt, Technologie und Organisationsstruktur: Eine Analyse desKontingenztheoretischen Ansatzes.* Bern: Haupt.

Segers, J. H. G. (1982), Het para-universitaire onderzoek: Positie en knelpunten [Para-academic research: Position and problems]. In: Segers, J. H. G., Snellen, I. Th. M., Vissers, A. C. M., *Stagnatie en bezinning: Sociaal-wetenschappelijk onderzoek en beleid in de jaren '80* [Stagnation and reflection: Research and policy in the social sciences in the 80s]. Tilburg: Inst. of Labour Issues, 57–79.

Thompson, J. D. (1976), *Organizations in action.* New York: McGraw Hill.

Ven, A. H. v. d., Emmett, D. C., Koenig, Jr., R. (1975), Frameworks for interorganizational analysis. In: Negandhi, A. R. (Ed.), *Interorganization theory.* Ohio: State University, 19–39.

Wamsley, G. H., Zald, M. N. (1976), *The political economy of organizations: A critique and approach to the study of public administration.* Bloomington: Indiana University Press.

Warren, R. L. (1967), The interorganizational field as a focus for investigation. *Administrative Science Quarterly,* **12**, 396–419.

Warren, R. L. (1972), The concerting of decisions as a variable in organizational inter-action. In: Tuite, M. (Ed.), *Interorganizational decisionmaking.* Chicago: Aldine.

Wassenberg, A. (Ed.) (1980), *Netwerken: Organisatie en strategie* [Networks: Organization and strategy]. Assen: Boom.

Weick, K. E. (1976), Educational organizations as loosely coupled systems. *Administrative Science Quarterly,* **21**, 1–20.

Wetenschappelijke Raad voor het Regeringbeleid [Academic Council on Government Policy]. *Plaats en toekomst van de Nederlandse industrie* [Position and future of Dutch industry]. Report 18. The Hague: Staatsuitgeverij.

White, P. E., Levine, S., Vlasak, G. J. (1975), Exchange as a conceptual framework for understanding interorganizational relationships: Application to non-profit organizations. In: Negandhi, A. R. (Ed.). *Interorganization theory* Ohio: Kent State University, 167–182.

Woodward, J. (1965), *Industrial organization: Theory and practice.* London: Oxford University Press.

Yuchtman, E., Seashore, St. (1967), A system resource approach to organizational effectiveness. *American Sociological Review,* **32**, 891–903.

Zwaan, A. H. v. d. (1980), De ruiltheorie toegepast opsamenwerkingsvormen in de gezondheidszorg [The exchange theory applied to forms of cooperation in medicare]. In: Greve, W. B. de, Vrakking, W. J. (Eds.), *Strategie van samenwerking tussen organisaties in welzijns- en gezondheidswerk* [Strategy of cooperation in organizations in social welfare, mental-health care and medicare]. Lochem: De Tijdstroom, 52–76.

Handbook of Work and Organizational Psychology
Edited by P. J. D. Drenth, H. Thierry, P. J. Willems and C. J. de Wolff
© 1984, John Wiley & Sons, Ltd.

5.2. Social indicators

Harry Zanders

Social systems are complex systems, in which many participants try to realize various ideas or objectives by way of a varied number of means. When the system is limited in size and when the number of objectives and means remains restricted and rather stable as well, such a system can be surveyed. If a system becomes more voluminous and complex, however, it will be necessary that systematic information on the system's development become available. This holds for, for example, modern society. The number of objectives which is pursued in it is particularly large as well as the number of means with which persons or groups try to realize their objectives, and the means are often very changeable in present society. The consequence of this is that new information will have to become available continually on the situation in and the developments of the system.

However, what kind of information do we have to gather? From where and how do we have to obtain data that offer us a clear and reliable picture of the conditions and processes in society? From various scientific disciplines, these questions have been raised for a long time already. Especially in economics they have also been worked out in operational models (Fox, 1974). There the development of indicators and standards for economic quantities was started. Models drawn up which allowed the mutual relations between the quantities to be studied. Such models were developed for the first time in the thirties on the basis of the application of mathematics in economics. The rise of the computer, after World War II, made it possible to tackle and work out more complicated models.

Today, such economic models are generally applied at macro-level. In The

Netherlands this is done by, for example, the Central Planning Office (Centraal Plan Bureau). These models are, however, completely economic in nature, i.e. the factors that are implied in such a model all refer to economic quantities, such as wage costs, prices of raw materials and capital costs. Just because the economic models describe and analyze only a part of social reality, one has come to see the limitations of such an approach. Especially in the sixties and seventies, when attention began to shift increasingly from the emphasis on material to more immaterial aspects in social intercourse, the demand for information other than strictly economic strongly came to the fore. With the help of economic models and, on the basis of presuppositions, it could indeed be calculated to what degree national production was going to increase, but the meaning of this for non-economic quantities was a matter that was hardly or not mooted. Such information, however, is urgently needed in order to pursue a justified policy. Therefore it was necessary to start to develop standards, with which certain social developments in society could be registered. Such standards may be called *social indicators*. Those social indicators are used in the first place to describe a social system. The next step is to draw up models on the basis of these social indicators, models in which the *mutual relations* between the indicators are analyzed.

Social systems and society have been mentioned several times in this introductory text. From this terminology it may already be concluded that this contribution will emphasize the developments around social indicators at the macro-level. However, also at the meso-level there is an increasing demand for indicators that mainly refer to the immaterial output of organizations (Dierkes and Bauer, 1973). In this context a reference to the introduction of the concept of well-being in the new Dutch Working Environment Act ('Arbeidsomstandigheden-wet') seems appropriate. The process of socialization of organizations leads to having to account both internally and externally for the policy pursued and the strategies to be followed. For this, systematically gathered information is necessary that will have to rest on indicators, about which there is at least some consensus.

What should we understand by social indicators? This question is central in the first part of this contribution in which the contents and meanings that are attributed to social indicators in the literature are gone into. Next it will be considered from which backgrounds and at which point in time the interest for social indicators developed. Finally, several large international projects will be discussed that demonstrate the recent activities and possibilities of the construction of social indicators. Several brief remarks on a number of discussions about social indicators will conclude this chapter.

DESCRIPTIONS AND DEFINITIONS

Indicators are used to build a bridge from theory to empiricism on which we want to give our opinion via research. They play a role in the process of translating theoretical concepts into empirically observable phenomena; they are the operationalized variables of theoretical concepts (Boesjes-Hommes, 1973; Segers, 1975). A definition of social indicators is given in Bauer's standard-work: 'Social indicators (are) statistics, statistical series, and all other forms of evidence that enable us to assess where we stand and are going with respect to our values and goals, and to evaluate specific programs and determine their impact' (Bauer, 1966). From this very broad description three types of indicators can be distilled.

First of all, social indicators can be used for the *description* of systems and developments in it. We can also relate them to certain norms or standards for the *evaluation* of social phenomena. In the third place, the information that social indicators offer may be used to *predict possible* future events. The question whether an indicators is qualified as descriptive, evaluative or predictive depends on the way in which the indicator concerned is applied. An example will make this clear. When we take as an indicator the figure that indicates the officially registered labour reserve, this unemployment figure can be looked at in different ways. We can use it rather neutrally as a figure that describes the situation on the labour market. We may also contrast the figure with a certain standard, by which the indicator is evaluative in character. In the third place, we can make pronouncements on other social phenomena, as on, for example, psychosomatic complaints or on voting behaviour, via the unemployment rate given. This third predictive application in that case demands a theoretical framework that offers the basis for making connections between social phenomena.

Bauer's definition is only one from the multitude we find in literature. The most important common characteristic of all descriptions and definitions is that social indicators are looked upon as quantitative standards relating to socially relevant aspects of society. Further, it may be observed that the demands made on the qualification as social indicator may vary strongly. Especially Land (1971) has argued that the term 'social indicator' should not be equated with all the forms of statistical information in the social field. He proposes to award the qualification 'social indicator' when (a) the indicators concerned are part of a social system model, (b) when they can be gathered and analyzed at different points of time and can be included in time series, and (c) when they may be aggregated and desaggregated according to levels that the model requires. So Land's starting point is a model in which the social indicators have their place. From this it can be decided what informative value the social indicators qualified possess.

Land (1975) has presented his train of thought by way of a scheme, that is partly represented here (Figure 1). The schematic presentation is based on a distinction frequently found in the literature on social indicators, in which case one proceeds from the trilogy 'input-system-output'. In the diagram's left column, which refers to the input of the system, two types of indicators are distinguished which refer to factors that can be manipulated by the policy and to factors that are fixed data for the policy, respectively. A corresponding division is found in the last column of the diagram, in which the implementation is discussed.

A distinction is made between intended effects and non-intended or side-effects.

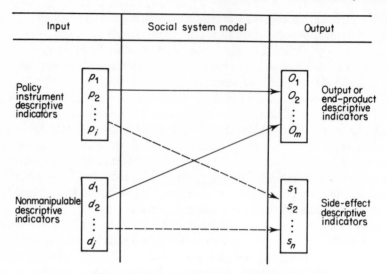

Figure 1. Relations between indicators.

Land points to the education process as an example. Input-data to be manipulated, which can be changed through the policy, may be: financial means, material equipment, manpower. Data that cannot be manipulated are, according to Land, for example, individual abilities, especially intelligence, and family situation. The results consciously selected and to be realized, the output, are in that case school achievement or study success. As examples of side-effects Land points to the occupational and income level that individuals may reach also by means of that education, to a way of life and to cultural orientation. The information on social processes in a certain field (e.g. education) may be structured with the help of this outline. But it also clearly appears that the distinctions made are relative and are determined in the first instance by the particular perspective on social processes. In many cases, things like occupational level and cultural orientation will certainly not be considered as side-effects of education, but rather as consciously chosen and intended end-results.

BACKGROUNDS AND DEVELOPMENTS

The need for information on a wide range of social phenomena and processes is the root of the social-indicator movement. Social indicators are the standards through which social phenomena and developments may be described and analyzed. The need to develop social indicators arose particularly in the sixties. Both in political circles and scientific quarters it was admitted more and more freely that too little information was available to come to planning and guiding social developments. To meet the need for information, new standards ought to be designed, in which not only the quantity but especially the quality of social developments could be expressed. As examples the fields of health and education may be mentioned. Not only the number of medical doctors or hospitals and not only the number of teachers and schools determine the quality of those sectors. Different criteria are necessary, with which the qualitative aspects can be recorded and analyzed. Especially the subjective appreciations of persons who get involved with certain provisions are relevant.

From the increasing number of activities concerning the registration of social developments the so-called 'social-indicator movement' originated in the sixties. Yet, the origin of the movement to trace and quantify social developments via indicators lies in an earlier period. Usually, the extensive 1933 report 'Recent Social Trends' of the Research Committee on Social Trends is considered to be its herald. This committee, formed in 1929 by order of president Hoover, had the task to study the social consequences of the economic crisis at that time and to establish national priorities. At the same time, an effort should be made to sketch an overall picture of the situation, rather than make a series of detailed studies. The emphasis on the aim to atain an overall picture of social developments was to remain a main characteristic of the social-indicator movement. A great part of the many themes discussed in the report of the committee, led by Mitchell and Ogburn, today are still themes for research (Report of the President's Research Committee on Social Trends, 1933). As examples may be mentioned: changing social attitudes and interests, the family and its functions, changing occupational patterns, women working outside the home, recreation and spare time, consumer behaviour, welfare activities, administration and society. This report laid the basis for the development of social indicators. Until about 1960, however, interest remained rather latent.

In the middle of the sixties, the trend was resumed again by Bauer (1966) with the publication of *Social Indicators*. Bauer did research by order of the National Aeronautic Space Administration (NASA) to trace the effects on American society of the rapid technological developments, especially of the space program. Such an approach, that is based on systematic and integrated research into the direct and indirect effects of the introduction of a new technology, is known nowadays as 'technology assessment' or effects-research. In this case, the study of possible side-effects of technological developments is emphasized. In his project Bauer speaks of 'second order consequences', i.e. consequences of certain technological innovations, without these consequences being directly intended or foreseen. An example may be the introduction of the automobile as a means of transport. Only later it appeared that this involves radical changes in, for example, the field of recreation, living environment (suburbanization), and even sexual values and norms. At this moment, 'technology assessment' is also given very much attention in The Netherlands. This can be ascribed especially to the rapidly increasing clamour for information on the possible effects that micro-electronics may come to have on our society (Rathenau, 1980).

A strong point of Bauer's project is that the question departed from was not restricted to the side-effects of technology. Together with Biderman and Gross, he made a broader program for measuring social developments and for relating them to social objectives. Illustrative of the lack of data is Biderman's contribution in which is was proved that for only half of the objectives formulated by the American government statistical data were available, especially in the field of cultural developments. Such a lack of data makes an evaluation of social developments hardly possible. There are, then, hardly any perspectives for a rational planning in the social field.

In 1966, the report of the presidential committee on *Technology, Automation and Economic Progress* was published in the U.S.A. In it a plea is made for, among other things, the development of a system of social accounts that was to give a more ample and balanced impression of the meaning of social and economic progress, also on the basis of a cost-benefit analysis. Such social accounts were designed analogous to the usual financial accounting systems. The wish to use social indicators got a strong impulse from political circles in 1967, when the so-called 'Full Opportunity and Social Accounting Act' was proposed at the initiative of the then senator Mondale and others. This would oblige the president to present a Social Report to the American Congress every year. Also in 1967, *Social Goals and Indicators for American Society* appeared, edited by Bertram Gross and containing several articles contributing to the discussion of social indicators.

In 1968 Sheldon and Moore published *Indicators of Social Change, Concepts and Measurements*, the first publication within the framework of the 'Monitoring of Social Change Project' of the Russell Sage Foundation. In this Publication emphasis was put on structural and institutional changes in fields like population development, spare time, the professional population. Next, *Toward a Social Report* was published in 1969 by the Department of Health, Education and Welfare. In this report, figures are presented only to a limited extent, because many necessary data were lacking. This study meant an important step in the development of a system of periodical social reports. Various social fields were scrutinized, and then what was known at that moment of the progress towards generally accepted objectives was examined. Health, social mobility, physical environment, income and povery, law and order, education, participation and alienation were discussed.

We cannot dwell here extensively on the contests of the publications and projects mentioned. The survey was meant to mention a number of starting points from the American history of social indicators. The most important conclusion we can draw from these publications up to the end of the sixties is that, clearly, a shift of accent took place in the perspective from which social phenomena and changes are approached. The primacy of economic and technical information on social developments was broken, because social factors too began to play a part in the information process.

At first this was still a derivative, 'second-order' role, but very soon an independent role was awarded to information on social factors. Seen from that perspective, measuring and evaluating social developments ought to get at least an equal role, along with the analyses of economic and technical developments. In the seventies, the activities around the development of measures and systems for registering and analyzing social developments have been carried on with vigour in the U.S.A. A limited selection from the literature published, furnished with a concise characterization follows.

1972: Leslie D. Wilcox and Ralph M. Brooks (Eds.), *Social Indicators and Social Monitoring; an Annotated Bibliography*. Besides a historical survey and a discussion of social indicators by E. Brooks, an annotated bibliography of more than 600 titles is presented.

1972: Angus Campbell and Philip E. Converse (Eds.), *The Human Meaning of Social Change*. This publication, like that of Sheldon and Moore, appears within the framework of the Russell Sage Foundation's Monitoring of Social Change Project. In this study a plea is made especially for the development of subjective indicators, i.e. indicators that proceed from personal appreciations and judgments.

1973: Executive Office of the President, Office of Management and Budget, *Social Indicators 1973*. The first American attempt to present an extensive collection of statistical data for the description of social conditions and developments in the United States. A large quantity of data is presented without comment.

1974: Karl A. Fox, *Social Indicators and Social Theory. Elements of an Operational System*. On the basis of concepts and starting points from different social sciences, such as psychology, sociology, economics and econometrics, it was attempted to construct operational models. E.g. Tinbergen's theory on economic policy is taken as a starting point in building quantifiable systems.

1975: Nestor E. Terlecky. *Improvement in the Quality of Life: Estimates of Possibilities in the United States, 1974–1983*. An attempt to develop a framework to determine the possibilities for the improvement of the quality of life in the United States. It was attempted to define explicitly national objectives and priorities, to determine the progress made towards the objectives and to determine the costs attached to the wish to come closer to the objectives set.

1975: Judith Innes de Neufville, *Social Indicators and Public Policy. Interactive processes of Design and Application*. Apart from an extensive survey of the development of the social-indicator movement and the origins of some indicators, e.g. the unemployment figure, De Neufville outlines the political meaning of social indicators and the relation between political decision-making processes and the availability of information.

1975: Kenneth C. Land and Seymour Spilerman (Eds.), *Social Indicator Models*.

In 14 articles, various strategies and applications of social indicators are demonstrated. The emphasis is on proving the inter-relations between social indicators, whereby the meaning of both replication studies and the design of longitudinal and dynamic strategies are indicated.

1976: U.S. Department of Commerce, Office of Federal Statistical Policy and Standards and Burea of the Census, *Social Indicators 1976*. After the 1973 report the second collection of statistical data on social conditions and social trends in the United States. No comment is added to the data.

1976: Frank M. Andrews and Stephen B. Whitney, *Social Indicators of Well Being: American Perceptions of their Life Quality*. Starting points for this study are subjective or perceptual indicators, by means of which the opinions and ideas of the Americans with regard to a large number of social developments are measured.

1976: Agnus Campbell, Philip Converse and Willard L. Rodgers, *The Quality of American Life; Perceptions, Evaluations and Satisfactions*. Just as with Andrews and Whitney, the emphasis is on the development of subjective indicators. The authors build on Campbell and Converse's work of 1972.

1978: Robert Quinn and Graham Staines, *The 1977 Quality of Employment Survey*. Institute for Social Research, Ann Arbor, Michigan. This is the third extensive ISR-survey in which, on the basis of a representative random sample of the American occupational population, data are presented on the characteristics and appreciation of labour. The first project was in 1969 (Quinn, 1971); the second in 1973 (Quinn and Shepard, 1974).

1978: Conrad Taeubner (Ed.), *America in the Seventies: Some Social Indicators*. In: *The Annals of the American Academy of Political and Social Science*, Vol. 435, January 1978. In this publication the text and comment can be found which is wanting in *Social Indicators 1976*. More than twenty authors give their opinion on the developments that can be distilled from the data of *Social Indicators 1976*.

1979: Kevin J. Gilmartin *et al.*, *Social Indicators: an Annotated Bibliography of Current Literature*. The bibliography includes 316 entries with sections on key historical works, state-of-the-art reviews, the theoretical and methodological approaches, analyzing and reporting social indicators.

1980: Robert J. Rossi and Kevin J. Gilmartin, *Handbook of Social Indicators: Sources, Characteristics and Analyses*.

1980: Alex C. Michalos, *North American Social Report: a Comparative Study of the Quality of Life in Canada and the U.S.A. from 1964 to 1974*. (Volumes 1 and 2

1980: Alexander Szalai and Frank M. Andrews (Eds.), *The Quality of Life, Comparative Studies*. This study consists largely of workshop papers presented in

1978 at the meeting of the International Sociological Association in Uppsala. The editors chaired the ISA symposium on 'comparative studies of life quality' and have assembled in this reader contributions from scholars from a dozen—mainly Western and East-European—countries.

1981: Conrad Taeubner (Ed.), *America Enters the Eighties: Some Social Indicators.* In: The Annals, Vol. 453, January 1981. Comments and interpretations are given about the data summarized in the report of the U.S. Department of Commerce: *Social Indicators III.* It is the fourth time the Annals have devoted an issue to the subject of social indicators.

1981: Angus Campbell, *The Sense of Well-Being in America: Recent Patterns and Trends.* Campbell presents a survey of the nature and distribution of well-being and comments on the significance of that knowledge.

1981: Thomas Juster and Kenneth C. Land, *Social Accounting Systems: Essays on the State of the Art.* A publication, with the papers of a Social Accounting Workshop in 1980, on developing objectives for future work on social accounting and recommendations for achieving them through the evaluation of existing social accounting schemes.

The increasing need for social information was of course not only an American affair. In other countries, many activities have been developed meanwhile that have made the social-indicator movement an international undertaking. Since the early seventies, periodical reports are published by the governments of most of the industrialized countries, in which voluminous quantities of data on recent social developments are summarized. Usually these data are grouped around themes that are closely connected with the existing administrative fields of care, like health, education, employment, social security. Since the beginning of the seventies we find such compendiums of statistical data in England (Central Statistical Office, 1970), France (Institut National de la Statistique et des Etudes Economiques, 1973), Germany (Bundesministerium für Arbeit und Sozialordnung 1974), Japan (Economic Planning Agency, 1973), and Canada (Statistics Canada, 1973).

An important impulse for initiating projects also started with international organizations, especially the OECD in Paris and the United Nations in New York. Various initiatives have been taken which have led to a number of results. In the United Nations especially the ideas of Richard Stone to set up a network of social-demographic statistics has been worked out (United Nations, 1975). The most famous international project was designed by the OECD. In the early seventies they started with a very ambitious program that in 1973 resulted in the first publication: 'The List of Social Concerns Common to Most OECD Countries'. We will return to this extensively in the following.

Expanding the concept 'prosperity' to include well-being, the acknowledgement of the one-sidedness of economic factors, the consciously or unconsciously accepted consequences of technological innovations—all these developments created, in The Netherlands too, a need for new and differently arranged information that might be used for social guidance. In The Netherlands, the first publication within this framework is *Systematische Maatschappij Informatie* ('Systematic Social Information'). This report, published in 1974, is the result of a work-group set up in 1971; its task was to investigate the possibilities for systematic social information. A number of objectives, starting-points and possible elaborations are presented. Central is the conclusion that it is necessary to have a theoretical framework that can be interpreted conceptually in only one way and by means of which the flood of potential data can be ordered. The emphasis therefore is on a theoretical-methodological discussion of the starting-points of systematic social information.

The wide perspective chosen by the work-group might create the expectation that a first concrete elaboration in the form of a social report for the Dutch situation could still take several years. Yet, we see in The Netherlands a development similar to the one we see everywhere else. The necessity to construct a general theoretical framework is recognized, but at the same time action is pragmatically initiated.

The Dutch social-indicator movement got an important stimulus in early 1974. Then the government founded the Social and Cultural Planning Bureau (Sociaal en Cultureel Planbureau). Already in 1975, this Bureau published its first and voluminous 'Social and Cultural Report' (*Sociaal en Cultureel Rapport 1974*). The objectives of this report are, as formulated in the introduction, to describe the state of affairs in the social and cultural fields as well as the developments taking place there. It may be described as a counterpart of the reports published by the Central Planning Office (Centraal Planbureau) in the field of economics.

The 1974 report was the first in a series. In the meantime the 'Social and Cultural Reports' for 1976, 1978, 1980 and 1982 have been published. These reports not only offer statistical figures, like the American *Social Indicators* and the English *Social Trends*, but extensive comments can also be found in them; these are rather descriptive in nature however. A few Dutch publications outside the government-sphere also may be mentioned, in which attempts are made to develop social indicators. In this connection may be mentioned the reports 'Satisfaction in Prosperity' (*Tevredenheid in welvaart*) and 'Quality of Employment, 1977' (*Kwaliteit van Arbeid*, 1977). For surveys with regard to social indicators by Dutch authors we refer to Swanborn (1974), Mootz (1975), Zanders (1975), Thierry (1977) and Van de Lustgraaf and Huigsloot (1979).

APPLICATIONS

We would like to use this section to go more specifically into several recent, large projects of the social-indicator movement. We will first pay attention to the social-indicator project of the OECD. In that project the emphasis is on the building up of an information-system via so-called objective indicators. Then we will deal with a few American projects in which the development of so-called subjective or perceptual indicators was preferred.

We chose two entries here, because several points with regard to the construction of social indicators which play an important role in the social-indicator movement come to the fore. This holds especially for the controversial points of view on the validity and reliability of so-called objective versus subjective indicators.

The basis for the OECD-project was laid in 1970, when that organization formulated the point of view that economic growth was no aim in itself, but an instrument with which to create better life-conditions. In order to determine the life-conditions of individuals in their social context, the qualitative aspects of prosperity growth also would have to be considered. First, however, the field that refers to welfare ('well-being') should be demarcated. This formed the first part of a three-phase plan by the OECD's Manpower and Social Affairs Committee. The following phases were distinguished: (I) the choice of sub-fields and subjects that are components of the concept of well-being; (II) the construction of measures for the indication of the relevant components; and (III) the actual measuring of the relevant social conditions and developments in it.

As a product of the first phase the 'List of Social Concerns Common to Most OECD Countries' (OECD, 1973), that has meanwhile become famous, was published. The central objective of the first phase of the social-indicators project was, as we have seen before, directed to reaching agreement on the aspects and fields that are a part of the general and broad concept 'well-being' or, as it is also called: 'quality of life'. Starting from a pragmatic approach, the OECD stimulated a process of consensus-forming among the member-states on the selection of sub-fields and subjects. This resulted in the identification of the following eight primary goal areas: (1) Health; (2) Individual development through learning; (3) employment and quality of working life; (4) time and leisure; (5) command over goods and services; (6) physical environment; (7) personal safety and the administration of justice; and (8) social opportunity and inequality.

Within each of these primary goal areas distinctions have subsequently been made in which specific fields of attention ('social concerns') were designated. Such a 'social concern' may be described as an identifiable and definable aim or field which may be of fundamental and direct importance for human well-being. Matters that are of instrumental or indirect importance for welfare do not come under this heading. In the first phase of the OECD-project, 24 'social concerns' were distinguished. In illustration we mention the following:

Health
—the probability of a healthy life through all phases of the life cycles;
—the impact of health impairements on individuals.
Employment and quality of working life.
—the availability of gainful employment for those who desire it;
—the quality of working life;
—individual satisfaction with the experiences of working life.
Social opportunity and inequality
—the degree of social inequality;

—the extent of opportunity for participation in community life, institutions and decision-making.

In 15 of the 24 fields of attention, even more detailed distinctions have been made. These last distinctions are defined as 'sub-concerns' or sub-fields. A more detailed discussion of these is outside the scope of this chapter. The interested reader may find them in the 'List of Social Concerns' mentioned.

After defining and formulating primary goal areas, the fields of attention and the sub-fields, the first phase of the OECD social-indicator project was completed. The second phase aimed to develop a system of social indicators, meant to validly express the level of well-being for each field of attention and to register the changes in those levels in the course of time. During the second phase there also appeared to be a need to revise and amplify the already defined primary goal areas on a number of points. Thus the fifth sub-field, the availability of goods and services, was reformulated as: personal economic situation, and for administration of justice (under sub-field no. 7) policy on jurisdiction was substituted. Finally, a new category was added: social environment. The emphasis in this phase was on the development of indicators for the 24 fields of attention.

The indicators accepted have shortcomings and lack theoretical foundations on many points. Yet, it seems particularly useful that the indicators which have been pragmatically chosen are to some extent useful for policy, even though these indicators are still of a provisional nature. Because of the approach, the right questions on various fields of policy might come into view. The indicators developed until now nearly all refer to registering factual, objective data. For example, as indicators for registering working conditions were chosen: (a) the number of fatal accidents in industry, (b) the number of long-term injuries in industry, and (c) the number of short-term injuries in industry. Such standards may indeed say something about the quality of working conditions in industry, but it will be clear that which can be defined as quality of working life covers a much wider field than to which the indicators refer to. This is also discerned by the OECD. Thus the possibility of individuals registering their perception and experience of their own situation is referred to. The most important question of the subjective or perceptual indicators comes to the fore. The perceptions and experiences of individuals and groups are a necessary and important component of the social-indicator program as the OECD sees it.

The result of policy-processes is indeed also expressed in the degree to which persons confronted with the policy experience it as negative or positive. As long as there are no good methodologies and standards available for registering those personal experiences, insight into the effectiveness of the policy will remain limited. Subjective indicators will therefore have to be included also in the OECD-program. The OECD has not yet been able to draw up acceptable approaches to develop such subjective indicators (Barbash, 1976; Portigal, 1976; OECD, 1974).

For the developments in subjective social indicators we shall have to consult other projects or institutions. We will do this by means of a few projects in the United States that aim to measure perceptions, evaluations and satisfactions.

In nearly every publication on social indicators the advantages and disadvantages of registering social phenomena via objective or subjective indicators come to the fore as points of discussion. Subjective indicators refer to the perceptions, feelings, preferences, attitudes etc. of individuals. Objective indicators are quantifiable entities that are not based on individual experiences, such as crime, age, unemployment. Especially Andrews (1974) argued for avoiding the implicit 'bias' that evokes the contrast objective-subjective by using a more neutral terminology. Andrews rightly observed that often in defining the phenomenon to be quantified, many subjective choice-elements play a part in the so-called objective standards. Further, the adjective 'subjective' suggests that the so-called indicators are less valid and less useful than the indicators described as 'objective'. According to Andrews, a clear alternative terminology is not immediately available. As a kind of intermediate solution he proposes to replace 'subjective' by 'perceptual'. So perceptual indicators are based on individual perceptions, feelings, attitudes, etc.

Perceptual indicators play a central role in a number of investigations into the quality of life by the Institute for Social Research (ISR) of the University of Michigan. From the early seventies the ISR, with support from the Russell Sage Foundation and the National Science Foundation, has been designing and carrying out research on the quality of life. Two voluminous studies have been published in the meantime in which empirical research on subjective social indicators is reported. In 1976, Campbell, Converse and Rodgers published *The Quality of American Life ; Perceptions, Evaluations and Satisfactions.* Also in 1976 Andrews and Whitney published: *Social Indicators of Well-Being ; Americans' Perceptions of Life Quality.*

In both projects individuals were chosen as research-units. By means of detailed interviews data were gathered from the respondents, who were selected in such a way that they were a representative sample of the American population of 18 years and over. The contents of both studies cover a very wide field. Explicit attention is paid to, among other things, housing conditions, health, work-experiences, marriage and family-life, personal life and development possibilities, and national government. Both Campbell *et al.* and Andrews and Whitney take the measurements, made by means of perceptual indicators, of the subjective experience of well-being to be explorative. The instruments used will have to be tested by means of further investigations and analyses for validity and reliability. This certainly holds when such standards are used in international comparative research.

The project of Andrews and Whitney offers the best starting-points for giving a survey of a research strategy that is eligible when developing subjective social indicators. We therefore would like to mention that strategy briefly.

As a basis for their study, Andrews and Whitney worked out a conceptual model, which is summarized in figure 2. The argument that led to the construction of this model is the following. In every human existence various sub-fields or domains can be distinguished, that can be appreciated by means of certain criteria or values. Such domains and criteria may be arranged as schematized in figure 2. Domains may comprise things like: places, things, activities, people and roles. Criteria may be: values, standards, aspirations, objectives and, put generally, judgments on the output of the domains. The fundamental point now is to capture in the model those domains and criteria that are relevant for the study of populations. Once the scheme is completely filled in, indices may be constructed via aggregation (possibly after weighting) indicating the well-being with regard to certain domains or criteria (E_i or E_j) as well as an index that indicates general well-being ($E..$).

So first the scheme will have to be filled in and then the mutual relations in the scheme will have to be analyzed. The strategy chosen by the investigators to fill in the scheme is of an inductive nature. By means of a study of the literature, an analysis of research already done, and via a number of open interviews, attempts have been made to trace those domains and criteria that are distinguished in human life. Via this practical procedure the boundaries of the open system were traced. In this first phase more than 800 fields ('concerns') were identified. After a first cluster-

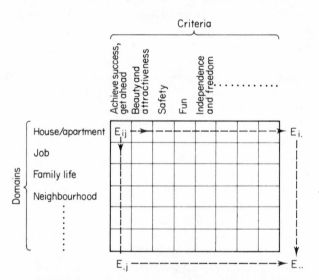

E_{ij} = Affective evaluative response to a particular domain with respect to a
    particular criterion

$E_{i.}$ = General affective evaluative response to a domain (across criteria)

$E_{.j}$ = General affective evaluative response to a criterion (across domains)

$E_{..}$ = General affective evaluative response to life-as-a-whole – i.e. perceived
    quality of life

Figure 2. The conceptual model of Andrews and Whitney.

analysis, in which special attention was paid to mutual overlaps, their number was reduced to approx. 60. Next, more than one hundred items were formulated in these fields which functioned as indicators for registering the state of affairs in the different fields. Of course, the appreciation of the different aspects was discussed extensively. An important part of the study was dedicated to both the development and the evaluation of standards or indicators that could possibly be used. A discussion of that would carry us too far. But we may mention a few general conclusions from the two ISR projects. They show in the first place that the, theoretically nearly unlimited number of fields, relevant to general well-being, can in fact be reduced to a few fields. This is an important conclusion to build on, for it prevents the discussions and the investigations on well-being being diverted to facets that in fact play a subordinate role.

The wide, comprehensive field has now indeed been explored and defined. Of course these conclusions only hold for the moment and only for the American situation. Longitudinal and comparative research will have to prove to what extent such conclusions will remain valid at different times and in different cultures (Cantril, 1965). Another main conclusion concerns the research instruments developed and evaluated. From the multitude of possible approaches and procedures a limited number of ways can be given on the basis of this research that indicate a valid and reliable course for further developments in the field of social indicators.

We have discussed the American projects because, starting from the individual or micro-level, they form a clear contrast with the projects developed by the OECD, in which representatives of national governments try to reach agreement on the elements that are part of the concept 'well-being' or 'quality of life'. The contrast in approach can be characterized as the individual versus the institutional approach. Both approaches have their restrictions and are one-sided.

The OECD-strategy used by institutes and organizations to develop social indicators may involve the danger that the indicators selected will be strongly biased. In this strategy, the process of decision-making on the choice of fields of attention with regard to well-being is for the greater part a process in which politicians, scholars and civil servants predominate. They determine the importance of certain facets for society's well-being. There is a large chance that only those aspects are thought to be important that are in agreement with the prevailing ideology. The individual approach may result in too little attention being paid to structural factors that have an important influence on the function of social systems.

CONCLUDING REMARKS

Social indicators are essential for the evaluation and guidance of social developments. Since the sixties research has extensively been carried out in which social indicators have been developed. Social indicators are the result of questions raised in politics and the social sciences. The consequence was that a pragmatic approach dominated when information systems were drawn up. The linking of the indicators to theoretical concepts often remained very limited. At first, expectations were raised that via social indicators comprehensive social models could be constructed, in which almost all social sectors could be taken into consideration simultaneously. In the meantime, emphasis is now put on the development of more limited models that start from the so-called 'middle-range' theories.

Still many questions remain to be discussed in the social-indicator movement. Briefly a few are:

— *The objective of social indicators.* Quite often it is argued that social indicators aim at measuring the output of social systems and not their input. The limits are often difficult to set, however, for certain phenomena; health, for example, may function both as output and input in different models.

— *The units of research.* Social developments are ultimately compared with individual judgments. Therefore individual persons will form the units of research in many cases. The results of research obtained in this way have to be considered in the social context of which the individuals are a part. Information about this context will have to be gathered too.

— *Comparability.* Especially the cross-cultural comparability of social information is relevant. Identical concepts might not always be indicated in different social systems in the same way.

— *Level of analysis.* In the social-indicator movement a striking distinction has grown between analyses at the macro- and micro-level on the one hand and at the meso-level on the other hand. In most of the literature on social indicators we find discussions and data that refer to social systems or certain social sectors, like health, employment, education etc. Moreover, many developments take place that aim to construct social indicators that refer especially to corporate systems; the term 'social accounting' refers to these activities (Knaapen, 1979). It seems desirable and useful to integrate the often separate developments of the various levels of analysis.

— *Accessibility of data.* The availability of infromation gives the power to guide and to control. Such power may not remain confined to specific groups or bodies. The access to the data that also steer social developments will therefore have to be open to all persons. Certainly in an era when the possibilities of manipulating data are strongly increasing, this aspect should be given special attention.

REFERENCES

Andrews, F. M. (1974), Social indicators of perceived life quality. *Social Indicators Research*, no. 1.

Andrews, F. M., Whitney, S. B. (1976), Social indicators of well-being. Americans' perceptions of their life quality. New York: Plenum Press.

Ballerstedt, E., Glatzer, W. (1975), *Soziologischer Almanach*. Frankfurt: Campus Verlag.

Barbash, J. (1976), *Job satisfaction attitudes surveys*. Paris: OECD.

Bauer, R. A. (Ed.) (1966), *Social indicators*. Cambridge (Mass.): MIT Press.

Biderman, A. D., Drury, Th. F. (Eds.) (1976), *Measuring work quality for social reporting*. New York: Halted Press.

Boesjes-Hommes, R. W. (1973), *De geldige operationalisering van begrippen*. [The valid operationalization of concepts]. Meppel: Boom.

Bundesministerium für Arbeit und Sozialordnung (1974), *Gesellschaftliche Daten*, no. 1. Bonn.

Campbell, A. (1981), *The sense of well-being in America: Recent patterns and trends*. New York: McGraw-Hill.

Campbell, A., Converse, Ph. (1972), *The human meaning of social change*. New York: Russell Sage Foundation.

Cantril, H. (1965), *The pattern of human concerns*. New Brunswick: Rutgers University Press.

Carley, M. J. (1979), Social theory and models in social indicator research. *International Journal of Social Economics*, **6**.

Central Satistical Office (1970), *Social trends*. London: Her Majesty's Stationery Office.

Delors, J. *Les indicateurs sociaux*. Paris: SEDEIS.

Dierkes, M., Bauer, R. A. (Eds.) (1973), Corporate social accounting. New York: Praeger.

Economic Planning Agency (1973), *Whitepaper on national life 1973. The life and its quality in Japan*. Tokyo: Japanese Government.

Executive Office of the President, Office of Management and Budget (1974), *Social indicators 1973*. Washington D. C.: U.S. Government Printing Office.

Fox, K. A. (1974), *Social indicators and social theory. Elements of an operational system*. Chichester: John Wiley.

Gilmartin, K. J., et al. (1979), *Social indicators: An annotated bibliography of current literature*. New York: Garland.

Gross, B. M. (1966), Social systems accounting. In: Bauer, R. (Ed.), *Social indicators*. Cambridge (Mass.): MIT Press.

Gross, B. M. (Ed.) (1967), *Social goals and indicators for American society*. Vols. I and II of the Annals of the American Academy of Political and Social Science, Vol. 371 (May 1967) and Vol. 373 (Sept. 1967).

Institute for Social Research, (1971), *A quarter century of social research*. Ann Arbor.

Institut National de la Statistique et des Etudes Economiques (INSEE) (1974), *Données Sociales 1973*. Paris.

Japanese Economic Council (1973), *Measuring the national welfare of Japan*. Report of the NWW Measurement Committee. Tokyo: Economic Council of Japan.

Johnston, D. F. (1978), Social indicators forecasting. In: Fowles, J. (Ed.), *Handbook of futures research*. London: Greenwood Press.

Juster T., Land, K. C. (1981), *Social accounting systems: Essays on the state of the art*. New York: Academic Press.

Knaapen, A. L. M. (1979), Social accounting. In: *Gids voor Personeelsbeleid, Arbeidsvraagstukken, Sociale Verzekering*. [Guide for Personnel Management, Labour Issues, Social Security], nos. 21, 22, 25.

Land, K. C. (1971), On the definition of social indicators. *American Sociologist*, **6**, 322–325.

Land, K. C. (1975a), Social indicator models: An overview. In: Land, K. C., Spilerman, S., *Social indicator models*. New York: Russell Sage Foundation.

Land, K. C. (1975b), Theories, models and indicators of social Change. *International Social Science Journal*, **27**, 1, 7–14.

Land, K. C., Spilerman, S. (Eds.) (1975), *Social indicator models*. New York: Russell Sage Foundation.

Lustgraaf, R. E. van de, Huigsloot, P. C. M. (1979), *Sociale indicatoren, een bewuste keuze?* [Social indicators, a conscious choice?]. Rijswijk: Social en Cultural Planning Bureau.

Michalos, A. (1980), *North American social report: A comparative study of the quality of life in Canada and the U.S.A. from 1964 to 1974.* Dordrecht: Reidel.

Mootz, M. (1975), Systematische maatschappij informatie in Nederland [Systematic social information in The Netherlands]. *Beleid en Maatschappij* [Policy and Society], November.

(v/h) Nederlandse Stichting voor Statistiek [(the late) Dutch Foundation for Statistics] (1974), *Tevredenheid in welvaart. Een bijdrage tot de ontwikkeling van subjectieve sociale indicatoren* [Satisfaction in prosperity. A contribution to the development of subjective social indicators]. Amsterdam/The Hague.

Neufville, J. I. de (1975), *Social indicators and public policy. Interactive processes of design and application.* Amsterdam/New York: Elsevier.

OECD (1973), *List of social concerns common to most OECD countries.* Paris: OECD.

OECD (1974), *Subjective elements of well-being.* Paris: OECD.

OECD (1977), *Measuring social well-being. A progress report on the development of social indicators.* Paris: OECD.

Portigal, A. H. (1976), *Toward the measurement of work satisfaction.* Paris.

Quinn, R. P., Shepard, L. J. (1974), *The 1972–73 Quality of Employment Survey. Descriptive statistics with comparison data from the 1969–70 survey of working conditions.* Ann Arbor: Institute for Social Research.

Quinn, R. P., Staines, G. L. (1978), *The 1977 Quality of Employment Survey: Descriptive statistics with comparison data from the 1969–70 and 1972–73 surveys.* Ann Arbor: Institute for Social Research.

Quinn, R. P., Seashore, S., Kahn, R., Mangione, T., Campbell, D., Staines, G., McCullogh, M. (1971), *Survey of working conditions. Final report on univariate and bivariate tables.* Washington D.C.: U.S. Government Printing Office.

Quinn, R. P., Mangione, T. W., et al. (1973), *The 1969–1970 survey of working conditions: Chronicles of an unfinished enterprise.* Ann Arbor: Institute for Social Research.

Rathenau, G. W., et al. (1980), *Maatschappelijke gevolgen van de micro-electronica* [Social consequences of micro-electronics]. The Hague: Staatsuitgeverij.

Report of the National Commission on Technology, Automation and Economic Progress (1966), *Technology and the American economy.* Washington D.C.: U.S. Government Printing Office.

Report of the President's Research Committee on Social Trends (1933), *Recent social trends.* Vols. I and II. New York: NcGraw-Hill.

Rossi, R. J., Gilmartin, K. J. (1980), *Handbook of social indicators: Sources, characteristics and analyses.* New York: Garland STPM Press.

Segers, J. H. G. (1975), *Sociologische onderzoeksmethoden* [Sociological research methods]. Assen/Amsterdam: Van Gorcum.

Sociaal en Cultureel Planbureau (1975, 1976, 1978, 1980, 1982), *Sociaal en cultureel rapport* [Social and cultural report] *1974, 1976, 1978, 1980, 1982.* The Hague: Staatsuitgeverij.

Statistics Canada (1974), *Perspective Canada. A compendium of social statistics.* Toronto.

Swanborn, P. G. (1974), Sociale indicatoren [Social indicators]. In: Swanborn, P. G. (Ed.), *Methoden en mensen* [Methods and people]. Rotterdam: Universitaire Pers.

Szalai, A., Andrews, F. M. (Eds.) (1980), *The quality of life. Comparative studies.* London/Beverly Hills: Sage Publications.

Taeubner, C. (Ed.) (1978), America in the seventies: Some social indicators. In: *The Annals of the American Academy of Political and Social Science,* **435**, January.

Taeubner, C. (Ed.) (1981), America enters the eighties: Some social indicators. In: *The Annals of the American Academy of Political and Social Science,* **453**, January.

Terleckij, M. E. (1975), *Improvement in the quality of life. Estimates of possibilities in the United States 1974–1983*. Washington D.C.: National Planning Association.

Thierry, Hk. (1977), Sociale indicatoren: Signalen voor samenlevings- en bedrijfsbeleid [Social indicators: Signals for social and industrial policy]. In: Thierry, Hk., *et al.*, *Sociale indicatoren in beweging* [Social indicators in action]. Deventer: Kluwer.

United Nations (1975), *Toward a system of social and demographic statistics*. Department of Economic and Social Affairs, Statistical Office, Studies in Methods, series F, no. 18. New York.

U.S. Department of Commerce, Office of Federal Statistical Policy and Standards and Bureau of Census (1976), *Social indicators 1976*. Washington D.C.: U.S. Government Printing Office.

Walker, K., Shore, R. (1977), Towards a policy for life at work. In: OECD, *Policies for life at work*. Paris: OECD.

Wilcox, L. D., Brooks, R. M. (Eds.) (1972), *Social indicators and social monitoring. An annotated bibliography*. Amsterdam/New York.

Werkgroep SMI (1974), *Systematische maatschappij informatie. Een aanzet tot discussie* [Systematic social information. A starting point for discussion]. Voorburg: Central Bureau of Statistics.

Zanders, H. L. G. (1975), Sociale indicatoren: Meetinstrumenten voor de maatschappij [Social indicators: Measuring instruments for society]. In: Gils, M. R. van (Ed.), *Werken en niet-werken in een veranderende samenleving* [Working and not-working in a changing society]. Amsterdam: Swets & Zeitlinger.

Zanders, H. L. G., Büchem, A. L. J. van, Berkel, J. J. C. van (1977), *Kwaliteit van arbeid, 1977. Een onderzoek naar kenmerken van en opvattingen over arbeid en arbeidsomstandigheden* [The Quality of Employment in the Netherlands 1977; a survey on objective and subjective social indicators of labor and other domains], The Hague Ministry of Social Affairs/Institute for Social Research of the Tilburg University.

Zapf, W. (Ed.) (1974/5), *Soziale Indikatoren: Konzepte und Forschungsansätze, I, II, III*. Frankfurt: Herder & Herder.

Zuthem, H. J. van (1980), Instituties en het process van humanisering van de arbeid [Institutions and the process of humanizing work]. In: Galan, C. de, Gils, M. R. van, Strien, P. J. van (Eds.), *Humanisering van de arbeid* [Humanizing work]. Assen: Van Gorcum.

Handbook of Work and Organizational Psychology
Edited by P. J. D. Drenth, H. Thierry, P. J. Willems and C. J. de Wolff

5.3. Organization and building—some contributions from architectural psychology

Herbert van Hoogdalem

1. INTRODUCTION

When an architect is asked to design a building for an organization, he will quite soon find himself asking the following questions:
who (what persons, groups, departments . . . ?) should *do what* (what activities and processes take place?)
where (how many and what kind of spaces, how are these situated with respect to each other?)
and *when* (how are these activities/processes patterned in time?)

Besides these questions, he will often want to know the background. *Why* should the principal mainly want bedrooms-for-four in his new hospital? Why should he want his psychiatric patients to sleep, eat and have recreation collectively in such big rooms? And why should the hospital be situated in such nicely wooded surroundings but so very isolated from ordinary people? Why is he so determined to have 'landscaped' offices for his employees rather than some other type of building?

The architect may of course keep these *why*-questions to himself or he may not consider them at all. He may restrict himself to making an inventory of the organizational program and translating the information into numbers and types of rooms and square metres. He will then define the relations between the rooms and process all these data into a plan and subsequently into building materials. In doing this, he will, to a great extent, fix the working of the organization for a long time to come.

The architect's questions, however, may give the principal food for thought

Drs. Herbert van Hoogdalem. Delft Technological University, Dept. of Architecture.

about his organization. For, the idea to start (re)building seldom arises only from a pure lack of space, but usually also because the existing space is not well laid out, arranged, located or otherwise shows shortcomings with respect to the organization. Building usually coincides with (re)organization, and in fact is part of it.

In this chapter, some ideas, concepts and theories are discussed which have as their subject the close relation between organization and building. That is why a selection has been made, eclectic rather than systematic, from several disciplinary areas, particularly architectural or environmental psychology. This recent branch of pschology has so far hardly dealt with the 'environment' of work and organization. Besides, it shows a certain one-sidedness by studying mainly the interaction between individuals and their environment and to a much lesser extent the interaction between groups, organizations and the built environment (for a criticism, see Lipman and Harris, 1980, Duffy, 1974).

Two case studies will be discribed, illustrating the application of some of the concepts to be discussed in a concrete design/organization context. The chapter closes with a number of problems which require an interdisciplinary approach by architects as well as by experts in the field of work and organization.

Readers who wish to orient themselves further in the field of environmental psychology, are referred to the *Annual Review*-articles by Craik (1973) and Stokols (1978). Further to the volumes edited by Proshansky *et al.* (1970), the sociologists Michelson (1970) and Gutman (1972), Wohlwill and Carson (1972), Canter (1975), Altman and Wohlwill (1976), Stokols (1972), Proshansky and Altman (1979), and Rapaport (1976). For methods of research in this field: Michelson (1975), Altman and Wohlwill (1977), Steffen and Van der Voordt (1978), and Zeisel (1981).

2. INTERACTION BETWEEN MAN AND ENVIRONMENT

In most definitions of environmental psychology it is very much emphasized that there is an interaction between man and built environment. In other words: man does not experience his environment passively, but interprets, structures and changes it, whenever possible. Neither is the built environment a passive, motionless and dead thing, but it influences human behaviour actively as well (for a review of definitions see: Bell *et al.* 1978). Even if one could imagine all sorts of things with human behaviour in respect of their environment, it is, however, more difficult and more uncommon, other than in a metaphorical sense, to conceive of an 'acting' built environment.

In architecture one often speaks of the functions of a building, and this seems a suitable starting point for considering first what role a building plays in the presumed interaction, in what ways the shaping of this role is thought of in architecture, and then turning to the human actors and their roles in this combined action.

2.1. The functions of a building

The architectural theorists Hillier and Leaman (1976) distinguish four main functions of buildings in their interaction with man and society.
1. The building is a climate-regulator. It more or less acts as a complex set of filters and amplifiers between inside and outside and thus modulates sensory stimuli.
2. The building contains people and their activities, supports certain activities and inhibits others. Thus localizing people's behaviour and their mutual relations, it regulates social relations to a certain degree.
3. The building is a symbolic and cultural object and as such exercises a critical or supporting influence on cultural ideas and values.
4. The building adds to the value of raw materials and thus is a capital investment; it has an economic function.

Broadbent (1978) later split up the first function, pointing out that the building not only regulates the climate inside, but also influences the climate outside, exercising an 'environmental impact'. Thus, high buildings cast long shadows on their environment and frequently cause wind-turbulences and wind-nuisance.

In fact, Broadbent signalized only the top of the iceberg. In consequence of the other functions, too, one can speak of an 'environmental impact' particularly as a consequence of the activities which take place inside the building. For instance, think of the consequences of building a multiple store in a housing area: much more traffic (resulting in noise, pollution, parking problems, traffic dangers), disappearance of small tradesmen, change of value of surrounding houses and land, growing speculation, growing pressure to change local development plans, a changed population structure due to moving and—as a result—a changed social climate, etc.

Conversely, the functioning of a building is influenced by its location with respect to other buildings, transport systems, sources of environmental nuisance, and facilities (Harvey, 1972).

Besides these functions of a building for the benefit of human occupancy, it is also important how it stands up against the impacts of climate, nature and man; in other words, how it functions physically and constructionally.

Over against this analysis of what a building does—whether the designer has intended this or not, and whether he has it under control or not—it is interesting to see in what ways architects interpret these functions and to what forms this may lead. We will restrict ourselves to the various forms of 'functionalism'. They have in common a preoccupation with the way buildings function—act, so to speak—in practice... The differences are duo to accentuating different kinds of functions.

2.2. Functionalistic trends in architectural design

Handler (1970) distinguishes at least six functionalistic trends:
—'*The functional as the uilitarian*', with the motto: 'From follows function'.

Everything in the design should be based on its use. All that is useful is permitted. The differentiation of the parts of the building ought to harmonize with the objectives. Buildings ought to be designed corresponding to human needs and wishes and not in accordance with a certain form-principle or some geometric pattern. That is why symmetry, if it does not follow from the use, should be rejected as an artificiality. — From this basic type of functionalism all sorts of other variants have developed.

—'*Functionalism as constructivism*', with the motto: 'Form follows structural functioning'. The form of a building is above all decided by the way it is constructed and the materials used. These should be used 'honestly' and not hidden from view by useless i.e. non-constructional additions. Everything should look clear and natural. Buildings should bear witness of man's power over matter. The architect should be a structural virtuoso, who uses the construction because of its own aesthetics.

—'*The functional as the expressive*', with the motto: 'Exhibit use and/or structure'. The objective of the building should be exhibited clearly; it should be clear at a glance, for what purpose it is intended and what activities will take place there. The form should symbolize the functions and represent the use, without direct reference—e.g. in the form of inscriptions or signs—being necessary. The structure, the materials and even the mechanical installations should not only be clearly shown but even be emphasized, to a degree of structural and mechanical exhibitionism (a particularly pure example of this is the 'Centre Pompidou' in Paris).

—'*The functional as the geometric*', with the motto: 'Form precedes function'. Use as a starting-point is mainly denied here. One concentrates on the way in which the geometry of the building functions visually. A vocabulary of forms should be developed not so much in accordance with new objectives, but in such a way that these may be fitted in. Simplicity is the seal of truth; no ornaments. Large smooth planes are used, in unfinished material. Geometrical arrangement should dominate, beauty is derived from the connection of geometrically specified planes and volumes.

—'*The functional as the organic*', with the motto: 'Form and function are identical'. Here the directive holds: work together with nature, don't oppose it, but adapt yourself. Fit buildings into the landscape, use natural materials from the environment. Use the 'wisdom of nature' and learn from the unity in the design of living forms and the systematics hidden within. Be guided by knowledge of natural sciences and by observing living things. There one can find innumerable examples of a perfect amalgamation of form and function. Form should be understood as a process. External form is only a reference to internal functioning, the form is the functioning of the whole. A building is not a simple concatenation of parts, but all the parts are inter-related. They are subject to a dominating unit, which is more than the sum of the parts.

—'*The functional as the efficacious*'; a motto for this variant might be: 'Use appropriate means'. For this counts: use the means economically. Experiment in order to find the best and most efficient solution to the problem posed. Use rational methods and procedures in the process of building and design. Emphasize internal logic or consistency of the design. The solution should be derived from conditions in the situation, without inserting arbitrary elements.

The wording of this summary is somewhat normative and dogmatic. Architects, indeed, are often harrassed during their training with this kind of exhortations and doctrines, which also function as standards for the critcism of each other's work. Often schools, which fiercely fight each other, centre round one of the above-mentioned starting points. In the practice of building, however, pure examples of a particular point of view but seldom occur.

2.3. Human behaviour in relation to its environment

As we have put the question before: 'What does the building do?' so we may also ask: 'What does man do?' when the physical environment is not adequately attuned to the activities he wants to perform.

McLoughlin (1970), a planner, distinguishes 'spaces' in the environment, areas where activities take place, and 'channels', traffic-lines connecting the 'spaces' and by which communication takes place. The ecological system of space/activities and channels/interactions finds itself in a dynamic balance. Disturbing this may lead to three main forms of human interference. This interference can be aimed at the 'spaces' as well as at the 'channels'. Schematically:

	Behavioural	Locational	Developmental
Spaces	reorganize activities	move activities to other space	modify or build new spaces
Channels	change mode of transport	take another route in existing network	have a telephone installed, build a flyover etc.

The essence of 'behavioural responses' is, that man adapts his behaviour and activities to the possibilities of the physical environment. With 'locational responses' he makes a choice from a number of different physical environments and shifts his activities to 'spaces' and 'channels' which are more appropriate. 'Developmental responses', finally, imply an active change of the physical environment, e.g. by building or rebuilding 'spaces' and 'channels'. In all cases the responses are directed at neutralizing the disturbance in the relation between man and environment by creating a new equilibrium.

McLoughlin's ecological model of systems may be used to make changes in reality visible and open to discussion. An illustration is to be found in an architectural-historical research by the sociologist King (1976). This study describes and analyzes changes of English army camps in British India during the previous century.

The 'disturbance' of the ecological system was, in this case, the high death rate of soldiers from malaria. For an adequate solution, according to King, knowledge of the possible causes of the disturbance is necessary. In those days, medical theory held that the incidence of malaria was favoured by three environmental factors: heat, humidity and decaying garbage. This theory led to a number of measures, which could be classed as behavioural, locational and developmental, respectively.

In order to prevent infection because of 'bad air' one chose locations high up in the mountains, on the windside of native villages or swamps. Instead of one large building several barracks were built, which were well spaced out. The amount of available air per soldier was drastically increased by means of high roofs and high windows; all this to promote the ventilation in and around the buildings as well as possible. This striving to maximize air supply even manifested itself in the design of a helmet, which left much room for the hair and allowed for ventilation through holes. Personal hygiene and physical resistance were promoted by making bathing obligatory and restricting the use of alcohol. Social contacts, including sexual contacts, with natives were discouraged or prohibited. When visiting native villages, the white soldiers had 'protective spaces' made around themselves by native soldiers. In order to fight the increasing boredom among the men, new forms of recreation were introduced, like sports and (visits to) libraries. These again led to a demand for new spaces.

King distinguishes a physiological and a cognitive level within 'behavioural responses'. In his adapted model he places man, who represents these levels, with the other parts of the total system. Then, it is not only interesting that locations are chosen, buildings are designed, built, and maintained, but also that the occupants/users are visualized as beings with a malleable body and mind. Environmental and behavioural designs complement each other in the 'total design' of a man-environment system.

The picture evoked here of an almighty sculptor, who models an apparent will-less and inert mass to his visions, ideas and norms, is perhaps applicable to the situation in the 19th century as described by King. Here the power of the colonial army-command, together with the rising authority of medical science, occupies a similar position with respect to its natural, built and human 'environmental material'. When developing a model of man-environment interaction one should, however, take into consideration that the occupants/users do not always off-hand accept the architectural and organizational structures, together forming the environment, that are imposed on them from higher up or from outside. The inhabitants will interpret, use and, if possible, try to change this environment according to their own, sometimes conflicting opinions, ideas and values.

In his model, King represents only part of the social-cultural system—i.e. the whole complex of positions and mutual relations, of knowledge, ideas, norms, and values—namely, that part that is internalized in the cognitive system of the individual human being. In the conceptual model to be described below the social-cultural system is clearly distinguished from the individual cognitive system as being an independent supra-individual entity.

2.4. The man-environment system as a structure of interacting control systems

A distinction may be made between natural environment (geological, climatic, biological, etc.) and cultural environment (changed, arranged, produced, etc. as a result of human interference). Within this cultural environment yet another distinction could be made between material culture (objects, tools, buildings, etc.) and immaterial culture (knowledge, laws, norms, social structures, organizations and institutions, etc.). In the following, we shall mean by 'environment' the cultural environment in particular, i.e. the material as well as the immaterial enclaves in the natural environment as designed and produced by man. Within man, who is both the producer and the occupant as well as the user of his environment, a material and an immaterial aspect may be distinguished also. This was indicated by King as the physiological and cognitive levels of human behaviour, respectively (see above).

The distinctions made here can again be found in the conceptual model of the man-environment system (van Hoogdalem, 1977), shown in figure 1. Every subsystem in this model is shown as a so-called TOTE-unit (Miller et al., 1960), see figure 2.

According to the TOTE-model, behaviour is goal-directed; this goal-directedness is watched over in the Test-phase; deviations from the course (incongruity) are signalized here and counteracted in the Operate-phase, until in the Test-phase an agreement is reached between the real and the intended course (congruity). The arrows in the TOTE-system symbolize the transfer of energy, information, or control: of all three, when, for instance, we describe a physiological reflex or a technical instrument such as thermostat; transfer of only control and information, when we describe cognitive or social-psychological processes. Such a concept, applicable to all four systems we distinguished, enables us to present a certain man-environment system like in figure 1.

The basic idea underlying such a representation of the man-environment system is the pursuit of an optimum balance. This would be achieved when in all subsystems the real and the desired courses would agree and the desired courses of all subsystems would converge.

In this model, one can recognize a conceptual distinction between goals and means, in which the means are the operations of the various subsystems carried out to achieve certain test values of the subsystem and, with that, of the total system. By connecting the various subsystems by a common Test-part it is implicitly suggested that, to attain a balance, different combinations of means may be applied.

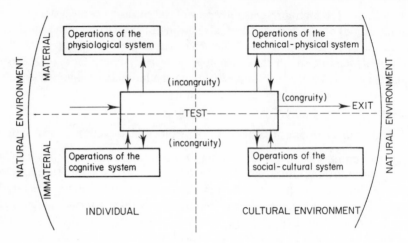

Figure 1. Conceptual model of the man-environment system.

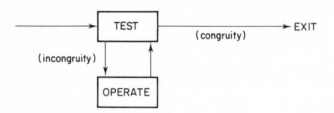

Figure 2. Diagram of a TOTE-unit.

These abstract notions and the application of the model as a means for analysing the complex man-environment systems may be illustrated by the following example, showing the essential complexity of any task designers and researchers have to deal with. A football match may be analyzed into the following subsystems:
—a certain number of players selected on 'physiological' characteristics (size of body, strength, age, sex, etc.) and cognitive characteristics (game tactics, experience, specialization).
—a certain role differentiation within each team and between the teams, a set of rules of the game and a referee in the role of the impartial guardian of these rules (social-cultural system).
—finally, an accurately defined space (dimensions and kind of field) and time, within which the match takes place (temporal-spatial or physical system).

For an exciting and fair course of the match and for comparability of matches it is necessary that one adheres to this customary practice of balanced combinations of mutually attuned environmental systems. An indication for this mutual attuning is, for example, that for junior football-players the match is shorter. In principle the field, too, could be smaller for them or they might play in teams of fifteen.

3. DIFFERENT APPROACHES OF THE MAN-ENVIRONMENT SYSTEM

Within the pattern of possible relations among the above distinguished subsystems, several partial approaches of man-environment systems may be typified by those relations, which they primarily examine.

3.1. The approach of human biotechnology

This approach focuses in particular on the relation between the subsystems that were characterized above as material. Applied research of disciplines like bio-dynamics, anthropometrics, (sensory-)physiology and ergonomics aims to formulate the conditions, criteria, demands, and norms (in terms of the model: test values), which a building should meet. Specialized fields of research deal with:
—natural and artificial lighting, acoustics;
—composition of the air, relative humidity, velocity of the air (sufficient ventilation, avoiding symptoms of draught), temperature;
—spatial and mechanical dimensions of parts of the building and furniture, based on anthropometric measurements of individual and group activities.

For a review of the research on the influence of light, temperature and acoustics, see Canter (1975); for measures and dimensions, see Neufert (1981); and for a comprehensive treatment of all these factors see Grandjean (1973).

The results of this research function as a guide to designers of buildings and also form the basis of law-enforced design directives, e.g. model-building ordinances and regulations of the Labour Inspection. The experience, which may or may not be based on systematic research, the insights and ideas, deposited in this obligatory norm system, exercise strong influence on the design of the built environment. The historical background of many regulations and requirements is highly coloured by medical-hygienic ideas and views, which in turn have very strongly influenced architecture and town-planning, particularly since the beginning of this century. A well-known motto, dating back to those days is: 'Light, air and space', see also the above-mentioned case study by King. Town-planning conceptions, distinguishing between working, living, traffic and recreation as the primary functions of a city, have, under the impetus of this motto, led to an actual spatial disentanglement of these functions in our cities of today.

3.2. Environmental-psychological approach

The approaches that go by the names of environmental psychology, architectural psychology, ecological psychology, etc., and that pay more attention to the relations between the material environment, the cognitive system and the social cultural system, respectively, date from the early sixties. According to emphasis, one can distinguish between an individual and a social-psychological approach.

—In the *individual psychological approach* the emphasis of research and theory is on the relation between the cognitive system and the material environment. One is interested in the way in which individuals, who may or may not be differentiated according to individual differences, perceive the material, built environment (especially visually), form a picture of it, a cognitive or mental map, what attitudes and preferences they develop with respect to the environment or elements of it. In such research, the influence of social-cultural factors on these cognitive processes is not explicitly studied. For a theoretical analysis of and research on the development of cognitive or 'mental maps' see Downs and Stea (1977).

—The *social-psychological approach*, on the other hand, emphasizes the relation between the spatial environment and the social-cultural environment and the influence they have on the relations between individuals and groups. Altman (1975) gives a detailed review of the research done in the framework of the social-psychological approach of the man-environment system, which is highly recommended as an introduction to this field. He arranges the various studies under four concepts: privacy, personal space, territoriality and crowding. Altman describes the relation between these concepts as follows: 'It will be proposed that privacy is a central regulatory process by which a person (or group) makes himself more or less accessible and open to others and that the concepts of personal space and territorial behaviour are mechanisms that are set in motion to achieve desired levels of privacy. Crowding will be described as a social condition in which privacy mechanisms have not functioned effectively, resulting in an excess of undesired social contact'. This description fits quite well with the above model of the man-environment system, as the summary in figure 3 shows.

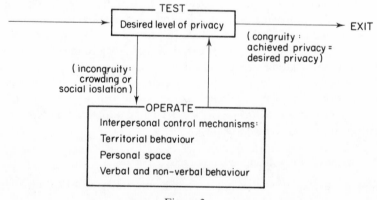

Figure 3.

We will now discuss some of these concepts.

Privacy. Altman remarks, that hardly any empirical research has been done on the concept of privacy, but that a number of conceptual analyses have been proposed by different disciplines like sociology, anthropology, jurisprudence and psychology. This contrasts sharply with the many empirical studies of the other concepts in figure 3.

Privacy appears to be a theoretical concept that meaningfully connects and explains various forms of observable interpersonal behaviour, including the use of the material environment. It refers to the assumed need for 'identity' of an individual, group or other social structure, by controlling the boundaries with others. In Altman's words: '... It is the ability to regulate contact when desired. If I can control what is me and not me, and if I can observe the limits and scope of my control, then I have taken major steps towards understanding and defining what I am. Thus privacy mechanisms serve to help me define myself. Furthermore, the peripheral functions towards which control is directed—regulation of interpersonal interaction and self/other interface processes—ultimately serve the goal of self identity' (p. 50).

Just as with other needs we may assume that the need of privacy varies greatly per person, situation and in time. Moreover, because of the interpersonal aspect, this need is very much influenced by the ideas, norms and values of the social-cultural system of which one is part, and depends on one's position in it. For, someone's 'ability to control' the material and immaterial environment is pre-eminently determined or limited by the 'power' of others in that environment.

Personal space. This concept refers to the phenomenon that, in most situations people keep at a certain distance from one another. When one crosses the imaginary borderline, the person approached will feel threatened, uneasy and will attempt to restore this distance by moving up, sitting down else where or by verbally or non-verbally (turning away, ignoring the other) making the intruder retreat.

Since Hall (1966) and Sommer (1969) introduced this phenomenon, which had already been described by ethologists, in environmental psychology, an elaborate 'measuring-programme' has been carried out in order to see to what extent this distance varies with personality factors, the nature of social relations (family, friendships, authority), situational factors (private-public, informal-formal), sex differences and (sub-)cultural differences. The methods of research range from having subjects arrange little figures or dolls said to stand in a certain relation to each other, via similar research with real people under laboratory conditions, to observing in 'natural' situations. A frequently used technique is that of 'space intrusion' in which one has an assistant deliberately intrude on someone's 'personal space' and then observes how the subject reacts. Altman summarizes a number of findings as follows:

—People with personality defects often show abnormal spatial behaviour; either they come too close or they keep at too great a distance.

—Children learn to 'keep the correct distance' gradually, parallel to the development of other social skills. In conformity with this girls learn to keep the 'correct' distance sooner than boys do.

—As regards sex differences no general conclusions can be drawn as yet.

—The same holds for cultural differences; often, research on this becomes the more complicated because of socio-economic variables closely connected with cultural factors.

—Distance between friends and persons regarded favourably is less than between strangers and persons regarded unfavourably.

As was noted above, avoiding eye contact and/or completely or partly turning away from the other is a compensation for too short a distance and the thus increased awareness of the other's presence. The combination of these behavioural mechanisms probably underlies the arangement of furniture, its (in)formal character, and the preference, based on the relation to the social partner, for a particular configuration. (Future) leaders of a group often occupy the head of the the table (Sommer, 1969), like many fathers at the family table. In relations which are informal and based on equality among partners, they tend to sit closer together or next to each other or at the corner of the table, whereas in a hierarchical or competitive relation the partners are seated opposite each other at a greater distance; sometimes the person lower in rank even remains standing. (A situation typical, for instance, for the judge and the accused. Moreover, a judge is often seated on a podium.) Sommer (1966, 1974) discusses a great number of interesting examples, particularly from the realm of public buildings, schools and psychiatric hospitals, where the arrangement of furniture cannot or can hardly be influenced (because it is fastened to the floor) or where its users are not allowed to interfere with it (because it is forbidden). He shows that because of this, interaction between people comes about with great difficulty or not at all. Furthermore, he refers to the fact that in these situations certain arrangements of furniture are determined by considerations of efficient maintenance and ideas of 'order and neatness' rather than by their real purpose, i.e. to offer users a choice in obtaining the desired individual or group privacy by spatial and physical means.

Territorial behaviour. As is the case with personal space, the study of human territorial behaviour, too, is inspired by the study of animals. In many species of animals territorial behaviour has been observed and found to be essential for their survival. The marking and defending of their territorial boundaries are a condition and guarantee for a relatively undisturbed course of vital functions such as feeding, mating and rearing their young.

The marking of territorial boundaries, which sometimes coincide with elements already present in the area, takes place in many different ways: by scent-, sound- or visible markings or by threatening behaviour. These signals are in the first place, meant for members of their own species and are respected by them. Consequently, real aggression and fights decrease once the boundaries are marked. Besides, animals seem to have the advantage over possible intruders when they are on their own territory. 'Home matches' are generally won. It is believed, that the territorial behaviour of animals is of vital importance for regulating social contacts and for the stability of the social system.

Inspired by these animal studies, human territorial behaviour has been observed and more closely examined as well. In a series of experiments Altman and his assistants have examined the connection between territorial behaviour and the social relation between pairs of volunteers from the navy. Under the pretence of testing a simulated stay in a submarine space, the two volunteers of each pair, until then complete strangers, were brought together in a socially entirely isolated space for a period of eight to ten days. The pairs were formed on the basis of test scores on dominance (i.e. the inclination to influence and control others). Pairs were composed either of people who both had high scores or by people of whom one scored high and the other low. Territorial behaviour was defined as the exclusive appropriation of a certain chair, bed, part of the room, etc., as opposed to a joint use of space and the objects in it by both partners. In accordance with the expectations, there were more verbal and physical skirmishes in the situation in which both were dominant, the tasks to be performed were badly carried out and there were more signs of stress and emotionality. What's more, in this situation fewer people endured the entire experiment. With these pairs, no clear territorial defining took place during the first days, but usually only at the end of the test period. With the dominant/non-dominant pairs the territorial defining was settled almost immediately, the same as with agreeing on the daily schedule, when to eat, work, and sleep. With these pairs in particular the territorial behaviour decreased during the test period. It was as if, as soon as these pairs noticed that they got on well, they attached less value to exclusive territories. Contrary to this the dominant couples, because of their problems to attune mutually to a flexible behaviour, resorted to territorial behaviour.

These and other studies of human territorial behaviour, make clear that man disposes of more forms of behaviour than animals in order to achieve a certain stability in his societal patterns. The spatial boundaries of human territories are therefore usually more flexible and open, although they do have to meet social-cultural (immaterial boundaries) conditions.

With this we come to an essential problem for architecture as well as environmental psychology, namely how material and immaterial 'resources' combine in the arrangement of human activities.

4. BUILDING AND ORGANIZING AS A PURPOSEFUL ARRANGE- MENT OF HUMAN ACTIVITIES IN SPACE AND TIME

We may illustrate this statement with the following experiment. A subject is given the matrix represented in figure 4 and asked to arrange per row the activities

activity	matches best with						matches least with
1. sleeping/parents							
2. sleeping/children							
3. sitting							
4. eating							
5. cooking							
6. bathing							
7. entrance							
8. toilet							

Figure 4. Matrix of activities.

consecutively, according to the degree to which they may or may not be linked best to the first activity.

The activities thus arranged were numbered (1 = best matching, and 7 = least matching) and on the resulting row-conditional distance-matrix, multi-dimensional scaling analysis was applied[1] and the two-dimensional solution of figure 5 obtained. The activities, indicated by dots, are arranged in such a way that two dots are situated more closely together, as, according to the subject, the activities match better. The interpretation of this configuration is that the subject arranges the various activities along a 'day-night' and a 'front-back' dimension.

The 'front-back' dimension is described in detail by Goffman (1959) in terms of 'on-stage' and 'off-stage' behaviour. In front of the décor people play their roles according to social expectations; behind it they drop their masks and feel free to behave as they please.

The arrangement according to the 'day-night' dimension (in the traditional Dutch low-rise house, this corresponds to the spatial distribution 'downstairs-upstairs'), refers to motives to connect activities spatially which succeed each other or overlap in time, and do match. When, however, they do not match (like

[1] The data were analysed by means of the SMACOF-I programme of dr. W. Heiser, University of Leiden, Dept. of Data Theory.

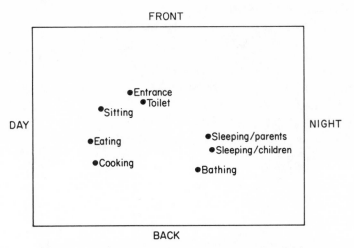

Figure 5. Two-dimensional representation of activities.

sleeping children and parents receiving visitors; in the sitting room) they should spatially be separated.

Beside a similar, more or less static, abstract spatial pattern—in which one may imagine walls and floors, windows and doors as partitions and connections, like a kind of filters between the various activities—there are, per household and (sub)culture varying norms and ideas about who is permitted to do what, where and when in such a spatial pattern. In this case, one could consider these norms and ideas as immaterial filters. The joint activity of both kinds of filters, material and immaterial, results in a certain grouping of people and their activities in time and space, as illustrated in figure 6. It should be noted that material filters very often act like immaterial filters as well, in that they symbolize or refer to social norms etc.

We will now turn to two illustrations of architectural-psychological applications of some of the ideas developed so far.

4.1. A translation of organizational relations into spatial relations

One may replace the residential activities from the above example (figures 4,5) by individuals, groups or sections within an organization. One may then ask these individuals etc. to state how close their relation with the other individuals, groups, sections within the organization is or should be. As a measure of the strength of a relation one may take, for instance, the number of verbal contacts per day, the volume of mail or goods traffic, the importance of contacts, etc. or some weighted score of all these measures. In the example described below, persons were merely asked to order the other sections on the scale: 'much, little or no relation'.

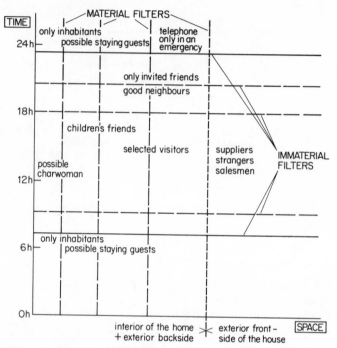

Figure 6. The ordering people in time and space by means of a combination of both material and immaterial filters.

The organization in question had two buildings at its disposal. The one building housed the production sections, headed by a production manager, the other the 'office sections' and the managing directors. The management had decided to put all sections together in a new building in a town 15 kilometres from the then place of business.

The motives were mainly economical; the production sections had been much reduced, which caused their building to be empty for the greater part. The traffic between the two buildings was maintained by spacial messengers.

The employees were confronted with an accomplished fact; they would have to travel longer in order to get to their work. Also, they did not agree with some of the lay-out plans for the new building, made by an architect following the board's suggestions. Anyhow, they wanted to be involved in these plans, to decide about the number, the size and further lay-out of the rooms for their own department and their location relative to other departments, the canteen and the meeting-room. At that moment, the present author was invited by the board of directors to organize and to round off this 'participation' of the employees in a week's time. The building schedule was very tight, as usual.

Per department, under the leadership of the head of the department, a form was filled out to arrange the other departments according to the degree of their relation with the own department. The board, too, filled out a similar form. They were also asked to place themselves in the position of each of the other departments and to arrange the remaining departments from that position.

In this way, two configurations were obtained,[2] one based on a combination of the arrangement of the departments (circles in figure 7) and one based on the board's assessment of these separate arrangements (dots in figure 7; for both configurations the dot and circle representing the board/secretary/typing-room merge).

The dot and circle representing one and the same department in both configurations are connected by a line. The length of this line indicates the discrepancy between the 'image' of the employees and that of the board. Roughly, these 'images' agree fairly well. In both configurations, all production sections are situated on the left (of the broken line), the office sections on the right. Both left and right, the partial configurations correspond rather well. In the discussion of these configurations with employees and board a few interesting aspects emerged. In the first place, it turned out that they were quite able to recognize and interpret this abstract 'picture' of their own organization. In the second place, the widest discrepancies between the two configurations, viz. with regard to the location of the canteen, the sales-groups and, to a lesser extent, the meeting-room, did turn out to be exactly those points which the employees had criticized in the first lay-out plans.

In the old situation, there had only been a canteen in the production building, which the employees often used in the evenings as well to play cards or to give parties. The production staff considered this canteen its favourite and exclusive territory.

The office staff had never had a canteen of their own, nor did they want one in the new building. They had their breaks in small, close-knit groups in their rooms, went for a stroll or had lunch at home. The board had very pronounced ideas about the location and function of the canteen in the new building. They wanted to make it into a meeting-place for both office and production staff and therefore to situate it half-way the production and office departments.

As to the relative location of the sales groups, this department was until then regarded—and regarded itself—as the most important department of the organization. The board, however, was working at reorganization plans which had not yet been made public. In this plan, the projects department in particular would play a more important role than it had done so far and would collaborate more closely with the board. The sales departments would loose their relative importance. Finally, as regards the position of the meeting room, the board wanted to link it to the office of the board of directors. In the existing office building the meeting room was situated far away from their department and the board expected to reduce the number and duration of meetings by exercising close supervision and control.

---

[2] Analysed also by means of the SMACOF-I programme (see footnote 1).

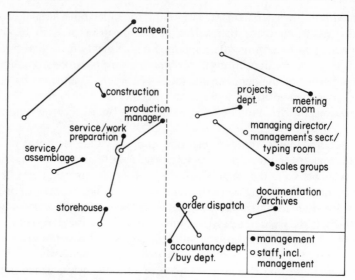

Figure 7. Configurations of departments (dots in circles) and managements (dots).

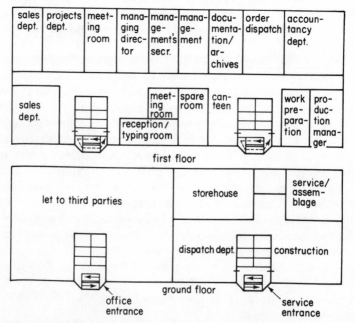

Figure 8. Lay-out of the new building.

The final outline of the lay-out of the new building is shown in figure 8. The production departments concerned with the supply and dispatch of goods are situated on the ground floor. Management, work preparation, canteen, and all office departments are situated on the first floor. The staircase on the right serves as the internal connection between both floors.

4.2. Spatial differentiation in agreement with the nature of work.

The 'landscaped' office is an exception to the rule that work- and organization environments have so far enjoyed little attention in architectural psychology (for reviews, see Heimessen, 1968; van Hoogdalem, 1980). One of the major problems experienced by many in the 'landscaped' office is that of doing work that requires a great deal of concentration. That is why in the firm where this case study was carried out many people regularly worked at home. The firm had once before held a special inquiry among these 'home workers', asking questions like: 'What do you think is the disadvantage of working at home?' 'How should a "landscaped" office be changed so as to make it pleasant to work in?' Answers to the first question were: 'you always have to carry your things about', 'you don't have reference books and documentation available at home', 'at home you're out of reach for colleagues', 'it makes an unfavourable impression on the firm's clients', 'it is not fair on colleagues who are not able (or allowed) to work at home', 'it is bad for the team spirit'. In short, this 'locational response' was not considered the perfect adjustment of worker and work environment.

In a series of interviews with the members of a department that had many 'home workers', one question in particular was emphasized: 'To which of your activities is the present environment favourable and to which is it unfavourable?' The various answers to this question could be arranged according to the different phases of a problem-solving process, whereas the impact of the 'landscaped' office was worded mainly in terms of a varying need of communication; see the scheme below.

Phase in the problem-solving process	*Characteristics of the need of communication*
I. *Defining-the-problem phase* In this phase, a question or a task should be translated into a solvable problem. Broad orientation, clarifi-tion, delineation in the field of the problems and their potential solutions.	I. The need of communication is great-est in this phase. One consults col-leagues, asks for advice and suggestions, wants to 'brain-storm'. Discussions may take rather long and 'run amok'. It is noticed that discussions overheard earlier (which was experienced as disturbing at the time) proved useful for the work in this phase. This is why one knows rather well who was dealing when with what subject.

II. *'Routine phase'*
In this phase, the solution and ela-boration of (partial) problems which are now formulated more clearly, is worked upon. Gathering literature and information. working out the material according to more or less familiar procedures. Because the work is now more structured, it requires average concentration. Moreover, it is possible to take up the thread rather quickly again after disturbances and interruptions.

II. In this phase, the need of communication is more purposeful. One knows more clearly, whom and what one needs for which specific task. On the other hand, the work is less sensitive to interruptions in this phase.

III. *Integration phase*
In this phase a paper (design, report, conclusion, recommendation) should be written based on previously worked out parts. The construction of an argumentation and adherence to this line of thought require a great deal of concentration. One builds up 'pressure'; after every interruption a relatively long time is required to take up the thread.

III. There is little need of communication. At most, one requires very specific information from others and one does not like to be confronted with questions or problems of others. Possible contacts with others are directed rather at recreation and at affirmation of the line one follows oneself. Some people literally arrange all separate parts of their work spatially and use this configuration as external support of the mental picture or concept they are working out.

On grounds of this inventory and summary it was proposed to split up the available space, which up to that moment had been equally divided between all members (each had about the same space and found himself so to speak, in the middle of it), in three clearly distinguishable zones:

—A *'quiet zone'*, meant for work in phase III. This zone, surrounded by tall filing cabinets, should only have long desks alongside the walls. Someone sitting there, should absolutely not be disturbed; furthermore, no conversation was permitted.

—The *'primary working zone'* for work in phase II. The existing work places were to be concentrated in this zone. In order to gain space to create a 'quiet zone', there had to be a two-way condensation: by having self-selected groups of two or three persons move their desks together, and by having the second lay-out table, that everybody had in the present situation, replaced by a filing cabinet of 1.50 meter high. Apart from saving space, this cabinet would also create a visual separation. Calls for people who are working in the 'quiet zone', are taken by the 'neighbours'. Long internal discussions and discussions with visitors should take place somewhere else, preferably in the discussion zone.

—The *'discussion zone'*, for work in phase I. This zone preferably to be situated at the entrance of the department area, would provide for one or more seats or tables, surrounded by partitions or cabinets of 1.50 metre high.

The staff accepted both the analysis of their activities and the spatial-organizational plan, but thought a special discussion zone was superfluous. In order to get an indication of the required number of seats in the *'quiet zone'* everybody kept a time diary, to account for their activities in terms of phase I, II and III. This took place over a period of one month. The results of the entire department were:

work in phase I: 18%; work in phase II: 43%;
work in phase III: 30%; work elsewhere: 9%.

On the basis of this outcome, three chairs were provided in the *'quiet zone'* for every ten workers. Subsequently, with the help of a scale model of 1:50, the employees worked at new lay-out and the formation of (sub)groups. The department itself requested the high filing cabinets from the management.

The new lay-out by now exists well over two years and functions according to expectations. The *'quiet zone'* is made full use of and people stick reasonably well to the 'quiet'-rules, while visitors and telephone-calls are duly received and filtered in the *'primary working-zone'*. Whether the amount of working at home has really decreased, has not been checked, due to, among other things, a considerable number of staff mutations in this department.

In other 'landscaped' offices there are often special 'quiet' spaces; a disadvantage is, however, that they are often situated at some distance from the departments and managed from a central point. They have to be reserved in advance and for a certain length of time. The solution realized here (decentralized, direct accessibility, group control, consensus on rules of conduct) does not have the concomitant 'tuning' problems.

5. BUILDING AS AN INTERDISCIPLINARY APPROACH

By way of conclusion we will mention, following Duffy and Worthington (1977), a number of organizational problems, which are closely connected with characteristics of buildings and therefore require an interdisciplinary approach in the design process of work- and organizational experts and architects.

1. How and how fast does the size of an organization as a whole and of its parts change? This growth-pattern has consequences for the extent to which the building ought to offer possibilities for enlarging or reducing it. Can the building be subdivided in such a way that parts may be let to third parties?
2. What is the distribution of group sizes of the work-units? What is—and under what conditions—the optimum size of groups? With this knowledge the architect will be able to design a dimensional structure, which will offer the correct lay-out and possibilities of subdivision.
3. Into what units or departments is the organization divided (differentiation) and in what way are they again integrated? How does communication and decision-making take place in the organization? To what extent can the building support the communication processes (see Duffy, 1974)?

4. What is the relation between organization and environment? Where should one situate the building or buildings? This is important in connection with the way clients and employees get to the building, with the supply and dispatch of goods, and the location of other organizations. What impression does the organization wish to make on its environment? Should accessibility be increased by providing more than one entrance, or does this present difficulties in management and surveillance activities?

5. Who within the organization makes the decisions on the designs? Is the final decision in one hand or is it spread over several persons? Obviously, this has major consequences for the task of the architect and for his possibilities to bring unity in his design.

REFERENCES

Altman, I. (1975), *The environment and social behavior*. Belmont (Cal.): Wadsworth.

Altman, I., Wohlwill, J. F. (1977), *Human behavior and environment, Vol. 2*. New York/London: Plenum Press.

Bell, P. A., Fischer, J. D., Loomis, R. J. (1978), *Environmental psychology*. Philadelphia: W.B. Saunders.

Broadbent, G. (1978), The rational and the functional. In: Sharp, F. (Ed.), *The rationalists. Theory and design in the modern movement*. London: The Architectural Press.

Canter, D. (Ed.) (1975), *Environmental interaction*. Surrey University Press.

Craik, K. H. (1973), Environmental psychology. *Annual Review of Psychology*, 24, 403–422.

Downs, R. M. Stea, D. (1977), *Maps in minds. Reflections on cognitive mapping*. New York: Harper and Row.

Duffy, F. (1974), *Office design and organization*. Environment and Planning B, Vol. 1, no. 2.

Duffy, F., Worthington, J. (1977), Organizational design. *Journal of Architectural Research*, 6, no. 1. (March).

Goffman, E. (1959), *The presentation of self in everyday life*. Harmondsworth: Penguin (repr. 1971).

Grandjean, E. (1973), *Wohnphysiologie. Grundlagen gesunden Wohnens*. Züricht: Artemis Verlag.

Gutman, R. (1972), *People and buildings*. London/New York: Basic Books.

Hall, E. T. (1966), *The hidden dimension*. New York: Doubleday.

Handler, A. B. (1970), *Systems approach to architecture*. New York: American Elsevier.

Harvey, D. (1972), *Society, the city and the space-economy of urbanism*. Washington, D.C.: Association of American Geographers.

Heimessen, C. F. H. (1968), *Opinie-onderzoek in kantoorruimten* [Opinion survey in office spaces]. Delft: Delft University of Technology, Centre of Architectural Research.

Hillier, B., Leaman, A. (1976), Architecture as a discipline. *Journal of Architectural Research*, 5, no. 1 (March).

Hoogdalem, H. van (1977), Some conceptual tools for the analysis of man-environment systems. *Delft Progress Report 2*, 249–256.

Hoogdalem, H. van (1980), Onderzoek naar ervaringen met kantoortuinen [Investigation of experiences with landscaped offices]. In: *Kantoortuinen of cellenkantoor, hoe maken wij een keuze?* [Landscaped offices or an office in cells: how do we choose?]. SER-Publication Deventer: Kluwer/Ten Haagen.

Jonge, D. de (1960), *Moderne woonidealen en woonwensen in Nederland* [Modern ideals and desires with regard to living in The Netherlands]. Arnhem: Vuga.

King, A. D. (1976), Values, science and settlement: A case study in environmental control. In: Rapaport, A. (Ed.), *The mutual interaction of people and their built environment*. The Hague/Paris: Mouton.

Lipman, A., Harris, H. (1980), Environmental psychology: A sterile research enterprise? *Architectural Psychology Newsletter*, **10**, no. 2 (June), 18–28.

McLoughlin, J. B. (1970), *Urban and regional planning: A systems approach*. London: Faber and Faber.

Michelson, W. (1970), *Man and his urban environment: A sociological approach*. Reading (Mass.): Addison-Wesley.

Michelson, W. (1975), *Behavioral research in environmental design*. Stroudsburg (Penn.): Dowden, Hutchinson and Ross.

Miller, G. A., Pribram, K. H., Galanter, E. (1960), *Plans and the structure of behavior*. New York: Holt, Rienhart and Winston.

Neufert, E. (1980), *Architects' data*. 2nd (International) English edition, ed. by V. Jones. London: Granada.

Prak, N. L. (1973), *De visuele waarneming van de gebouwde omgeving* [Visual perception of the built environment]. Delft: University of Technology, Dept. of Building Engineering.

Proshansky, H. M., Altman, I. (1979), Overview of the field. In: White, W. P. (Ed.), *Resources in environment and behavior*. Washington, D.C.: American Psychological Association.

Proshansky, H. M., Ittelson, W. H., Rivlin, L. G. (1970), *Environmental psychology. Man and his physical setting*. New York: Holt, Rinehart and Winston.

Rapaport, A. (Ed.) (1970), *The mutal interaction of people and their built environment*. The Hague/Paris: Mouton.

Sommer, R. (1969), *Personal space. The behavioral basis of design*. Englewood Cliffs (N.J.): Prentice-Hall.

Sommer, R. (1974), *Tight spaces. Hard architecture and how to humanize it*. Englewood Cliffs (N.J.): Prentice-Hall.

Steffen, C., Voordt, D. J. M. van der (1978), *Belevingsonderzoek stedelijk milieu* [A study of how the urban environment is experienced]. Delft: University of Technology, Centre of Architectural Research.

Stokols, D. (1977), *Perspectives on environment and behavior. Theory, research and applications*. New York: Plenum Press.

Stokols, D. (1978), Environmental psychology. *Annual Review of Psychology*, **29**, 253–295.

Wohlwill, J. F., Carson, D. H. (Eds.) (1972), *Environment and the social sciences: Perspectives and applications*. Washington, D.C.: American Psychological Association.

Zeisel, J. (1981), *Inquiry by design. Tools for environment-behavior research*. Monterey (Cal.): Brooks/Cole.

Handbook of Work and Organizational Psychology
Edited by P. J. D. Drenth, H. Thierry, P. J. Willems and C. J. de Wolff
© 1984, John Wiley & Sons, Ltd.

5.4. European industrial relations in a time of crisis

W. Albeda

1. INTRODUCTION

Since 1973 the Western world has been experiencing a depression, comparable only to the depression of the 1930s. Economic growth rates went down from a comfortable five or six per cent in the sixties to one or two per cent, and several countries have reached negative figures for the GNP development already. After so many prosperous years, after having had full employment during such a long period, this is a very traumatic experience, influencing each sector and every aspect of society. Of course, labour relations are not excluded.

No-one could say that the years between 1945 and 1973 were easy years for trade union leaders and employers. Labour relations deal with the social aspects of economic change. And economic growth implies very important economic changes, as economic history clearly shows. From the point of view of labour relations the most important changes were as follows:
—A period of mass consumption developed after the period of recovery from the war.
—Full employment changed the power relationships within the labour relation systems.
—The new wealth led to an important development in the field of education. New workers have had a better education, and have higher qualifications when entering the labour market.
—Within the labour force, the relative importance of clerical and professional workers on the labour market increased. The shift from manufacturing to

Dr. W. Albeda, Rijks Universiteit Limburg, Algemene Faculteit, 6200 MD Maastricht.

services, predicted by authors like Colin Clark and Jean Fourastie, took place indeed.

Such changes cannot leave the labour relations system unaffected. It seems appropriate to first pay some attention to the important changes in labour relations.

2. CHANGING SYSTEMS

In a sense, it is an heroic venture to speak of a European 'labour scene'. Although the various economic systems in Western Europe share many basic characteristics, the social and cultural climate differs widely from country to country. It is well known that the European trade union movement, although certainly not a unitary movement, has characteristics that are sharply opposed to those of the American trade unions. This difference has been explained by Reichhold in his basic study on the European labour movement (1953), by taking into account the different developments that took place on both sides of the Atlantic during the 19th and the beginning of the 20th century. During the 'formative' years of the American labour movement, labour was scarce and American industry had to draw upon the world market for skilled labour. Moreover, industry had to compete with agriculture: workers had the alternative to 'go west' and to become independent farmers. This reality of the beginning of this century became the myth of the present: the American workers have always thought that the laws of capitalism worked in their favour. Therefore, the trade unions (after a short period of radicalism) tried to utilize capitalism instead of fighting it. The basic attitude of the American unions (job control rather than control of the work organization or the economy) may be explained in this light.

In contrast, the European trade union movement has always remembered that the origins of industrialism in Europe were characterized by an abundance of labour and a shortage of capital. The laws of capitalism, therefore, worked against labour during the years capitalism developed in Europe.

This could explain the basically anticapitalist attitude of the European labour movement and the close ties between socialist ideology and the unions in most European countries. Generally, European workers still suspect that the system works against them. This attitude is basic even in those countries we call 'integrating'. The difference between 'polarization' and 'integration' is, perhaps, one of method rather than one of principle.

It is necessary to keep in mind this basic state of affairs, when postwar developments in Western Europe are to be discussed. It can explain the ongoing flow of ideas from the radical South to the pragmatic North. It also explains why full employment and the improved standard of living did not, up to now, undermine the influence of socialism in European politics.

With regard to the labour relation system, the European countries may be divided into two main groups: the Latin countries with their polarizing system and the northwestern part of the continent with its integrating system.

a) As the name indicates, *polarizing* systems are characterized by a high degree of labour unrest, uncooperative trade unions, rather conservative and inflexible employers, and a high level of strike activity. The trade unions in these countries have strong, ideological objections against private enterprise; they are more interested in the possible changes in the economic system than in short-term improvements. Because of their rejection of the system as such they are not impressed by the fact that there are economic limits to their demands. The employers respond to this attitude by resisting trade union demands whenever possible (thus reinforcing the union position and show little willingness to compromise vis-à-vis the trade unions. the unions are characterized by a high degree of spontaneity and decentralization, but have eternal financial and organizational problems: they are a movement rather than an organization.

b) The *integrative* systems are characterized by cooperative trade unions and employers who are prepared to recognize them and to work towards compromises; as a consequence, there is a high degree of peace in the labour relations system. The trade unions are well organized and relatively well funded, but tend toward bureaucratization. They are an organization rather than a movement.

The differences in the characteristic features of the trade unions are summarized in table 1. Although this tabulation may seen a bit simple, it is well documented in a number of studies (e.g. Jacobs, 1973; Ross and Hartman, 1960). In their interesting comparative study on patterns of industrial conflict in the world, Ross and Hartman make a distinction between, among other things, a northern-European type of industrial relations and a mediterranean system. In the European Economic Community, the northern-European system is to be found in West Germany and The Netherlands is characterized by few strikes, in which relatively few workers are involved and few working days are lost. The mediterranean system, as found in France and Italy, is characterized by many strikes of short duration, involving many workers. Belgium can be considered as an intermediate between these two extremes. Ross and Hartman list the following important factors explaining these differences:

—the different roles of the governments in the socio-economic sphere,
—the more or less sophisticated policy of the employers,
—the degree of centralization in the bargaining system,
—the existence of class contrasts.

In a number of countries, the trade unions are divided along ideological or religious lines. Belgium, The Netherlands, and Switzerland have denominational trade unions alongside socialist and liberal trade unions. France and Italy each have a communist trade union. The existence of communist trade unions may be an indication of the fact that major groups of workers feel left behind in the process of modernization. In Italy the existence of the underdeveloped 'mezzogiorno' of course strengthens such feelings. Although the communist trade unions are the strongholds of polarization, it is the polarization of the

Table 1. Characteristics of two types of trade unions.

	POLARIZING	INTEGRATING
Character of organization	ideological movement	bureaucracy
Union attitude toward society	hostile	accepting, compromising
Union attitude	revolutionary	reformist
Bargaining	unequal struggle	bargaining as equals
Influence on decision making	use of power in factory and on the street	input at the conference table
Strikes	often	seldom
Organizational structure	weak	strong
Unity	fragmented	tight
Finance	poor	good

society itself that lies at the root of this attitude among workers. It is interesting to note that in both Italy and France the relative importance of agriculture within the labour force is higher than in the other European countries. Revel (1981) pointed out recently that in the elections of 1981 in France only the most 'archaic regions voted communist. 'The map of industrialization in France does not coincide with the map of the communist vote' and the communist-inspired CGT has been losing members since 1977.

Unlike their counterparts in northwestern Europe, the French trade unions have never believed in the slow process of piecemeal changes to adapt the capitalist system to the 'humanistic' ideas of the labour movement. As a consequence, collective bargaining never developed like it did in northwestern Europe. At the same time one should be aware that the attitude of the employers in more than one sense mirrors the attitude of the trade unions. The 'patronat français' is a powerful, but rather conservative movement, less open to change than are northwest-European or American employers.

Whereas trade unions in northwestern Europe are well organized, well funded, and well staffed, the trade unions in Italy have permanent financial problems leading to difficulties in the field of staffing. Trade unions are having a hard time because of their unstable membership, low dues, and the dependence of their officers upon part-time, and politically bound jobs. Only in some branches, such as the metal and chemical industries, are the three federations strongly organized. The Italian trade unions, however, are well known for the number of innovative ideas which they develop. Especially during the sixties, new impulses often originated in the CGIL and CISL. The communist CGIL is much less dogmatic and far more innovative than its French counterpart. Many new ideas, such as the introduction of bargaining for jobs or for the quality of work, originated in Italy.

Until 1933, the German trade union movement, divided into denominational, social-democratic, and conservative unions, had set the example for the rest of Europe. Germany developed the industrial union, comprising all trades, instead of the craft unions of Britain. The well-organized, rather pragmatic German trade unions established the pattern for the set-up and organization of trade unions all over northwestern Europe. After the war, the German trade unions were in a position to make a completely new start. The denominational trade unions never regained their strength. The DGB has become the most important trade union organization in Western Europe, with its six million members organized in a few powerful unions, and with a rather conservative leadership. The unique system of 'Mitbestimmung' (codetermination) in the mining and steel industries and the 'Betriebsverfassung' in other inudustries played an important role in integrating the workers and, by implication, the trade unions in postwar German society.

The Dutch trade unions played a unique role in the years immediately after World War II. As a consequence of the general conviction that only a policy of low wages could bring about full employment, employers and trade unions decided to support a government-controlled wage policy. For almost 20 years (1945 to 1963/4) the government had the power to fix wage rates for all industries, advised of course by the central federation of employers and trade unions, cooperating within the 'Stichting van de Arbeid' (Foundation of Labour). During this period an attempt was made to base wage developments on the results of economic studies rather than on the power relations at the bargaining table. The system collapsed in 1963 (the so-called wage explosion), when scarcity on the labour market led to regional developments totally contrary to the national agreements.

In the Scandinavian countries, after the prewar years of centralized bargaining systems based upon a master agreement (in Sweden the so-called Salsjöbaden-agreement of 1938), the development was carried to its logical conclusion: bargaining at the national level for the national wage level, with governments which, although of course very interested in the outcome, never played such an active role as the Dutch government.

3. DEVELOPMENTS IN THE SIXTIES

In the postwar period, especially in the northwestern European countries, the 'anticapitalist trauma' could have been expected to disappear under the influence of full employment and the rising standard of living. In the years before 1960, in the worldwide mood known as 'the end of ideology' (Bell, 1973), the 'law of increasing peace' in industrial relations was postulated, not quite in earnest, but nonetheless not as a joke either. Several studies hypothesized that as industrial society 'matured' (indicated by rising wages and fewer working hours), workers would learn to accept their dependence, their lack of autonomy, and their unchallenging jobs. The following factors were supposed to work in this direction:

a) Increasing organizational stability. The trade union movement is consolidated in one or more federations that are recognized as important and basic elements in the societal organization.

b) Increasing sophistication of employers. Union-management relations arrive at a stable pattern of collective bargaining at an ever more central level.

c) Connections between unions and powerful political parties.

d) Increased governmental activities in the field of labour relations; moreover, the government feels rather sympathetic towards the trade union movement.

It was possible to perceive such a development particularly in the northwestern parts of West Europe. In the Scandinavian countries these conditions were already present and relative peace in labour relations seem to be result.

However, in the sixties two new developments changed this rather appealing future:

1) The development and persistence of high inflation rates.

2) The development of new (and partly the resurrection of old) ideologies after that postwar period when ideologies appeared to be dead or slumbering.

ad 1: The unique economic developments of the fifties and sixties caused scarcities on the regional and national labour markets. Phillips curves describe the process of wages being pushed up by the trade unions or by groups of workers exploiting the scarcity of certain skills, while at the same time the resistance of employers, competing for the last worker on the labour market, weakens.

At the same time, governments all over Europe constructed comprehensive and generous systems of social security. They pursued regional economic policies to overcome the persistence of regional unemployment even during national full-employment situations. All over Europe, people entered the automobile-age and consumption was rising to ever higher levels. In a number of countries, the trade unions try to protect their members against the dangers of inflation, which would take away their purchase power, by introducing automatic price index clauses in collective agreements. Such arrangements will reinforce already inherent inflationary tendencies. International monetary developments add to this worldwide inflation.

ad 2: In the sixties, Europe experienced a kind of a 'cultural revolution', just like North America. Although this revolution did not find its origin in labour relations, it did influence labour relations. This 'cultural revolution' started at the universities, when the student movement protested against what they perceived as authoritarian attitudes and bureaucratic structures. They turned to neo-marxist thinking which considers the 'consumption society' of both the capitalist West and the communist East as the explanation for a perceived lack of freedom and insufficient economic and social democracy. Economic growth was not praised as a source of the rising standard of living, but was criticized for the damage it did to the environment, to the quality of life in general, and to working life in particular.

This new ideology is calling for 'democratization' and power distribution. It may be seen as a reaction against the unmistakable development of strongly bureaucratic, technocratic elements both in government and in business. In a sense, modern socialism suffers from a paradox. The demand for a well-organized, just, and secure society has fostered the development of technocracy and bureacracy. At present, this same socialism is asking for individual freedom, for the self-government of small groups (geographical and functional), and for 'workers control'. This new ideology did not fail to influence the trade union movement: a radicalization of their theoretical stance and, later, of action took place, first in the south and later in the north of West Europe. This radicalization has the following characteristics (see also Barkin, 1975):

1) A new and more strongly anticapitalist position.

2) A new interpretation of socialism: highly decentralized and characterized by democratic planning and workers' control.

3) This new ideological attitude leads to a 'harsher' attitude, using the weapon of strikes more easily than before, and accepting also the more radical weapon of the occupation of plants (Crouch and Pizzorno, 1978).

4) A new emphasis on trade union activities at the shopfloor rather than mainly at the national or industrial level.

5) More emphasis on 'non-wage' issues in the bargaining process, including industrial democracy and codetermination.

This development may be documented as follows: perhaps the most spectacular development occurred in 1970 when everywhere in Europe, from Britain to Poland and from Sweden to Italy, wild-cat strikes took place. The explanation should be two-fold. On the one hand the tense labour markets gave rise to a power shift within the trade unions. Given local shortages of labour, groups of determined workers were able by means of strikes, to gain wage increases which their unions could never have managed by bargaining The revolt of Paris in 1968, which was initiated by students but taken up by the trade unions, and the 'hot autumn' in Italy in 1969 triggered off such developments in many other countries (Spitaels, 1972). The seventies witnessed interesting new achievements in the field of codetermination, industrial democracy, and safety and health, which were a response to this development.

The denominational trade unions in The Netherlands and Belgium were not immune to these developments. The Dutch Catholic unions underwent a radicalization that facilitated the merger of that trade union movement with the social-democratic NVV (Nederlands Verbond van Vakverenigingen) into the FNV (Federate Nederlandse Vakbeweging) in 1976. Although the Belgium ACV (Algemeen Christelijk Vakverbond) has accepted the idea of 'workers self management', its position vis-à-vis the socialist ABVV (Algemeen Belgisch Vakverbond) remain clear and uncompromising.

With respect to codetermination, the German system was extended to encompass the steel and coal industries. At the same time, employers saw their chance to retreat a little from the 50–50 ratio the 1951 law provided the workers. In The Netherlands, Sweden, and Norway forms of codetermination were introduced (new legislation broadening the scope of works councils, and new legislation with regard to workers' rights to appoint members to supervisory boards). This development was confined to the countries of northwestern Europe. In the polarizing systems of France and Italy and in the British system, attempts to change the organizational structures have barely had a chance. The distrust of the trade unions as regards the functioning of private enterprise economies is too great to interest them in such changes that concentrate on democratization of private companies within the existing system. Trade unions in France and Italy wish to change the system as such. Martinet (1979) says: 'because they are rich and powerful, and because they are reformist, the trade unions of Northern Europe have no fear of entering the super supervisory board of private companies. Because they are relatively poor and also in view of their revolutionary tradition the trade unions of Southern Europe (outside the public sector) restrict themselves to claiming control'.

The British trade unions take up a somewhat different position: they distrust forms of democratization which develop outside the trade union structures. They see only 'one unique way' or workers' influence: through their unions. The British trade unions, therefore, have always preferred strong trade union representation on the shopfloor (the shop-steward system) over forms of formal democracy within private companies.

In the field of the quality of work, safety, and health, new developments took place all over Europe (Hetzler, 1980). Italian trade unions played a pioneering role by introducing issues like content of the job, functioning of the assembly line, speed of work and so on, into their bargaining process, applying the results of American studies in a marxist environment. Later, in France and elsewhere in Europe, elements of the 'quality of work' were introduced into the bargaining (e.g. changes in the speed of the assembly line or proposals to abolish the assembly line altogether). In several countries, governments have introduced new legislation in this field (Sweden, Norway, The Netherlands). In these cases, the workers' and trade unions' influence was strengthened in this respect. In

France, the trade unions opposed the existing piece-work systems. In labour conflicts, matter like working pace and the abolition of the assembly line played a role. The shift system was attacked everywhere. Instead of the four-shift system, the five-shift system was proposed by the unions. In general, workers resisted working-time schedules, that interfered with their family life and leisure time. In several cases of 'productivity bargaining' in Britain, changes in the content of the job were introduced. In their 1974 Report on Industrial Democracy the TUC asked for an extension of the bargaining process that would lead to 'joint control over non-wage areas and work organizations'. In Germany and The Netherlands works councils now have new responsibilities in these fields.

'Shopfloor' democracy was promoted in different forms by employers and trade unions alike in various European countries. Well known are the Norwegian experiments in which the government, employers, and labour unions jointly sponsor the Norwegian National Participation Council, an organization encouraging experimentation in the design of work. In Great Britain quite some experience existed in this field as a result of the longstanding research of the Tavistock Institute. This research played a major role in the Norwegian developments. In Sweden, a task force made up of trade unions and employers' organizations sponsored independent research projects on several aspects of industrial democracy (Björk, 1975). In Germany, the Institute for Applied Social Sciences (Infas) made, at the request of the Minister of Labour, an investigation of labour satisfaction which led to various proposals for improvement and legislative actions.

Examples from other countries could be cited as well. The sixties and seventies saw a new 'mood' in Europe. It would be misleading to say that workers were no longer interested in wages and had shifted their attention to shopfloor democracy and the quality of working life. But it is unmistakably true that as a result of the new mood', these elements came to play more of a key-role in trade union activities and political discussions.

The European trade union movement is not a unitary organization. This means that different developments may take place simultaneously. Although most trade union activities take place at the bargaining table, and most trade unions are involved in the process of bargaining, in some countries a radical wing came into existence that rejected any form of cooperation with employers or with 'capitalist' governments (Crouch and Pizzorno, 1978). In general, this development did not influence the day-to-day functioning of the trade union movement in most countries. It is true, however, that most European trade unions have reaffirmed their belief in (some form of) socialism as their long-term objective.

The problem is, of course, what exactly 'socialism' means here. Is it some version of state socialism, as was introduced in France? Or rather a form of 'a worker-controlled company' in a planned economy? In all likelihood the latter ideal plays a predominant role in the policy and goals of many trade unions (Myrdal, 1980).

Employers in the private sector in Western Europe have a higher degree of organization and of joint action, than their counterparts in the U.S. or Japan (ILO, 1974). In Europe, although the figures differ per country, employers are well organized and they are willing to delegate important functions in the area of industrial relations to employers' organizations. As economic and industrial relations problems have become more and more complicated, many employers no longer command the expertise necessary for handling such problems. Moreover, given the more active role of governments in economic life, there is a growing need for representation of employers both at the industrial and at the central (= all-industry) level.

Employers' organizations span a range of functions at least as wide as those of unions. The ILO study 'Collective bargaining in industrialised market economies' sums them up as follows:

'They engage in important representational and lobbying tasks in relation to the legislative and administrative branches of government; their public information and public relations services are designed for the effective dissemination of employers' views; they often maintain research and data-gathering departments, and they may offer their constituents limited specialized legal services; and a number of them also assume responsibility for training and apprenticeship in their economic branches and seek to promote further development in their particular industrial sectors or geographical areas. Closer to the subject of labour-management relations, employers' associations engage in a wide variety of tasks which may include the formulation of common personnel policies for their members, the analysis of the collective bargaining proposals of unions, the research required for the adoption of a uniform employer position on union negotiating demands, and the actual conduct of collective agreements that are in force and the determination of employer strategy in the event of open industrial conflict.'

In a number of countries, for instance the Federal Republic of Germany, Sweden, and Great Britain, the necessity to counterbalance the power of highly concentrated labour unions led to the development of multi-industry associations, covering several large industries. These associations have a major say in the respective national confederations of employers' organizations.

It may be said that employers' organizations were set up as a response to the actions of the trade unions. In that sense, highly centralized trade union movements (like the Scandinavian TU for example) are confronted with highly centralized employers' organizations. In the same sense, it can be said that, like their bargaining partners, the trade unions, the employers' organizations fit in the national industrial-relations systems. The aggressive and revolutionary trade unions of France are faced with rather conservative employers: 'the employer in France is the patron, his national association is the patronat, and in these words is embodied an almost feudal flavour which contrasts strangely with our modern age' (Kendall, 1975).

In the Scandinavian countries and in The Netherlands employers' organizations have generally supported the development of centralized collective bargaining. In Germany the employers' organizations have resisted government interference with the process of collective bargaining, just like their counterparts of the DGB. Although in The Netherlands employers have sometimes asked for such interference, they joined the trade unions in their complaints before the ILO in 1981.

4. EUROPEAN INDUSTRIAL RELATIONS AND THE DEPRESSION

4.1. Trade unions and government policies

Since 1973 Western Europe has been suffering a depression whose scope and depth are comparable only to the depression of the thirties. Growth rates have come down from the average of five to six per cent in the sixties to one or two per cent or even negative values at the end of the seventies and the beginning of the eighties. At the same time, high inflation rates persist and unemployment is back at prewar levels.

As Dahrendorf (1981, p. 23) rightly remarked, the seventies were a breaking point in the upward trend. In many respects, the West-European welfare states were constructed under the assumption that economic growth rates of five per cent or more are normal and could be expected to continue. When growth rates start falling short of this percentage, many of the provisions of the welfare state are endangered: old age pensions, social provisions, sickness benefits and unemployment allowances, subsidies for housing and education—all have their own growth rate which, as economic growth slows down, will accelerate (especially unemployment allowances) rather than decelerate.

This means that the depression is a threat not only to the employment and standard of living of the working part of the population, but also to the incomes of an increasing part of the unemployed population. Although, generally speaking, West-Europeans still enjoy a rather high standard of living, confidence that this standard will continue is being undermined; job security and income security alike are in jeopardy.

International cooperation seems the most promising policy to end the economic depression. However, governments have very different ideas about what is a desirable policy. The monetarist governments (Great Britain and The Netherlands) want to reduce overall government spending and more particularly spending in the field of social security. All governments wish to limit wage increases. The socialist government of France initially followed a different path than other European countries. It nationalized an important part of industry, increased its spending in social security, and accepted Keynesian policies. Moreover, it supported the trade union demand for work sharing. However, the adverse effects of the expansion of government expenditure on its financial position within Europe forced the French government to limit its expenditure.

Trade unions in general favour Keynesian policies. This leads to ongoing conflicts between governments and trade unions. Most governments see no chance to avoid substantial savings on their budgets in general and on their social programmes in particular. At the same time, governments want to curb inflation and improve their competitive position on the world market by freezing wages. The often existing automatic price index clause of course makes such a policy yet more difficult.

Great Britain is an interesting example of the problems that may arise between government and trade unions (Barnes and Reid, 1980). Between 1972 and 1974, The General Council of the TUC and politicians of the Labour Party reached an agreement on the policies to which a next Labour government should commit itself. This agreement did not include voluntary wage restraint or forms of statutory wage controls. The role of wages in economic developments was played down. The manifesto, published by the party, strongly emphasized the ability of Labour to work with the unions. A labour government would 'control prices and attack speculation and set a climate fair enough to work together with the unions'.

In its first years the Wilson government had some success in convincing the trade unions of the necessity to moderate these wage clauses. But when in 1978, in its White paper 'Battle against Inflation', the government challenged the traditional concept of free collective bargaining and proposed a permanent income policy 'by implementation' (Barnes and Reid, 1980, p. 214), this led to a conflict with the TUC. In the words of Barnes and Reid, Callaghan (Wilson's successor) finally had to raise the question 'How can any government govern the country without provoking a destructive reaction from the trade unions?'. The TUC insists on the importance of free collective bargaining. Moreover, in the case of voluntary wage restraint, the TUC has in sufficient authority over the affiliated unions. Barnes and Reid conclude:

'It is true that the trade union movement is not the only pressure group whose activities cause inflation, or the only pressure group to compel governments to change or abandon policies. It has, however, special characteristics which distinguish it from others. It is a "mass" group—it claims to speak for millions and to have a continuing mandate which overrides that of either of the political parties. It exerts its pressure on governments in full view of the public; and often by means which cause serious public inconvenience and hardship...'.

The traditional view the union movement has of itself as being 'outside the law' and of being committed to changing the system in which it operates has persisted, regardless of the effective industrial and political power it now exercises within that system.

The British trade unions are having a hard time in the present depression. Figures from the January (1983) issue of the Department of Employment Gazette show that, taking 1980 and 1981 together, union membership fell by 9.4% whilst employment fell by 7.6%. The loss of membership therefore is not merely the result of loss of employment. Many unions experience difficulties in recruiting young members, notwithstanding their vulnerable position on the labour market.

With respect to the *French* situation, Landier (1981) concludes that, as a result of the crisis, the trade unions, and especially the more radical ones (CGT, CFDT), are losing members. Accounting do informations, available at FMV headquarters in Amsterdam, the official membership went as follows.[1]

	CGT	CFDT
1977	1 mln.	820.000
1978	1 mln.	1077.000
1079	1 mln.	1079.000
1980	905.000	1048.000
1981	905.000	970.000
1982	905.000	970.000

Loss of members leads, of course, to serious financial problems for the unions. Landier shows that, unlike the two radical trade unions in France, the more moderate organizations (CFTC, CGT-FO) are slowly growing. He even predicts 'marginalization' of the two radical unions.

He notes a decrease in the number of strikes in France since 1975. Relatively more strikes occur because of dismissals rather than wages: the trade unions are on the defense. The real problem of these unions is that (like so many governments) they have no real solution for the depression. They differ from the British unions in that the power they command is much less convincing than that of their British counterparts. The movement is too deeply divided. They are at present too far removed from the center of political power to have any real influence.

It is as yet[2] too early to evaluate the influence of the coming into power of the socialist government of Mitterand. The trade unions themselves expect their influence to be reinforced. Only the CFDT seems willing to change its policy, as the new government appears to sympathize more with the trade union movement. The others take a more cautious attitude.

[1] Membership figures for french trade unions are not readily available. These figures are based upon the data given by the trade unions themselves.

[2] September 1982.

The *German* trade unions have accepted, perhaps more so than the other unions in Europe (except for the Austrian and Swiss unions), voluntary wage restraints. Here, as in Great Britain, the 'colour' of the government has influenced the attitude of the trade unions. However, the lack of results in terms of an increase of employment rates caused difficulties within the DGB itself. Of course, one should keep in mind that, the proportion of unemployed being close to 10%, the power of the trade union movement to attain more than minimal wage increases should not be overestimated.

The tendency for trade unions to lose members during this period of increasing unemployment is almost universal in Western Europe. The trade unions' vulnerable position limits the possibilities for governments to obtain the support of the trade unions for their policies. These policies mostly imply the reduction of government expenditures and, more particularly, restrictions on the expenditures on social security. Such policies cannot but entail fundamental problems for the trade unions.

The trade unions react in different ways. In The Netherlands, for instance, the trade unions are well known for their cooperative attitude. However, the attempts of successive cabinets to establish some form of 'social contract' did not meet with success. The one exception, the social contract for 1973, could not preclude a nation-wide conflict on the issue of the limitation of wage differentials in that year. Later attempts have all failed. However, in some cases the yearly rounds of central collective bargaining led to a so-called 'quasi-agreement': the uncompleted central bargaining sets the boundaries for the decentralized bargaining in trade and industry. In 1979 the central bargaining had almost reached a broad agreement on wages, labour market policy, and work sharing, but at the last moment negotiations broke down.

Dutch law allows the government to regulate wages in case of an economic emergency. Although according to that criterion the government could use its power every year again, the trade unions mostly try to convince parliament not to consent to such a policy. However, one of the consequences of the unions' loss of power on the labour market is that they are in no position to successfully oppose the government's attempts at wage control, once the parliament has accepted such a policy. As a consequence, the Dutch government has, over the last nine years, more often than not imposed wage freezes on the trade unions and employers. The relationship between the trade unions and the government is worse than ever. Although the 1982 political crisis in The Netherlands did not originate from the attitude and actions of the trade unions, the continuous controversies between the FNV and the Dutch socialist partly played an important role in it. In November 1982, however, the central organizations of the trade unions reached a global agreement on the desirability of introducing a reduction of working hours, to be financed through a partial or complete supression of the wage increases resulting from the automatic compensation of the cost of living. The Dutch government has since assumed a strongly favourable attitude towards the necessity of forms of work sharing.

Wage controls are, of course, not limited to The Netherlands. In 1980, Belgium imposed a wage freeze on the social partners for the first time.

The attempts of several governments to reach some form of voluntary central agreement with the central organizations of employers and trade unions are, of course, a much better alternative for attaining moderation of wage developments than are statutory measures. In different countries (The Netherlands, Norway, Finland, Ireland) experience has shown that, in order to convince the workers of the advantages of a social contract, it is necessary to introduce compensatory advantage (Wage policies and collective bargaining development, 1979). Such advantages may be provided through government price policies, fiscal policies, or subsidies. Tax reductions, social policy measures, and schemes to create employment are used as a *quid pro quo* for the limitation of wage increases.

It is clear that, from a political point of view, the social agreement approach is much more attractive than one-sided wage control. The feasibility of this approach is determined by institutional factors such as the existence of central bargaining mechanisms. Central bargaining is excluded when the central organizations lack control over the affiliated organizations. Such control is, of course, not possible in the Sothern European countries or in Great Britain. In Germany, the autonomy of the social partners is an almost sacred priniciple and the government's reluctance to enter the field of wage negotiations is well known. As a consequence, only the smaller countries (those in Scandinavia and the Benelux, and Ireland) have any experience at all in this field.

Trade unions may be interested in this approach because they are aware of the dangers of wage increases in a time of depression. More important, however, is the consideration that decentralized bargaining with employers may fix wage rates, but cannot determine purchasing power. Given the importance of taxes and social security payments, bargaining with the government opens up perspectives of getting a better hold on net-incomes.

In the central bargaining process the tradition of automatic indexation of wages receives a lot of attention. Indexation of wages removes the downward pressure of the labour market. Governments attempt to substitute tax reductions for index clauses. Norway and The Netherlands are examples of governments attempting to convince the trade unions of the attractiveness of this form of trade-off. The Norwegian government has been more successful than the Dutch government in reaching an agreement of this kind. In The Netherlands such a deal was introduced by law in 1981. In March 1981 the Belgian government fell over a plan, proposed by Prime Minister Martens, to put a complete freeze on the cost-of-living indexation system. Marten's successor Eyskens ruled out any immediate changes in the system. However, in spring 1982, the Belgian government introduced legislation to put restrictions on the system of automatic indexation.

Where attempts to conclude such agreements have succeeded, experience shows that governments have to accept rather comprehensive deals including different policies. From a political point of view, however, the advantages of voluntary agreement over wage controls are so important, that governments are often prepared to go out of their way to satisfy the unions. However, even the French Mitterand-government introduced legislation to implement a wage freeze, which was done on the occasion of the devaluation of the French franc (June, 1982).

4.2. Bargaining and legislation during a depression[3]

The current depression influences the process of collective bargaining in more than one way. In the first place, rising unemployment figures and the difficult economic position of many enterprises have their effects on the power relations. As union members are reluctant to strike in an enterprise that already is in difficulties, trade unions are losing an important part of their bargaining power. On the other hand, the same difficult economic position may diminish the employers' power to oppose a strike. This limits the employers' possibilities to strengthen their position during a depression. To give an example: in 1977, the Dutch employers tried to get the automatic indexation clauses abolished, but lost the subsequent struggle in a general wave of strikes. Trade unions presently are more successful in resisting inroads on existing rights than they are in acquiring new rights.

The hope that, at least in some sectors of the economy, there is still something to gain and the attempt to get rid of government control brings about a movement towards decentralized bargaining. Examples are: Denmark, Belgium, Ireland, Norway, Sweden, and The Netherlands. Decentralization may also be inspired by a lack of confidence in the effectiveness of government policies.

The depression furthermore introduced some new elements into collective agreements. In Denmark, Norway, and The Netherlands the days of agreements covering more than one year seem to be over. Growing uncertainty about economic developments led bargainers in Norway and Spain to introduce mid-term wage increases and in Ireland and Spain 'inability to pay' clauses were introduced. Productivity-linked wage increases in Spain, based on the 1980/1981 central contract between Spain's main private-sector employers' federation and the second largest trade union federation, the UGT, seem to have a similar background.

In many cases the trade unions tried to introduce forms of work sharing. The European Trade Union Federation proposed a 10% reduction in working hours. In general, employers and governments were reluctant to accept proposals to reduce the number of hours worked per day. Only the Mitterand-government in

[3] Most facts in this section can be found in the *European Industrial Relations Review*, 1980, 1981, 1982 (London).

France took the initiative to propose a shorter working week. The French government has introduced legislation to offer governmental support to employers who create new jobs by reducing working time. Governments in Austria, Ireland, Italy, and Denmark also took a positive attitude towards a reduction of working time, whereas strong opposition existed within the governments of Spain, Great Britain, and Sweden. In The Netherlands, the unions consider the five-shift system as a vehicle both for creating new jobs and for reducing health risks for shift workers. A few firms (public utilities, petrochemical sector) have recently adopted this system, which entails a reduction of the average working week to 33.6 hours. The central agreement on the reduction of working time leaves room for decentralized implementation.

In its report 'Collective bargaining in Western Europe 1981 and prospects for 1982', the European Trade Union Institute points to the continuing trend towards reduction of weekly working hours. The average, collectively agreed working week in ten West European countries (with slight variations according to economic sector) is already significantly below the 40-hours-per-week level, e.g. in Belgium 36–39 hours, Finland 35–40 hours, Ireland 35–40 hours, Italy 36–40 hours, Sweden 37.5–40 hours, France 36–39 hours, Greece 32–36 hours.

Progress has also been made in the area of annual leave. The average, collectively agreed annual leave in the Federal Republic of Germany is 5–6 weeks, in Sweden 5–8 weeks, in France 5–6 weeks, in Great Britain 4–6 weeks.

Early retirement schemes are more common than are shorter working weeks. For most workers in Denmark, France, Germany, The Netherlands, and Luxemburg, schemes for voluntary or even obligatory early retirement are currently applied. In Austria, new legislation in this respect is under way. The EEC is planning a directive on this matter. At the initiative of the European Commission a number of governments have introduced limits on overtime (Belgium and Denmark, legislation under way in The Netherlands).

In several countries, unions and governments have been taking measures to improve the rights of part-time workers in the process of collective bargaining or legislation. Spain introduced legislation in 1981. In the same year, in Belgium, the National Labour Council reached an agreement on detailed measures to improve the rights of part-timers. The agreement includes a number of regulations, such as the right to a written contract, conditions under which overtime work is allowed: prior right to be given full-time jobs if available. The EEC is preparing a directive on part-time work.

The increasing rigidity of the way in which labour markets function forms an element of the depression all European countries have in common. In some of them, employers have urged their government and trade unions to take joint action. Various examples of new regulations in collective agreements can be given. In Denmark, collective agreements cover re-training assistance and alterations in the placement process. In Spain and Sweden, collective agreements have opened up possibilities for more flexibility in recruitment.

CONCLUSIONS

The depression of the 1980s has a profound influence on industrial relations in Western Europe. Three factors play a major role:

1) The attempts of governments to regulate the process of collective bargaining and especially the wage level.

2) The changing power relations. Trade unions are losing their power on the labour market as well as in the political field. Their power on the labour market is undermined by the reluctance of workers to strike for the traditional reasons (wage increases). Only defensive actions appear to be successful (e.g. attempts to abolish the automatic index clauses).

3) The growing awareness of governments, employers, and unions alike that something should be done about the growth of employment and the rigidities of the labour market.

These factors may be observed all over Europe. They do, however, not change the existing underlying pattern of labour relations in the different countries. Although here and there the consensus underlying the system appears to be wavering (e.g. The Netherlands), the basic characteristics of the polarizing and integrating systems have, to this day, not changed in any significant way. There is no exception to the rule that governments have actually become more active in the field of collective bargaining.

REFERENCES

Barkin, S. (Ed.) (1975), *Worker militancy and its consequences 1965–1975*. New York: Praeger.
Barnes, D., Reid, E. (1980), *Governments and trade unions, the British experience 1964–1979*. London: Heinemann.
Bell, D. (1973), *The coming of post-industrial society*. New York: Basic Books.
Björk, E. (1975), An experiment in work satisfaction. *Scientific American*, **232**, no. 3 (March).
Clark, C. (1957), *The condition of economic progress. The economics of 1960*. London: MacMillan.
Grouch, C., Pizzorno, A. (1978), *The resurgence of class conflict in Western Europe since 1968*. 2 vols. London: MacMillan.
Dahrendorf, R. (Ed.) (1981). *Trendwende, Europas Wirtschaft in der Kris*. Vienna: Molden.
European Industrial Relations Review (1980, 1981, 1982). London.
Fourastié, J. (1950), *Le grand espoir duss siècle*. Paris: PUF.
Hetzler, H. W. (1980), *Arbeitsstrukturierung durch Verhandlungen*. Mannheim: Forschungsstelle für Betriebswirtschaft und Sozial-Praxis.
ILO (1974), *Collective bargaining in industrialised market economies*. Geneva.
Jacobs, E. (1973), *European trade unions*. London.
Kendall, W. (1974), *The labour movement in Europe*. London: Allan Lane.
Landier, H. (1981), *Demain, quels syndicats?* Paris: Livre de Poche.
Martinet, G. (1979), *Sept syndicalismes*. Paris: Seuil, p. 220.
Myrdal, H. G. (1980), The Swedish model—will it survive? *British Journal of Industrial Relations*, March.

Reichhold, X. X. (1953), *Die europäische Arbeiterbewegung.* Frankfurt a/M: Josef Knecht.

Revel, J. F. (1981), *La grace d'état.* Paris: Grasset.

Ross, A., Hartman, X. (1960), *Changing patterns of industrial conflict.* New York: Croom Helm.

Spitaels, G. (Ed.), Crisis in the industrial relations in Europe. *Cahiers de Bruges,* no. 28 (special issue). Bruges.

Wage policies and collective bargaining development in Finland, Ireland and Norway (1979) Paris: OECD.

Handbook of Work and Organizational Psychology
Edited by P. J. D. Drenth, H. Thierry, P. J. Willems and C. J. de Wolff
© 1984, John Wiley & Sons, Ltd.

5.5. Traffic and mobility

John A. Michon

1. INTRODUCTION

1.1. What is traffic?

Traffic can be described as the grand total of all displacements of people, goods, and messages, as they derive from the activities of the members of a society. Activities cannot normally be performed at a single location or at one time and they therefore create a need for mobility. This need is met by developing a transportation system, consisting of one or more transportation modes that tend to be fairly loosely connected. The use of this transportation system creates traffic.

This description covers all types of spatial displacement including, for instance, movements within the confines of hospitals or offices. Conventionally, however, the area that we know as traffic psychology deals only with human behavior in relation to road traffic. There is no particular reason why it should, although in fact other forms of traffic such as nautical and air traffic are largely restricted to professionals. Consequently, the captain's, the pilot's and the train engineer's performances are easily considered part of Human Factors in general, unlike the seemingly trivial efforts of ordinary people finding their way about.

Traffic psychology as it is understood here has long shown an almost exclusive concern for automotive problems. More recently, however, there have been two substantial additions to the field of topics under investigation. Attention has shifted to the problems of other categories of road users besides drivers, and now includes pedestrians, cyclists and handicapped people. Attention has also moved to different aspects of mobility, which has brought topics such as travel time budgets and travel mode choice within the psychologist's horizon.

The view has been accepted that human mobility is embedded in a social environment, and that traffic and transport should be treated in terms of the characteristics of a system in which the human being is only one of many components, albeit an important one.

The most characteristic feature of the human component in this system is its behavior as a (fallible) problem solver. Taking that point of view, one can outline a descriptive framework that enables one to specify a number of basic tasks that together constitute the set of relations between people and the environment in which they attempt to satisfy their mobility needs.

One may distinguish four stable levels at which the human being appears in a systematic relation to the transport and traffic system (Michon, 1976; Michon and van der Molen, 1976). These levels may be defined by reference to a person's role as an active road user, as a transportation consumer, as an active social being and as a psycho-biological organism satisfying a number of needs, respectively. Table 1 specifies these four functional levels relative to the (problem-solving) context in which they appear. One should keep in mind that these levels are coupled in what can probably best be described as a nested hierarchy.

In the following sections I shall loosely follow this distinction, combining the second and third levels because activity pattern and travel choice are easiest to discuss together. The fourth level is closely related to the field of environmental psychology, and problems in that field are much the same, whether they result from the transport system or from industrial or home activities. For that reason I shall refer only briefly to this level.

Table 1. Schematic representation of the four levels at which humans are dealing with the traffic and transport system. What is available as a 'task aid' for solving the characteristic problems at that level splits into 'task aid' *plus* task environment at the next lower level.

Level	I	II	III	IV
Human 'role'	road user	transport consumer	social agent	psycho-biological organism
Characteristic problem	maintenance of speed and heading	trip making	patterning of social activities (communication)	need satisfaction (health and well-being)
Task environment	road	road network (geographical structure)	land use (socio-economic structure)	nature, environment
Task aids	vehicle, signs, lighting	transport modes	transport system	'culture' (technology)

The psychologist investigates each and all of these four levels, both in terms of people's normal functioning and in terms of the system's pathology. Thus, at the first level, research may be directed at traffic flow as well as at traffic (un)safety; similarly, at the second level, research will deal with trip and mode choice as well as with underprivileged travelers, such as the handicapped and those who have no access to automobiles or public transport.

This chapter is approach-oriented rather than fact- or problem-oriented. Although there is much to be said for either alternative, I have chosen for the first option for two reasons. The first is that a large proportion of the facts of traffic psychology coincides with facts known from other domains of ergonomics and psychology. The second is that a separate treatment of the various problem areas easily leads to a rather disconnected and piecemeal discussion of issues that are relevant only to tiny fractions of the population. Only as the recent trends in traffic psychology as I shall outline them develop further, a proper framework for both problem areas and facts will eventually crystallize.

1.2. The task of transport and traffic psychology

Transport and traffic studies have a solid basis in the technical sciences and in economics. As a result there is a core of well established knowledge, lore and insight on which research in this field can rely. Transport and traffic are treated as supra-individual technical and social systems in which the *trip* is, in a way, treated as the elementary or primitive element. A trip can be defined as 'the one-way travel from one point to another for a particular purpose' (Lane *et al.*, 1971, p. 39). Of course, it is assumed that trips are made by real people, but conventionally transport and traffic scientists have not gone so far as to attempt to *explain* these trips in terms of the underlying psychological process that are presumably causing them. This position is similar to that of linguistics: linguists actually study language as *competence*, that is, as a supra-individual social system without reference to actual speakers or listeners. Psychologists, on the other hand, are there to explain people's behavior, their *performance* in as far as it pertains to mobility (or language). This raises the question of the nature of psychology's task in the field of transport and traffic: is it to serve as an aid or as a guide (Michon, 1980a)? If it is the first, the role of the psychologist is that of a consultant who offers his or her best advice within the established technological and economic perspectives. If psychology is capable of offering guidance rather than advice, then we should expect psychological theories about, for instance, information processing or motivation to provide a new and different way of functionally describing the problem area. Both approaches—advice and guidance—can be found in actual practice, but usually they remain implicit. The second approach seems to be conducive of considerable and occasionally grotesque confusion and misunderstanding between the established disciplines and psychology: apparently a psychologically relevant partitioning of the problem area is not necessarily isomorphic with the way transport and traffic engineers tend to decompose their field.

2. THE ROAD USER

To the extent that we consider road users as components of the traffic system, their task can be described roughly as: maintaining course and speed while avoiding obstacles, within the constraints of the actual traffic environment. These constraints are imposed partly by the vehicle and the road environment and partly by the road users themselves. The road environment is taken to comprise the organization and the legal constraints (regulations).

2.1. The classical approach

From the beginning of the twentieth century psychologists have studied road users in ways that by and large reflect the development of psychology in general. I shall follow this development in broad outline. The major questions psychologists asked in the early years have changed in their wording rather than their content. For a long time these questions were:
—what is correct traffic behavior and how can it be taught;
—is it possible to distinguish between good and bad road users.

2.1.1. THE EARLY PERIOD

Among the very first to engage in empirical studies that we recognize as traffic psychology was Hugo Munsterberg (Dorsch 1963). He believed that reaction time would be a good predictor of one's performance as a tramway motorman and tested his belief in several laboratory studies.

Only in the 1920s we may speak of a real start. At that time the selection of suitable candidates for professional jobs as drivers and vehicle engineers became a serious matter. At the same time the mirror image of this issue attracted considerable interest: is it possible to eliminate the least competent road users (drivers) by means of psychological assessment? The latter question raised an ethical discussion; in principle, citizens should be free to use the public road in any way they like within the limits of the law, and yet there may be serious reasons to prevent this. One such reason would be a person's permanent disposition to get involved in a disproportionate number of accidents. And so the search for the born accident-prone road user began.

The first attempt to identify the predisposed accident-prone driver was based on a familiar statistical misunderstanding. Those road users who, over a period of two or three years, are involved in a high number of accidents are supposed to be the ones that will also stand out in a next period, for reasons that may range from Freudian death wishes to permanent neuro-physiological disorders.

However, it may well be that a high incidence of accidents in one period is actually not at all predictive of the incidence in the next period, as one would expect if accidents are distributed stochastically according to, for instance, a Poisson process (Greenwood and Yule, 1920).

Numerous studies have been carried out with this question in mind. The most extensive data were obtained by Campbell and Levine (1973) among over 2 1/2 million drivers in North Carolina. They showed that the degree of accident involvement (0 to 5 + accidents) in one period of two years was essentially independent of the involvement in a next period of two years. Thus these authors confirmed several earlier studies showing that it is impossible to select accident-prone road users on the basis of accident involvement as such. Yet, the attractiveness of the concept seems to be so high that occasionally a revival of the concept can be observed; sometimes such reanimation is due to old believers (e.g. Häkkinen, 1982), sometimes new arguments are brought to bear on the issue (McKenna, 1983).

2.1.2. TESTS

The rapid development of psychological testing in the thirties and forties did not leave traffic psychology uninfluenced. There have been many attempts to answer the two major questions, selection of professionals and predisposed bad road users, by means of a wide range of tests. Such attempts have had limited success, particularly if they involved tests that bear little resemblance to the actual traffic task, that is driving (see e.g. Haddon et al., 1964).

The ultimate defeat of the classical testing approach is found in the study by Conger et al. (1959), who correlated the results of no less than 52 psychological tests with several driving safety criteria. The number of correlations that were found to be significant turned out to be exactly at chance level, showing that reaction times, scales of neuroticism, the ability to catch sticks that unpredictably drop from the ceiling, or the imagination to interpret Rorschach inkblots, are insufficient grounds for predicting (safe) driving behavior. It should be added in passing, however, that tests may have some limited usefulness for selection purposes if one needs to select a small number of drivers from a large population of candidates (e.g. Shaw and Sichel, 1971). And finally, it may be mentioned that tests for predicting traffic violations (rather than accident involvement as usual) have fared but slightly better (Miller and Schuster, 1983).

2.1.3. ASSESSMENT NOW

As a result of the failure to base driver performance assessment on tests from the psychological laboratory, interest in road user testing declined without, however, disappearing altogether from the traffic psychologist's perspective. If one thing has become clear, it is that tests will not fare too well if they are developed without consideration for the criteria to which they apply. Several alternative approaches have been attempted in more recent years, and some moderate success has been claimed for these alternatives.

a) Fleishman (1967, 1975) developed a factorial model for cognitive and motor skills. According to his model, such skills result from the combination of a small number of elementary aptitude factors (e.g. reaction speed, spatial orientation). These combinations can be represented as vectors in a multidimensional space. As a result of development or learning the dimensional structure of this space will change. When practising a manual skill, for instance, the aptitude for verbalizing one's behavior will gradually become less important and may finally even disappear from the factor structure for that skill. The latter will be the case when performance attains a state of automaticity. One of Fleishman's concerns has been automobile driving, although he never studied this task over time as a function of training on experience.

b) Quenault (1967; Quenault et al., 1968) developed a techique for systematic observation under fairly unconstrained normal driving conditions. He had his subjects drive along a predetermined standard route. An observer possessing detailed knowledge of this route would accompany the subject and make a detailed protocol of a semi-quantitative nature involving both the situation on the road and the behavior of the driver. On the basis of a number of summary scores derived from the protocols, Quenault was able to distinguish between four types of driver: the safe driver, the injudicious driver, the dissociated active driver and the dissociated passive driver. The descriptions of these four types have a very high face validity, but there is, unfortunately, little empirical support for them. There has been some application of this technique as a means of selecting candidates for a differentiated program of remedial driver training.

c) Accident frequency. Several authors have attempted to develop selection and evaluation criteria on a healthier basis than the initial attempts to identify the accident-prone driver. This procedure is based on principles that are commonly used in industrial quality control procedures (Shaw and Sichel, 1971). This procedure uses the time intervals between successive accidents or critical events. The assumption is that for each individual, intervals between stochastically independent critical incidents will show a distribution whose parameters will remain stationary as long as the underlying generating processes remain stationary too. Stress, disease and other causes may, however, induce changes in the parameter settings. This will alter the average interval between successive incidents or their variance, or both. If such changes are observed, the employer or other authorities may intervene systematically, at least if the relation between these changes and their causes is known.

It will be evident that incident records need to be extremely detailed and complete in order for such a method to be of any practical use. This condition will be fulfilled only in professional transport companies that keep their employees under close observation.

2.1.4. ACCIDENT PRONENESS AS A TEMPORARY DISPOSITION

The methods reviewed in the previous section entertain the hypothesis that accident-proneness is not a chronic but a temporary disposition. Any road user can contract this condition whenever a combination of conditions is fulfilled (Koornstra, 1973a, 1973b). Age, experience, the menstrual cycle, stress in personal life, the first and last days of a vacation are among the conditions that influence a person's chances of getting involved in an accident or accidents (see e.g. Burg, 1972; Evans and Wasielewski, 1982; Goldstein, 1962; Liskey, 1972; McGuire, 1976; Shaw and Sichel, 1971). Enough support, perhaps, for the suggestion recently put forward by McKenna (1983) to accept the reality of the concept 'differential accident involvement' as a phenomenon worth studying without reference to the implications that are suggested by the term 'accident proneness'.

2.1.5. LEARNING AND PERSUASION

Educational programs for road users, in particular for drivers, have a fairly long history. In 1936 already, driver education was introduced as a regular topic in the US high school curriculum. Usually the school program includes a number of exercises in a driving simulator, some on-the-road driving lessons, and classroom teaching that involves not only knowledge of signs and regulations but also some background to the general aspects of traffic and transportation, and sometimes car maintenance as well.

Another classic program is known as the Defensive Driving method. It is based on the assumption that road users must anticipate potential hazards, particularly those that derive from the activities of the other road users.

The effectiveness of such driver education programs have long remained in doubt (Goldstein, 1973). However, a large scale evaluation program carried out by the National Highway Safety Administration in the State of Georgia, involving more than 25,000 highschool students showed some consistent but modest effects. (NHTSA, 1984 forthcoming). Students who completed such a course were shown to be somewhat less involved in traffic accidents within the first six months of licensed driving and to have fewer citations for traffic violations during the first year. After that no differences between those students and a central population could be found.

The same can be said of the classical approach to media campaigns. The conventional approach adopted in this case was to influence attitudes and motivations (rather than to *inform* people, as is now common practice). The textbook example of this type of campaign in The Netherlands used the slogan 'Be a gentleman on the road' ('Wees een heer in het verkeer'). The slogan itself has proved quite powerful: it has in fact become a standard colloquial expression. For its intended purposes, however, it has been less than ideal. (This need not surprise us: ladies are not addressed at all; most men will entertain the notion that they are gentlemen anyway and consequently will not feel addressed; those who couldn't care less about chivalry will not pay attention; and the sporadic individual who takes the hint is not told what he should do to become a gentleman.) Only in recent years, insights from cognitive and instructional psychology have been systematically applied to education of and campaigns for road users.

2.2. The systems approach

The age of disappointment with the classical approach coincides with the rise of the ergonomic or human factors approach. This, added to the sudden, almost explosive growth of motorized traffic, underscored the man-machine character of modern road user behavior. The 'functionalistic' experimental psychological approach—in particular the information processing approach—began to dominate the field of traffic psychology around 1955.

2.2.1. THE INFORMATION CYCLE

The common theoretical assumptions of the 'modern' view of road user behavior are contained in the well-known information cycle

$$\rightarrow perception \rightarrow processing \rightarrow decision\ making \rightarrow action \rightarrow$$

In the earliest attempts at interpreting this processing cycle there is a heavy bias towards perception. Allen (1970), for instance, represents the road user as little more than a hypertrophic eyeball. Only gradually attention shifted in the direction of higher mental processes, and only after most of the relevant perceptual problems had found an approximate solution. Visibility, legibility, conspicuity, brightness, irradiation, straylight, the effects of blind angles and curved mirrors have become fairly standard fare in ergonomic texts.

Vehicle handling (control) has undergone a more or less parallel development. Research in this area derived its momentum from the advances in the theory of control systems in the fifties and early sixties. Some psychologists were able to adopt the relevant formalisms and to launch cooperative projects with technologists (Reid, 1983). The two fields—perception and vehicle control—are still lacking a theoretically sound integration. Combining them would constitute a major breakthrough.

The student of road user perception is able to provide a description of the ways in which the subject filters and reduces the inputs from a complex, dynamic environment, thus obtaining the required information about course, speed and acceleration (e.g. Koenderink en van Doorne, 1978; Riemersma, 1981). In these perceptual models, the observer has little use for the information obtained: he remains, as it were, 'buried in thought'.

On the other hand, models of vehicle control behavior are actually quite appropriate for dealing with complex inputs, but in actual practice they usually do not go beyond very simple, abstract representations of a dynamic (visual) environment (e.g. Crossman and Szostak, 1968).

The combination of the two problem areas would provide an integrated model of the way in which visual impressions of a complex environment are transformed into control movements which in their turn influence these impressions. Such a combination has not yet been achieved in a psychologically convincing way, even though Reid (1983) reports several recent attempts to deal with some of the crucial information processing aspects involved. It seems likely though, that the increasing importance of robotics will provide a new impulse for this problem, because here the connection of intelligent sensors and decision procedures with highly flexible effectors is of fundamental concern.

2.2.2. INFORMATION PROCESSING: THE COGNITIVE APPROACH

In the early seventies we see among traffic psychologists a considerable shift of attention in the direction of cognitive issues, like everywhere else in psychology. This new approach seems, at first sight, less appropriate for a further expansion of those models that, more or less, bear the character of a control model. Cognitive models are of a 'discrete' nature and less directly aimed at the elementary perceptual-motor skills which have long been central to the considerations of ergonomists and performance theorists. Instead, the cognitive approach is more concerned with the tactical and strategic aspects of road user behavior. By 'tactical' we mean the manoeuvring behavior, such as overtaking or gap acceptance, by 'strategic' such behaviors as route choice and time budgeting (Michon, 1971).

Yet, control models are now bearing the marks of the cognitive revolution as well. They incorporate components with labels like 'representation' or 'environmental model'. This reflects the (cognitivistic) assumption that control of external variables is based on information about the external world that the system already possesses. Actually, this trend towards a more cognitive view is not arbitrary; Wonham's 'Internal Model Principle' states that any system of sufficient complexity that (1) shows control of external variables and (2) maintains a stable internal structure, must necessarily contain a feedback loop of which a sufficiently complex model of the controlled environment is an intrinsic part (Wonham, 1976).

As a result of the cognitive approach, several research options have evolved. Among these recent topics we find, in the first place, issues of spatial representation in combination with cognitive strategies for route choice and route guidance. Secondly, there has been an increasing interest in perceptual and cognitive aids for facilitating the road user's tasks. In the third place, there is a renewed interest in learning and development of knowledge and skills in traffic, particularly in an instruction-technological frame of reference.

a) Geographical representation, cognitive strategies and route guidance. One of the conditions for properly facing the road user's primary concern—go from A to B without swerving off the road or hitting an obstacle—is the possibility of orienting oneself with respect to the relative locations of A and B, to choose the right direction at nodes in the road network, and to find (or at least consider) an alternative route if there is an obstruction of the regular route.

An important impulse for this line of research were *The Image of the City* by Kevin Lynch (1960) and the more recent volume of studies on 'mental maps' by Downs and Stea (1973). This last work has had considerable impact on the ideas about and practice of road signing, both in rural and urban situations (e.g. Stichting Verkeerstechniek, 1980).

Relatively much research effort has gone into drivers' mental representations of their local topographical environment. One of the most interesting studies involves an elaborate analysis of the Paris taxi driver by Pailhous (1970). The study shows that it is indeed possible to give a nearly exhaustive description of route choice in terms of cognitive strategies. In this particular case one can identify three such strategies:

—use of a 'primary grid', of which each point (location) is immediately available in relation to every other point (in other words, a true mental map);

—a secondary, associative and highly fragmented grid, parts of which are generated on the basis of local external cues;

—implicit knowledge about the global orientation of areas and characteristic points (landmarks) relative to one's own position and related to the compass.

b) To the extent that the insights from the studies mentioned in the previous paragraphs have been applied, the field of application has been restricted to so-called *passive* information systems. There is, however, a rapid development towards more dynamic information systems that, in principle, will have a tremendous impact on traffic and on the road user's various tasks. On the one hand, we may expect the development of personalized road-to-car and car-to-road messages by means of telecommunication techniques, and road signs that are responsive to the environment (weather, traffic flow, etc.). On the other hand, there exist several experimental systems which take away the driving task from the driver altogether. The fast pace at which micro-electronics and telecommunication technology are developing at present suggests that we have barely begun to fathom this potential.

The various types of aiding system can be classified according to the degree to which they interfere—or intervene—with human task performance (Michon, 1973). Given the differences between normal participation in traffic, as a mostly non-professional activity, and controlling or navigating a ship, airplane or train, as a professional skill, the transfer of insights and experiences from the latter to the first category of skills is not easy. Consequently, the large number of studies in these fields can only partly be brought to bear on road user performance.

These developments are part of a more general trend towards the automation and 'informatization' of work. The necessity of ergonomically and psychologically supporting research into the field of intelligent job aids is underscored explicitly by the increasing demand from society that such systems be 'user friendly'.

c) The cognitive trend in traffic psychology has resulted in a renewed interest in such matters as traffic education, training and enforcement. The approach now includes the new insights in the ways people represent traffic situations, spatial orientation, the hierarchical structure of behavioral rules and the acquisition of cognitive skills.

Without any doubt, the educational methodology has improved considerably over the last 15 or 20 years: instructional psychology and computer assisted instruction are making significant contributions in this field. Goldstein's negative opinion—already quoted in section 2.1.4—should be revised in the light of recent achievements. Similarly, operant conditioning has made us more sensitive to the difficulties of defining the 'true' discriminative stimuli in a learning situation, that is, those stimuli that indeed inform a person about the success of his or her actions (Hurst, 1980; Van Houten et al., 1980). An example is Hurst's proposition to revoke reckless young drivers' licenses more frequently than is customary. A majority of the people whose licenses are revoked will drive just the same. This very fact will replace the original driving machismo. Staying out of the hands of the police replaces the original 'bad behavior' and requires in fact a more conventional, that is, less conspicuous driving style (Hurst, 1980).

In addition, research on language comprehension and semantic memory has added considerably to our understanding of the ways in which learning materials ought to be structured such that storage and application of knowledge and skills are made easier. Various forms of task analysis have been designed for this purpose (e.g. van der Molen et al., 1981; Veling, 1982). Integrative approaches along these lines are still very rare, however. One of the very few programs in which a genuine effort was made to integrate the study of *process* (functions), *product* (behavior observations), and *instruction* (learning program), is the project on traffic education for young children of the Traffic Research Center in Groningen (see Michon, 1981; Rothengatter, 1981; van der Molen, 1983; van der Molen et al., 1981).

2.3. Dealing with danger

A fundamental concern of traffic psychology is *traffic safety*. Apparently, it has been so fundamental in the past that theory on traffic psychology is almost synonymous with theory about behavior under dangerous circumstances. There are several models to account for unsafe behavior on the road, and it is possible to distinguish two major model types: compensation models and threshold models.

2.3.1. COMPENSATION MODELS

One of the first formulations of the risk compensation principle is Taylor's 'risk-speed compensation model' (Taylor, 1964). Its basic tenet is: the greater the perceived risk, the lower a driver's chosen speed will be. In short: the product of perceived risk and speed is constant. The accepted level of risk is individually determined, partly on the basis of external factors (time pressure) and partly on internal factors (age, perhaps neuroticism, etc.).

Taylor has tested his model by measuring the galvanic skin response (GSR), assuming that this variable is a physiological indicator of tension and perceived risk. The GSR scores were compared with vehicle speed under two conditions. In one case subjects drove in busy traffic, in the other they drove along a very quiet highway. In the first condition a driver must maintain a forced, more or less constant speed. Consequently, the GSR level is expected to vary with the perceived risk (tension) of the momentary situation. Under free driving conditions, as in the second condition, drivers supposedly keep their levels of perceived risk constant by varying their speed accordingly. This expectation was indeed borne out by Taylor's experiments.

Taylor's model is purely descriptive and makes no claim about the internal processes that play a role in compensatory behavior. In particular, it remains unclear what in fact is the effective stimulus determining the level of risk perceived.

An extension of the principle that drivers attempt to establish a balance between progress on the road and their level of acceptable subjective risk can be found in Wilde's 'risk compensation model' (Wilde, 1978). It dresses Taylor's framework with internal cognitive and motivational processes. Wilde's model assumes that the level of accepted subjective risk is a more or less stable personal disposition. Consequently, it predicts that attempts to increase traffic safety by improving roads, vehicles, or even driving competence (training and experience) are likely to fail. Almost any improvement will in fact be compensated by faster or less cautious driving. Wilde's model stipulates instead the necessity of designing measures that will lower the level of accepted subjective risk permanently, and thus leans heavily on the assumption that effective means of persuasion and enforcement can be found.

There is one more factor to be taken into account in compensation-type models: what is an acceptable risk is not judged by the individual road user alone. It is likely to be influenced to an appreciable extent by the level of risk acceptance of the community at large. In countries or regions where violence is comparatively high, traffic safety indices tend to be low (e.g. Adams, 1972; Näätänen and Summala, 1976; Shinar, 1978). It seems likely that traffic safety is closely related to the general level of lethality and morbidity in a society. If this is indeed the case, then risk compensation may be assumed to incorporate both an individual and a supra-individual feedback mechanism (Michon, 1976b).

2.3.2. THRESHOLD MODELS

Klebelsberg (1971, 1977) adopted a somewhat different view by postulating a control process that enables a driver to maintain a stable balance between *subjective*, perceived safety (S), and *objective*, physically or statistically determined safety (O). If the system settles at a level where S = O an ideal situation ensues. Traffic behavior is exactly commensurate with the prevailing circumstances, and improvements in O, whenever they are perceived, will result in an amelioration of S.

Individual road users differ in their personal balance between S and O for a variety of reasons, cognitive, motivational, as well as physiological. Dangerous is any equilibrium where S > O, that is when the road user tends to judge situations safer than they in fact are. On the other hand, of S < O there is a surplus safety margin.

The most important and seemingly very practical consequence to be derived from this model is the following. An *apparent* decrease in the level of objective safety, which actually leaves O unaffected, must lead to a corresponding decrease in S and as a result behavior should become safer. One might, for instance, consider the possibility to arrange street lighting fixtures along a curve in the road in such a way that drivers would get the impression of a sharper curvature than would actually be there. As a result, they would then negotiate that curve at a lower speed than they would otherwise.

This argument has a certain popularity among traffic practitioners, but actually it is worse than useless: it is dangerous. The reason is simple: as long as we do not know which characteristics of a traffic situation are the effective stimuli for our perception of risk and danger, we will be unable to introduce a reliable apparent reduction of O into the situation. Very likely there are tremendous individual differences in the way people form their impressions of a risky situation. Providing inaccurate cues about O in a systematic but incomplete and unreliable way will necessarily lead to suspicion, insecurity, and even a dangerous underestimation of risk in other places where objective safety and perceived safety do in fact match.

A more complete threshold model was proposed by Näätänen and Summala (1976). Their 'subjective risk control model' states that perceived risk (R) in traffic depends on both the level of subjective probability of a hazardous event (P) and the subjective importance of the consequences (B) of the event and, more specifically, on the product of these two factors: $R = P \times B$. Behavior is assumed to be directly related to the level of R.

In most circumstances, R is perceived to be actually equal to zero, that is, under normal road conditions traffic participants feel and act as if they are not running any 'real' risk at all. In other words, there is a threshold for risk perception, and only if that threshold is exceeded, risk compensation mechanisms are called upon in an attempt to lower the risk level. This threshold is the crucial control point in Näätänen and Summala's model. The authors argue that in many road users it is permanently too high—again, for a variety of reasons, cognitive, motivational, or physiological.

In contrast with Wilde's position, Näätänen and Summala consider their model to indicate that methods of influencing people by education, campaigns or enforcement are not effective. The risk perception threshold turns out to be highly resistant to such influences. Consequently, a genuine improvement of traffic safety is to be expected only from better vehicles and better roads.

Thus, Wilde (1978, 1982) and Näätänen and Summala (1976) yield countrary recommendations. This derives from the fact that Wilde assumes a continuous compensation of deviations from an accepted level of subjective risk, while Näätänen and Summala do, in fact, start from quality control assumptions: only if a tolerance limit is exceeded, compensatory mechanisms are put in operation. While Wilde concludes that environmental changes will have little effect because they call for behavioral adaptations that neutralize these changes, the other authors predict that such changes will be effective since they reduce the likelihood that the road user will incorrectly act *as if* the risk were effectively equal to zero. The difference between these two models can, in principle, be subjected to empirical test. Until now, however, no such attempts have been made. Perhaps we should not expect too much from such a test; we may in fact be dealing with two 'coping strategies' that are used by different road users under different circumstances.

2.4. The social psychological approach

Road users interact, even if it sometimes may seem otherwise. Close scrutiny reveals that these interactions are mediated by distinctive cues, often of a rather subtle nature such as the way cars approach the midline of a street when preparing to make a left turn (Shor, 1964; see further Knapper et al., 1980; van der Molen, 1983). Perhaps one may even distinguish several types of road users according to their stereotypical approach of other traffic participants (Bliersbach and Dellen, 1980), although the available evidence for this conjecture is still rather sparse. When the purpose is to improve the behavior of road users with respect to each other—assuming that unsafe traffic is at least in part the result of malice, aggression and simple misunderstanding—then the crucial question is whether the explication of these misperceptions and negative attitudes can help fulfill that purpose. This question reduces to another one: are there methods that enable us to provide road users with better insight (i.e. better information) about the distinctive cues that effectively reveal the intentions of the other road users. Psychologists have entertained a considerable amount of doubt with respect to this approach. However, not so long ago Fishbein and Ajzen (1975; also Ajzen and Fishbein, 1977) proposed a theoretical framework and empirical support for a more optimistic view on this matter. Since then, studies of attitudes and beliefs and their interactions with behavior and behavioral intentions have regained their prominent status.

The success of applications of a model such as Fishbein and Ajzen's depends on the possibility to incorporate them into an adequate cognitive frame of reference. This, in other words, requires that a causal process description be given in such terms that road users are willing and capable of accepting that description as a plausible theory about their behavior. This, however, tends to be problematic; in fact, it harks back to the discussions about the significance of introspective statements about mental activity. As it stands, these discussions were recently reactivated by Nisbett and Wilson (1977), and later by Ericsson and Simon (1980). For a recent review see Hastie (1983). Given this discussion it seems possible, at least in principle, to formulate an effective and plausible theory of road user behavior in information processing terminology. An additional question that remains is whether such a theory can be incorporated into an effective educational procedure (Michon, 1980b; Rothengatter, 1981).

A good example of these issues is the frequently discussed but ill-understood phenomenon of aggressive behavior in traffic (a.o. Hauber, 1977). In this context Bliersbach and Dellen (1980) reported that road users are able to discuss their emotions, but fail to understand the intensity of their feelings. A process description that appears to be applicable to traffic aggression is provided by Mandler (1975). Interruptions of an activity, according to Mandler, can be experienced as emotionally pleasant or unpleasant. Usually, however, they carry negative emotional significance: they tend to interrupt precisely those activities which are the most adequate under the given circumstances. Assuming that traffic behavior is, first and most, directed at going somewhere, an interruption of that goal-directed behavior is most likely to release strong negative affect.

If a theory of road user behavior is to be both effective (as a means of influencing people's behavior) and plausible (as a 'universe of discourse' for the road users themselves), we should look for a descriptive frame of reference which incorporates cognitive and motivational processes and, at the same time, a taxonomy of distinctive features (discriminative stimuli) which helps road users to recognize the occurrence of these processes, both in others and in themselves. This requires, in the last instance, a fortuitous combination of a process model and ethological observations of traffic behavior (van der Molen, 1983).

2.5. Conclusion

In retrospect, the domain of the traffic psychologist seems to have evolved from assessment and selection of drivers to the more general issues of ergonomics and cognitive psychology as applied to road users in general. Although we have not discussed this very explicitly, this evolution has brought along a considerable widening and deepening of the field: the almost exclusive concern for driving behavior has given way to interest in other categories of road users as well: pedestrians, (motor-)cyclists, and certain high-risk groups such as older people, children and the handicapped. The present framework of traffic psychology as it has developed in recent years actually offers a fairly unbiased potential for studying road users and traffic conditions in general, thus opening a gate to a more coherent theoretical substratum than was available in the past.

There have also been external factors that have facilitated the expansion of traffic psychology in the past two decades. One is the advent of micro-electronics which has made the construction and use of instrumented vehicles for on-the-road experiments appreciably simpler. As a result, almost any road user behavior can be measured under practically 'natural' conditions, with on-line recording and processing of a large number of behavioral and vehicular variables. Consequently, studies of long driving hours, fatigue, alcohol effects and drug use have become feasible. Furthermore, the vehicle simulator has become a standard research tool, in particular for experiments under conditions that for ethical or technical reasons cannot be carried out on the road. Unfortunately the cost of construction and operation of advanced simulators is so high that only few investigators have access to one.

Finally, behavior observations have profited tremendously from the availability of advanced video-recording techniques, and especially from electronic frame interpretation which allows rapid processing of large quantities of observational data.

3. MOBILITY

3.1. What is mobility?

This part of the chapter deals with people as transport consumers and performers of more or less integrated patterns of activities. Although it has long been common practice to treat travel choice problems in isolation, it is now accepted that social activities are in fact the driving force behind these choices. This is a sufficient reason for combining them in what follows.

Unlike traffic, mobility is difficult to define unambiguously. Confusion prevails in political as well as in scientific discussions. One can distinguish at least three different meanings of the term 'mobility, the use of which depends on one's pragmatic intentions:

—mobility considered as *travel need*, the necessity or desire to move from one place to another;

—mobility considered as *travel opportunity*, the actual or perceived possibilities that people have for (unconstrained) travel and that satisfy their mobility needs;

—mobility considered as the actual *travel behavior*, the number and nature of the trips made, in short, the amount of travel of the individual and perhaps also of society as a whole.

In what follows I shall use the term in the latter sense.

3.2. Aggregate models

Psychological investigation of transport behavior is relatively new. It emerged as a concomitant of the changing political and social views on transport and traffic as they occurred towards the end of the sixties. Between 1950 and 1970 traffic increased stupendously: in many parts of the world—including Western Europe—the number of automobiles doubled every five years. Until 1970, government policies tended to follow the increasing demand for infrastructure and consequently planning consisted mostly of predictions of the provisions to be made to meet this growing demand. Planning relied on modeling techniques that use large-scale aggregated zonal data, that is, data which are based on the average characteristics of all inhabitants of areas that are determined by geographical criteria. A popular kind of aggregate model is the 'gravity model', which states that the amount of traffic generated between two zones is inversely related with the square (or perhaps another function) of the distance between these zones. Predictions are then based on expected changes in the composition of the zones. Changes in, for example, the number of shops or private homes, the closing of a school, new shops, or the aging of the residential population, are likely to alter the mutual attraction between zones, and the way in which such changes affect the predicted traffic volumes directly follows from the distance relations between all zones (Wohl and Martin, 1967; Lane et al., 1971; Hamerslag, 1980).

Unfortunately, planning on the basis of data at a high level of aggregation succeeds only if government policy is essentially of the compliant sort (or, otherwise, if the area under concern is small and demographically and urbanologically stable). As soon as government switches to a policy of control—as it did in many countries after 1970—different planning procedures are called for. Control irrevocably implies intervention in the citizen's personal freedom of choice with respect to the when, the how, and sometimes even the why of making trips. Therefore it is hardly surprising that the early seventies showed a crisis in classical transport planning and a vigorous search for new and more appropriate techniques.

3.3. Disaggregate models

An important breakthrough occurred with the introduction of disaggregate models. Unlike the aggregate models, they are based on individual travel data. Data from a representative sample of the population under concern are collected and individual utility functions determined. These functions are estimated on the basis of shifts in preference or actual travel behavior when one or more attributes (characteristics) of one or more travel alternatives are changed. Individual choices involve the choice alternative which, under the given circumstances, yields the highest weighted sum of attribute values. The first disaggregate model, known as the multinomial logit model (Richards and Ben-Akiva, 1975) was followed by a veritable avalanche of similar and not quite so similar models (Richards, 1976; Hensher and Stopher, 1979; Stopher et al., 1981). These later models differ in at least two important respects from the original model.

a) Psychologically most interesting are the assumptions which different models make with respect to the choice process. Is the decision maker seen as rational or as subject to 'bounded rationality', in other words are we dealing with utility maximizing or only with satisficing? What are the assumed relations between probability and utility; next to the logit model we now have probit models and, more recently, dogit models. The latter group attempts to deal with a rather severe psychological shortcoming of the earlier models which required that the assumptions of Luce's choice axiom be met. This axiom states that the ratio of the choice probabilities of two alternatives in a choice set is independent of the other items in the set. The 'axiom' is frequently not met in field situations. There are several reasons for this: the choice alternatives in a real transport system are usually not quite independent. Another reason is that the choice set will hardly ever be exhaustive; after all, you might choose to borrow a skelter from that kid around the corner for tomorrow's trip to work.

A further psychologically relevant reason for continually improving on the existing models derives from the wish to obtain more detailed insight in the structure of the decision process. Decisions about trip making consist of a number of more elementary decisions: one must choose a destination, a time of departure, a time of arrival, a route and a mode (vehicle). An important question is how these constituent decisions relate and how they ultimately generate the compound decision; whatever the answer, it is unlikely that they are just a string of sequential and independent decisions leading up to a grand finale: the actual trip chosen.

b) Other reasons for developing alternative and more refined models have a methodological or statistical background. Sampling theory and assumptions about the distributions involved will dictate certain model constraints. Although the resulting models can be of a rather stunning mathematical elegance, they tend to produce results that are almost indistinguishable from the results obtained with much less adequate and more primitive models. In short, disaggregate models as we know them today are robust against violation of their assumptions and not sufficiently robust against a few deviant data points in a large set of data.

3.4. Psychological models

In the discussions about psychological determinants of mobility one can trace three types of model, correlation models, input-output models, and process models (Michon and Benwell, 1981).

a) *Correlation models* express relations between observable and hypothetical entities in terms of correlation coefficients. Fishbein and Ajzen's (1975) model, for instance, relates (hypothetical) belief structures, attitudes and norms with actual behavior (see e.g. Held, 1981). The principal difficulty with these models is that the causal relations between the variables remain unspecified. Other problems derive from their static character, from the fact that they do not have an intrinsic error theory and, in particular, from the fact that they cannot in their present form deal with mobility constraints; if a choice is to be made between several alternatives they assume unlimited availability of every alternative. In actual practice, however, this is a very implausible assumption.

Most of these objections are not pernicious and can be met by making more adequate and advanced models (see various chapters in Stopher et al., 1981).

b) *Input-output* models are known to the psychologist as S-R models. Most disaggregate choice models belong in this category. Psychologically these models derive their meaning largely from the context in which they can be applied, for instance if they are related to attempts to change travel behavior by means of operant conditioning. In recent years, several more or less systematic beginnings have been made in this direction (Cone and Hayes, 1977; Everett et al., 1974). The most persistent problem in this context is the difficulty of determining what discriminative stimuli effectively influence the traveler's behavior and what aspects of behavior are to be reinforced. Also, realistic reinforcement schedules tend to be rather costly.

c) *Process models* make explicit assumptions about the information processing going on—consciously or automatically—while a choice is being made. Within this class of models the crucial distinction is that between simultaneous and sequential models (Foerster, 1981; Golob and Richardson, 1981). Simultaneous (or compensatory) models start from the assumption that choices are based on a weighed evaluation of all relevant qualifying aspects (attributes) of the various alternatives, all at the same time. Such a procedure would seem to require a high degree of experience and automationN of the choice process, and would therefore be expected to be characteristic of experienced travelers or of local people who know the 'ins and outs' of the available options.

Sequential models, on the other hand, assume that choices are based on the successive elimination of alternatives on the basis of one criterion at a time. The latter procedure imposes a much lighter load on the traveler's memory and can also explain the disproportionate attention that inexperienced travelers (or strangers) tend to pay to salient, but not necessarily important attributes of an alternative.

Both approaches to the choice process have to deal with a number of methodological issues. These can be subsumed under four headings (Michon and Benwell, 1981).

a) How well can a model deal with the dynamic character of mobility, that is, how robust is it with respect to variations in time, geographical location, and situation? To what extent can it deal, among other things, with fashionable trends which can make a travel alternative popular or impopular almost overnight?

b) How well can a model deal with the various kinds of restrictions (constraints) that can be imposed on the free choice of travel alternatives (see e.g. Heinze, 1978). Some constraints are absolute (and therefore not really problematic); thus, only 24 hours are available per day. Other constraints are more problematic, however, especially some that may be considered artifacts of the model. Models of the amount of time people spend traveling—the so-called travel time budget—have sometimes produced strange results (and in a few cases also strange transport policies), because the investigators did not consider the many very short trips on foot people make in the course of a day as trips at all. Neglecting these micro-trips will actually lead to a rather peculiar picture of the amount of travel in a community.

Other constraints are of a more realistic and socially important nature; they need to be considered with equal care. If policy decisions are made by the authorities to influence the travel behavior of a population, then the net effect of these decisions is not going to be very impressive if it turns out (as it did in a particular case in the German Federal Republic) that 85% of the target population has no real alternatives that would make it possible for them to comply with that policy (Bròg, 1979).

A last important category of constraints, one we still know very little about, is of a psychological nature. Even if travel conditions are improved, for instance by running a clean, modern bus line that stops within a few hundred yards from their homes, car travelers are not quick in seriously considering the new alternative. In other words, there are thresholds—sometimes substantial ones—that tend to refrain people from changing their travel behavior adaptively and smoothly. Not only do they not react to changing circumstances, they even tend to avoid pertinent information that might influence their travel habits (and thereby perhaps make life temporarily more insecure or dissonant). One line of research is specifically directed at attempts to overcome such resistance. The general approach here is to define the subsets (segments) of the population indicated as 'potential switchers'. Potential switchers can be defined as those travelers who are almost indifferent with respect to their usual means of transportation or the alternative to which the authorities wish to convert them (Gensch and Torres, 1980). An analysis of their preferences and actual choice behavior makes it possible to design measures that are optimally directed at slighting whatever (already low) subjective thresholds may still be in effect by improving the alternative that is to be promoted exactly on those points the potential switcher values least in that alternative.

3.5. Activities and dynamic behavioral stability

A quite different approach to human mobility is taken in the analysis of the space-time structure of activity patterns. The aim here is to define clusters or sequences of activities that are characteristic of certain subgroups in the community, and also to define stable parameters that characterize the mobility of those groups.

3.5.1. ACTIVITY PATTERN ANALYSIS

In the past two decades, considerable attention has been devoted to the ways in which people in different cultures and countries use the 24 hours of the day (Szalai, 1972; Vidakovic, 1980; Zahavi, 1979). Fairly recently the spatial aspect was added and this has widened the possibilities for activity pattern analysis quite considerably: the relation between where and when is, after all, almost by definition of crucial importance when studying mobility (see Russell and Ward, 1982, for a review). The activity pattern someone displays in the course of a day can be described by a trajectory in a space-time diagram. Also the influence of staggered work times, traffic congestions, service schedules and other factors on these trajectories can be represented by means of such diagrams (e.g. Carlstein et al., 1978; Burns 1979).

For a long time the analysis of space-time trajectories used to be purely qualitative; analytic procedures and parameters that summarize the characteristics of various types of trajectories have been slow in coming. Burns (1979) was one of the first to provide a more sophisticated framework for the space-time analysis of activity patterns. A central concept in the way analysts now look at trajectories is the *space-time prism*. A space-time prism is a polyhedron in space-time whose shape is determined by the fastest speed at which one can travel away from one's point of departure in any direction, and the fastest speed at which one can approach one's destination from any direction. Travelers are caught within these prisms and must make their trips within a prism's confines. Shape and localization of space-time prisms can be systematically influenced by manipulation of the spatio-temporal properties of the transport and traffic system.

When factors like speed limitation or energy start dominating a policy, thereby preventing the full deployment of the potential of a transport system, steering mobility by means of 'temporal strategies' becomes more and more attractive. Such strategies involve staggered working hours, optimalization of schedules, free transit lanes and preferential traffic lights for public transport, and flexitime schedules for shops and public services. These should result in more adequate space-time prisms that suit more people more of the time.

Activity pattern analysis is developing along less formal lines as well. A number of rather simple simulation-gamelike techniques has been developed in recent years. They make it possible to obtain a fairly detailed overview of the activity pattern of a person or a household in a relatively short time, say one or two hours. The *Household Activity and Transport Simulator* (HATS), developed by the Transport Studies Unit of the University of Oxford, consists of a 'game board' on which a topographical map of the area is fitted. Below the map one finds a number of strips each representing the 24-hour day, one strip for each household member. In the course of a group discussion the members of the household determine how they relate their travel patterns to their own activities and to those of the others on which they depend (Jones, 1981). The attractive aspect of such methods is that the investigator can get a firsthand impression of the (likely) consequences if abrupt changes were to be introduced in the transport system. The effect of skipping a few runs in a bus service, the availability (of a new supermarket in the neighborhood, or abandoning the family car can be discussed with the family members in a well-structured interview situation. The importance of such simulation techniques for a better and psychologically relevant insight in travel patterns is still under discussion, primarily since there are no systematic procedures (protocol analysis methods) available for adequately summarizing the results obtained. At best they can serve, at present, as a catalyst and reference in group discussions. It seems likely that such discussions will become more and more a regular source of policy-relevant information. The further development of HATS-like techniques seems therefore an important issue. In order to be successful as aids for planning and evaluation they depend on the availability of methods for turning the 'soft' contents of these discussions into formally more robust data.

3.5.2. DYNAMIC STABILITY: THE TIME BUDGET

Mobility needs are surprisingly flexible and usually adapt quickly to the actually available means of transportation. This indicates that the satisfaction of mobility needs may be considered as a control process: people apparently search for an equilibrium under the circumstances in which they are living. Consequently, we can treat mobility needs as setpoints in a control system, that is, those stable values of environmental and behavioral variables that people attempt to attain or to maintain while performing their activities. To the extent that they strive for explicit setpoints we may say that they entertain a pronounced lifestyle.

What are suitable characteristics of people's travel behavior and opinions that we might treat as setpoints and control variables in the intended sense? In particular those characteristics that we have already met as *constraints* in section 3.4 of this chapter; among them we have the accessibility of particular transport modes and their comfort, travel time, safety, and costs. In the past, such factors used to be treated as constants. In fact, however, they are highly dynamic factors which serve as the means by which people attempt to keep the performance of the transport system—and thereby their individual mobility pattern—in balance (Heinze, 1978).

The factors just mentioned, that is, accessibility, comfort, time, safety and costs, are highly generalized quality characteristics. Can they indeed be considered as variables that individuals try to control or stabilize at a particular level? And if so, how should we influence them if we want to modify habitual travel patterns? An illustration of the considerations that derive from such questions is the 'law of constant travel time' (Hupkes, 1979; Zahavi, 1979). This 'law' states that people will stabilize the total time spent on traveling at roughly 400 hours per year, or 1.1 hours per day, irrespective of the circumstances under which they live. Considerable empirical support has accrued over the past ten years, and the law seems to hold under very different social, cultural and economic conditions. Of course, people will frequently be unable to obey this 'law of nature', but if they have to function under circumstances that push them too far away from the point of equilibrium, tensions will build up that counteract the forces causing the disequilibrium. These tensions may be relieved in various ways, depending on the prevailing constraints. In big cities, such as Tokyo, the daily work trip may take several hours and under such conditions substitute behavior may be displayed. In their own cars people will create a cozy atmosphere by taking along newspapers, electric razors and coffee machines, or they will prepare for meetings or dictate letters. In commuter trains stable social groups may evolve displaying, among other things, adaptive territorial behavior. If such substitute behavior is not possible, tensions may be relieved by looking for another job, moving, or social action (e.g. for a free bus lane).

Analogous to the risk compensation principle discussed in section 2.3, the 'law of constant travel time' does explain why modifications in the attributes of the transport system or the external circumstances frequently have little effect on the general mobility pattern: the basic need to travel 70 minutes per day is not affected by such changes. The question then is whether this need can be changed at all, a question that, unfortunately, has no good answer yet. In the first place, there are serious doubts about the actual constancy of what seems to be a constant travel time budget (e.g. Bròg, 1979; de Wit, 1980; Supernak, 1984). Theoretically more interesting, however, is the unfinished discussion as to whether a more or less constant travel time budget is only a derivative of an economic process of utility maximization, or whether we should look at it as a more fundamental biological need of human beings to move about the explore the environment, a basic need which they would share with many other species (Hupkes, 1979; Rachlin et al., 1981).

3.6. Conclusion

The contribution of behavioral science to the study of mobility and transport is barely ten years old, and its impact has been commensurate: there are many beginnings and little has crystallized. Nevertheless there are several points from which crystallization may proceed in the near future.

In the first place, much more research on the causal relations between beliefs and attitudes on the one hand, and behavior on the other seems to be called for. A second important problem kernel concerns the representations and cognitive processes that underlie travel choices. And, finally, the mobility budget and its conceptualization as a control system appears to be a theoretically very important issue; moreover, it appears to be a 'hot' issue, currently attracting considerable attention in economic psychology (Scitovsky, 1976; Lea, 1978) as well as in comparative psychology (Rachlin *et al.*, 1980; Rachlin *et al.*, 1981).

4. THE IMPACT OF TRANSPORT AND TRAFFIC SYSTEMS ON WELL-BEING

The discussions in the previous sections had as their natural limits the boundaries of transport and traffic systems. We have looked at the internal structure and functions of those systems to the extent that human beings play an active role in them. However, the universe is larger than this and the transport and traffic system taken in the generic sense will therefore exert influence on other parts of the social fabric. Effects on health, the environment and well-being have attracted considerable attention in the last ten or fifteen years, particularly the negative effects: exhaust fumes, noise, vibrations, severance of the visual environment and the impossibility for children to play outdoors in the street. Such impacts are gradually subsumed under the main headings of 'livability', and 'subjective safety' or rather the lack thereof (e.g. Stringer and Wenzel, 1976, and more generally, Altman and Wohlwill, 1976, 1977).

Politically these topics tend to be rather conspicuous. Sometimes behavioral scientists are asked to provide normative statements about the (un)acceptability of certain side effects of traffic. Expectations of this nature are bound to be frustrated and psychologists should carefully avoid raising them. Only a few (physiological) limits can be specified in a sufficiently explicit way, noise and toxicity of carbon monoxide being among them. In most cases, comparative judgments are the best one may offer in this context.

4.1. Environmental psychology

The side effects of transport and traffic have been studied mostly in two theoretical frameworks: the theory of motivation and the information processing approach.

4.1.1. THE MOTIVATIONAL APPROACH

Public attitudes and (dis)satisfactions with respect to the side effects of traffic have kept behavioral scientists disproportionally busy. No doubt this is partly a consequence of the interest authorities tend to have in the impact of their policies on their electorate; the theoretical significance of the majority of such studies is so small that this alone would not keep the interest of the scientific community going.

Of course there are also studies that *do* have scientific meaning because they attempt to relate impact data to theoretical concepts. Several studies have connected such data to Maslow's motivational hierarchy, but their explanatory value remains doubtful. A much more promising line was taken a few years ago by Mehrabian and Russell (1974). These authors have tried to provide a coherent description of the relation between behavior and the individual's habitat in terms of the approach-avoidance polarity. In their opinion, the interaction between information from the environment and personality characteristics (i.e. motivations) will determine the levels of a small number of 'primary emotional responses' which manifest themselves in the observable dynamics of approach and avoidance. Although Mehrabian and Russell have attempted to create a general framework for an empirical environmental psychology, they have devoted relatively much attention to the impact of transport and traffic. Their principal methodological tool is the semantic differential which serves as the quantifier for the primary emotional responses, pleasure, arousal and dominance.

4.1.2. Information processing

A good deal is known about the effects of stress inducing factors, sources of irrelevant and generally obnoxious information. They can take the form of disorientation, slips of performance, lapses of attention, psychosomatic disorders and functional defects. Milgram (1970) extrapolated these rather basic phenomena toward the general thesis that modern urban society suffers from a permanent overload of information. Of course, this burden is not imposed on us by the traffic system alone, although it does play a considerable role. As a result of this permanent bombardment with largely irrelevant information various defensive mechanisms are put in effect, including xenophobia, withdrawal and depressed feelings. The fact, however, that these effects occur in some cities (New York, Amsterdam) and not in others (Tokyo), demonstrates that at least a number of other conditions need to be fulfilled. Consequently it seems preferable to postpone serious attempts to construct such far-reaching theories, even if they succeed in striking many people's fancy. Indeed, more recently, theorists dealing with environmental issues have stepped down somewhat. Although the search for very general theoretical schemes and taxonomies is still going on, much more prudence and care are exercised in drawing conclusions from them (see Russell and Ward, 1982). In practice, however, the concerns tend to be much more mundane: there is much interest in practical issues such as the layout of 'livable' residential areas, the freedom of movement for children and handicapped people, optimalization of bicycle routes and several others. Each of these themes involves aspects of visual impact, the ability of people to readily obtain relevant information, and the load imposed on the organism when performing particular tasks under various environmental conditions.

4.2. Risk analysis

The initial enthusiasm for the application of environmental psychology to traffic situations has passed its pinnacle, perhaps as a result of the impossibility of providing normative indications for traffic and transport policies. The prevalence of environmental issues remained, however. In that context issues of risk and system safety have attained a central position. Following technical risk analysis the description and evaluation of subjective risk has become a popular research topic (Slovic *et al.*, 1974; Slovic *et al.* 1977; Vlek and Stallen, 1980, 1981; Wagenaar, 1983), although in traffic research it is still in its infancy. 'Subjective safety' certainly carries considerable political weight, but at present it has no operational definition. This will change in the coming years as efforts will increasingly be made to control the various risks that the major technological systems of our society, traffic and transport systems among them, impose on ordinary people.

The following examples illustrate two approaches to this problem field. Although they are oversimplified, they demonstrate one general premise of applied research: an empirical relation, however strong, remains weak if it is not carried by theoretical insight, however weak. In fact, the first example leads to nothing, while the second still retains a latent meaning surplus.

4.2.1. SMEED'S RULE

In 1949 Smeed published a study which showed that for some 20 countries the number of deaths on the road could be described by the equation $D = 0.0003$ $(NP^2)^{1/3}$, in which N represents the number of motorized vehicles (automobiles) and P stands for the size of the population (Smeed, 1949). About twenty years later Smeed produced even more impressive evidence showing that his rule applied to some 70 countries and held up over periods of 40 years or more (Smeed, 1972, 1974). The robustness of this empirical 'law' was put in serious jeopardy, however, after 1972. In a majority of the developed countries we observe at that time a reversal of the numbers of traffic deaths, a trend which actually antedated the energy crisis and which has now lasted approximately 10 years in succession. As a result Smeed's Rule has lost much of its value as a descriptive rule, and gained only in its major characteristic, its incomprehensibility. It has remained a mystery why it performed so well for such a long time, although it is possible, of course, to sum up any number of factors that play or should play a role in establishing the observed relation.

4.2.2. RISK AS THE PRODUCT OF PROBABILITY AND SERIOUSNESS

Accidents can be considered as the coincidence of a number of stochastically independent events which lead to an accident only because of their simultaneity. Accidents therefore tend to happen more or less randomly. The probability (i.e.

the inverse of frequency) of a serious accident is, fortunately, smaller than the probability of a minor accident. This relation can be expressed as Risk = Probability × Seriousness; it is in fact equivalent with the expression for expected value in decision theory (Vlek and Wagenaar, 1979).

The equation for Risk has a subjective counterpart, in which perceived risk (R) is expressed as the product of estimated probability (P) and expected seriousness of the consequences (S). Sometimes this subjective relation is expressed as $R = P \times S^a$. The exponent a allows the assignment of a greater ($a > 1$) or smaller ($a < 1$) weight to the consequences, relative to the estimated probability of occurrence. Empirically it has been established that risk perception in daily life is largely based on just the imaginability of the consequences, and hardly on the probability of an accident (see e.g. Tversky and Kahneman, 1974; Wagenaar, 1983): in other words, the value of the exponent a is much larger than 1.

Since authorities tend to comply with this socially accepted criterion, safety measures are mostly directed at reducing the frequency of accidents with the conceivably most serious consequences. If, however, the total safety effort remains constant (which in a period of economic depression may be the best we can hope for), then we would expect an increase in the probability of less serious accidents. Although we must consider this an undesirable concomitant of safety policies directed at the prevention of the very serious accidents, it is in fact what we do observe in practice. The most important indicators of traffic unsafety have been the numbers of people killed or seriously injured in traffic accidents. These numbers have, fortunately, decreased consistently and fairly dramatically over the last ten years (in The Netherlands half as many people were killed on the road in 1982 as in 1972, the worst year in history). At the same time one may observe an increase in the number of less serious accidents and also a larger number of non-critical injuries. A well-balanced policy should therefore aim at accident prevention in general.

4.3. Conclusion

While the initial enthusiasm for environmental psychology as a carriage for research concerning the (ill) effects of the traffic system has faded, a genuine interest in the perception of risky situations has emerged and is still growing. Cognitive psychology and psychophysiology should be capable of providing a much clearer picture of the impact of the traffic and transport system on the psycho-biological integrity of the human organism. Such research will eventually contribute to a better understanding of what presently are only fuzzy concepts: 'livability', 'subjective safety' and 'well-being'. The appropriate research methodology needs to be developed in greater detail, although considerable progress has been made in recent years, particularly in behavioral decision theory (Einhorn and Hogarth, 1981), and the theory of stress coping (Ursin et al., 1978; see also Miller, 1983).

REFERENCES

Adams, J. R. (1972), Psychosocial factors and accidents in the highway transportation system. In: Forbes, T. W. (Ed.), *Human factors in highway traffic safety research*. New York: Wiley-Interscience, 331–347.

Ajzen, I., Fishbein, M. (1977), Attitude-behavior relations: A theoretical analysis and review of empirical research. *Psychological Bulletin*, **84**, 888–918.

Allen, M. J. (1970), *Vision and highway safety*. Philadelphia: Chilton.

Altman, I., Wohlwill, J. F. (1976), *Human behavior and environment: Advances in theory and research. Vol. I*. New York: Plenum.

Altman, I., Wohlwill, J. F. (1977), *Human behavior and environment: Advances in theory and research. Vol. II*. New York: Plenum.

Bliersbach, G., Dellen, R. G. (1980), Interaction conflicts and interaction patterns in traffic situations. *International Review of Applied Psychology*, **29**, 475–490.

Brög, W. (1979), Mobility and lifestyle: Sociological aspects. In: *Transport and the challenge of structural change*. Proceedings of the 8th International ECMT Symposium on Theory and Practice in Transport Economics, Istanbul, 1979.

Burg, A. (1972), Characteristics of drivers. In: Forbes, T. W. (Ed.), *Human factors in highway safety research*. New York: Wiley, 74–94.

Burns, L. D. (1979), *Transportation: Temporal and spatial components of accessibility*. Lexington (Mass.): Lexington Books/Heath.

Campbell, B. J., Levine, D. (1973), Accident proneness and driver license programs. In: *Proceedings of the First Conference of the International Driver Behavior Research Association*, Zurich, 1973; PS3. Paris: IDBRA, 1–12.

Carlstein, T., Parkes, D., Thrift, N. (Eds.) (1978), *Human activity and time geography Vol. 2 Timing space and spacing time*. London: Arnold.

Cone, J. D., Hayes, S. D. (1977), Applied behavior analysis and the solution of environmental problems. In: Altman, I., Wohlwill, J. F. (Eds.), *Human behavior and environment. Vol. 2*. New York: Plenum.

Conger, J. J., Gaskill, H. S., Gladd, D. D., Hassell, L., Rainey, R. V., Sawrey, D. W. L. (1959), Psychological an psychophysical factors in motor vehicle accidents. *Journal of the American Medical Association*, **169**, 1581–1587.

Crossman, E. R. F. W., Szostak, H. (1968), Man-machine models for car steering. In: *Proceedings of the Fourth Annual Conference on Manual Control*. NASA Report SP 192. Washington DC, 171–195.

Dorsch, F. (1963), *Geschichte und Probleme der angewandte Psychologie*. Bern: Huber.

Downs, R. M., Stea, D. (Eds.) (1973), *Image and environment: Cognitive mapping and spatial behavior*. Chicago: Aldine.

Einhorn, H. J., Hogarth, R. M. (1981), Behavioral decision theory: Processes of judgment and choice. *Annual Review of Psychology*, **32**, 53–89.

Ericsson, K. A., Simon, H. A: (1980), Verbal reports as data. *Psychological Review*, **87**, 215–251.

Evans, L., Wasielewski, P. (1982), Do accident-involved drivers exhibit riskier everyday driving behavior? *Accident Analysis and Prevention*, **14**, 57–64.

Everett, P. B., Hayward, S. C., Meyers, A. W. (1974), The effect of a token reinforcement procedure on bus ridership. *Journal of Applied Behavior Analysis*, **7**, 1–9.

Fishbein, M., Ajzen, I. (1975), *Belief, attitude, intention and behavior: An introduction to theory and research*. Reading (Mass.): Addison-Wesley.

Fleishman, E. A. (1967), Performance assessment based on an empirically derived task taxonomy. *Human Factors*, **9**, 349–366.

Fleishman, E. A. (1975), Toward a taxonomy of human performance. *American Psychologist*, **30**, 1127–1149.

Foerster, J. F. (1981), Non-linear and non-compensatory perceptual functions of evaluation and choice. In: Stopher, P. R., Meyburg, A. H., Brög, W. (Eds.), *New horizons in travel-behavior research*. Lexington (Mass.): Lexington Books/Heath, 335–352.

Forbes, T. W. (Ed.) (1972), *Human factors in highway traffic safety research*. New York: Wiley-Interscience.

Gensch, D. H., Torres, P. T. (1980), *A perceived difference segmentation model for mass transit marketing*. Paper presented at the 59th Annual TRB Meeting, Washington, 1980, School of Business, University of Wisconsin, Milwaukee, Wisc.

Goldstein, L. G. (1962), *Human variables in traffic accidents: A digest of research*. Highway Research Board Bibliography nr 31, 1962.

Goldstein, L. G. (1973), *Driver improvement: A review of research literature*. Sacramento (Cal.): California Department of Education.

Golob, T. F., Richardson, A. J. (1981), Noncompensatory and discontinuous constructs in travel-behavior models. In: Stopher, P. R., Meyburg, A. H., Brög, W. (Eds.), *New horizons in travel-behavior research*. Lexington (Mass.): Lexington Books/Heath, 369–384.

Greenwood, M., Yule, G. U. (1920), An inquiry into the nature of frequency distributions representative of multiple happenings with particular reference to the occurrence of multiple attacks of disease and/or repeated accidents. *Journal of the Royal Statistical Society*, **83**, 255–279.

Haddon, W., Suchman, E., Klein, D. (1964), *Accident research*. New York: Harper and Row.

Häkkinen, S. (1979), Traffic accidents and professional driver characteristics: A follow-up study. *Accident Analysis and Prevention*, **11**, 7–18.

Hamerslag, R. (1980), Spatial development, developments in traffic and transportation, and changes in the transportation system. In: Polak, J. B., Kamp, J. B. van der (Eds.), *Changes in the field of transport studies*. The Hague: Nijhoff.

Hastie, R. (1983), Social inference. *Annual Review of Psychology*, **34**, 511–542.

Hauber, A. (1977), *Gedrag van mensen in beweging: Onderzoek naar agressie in het verkeer en fraude bij het openbaar vervoer* [Behavior of people on the move: research on aggression in traffic and fraud in public transport]. Leiden University of Leiden (dissertation).

Heinze, G. W. (1978), *Verkehr schafft Verkehr: Ansatze einer Theorie des Verkehrswachstums als Selbstinduktion. Berichte zur Raumforschung und Raumplanung*. Wien: Oesterreichis che Gesellschaft für Raumforschung und Raumplanung.

Held, M. (1981), Some thoughts about the individual's choice among alternative travel modes and its determinants. In: Stopher, P. R., Meyburg, A. H., Brög, W. (Eds.), *New horizons in travel-behavior research*. Lexington (Mass.): Lexington Books/Heath, 155–170.

Hensher, D. A., Stopher (Eds.) (1979), *Behavioral travel modeling*. London: Croom Helm.

Houten, R. van, Nau, P., Marino, Z. (1980), An analysis of public posting in reducing speeding behavior on an urban highway. *Journal of Applied Behavior Analysis*, **13**, 383–395.

Hupkes, G. (1979), Nieuwe ontwikkelingen rond de BREVER-wet [New developments around the BREVER-law]. *Verkeerskunde*, **30**, 363–369.

Hurst, P. M. (1980), Can anyone reward safe driving? *Accident Analysis and Prevention*, **12**, 217–220.

Jones, P. M. (1981), Activity approaches to understanding travel behavior. In: Stopher, P. R., Meyburg, A. H., Brög, W. (Eds.), *New horizons in travel-behavior research*. Lexington (Mass.): Lexington Books/Heath, 253–265.

Klebelsberg, D. (1971), Subjektive und objektive Sicherheit im Strassenverkehr als Aufgabe für die Verkehrssicherheitsarbeit. *Schriftenreihe der Deutschen Verkehrswacht*, **51**, 3–12.

Klebelsberg, D. (1977), Das Modell der subjektiven und objektiven Sicherheit. *Schweizerische Zeitschrift für Psychologie und ihre Anwendungen*, **36**, 285–294.

Knapper, C. K., Leplat, J., Michon, J. A. (Eds.) (1980), Special issue on driving behavior. *International Review of Applied Psychology*, **29**, 397–528.

Koenderink, J. J., Doorne, A. J. van (1978), How an ambulant observer can construct a model of the environment from the geometrical structure of the visual inflow. *Kybernetik*, **19**, 224–247.

Koornstra, M. J. (1973a), A model for estimation of collective exposure and proneness from accident data. *Accident Analysis and Prevention*, **5**, 157–174.

Koornstra, M. J. (1973b), Empirical results on the exposure-proneness model. *Accident Analysis and Prevention*, **5**, 55–66.

Lane, R., Powell, T. J., Smith, P. P. (1971), *Analytical transport planning*. London: Duckworth.

Lea, S. E. G. (1978), The psychology and economics of demand. *Psychological Bulletin*, **85**, 441–466.

Levin, I. P. (1981), New applications of attitude measurement and attitudinal-modeling techniques in transportation research. In: Stopher, P. R., Meyburg, A. H., Brög, W. (Eds.), *New horizons in travel-behavior research*. Lexington (Mass.): Lexington Books/Heath, 171–188.

Liskey, N. E. (1972), Accidents, a rhythmic threat to females. *Accident Analysis and Prevention*, **4**, 1–12.

Lynch, K. (1960), *The image of the city*. Cambridge (Mass.): MIT Press.

McGuire, F. L. (1976), Personality factors in highway accidents. *Human Factors*, **18**, 433–442.

McKenna, F. (1983), Accident proneness: A conceptual analysis. *Accident Analysis and Prevention*, **15**, 65–72.

Mandler, G. (1975), *Mind and emotion*. New York: Wiley.

Mehrabian, A., Russell, J. A. (1974), *An approach to environmental psychology*. Cambridge (Mass.): MIT Press.

Michon, J. A. (1971), *Psychonomie onderweg* [Psychomics underway]. Groningen: Wolters-Noordhoff.

Michon, J. A. (1973), Deelnemen aan het verkeer [Taking part in traffic]. *Verkeerstechniek* [Traffic Technology], **23**, 562–569.

Michon, J. A. (1976a), The mutual impacts of transportation and human behavior. In: Stringer, P., Wenzel, H. (Eds.), *Transportation planning for a better environment*. New York: Plenum Press, 221–236.

Michon, J. A. (1976b), Waarnemen en informatie in het verkeer [Perception and information in traffic]. *Natuurkundige Voordrachten* [Natural Science Lectures], New Series, **55**, 173–184.

Michon, J. A. (1980a), Psychology: Aid or guide for travel demand analysis? In: Polak, J. B., Kamp, J. B. van der (Eds.), *Changes in the field of transport studies*. Den Haag: Nijhoff, 160–174.

Michon, J. A. (1980b), Telling road users who they are and what they do: Can they profit? *International Review of Applied Psychology*, **29**, 399–414.

Michon, J. A. (Ed.) (1981), Traffic education for young pedestrians. *Accident Analysis and Prevention*, **13**, nr. 3 (Special issue), 161–268.

Michon, J. A., Benwell, M. (1981), Travelers' attitudes and judgments: Application of fundamental concepts of psychology. In: Stopher, P. R., Meyburg, A. H., Brög, W. (Eds.), *New horizons in travel-behavior research*. Lexington (Mass.): Lexington Books/Heath, 189–203.

Michon, J. A., Molen, H. H. van der (1976), *Sociale verkeerskunde: Verslag van het symposium gehouden in Groningen* [Social traffic science: Report of the symposium held in Groningen], November, 1974. The Hague: ANWB.

Milgram, S. (1970), The experience of living in cities. *Science*, **167**, 1461–1468.

Miller, N. E. (1983), Behavioral medicine: Symbiosis between laboratory and clinic. *Annual Review of Psychology*, **34**, 1–32.

Miller, T. M., Schuster, D. H. (1983), Long-term predictability of driver behavior. *Accident Analysis and Prevention*, **15**, 11–22.

Molen, H. H. van der (1983), *Pedestrian ethology: Unobtrusive observations of child and adult road-crossing behaviour in the framework of the development of a child pedestrian training programme*. Haren, Neth.: Traffic Research Center, University of Groningen.

Molen, H. H. van der, Rothengatter, J. A., Vinjé, M. P. (1981), Blueprint of an analysis of the pedestrian's task—I. Method of analysis. *Accident Analysis and Prevention*, **13**, 175–192.

Näätänen, R., Summala, H. (1976), *Road user behavior and traffic accidents*. Amsterdam: North-Holland.

Nisbett, R. E., Wilson, T. D. (1977), Telling more than we can know. *Psychological Review*, **84**, 231–259.

Pailhous, J. (1970), *La représentation de l'espace urbain*. Paris: Presses Universitaires de France.

Quenault, S. W. (1967), *Driver behavior, safe and unsafe drivers*. Crowthorne, U. K.; Transportation and Road Research Laboratory, Report Nr. LR 70.

Quenault, S. W., Golby, C. W., Pryer, P. M. (1968), *Age groups and acident rate—driving behavior and attitudes*. Crowthorne, U. K.: Transportation and Road Research Laboratory, Report Nr. LR 167.

Rachlin, H., Battalio, R., Kagel, J., Green, L. (1981), Maximalization theory in behavioral psychology. *The Behavioral and Brain Sciences*, **4**, 371–388 (with commentaries 388–418).

Rachlin, H., Kagel, J. H., Battalio, R. C. (1980), Substitutability in time allocation. *Psychological Review*, **87**, 355–374.

Reid, L. D. (1983), Survey of recent driving steering behavior models suited to accident investigations. *Accident Analysis and Prevention*, **15**, 23–40.

Richards, M. G. (1976), Gedisaggregeerde modellen [Disaggregate models]. *Verkeerskunde*, **27**, 121–123, 162–165, 310–314.

Richards, M. G., Ben-Akiva, M. E. (1975), *A disaggregate travel demand model*. London: Saxon House/Heath.

Riemersma, J. B. J. (1981), Visual control during straight road driving. *Acta Psychologica*, **48**, 215–225.

Rothengatter, J. A. (1981), *Traffic safety education for young children, an empirical approach*. Lisse: Swets and Zeitlinger.

Russell, J. A., Ward, L. M. (1982), Environmental psychology. *Annual Review of Psychology*, **33**, 651–688.

Scitovsky, T. (1976), *The joyless economy: An enquiry into human satisfaction and consumer dissatisfaction*. Oxford: Oxford University Press.

Shaw, L., Sichel, H. (1971), *Accident proneness*. Oxford: Pergamon Press.

Shinar, D. (1978), *Psychology on the road: The human factor in traffic safety*. New York: Wiley.

Shor, R. E. (1964), Shared patterns of nonverbal expectations in automobile driving. *Journal of Social Psychology*, **62**, 155–163.

Slovic, P., Fischhoff, B., Lichtenstein, S. (1977), Behavioral decision theory. *Annual Review of Psychology*, **28**, 1–39.

Slovic, P., Kunreuther, H., White, G. F. (1974), Decision process, rationality and adjustment to natural hazards. In: White, G. F. (Ed.), *Natural hazards, local, national, and global*. Oxford: Oxford University Press, 187–205.

Smeed, R. J. (1949), Some statistical aspects of road safety research. *Journal of the Royal Statistical Society*, **112(A)**, 1–23.

Smeed, R. J. (1972), The usefulness of formulae in traffic engineering and road safety. *Accident Analysis and Prevention*, **4**, 303–312.

Smeed, R. J. (1974), The frequency of road accidents. *Zeitschrift für Verkehrssicherheit*, **20**, 95–108.

Stichting Verkeerstechniek [Foundation for Traffic Technology] (1980), *Stadsbewegwijzering* [Urban road signing]. Arnhem: Foundation for Traffic Technology.

Stopher, P. R., Meyburg, A. H., Brog, W. (Eds.) (1981), *New horizons in travel-behavior research*. Lexington (Mass.): Lexington Books/Heath.

Stringer, P., Wenzel, H. (Eds.) (1976), *Transportation planning for a better environment*. New York: Plenum Press.

Supernale, J. (1984), Travel regularities and their interpretations: a discussion paper. Paper read at the 63rd Annual Meeting of the Transportation Research Board, Washington D.C. Drexil University, Philadelphia.

Szalai, A. (Ed.) (1972), *The use of time*. The Hague: Mouton.

Taylor, D. H. (1964), Drivers' galvanic skin response and the risk of accident. *Ergonomics*, **7**, 439–451.

Tischer, M. L. (1981), Attitude measurement: Psychometric modeling. In: Stopher, P. R., Meyburg, A. H., Brog, W. (Eds.), *New horizons in travel-behavior research*. Lexington (Mass.): Lexington Books/Heath, 111–138.

Tversky, A., Kahneman, D. (1974), Judgment under uncertainty: Heuristics and biases. *Science*, **185**, 1124–1131.

Ursin, H., Baade, E., Levine, S. (1978), *Psychobiology of stress: A study of coping men*. New York: Academic Press.

Veling, I. (1982), Measuring driving knowledge. *Accident Analysis and Prevention*, **14**, 81–86.

Verkeerskunde [Traffic Science].

Vidakovic, V. (1980), *Mens—tijd—ruimte: Uit de dagboeken van 1400 Amsterdammers* [Man—time—space: From the diaries of 1400 Amsterdammers]. Amsterdam: Dept. of Urban Planning.

Vinje, M. (1981), Children as pedestrians. *Accident Analysis and Prevention*, **13**, 225–240.

Vlek, C. A. J., Stallen, P. J. M. (1980), Rational and personal aspects of risk. *Acta Psychologica*, **45**, 273–300.

Vlek, C. A. J., Stallen, P. J. M. (1981), Judging risks and benefits in the small and in the large. *Organizational Behavior and Human Performance*, **28**, 235–271.

Vlek, C. A. J., Wagenaar, W. A. (1979), Judgment and decision under uncertainty. In: Michon, J. A., Eijkman, E. G. J., Klerk, L. F. W. de (Eds.), *Handbook of psychonomics, Vol. 2*. Amsterdam: North-Holland, 253–345.

Wagenaar, W. A. (1983), *Menselijk falen* [Human failure]. Leiden: University of Leiden.

Wilde, G. J. S. (1978), Theorie der Risikokompensation der Unfallsverursachung und ihre praktische Folgerungen für die Unfallverhütung. *Hefte zur Unfallheilkunde*, **130**, 134–156.

Wit, J. G. de (1980), De wettelijke aanspraken van BREVER: Methodologische exercities met een gedragstheorie [The legal claims of BREVER: Methodological exercises with a behavioural theory]. *Verkeerskunde*, **31**, 354–357, 415–418.

Wohl, M., Martin, B. V. (1967), *Traffic systems analysis for engineers and planners*. New York: McGraw-Hill.

Wonham, W. M. (1976), Towards an abstract internal model principle. *IEEE Transactions on Systems, Man, and Cybernetics*, **6**, 735–740.

Zahavi, Y. (1979), *Travel over time: Final report*. Federal Highway Administration Report Nr. P.–79–004. Washington DC.: US Department of Transportation.

5.6. Work and organizational psychology in cross-cultural perspective

P. J. D. Drenth and B. Groenendijk

1. INTRODUCTION

One may wonder why a whole chapter in this handbook is devoted to the cross-cultural aspects of organizational psychology. Before the problems and research results of this relatively new research field are taken up, this question will be briefly handled.

More and more frequently it is recognized that the activities of organizations are not restricted to any one country. There is an increasing number of contacts between organizations in various countries. Large organizations often have establishments in more than one country. Even the goals of some organizations are international in character; as an example one can think of the various organizations within the framework of the United Nations.

The international orientation of some organizations raises a number of questions, for example:

—What should be paid attention to in the training of organization members who will be assigned abroad or who will maintain regular contacts with persons or organizations in other countries? In which way should certain cultural idiosyncracies or relationships between persons and groups of persons different from those of the country of origin be taken into account?

—Does the culture of a country influence the manner in which an organization functions? Is it primarily the organizational structure which is influenced or rather the way in which various informal processes occur? Or is cultural influence

Prof. dr. P. J. D. Drenth and Drs. B. Groenenijk, Subfaculteit Psychologie der Vrije Universiteit De Boelelaan 1081, 1081 HV, AMSTERDAM.

perhaps restricted to the attitudes, values and norms of organization members, without affecting the manner in which organizations function?

—Do organization principles which have contributed to a more effective functioning in a given country have the same results in other countries, as for instance Negandhi (1979) suggests? Or are organizations in different countries effective in different ways, as for instance Cole (1973, 1979) has shown in a comparative study of Japanese and American organizations?

Considering this background, the fact that so much research restricts itself to organizations in only one country is perhaps more surprising than the existence of cross-cultural research. In any case the implicit or explicit assumption of much of this research, that the research results are supposed to have general validity, should be received with reserve. Research which has the pretention of leading to statements about organizations in general cannot remain restricted to organizations in one given country.

One important reason for the reluctance to carry out cross-cultural research is perhaps the large number of methodological problems inherent in this type of study. These problems will be discussed in section 2. The problems do not exclusively occur in cross-cultural research. They often play a role in non-cross-cultural research as well, though the researcher is often less aware of it. Thus, cross-cultural research also can lead to a clarification of previously often 'automatic' applied concepts and to nuances in traditional interpretations of work and organizational psychology in general.

In the economic history of the last centuries, one sees that with increasing industrialization more and more people are spending a very important part of their lives in work organizations. Great differences occur in the way in which organizations exercise influence on the attitudes and behaviour of their employees. Many of these differences seem to be connected to national or cultural differences. In order to imagine this, one only has to think of the differences between the American or West European production worker on the one hand and his Japanese counterpart on the other (see for example Dore, 1973; Cole, 1979). It is obvious that the study of interactions between work organizations and the behaviour of employees is an interesting area of research, especially when these interactions are placed against the background of intercultural differences.

In organizational psychology two main questions are dominant:

—*First*, what are the interactions between organizational characteristics and processes on the one hand and attitudes, work behaviour and performance of people working in these organizations on the other? We used the term 'interactions', i.e. reference is made to the effects of organizational variables on the behaviour and attitudes of organization members as well as to the effects of behaviour and attitudes on (certain characteristics of) the organization.

—*Second*, under which conditions are certain organizational characteristics and processes related to certain attitudes (for example commitment to the organization, satisfaction) or to certain work behaviour (for example productivity, effort, absenteeism, personnel turnover)?

The first question is aimed at a *direct* causal relationship between organization and human behaviour. The second question is the so-called *contingency question*. Many of the assumed conditions (also called contingent factors) in this second question are possibly embedded in the organization itself. Technology, nature of the work and product, size, centralization, formalization, specialization etc. come to mind (see Veen in this Handbook, ch. 4.1). Other contingent factors may be found in the individual or the group itself, such as age, sex, social-economic level, rank in the organization and education. Others are to be located in the broader physical and social environment, such as geographical conditions, political structure of the country, level of the country's development, unemployment level, and the dominating value system.

Now, considering the above definition of organizational psychology, the question of what is the subject matter of cross-cultural research in organizational psychology still remains to be answered. Translated into cross-cultural perspective, one could formulate questions just designated as follows (see figure 1, in which the numerals refer to sub-questions to be mentioned below):

1. Can the interaction between organizations and individuals be *explained* in terms of cultural factors?— This problem can be further split into two sub-questions:

1a. Can the organizational characteristics, which might influence the work behaviour and performance of people in organizations, be explained by cultural factors? The answer to this question should be given in two stages. Whether organizations per culture exhibit differences has to be examined in the first stage. Next comes the question whether these differences can be explained in cultural terms.

1b. Can certain differences in the attitudes and behaviour of people in

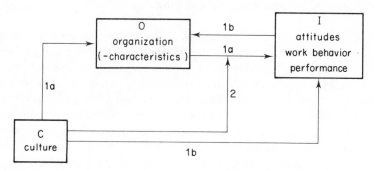

Figure 1. Hypothetical relationships between culture, organizations and individuals.

organizations, which might influence the various aspects of the organization, be explained in terms of cultural factors?

2. Is culture perhaps a *contingent* factor in the relationship between organization and human behaviour?

This second problem pertains to the question whether the relationship between certain organizational characteristics (climate, size, formal characteristics etc.) on the one hand and certain attitudes or certain work behaviour of the employees (job satisfaction, participative style, performance etc.) on the other hand differs from one culture to the other.

The word 'cultural' has already been used several times above. Of course not all national differences are cultural differences, although this is indeed suggested by the fact that in many publications the words 'cross-cultural' and 'cross-national' are used synonymously. There are differences in language, law, religion, geographical and climat's variables, economic and technological factors and the like. Some of these aspects are influenced by or even have influence on cultural factors, but this still does not mean that they can be just simply equated with culture. On the other hand there is a tendency to consider 'culture' as a sort of 'residue factor'. Everything which cannot be explained on the basis of other identifiable factors is called 'culture'. This kind of approach does not have much explanatory power. Therefore, a further definition of what is meant by 'culture' is appropriate (see also Child, 1981).

According to us, the concept 'culture' should be thought of as the pattern of attitudes, values and norms in a given society which in part influences the behaviour of population groups. This pattern exhibits a certain stability over generations, although it does adapt itself to changing social and physical conditions. This definition is in agreement with the much quoted definition of Kluckhohn (1951), who defines the concept as 'Patterns of behaviour of human groups acquired and transmitted by symbols; the essential core of culture consists of traditional ideas, and especially their attached values'. Kroeber and Parsons (1958) defines this concept a bit more sharply as 'patterns of roles and norms embedded in certain paramount values'.

In the following section the methodological problems which occur in the area of cross-cultural research in work and organizational psychology will be discussed (section 2). Then a section will be devoted to research on cross-cultural differences in the attitudes of organization members (section 3). After this, the organization itself will be accentuated. First, the question whether cross-national differences exist will be examined (section 4) and next the possibility of culture as an explanatory factor (section 5). In addition, the question whether there is any support for the proposition that cultural differences will disappear with further increases of advanced technology in work organizations will be discussed (section 6). In the final section figure 1 will be briefly handled again, while attempting to indicate how the most probable causal lines run.

2. METHODOLOGICAL PROBLEMS

The difficulties in cross-cultural research caused by the large number of methodological problems have been described in more or less detail by many authors (Andriessen 1979; Berry, 1980; Brislin et al., 1973; Elder, 1976; Przeworski and Teune, 1970; Roberts, 1970). In this section the following will be successively discussed: problems of translation, equivalence of concepts, differences in relationships, problems with response-sets, sampling difficulties, and finally the choice of the appropriate level of aggregation

Translation

In many cross-cultural studies use is being made of a questionnaire or interview form. These are very often formulated in the mother tongue of the respondent. This is however not always the case: sometimes English questionnaires are used in other language areas. Apart from the problem that the questionnaire can be only used on that part of the population with an adequate command of English, the question still remains whether the applied words and expressions have the same meaning for respondents outside of English language countries as for people who use English as the daily vernacular. The simple utilization of English questionnaires outside of English language areas should be discouraged as a rule. Naturally, this applies for other languages as well.

New problems naturally occur in translation. How is a comparable translation obtained? The so-called 'back translation' is a frequently applied technique which is considered by Roberts (1970) and others as the minimum condition for cross-national comparative research. This technique involves the independent translation of the translated version back into the original language. The back translation and the original are compared and then, if necessary, the translation is adjusted. This method is also not without problems (see for example Bennett, 1977a). For many words, there are simply no good translation equivalents, especially when they have to be translated out of context (Osgood, 1967).

The so-called 'decentering' method is an improvement of this technique (Brislin et al., 1973; Brislin, 1976). In this method, which is an extension of 'back translation', the original version is not taken as the only criterion. After the back translation, the original version can be so altered that it is 'translatable'. In this way the translated version is a more equivalent alternative for the original version. For an example the reader is referred to Katerberg et al. (1977). The literal translatability is the criterion here just as with ordinary back translation. However, this is not the only possible criterion. Even well translated questionnaires cannot always be considered to actually measure the same things (possess functional equivalence). Functional equivalence, as a rule, is considered to be the ultimate goal of the translation or adaptation (Andriessen, 1979; Elder, 1976; Osgood, 1967; Przeworski and Teune, 1970).

Conceptual, functional and score equivalence

The term 'conceptual equivalence' relates to the question whether a concept used to study differences between cultures has the same meaning in those different cultures. Thus, in an industrialized society the concept 'work' will have as a rule an entirely different meaning than in a classical agrarian society. In itself this can be indeed an interesting subject for research (see for example the international comparative study on 'the meaning of working', MOW, 1981). A cross-cultural comparison always involves a comparison in terms of concepts which should have the same meaning in different countries (conceptually equivalent concepts).

For these equivalent concepts one should have instruments (indices, scales, tests) which are sufficiently *functionally equivalent*; i.e. measure the same thing in the different populations (Poortinga, 1975; Przeworski and Teune, 1970). If there is more than one instrument meeting this requirement, functional equivalence can be made plausible. If one can assume that the relationships between the variables measured by the instruments are identical in the different cultures, the requirement of functional equivalence leads to the testable condition that the correlations between the various instruments must be the same.

Moreover, when average scores in different populations are compared, there is an even more rigorous requirement for comparability: the scale values must be comparable (*score equivalence*). However, the testing of both kinds of equivalence is only possible when there is some a priori knowledge concerning the relationships between the variables in question and when the measuring instruments are sufficiently precise. In individual psychology it seems that the requirements above are only met in the case of experimental psychological measures that are easy to operationalize (Poortinga, 1971; Drenth and van der Flier, 1973).

In cross-cultural research in organizations, the requirements mentioned above are often neither met in the measurement of individual attitudes and values nor in the measurement of organizational characteristics. The more rigorous requirement of score equivalence especially presents problems. We will return to this point in the following section.

Score equivalence and differences in relationships

By far the largest part of cross-cultural research is concerned with score differences on one or more variables. This type of research will be handled in detail in this chapter. Nevertheless, from the discussion in the previous section it became clear already that such comparisons between scores are not without problems. For Przeworski and Teune (1970) the fact that score equivalence of the applied instruments is very seldom demonstrated is a reason to emphasize the differences in *relationships* between variables instead of simple differences in *level*. For such differences in relationship 'only' the requirement of functional equivalence is to be met. Przeworski and Teune also propose an analysis strategy that should prevent a premature explanation of differences between organizations in terms of factors on a higher system level such as 'culture'. They advise to examine first to what extent variables on a lower level, 'individual variables' to start with, could explain the discovered differences.

It should be noted that research which satisfies all the criteria of Przeworski and Teune is not easy to do. For example, in organizational psychology there is relatively little research in which differences in relationships are sought and found. An example of this kind of research is that of Bennett (1977b), who studied the relationship between leadership characteristics and effectiveness of managers in Hong Kong and the Philippines. The 'Least Preferred Coworker' scale of Fiedler (1967) was one of the instruments used. A low LPC-score is supposed to show that the manager is task oriented while the manager with an high LPC-score is more oriented towards social relationships. It turns out that Filipino managers with a high performance appraisal have a relatively low LPC-score, while in Hong Kong a low LPC-score is found with managers with a low performance appraisal. A second instrument used by Bennett was the 'Self Description Inventory' of Ghiselli. In both countries he found the expected positive correlations with leadership effectiveness (performance assessments) for a number of scales on the SDI. For two scales which were conceptually related to the LPC-scale namely 'Working Class Affinity' and 'Maturity', clearly contrary relationships were found. These scales correlated positively with the performance assessments in Hong Kong and negatively in the Philippines, which corresponds with the results found for the LPC-scale.

The discussion of differences in level and differences in relationships seems to lead to an unsatisfactory conclusion. If the confirmation of differences in level must strictly meet the high requirements proposed, for example, by Poortinga (1975) and Przeworski and Teune (1970), such differences will be very seldom determined. Indirectly it can still be attempted to make such differences plausible. One possibility is to use several different methods to measure the same phenomenon, as in the study of Bennett discussed above. Moreover, the use of techniques other than the usual questionnaire method can contribute to the plausibility of the conclusions (for example games or simulations, see Bass, 1977 and Bass and Eldrige, 1973).

The problems which occur in research on differences in score level should, of course, also be discerned in an evaluative discussion of such research. In such a case there is an extra possibility to test certain conclusions regarding differences between cultures. In fact, the results of various studies in which comparable concepts were investigated can be compared to each other. If the conclusions of the various studies are in agreement, they become more convincing. We will make use of this possibility especially in section 4.

Faking and response sets

The problem of 'faking' is a difficult obstacle in intra-cultural research. With this concept we are not exclusively thinking of the conscious distortion and embellishment of responses but of a much more broadly conceived phenomenon, whereby a respondent presents himself other than he really is or expresses opinions other than those he really entertains, mostly on the basis of a subjective evaluation of the goal of the research situation (for an analysis of faking on questionnaires see van Esbroeck, 1982). In cross-cultural research this phenomenon can determine a still much larger part of the variance. In some cultures (Japan, China, Indonesia) the tendency 'to please' the interrogator is perhaps a lot stronger then in other cultures. This 'pleasing' will result in highly colored responses, according to a subjective estimate of what the researcher would like to hear.

Something like the above probably applies to the general social desirability. In some cultures the tendency to give socially desirable answers due to upbringing and tradition is stronger than in other cultures. Notably in cross-cultural research these differences in social desirability could seriously damage the comparability of the scales.

This reasoning also applies to the different kinds of response-sets. For example, the acquiescence-set can be furthered as well in East Asian countries by the 'courtesy bias' mentioned (Elder, 1976). The response-set problem also can be encountered in all kinds of other and more subtle variations. Response categories such as 'often', 'sometimes', etc. can vary widely in meaning, especially when the circumstances are rather diverse. This definitely plays a role in cross-cultural research. In a plant in a developing country an occasional consultation by the manager is perhaps experienced as 'often', while in a Scandinavian concern it will evaluated as 'seldom'. It is, therefore, important to formulate the response categories as concrete as possible.

Finally, one must not forget that large differences between countries exist as to what one considers a proper and acceptable question. Deutscher (1973) points out that questions about income, family life, leisure and the like are considered as a much greater breach of 'privacy' in some countries than in others. That this will color reactions does not need an argument.

Selection of countries, organizations and respondents

The selection of the countries to be involved in the research and the compilation of the samples, organizations and persons within the country should be based on theoretical and methodological considerations. In fact, the solution is often highly influenced by practical conditions.

As for the choice of the countries, there are two approaches to choose from, depending on the question:

a. Maximum *similarity* between the countries; this model is justified when one wants to examine the influence of a certain independent variable on organizational characteristics. As an example one can think of the influence of the independent variable 'capitalism versus socialism' on the extent of democratization in industrial organizations. In an ideal case one chooses countries which greatly differ on the designated dimension, but are as similar as possible for the remainder. The weakness of this approach is that the last requirement is hardly ever satisfied. Countries differ as a rule on a number of other features, on the basis of which plausible alternative explanations could be generated.

b. Maximum *differences* between the countries; this model is desirable when the establishment of a theoretical or causal relationship is involved. If, for example, one wants to demonstrate that the level of social security or the percentage of unemployment in a country influences absenteeism or personnel turnover, one does well in choosing a set-up with countries as different as possible. In making generalizations, clearly different cases ('case independence', Elder, 1976) in the sample are very important.

As has already been said, pragmatic considerations and questions play an important part in the selection of the countries (can qualified co-workers for the project be found in the country involved, is there entry to the companies and cooperation on the part of the authorities, is there sufficient subsidy and the like). Because of these reasons cross-cultural research is often restricted to a very small number of, often even two, countries.

The selection of organizations also is often not made according to the rules. Ideally, one chooses a sample in each country which is as comparable as possible with samples in other countries on aspects as technology or size of the organization (see for example IDE, 1981a). In practice, this selection of organizations is often problematic. Here also the sampling is often determined by practical considerations. Admission to companies is not always easy to obtain, especially when rather time-intensive research is involved. In addition, the concept 'organization' itself is not always uniform in different countries. The structure of organizations, their financial and organizational relationship to the mother company or the financial holding can vary widely.

Once the selection of the company has been made, it is often less difficult to make a selection of respondents (IDE, 1981a) groups or work units (Koopman *et al.*, 1981), decisions (DIO, 1983) or whatever the unit of analysis might be.

In the foregoing it was assumed that the choice of certain countries is made first, that subsequently organizations within the countries are chosen and that finally the selection of respondents within the organizations takes place. Sometimes another route is actually followed. For instance, Hofstede (1979, 1980) compared the subsidiaries of the same multinational in 39 countries. One could say that the choice of the organization preceded the choice of countries and for a large part also determined the latter choice. This method has the important advantage that the organizations will not vary too much regarding salient characteristics. A disadvantage is that the research is restricted to the one multinational concern and the generalizability is more limited.

Finally, we mention another, less well justified procedure which is often encountered in cross-cultural research in organizational psychology, particularly in research on attitudes of organization members. We have in mind research that is based on sample of persons who accidently(?) participate in workshops or courses (see for example Barrett and Bass, 1976).

Level of aggregation

One last difficulty to be discussed concerns the level of observation and analysis. In cross-cultural organizational psychology this is naturally often the level of organization. This entails two problems: first, the number of observations; second, the distinction individual-aggregated data.

If one wants to collect a rather fair amount of data per organization, it is often difficult to involve an adequately large number of organizations in the various countries in the research. The total number of organizations in the IDE-research amounted to 134, a proportionately extensive sample. However, in total there were 7,832 individual respondents involved in the research.

In the second place, attention is drawn to the distinction individual-aggregated data (Scheuch, 1966). When the level of analysis is the same as that of observation, the data are individual (this can be the level of persons, but also the level of decisions, departments and organizations). Data are aggregated when the analysis level is higher than the observation level. This occurs, for example, when the analysis is done on the level of the department or organization, while the data consists of averaged scores of members of the department or organization.

Such changes in level are seen relatively often in cross-cultural research in organizational psychology. A few examples: the concepts 'division of power' and 'total amount of power in the organization', as developed by Tannenbaum, are repeatedly used in cross-cultural comparative research between organizations (Tannenbaum, 1968; Tannenbaum et al., 1974; Tannenbaum and Cooke, 1979). In fact, this involves aggregated measurements based on average scores for the various hierarchical levels. Hofstede (1980) also makes use of aggregated data for each of the subsidiaries investigated by him.

A warning not to lose sight of this difference in level seems appropriate. Robinson (1950) long ago pointed out the danger of these, what he calls, 'ecological' correlations. It is not admissible to draw conclusions from correlations on a high level of aggregation about relationships on an individual level and vice versa. A relationship between the degree of unionization and the level of activity of the works council, established on the organization level, cannot simply lead to the conclusion that this relationship also exists on the individual level. It could very well be that trade union members are not active on the works council, but that with an increasing union membership precisely non-trade union members become more active on the works council. Similarly, a correlation on the individual level can disappear on the organization level (the 'Durkheimian Fallacy', Blalock, 1961).

Ecological correlations are often higher than individual ones; because of the process of averaging, part of the error variance drops out of the individual data.

One does well to view these various kinds of correlations as separate realities and to be careful with interpretations at other levels of analysis.

Mutatis mutandis that we have said above is also valid for an aggregation at a still higher level, namely that of the country itself. One could establish average organization scores at the country level and relate these to socio-political norms, cultural factors and the like. From the foregoing it will be clear that relationships on this level neither are to be simply extrapolated to the level of the organization.

3. CULTURE AND ATTITUDES

By far the greatest part of cross-cultural research in organizational psychology pertains to attitudes, needs, expectations and norms of organization members. In this chapter this literature will not be extensively discussed. On the basis of the most cited study in this area, that of Haire, Ghiselli and Porter (1966), we will indicate the limitations and possibilities of this type of research. The research of Haire *et al.* was carried out on a sample of ± 3,600 managers from 14 different countries. They found a large number of differences between the 14 countries, especially pertaining to attitudes and assumptions underlying management practices. The most striking result of the research was the clustering of countries in the following five groups:
1. Northern Europe (Norway, Sweden, Denmark and West Germany).
2. Latin Europe (Spain, Italy, France and Belgium).
3. Anglo-American (United Kingdom and United States).
4. Developing countries (India, Argentina and Chili).
5. Japan.

Besides the fact that systematic differences between the clusters exist, it is important to know in which respect they are different. Here, the enumeration will be restricted to a small number of striking and consistent differences between the clusters.

In the first place, these differences concern ideas about leadership. In general, it seems that managers do not have a high opinion of the 'capacity for leadership and initiative' of most people. Respondents from Europe (Northern and Latin) have still less confidence in those capacities than managers from other countries. This difference was not found on three other dimensions which concerned attitudes with respect to participative leadership. Here the developing countries stood out from all the other countries (therefore Europe also) due to negative attitudes. Further, 'to direct' seemed to have a more positive meaning than 'to persuade' in all countries. This difference was by far the greatest in Northern Europe, especially West Germany.

Secondly, there are differences in the extent of satisfaction of a number of needs within the Maslow hierarchy (somewhat modified by Haire *et al.*). Especially the developing countries, but also the Latin European countries, were conspicuous for their low level of satisfaction. In Northern Europe satisfaction is high. These needs were found to be the most important in the developing countries, the least in Northern Europe.

The discussed study of Haire *et al.* is illustrative for the enormous amount of research in relation to attitudes, values, norms and opinions of organization members. Most of this research is discussed by Roberts (1970), Barret and Bass (1976), Tannenbaum (1980) and Bhagat and McQuaid (1982). One study which is not mentioned in these survey articles is that of Redding and Casey (1976), a direct extension of the study of Haire *et al.* to a number of countries in Southeast Asia. Further, there is research carried out on the motives of employees (Ronen, 1977, 1979), on the 'modernity' of values in three developing countries (Fliegel *et al.*, 1979) and on opinions about the meaning of working (MOW, 1981).

The research of Haire *et al.* has a number of limitations which are also applicable to most of the other studies in this area. In the first place, one may wonder to what extent the observed differences between the countries are due to differences in the designated variables or to differences in the *meaning* of the concepts used. The differences found in attitudes towards participation could also be, for example, the result of the different meanings attached to the concept 'participation'. Thus, Martyn-Johns (1977) questions the applicability of the Western concept of participation for the more cooperative decision-making processes which occur in Java (see also Hofstede, 1980, p. 113).

In the second place, this concerns mostly cross-cultural research in relation to organizations, in which the organization itself is not studied. It is obvious that such research only can give a limited answer to our questions. For this reason the remainder of this chapter will emphasize research that is directly concerned with characteristics of organizations. In the third place, one can ask to what extent the differences found really reflect 'cultural' differences. However, this question is often tautological. Culture, as a rule, is defined in terms of values, norms, opinions and attitudes. If, then, an attempt is made to explain the differences in values and the like by means of 'culture', the risk of circular reasoning is not imaginary.

In each study in which differences between countries are found, one can ask to what extent these differences actually reflect cultural differences. In the case of the study of Haire *et al.*, there are two arguments which plead for such a conclusion:
1. The clustering into five groups of countries shows a culturally meaningful picture. Culturally related countries often seem to go together in the same cluster. In addition, it seems that the clustering of the countries also follows an economic logic.
2. This picture is confirmed in a follow-up study by Ajiferuke and Boddewijn (1970), who related the data of Haire *et al.*, to a number of socio-economic indicators on the macro level. The level of education proved to be an important predictor of attitudes and assumptions underlying management practices. The importance of the needs is predicted best from life-expectations, but the percentage of Roman Catholics and the average degree of urbanization are also important

predictors. Need fulfillment and, especially, satisfaction could be predicted from the percentage of Roman Catholics and the percentage of illiterates. Ajiferuke and Boddewijn agree with the emphasis of Haire *et al.* on economic as well as cultural explanations. They also point out that the variables themselves are more important than their labels, such as cultural, psychological, sociological or economic.

In addition, Ajiferuke and Boddewijn indicate a possibility to avoid the tautology problem. By defining culture on the macro level, a clear distinction can be made between culture on the one hand and attitudes, values, norms and opinions on the other hand. Another solution would be to define culture on the personal level, but simultaneously to distinguish which values, attitudes, norms and opinions are to be considered as 'culture' and which not. In this approach one defines some personal characteristics, aggregated for certain cultural groups, as 'culture' and distinguishes these from other personal variables which could hold as 'effects of culture'. In any case, it should be true of the former that (a) they are relatively stable through time and that (b) they give a more integrated picture of behavior and attitudes in various situations. Attitudes which exclusively concern the work situation will not be considered as a rule.

It is really surprising that so many organizational psychologists search for 'cultural' differences between countries without bothering about the definition of culture. One would expect more attention to be paid to this problem of conceptualization and definition precisely by psychologists.

4. DIFFERENCES BETWEEN ORGANIZATIONS IN DIFFERENT COUNTRIES

In section 3 it was already pointed out that many cross-cultural studies in organizational psychology are restricted to attitudes, needs, norms and values of organization members. A result of this is that much greater attention can be observed for the relationship between culture and behavior (in a broad sense) of individuals (1b in figure 1) than for the relationship between culture and organizational characteristics (1a in figure 1). In relation to the third possibility this figure, cultural differences in relationships between characteristics of organizations and the behavior of persons (2 in figure 1), research is even more scarce. An exception to this is the recent study of Sekaran and Mowday (1981), which among other things is concerned with the relationship between certain characteristics of work and 'job involvement' in India and in the United States. One of the conclusions is that this relationship is generally less strong in India than in the United States. As yet it is not clear to what extent cultural factors are responsible for this.

In view of the importance that we attach to cross-cultural research in which organizations are examined, two sections in this chapter are devoted to this subject. In the present section the question whether there are differences between organizations in different countries will be handled. This discussion will focus on the variables mentioned in the summary chapter of Lammers and Hickson's volume (1979), which are examined in various studies in this area. These variables, which are often related, seem to reflect the main stream of existing cross-cultural research of organizations. The explanation of the observed differences will not be handled in this section. The question to what extent these differences may be considered as 'culturally determined' will be discussed in section 5.

Social distance and power

In the 1950s the French sociologist Crozier studied the phenomenon 'bureaucracy' in government organizations in France. Here, attention was especially paid to the dysfunctional aspects of bureaucracy. After a comparison with organizations in the United States and in the Soviet Union, Crozier (1964) concluded that these dysfunctional characteristics are for a large part to be ascribed to French culture. Clark (in Lammers and Hickson, 1979, chapter 14) embroidered further on Crozier's study of the nationalized French tobacco industry by examining to what extent the dysfunctional characteristics of bureaucracy mentioned by Crozier can also by found in three factories in the English tobacco industry (not state-owned). Both types of organizations have a comparable market position (practically a monopoly), are approximately of the same size and use the same technology. Clark observed a large number of differences between the French and English factories. In the first place, French bureaucracy was typified by a large number of impersonal rules, drawn up by people who are not directly involved in the daily operations of the factory. In England the existing rules are made by both management and the trade-union representatives within the factory. In addition, the rules in England are often not aimed at covering all possible situations and their application is often open to interpretation by the managers and trade-union representatives. In the second place, there is a highly stratified social structure in France, while in England the social classes are less highly isolated. In the third place, local management in England is more autonomous with respect to the mother organization. Finally, in France the uncertainty which comes about when everything cannot be laid down in rules more often leads to conflicts between the various groups within the organization. This is much less the case in England, which for example, is evident from the more flexible manner in which machine stoppages are handled.

Lammers and Hickson (1979) distinguish at least two types of organization: a *classical* bureaucracy which occurs especially in Southern Europe and more *flexible* type of bureaucracy which is supposed to be dominant in Northern Europe and in North America. In developing countries the so-called 'traditional organization' (which is in fact very similar to the Latin type) is supposed to be prevailing. This classification is supported by the results of the various studies in the book of Lammers and Hickson.

The study of Gallie (1978) on two French and two English oil refineries is comparable to that of Clark. In France he found more social distance between workers and middle management. This result agrees with the more rigid stratification found in France by Clark. Further, Gallie observed a less unequal distribution of power in England. The larger number of conflicts in the French oil refineries is ascribed to, among other things, these two differences between the organizations. In the study of Maurice (Lammers and Hickson, 1979: chapter 3; see also Maurice et al., 1980), organizations in France and West Germany are compared to each other. The results show a less rigid stratification in West Germany than in France. In this respect, West Germany is more similar to England than to France. This was confirmed by the results of Hofstede (1979, 1980) in relation to power-distance. The index for this, the PDI (Power Distance Index), consists of three items, which can be briefly typified as follows (the descriptions are characteristic for a high PDI-score):

1. Non-managerial employees' perception that employees are afraid to disagree with their managers (this question is considered by Hofstede to be the core of his PDI).

2. Subordinates' perception that their boss tends to make decisions in an autocratic or persuasive/paternalistic way.

3. Subordinates' preference for anything but a consultative style in their boss: that is, for an autocratic, a persuasive/paternalistic, or a democratic style (Hofstede, 1980, p. 103).

Hofstede compared 39 subsidiaries of a multinational concern[1] in relation to the PDI. The results point in the direction of a North-South distinction. English language countries, Scandinavian countries, West Germany, Austria and Israel have a relatively low PDI-score. In contrast, Latin Europe, Latin America and a number of Asian countries have an high PDI. Separate date (not from the same concern) for Yugoslavia prompt the surmise that this country belongs to the second group. Thus, West Germany and England are in the same group and even have the same PDI-score. This result agrees with the findings of Maurice described above.

Here, it should be noted that in our opinion the power-distance of Hofstede, in contrast to what the words suggest, does not reflect real differences in power. Interpretation of the questions in the index would rather lead to lables such as 'participative climate' or 'social distance'. The results are accordingly completely in agreement with the results of Clark and Gallie concerning rigid stratification and social distance. The differences in stratification found by Maurice are considered to be consequences of differences in 'power-distance' by Hofstede. The results of Hofstede are, however, not in agreement with the results of Tannenbaum et al. (1974) in relation to the distribution of influence within organizations in five countries.

In the IDE study (1979, 1981a) differences between predominantly West European countries were found, using a measure for the distribution of influence

---

[1] In section 2 several observations have been made already on this sample. The companies are maximally comparable, but the generalizability can be questioned.

derived from the study of Tannenbaum. Since all of these twelve countries were represented in the study of Hofstede, a direct comparison can be made. Then it turns out that e.g. in Israel, which had the lowest PDI score among the twelve countries, the greatest differences in influence exist between top management and workers! Yugoslavia, the country with the highest PDI-score, has the smallest differences in influence. In any case, there seems to be no relationship between Hofstede's PDI and influence differences in the IDE study. Hofstede (1980, p. 118) explains these differences between his own results and those of Tannenbaum *et al.* (we assume that this is also valid for the IDE results) concerning the distribution of power by suggesting that the PDI measures *informal* elements of hierarchy, while the influence question of Tannenbaum *et al.* is supposed to measure *formal* elements of hierarchy. He points to the relationship between the PDI results and the results of Tannenbaum *et al.* with respect to 'informal participation'. This concept was measured by Tannenbaum *et al.* using some five questions, among which:
—does your immediate supervisor tend to take into account your suggestions and opinions?
—do you trust your immediate supervisor?
The questions are indeed very remindful of those from Hofstede's PDI. A comparison of the results for four of the five countries from the study of Tannenbaum *et al.*,[2] however, does not yield an unambiguous agreement. In table 1, the rankings of the countries are reported for the PDI of Hofstede and for 'informal participation' of Tannenbaum for relatively large and small organizations.

The PDI still seems to show more agreement with Tannenbaum's 'informal participation' than with his 'influence differences'. This, however, hardly supports Hofstede's interpretation of the PDI, because according to Tannenbaum *et al.* this 'informal participation' reflects the climate within the work group rather than differences in power. Differences in power can even sometimes go together with *more* 'informal participation', the latter as an attempt to soften the negative

Table 1. The PDI and informal participation. Rankings for four countries. (1 = low PDI = high informal participation).

	Informal participation (small organizations)	Informal participation (large organizations)	Power distance (Hofstede)
United States	1	1	2
Austria	3	2	1
Yugoslavia	2	3	4
Italy	4	4	3

[2]The results from Israel are not comparable, since they refer to kibbutzim.

consequences of hierarchy (Tannenbaum *et al.*, 1974). Therefore, it is somewhat surprising that Hofstede (1979, 1980) views his PDI as conceptually related to the Aston dimension 'centralization' (see this Handbook, ch. 4.1). Mintzberg (1979) among others indicates that in this concept the formal side of the decision process is emphasized too much. It seems, therefore, that this concept has even less in common with the PDI—which should measure precisely the informal aspects of participation—than Tannenbaum's influence differences.

The research results discussed in this section prompt the surmise that the North-South distinction of Lammers and Hickson in the first instance refers to a dimension that could be described as 'rigid stratification', 'social distance' or 'informal participation'. The data of Clark, Gallie, Maurice, Hofstede (PDI) and Tannenbaum (partly) fit in this picture. Probably this dimension reflects no differences in the division of power within organizations. Regarding such differences in power, as studied by Tannenbaum *et al.* and in the IDE research, the distinction North-South is less adequate (see also table 3).

Formalization and bureaucratic control

In the beginning of this section the study of Clark (1979) was discussed, who observed a number of differences between the French and English tobacco industry. One of these differences referred to the application of impersonal rules. In this section we will examine the extent to which also other research results on the presence and use of impersonal rules fit into the North-South distinction discussed in the previous section. The study of Aiken and Bacharach (in Lammers and Hickson, 1979, chapter 12) is interesting in this respect: a comparison was made between the local authorities in both the French and Dutch language areas of Belgium. Four important differences were found:
1. Social control in Flanders is more often based on interpersonal contact (such as direct supervision) and in Wallonia more often on impersonal rules (bureaucratic control).
2. Still, respondents in Flemish organizations more often reported the presence of written documents such as job descriptions and documentations of the chains of command (formalization, see also Hickson *et al.*, 1974).
3. The Flemish often follow shorter routes in order to accomplish something than those indicated by the formal prescribed procedures. This fact could explain why the greater formalization in Flanders does not lead to stronger bureaucratic control. Apparently the rules are applied with more flexibility.
4. The Flemish report more often that they have varied work, while respondents in Wallonia more often called it routine work.

This observation is in agreement with the North-South distinction as sketched by Clark for Great Britain (North) and France (South). Child and Kieser (in Lammers and Hickson, 1979, chapter 13; see also Child, 1981) find that the role of the manager in the English organizations studied by them is more formalized than in West German organizations. Further, the West German managers more often view their work as less varied and as routine work. Other relevant research results in this connection are those of Tannenbaum *et al.* (1974) concerning 'opportunities provided by the job'; these are greater in the United States on all levels of the organization than in Italy, Yugoslavia and Austria. If one views the United States as related to Great Britain and Flanders, Austria as related to West Germany, and Yugoslavia and Italy as related to France, these results are in agreement with those of Clark, Child and Kieser, and Aiken and Bacharach.[3]

Confirmation of this picture is found in the study of Hofstede (1980), which is contrast to the studies just discussed involved a large number of countries. His dimension 'uncertainty avoidance' is conceptually related to 'bureaucratic control'. The UAI (Uncertainty Avoidance Index) consists of three items, among which the question if respondents find that company rules should not be broken—even if the employee thinks it is in the company's best interest. The results show that respondents from Latin coutries in Europe and America score relatively high on this dimension and, therefore, have a strong tendency to avoid uncertainty. Scandinavian countries, The Netherlands and, especially, English-speaking countries score low on the UAI. West Germany, Austria and Switzerland (the latter the least clear) show a lower score than Latin countries but a clearly higher score than other 'Northern' countries. The Asian countries in the sample have scores which vary from very high (Japan) to very low (Singapore). In general, especially the South-East Asian countries score rather low on this index. In table 2, the results of Clark, Tannenbaum, Child and Kieser, and Aiken and Bacharach are briefly summarized and compared with Hofstede's results on the UAI.

Table 2. A comparison of three groups of countries on the variables 'formalization', 'bureaucratic control', 'routine work' and 'uncertainty avoidance'.

	Formalization	Bureaucratic control	Routine work	Uncertainty avoidance
Great Britain	+ (Clark, Child & Kieser)	− (Clark)	− (Clark, Child & Kieser)	− (Hofstede)
USA			− (Tannenbaum)	− (Hofstede)
Flanders	+ (Aiken & Bacharach)	− (Aiken & Bacharach)	− (Aiken & Bacharach)	
France	− (Clark)	+ (Clark)	+ (Clark)	+ (Hofstede)
Italy			+ (Tannenbaum)	+ (Hofstede)
Yugoslavia			+ (Tannenbaum)	+ (Hofstede)
Wallonia	− (Aiken & Bacharach)	+ (Aiken & Bacharach)	+ (Aiken & Bacharach)	
Germany	− (Child & Kieser)		+ (Child & Kieser)	± (Hofstede)
Austria			+ (Tannenbaum)	± (Hofstede)

[3] Maurice *et al.* (1980) report another picture of the position of Germany with respect to 'routine work'. However, in their description it is not quite clear how they have come to their conclusion.

The results in this table reasonably agree for three of the four variables. Hofstede's UAI seems to be a good indication of what is described as 'bureaucratic control' in other studies. Also the extent of variation in the work seems to be connected to this.

Besides, Hofstede (1979, 1980) states that his UAI is conceptually related to the Aston dimension 'structuring of activities' (see also Hickson *et al.*, 1974; Mintzberg, 1979). 'Formalization' is a component of this dimension. We have already seen in the research of Aiken and Bacharach and in that of Child and Kieser that a high degree of formalization does not always go together with a high degree of bureaucratic control and routine work. The assumption of Hofstede is also not in agreement with the results of McMillan *et al.* (1973) who found less formalization in England than in the United States and Canada.

A more systematic comparison between the UAI and formalization can be made with the aid of formalization scores for 12 countries, as collected in the IDE research (1981a). In this research, the Aston measure for formalization was used. The UAI scores for these 12 countries are also available. The results are reported in table 3 and show two things:
1. There is hardly a relationship between formalization (Aston) on the one hand and bureaucratic control (UAI) on the other.
2. The results in relation to formalization do not seem to behave according to a 'culturally sensible' pattern.

In addition to the results for the UAI (Hofstede) and formalization (IDE), table 3 also shows the results on the PDI (Hofstede) and power distribution (IDE). It seems therefore that neither the PDI and power differences nor the UAI and formalization cover each other. Hofstede's PDI is, as already demonstrated, more

Table 3. Ranking of 12 countries on four variables. (1 = little power inequality (IDE), low PDI (Hofstede), low UAI (Hofstede), little formalization (IDE).

	Inequality power distribution	PDI	UAI	Formalization
Great Britain	6	6/7	3	10
Norway	2	3/4	4	5
Denmark	4/5	2	1	7
Finland	7/8	5	6	9
Sweden	3	3/4	2	11
West Germany	9	6/7	7	6
Israel	12	1	9	2
The Netherlands	4/5	8	5	4
Belgium	10/11	10	12	8
Itlay	7/8	9	8	1
France	10/11	11	10	3
Yugoslavia	1	12	11	12

related to concepts such as participative climate, rigid stratification and social distance, and his UAI is more in agreement with bureaucratic control and routine work.

5. IS IT CULTURE?

The fact that differences exist between organizations in different (groups of) countries does not always mean that these differences are cultural in nature or culturally determined. There are various ways to investigate this. In the first place one can think of hypothesis testing research, as advocated by Triandis (1972) and Child (1981). This possibility is especially attractive when there is a clear expectation with respect to such a role for cultural factors, which may be based on previous research and/or a theory. Hypothesis testing cross-cultural research in organizational psychology is, however, rather rare. The reader is referred to Triandis and Vassiliou (1972) for an example.

A second route to make it plausible that we really deal with cultural differences is the one followed by Ajiferuke and Boddewijn in their study of attitudes (see section 3). Likewise, one may relate the differences between the organizations on the country level to macro-level variables such as the dominant religion or income inequality. It will be obvious that a relatively large sample of countries is needed for such an analysis. Nevertheless, some evidence has been collected in this manner in relation to three dimensions discussed in section 4. It concerns the PDI (interpreted by us as 'social distance'), the UAI (uncertainty avoidance) of Hofstede and the power distribution as measured by Tannenbaum *et al.* and in the IDE-research. This research will be discussed in this section. A disadvantage of this approach is that really unique features of a given culture cannot be studied. Perhaps a more descriptive type of research is appropriate in relation to the influence of such unique characteristics. Such an approach, for example, was followed by Dore (1973) in his comparison of two Japanese and two English factories. Gallie also follows such an approach (see the end of this section).

Hofstede examines to what extent certain geographical, economic and demographic indicators explain the differences found for the two variables PDI and UAI.[4] Besides, a number of possible political, religious and historical determinants are sought for these dimensions.

In the analysis of geographical, economic and demographic factors, the PDI seems to correlate the most with Gross National Product per capita, latitude (distance to the equator) and population growth, three highly connected variables. Latitude, the size of the population (thus not the growth) and GNP can together, in this sequence, explain almost 60% of the differences between the countries in the

---

[4]For completeness it is to be noted that Hofstede identifies two other dimensions: individualism (correlated very negatively with PDI) and masculinity; these two will not be considered in this chapter.

PDI. This agrees with the North-South distinction sketched in section 4. In the second place, there seems to be a strong connection between the PDI and income inequality in the society. In addition, countries with a low PDI seem to have more often a balance of power in government. This involves regular elections and peaceful changes in coalitions. There is more often political violence in countries with a high PDI. Therefore, the PDI is strongly connected to processes which are prevalent in the society as a whole. This points to the influence of cultural factors along with economic and physical-geographical factors.

With respect to the UAI it is first of all striking that this index shows a less strong relationship to the geographical, economic and demographic indicators. There is, however, a significant relationship to the GNP but much less strongly than for the PDI. In addition, Hofstede makes an interesting comparison with the data of Lynn and Hampson (1975) concerning a number of medical and related indicators. Lynn and Hampson found, in an ecological factor analysis in 18 developed countries, two factors which they called 'neuroticism' and 'extroversion'. Their first factor, on which for example the indicators for suicide and alcoholism have a high loading, appears to be strongly related to Hofstede's UAI. A third analysis of Hofstede concerns religious factors. In a sample of 29 predominantly christian countries, he found a strong relation between the percentage of catholics (Roman and Orthodox) and his UAI. There is a stronger tendency to avoid uncertainty in more catholic countries. Obviously, the UAI is related to that which prevails in the society as a whole, geographical, economic and demographical factors play a less predominant role than with respect to the PDI.

In a study of Tannenbaum *et al.* (1974) differences in the degree of power inequality were found between a number of comparable enterprises in Italy, Austria, the United States, Yugoslavia and Israel (kibbutz). In Yugoslavia and Israel (kibbutz) the difference in influence between the workers and top management is smaller than in Italy, Austria and the United States. The results concerning the distribution of power were interpreted as related to the existing ideology and the formal rules in the kibbutzim and in Yugoslavia. Such an interpretation does not exclude a cultural explanation. Ideologies as well as formal rules could reflect very well certain cultural values and norms. But it is true that the results do not fit the classification of countries in a Northern and Southern group (section 4). As far as cultural factors play a role here, they are probably cultural factors which are specific for certain countries and not for the groups of countries found by Hofstede and Lammers and Hickson. In addition, the interpretation of Tannenbaum *et al.* emphasizes more the possibility of influencing the division of power than a cultural explanation would do.

In the IDE research (1979, 1981b), it seems that the found differences in power distribution between 12 countries are in great part to be explained by the existence of formal rules for participation. This is understood by the researchers as all formal, written regulations and rules aiming at the support and promotion of employees' participation in organizations. These include not only legal regulations but also the results of collective bargaining and of the policy of management. Just as Tannenbaum *et al.* the IDE researchers emphasize the possibility of human intervention in the power division. Power (in)equality is not, therefore, seen as a permanent and stable cultural fact or as the unavoidable result of technological developments.

This interpretation is supported by an analysis of the data from the IDE study, in which an attempt was made to find an explanation for the observed differences in *formal rules* on participation as described above (IDE, 1981b; Drenth, 1983). Three kinds of explanatory factors have been proposed: economic, cultural and structural. The reasoning behind the *economic* explanation is that one can permit 'participation' only under economically favourable conditions. It could be also defended that in technologically advanced (rich) countries more contributions from the personnel are necessary in the decision making. An index of economic growth and the national income per capita in 1975 were used as indices for the economic factor.

The *cultural* explanation arises from idea that employees' participation laws are rooted in attitudes and values in relation to cooperation, distribution of power and the like. Three indices were used: political democracy, economic equality (ranking as far as income level is concerned) and cooperation orientation (ranking in terms of days lost due to strikes during the period 1967–1976).

Finally, the *structural* explanation is based on the idea that a system of employees' participation will be developed only in cases where there is the combination of a strong position for both employees and employers. The strength of both positions was derived from a historical analysis of the system of industrial relationships in the country concerned.

In table 4 the countries are ranked according to three criteria for employees' participation regulations (direct, indirect and by representation on the board of directors or council of commissioners). Further, the results are presented in relation to the various indices mentioned above for the three explanation alternatives. From this analysis it seems that the cultural explanation is the weakest.[5] The economic explanation also seems to be not very solid. There is a relationship with economic growth but not with prosperity.[6] The structural explanation finds the most support. A strong position and organization of both employers and employees seem to form a favourable condition for the promotion of legislation in the area of employees' participation in industrial organizations.

---

[5] Again, this illustrates all the more the difference between power inequality and formal rules in relation to participation on the one hand and Hofstede's PDI on the other. Two of the culture indices (political democracy and income level) agree with indices which are connected to the PDI.

[6] For Hofstede's PDI this is precisely the opposite: a relationship with GNP but not with economic growth.

Table 4. Formal rules in relation to participation and a number of possible determinants (1947–1975).

	Formal rules (1)	Position trade union (2)	Position management (2)	Economic growth (3)	Prosperity level (4)	Cooperation orientation (4)	Economic equality (4)	Political democracy (4)
Yugoslavia	A	?	?	1	3	1	1	?
West Germany	A	1	1	1	1	1	2	3
Sweden	A	1	1	1	1	1	3	1
Norway	B	1	1	1	1	2	2	1
The Netherlands	C	2	2	1	2	1	2	2
France	C	2	2	1	2	2	3	1
Belgium	D	2	2	1	2	2	2	2
Finland	D	2	1	1	2	3	2	1
Israel	D	1	3	1	3	2	1	3
Denmark	D	2	2	2	1	3	3	2
Italy	E	2	3	2	3	3	3	3
Great Britain	E	2	3	2	3	3	1	2

(1) A = many formal rules in relation to participation, E = few formal rules.
(2) 1 = strong, 2 = average, 3 = weak.
(3) 1 = quick, 2 = slow/stagnation.
(4) relative rank from 1 to and including 3.

The regulatory sketched here (strong position trade union and management →formal rules→more equal power distribution) can definitely not explain all the differences between countries. From a comparison between France and England it seems, for example, that a smaller number of rules and a weak position of management accompany a more equal power distribution in England. A possible explanation for this is perhaps the interpretation of Gallie (1978), who ascribes the greater social integration in English oil refineries to the strivings of the English trade unions for more control over the immediate work situation. At the organizational level, the unions were rather successful in obtaining such influence. Relatively few formal rules are involved here. In contrast, the French unions have always been more oriented towards making the working class more conscious of its position and opportunities. They also have not been without success. The aspirations of French workers are higher than those of English workers, as far as the reformation of society as a whole is concerned. But they have less influence on the daily operations within the organization, partly because control over the immediate work situation is less strongly pursued and partly because of the unwillingness of French management to allow for such influence. The historical development of the system of industrial relations in both countries is considered of great importance by Gallie. This explanation emphasizes cultural elements which are specific in each of the two countries.

The conclusion could be that, as far as there is cultural influence on the (in)equality of power distribution, it should be perhaps sought in cultural characteristics which are *specific* for a given country. General cultural explanations such as those of Hofstede seem to have little applicability here. Such explanation could, however, be quite valid in trying to understand the differences in social distance (PDI) and, especially, differences in the avoidance of uncertainty (UAI).

6. CONVERGENCE?

In this section attention is drawn to a thesis which rather deviates from what was discussed in the previous three sections. It pertains to what is called the *convergence hypothesis*. This hypothesis presumes that increasing industrialization has more influence on organizations than cultural factors. The reasoning is that as a consequence organizations in different countries will become more and more alike and that cultural differences, if existent, slowly disappear. This convergence hypothesis, which is extensively discussed by advocates as well as opponents (Child and Kieser, 1979; Child, 1981; Cole, 1973; Dore, 1973; Fliegel *et al.*, 1979; Maurice, 1979; Negandhi, 1979; Pascale, 1978), can be schematically represented as in figure 2. For reasons of clarity the diagram is limited to two countries with different cultures.

The convergence hypothesis is based on a number of assumptions. The first

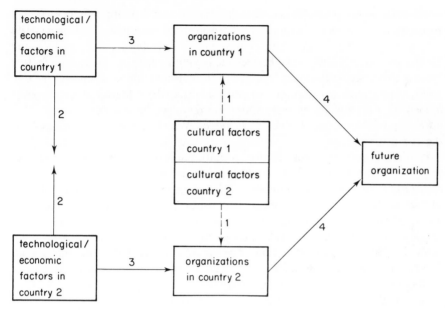

Figure 2. Schematic representation of the convergence hypothesis. The assumptions on which the hypothesis is based are indicated by numerals. The numerals are referred to in the text.

one (1 in the diagram) is related to the role of cultural factors. In the convergence hypothesis it is assumed that these factors exercise a *less great* influence on organizations than economic and technological factors. The differences between organizations in different countries discussed in the previous sections are in themselves no strong argument against the convergence hypothesis. In this hypothesis it is proposed that the differences *decrease* because other factors are more important than cultural factors, and not that there are no differences. But the differences found between technologically very advanced organizations in different countries (Gallie, 1978) leads one to suspect that the cultural differences are quite persistent. Form (1979) and Negandhi (1979) consider research in which no differences between countries were found as one of the arguments for the convergence hypothesis. This argument is actually even weaker than the one just mentioned, since a null hypothesis does not have the same status as an alternative hypothesis. The fact that a null hypothesis cannot be refuted does not imply that the hypothesis is correct!

The second assumption involves the convergence of economic and technological factors themselves (2). Strictly speaking, the convergence hypothesis also holds that *no* convergence will occur if these factors do not tend to develop similarly in the different countries. This last possibility is only seldom taken into account by the supporters of the convergence hypothesis.

The third assumption (3) is that technological and economic factors exercise *strong influence* on organizations. This proposition was studied by Form (1979) among others, who occupies himself especially with technological variables, and by Negandhi (1979), who emphasizes the economic factors. That these factors exercise influence on that which occurs in the organization is, of course, beyond doubt. The fourth assumption, which holds that these factors have *the same* influence on organizations everywhere and therefore have a 'converging' effect upon organizations, is quite debatable, indeed. We will come back to this point at the end of this section.

It will be clear that a cross-cultural longitudinal study is necessary in order to test this pretentious model. A somewhat more modest test was done by Fliegel *et al.* (1979). In this study a number of values were studied, which are considered to vary with technology: the more capital-intensive the technology, the more 'modern' the values. The authors studied these values in people who were employed in sectors at four levels of technological development in three different countries (Brazil, Ghana and India). The hypothesis says that, if the convergence hypothesis is correct, the differences in values between the countries should be smaller for capital-intensive industries than for labour-intensive sectors. However, the expected convergence was not found in this study.

The most important problems in connection with the convergence hypothesis lay, in our view, on the conceptual level. Two questions are important:

1. To what characteristics of organizations and of people within organizations does the convergence hypothesis apply? Also, supporters of the convergence hypothesis think that it is possible that certain attitudes are influenced by cultural factors. They think thereby for example of ideologies (Form, 1979) and morale (Negandhi, 1979) of employees. In this respect, the contrast between the 'culture thesis' and the convergence hypothesis seems to be less sharp than at first sight. However, it is not always clear to which variables the convergence hypothesis applies and to which it does not. Negandhi (1979) observes for example that there is a social-cultural influence on interpersonal relationships. Form, another supporter of the convergence hypothesis, thinks that interpersonal interaction at work is determined by technological factors.

2. Are economic and technological factors so sharply in contrast to cultural factors as is assumed by the advocates and opponents of the convergence hypothesis? The fact that both kinds of factors are related to climate leads one to surmise otherwise. Perhaps research on the question of the relationship between these factors and the manner in which they interact is more important than research in which it is assumed that they are directly opposed to each other.

In connection with this last question, perhaps the literature on the relationship between mechanization and automation on the one hand and organization characteristics and characteristics of work on the other hand is also relevant. This literature shows an interesting development. In the 1960s general principles were emphasized, such as: mechanization leads to alienation, but automation leads to a return of meaningful task content (Blauner, 1964; Faunce, 1970). This approach has made room for a more pessimistic vision on the consequences of automation which, among others, recurs in a report of the Social Economic Council (Ekkers *et al.*, 1980) and in a report commissioned by the Scientific Council for Government Policy (de Sitter, 1981). The most interesting development is that in a number of cases the recognition of the importance of technological factors is coupled with an emphasis on the various choice options (van Assen and den Hertog, 1980; Ekkers *et al.*, 1980; de Sitter, 1981; see also Algera and Koopman in this Handbook). In the socio-technical systems approach (Davis and Taylor, 1976; Cummings, 1978; see also van Dijck in this Handbook), one could encounter a similar approach earlier. It will be clear that such a standpoint leaves more room for the possibility of cultural factors than the technological determinism of the convergence hypothesis.

7. SUMMARY AND CONCLUSIONS

Finally, we would like to place a number of points at issue, which were discussed in this chapter, into a somewhat more comprehensive perspective. In section 2 it was mentioned that there are important methodological advantages in studying differences in *relationships* between variables in different countries. Such research, however, is rather rare. For this reason attention was predominantly paid to differences in *level* in this chapter; this also being true of this closing section.

The greatest part of cross-cultural research on organizations is concerned with differences in attitudes, needs, expectations and opinions of organization members. Such research is definitely important, but the risk of circular reasoning is not imaginary. The concept 'culture' itself is mostly defined in terms of attitudes, opinions, values and norms (see section 1). Consequently, a more clear delineation of the concept 'culture' was advocated in section 3. That such personal characteristics are 'cultural' in nature can be made plausible by relating them to variables at the system level, such as the variables used by Ajiferuke and Boddewijn (1970) and Hofstede (1980).

With regard to formal organizational characteristics, such as the well-known Aston dimensions, there is little reason to assume that cultural factors exercise influence here. This does not mean that in this respect no differences between countries exist, but it is difficult to observe a culturally meaningful pattern in these differences. Organizations do not only have *formal* characteristics but they are also characterized according to the way in which they function. Such characteristics can be distinguished from formal characteristics because they are more related to the daily operations of the organization, which do not always have to be in agreement with formally prescribed rules. In order to distinguish such organizational characteristics from formal organizational characteristics, they are sometimes called '*organizational processes*' (see for example Aiken and Bacharach, 1979).

Perhaps this distinction can be illustrated by two examples. 'Formalization' (= the presence of written rules) is a formal organizational characteristic. The extent to which and the manner in which organization members follow these rules could be designated as organizational processes. 'Centralization' (= the extent to which formal authority for decision making is localized at the top of the organization) is a formal organizational characteristic. The degree to which various groups within the organization exercise influence on that which occurs in this organization and the manner in which this happens again are to be conceived as organizational processes.

Organizational processes cannot be sharply demarcated from the behavior of organization members. If members of a given organization behave themselves systematically differently from members of other organizations (for example in following the instituted rules), then there is a question of differences in organizational processes. A clear distinction can be made, however, between organizational processes and *attitudes* ('that which is going on in their heads'). Figure 3 contains a schematic representation of the research area, which in comparison to figure 1 (section 1) contains a few new elements.

In the first place, the concept 'organizational processes' discussed above is integrated in the scheme. The two part-classification 'individual-organization' has been substituted by the given three-part classification. In addition, the possibility to distinguish 'cultural individual variables' from other individual variables proposed in section 3 is taken into consideration. Such a description of culture in terms of attitudes, values, norms and opinions is closely connected to the definition of Kluchkohn (1951) mentioned in section 1, in which ideas and, especially, the related values are considered to be the core of the culture concept. In order to make plausible that the individual variables under consideration are cultural in nature, an attempt could be made to relate them to system level variables such as political and religious variables (Ajiferuke and Boddewijn, Hofstede, IDE, see sections 3 and 5). The research discussed in sections 4 and 5 can be easily placed in this scheme. Cultural factors seem to have only little

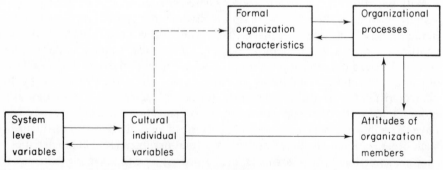

Figure 3. A further demarcation of the research area.

influence on formal organization characteristics. There is, however, a rather strong relationship between culture on the one hand and attitudes of organization members on the other. Some organizational processes are predominantly determined by formal organizational characteristics. The discussion in section 5 for example, showed that the power distribution within an organization is largely determined by formal regulations regarding employees' participation. Other organization processes seem to be related to 'culture'. In this connection, two dimensions were mentioned in section 4: the first one can be described as 'rigid stratification/social distance' and is related to the 'power-distance' index of Hofstede. The second dimension can be called 'bureaucratic control/routine work' and is related to Hofstede's index for 'uncertainty avoidance'. The relationships between these two dimensions on the one hand and the more (but not exclusively) attitude-oriented indices of Hofstede on the other hand strengthen the conviction that cultural influence on organizations predominantly occurs via attitudes and values of organization members.

Here, we would like to make two restraining observations regarding this classification into two dimensions. The first one concerns the sample of countries on which this classification is based. In general, it should be pointed out that research involving non-Western countries is scarce. There are exceptions such as the studies of Fliegel *et al.* (1979), Gruenfeld and McEachern (1975), Hofstede (1980) and Negandhi (1979), who (also) have included developing countries in their samples. Research which includes East European Countries is possibly even more scarce. To this rule the research of Granick (1979) and a recent extension of the research of Tannenbaum (see Tannenbaum, 1980) are exceptions. The classification sketched in section 4 is also almost exclusively based on Western countries and it is still the question to what extent the classification is meaningful outside of this area.

Japan is one of the non-Western countries on which a reasonable amount of comparative research exists. According to Hofstede (1980) this country is typified by a high PDI-score and, especially, a high UAI-score. In the first place, it can be noted that the Japanese system of participation can be portrayed as 'paternalistic', which agrees with the relatively high PDI-score. On the other hand, Dore (1973) reports that stratification in Japan is even less rigid than in Great Britain. The stronger commitment of the Japanese employee to the organization can be considered as an indication of avoidance of uncertainty. The emphasis on the use of formal rules in organizing the work mentioned by Dore (1973) also points in this direction. Cole (1979) observed that the splitting of functions into different sub-functions is much less strong in Japan than in the United States. Fassin (1982) also noted that the division of tasks and specialization is less advanced in Japan and that functions in Japan are less accurately described. It is, therefore, improbable that work in Japan is more routine, as one would expect on the basis of the relationship between uncertainty avoidance and routine work sketched in section 5. These results once again confirm that it is unwise to generalize relationships observed in Western countries to non-Western countries without a further verification.

The second restraining observation concerns the manner in which the classification sketched in section 4 is compiled. This classification is based on a post-hoc comparison of a number of different studies, in which grateful use was made of the variables discussed by Lammers and Hickson (1979). This way it seemed possible to compose a rationally satisfactory 'picture' which in any case is in agreement with the results of past research. There is still the question whether this 'picture' will remain intact in future research, especially when non-Western countries are more often included in the research. The somewhat pragmatic exploratory approach followed is in contrast to the more controlled, hypothesis testing research as advocated for example by Traindis (1972) and Child (1981).

Herewith we have reached a classic but in this case very relevant point: more research is needed. However, not every cross-cultural study is equally welcome. There is need for research based on clear concept demarcation. This is true for the concept of culture itself as well as for the variables or dimensions on which cultural differences could manifest themselves. Only then will there be clarity on the question of the nature and determinants of differences between countries in organizational characteristics and processes.

REFERENCES

Aiken, M., Bacharach, S. B. (1979), Culture and organizational structure and process: A comparative study of local government administrative bureaucracies in the Walloon and Flemish regions of Belgium. In: Lammers, C. J., Hickson, D. J. (Eds.), *Organizations alike and unlike*. London/Boston/Henley: Routledge & Kegan Paul.

Ajiferuke, M., Boddewijn, J. (1970), Socio-economic indicators in comparative management. *Administrative Science Quarterly*, **15**, 453–458.

Andriessen, J. H. T. (1979), *Cross-cultureel onderzoek. Problemen en oplossingen* [Cross-cultural research. Problems and solutions]. Amsterdam: Free University (unpubl. paper).

Assen, A. van, Hertog, J. F. den (1980), Werkbeleving en werkstructurering [Work satisfaction and job design]. In: Galan, C. de, Gils, M. R. van, Strien, P. J. van (Eds.), *Humanisering van de arbeid* [Humanizing work]. Assen: Van Gorcum.

Barrett, G. V., Bass, B. M. (1976), Cross-cultural issues in industrial and organizational psychology. In: Dunnette M. D. (Ed.), *Handbook of industrial and organizational psychology*. Chicago: Rand McNally.

Bass, B. M. (1977), Utility of managerial self-planning on a simulated production task with replications in twelve countries. *Journal of Applied Psychology*, **62**, 506–509.

Bass, B. M., Eldridge, L. (1973), Accelerated managers' objectives in twelve countries. *Industrial Relations*, **12**, 158–171.

Bennett, M. (1977a), Testing management theories cross-culturally. *Journal of Applied Psychology*, **62**, 578–581.

Bennett, M. (1977b), Response characteristics of bilingual managers to organizational questionnaires. *Personnel Psychology*, **30**, 29–36.

Berry, J. W. (1980), Introduction to methodology. In: Triandis, H. C., Berry, J. W. (Eds.), *Cross-cultural psychology*, 2. Boston: Allyn and Bacon.

Bhagat, R. S., McQuaid, S. J. (1982), Role of subjective culture in organizations: A review and directions for future research. *Journal of Applied Psychology* (monograph), **67**, 5, 653–685.

Blalock, H. M. (1961), *Causal inferences in non-experimental research*. Chapel Hill: University of North Carolina Press.

Blauner, R. (1964), *Alienation and freedom*. Chicago/London: University of Chicago Press.

Brislin, R. W. (1976), Comparative research methodology: Cross-cultural studies. *International Journal of Psychology*, **11**, 215–229.

Brislin, R. W., Lonner, W. J., Thorndike, R. M. (1973), *Cross-cultural research methods*. New York: John Wiley.

Child, J. (1981), Culture, contingency and capitalism in the cross-national study of organizations. In: Cumming, L. L., Staw, B. M. (Ed.), *Research in organizational behavior*. Volume 3. Greenwich: JAI Press Inc.

Child, J., Kieser, A. (1979), Organization and managerial roles in British and West German companies: An examination of the culture-free thesis. In: Lammers. C. J., Hickson, D. J. (Eds.), *Organizations alike and unlike*. London/Boston/Henley: Routledge & Kegan Paul.

Clark, P. (1979), Cultural context as a determinant of organizational rationality: A comparison of the tobacco industries in Britain and France. In: Lammers, C. J., Hickson, D. J. (Eds.), *Organizations alike and unlike*. London/Boston/Henley: Routledge & Kegan Paul.

Cole, R. E. (1973), Functional alternatives and economic development: An empirical example of permanent employment in Japan. *American Sociological Review*, **38**, 424–438.

Cole, R. E. (1979), *Work, mobility and participation: A comparative study of American and Japanese industry*. Berkeley: University of California Press.

Crozier, M. (1964), *The bureaucracies phenomenon*. London: Tavistock.

Cummings, T. G. (1978), Self-regulating workgroups: A sociotechnical synthesis. *Academy of Management Review*, **00**, 625–634.

Davis, L. E., Taylor, J. C. (1976), Technology, organization and job-structure. In: Dubin R. (Ed.), *Handbook of work, organization and society*. Chicago: Rand McNally.

Deutscher, L. (1973), Asking questions cross-culturally. In: Warwick, D. P., Osherson, S. (Eds.), *Comparative research methods*. Englewood Cliffs: Prentice-Hall.

DIO, International Research Team (1983), A contingency model of participative decision making: An analysis of 56 decisions in three Dutch organizations. *Journal of Occupational Psychology*, **56**, 1–18.

Dore, R. (1973), *British factory—Japanese factory*. London: Allen & Unwin.

Drenth, P. J. D. (1983), Cross-cultural organizational psychology: Challenges and limitations. In: Irvine, S. H., Berry, J. (Eds.), *Human assessment and cultural factors*. London: Plenum Press.

Drenth, P. J. D., Flier, H. van der (1973), Culturele verschillen en de vergelijkbaarheid van test prestaties [Cultural differences and the comparability of test performance]. In: Drenth, P. J. D., Willems, P. J., Wolff, Ch. J. de (Eds.), *Arbeids- en organisatiepsychologie* [Work- and organizational psychology]. Deventer: Kluwer.

Ekkers, C. L., Brouwers, A. A. F., Pasmooy, C. K., Vlaming, P. M. (1980), *Mens en arbeid: Effecten van automatisering* [Man and work: Effects of automation]. SER (Socio-economic Council).

Elder, J. W. (1976), Comparative cross-national methodology. *Annual Review of Sociology*, **2**, 209–230.

Esbroeck, R. van (1982), *Analyse van 'faking-gedrag' bij adolescenten in beroepsinteressen vragenlijsten* [Analysis of 'faking behaviour' in adolescents in vocational interest questionnaires]. Brussels: Free University.

Fassin, Y. (1982), Management in Japan [in Dutch]. *Tijdschrift voor Organisatiekunde en Sociaal Beleid* [Journal of Organization Science and Social Policy], (*M & O*), **36**, 151–163.

Faunce, W. A. (1970), Automation and the division of labor. In: Marcson, S. (Ed.), *Automation, alienation and anomy*. New York: Harper & Row. Also in: *Social Problems* (1965), **13**, 149–155.

Fiedler, F. E. (1967), *A theory of leadership effectiveness*. New York: McGraw-Hill.

Fliegel, F., Sofranko, A. J., Williams, J. D., Navin, C. S. (1979), Technology and cultural convergence: A limited empirical test. *Journal of Cross-cultural Psychology*, **10**, 3–22.

Form, W. (1979), Comparative industrial sociology and the convergence hypothesis. *Annual Review of Sociology*, **5**, 1–25.

Gallie, D. (1978), *In search of the new working class. Automation and social integration within the capitalist enterprise*. Cambridge: Cambridge University Press.

Gruenfeld, L. W., MacEachern, A. E. (1975), A cross-national study of cognitive style among managers and technicians. *International Journal of Psychology*, **10**, 27–55.

Haire, M., Ghiselli, E. E., Porter, L. W. (1966), *Managerial thinking, an international study*. New York: Wiley.

Hickson, D. J., Hinings, C. R., McMillan, C. J., Schwitter, J. P. (1974), The culture-free context of organization structure: A tri-national comparison. *Sociology*, **8**, 59–80.

Hofstede, G. (1979), Hierarchical power distance in fourty countries. In: Lammers, C. J., Hickson, D. J. (Eds.), *Organizations alike and unlike*. London/Boston/Henley: Routledge & Kegan Paul.

Hofstede, G. (1980), *Cultures consequences: International differences in work-related values*. Beverly Hills: Sage Publications.

IDE-International Research Group (1979), Participation: Formal rules, influence and involvement. *Industrial Relations*, **18**, 273–294.

IDE-International Research Group (1981a), *Industrial democracy in Europe*. Oxford: Oxford University Press.

IDE-International Research Group (1981b), *European industrial relations*. Oxford: Oxford University Press.

Katerberg, R., Smith, F. J., Stephen, H. (1977), Language, time and person effects on attitude scale translations. *Journal of Applied Psychology*, **62**, 4, 385–391.

Kluckhohn, C. (1951), The study of culture. In: Lerner, D., Lasswel, H. D. (Eds.), *The policy sciences*. Stanford: Stanford University Press.

Koopman, P. L., Drenth, P. J. D., Bus, F. B. M., Kruijswijk, A. J. Wierdsma, A. F. M. (1981), Content, process, and effect of participative decision-making on the shop floor: Three cases in The Netherlands. *Human Relations*, **34**, 657–676.

Kroeber, A. L., Parsons, T. (1958), The concepts of culture and of a social system. *American Sociological Review*, **23**, 582–583.

Lammers, C. J., Hickson, D. J. (Eds.) (1979), *Organizations alike and unlike*. London/Boston/Henley: Routledge & Kegan Paul.

Lynn, B., Hampson, G. L. (1975), National differences in extraversion and neuroticism. *British Journal of Social and Clinical Psychology*, **14**, 223–240.

McMillan, C. J., Hickson, D. J., Hinings, C. R., Schneck, R. E. (1973), The structure of work organizations across societies. *Academy of Management Journal*, **16**, 555–569.

Martyn-Johns, T. A. (1977), Cultural conditioning of views of authority and its effect on the business decision-making process with special reference to Java. In: Poortinga, Y. H. (Ed.), *Basic problems in cross-cultural psychology*. Amsterdam/Lisse: Swets & Zeitlinger.

Maurice, M. (1979), For a study of 'the societal effect': Universality and specificity in organization research. In: Lammers, C. J., Hickson, D. J. (Eds.), *Organizations alike and unlike*. London/Boston/Henley: Routledge & Kegan Paul.

Maurice, M. Sorge, A., Warner, M. (1980), Societal differences in organizing manufacturing units. A comparison of France, West Germany and Great Britain. *Organization Studies*, **1**, 59.

Mintzberg, H. (1979), *The structuring of organizations*. Englewood Cliffs: Prentice-Hall.

MOW International Research Team (1981), The meaning of working. In: Duglos, G., Weierman, K. (Eds.), *Management under different value systems*. Berlin: De Gruyter, 565–630.

Mulder, M. (1972), *Het spel om macht* [The power game]. Meppel: Boom.

Mulder, M. (1980), *Omgaan met macht. Ons gedrag met elkaar en tegen elkaar* [Managing power. Our behaviour with each other and against each other]. 2nd ed. Amsterdam/Brussels: Elsevier.

Negandhi, A. R. (1979), Convergence in organization practices: An empirical study of industrial enterprise in developing countries. In: Lammers, C. J., Hickson, D. J. (Eds.), *Organizations alike and unlike*. London/Boston/Henley: Routledge & Kegan Paul.

Osgood, C. E. (1967), On the strategy of cross-national research into subjective culture. *Social Science Info*, **6**, 5–37.

Pascale, R. T. (1978), Communication and decision-making across cultures: Japanese and American comparison. *Administrative Science Quarterly*, **23**, 91–110.

Poortinga, Y. H. (1971), *Cross-cultural comparison of maximum performance tests: some methodological aspects and some experiments with auditory and visual stimuli*. Johannesburg: National Institute for Personnel Research.

Poortinga, Y. H. (1975), Limitations on intercultural comparison of psychological data. *Nederlands Tijdschrift voor de Psychologie* [Dutch Journal of Psychology], **30**, 23–39.

Przeworski, A., Teune, H. (1970), *The logic of comparative social inquiry*. New York: John Wiley.

Redding, S. G., Casey, T. W. (1976), Managerial beliefs among Asian managers. *Proceedings of the Academy of Management Journal*, 351–355.

Roberts, K. H. (1970), On looking at an elephant. *Psychological Bulletin*, **74**, 327–350.

Robinson, W. S. (1950), Ecological correlations and the behaviour of individuals. *American Sociological Review*, **15**.

Ronen, S. (1977), The university of work motivation theory. In: Poortinga, Y. H. (Ed.), *Basic problems of cross-cultural psychology*. Amsterdam/Lisse: Swets & Zeitlinger.

Ronen, S. (1979), Cross-national study of employees' work goals. *International Review of Applied Psychology*, **28**, 1–11.

Scheuch, E. K. (1966), Cross-national comparisons using aggregate data: Some substantive and methodological problems. In: Merritt, R., Rokkan, S. (Ed.), Comparing nations: *The use of quantitative data in cross-national research*. New Haven (Connecticut): Yale University press.

Sekaran, U., Mowday, R. T. (1981), A cross-cultural analysis of the influence of individual and job characteristics on job involvement. *International Review of Applied Psychology*, **30**, 51–64.

Sitter, L. U. de (1981), *Op weg naar nieuwe fabrieken en kantoren* [Towards new factories and offices]. Deventer: Kluwer.

Tannenbaum, A. S. (1968), *Control in organizations*. New York: McGraw-Hill.

Tannenbaum, A. S. (1980), Organizational psychology. In: Triandis, H. C., Brislin, R. W. (Ed.), *Handbook of cross-cultural psychology*, 5. Boston: Allyn & Bacon.

Tannenbaum, A. S., Cooke, R. A. (1979), Organizational control: A review of studies employing the control graph method. In: Lammers, C. J., Hickson, D. J. (Eds.), *Organizations alike and unlike*. London/Boston/Henley: Routledge & Kegan Paul.

Tannenbaum, A. S., Kavcic, B., Rosner, M., Vianello, M., Wieser, G. (1974), *Hierarchy in organizations*. San Francisco: Jossey-Bass.

Triandis, H. C. (1972), *The analysis of subjective culture*. New York: Wiley.

Triandis, H. C., Vassiliou, V. (1972), Interpersonal influence and employee perception in two cultures. *Journal of Applied Psychology*, **56**, 140–145.

Author Index

Subject Index

S1

DATE DUE